Accounting and Tax Principles for Legal Professionals

DELMAR LEARNING

Options.
Over 300 products in every area of the law: textbooks, CD-ROMs, reference books, test banks, online companions, and more – helping you succeed in the classroom and on the job.

Support.
We offer unparalleled, practical support: robust instructor and student supplements to ensure the best learning experience, custom publishing to meet your unique needs, and other benefits such as West's Student Achievement Award. And our sales representatives are always ready to provide you with dependable service.

Feedback.
As always, we want to hear from you! Your feedback is our best resource for improving the quality of our products. Contact your sales representative or write us at the address below if you have any comments about our materials or if you have a product proposal.

Accounting and Financials for the Law Office • Administrative Law • Alternative Dispute Resolution • Bankruptcy • Business Organizations/Corporations • Careers and Employment Civil Litigation and Procedure • CLA Exam Preparation • Computer Applications in the Law Office • Contract Law • Court Reporting • Criminal Law and Procedure • Document Preparation • Elder Law • Employment Law • Environmental Law • Ethics • Evidence Law • Family Law • Intellectual Property • Interviewing and Investigation • Introduction to Law Introduction to Paralegalism • Law Office Management Law Office Procedures Legal Nurse Consulting • Legal Research, Writing, and Analysis • Legal Terminology • Paralegal Internship • Product Liability • Real Estate Law • Reference Materials • Social Security Sports Law • Torts and Personal Injury Law • Wills, Trusts, and Estate Administration

Delmar Learning
5 Maxwell Drive
Clifton Park, New York 12065-2919

For additional information, find us online at:
www.delmarlearning.com

Accounting and Tax Principles for Legal Professionals

BETH WALSTON-DUNHAM

THOMSON
DELMAR LEARNING

Australia Canada Mexico Singapore Spain United Kingdom United States

THOMSON
DELMAR LEARNING

ACCOUNTING AND TAX PRINCIPLES FOR LEGAL PROFESSIONALS

Beth Walston-Dunham

Career Education Strategic Business Unit:
Vice President:
Dawn Gerrain

Director of Learning Solutions:
John Fedor

Acquisitions Editor:
Shelley Esposito

Managing Editor:
Robert Serenka, Jr.

Editorial Assistant:
Melissa Zaza

Director of Content & Media Production:
Wendy A. Troeger

Senior Content Project Manager:
Betty L. Dickson

Art Director:
Joy Kocsis

Director of Marketing:
Wendy Mapstone

Marketing Manager:
Gerard McAvey

Marketing Coordinator:
Jonathan Sheehan

Library of Congress Cataloging-in-
Publication Data

Walston-Dunham, Beth.
  Accounting and tax principles for legal
professionals / Beth Walston-Dunham.
    p. cm.
  ISBN-13: 978-1-4180-1107-9
  ISBN-10: 1-4180-1107-X
1. Lawyers--United States--Accounting.
2. Accounting--Law and legislation--United
States. 3. Income tax--Law and legislation--
United States. I. Title.
  KF320.A2W35 2008
  657.024'34--dc22
                                    2007032086

NOTICE TO THE READER

Dedication

This book is for my father
Keith Walston, C.P.A.,

For always holding me accountable
on the books and off.

Contents

CHAPTER 3   Concluding the Financial Reporting Period 50

CHAPTER 4   Accounting in the Law Office 62

CHAPTER 7 Commonly Encountered Information Documents

CHAPTER 8 **Common Federal Income Tax Individual Forms** 211

Table of Exhibits

Preface

In recent years, the legal profession has been faced with an increasingly competitive market in an ever-changing legal system. As a result, the need for attorneys and paralegals alike to maintain competence and a widening grasp of knowledge has grown. One of the more significant changes in the law relevant to the field of taxation is the remodeling of the Bankruptcy Code. Under the new provisions, bankruptcy applicants must have current returns on file before establishing their estate in bankruptcy. Additionally, many clients of the various types of law firms prefer their own attorney to prepare the individual return as opposed to a commercial firm. This is because the attorney often has intimate knowledge of the financial situation of the client and the methods of return preparation that would best serve the client. By offering this service, the law firm also can generate revenue.

To obtain a competitive edge in the market, law offices must have the ability not only to increase revenue but to contain costs as well. A well-trained paralegal or attorney often can perform many, if not all, of the accounting functions previously delegated to private accounting firms. This text is designed to assist the paralegal or attorney develop valuable skills that have a very real impact on the bottom dollar of the business of practicing law. The successful completion of the text should provide the student/practitioner with several new marketable skills associated with the law office environment. These include, but are not limited to, essential accounting, bookkeeping and payroll functions relevant to an administrative position within a law office. The reader also will be armed with basic skills for tax preparation of governmentally required documents such as payroll reports. Finally, the text provides the information to develop knowledge to prepare commonly required court accounting reports as well as basic individual and small business tax returns.

With respect to the construction of the text, it is divided into distinct components. First is a basic introduction to general accounting concepts, followed by chapters that address elemental tax issues. The two sections are intended to complement one another and assist the legal professional in the day-to-day business operations as well as relevant tax consequences for the law office and clients. More specifically, the early chapters are intended to familiarize the novice with general accounting terminology, basic concepts, ordinary business accounting documents, and office accounting procedures commonly used in the private practice setting. The latter chapters are intended to familiarize the novice with general procedures regarding periodic and annual taxation on income and transactions that affect the law office.

Features of the text include a generous use of illustrations of commonly used accounting formats as well as government documents. Each chapter provides incremental assignments and realistic applications of the principles discussed. Both the accounting and taxation portions of the text are culminated with comprehensive assignments that allow the student to integrate the various matters addressed within the chapters. Importantly, each chapter is concluded with an ethical perspective on the subject matter and review of relevant terminology.

It is well established that the independent law office must maintain a continuing effort to remain competitive in the marketplace. When this is considered in conjunction with the efforts of the governmental entities to encourage mass online filing of tax returns and changes in law such as the Bankruptcy Code, there is an obvious opportunity both for client service and increased revenues. The legal professional with skills to assist the law firm in taking advantage of this opportunity is in an enviable position.

Introduction to Accounting

After completing this chapter, you will be able to:

❑ Explain the function and purpose of accounting in the law office

❑ Discuss the role of accounting in a profit-based business

❑ Describe how accounting is beneficial to employers

❑ Define the fiduciary relationship

A. WHAT IS ACCOUNTING?

In any type of business, it is necessary to keep track of the incoming and outgoing sources of monetary wealth in order to determine the value of the business and its degree of success. The process used for this is accounting. The term **accounting** is described in the following way:

"A system of setting up financial record books, especially for tax purposes . . . a full explanation of a transaction or of an entire business."

Accounting is much more involved than simple math computations or lists of product inventory in a retail business. The information produced through accounting is used to create a realistic and understandable representation of the overall health of a business enterprise. It provides information that allows informed decisions for

ACCOUNTING

A system of setting up financial record books, especially for tax purposes; a full explanation of a transaction or of an entire business

the future growth or direction of the business. It generates the necessary information for required periodic reporting to various government entities with regard to financial transactions and potential tax consequences. It is also an invaluable tool at the end of the life of the business to establish values for sale or liquidation of the interests of the business.

An important note at the outset is that much of traditional accounting has been replaced with highly sophisticated computer software. In today's job market, to be competitive as one capable of performing accounting functions and having a working knowledge of one or more of the more commercially popular programs is essential. However, without a basic understanding of the underlying processes, even one who is fluent in accounting software is destined to encounter disaster when problems arise. Consider the skill of research ability. Much of this has become a computerized process. However, without a basic knowledge of how and where information is organized, computer research can be frustrating and fruitless.

As can be seen from Application 1.1, there are numerous issues to be addressed when managing the money of a business even in its infancy stage. An individual is accountable only to him or herself. In other words, that person manages incoming and outgoing funds for a single entity—the individual. However, even the smallest law practice has a number of responsibilities with respect to financial activity. A business like this has both legal and ethical duties toward clients with regard to money. Additionally, employees and owners also expect and deserve responsible financial behavior. Finally, government reports and tax documents require periodic and detailed information with regard to certain aspects of the financial activity of the business. As a result, accounting is a key element of any law practice.

APPLICATION **1.1**

Joe and Mark are recent law school graduates. On passing the bar, they want to set up their own law practice. Part of this process requires them to set up a bookkeeping system. To start, Joe and Mark create accounts for incoming money from clients, accounts to record any money they personally contribute to start the business, and a separate account for client funds that might be held on behalf of clients. The next step is to set up a journal that details how incoming and outgoing money is attributed to the various areas of the business, such as client payments, utilities, supplies, advertising, miscellaneous expenses, and so on. By setting the system up using a software program that automatically calculates and transfers data to appropriate accounts after the initial journal entry, numerous time-consuming steps are eliminated and the potential for error is greatly reduced. However, failure to know which accounts are necessary for a particular business, for example, accruing expenses such as taxes, insurance, and so on, could cause amounts to appear by default in the wrong general accounts, for example, in the cash account, although those amounts were not really available to spend.

B. WHAT ROLE DOES ACCOUNTING PLAY IN THE LAW OFFICE?

Although any business organization, large or small, must track financial activity, accounting plays a particularly important role in the practice of law. In addition to regular business operations, a law practice frequently uses accounting for specific purposes, for example, when managing the assets of other individuals or businesses who may be clients. As with most business organizations, a law practice typically has employees and therefore must provide proper accounting for the payment of wages and related taxes for them. However, unlike many other types of businesses, law practices often also employ regular employees, periodic employees, and independent contractors who are working on behalf of specific clients. The payments to periodic employees and independent contractors must be properly chronicled as well. The following discussion provides a more thorough explanation of how these various functions affect the law practice from the standpoint of accounting.

1. As a Business

The practice of basic accounting principles is essentially the same for any business. There are established standards and accepted rules of practice to which all businesses should adhere. These standards and rules allow businesses to deal with each other on a common ground. The more complicated that the transactions of the business are will dictate how complex the accounting processes for the business become. But the essential elements of tracking incoming and outgoing funds, detailing the types of transactions conducted, and billing and collection records generally are similar regardless of the type of business.

For the law office, accounting is an essential element. Because attorneys are subject to codes of professional conduct, laws of licensure, and public scrutiny as well, the need to follow accepted rules of procedure for the internal controls of the business is paramount. This includes appropriate tracking of incoming and outgoing funds. Specifically, proper and detailed documentation of all monies associated with law firm accounts should be maintained and current at all times. This helps to satisfy a cardinal ethical canon for attorneys, which is to avoid even the appearance of impropriety.

2. As An Employer

There are numerous accounting functions associated with a business that employs others. In the 1800s, an employee often worked with little other formality than a verbally agreed-on wage. At the end of a period (often weekly), that employee would be given an amount of cash equal to the earned wage. Thus, bookkeeping for employees was a relatively simple task. Today, that process has become much more complicated as the result of wage and hour laws, tax laws, employment benefits converted to cash, and various other considerations that range from retirement plans to garnishments. Much of this will be explored in greater detail in subsequent chapters. However, for the purposes of this introductory chapter, the accounting practices for an employer will be briefly discussed.

A law firm often has numerous types of employees. There are owners whose wages are tied directly to the profit or loss of the business. These individuals may be compensated as employees or as self-employed individuals, based on the type of business organization under which the law practice operates.

One or more individuals may be employed as support staff. It is necessary to keep track of the wages and hours worked by these regular employees. Any other payments, for example, overtime, may require a different rate of pay. Once the amount earned has been determined, it is necessary to calculate any withholding for state and federal obligations such as taxes, Social Security, and Medicare. The value of optional benefits also must be calculated to determine the effect on the employee's compensation.

APPLICATION 1.2

Joan is in charge of the accounting functions for a law office of 30 attorneys and a support staff of an additional 25 people. Maxine is in charge of accounting functions for a law office of three attorneys and a support staff of three. Both Joan and Maxine are required to keep records for the financial transactions of their practice. Some of the duties common to both types of practice include:

1. Record all incoming funds with regard to the particular client account, including the reason for the receipt, such as payment of a client bill, settlement of a client's case, reimbursement for expenses paid on behalf of the client, and so on.

2. Record all outgoing funds with regard to the specific account from which the funds are extracted, the purpose of the expenditure, including payments of expenses related to client cases, general office operating expenses, payments to attorneys, payments to independent contractors, payments to employees, tax payments, and so on.

3. Billing and collections of accounts within the office.

4. Periodic summaries (monthly, quarterly, annually) in the form of financial reports, and statements that detail the activity of the various types of accounts including billing, collections, assets and expenses of the business, and payroll information.

5. Periodic governmental reports including tax returns, employment taxes, and so on, for both state and federal governments as required by law.

Independent contractors typically are paid gross sums without deductions for taxes or benefits. They are not considered part of the regular payroll. Payments to independent contractors usually are made on behalf of a client. The same may be true for a periodic employee hired to work on a particular case for a specified period of time. These employees may or may not be subject to tax withholding, depending on their employment status. However, they are typically not eligible for benefits. Nevertheless, the payments to independent contractors and periodic employees also must be properly recorded in order to issue the correct documents for tax purposes at year-end. A record also should be kept to show how much was spent on these types of services.

3. As A Fiduciary

a. What Is a Fiduciary?

The term **fiduciary** is one that is broadly used in business and law. It can be applied in several contexts. However, it can be most broadly defined as follows:

"Any relationship between persons in which one person acts for another in a position of trust."

It is somewhat obvious that a lawyer who represents a client acts as a fiduciary with respect to that client's legal rights. However, that is not usually the full scope of the relationship. The delivery of legal services is one of professional skill. Usually, the delivery of services and payment for those services is measured in two ways: time and results. If a client retains an attorney for representation, the parties enter into a

FIDUCIARY

Any relationship between persons in which one person acts for another in a position of trust

---

APPLICATION 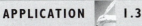 **1.3**

Maxine is preparing to issue the semimonthly payroll for the law office in which she is employed as the accountant. There are five employees in addition to the attorneys. Maxine must calculate the wages earned by each of the employees and any deductions that must be applied to those wages. The wages and deductions must be recorded appropriately. The payments must be prepared in the form of paychecks along with statements that detail the deductions applied for each employee. This information also must be retained by the business in a cumulative form to enable Maxine to prepare financial statements and any required documentation and periodic tax payments. Maxine has a computer software program that assists her in the calculations. However, she must input all of the information for each employee properly. Additionally, the firm has employed an independent legal investigator to work on a particular case. That contractor also must be paid and the payment properly recorded with respect to the client for whom the work is performed. A business record of the payment also must be kept for that specific contractor in order to properly report all payments to the contractor at the end of the year for tax purposes.

contractual relationship. The attorney is obligated to utilize his or her best professional skills and ability to represent the interests of the client. The client in turn agrees to compensate the attorney for the time spent and/or results produced. The client trusts the lawyer as a fiduciary in a legal sense. But the client also often entrusts financial resources to the attorney. The attorney has a corresponding obligation to protect those resources.

The obligation of the attorney as a fiduciary is not only monetary. There also is the requirement that the client's best interest be placed above the interests of others by the attorney. This includes the attorney's own interests. For example, if an attorney represents a client with respect to investments, the attorney cannot become involved in those investments personally to the detriment of the client. Similarly, if a client contracts with an attorney for representation, the attorney must decline all representation of others with interests that could in any way be in conflict with the interests of the existing client. This is true even though there might be a risk of substantial financial loss for the attorney. The role of fiduciary with respect to the client is paramount to any other interests of the attorney, either professionally or personally.

b. The Fiduciary Relationship with Clients.

As a financial fiduciary, an attorney may act in a variety of ways. A client may deposit funds with the attorney as a retainer. This is an amount of money to be drawn on as the services of the attorney are rendered. Another circumstance occurs when an attorney holds funds in escrow such as that described in Application 1.4. In this situation, two or more parties have a potential claim to a sum of money. Until the issues between the parties are brought to resolution, the attorney acts as an objective third party and holds the funds. Another situation occurs when a sum of money is

---

APPLICATION **1.4**

James is an attorney practicing law in a small community. He frequently is involved in local real estate transactions. Wilford Beaumont owns 3,500 acres of farmland. Wilford is preparing to retire and wishes to sell off much of the land to several different individuals. Wilford plans to sell the property by accepting monthly payments from the individuals at the current rate of interest until the property is paid off. James has been hired to prepare all the proper documentation to complete the transaction. Wilford also has required a good faith deposit from each of the potential purchasers while the documents are prepared. When all of the proper documentation is signed, the amount deposited will be applied toward the sale. However, until that time, it is to be held by a third party. James has been retained to hold the money because he is already involved in preparation of the legal documents. Thus, James is a fiduciary of Wilford with regard to the attorney-client relationship, and he also is a financial fiduciary to Wilford and the purchasers. James not only is responsible to act in Wilford's best interest legally, he also must protect the financial assets placed in his care.

received from an opposing party in litigation. The attorney is responsible to see that any outstanding expenses of the client in litigation, as well as any attorney's fees due, are satisfied and the remainder given to the client. Some attorneys hold funds in "trust" for clients; in this situation, the attorney manages money for the client in accordance with a legal trust document. Trusts often are used for the benefit of minors, incapacitated adults, and others who may not be capable of acting in their own best interest with regard to financial matters.

In each of these instances, and in any other situation in which an attorney holds funds on behalf of a client, the attorney is obligated to honor the trust of that client. This is accomplished in a variety of ways. First, a client's funds cannot be commingled with the funds of the attorney. The attorney may not borrow or in any other way access the client's funds for use not directly benefiting the client and/or for specifically agreed-on purposes. A proper accounting of the safekeeping and disposition of the funds is due to the client who has placed his or her trust in the attorney.

Although the obligation of a fiduciary is one based on trust and is, in turn, a matter of ethical conduct, for the law firm it is also a matter of a legal obligation. Over the years, a number of attorneys have been on the receiving end of severe disciplinary action and even criminal charges as a result of mishandling client funds. Exhibit 1–1 is an excerpt from the New York Lawyer's Fund for Client Protection. This excerpt includes common requirements found in most jurisdictions with regard to handling of client funds.

EXHIBIT 1–1   WHAT ARE A LAWYER'S ETHICAL OBLIGATIONS REGARDING CLIENT FUNDS?

A lawyer in possession of client funds and property is a fiduciary. The lawyer must safeguard and segregate those assets from the lawyer's personal, business or other assets. A lawyer is also obligated to notify a client when client funds or property are received by the lawyer. The lawyer must provide timely and complete accountings to the client, and disburse promptly all funds and property to which the client is entitled. A client's non-cash property should be clearly identified as trust property and be secured in the lawyer's safe or in a safe deposit box. These fiduciary obligations apply equally to money and property of non-clients that come into a lawyer's possession in the practice of law.

What is an attorney trust account?

It is a "special" bank account, usually a checking account or its equivalent, for client money and other escrow funds that a lawyer holds in the practice of law. A lawyer can have one account, or several, depending on need. Each must be maintained separately from the lawyer's personal business accounts, and other fiduciary accounts, like those maintained for

(continues)

EXHIBIT I–I   WHAT ARE A LAWYER'S ETHICAL OBLIGATIONS REGARDING CLIENT FUNDS? *(continued)*

estates, guardianships, and trusts. Attorney trust accounts must be maintained in banking institutions located within New York State, that is, a "state or national bank, trust company, savings bank, savings and loan association or credit union". Out-of-state banks may be used only with the prior and specific written approval of the client or other beneficial owner of the funds. In all cases, lawyers can only use banks that have agreed to furnish "dishonored check notices" pursuant to new statewide court rules. These new rules also require lawyers to designate existing or new bank accounts as either Attorney Trust Account, Attorney Special Account, or Attorney Escrow Account, with pre-numbered checks and deposit slips imprinted with that title.

What is the purpose of an attorney trust account?

To safeguard clients' funds from loss, and to avoid the appearance of impropriety by the lawyer-fiduciary. The account is used solely for funds belonging to clients and other persons incident to a lawyer's practice of law. Funds belonging partly to a client and partly to the lawyer, presently or potentially, must also be deposited in the attorney trust account. The lawyer's portion may be withdrawn when due, unless the client disputes the withdrawal. In that event, the funds must remain intact until the lawyer and client resolve their dispute. Withdrawals from the attorney trust account must be made to named payees, and not to cash. And only members of the New York bar can be signatories on the bank account.

What about bank service charges?

A lawyer may deposit personal funds into the attorney trust account that are necessary to maintain the account, including bank service charges.

Should interest-bearing accounts be used?

Lawyers, as fiduciaries, should endeavor to make client funds productive for their clients. By statute, every lawyer has complete discretion to determine whether client and escrow funds should be deposited in interest-bearing bank accounts. For funds nominal in amount, or which will be held only briefly by a lawyer or law firm, the statute authorizes their deposit in so-called IOLA bank accounts. But lawyers may also establish interest-bearing accounts for individual clients. For all client funds, lawyers may use pooled accounts in banks which have the capability to credit interest to individual client sub-accounts. A lawyer or law firm may also do the calculations necessary to allocate interest to individual clients or other beneficial owners.

(continues)

EXHIBIT 1-1   WHAT ARE A LAWYER'S ETHICAL OBLIGATIONS REGARDING
CLIENT FUNDS? *(continued)*

How should large trust deposits be handled?

When a client's funds and the anticipated holding period are sufficient to generate
meaningful interest, a lawyer may have a fiduciary obligation to invest the client's funds in an
interest-bearing bank account.In that case, prudence suggests that a lawyer consult with the
client or other beneficial owner. And when dealing with large deposits and escrows, lawyers
and clients should be mindful of federal bank deposit insurance limits.There may also be
income tax implications to consider. Using the law client's social security or federal tax
identification number on the bank account can avoid unexpected tax problems for
the lawyer.

May a lawyer retain the interest on an attorney trust account?

No. A lawyer, as a fiduciary, cannot profit on the administration of an attorney trust
account. While a lawyer is permitted to charge a reasonable fee for administering a
client's account, all earned interest belongs to the client. Legal fees cannot be pegged to the
interest earned.

Are there special banking rules for down payments?

Yes. A buyer's down payment, entrusted with a seller's attorney pending a closing, generally
remains the property of the buyer until title passes. The lawyer-escrow agent is serving as a
fiduciary, and must safeguard and segregate the buyer's down payment in a special trust
account. The purchase contract should make provisions for depositing the down payment in
a bank account, the disposition of interest, and other escrow responsibilities. A 1991 statute
codifies the fiduciary obligations of lawyers and Realtors who accept down payments in
residential purchases and sales, including condominium units and cooperative apartments.
This statute requires that the purchase contract identify: (1) the escrow agent and (2) the
bank where the down payment will be deposited pending the closing. There are also special
rules, promulgated by the New York State Department of Law, where escrow accounts are
established in connection with the conversion of buildings into condominiums and
cooperatives.

Are other bank accounts needed?

Yes. A practitioner needs a business account as a depository for legal fees, and to pay
operating expenses. A typical designation is Attorney Business Account. Lawyers also need
special bank accounts when they serve as fiduciaries for estates, trusts, guardianships, and
the like.

(continues)

EXHIBIT 1–1   WHAT ARE A LAWYER'S ETHICAL OBLIGATIONS REGARDING CLIENT FUNDS? *(continued)*

Where are advance legal fees deposited?

This depends upon the lawyer's fee agreement with the client. If the advance fee becomes the lawyer's property when it is paid by the client, the fee should be deposited in the business account, and not in the attorney trust account. If, on the other hand, the advance fee remains client property until it is earned by the lawyer, it should be deposited in the attorney trust account, and withdrawn by the lawyer or law firm as it is earned. In either event, a lawyer has a professional obligation to refund unearned legal fees to a client whenever the lawyer completes or withdraws from a representation, or the lawyer is discharged by the client.

And advances from clients for court fees and expenses?

This also depends upon the lawyer's fee agreement with the client. If the money advanced by the client is to remain client property until it is used for specific litigation expenses, it should be segregated and safeguarded in the attorney trust account, or in a similar special account.

How are unclaimed client funds handled?

If a lawyer cannot locate a client or another person who is owed funds from the attorney trust account, the lawyer is required to seek a judicial order to fix the lawyer's fees and disbursements, and to deposit the client's share with the Lawyers' Fund for Client Protection.

What happens when a sole signatory dies?

The Supreme Court has authority to appoint a successor signatory for the attorney trust account. The procedures are set forth in court rules adopted in 1994.

What accounting books are required?

No specific accounting system is required by court rule, but a basic trust accounting system for a law firm consists of a trust receipts journal, a trust disbursements journal, and a trust ledger book containing the individual ledger accounts for recording each financial transaction affecting that client's funds. At a minimum, each client's ledger account should reflect the date, source, and a description of each item of deposit, as well as the date, payee, and purpose of each withdrawal. Many practitioners find that the so-called "one-write" or "pegboard" manual systems provide an efficient and economical method of trust accounting.

(continues)

EXHIBIT 1–1   WHAT ARE A LAWYER'S ETHICAL OBLIGATIONS REGARDING
CLIENT FUNDS? *(continued)*

There are also approved computer software packages for law office trust accounting. Whether it be an attorney trust account or the lawyer's operating account, each should be maintained daily and accurately to avoid error. All source documents like duplicate deposit slips, bank statements, canceled checks, checkbooks and check stubs must be preserved for seven years.Internal office controls are essential. It is good business practice to prepare a monthly reconciliation of the balances in the trust ledger book, the trust receipts and disbursements journals, the bank account checkbook, and bank statements.

What bookkeeping records must be maintained?

Every lawyer and law firm must preserve, for seven years after the events they record, copies of all:

- books of account affecting all attorney trust and office operating accounts.

- checkbooks and check stubs, bank statements, pre-numbered canceled checks and duplicate deposit slips.

- client retainer and fee agreements.

- statements to clients showing disbursements of their funds.

- records showing payments to other lawyers or non-employees for services rendered.

- retainer and closing statements filed with the Office of Court Administration.

- In the event a law firm dissolves, appropriate arrangements must be made for the maintenance of the firm's records, either by a former partner or the successor law firm. In the absence of an agreement, the local Appellate Division has the authority to impose an arrangement.

How are these rules enforced?

A violation of a Disciplinary Rule constitutes grounds for professional discipline under section 90 of the Judiciary Law. Also, the accounts and records required of lawyers and law firms by court rule may be subpoenaed in a disciplinary proceeding.Lawyers are also required to certify their familiarity and compliance with Disciplinary Rule 9-102 in the biennial registration form which is filed with the Office of Court Administration.

New York Lawyer's Fund For Client Protection

APPLICATION 1.5

Sharon suffers from extreme bipolar disorder. She receives money from various sources each month in amounts that are more than sufficient to meet her basic needs. However, when in a manic phase of her mental illness, she is prone to spending great sums of money at the local discount store. She then promptly donates the purchases to a charity. This often leaves her unable to pay her living expenses. As a result, she has placed her income into a trust account. A local attorney and friend manages the account, pays Sharon's bills, and issues her a weekly allowance. Although the attorney has done this for several years, he has never kept any formal records with regard to his management of the account. Recently, Sharon married a man she met online a few months ago. He brings ethical charges against the attorney and obtains strong disciplinary action against the attorney including a nine-month suspension from practicing law. Although the attorney has never abused his access to Sharon's money, without any proper accounting he is unable to prove this and his careless recordkeeping is in and of itself a serious violation of legal and ethical standards, whether or not he injured Sharon.

ASSIGNMENT 1.1

Consider the following that occur within a normal month of business and determine whether they would most specifically impact the accounting function of a law firm as (A) a business; (B) an employer; (C) a fiduciary or (D) none of the above. More than one choice may be appropriate. Explain your answer.

1. Anne is paid hourly and works 43 hours in one week.

2. Mike is a legal investigator and wants to be paid for 12 hours of interviews that he conducted. These interviews were conducted on behalf of Client L.

3. A check for $346 dollars is issued to Office Buddies Supply Company.

4. A check for $3,890 is issued to Client X as his share of a settlement received in a lawsuit.

5. The decision is made to fire George the next time he is caught using company property for personal use.

6. Madeline has been fired and her final check needs to be prepared.

7. Client M has sent in a $2,500 retainer.

8. Office Buddies Supply Company has issued a credit for $137 in returned office supplies.

(continues)

ASSIGNMENT **1.1** *(continued)*

9. Your Local Power Company has adjusted your budget billing monthly electric bill for the year. It has been increased from $452 to $478 per month.

10. AMC, the malpractice insurance company, has issued a premium refund of $345 for the unused portion of an insurance policy on an attorney who left the firm.

11. The law firm changed the company that provides cellular service.

12. An invoice is received for office stationary that was recently ordered.

13. An invoice is received for business cards recently ordered for the attorneys.

14. Joe's income for this year means that he is no longer required to pay into Social Security.

15. Mara has recently returned from maternity leave and currently has no unused sick time.

16. Roberta turns in an hourly report for trips to court on behalf of Client Y.

17. A check is written to Super Subs for sandwiches delivered to the monthly staff meeting.

18. Mark turns in a statement requesting that his bar association dues be paid. The firm pays all bar association dues for its attorneys as a job benefit. Mark is the senior partner in the firm. Bar association membership is required as part of state licensure.

19. Susan requests mileage reimbursement. She is the office runner who carries out all deliveries and pickups for the office.

20. An invoice is received from an expert witness who has testified in the case of Client O.

ASSIGNMENT **1.2**

In the following case, detail the proper process necessary for the defendant to have avoided ethical charges and subsequent disciplinary action.

JUDICIAL OPINION
STATE V. CLOWER, 831 A.2D 1030 (D.C. APP. 2003).

Respondent represented Claudia Bradford in a personal injury action against the District of Columbia. In connection with that action, respondent and Ms. Bradford executed an "authorization and assignment" agreement with Nathaniel Randolph, who was Ms. Bradford's physical therapist. The agreement obligated respondent to pay Mr. Randolph's fees from the proceeds of any recovery in the personal injury action. Mr. Randolph thereafter continued to provide therapy to Ms. Bradford and testified on her behalf at trial. The jury returned a verdict in Ms. Bradford's favor for $192,000, and the District of Columbia noted an appeal.

Two years later, while the appeal was pending, the District of Columbia and Ms. Bradford agreed to settle. On May 7, 1996, the District forwarded to respondent a $100,000 settlement draft payable to Ms. Bradford and respondent. Respondent deposited the draft into his escrow account and prepared a settlement and disbursement statement for his client's approval. The statement allocated $5,499 of the settlement to Mr. Randolph. The statement further provided that respondent would receive $35,496.10 ($33,000 in attorney's fees and $2,496.10 for costs that respondent had advanced). Except for a few hundred dollars payable to Suburban Credit, Ms. Bradford was allocated the balance of the settlement, $58,565.64.

Ms. Bradford approved the proposed distributions and, for personal reasons, requested that respondent defer distributing her share of the settlement proceeds to her. As an accommodation to his client, who was disabled, respondent agreed to continue to hold Ms. Bradford's portion of the settlement funds in his escrow account. In accordance with the settlement and disbursement statement, respondent paid himself and Suburban Credit. He did not, however, pay Mr. Randolph.

On May 9, 1996, respondent prepared a letter to Mr. Randolph advising him that the lawsuit had been settled and asking him to accept a fifty percent reduction in his fee. The letter stated that the full $5,499 due Mr. Randolph would be held in escrow for him. For unknown reasons, this letter was never sent. Mr. Randolph did not learn of the settlement until he made inquiry of respondent over two years later, in September 1998. Meanwhile, between July 1996 and September 1998, respondent issued a series of checks distributing the remaining settlement funds to Ms. Bradford herself and to three payees who were not listed on the settlement and disbursement statement. Until August 1998, respondent still held sufficient funds in his escrow account to pay Mr. Randolph the $5,499 that the statement showed he was entitled to receive. By then, however, respondent had forgotten about his obligation to pay Mr. Randolph. In August and September 1998, respondent distributed the last of the settlement funds in his possession. Respondent never checked his records before making these distributions to ensure that he had made all the payments called for on the settlement and disbursement statement.

(continues)

JUDICIAL OPINION
STATE V. CLOWER, 831 A.2D 1030 (D.C. APP. 2003). *(continued)*

When Mr. Randolph finally contacted respondent in September 1998, respondent informed him that Ms. Bradford's case had been settled and that all of the settlement funds had been distributed. Mr. Randolph complained to Bar Counsel that respondent had failed to pay his bill as required by the authorization and assignment agreement that respondent and Ms. Bradford had signed. Bar Counsel opened an investigation.

In the course of the investigation, Bar Counsel requested records demonstrating that Ms. Bradford had authorized the payments from her settlement funds to the several persons who were not listed on the settlement sheet. In response to that request, Ms. Bradford provided a letter confirming that respondent had made those payments with her knowledge and consent. However, respondent had no contemporaneous written records evidencing his client's authorization or explaining why he made the disbursements from her funds in his escrow account.

By virtue of the authorization and assignment agreement, Mr. Randolph had an interest in the settlement proceeds. Rule 1.15(b). therefore required respondent to "promptly notify" Mr. Randolph upon his receipt of those proceeds and to "promptly deliver" to Mr. Randolph the funds he was entitled to receive. The Board on Professional Responsibility found, and respondent does not dispute, that respondent violated these requirements. See In Re Shaw, 775 A.2d 1123 (D.C. 2001). We agree. We also note that while respondent's failure to notify and pay Mr. Randolph was, in the Board's words, "a negligent oversight," respondent prolonged his failure to pay even after Mr. Randolph brought the oversight to respondent's attention. Mr. Randolph still had not been paid by January of 2000, when he appeared before the Hearing Committee in this matter.

The Board concluded that respondent also violated Rule 1.15 (a) and D.C. Bar R. XI, § 19(f), by failing to keep "complete records" of the settlement funds he held for Ms. Bradford between May 1996 and September 1998 The Board found that respondent's records were incomplete because they were "devoid of any written explanation as to why he was distributing his client's funds to various third parties" whose names were not shown on the settlement and disbursement statement his client had approved. The Board explained its interpretation of the "complete records" requirement as follows:

Rule 1.15(a) provides in pertinent part as follows:

(a) A lawyer shall hold property of clients or third persons that is in the lawyer's possession in connection with a representation separate from the lawyer's own property. Funds shall be kept in a separate account. . . .. Complete records of such account funds . . . shall be kept by the lawyer and shall be preserved for a period of five years after termination of the representation.

(continues)

JUDICIAL OPINION
STATE V. CLOWER, 831 A.2D 1030 (D.C. APP. 2003). *(continued)*

Section 19 (f) of D.C.App. Rule XI similarly provides in pertinent part as follows:

(f) Required records. Every attorney subject to the disciplinary jurisdiction of this Court shall maintain complete records of the handling, maintenance, and disposition of all funds . . . belonging to another person . . . at any time in the attorney's possession, from the time of receipt to the time of final distribution, and shall preserve such records for a period of five years after final distribution of such funds. . . ..

Bar Counsel contended that the "complete records" requirement imposed a duty on respondent to maintain contemporaneous written authorizations from his client for each disbursement from the settlement proceeds. The Board was "not convinced that a contemporary written authorization by the client is the only method for making 'complete records.'"

The Rules of Professional Conduct should be interpreted with reference to their purposes. The purpose of maintaining "complete records" is so that the documentary record itself tells the full story of how the attorney handled client or third-party funds and whether the attorney complied with his fiduciary obligation that client or third-party funds not be misappropriated or commingled. Financial records are complete only when documents sufficient to demonstrate an attorney's compliance with his ethical duties are maintained. The reason for requiring complete records is so that any audit of the attorney's handling of client funds by Bar Counsel can be completed even if the attorney or the client, or both, are not available.

In this matter, had Respondent or Ms. Bradford not been available to testify that Respondent's checks disbursing her settlement funds to unknown parties were properly issued, the documents maintained by Respondent would not have been sufficient to establish that Respondent was in compliance with his fiduciary duties. Absent proof that the checks issued to Ms. Bradford's acquaintances were properly issued, the Clients' Security Trust Fund might have been required to compensate Ms. Bradford's heirs. See D.C. Bar R. XII, § 3, "Purpose of Trust Fund."

We agree fully with the Board's reasoning and its conclusion that respondent violated his duty to maintain "complete records" of the account in which he held his client's settlement proceeds. Respondent argues that the Board adopted a novel interpretation of a vague requirement——the Rules do not define the term "complete records"——and that it is unfair to hold him accountable under a more rigorous record keeping standard than was in place at the time he disbursed Ms. Bradford's funds. Respondent emphasizes that he did maintain records that showed each disbursement he made and that identified each payee. In re Choroszej 624 A.2d 434, (D.C. 1992). (holding that attorney failed to maintain complete records in violation of Disciplinary Rule [DR] 9-103(B)(3), the predecessor to Rule 1.15(a),

(continues)

JUDICIAL OPINION
STATE V. CLOWER, 831 A.2D 1030 (D.C. APP. 2003). *(continued)*

where he could not produce a ledger of the checks he had written on a client trust account or bank statements and accounting records showing what was paid to or received from his clients).

We reject respondent's argument. The Board's interpretation of the "complete records" requirement strikes us as only common sense, and it is not novel. See In re Jones, 521 A.2d 1119 (D.C. 1986). (adopting Board report finding a violation of DR 9-103(B)(3) where attorney could not furnish documentary justification for disputed disbursements); see also the Model Rule on Financial Record keeping adopted by the American Bar Association in 1993, that lists in detail the records a lawyer should keep. Moreover, the gaps in respondent's records were blatant: his settlement and disbursement statement purported to list the persons entitled to shares of the settlement proceeds, but he made payments to persons who were not listed and failed to pay one person who was listed. Nothing in respondent's records explained these obvious discrepancies.

The Board recommends a public censure as the appropriate sanction for respondent's failures to notify and pay Mr. Randolph promptly and to maintain complete records of client funds. Respondent argues that a public censure is too harsh and is inconsistent with sanctions imposed in similar cases; he asks us to consider an informal admonition instead. Our Rules provide that we "shall adopt the recommended disposition of the Board unless to do so would foster a tendency toward inconsistent dispositions for comparable conduct or would otherwise be unwarranted." D.C. Bar R. XI, § 9(g)(1). "Although the ultimate choice of a sanction rests with this court, we are obliged to respect the Board's sense of equity in these matters unless that exercise of judgment proves to be unreasonable." In re Ross, 658 A.2d 209 (D.C. 1995). (internal quotation marks and citations omitted). Based on the gravity of respondent's prolonged failure to notify or pay Mr. Randolph (which was exacerbated by respondent's failure to pay even after the omission was brought to respondent's attention), respondent's disbursement to others of the funds in which Mr. Randolph had an interest, the sizable amount at stake, and the absence of mitigating factors, we cannot disagree with the Board that a public censure is appropriate and consistent with the sanctions imposed in similar cases. See, e.g., In Re Shaw 775 A.2d 1125 (imposing public censure on attorney who failed to pay a third-party medical provider and charged an excessive legal fee); In Re Mitchell, 727 A.2d. 308 (D.C. 1999). (public censure for failure to deliver client funds to client in conjunction with other ethical violations).

For the foregoing reasons, we adopt the recommendation of the Board that respondent Donald A. Clower be publicly censured for violating Rules 1.15(a) and 1.15(b) of the District of Columbia Rules of Professional Conduct and D.C. Bar R. XI, § 19(f).

So ordered.

ETHICAL QUESTION

Mary Jo has deposited a $3,000 down payment on a real estate transaction to be held in escrow by Attorney Jenkins. There is a contract that specifies that this money is to be held for the buyer and seller until the contract of sale is completed. If the sale is not completed, the terms of the contract address various circumstances that might occur and how the money is to be handled in the event of an incomplete contract. If the contract is completed, the money will be disbursed to Mary Jo. However, Mary's mortgage payment on the property will be delinquent after February 14. She is already behind and this is her final date to pay and avoid foreclosure proceedings. The closing is not scheduled until February 20. Everything is in order for the sale, and all that is left is for the buyers to come into town on the 17th, sign, and provide final payment. As a result, Mary calls Attorney Jenkins on February 13 and asks that the $3,000 be paid on the 14th to the bank holding the mortgage on the property.

What would be the potential ethical issue for Attorney Jenkins if the money is disbursed prematurely as Mary Jo has requested?

SUMMARY

In this chapter, the basic purpose of accounting within the law practice has been introduced. As discussed, accounting is an integral part of any business, but there are particular concerns and applications in law offices. The law firm must operate under the same general accounting principles and standards of any business for the purpose of tracking profit, loss, general business health, and government required record keeping and reporting. However, the practice of law also brings additional concerns for the accounting process. There often are a variety of individuals compensated by the law practice, including owner/partners, employees, periodic employees, and independent contractors. Additionally, the law practice often is responsible not only for its own financial transactions but also for those of its clients. This requires both ethical and legal compliance with established rules that detail the nature and process of accounting to be used. All in all, the number of accounting issues that face the typical law firm are complex and require substantial professional skill.

KEY TERMS

Accounting   Fiduciary

For additional resources, visit our Web site at www.westlegalstudies.com

CHAPTER 2

Accounting Foundations

After completing this chapter, you will be able to:

❏ Explain basic accounting terms

❏ Distinguish the fiscal and calendar year methods in accounting

❏ Distinguish Permanent and Temporary accounts

❏ Discuss the Double Entry bookkeeping method

❏ Describe the commonly used accounting documents

A. ACCOUNTING TERMINOLOGY

Like most professions, accounting has a language of its own. There are a large number of terms, some unique and some that have both generic definitions and those specific to accounting. These terms are employed by individuals and businesses engaged in accounting practices. This language of accounting allows businesses and individuals to communicate more effectively with one another and with government entities as well. Without such terminology, much more detailed explanations would be necessary and the opportunity for miscommunication would increase dramatically. As a result, relevant terms make the practice of accounting more efficient and accurate. A number of terms that are frequently used in accounting and often seen in the running of a professional business such as a law office are described in this chapter (see Exhibit 2–5 on pg 39-47). In the example that follows, the danger of inadequate knowledge is demonstrated.

APPLICATION 2.1

Nancy was a recent law school graduate. She had returned to school after raising her family and now wanted to start her own law practice. She received her license in the fall and planned to open her new practice on the first of January. To save money on start-up expenses, Nancy hired her 19-year-old daughter, Sara, to do the daily bookkeeping for the business. At the end of the first year, Nancy took the bookkeeping to an accountant in town for preparation of the necessary tax forms. In order to begin preparation of the tax documents and to set up a file for future use, the accountant submitted a list of questions and requests for information to Sara. Specifically, the accountant requested the following:

- Ledger Balances
- Basis, % of use, and accumulated depreciation or amortization schedules for all new and converted capital assets
- Chart of Accounts
- Monthly Financial Statements including Income Statements and Balance Sheets
- Current and Projected Retained Earnings and Draw accounts
- Payroll account balances
- Quarterly Tax Documents for payment of estimated income, and employment taxes

Sara had no formal training in accounting. Furthermore, she and her mother did not see the need for anything fancy because the business was just starting out. Sara opened a checking account and kept a regular checkbook. Any time she or her mother wanted to take money out of the business, they would deposit checks from clients into their personal accounts for the rather than passing them through the business account. Each client's record of payments and charges was kept on a piece of note paper in that client's file. No quarterly tax documents were filed of any kind. None of the other documents requested by the accountant even existed, just a drawer full of receipts and monthly bank statements (which did not include canceled checks).

Because Sara and her mother did not have an understanding of basic accounting principles and terminology, the necessary information to properly record the activities of the business were in complete disarray. A tremendous amount of time and expense was necessary to recreate an entire year of the business. In addition, the handling of client funds was, at the least, ethically questionable, and there was potential for substantial tax penalties.

B. THE FISCAL/CALENDAR YEAR

At first glance, it may seem foolish to dedicate a portion of the text to the definition of what constitutes a year. This would seem obvious to the average individual. However, the definition of a year and its components in accounting and tax terms may be quite different. Of course, in the United States, generally a year is calculated by using the traditional **calendar year**, which begins on January 1 and ends on December 31. There is a growing trend among businesses to use the calendar year for accounting as well as for tax purposes. This is done to measure the financial status of a business over a given period of time. Yet many businesses, and even some government entities, compute their year for accounting purposes using a different calendar. It is also wise to note that, although a company may use one time period for accounting purposes, another may be employed to satisfy governmental reporting requirements.

A business may elect to use a period for accounting that is different from the traditional calendar year. This is not a matter of consequence, as long as the period of accounting and reporting is in fact 52–53 weeks or 12 months. Until such time as a formal change is adopted and approved by appropriate authorities, the same fiscal year should be used each time. For example, a business may begin operations on July 1 and conclude the business accounting for the year on the following June 30. This is entirely acceptable and can continue each year thereafter until, if and when, the business would notify all interested parties that the fiscal year is to be changed to a different 12-month period. If the business uses the same period for tax purposes, the change to the **tax year** also must be approved by the government.

There is also a period known as a **short year**. In the short year, circumstances require that the accounting cycle of a business occur for a period of less than 12 months. This might occur if there is a change in ownership, a change in the dates elected for the fiscal year, the end of the business entity before the completion of a fiscal year, or in any other situation that would cause a substantial interruption in the normal business operations. Another example might be if a business begins during the year but wishes to use a calendar year for all future accounting and tax years. When a short year occurs, all of the same accounting records and tax documents are prepared as in a normal full year accounting cycle. However, they are prepared for the shortened period of time.

The tax year is the period of time covered by an annual return filed with state and local governments and reflecting business activity. If a business is on a calendar year, the tax year is the period covered by January 1–December 31. If a business is on a fiscal year, the tax year is typically the same one year period (52–53 weeks) defined by the stated fiscal year. A business may elect, however, to use the calendar year for tax purposes and a different fiscal year. This can create additional work, in that the business activity must be tracked for both the calendar year for taxes and for the fiscal year for business purposes. As a result, businesses generally follow the same tax year as fiscal year. Typically, the tax year is adopted officially with the filing of the first full year tax return. With respect to the tax year, the annual return for the business is

CALENDAR YEAR

Begins on January 1 and ends on December 31.

TAX YEAR

An annual accounting period for keeping records and reporting income and expenses. An annual accounting period does not include a short tax year. A tax year can be based on either the calendar year or the fiscal year.

SHORT YEAR

An accounting cycle of a business that occurs for a period of less than 12 months.

generally due no later than the 15th day of the fourth month after the end of the tax year. For example, if a business ends on a calendar year, the annual return is due on April 15. An exception applies to tax-exempt organizations. They must file an annual return by the 15th day of the fifth month after the end of the tax year. Once a tax year is adopted, the same tax year must continue to be used unless permission is received from the Internal Revenue Service (IRS) to alter the tax year, or if a short year occurs. A business is subject to a "required tax year" if the tax year for the particular type of business is required under the Internal Revenue Code and the Income Tax Regulations. A business has not adopted a tax year if it merely did any of the following:

- Filed an application for an extension of time to file an income tax return
- Filed an application for an employer identification number (EIN)
- Paid estimated taxes for that tax year

Even though a business may be on a fiscal and tax year schedule that differs from the regular calendar year, certain government documents must be filed according to the calendar year, an example of which is quarterly reports filed by employers. If a business employer does not have agricultural employees, it will file the quarterly reports that reflect the identity of employees, wages paid, various types of taxes withheld, and so on. It is necessary to file such reports quarterly and on the calendar-year basis for the benefit of the employees. Individuals follow the calendar year for tax purposes and as such must have their income reported according to that schedule. With this reporting requirement for businesses, governmental agencies are able to record wages properly for purposes of income tax issues, unemployment, Social Security, and so on. A great deal more of this discussion is provided with respect to periodic reporting in subsequent chapters. For the purpose of this chapter, it is important to note the various types of tax years that can be employed by a business when preparing accounting documents. Another widely accepted method of reporting transactions, known as **double entry**, is discussed in the following section.

DOUBLE ENTRY

A method of bookkeeping that records both the credit and debit elements of each financial transaction affecting a business.

APPLICATION **2.2**

Adam and Millie decide to open their own business. They incorporate and officially start business on June 30. Their attorney advises them that they need to make a choice of their tax and fiscal year and prepare accounting and governmental returns accordingly. They elect to use the calendar year. On September 15, they file a quarterly report with respect to wages paid the employees of the business. On December 31, they close the books for the year, declaring a short year. On April 15, they file the first annual return for the corporation. Even though business was only conducted for four months, it is treated as an annual return for a short year. The next return will be due in one year and will record activity for the period January through December.

(continues)

APPLICATION **2.2** *(continued)*

Consider the following: Adam and Millie decided to adopt a fiscal year beginning on September 1. In that instance, they would still file quarterly employee reports. However, nothing would be due in September because no business was transacted in the preceding quarter. The annual return would be filed in the appropriate time, following the close of business on August 31.

C. DOUBLE ENTRY ACCOUNTING

Every financial transaction of a business creates two effects: something is coming into the business and something is going out. For example, in a law office, legal services are outgoing to clients in exchange of payment or promise of payment coming in. In a retail business, a product from the inventory is outgoing in exchange for incoming cash or promise of payment. Whether or not the business trades in services or products, there is still an effect on two aspects of the business. Even as a business starts up, owners contribute capital assets such as cash, credit, furnishings, and so on in exchange for a share of ownership. As a result, it is necessary to record both elements of each financial transaction affecting a business. This is referred to as **double entry accounting** or double entry bookkeeping. Without the double entry system, an accurate picture of the overall health of the business would be difficult, if not impossible.

In larger businesses, the process of double entry accounting is often dispersed among different individuals. One may be responsible for recording the incoming aspect of the transaction, whereas another records the outgoing aspect. This is a safeguard for accuracy and honesty known as an **internal control**. In smaller

▇ **DOUBLE ENTRY ACCOUNTING**

Recording both elements of each financial transaction affecting a business.

▇ **INTERNAL CONTROL**

A safeguard for accuracy and honesty.

ASSIGNMENT **2.1**

For the following situations, determine when the next annual return would be due.

   a. A new business on a calendar year basis starts operations on July 15, 2006.

   b. An existing business on a calendar year basis filed a short year return on April 15, 2007.

   c. A new business on a fiscal year from the start of business begins operations on July 15, 2007.

   d. A tax-exempt organization starts business on May 1, 2006, and elects a calendar year.

   e. An existing business on a calendar year ends all business operations on February 1, 2006.

businesses, one individual may be responsible for both aspects of entering the transaction into accounting records. Even this provides some degree of safety, in that if one part of the two entries is recorded in error, it will show up when the balances do not correspond. However, if one person is in charge of both entries, it is important to have them reviewed periodically by someone else to ensure that the individual is not engaged in any sort of deliberate or careless misrecording of accounts.

DEBIT

A "to" or "plus" entry.

CREDIT

A "from" or "minus" entry.

When entries are made in a double entry system, each entry is listed as a **Debit** as well as a corresponding **Credit**. A Debit may be thought of as a "to" or "plus" entry. The debit is entered in the left-hand side of the column for the account that is somehow increased by the transaction. The corresponding Credit is a "from" or "minus" entry. It is recorded on the right-hand side of the column. It can be difficult to keep debit distinguished from credit. This is especially so because a credit usually is thought of as a positive rather than a negative. A simple way to keep them separated in one's mind is to think of a debit as a deposit. A debit increases a balance. In the event of an expense account, it increases the expenses or associated debt. In the event of an asset account, it increases the value of the asset.

APPLICATION **2.3**

Sam is in charge of bookkeeping for a small law practice. On September 15, one of the attorneys turns in a receipt indicating that she made several purchases for the firm at an office supply outlet. The purchases include a $2,000 desk, a $1,000 filing cabinet, and $500 in consumable office supplies such as printer cartridges, file folders, paper, and so on. Sam records in accounts payable the amount of $3,500 to be paid to the attorney. He similarly records increases in the capital assets account $3,000 for office furnishings, and in the office supplies account $500. At the end of the month, the decrease in cash will correspond to the increase in other assets, namely, furnishings and supplies.

Now assume that Sam erroneously recorded $2,000 rather than $3,000 in the capital assets account. At the end of the month, the balances of assets against outgoing funds will not match by $1,000. In a review of the financial transactions for the month of September, it is clear that on September 15, $3,500 went out but only $2,500 came in. Further investigation can reveal the entry error. Without balancing accounts, this might not be discovered and the assets of the business would be understated.

Finally, assume that Sam was in the business of taking self-appointed raises. On September 15, he recorded an increase in capital assets in the amount of $4,000. He also recorded outgoing funds in the amount of $4,000 (a $3,500 check to the attorney and $500 in cash also noted for the attorney). Technically, the books would balance and there would be no cause for question if the periodic accounting documents showed balancing entries. However, the disbursement of part cash and part check would likely appear somewhat unusual to one reviewing the books of the business. And in an audit in which invoices and receipts were matched to accounting entries, the figures would not match.

In order to create the equal balance of double entry accounting, it is necessary to have an equation that is used consistently to represent the various entries, regardless of the specific accounts in which they are recorded. This universally accepted equation is as follows:

ASSETS = LIABILITIES + EQUITY

When thought through, this equation makes perfect sense. The assets are the items of value owned by the business itself. It is necessary, however, to take into account any items that involve a lien or debt of the business that affect the actual percentage of ownership. The difference between assets and liabilities is the amount owned outright and that is known as equity, represented by the ownership interest and the debts of the business. Consider the following. A car is purchased for $10,000. The owner of the car pays $4,000 and borrows the remaining $6,000, thus creating a liability. The car is an asset. Its worth is $10,000, and that figure represents 100% of it as an asset. The figure also equals the percentage of ownership ($4,000 or 40%) plus the liability or debt ($6,000 or 60%).

In order to balance a double entry accounting system, the financial transaction is recorded as it affects the asset side of the equation as well as how it affects the liability or equity side of the equation. If something is bought 100% with borrowed money, it would be recorded as an increase in asset and an equal increase in liability. If it were to be paid for in cash, the transaction would be entered as an increase in asset and an equivalent increase in equity. If an asset were disposed of, there would still be a double entry. However, that entry would decrease on each side of the equation. The asset would be removed, as would the equity or liability of the asset. The entries are recorded in a general ledger that includes a description of all transactions and in the particular accounts that best represents the transaction. What follows are a few of the sample accounts that might be found under the various Assets, Liabilities, and Equity portions of the accounting books for a particular business such as a law practice.

ASSETS	LIABILITIES	EQUITY
Accounts Receivable	Accounts Payable	Owner A Capital
Cash	Taxes Payable	Owner B Capital
Electronic Equipment	Notes Payable	

D. PERMANENT VERSUS TEMPORARY ACCOUNTS

Within each of the primary three categories of the accounting equation are two distinct types of accounts. These are known as Permanent and Temporary Accounts. The permanent accounts carry balances forward from one accounting period to another.

APPLICATION 2.4

Assume that three practicing attorneys decide to form a partnership. In order to start up the business, they each make contributions. On April 16, Partner A contributes $30,000 in cash. Partner B contributes a computer system valued at $25,000. Partner C contributes his accounts receivable from his existing practice, valued at $45,000. In addition, the partners take out a $75,000 note payable in the form of a two-year business loan to cover start-up expenses, initial payroll, and so on. These transactions might be recorded in the following way.

1. $30,000 in the Equity column to capital account A, and $30,000 to the Asset column cash account.

4/16	Cash		30,000	
	Capital Account A			30,000

2. $25,000 in the Equity column to capital account B, and $25,000 in the electronic equipment account in the Asset column.

4/16	Equipment		25,000	
	Capital Account B			25,000

3. $45,000 in the Equity column to capital account C, and $45,000 in the Asset column under the accounts receivable column.

4/16	Accounts Receivable		45,000	
		Capital Account C		45,000

4. $75,000 in the liability column under notes payable and $75,000 in the Asset column under Cash or another asset account such as Loan Proceeds.

4/16	Cash		75,000	
		Notes Payable		75,000

An example would be an owner's capital account in the Equity column. The owner's percentage of ownership does not change simply because the books are closed out for the accounting period. Rather, that balance would be the final entry in accounting period and the first entry in the new accounting period. Permanent accounts are always reflected on the balance sheet for the business. The balance sheet is discussed in much greater detail later in this chapter and in subsequent chapters. It is necessary at this time only to know that the balance sheet is used to illustrate the accounting equation for a particular business on a particular date.

The other account is known as a temporary account. The rationale for these accounts is quite simple. A business may need to keep track of various short-term and subcategories of information within an accounting period. However, the account may not be used in the future, or it may be one of several similar accounts that can be reported together for the purpose of financial statements. With regard to temporary accounts, consider an account receivable for a particular client in a law office. That client may have one short-term legal issue, such as probate of an estate. Although it is important to keep track of each client's payments, and to keep them separate from other clients, it is not necessary to place each client in a permanent slot in the accounting books. Once a client's case is completed and payment has been fulfilled, that client's account is no longer required. It is also not necessary to report every single item of income individually at the end of the accounting period. For example, when an accounting cycle is completed, the total accumulation of all the accounts receivable can be reported as a single sum.

Other accounts include revenue and expense accounts. These accounts are used on the Equity side of the accounting equation. Such accounts increase (through revenues) or decrease (through expenses) the capital or value of the interest of the owners. At the end of an accounting period, the net increase or decrease of these accounts is reflected in a net increase or decrease in the equity portion of the accounting equation. Such short-term accounts are temporary. Often, they will have only a handful of entries necessary to show an increase or decrease over time. For example, at the end of a year, a computer system is worth less than it was at the beginning of the year. At that time, the expense account can be used to record a decrease in value equal to the amount of depreciation of the item.

ASSIGNMENT 2.2

Consider the transactions described here. For each, identify the proper side of the accounting equation in which the transaction should be recorded. Second, identify and explain whether the accounts used to record the transaction are likely to be temporary or permanent.

(continues)

1. A one-year note for a computer system is paid off.

2. A bill is received for the costs of a deposition of an expert witness in a client's case. By contract, the client is responsible for all attorneys' fees and expenses associated with the case.

3. New office furniture is purchased for the reception area.

4. A new partner is merged into the firm and brings both his accounts receivable and accounts payable from his former individual practice.

5. Quarterly payroll taxes (withheld from payroll checks and an accrued employer's share) are paid to the federal government.

E. BASIC ACCOUNTING DOCUMENTS

For each business, a series of documents are prepared that reflect the financial activity. The **General Journal** contains the **Chart of Accounts**, and a place in which the specific transactions are recorded by date, amount, and accounts affected. In addition, a ledger is kept for each of the individual accounts, in which the debits and credits for the particular accounts along with the date they occurred are recorded. Then, at the end of various accounting periods and the annual accounting cycle, these transactions are recorded, combined, and summarized in a variety of accounting documents such as the **Trial Balance**, **Balance Sheet**, **Income Statement**, government reports, and so on. The following discussion and subsequent chapters give a more thorough explanation of how each of these plays an integral role in the accounting process.

1. General Ledger/Journals

Ordinarily, a business will maintain a general journal. This is where all of the financial transactions are recorded. For example, at the end of the day in a law office, an entry in the general journal might be made that includes the date and debits the Cash account for an amount representing the payments that came in that day to increase the asset of Cash. The accounts receivable account also would be credited to show a decrease in the amount owed by clients. This is also an asset account and thus it does not affect the accounting equation of assets = liability plus equity. But, it does show a more accurate view of what the assets actually are. For that reason, it should be recorded.

Every accounting system, regardless of the type or size of business, maintains a Chart of Accounts in the General Journal. This is simply a listing of the accounts used to track financial transactions of the business. What accounts are created is largely

GENERAL JOURNAL

Contains the Chart of Accounts, and is a place in which the specific transactions are recorded by date, amount, and accounts affected.

CHART OF ACCOUNTS

A listing of the accounts used to track financial transactions of the business.

TRIAL BALANCE

The final tally or balance for every account in the Chart of Accounts.

dictated by the type of business. For example, a business whose primary commodity is service for fee such as a law practice will not typically maintain accounts for things such as inventory, raw materials, and so on. By contrast, a retail business typically will not maintain accounts for such things as professional liability (malpractice) insurance, escrowed funds, and so on. However, there are a large number of financial transactions that occur in all types of business and they contribute significantly to the usual Chart of Accounts that is established when a new business begins. There are no absolutes as to what should be included in a Chart of Accounts. Rather, thought should be given to the nature of the business, its sources of income, its assets, and its liabilities. Reference to general accounting texts, texts applied to accounting of specific businesses, and information required on relevant governmental tax forms can provide a great deal of guidance in the accounts that should be established.

Typically, the Chart of Accounts will be organized by grouping like accounts. For example, Asset accounts are listed under the Assets section; Liabilities and Equity accounts are organized similarly as well. There also may be an additional section to detail short-term or temporary accounts. These would be maintained under Revenue and Expense sections that increase and decrease the owner's capital accounts. Ultimately, the more detailed a Chart of Accounts, the easier it will be to prepare periodic financial statements, tax reports, and other documentation that may be required in the course of the business cycle. In addition to organizing accounts that are similar in purpose, it is also common to number accounts. For example, Asset accounts would be listed as a four-digit number beginning with 1xxx, Liability accounts would begin with the number 2xxx, Equity accounts would begin with 3xxx, and so on. By using a four-digit number, there is room for a business to grow. Using a number to represent the individual accounts also makes recording transactions much easier, as a four-digit number rather an entire account description can be used when transactions are initially recorded into the general journal. Exhibit 2–1 shows a sample Chart of Accounts.

BALANCE SHEET

The summary of all accounts of the business.

INCOME STATEMENT

Used to disclose the financial activity over a period of time.

EXHIBIT 2–1   CHART OF ACCOUNTS

A, B & C, LAW OFFICE

ASSET ACCOUNTS

1001 Checking Account

1002 Petty Cash

1003 Payroll Account

1004 Client Funds Escrow Account

1005 Investments

1006 Accounts Receivable

(continues)

EXHIBIT 2–1   CHART OF ACCOUNTS *(continued)*

1007 Other Receivable

1008 Allowance for Doubtful Accounts Receivable

1009 Prepaid Expenses

    1009.1 Insurance—premises

    1009.2 Insurance—worker's compensation

    1009.3 Insurance—professional liability

1010 Fixed Assets

    1010.1 Furniture

    1010.2 Equipment

    1010.3 Fixtures

    1010.4 Accumulated Depreciation

    1010.5 Land

    1010.6 Building

LIABILITY ACCOUNTS

2001 Accounts Payable

2002 Notes Payable

2003 Payroll Payable

2004 Payroll Taxes Payable

2005 Property Taxes Payable

2006 Real Property Taxes Payable

2007 Accrued Escrow Funds Payable

EQUITY ACCOUNTS

3001 Partner A Capital

3002 Partner B Capital

3003 Partner C Capital

3004 Capital Surplus

3005 Retained Earnings

(continues)

EXHIBIT 2–1 CHART OF ACCOUNTS *(continued)*

REVENUE ACCOUNTS

4001 Partner A Fees Generated

4002 Partner B Fees Generated

4003 Partner C Fees Generated

4004 Misc. Income

EXPENSE ACCOUNTS

5001 Advertising

5002 Amortization

5003 Auto Expense Reimbursement

5004 Bad Debt

5005 Bank Fees

5006 Charitable Contributions

5007 Depreciation

5008 Funds Advanced on Behalf of Clients

5009 Dues/Subscriptions/Professional Licensure

5010 Continuing Legal Education

5011 Employee Tax Withholding

5012 Accounting

5013 Postage

5014 Utilities

5015 Supplies

5016 Equipment

5007 Furnishings

5008 Telephone

5009 Wages

5010 Salaries/Draw to Professional Staff and Partners

5011 Misc.

Once the general journal has recorded entries, those entries also should be recorded in the specific accounts that are maintained in separate ledgers. Without this additional step, it would be impossible to know which specific accounts or clients have received debits or credits. It also allows for a periodic tabulation of the balance of each particular account. For example, a personal check register maintains an ongoing list of debits (deposits) and credits (withdrawals) for that particular bank account. In addition to balancing the register from time to time to check the accuracy of the recorded transactions, it also is necessary to keep in mind how those deposits and withdrawals affect other matters, such as the balance due on a bill, money transferred from other accounts, for example, savings, and so on. Most individuals engage in double entry accounting on a regular basis without ever realizing it.

2. Trial Balance

The first step in preparing a summary of the financial status of a business is to assemble a Trial Balance. This document is perhaps the most detailed of the financial statements. In a trial balance, the final tally or balance for every account in the Chart of Accounts is listed. Each account reflects either a debit or credit balance. When listed according to the accounting equation, the two sides should reflect equal amounts. Consider a personal check register. In one column, all of the deposits to the checking account are recorded. In the other column, all of the checks, withdrawals, service charges, and so on that represent money removed from the account are recorded. At the end of the month, when the statement is received, the balance is compared to the balance in the check register. A Trial Balance is essentially the same. All of the debit account balances are compared to all of the credit account balances. The two amounts should be identical. If they are not, then there is a recording error that must be discovered and corrected.

The Trial Balance is more detailed because it contains all of the balances in all of the accounts. For most individuals reviewing the financial status of the business, this is more information than is necessary. However, it is essential to prepare a trial balance first to ensure that all account balances are correct. Then, the individual accounts can be grouped in like accounts to present a more concise view of the financial status of the business. Exhibit 2–2 demonstrates a sample trial balance.

■ ADJUSTING ENTRIES

Often include items such as incorrect mathematical computations and improper recording of numbers such as transpositions.

3. Corrections, Adjustments, and Closing Entries

Once the trial balance is completed, **adjusting entries** may be necessary to correct errors in the original trial balance and make updates or changes in assets that are only recorded periodically. With regard to errors in the original trial balance, these often include items such as incorrect mathematical computations and improper recording of numbers such as transpositions. They simply require an entry showing

EXHIBIT 2–2   SAMPLE TRIAL BALANCE

A,B, & C LAW OFFICE

TRIAL BALANCE

DEBIT CREDIT

ASSET ACCOUNTS

1001 Checking Account 2,163

1002 Petty Cash 246

1003 Client Funds Escrow Account 11,259

1004 Investments 96,724

1005 Accounts Receivable 112,552

1006 Prepaid Expenses

    1006.1 Insurance - premises 852

    1006.2 Insurance - worker's compensation 233

    1006.3 Insurance - professional liability 4,580

    1007 Fixed Assets

    1007.1 Furniture 13,145

    1007.2 Equipment 18,221

    1007.3 Fixtures 6,541

    1008 Accumulated Depreciation 7,642

    1010.5 Land 55,400

    1010.6 Building 465,893

LIABILITY ACCOUNTS

2001 Accounts Payable 18,324

2002 Notes Payable 412,066

2003 Payroll Taxes Payable 4,557

2004 Real Property Taxes Payable 4,982

(continues)

EXHIBIT 2–2   SAMPLE TRIAL BALANCE *(continued)*

EQUITY ACCOUNTS

3001 Partner A Capital 36,409

3002 Partner B Capital 36,409

3003 Partner C Capital 36,409

REVENUE ACCOUNTS

4001 Partner A Fees Generated 78,848

4002 Partner B Fees Generated 79,911

4003 Partner C Fees Generated 72,252

TOTAL $787,809

CORRECTION

An additional entry made to amend an error and correct the affected accounts.

the **Correction**. Specifically, an additional entry must be made to amend the error and correct the affected accounts. Other and more significant adjustments include items such as depreciation of assets to reflect their change in value over time.

In a business, some items are consumable, for example, supplies such as paper, pens, staples, and so on. Other items are not consumable but deteriorate in usefulness and value over time. This includes furnishings, computers, office equipment, and even buildings. These things are not there one day and gone the next. In order to record their gradual decrease in value or depletion properly, the item periodically is reduced in its worth as an asset. This is done through depreciation or depletion. Typically, an asset that decreases in value will be depreciated on a schedule of time and percentage of loss set out by the IRS. Most businesses follow these schedules because it allows for simpler preparation of tax returns at the end of the year. For example, a computer system for an office costing $10,000 would be depreciated according to approved schedules over a five-year period.

There are very specific tables for the various types of assets. Each table is based on a number of factors, including when during the year the asset was purchased, over how many years the asset is depreciated, and the percentage of depreciation assigned for a particular year of ownership such as year 1, year 2, and so on. Depending on the type of item and table used, depreciation may be "straight-line," in which the same

---

ASSIGNMENT **2.3**

For each of the items listed in Exhibit 2–3, explain why it would have a debit or credit balance.

percentage is charged each year, or it may be "descending," in which a differing amount is charged each year. It is extremely important to use the proper table in order to record the depreciation accurately for tax purposes. There will be more discussion of this in subsequent chapters.

An adjusting entry for depreciation may record the amount that reflects the percentage of the original value that is being depreciated. For example, an asset that originally cost $5,000 that is depreciated in equal amounts over five years will be reduced by 20%, or $1,000, each year. The entry will charge depreciation as an expense of doing business. Because it increases the expense of the business, the depreciation expense account is recorded as a debit. Accordingly, the Accumulated Depreciation Account is credited or decreased to show the amount of depreciation left to be used in the future.

Finally, adjusting entries are made to reflect depletion of assets, loss, and any amounts earned, or increases in value that have not been yet recorded. Examples include a reduction in office supplies, furniture or equipment that becomes broken or unusable for some reason, and increases such as an increase in value of investments or property that appreciates over time, such as land. After the adjustments are identified, they are properly recorded in the general journal, specific accounts, and then an Adjusted Trial Balance is prepared.

Following the Adjusted Trial Balance, the books for the business are ready for closing for the particular accounting period. At this time, **closing entries** made. These are quite simple. All that is necessary is to close out all of the temporary accounts into the more general permanent accounts. An opposing entry is recorded for the balance of the temporary account. A corresponding opposing entry is made for the permanent account. For example, assume a business has three long-term notes for the building, equipment, and the original start-up costs. The balances of each of these are adjusted, closed, and then combined into the more general Notes Payable account. Also, the expense accounts are closed out and entered in the current liabilities. Revenue accounts are closed into the Equity accounts.

In some instances, an expense or revenue item covers more than one accounting period. In this event, a **reversing entry** may be required. For example, consider a note payable. The loan payment on the building is due on the 10th day of the month. The interest expense associated with the note is apportioned to 10 days of one month and 20 days in the previous month. It is necessary, then, when preparing to open the books for the next accounting period, to enter the portion of the expense attributed to the next accounting period to accurately reflect when the expense was actually incurred.

4. Balance Sheet

The balance sheet is an effective tool to track trends in the financial health of a business. If prepared on a regular basis, the balance sheet can reflect the overall changes occurring from period to period and in comparison with the past.

■ **CLOSING ENTRIES**

The closing out of all temporary accounts into the more general permanent accounts following the Adjusted Trial Balance.

■ **REVERSING ENTRY**

An expense or revenue item covering more than one accounting period.

For example, a balance sheet for each month in a year can establish if the business is experiencing consistent growth or decline. Comparing a balance sheet for the same period in previous years can clearly establish seasonal trends in the business, and it also can be useful for future planning with regard to growth, downsizing, and even budgeting.

Consider the law office that operates primarily on contingency fees. These firms often handle cases such as personal injury, malpractice, and so on. As a result, they frequently are engaged in litigation with parties represented by insurance companies. In turn, insurance companies on a calendar-year basis may have more incentive to close out cases at the end of the year to present a more desirable accounting to shareholders by demonstrating fewer claims pending. Because of this, it is not uncommon for there to be a surge in settlements reached at year-end. Consequently, a law office may experience a significant increase in assets such as cash at the end of the year. By identifying this trend, the office can plan accordingly for those periods when income typically wanes. Similar types of periodic upward and downward drifts are present in virtually all forms of business. Therefore, the balance sheet can be a concise but invaluable tool (see Exhibit 2–3).

EXHIBIT 2–3 BALANCE SHEET

A, B, & C LAW OFFICE

BALANCE SHEET

ASSETS

Long-Term Assets

　　Building 512,000

　　Land 78,000

Current Assets

　　Cash 23,000

　　Personal Property 18,000

　　Investments 92,000

　　Receivables 128,000

　　TOTAL 780,800

(continues)

EXHIBIT 2–3   BALANCE SHEET *(continued)*

LIABILITIES

LONG-TERM LIABILITIES

   Mortgage Payable 528,000

CURRENT LIABILITIES

   Accounts Payable 13,000

TOTAL LIABILITIES 541,000

EQUITY

Partner A Capital 95,920

Partner B Capital 71,940

Partner C Capital 71,940

TOTAL CAPITAL 239,800

TOTAL CAPITAL AND LIABILITIES 780,800

---

5. Income Statement

Unlike the Balance sheet, which gives an overview of the entire business at a particular moment in time, the Income Statement is used to disclose the financial activity over a period of time. An Income statement also may be referred to as a Profit and Loss Statement. Often, Income Statements are prepared at logical end points such as at the end of an annual accounting period. They also may be prepared more frequently depending on how closely the activity of the business is being tracked. Quarterly income statements can be helpful in making a determination of any required tax deposits such as payroll taxes. More specifically, the balance sheet is a summary of the accounts supporting the general accounting equation of Assets = Liabilities + Equity and thus demonstrates the overall financial health of a business. In comparison, the Income statement examines the revenues and expenses for a particular period of time. The Income Statement demonstrates the income equation that is stated as follows:

Income = Revenue - Expenses

In addition to the help it provides for tax purposes, the income statement also can be used to evaluate the ratio between income and expenses. This, in turn, allows the owners of the business to determine if there is a need to decrease certain expenses in order to maximize profits, or perhaps to use significant profits to reinvest and develop the business more aggressively (see Exhibit 2–4).

EXHIBIT 2–4   INCOME STATEMENT

A, B, & C LAW OFFICE

INCOME STATEMENT

Period of 01/01/2007 to 01/01/2008

REVENUES

Fees Collected 108,450

Settlement Income 21,550

Less Refunds 1,800

NET REVENUES 131,800

EXPENSES

Advertising 500

Amortization 300

Auto Expense Reimbursement 1,200

Bad Debt 600

Bank Fees 120

Charitable Contributions 0

Depreciation 560

Funds Advanced on Behalf of Clients 1,400

Dues/Subscriptions/Professional Licensure 300

Continuing Legal Education 100

Employee Tax Withholding 3,500

Accounting 900

Postage 450

Utilities 700

Supplies 1,600

Equipment 0

Furnishings 0

(continues)

EXHIBIT 2–4   INCOME STATEMENT *(continued)*

Telephone 2,100

Wages 47,600

Rent 6,000

Salaries/Draw to Professional Staff and Partners 39,000

Misc. 350

NET EXPENSES 107,280

NET INCOME 24,520

EXHIBIT 2–5   GLOSSARY OF ACCOUNTING TERMS

Above the Line: This term can be applied to many aspects of accounting. It means transactions, assets, and so on that are associated with the everyday running of a business.

Account: A section in a ledger devoted to a single aspect of a business (e.g., a bank account, wages account, office expenses account.)

Accounting Cycle: This includes opening the books at the start of the year, recording transactions, and closing the books at the end of the year.

Accounting Equation: The formula used to prepare a balance sheet.
Assets = Liabilities + Equity.

Accounts Payable: An account in the general ledger that maintains the current balance of all outstanding debts of the business.

Accounts Payable Ledger: A subsidiary ledger that holds the specific accounts of the suppliers to a business and any outstanding debt to each supplier.

Accounts Receivable: An account in the general ledger that contains the overall balance of the individual accounts within the accounts receivable ledger.

Accounts Receivable Ledger: A subsidiary ledger that holds the specific accounts of the customers of a business.

Accruals: If during the course of a business certain charges are incurred but no invoice is received, then these charges are referred to as accruals. Accruals also can apply to the income side, for example, client billing.

Accrual Method of Accounting: Most businesses use the accrual method of accounting. When you issue an invoice on credit (i.e., regardless of whether it is paid or not), it is

(continues)

EXHIBIT 2–5   GLOSSARY OF ACCOUNTING TERMS *(continued)*

treated as a taxable supply on the date it was issued for income tax purposes. The same applies to bills received from suppliers. (This does not mean that you pay income tax immediately. It is just that it must be included in that year's statement of profit or loss.)

Accumulated Depreciation. This is an account in the general ledger that contains the depreciation of a fixed asset until the end of the asset's useful life until it is disposed of. It is credited periodically with the amount of depreciation (decrease of value). Each fixed asset will have its own accumulated depreciation account.

Amortization Table: The schedule showing depreciation over a fixed period of time. The depreciation may be of an asset or a liability, for example, reduction of a debt.

Annualize: To convert anything into a yearly figure.

Appropriation Account: An account in the general ledger that shows the way in which the net profits of a business have been used.

Arrears: Bills that should have been paid. For example, if you have not paid your utility bill for the last two months, then you are said to be two months in arrears on the utility bill.

Assets: What a business owns or is due. Examples include equipment, vehicles, buildings, money in the bank, accounts receivable, petty cash, and so on.

Audit: The process of checking every entry in a set of books to make sure that they agree with the original paperwork (e.g., checking a journal's entries against the original purchase and sales invoices).

Bad Debt Accounts: a ledger account that records the value of unrecoverable debts from customers. Real bad debts or those that are likely to happen may be deducted as expenses against tax liability.

Bad Debt Reserve Account: An account used to record estimates of bad debts for the year (usually based on a percentage recorded in the past) and thereby helping to more accurately predict net profits. The amount estimated to be uncollectible has not yet occurred and so cannot be deducted against tax liability.

Balance Sheet: The summary of all accounts of the business. Usually prepared at the end of each financial year following the preparation of the Trial Balance.

Balancing Charge: When a fixed asset is sold or disposed of, any loss or gain on the asset can be reclaimed against (or added to) any profits for income tax returns. This is also referred to as a balancing charge.

Capital: The amount of money or items of value put into the business by an owner as opposed to money earned by the business.

(continues)

EXHIBIT 2–5   GLOSSARY OF ACCOUNTING TERMS *(continued)*

Capital Account: A term usually applied to show the owner's equity in the business.

Capital Gains Tax: When a fixed asset is sold at a profit, the profit may be subject to Capital Gains Tax.

Cash Accounting: This term describes an accounting method whereby only invoices and bills that have been paid are accounted for.

Cash Account: A journal in which the cash sales of a business are recorded.

Cash Flow: Shows the flow of money in and out of the business over a period of time. Usually issued in the form of a report at the same time that the other periodic financial documents are issued.

Chart of Accounts: A list of all of the accounts held in the ledger.

Closing the Books: A term used to describe the journal entries necessary to close the sales and expense accounts of a business at year-end by posting their balances to the profit and loss account, and ultimately to close the profit and loss account as well by posting its balance to another account such as capital.

Compensating Error: A double entry error that has the effect of canceling another double entry error.

Compound Interest: Apply interest on the capital plus all interest previously accrued as of a specific date, for example, quarterly.

Control Account: An account held in a ledger that summarizes the balance of all the accounts in the same or another ledger. Typically, each subsidiary ledger will have a control account that will be mirrored by another control account in the general ledger.

Cook the Books: Falsify a set of accounts.

Creative Accounting: A questionable means of making a company's figures appear more (or less) appealing to shareholders and other interested parties. An example is "branding," in which the value of a brand name is added to intangible assets, which increases stated value of shares. Capitalizing expenses is another method (i.e., moving expenses to the assets section rather than declaring them in the Profit & Loss account).

Credit: A column on the right side of a journal or ledger to record the "from" side of a transaction, for example, if you buy some gas using a check, then the money is paid from the bank account to the gas account. You would then credit the bank account when making the journal entry.

Creditors: A list of suppliers to whom the business owes money.

(continues)

EXHIBIT 2–5   GLOSSARY OF ACCOUNTING TERMS *(continued)*

Creditors (Control Account): An account in the general ledger that contains the overall balance of the Purchase Ledger.

Debit: A column in a journal or ledger on the left used to record the "to" side of the transaction. It records amounts going into an account.

Debtors: A list of clients or customers who owe money or assets to the business. When this is received, it is recorded as a debit on the left side of the accounting columns.

Deferred Expenditure: Expenses incurred that do not apply to the current accounting period. The expense is debited (having the effect of increasing) the proper accounts such as deferred expenses. When the expense becomes current, it can be transferred to a regular profit/loss account, e.g. prepaid insurance.

Depreciation: The value of assets usually decrease as time goes by. The amount or percentage it decreases by is called depreciation. In this way, the business can spread the cost of an item to the business over the period of time the item has a useful life.

Double Entry Bookkeeping: A system that accounts for every item affected by a financial transaction, including where it came from and where it went to. This is done through balancing entries called debits and credit.

Draw: The money taken out of a business by its owner(s) for personal use. This is different from the expense of wages paid to employees of a business.

Encumbrance: A liability (e.g., a mortgage) is an encumbrance or lien on a property (also included is money retained or set aside for a business purpose).

Entry: Part of a transaction recorded in a journal or posted to a ledger.

Equity: The actual value of the business owned outright, that is, represented by the difference between the business's assets and liabilities.

Error of Commission: A double entry term that means that one or both sides of a double entry has been posted to the wrong account (but is within the same class of account), for example, gas expenses posted to vehicle maintenance expenses.

Error of Omission: A double entry term that means that a transaction has been omitted from the books entirely.

Error of Original Entry: A double entry term that means that a transaction has been entered with the wrong amount.

Error of Principle: A double entry term that means that one or both sides of a double entry has been posted to the wrong account (and to a different class of account), for example, gas expenses posted to Fixtures.

(continues)

EXHIBIT 2–5 GLOSSARY OF ACCOUNTING TERMS *(continued)*

Expenses: Goods or services purchased directly for the running of the business. This does not include goods bought for resale or any items of a capital nature.

Fiscal year: The term used for a business's accounting year. The period is usually 12 months, and can begin during any month of the calendar year.

Fixed Assets: These consist of anything that a business owns or buys for use within the business and that retains a value at year-end, including major items such as land, buildings, equipment, and vehicles as well as smaller items such as tools.

Goodwill: An extra value placed on a business if the owner of the business decides the business as a whole is worth more than the value of its assets, usually included when the business is to be sold as a going concern.

Gross Loss: The balance of the trading account, assuming that it has a debit balance.

Gross Profit: The balance of the trading account, assuming that it has a credit balance.

Historical Cost: Assets, stock, and so on can be valued at what they originally cost rather than the current fair market value.

Income: Money received by a business from its commercial activities. See Revenue.

Insolvent: A company is insolvent if it has insufficient funds (all of its assets) to pay its debts (all of its liabilities).

Intangible Assets: Assets of a nonphysical or financial nature. An asset such as a loan or an endowment policy are good examples.

Inventory: A subsidiary ledger generally used to record the details of individual items of stock. Inventories also can be used to hold the details of other assets of a business.

Invoice: A term describing an original document either issued by a business for the sale of goods on credit (a sales invoice) or received by the business for goods bought (a purchase invoice).

Journal(s): A book or set of books in which your transactions are first entered.

Journal Entries: A term used to describe the transactions recorded in a journal.

K: A legally recognized abbreviation for the term "contract."

Ledger: A book that reorganizes entries posted from the journals into accounts in order to track particular aspects of the business.

Liabilities: This includes bank overdrafts, loans taken out for the business, and money owed by the business to its suppliers. Liabilities are included on the right-hand side of the balance sheet and normally consist of accounts with a credit balance.

(continues)

EXHIBIT 2–5 GLOSSARY OF ACCOUNTING TERMS *(continued)*

Long-Term Liabilities: These usually refer to long-term obligations such as loans that last for more than one year.

Management Accounting: Accounts and reports that are custom-made for the use of managers and directors of a business.

Matching Principle: A method of analyzing the sales and expenses that tie those sales to a particular period.

Maturity Value: The (usually projected) value of an asset on the date that it becomes due.

Memorandum Accounts: A name for the accounts held in a subsidiary ledger, for example, specific client accounts in the accounts receivable ledger.

Multistep Income Statement. An income statement (profit/loss statement) that has had its revenue section split up into subsections in order to give a more detailed view of income sources, for example, an income statement for a law firm that details the fees generated by each individual attorney.

Narrative: A comment appended to an entry in a journal. It may describe the nature of the transaction and, often, the other side of the double entry.

Net Loss: The value of expenses less sales, assuming that the expenses are greater.

Net Profit: The value of sales less expenses, assuming that the sales are greater.

Net Worth: Value of capital and asset accounts less all expense accounts.

Nominal Ledger: A ledger containing the nominal accounts of a business, for example, petty cash.

Normalize: This term can be applied to many aspects of accounting. It means to average or smooth out a set of figures so that they are more consistent with the general trend of the business.

Opening the Books: Each time that a business closes the books for a year, it opens a new set of books for the next accounting year. The new set of books must have balances transferred into them by reversing entries to start the new year with an accurate statement of accounts.

Ordinary Share: This is a type of share of ownership issued by a corporation.

Original Book of Entry. A book that contains the details of the day-to-day transactions of a business such as a journal.

Overhead: The costs necessary to run a business. This would include all expense accounts.

Petty Cash: A small amount of cash money held in reserve (usually applied to purchases of items of nominal value when a check or credit card is not suitable).

(continues)

EXHIBIT 2–5 GLOSSARY OF ACCOUNTING TERMS *(continued)*

Posting: The copying of entries from the journals to the ledgers.

Prepayments: One or more accounts set up to account for money paid in advance such as a retainer.

Profit Margin: The percentage difference between the costs of a product and the price at which it is sold.

Provisions: One or more accounts set up to account for expected future payments.

Purchase Ledger: A ledger that holds the accounts of each of the suppliers of a business. A single control account is held in the ledger that shows the total balance of all the accounts in the purchase ledger.

Real Accounts: These are accounts that deal with money such as bank and cash accounts. They also include those dealing with property and investments. In the case of bank and cash accounts, they can be held in the ledger or balanced in a journal.

Realization Principle: The idea whereby the value of an asset can only be determined when it is actually sold or otherwise disposed of. Only then is the actual value "realized."

Receipt: A term typically used to describe confirmation of a payment—if you buy office supplies, you normally will ask for a receipt to prove that the money was spent legitimately.

Reconciling: The procedure of checking entries made in a business's books with those on a statement sent by a third person, for example, bank statements.

Reserve Accounts: Reserve accounts usually are set up to make a balance sheet clearer by reserving or apportioning some of a business's capital against future purchases or liabilities such as equipment replacement, insurance, and so on.

Retained Earnings: This is the amount of money held in a business after its owners have taken their share of the profits to be reinvested and used for future expenses, growth, development, and so on.

Retainer: A sum of money paid in order to ensure that a person or company is available when necessary.

Retention Ratio: The proportion of the profits retained in a business after all the expenses (usually including tax and interest) are taken into account.

Revenue: The income from all sources for a business.

Self-balancing ledgers: A system that makes use of control accounts so that each ledger will balance on its own. A control account in a subsidiary ledger will be mirrored with a control account in the ledger.

(continues)

EXHIBIT 2–5   GLOSSARY OF ACCOUNTING TERMS *(continued)*

Self-employed: The owner (or partner) of a business who is legally and personally liable for the debts of the business.

Service: A term usually applied to a business that sells services rather than manufactures or sells goods.

Shares: These documents (also known as stock) are issued by a company to owners and represent a percentage of ownership.

Simple Interest: Interest applied to the original sum invested and not to any previously accumulated interest.

Single-Step Income Statement: An income statement in which all revenues are shown as one total rather than by the various sources of income.

Sole Proprietor: The self-employed owner of a business.

Source Document: Journal entry reference to an original invoice, bill, or receipt.

Stock: This can refer to the shares of a limited company or to goods manufactured or bought for resale by a business.

Stock Control Account: An account held in the ledger that holds the value of all the various types of goods for sale that are detailed in the inventory subsidiary ledger.

Straight Line Depreciation: Depreciating something by the same amount every year rather than as a percentage of its previous value.

Subsidiary ledgers: Ledgers opened in addition to a business's ledger. They are used to keep sections of a business separate from each other.

T Account: A particular method of displaying an account in which the debits and associated information are shown on the left, and the credits and associated information on the right.

Tangible Assets: Assets of a physical nature. Examples include buildings, vehicles, equipment, fixtures, and so on.

Transaction: Two or more entries made in a journal that, when looked at together, reflect an original occurrence such as a sale or receipt.

Trial Balance: A statement showing all the accounts used in a business and their balances.

Turnover: The income of a business over a period of time.

Undeposited Funds Account: An account used to show the current total of money received. The funds can include cash, checks, credit card payments, drafts, and so on.

(continues)

EXHIBIT 2–5 GLOSSARY OF ACCOUNTING TERMS *(continued)*

Wages: Payments made to the employees of a business for their work on behalf of the business. These are classed as expense items and must not be confused with "drawings" taken by owners and applied directly against revenues.

Work in Progress: The value of a partly finished revenue generating item.

Write Off: An asset that is reduced to zero in value such as with uncollectible receivable.

Zero-Based Account: Usually applied to a personal account (checking) in which the balance is kept as close to zero as possible by transferring money between that account and another account, for example, a savings account.

Zero-Based Budget: A budget that is started at zero; all costs that increase the budget must be justified.

ASSIGNMENT **2.4**

Consider the terms in Exhibit 2–5 and identify each one that most likely would not be used in accounting for a law practice. Explain your answers.

ETHICAL QUESTION

Mark is in charge of accounting and bookkeeping for the ABC Law Office. He is originally hired by attorneys A and B, for whom he has immense respect. About one year later, Partner C merges his private practice with A and B. Partner C comes to Mark and informs him that he wants his biweekly paycheck to be cut as two totally separate checks in equal amounts. Mark does as he is asked. Over time, he becomes aware from Partner A that Partner C only reports one-half of his income to his wife. The other one-half is kept separate and unknown to C's wife. Partner C prepares two tax returns each year. One with the inaccurate amounts is presented to and signed by his wife. The second with the actual amounts is prepared by C and filed electronically so that no signature is submitted to the IRS. About five years after joining the firm, Partner C and his wife are engaged in divorce proceedings. Mark knows the woman from social interactions and visits to the office, and he thinks very highly of her. After hours one evening, Mark reviews the divorce file and finds that the wife is not represented by her own attorney. The next time that she is at the office, he tries to bring up the subject by asking if he should be sending information to her attorney. She says that she sees no need, as Partner C has offered her more than one-half of their

assets and a generous maintenance agreement for one-half of his income (this is one-half of
the one-half paycheck that he has always brought home) for a period of several years. As an
employee of the firm, and as an accountant, does Mark have a legal and/or ethical obligation
to inform Partner C's wife of the years of deceit, resulting in hundreds of thousands of
dollars being diverted from the marriage and not considered in the settlement of the
marital assets?

Under the existing facts, although moral values may dictate a different result, Mark has
no obligation legally to disclose the information. To the contrary, he is an employee of the
firm and is bound by the rules of confidentiality, as Partner C in this circumstance is a client
as well as an employee. Ethically, he has no obligation as well. Rather, his ethical
requirements are to maintain the confidentiality of information about a civil case that he has
obtained as the result of his employment. It is the responsibility of Partner C's wife to seek
legal representation to protect her interests. If she did so, discovery would no doubt expose
the actual amounts paid to Partner C. As long as Mark does not engage in any activity to
assist Partner C in the settlement of the dissolution of marriage, he is not involved in
improper conduct. Mark may, however, discuss the matter with the other partners of the
firm. They, in turn, may have alternatives that Mark would not in terms of confronting
their partner.

SUMMARY

Throughout this chapter, the basic accounting process is explained. Universally
accepted terminology and basic procedures enable businesses to interact with one
another, as well as ease the process of filing necessary taxes, governmental reports
and returns. Double entry accounting is a valuable safeguard and reflects how each
transaction affects a business. The basic accounting equation of Assets = Liabilities +
Equity allows a determination of the financial health of a business. Periodic financial
documents such as the Trial Balance, Adjusted Trial Balance, and a Balance Sheet
ensure that financial transactions are accurately recorded. The Income Statement is a
useful tool to track the overall profitability of a business. All of these, used
cumulatively, can guide, and in some cases dictate, the future growth or decline of
a business.

■ KEY TERMS

calendar year	Debit	Income Statement
tax year	Credit	adjusting entries
short year	General Journal	Correction
double entry	Chart of Accounts	closing entries
double entry accounting	Trial Balance	reversing entry
internal control	Balance Sheet	

Concluding the Financial Reporting Period

■ OBJECTIVES

After completing this chapter, you will be able to:

❑ Explain the concluding aspects of periodic accounting procedures

❑ Discuss the procedures to close an accounting period

❑ Explain Adjusting, Closing, and Reversing Entries

❑ Describe the financial statements produced at the end of an accounting period

A. PERIODIC ACCOUNTING

In the preceding chapters, some discussion has been given to the need for **Periodic Accounting**. For any business to profit, it is essential that, from time to time, the financial status of the business be reviewed. Failure to do so could have disastrous results. Consider the individual who never balances a check register. At some point, the occasional errors or omissions in recording information either by the individual or from the bank as well as service charges and the like will compound to produce a balance that is not an actual reflection of the amount of money in the account. Even the most attentive accountant who checks every entry for each transaction would agree that it is important to balance the accounts. Even without errors, it is necessary to consider the overall financial status of a business regularly to make determinations about the need for growth or scaling back, for preparation of tax returns, and to report to the owners about the status of their investment in the business. For most businesses, to do this only once each year would present an almost insurmountable task given the sheer volume of transactions that occur within the normal course of an active business. As a result, most businesses will do a more frequent periodic accounting.

The frequency of periodic accounting is entirely at the discretion of the business. In fact, some businesses actually abide by only an annual accounting. However, the vast majority will conduct periodic accounting on a quarterly, monthly, and perhaps even more frequent basis. This has been made much easier with the advent of computer software programs that can update information automatically. Simply put, periodic accounting is the regular and systematic process of tallying the accounts and preparation of such documents as Worksheets, Trial Balance, Balance Sheet, and Income Statements for a specified period of time. Then, when each period is compared, it can be used to determine trends in the business cycle that guide business decisions ranging from growth, to savings, to the best time for purchases, staffing needs, and so on. The same is true whether the business is a large retail operation or a small law office. Listening to the news about the stock market on any given day will clearly demonstrate the impact of periodic accounting. When large corporations announce quarterly report information, the entire market may respond positively or negatively, as the reports are considered indications of economic trends.

PERIODIC ACCOUNTING

The regular and systematic process of tallying the accounts and preparation of such documents as Worksheets, Trial Balances, a Balance Sheet, and Income Statements for a specified period of time.

B. YEAR-END

Even though a business may conduct periodic accounting to provide a window of information about the business throughout the year, the most important financial analysis is the close of the fiscal year. As discussed previously, this may be at the end of a calendar year, or another date if the business follows a stated fiscal year other than January 1 through December 31. The dates are not significant. It is the process of closing the books for the entire accounting year and the summaries prepared that reflect business activity and influence the future of the business.

At the conclusion of a business year, the commonly used account balances are reduced to zero. This includes the temporary accounts, revenue, and expense accounts. The balances in these accounts are transferred into the permanent asset, liability, and equity accounts. The result is to create a final picture of the solvency as if the business were to cease operations on the closing date. This is accomplished through adjusting and closing entries.

The final adjusting and closing entries are necessary to bring the overall picture of the business into view. For example, supplies may be depleted on a daily basis. However, an entry is not needed every day to reflect the number of pieces of paper used. Similarly, a piece of equipment such as a computer decreases in its useful life on a daily basis. But it is only periodically that this accumulated decrease is reflected

YEAR-END

The process of closing the books for the entire accounting year.

in a debit entry to the accumulated depreciation account and decrease or credit in the asset account. Just as important, although accounts receivable reflect the amount owed to the business by third parties, typically less than 100 percent will actually be collected. As a result, it is necessary to reduce the amount of receivables considered collectible before recording it as a permanent asset periodically.

C. WORKSHEETS

WORKSHEETS OR WORKING PAPERS

Documents used to see the activity of the business, the net changes in the assets, liabilities, and equity, as well as the revenue trends.

It is helpful to be able to review the business from various perspectives. By combining the various financial statements into an overall document, one can see the activity of the business, the net changes in the assets, liabilities, and equity, as well as the revenue trends. The documents used to demonstrate these various aspects are known as **worksheets** or **working papers**. When preparing working papers, it is not uncommon to use a large spreadsheet with multiple columns and subcolumns. Each primary column is used to exhibit a different financial statement such as the Trial Balance, Income Statement, and so on. The subcolumns represent the debit and credit balances of the various accounts. Additionally, the proposed adjusting and closing entries can be shown on the worksheet and analyzed before permanently recording them in the accounts of the journal and ledgers. Exhibit 3–1 is an example of a Worksheet.

D. THE TRIAL BALANCE

In this section, the actual process to complete a Trial Balance will be explored. As stated earlier, the Trial Balance is prepared at the end of an accounting period to complete a summary of the financial activity throughout the period. The Trial Balance is the document used to present an overview of the activity within the individual accounts.

ABC Law Firm Month 2	TRIAL BALANCE DEBIT	BALANCE CREDIT	BALANCE SHEET DEBIT	SHEET CREDIT	INCOME STATEMENT Month 1	STATEMENT Month 2	STATEMENT Month 1	CAPITAL Month 2
CHECKING	36951		36951					
CASH	300		300					
CLIENT ESCROWED FEES	8290		8290					
ACCTS RECEIVABLE	98611		98611					
DOUBTFUL ACCOUNTS	13844		13844					
PREPAID EXPENSES Insurance								
Property	809		809					
Malp.	5401		5401					
Work Comp	401		401					
FURNITURE			7600					
EQUIPMENT			13650					
FIXTURES			4550					
ACCUM. DEPREC.				4030				
LAND	15000		15000					
BUILDING	110000		110000					
LIABILITY ACCOUNTS								
Notes pyble		47685		47685				
EQUITY ACCOUNTS								
A. Capital		100000		100000			10000	128910
B. Capital		90000		90000			90000	116019
Retained Earnings				73700				
REVENUE								
Partner A		36300			30400	36300		
Partner B		37400			37774	37400		
EXPENSES								
Advert.	468				(312)	(468)		
Utilities	541				(541)	(541)		
Supplies	329				(287)	(329)		
Wages	8442				(12974)	(8442)		
Partner Draw	8000				(10000)	(8000)		
Postage.	76				(76)	(76)		
Telephone	115				(115)	(115)		
Prof. edu/lic.	249				(249)	(249)		
Equip. maint.	303				(303)	(303)		
Auto reimb.	247				(150)	(247)		
TOTAL	308385	308385	315315	31315	43196	54930	190000	244929

EXHIBIT 3–1   Sample Worksheet

Recall the various stages of the accounting cycle:

1. Record the Transaction in the General Journal.
2. Post the Transaction in the Specific Ledger Accounts.
3. Prepare the Trial Balance.

As stated earlier, as each transaction occurs it should be recorded as a debit and a credit in the appropriate accounts. For example, a payment by a client on their account might first be recorded in a general journal in the following manner:

ACCOUNT	DEBIT	CREDIT
1001 -Cash	150.00	
1002-362 Accounts Receivable - Joe Smith		150.00

These entries also would be recorded in the ledger that is used to manage the funds for the particular accounts. Each transaction changes the balance of the affected accounts. An example for the entry to specific accounts might appear as follows:

1001 CASH ACCOUNT	DEBIT	CREDIT	BALANCE
3/03/06			4,546.00
3/04/06	150.00		4,696.00

1002-362 ACCOUNTS RECEIVABLE - JOE SMITH	DEBIT	CREDIT	BALANCE
			2,855.00
		150.00	2,705.00

The Trial Balance is the first test of the accounting equation. First, the debit column balance and the credit column balance in the general journal of transactions are totaled. Consider the example in Application 3.2. These two figures should be equal. If they are not, then there is an error in addition or in the recording of a transaction. This may seem simple enough to locate. However, some transactions are more complicated than two entries. For example, all of the income for a particular period, such as a day or week, may be recorded in a single entry: one to Cash and another to each of the specific accounts receivable or other income accounts affected. Similarly, a purchase of more than one category of item with the same check may be posted to a number of accounts. Any of these can result in an error. Once the journal debit and credit columns balance, it is necessary to balance the individual accounts. Fortunately, if amounts are entered properly, computer software eliminates virtually all of the computational errors that were once a common issue.

Moving to the chart of accounts, each account in the chart should be totaled for a balance. This consists of balancing the debit column, credit column, and then putting the columns together for a final debit or credit balance.

E. ADJUSTING ENTRIES

As discussed in Chapter 2, adjusting entries are made to bring account balances to a current and accurate reflection of the status of asset, liability, and equity accounts. Adjusting entries are used to show account balances that have increased or decreased incrementally over time. There are generally two kinds of adjusting entries. There are those that show an item that has accrued or built over time, and there are those that show an item that needs to be deferred to a future point. For example, an existing asset may decrease in value with use or time. As discussed

---

ASSIGNMENT **3.1**

Consider the following transactions; record them in a T account (showing a debit and credit column) as they would appear in a general journal on March 1, 2007. Then record them in an account with a debit, credit, and balance column for the particular accounts.

a. Martin Schmidt paid $300.00 on his account by check. His account balance before the payment was $2565.00.

b. An office supply order arrived COD (cash on delivery) in the amount of $176.00. The office supplies account had a balance before the delivery of $684.00.

c. Mary Hornsby delivered a $500 check for earnest money on a house she is purchasing to be held in escrow by the law firm until the purchase is completed.

d. Maggie Henson, an employee, was given an overtime payroll check for $544.00. $136.00 of the check was withheld for federal income taxes, $42.00 was withheld for the employer portion of Social Security/Medicare payroll taxes, $42.00 was withheld for the employee portion of Social Security/Medicare payroll taxes, and $16.00 was withheld for state income taxes.

e. A check was mailed to ACME Advertising for a shipment of new business cards for the attorneys in the office.

** Before all transactions, the checking account had a balance of $4,812.00; Client Escrow Checking had a balance of $5,178.00; Mary Hornsby did not have an escrow account balance; Accrued payroll had a balance of $12,105.00; Accrued employee federal income taxes for Henson was $942.00; Accrued employee state income taxes for Henson was $241.00; Accrued payroll employer FICA (Social Security/Medicare) taxes was $3,156.00; Accrued payroll employee FICA $3,156.00.

earlier, this change in value is reflected in depreciation accounts at the end of the accounting period. There are also assets purchased in advance such as insurance. Although the premium is paid in one accounting period, the actual insurance purchased may not be fully consumed until a subsequent accounting period. This would be a deferred item.

Many transactions occur all at once rather than over time. These are things such as monies received in accounts, the actual payment of expenses, and so on. The key to adjusting entries is to remember that they are used to record events that occur incrementally either in the past or in the future. For example, employees create a payroll liability for the business that increases daily. However, most businesses only enter payroll expense periodically. If a payroll period crosses over the end and beginning of accounting periods, it is necessary through adjusting entries to record the correct amount of payroll accrued in the proper accounting period. The same is true for other items that change by increase or decrease over time.

F. CLOSING AND REVERSING ENTRIES

When closing out a year of accounting and financial activity, it is necessary to clear the slate. Before the accounting period can truly be completed, or before a new period can begin, the temporary accounts used during the accounting period should

---

APPLICATION **3.2**

Mark is preparing to close the books for the quarter. As he reconciles the bank statements, he notes that $8.42 in interest was earned on the account in month 1 of the Quarter and paid into the account on the first day of month 2. A detailed adjusting entry for the quarter would appear as follows:

1/30	Interest Receivable	8.42	
	Interest Revenue		8.42
2/1	Cash		8.42
	Interest Receivable		8.42

Note that Interest revenue does not have a second entry. This will not throw the account out of balance. It was recorded on the Equity/Liability side of the accounting equation when the item originally occurred. Interest receivable and Cash are both asset accounts and therefore the two entries do not change the balance of the accounting equation. Rather, the second entry is merely to record the information in the proper account and thereby make the cash account used for spending more accurate.

*A less detailed entry might show only the Interest Revenue and Cash accounts affected.

ASSIGNMENT 3.2

Consider the following items and prepare the adjusting entries that would be recorded in the general journal and then posted to the ledger accounts.

a. The company-owned vehicle has depreciation for the year in the amount of $2,076. This would decrease the value of the asset and create an expense.

b. The annual office supply inventory purchases total $3,545. The end-of-year inventory reflects a value of $1,128.

c. The bank account has received interest for the year amounting to $121.

d. The mortgage interest paid for the year on the office building is $4,321. This creates an expense and reduces the amount of accumulated note payable interest.

e. The end of the year falls midway through a payroll period. There is an accrued payroll of $6,712 at the year end.

be taken to a zero balance. At first glance, this may seem impossible if the accounts that reflect things such as income or expense have a positive balance. However, it is important that these items remain confined within the accounting period to properly show the financial activity. Through the use of closing entries, these balances can be transferred into the permanent accounts of the accounting equation and better demonstrate the financial health of the business. To properly make closing entries, the balances of temporary accounts are transferred to an Income Summary Account. This account shows the difference in the amounts coming from the revenue side versus those coming from the expense side. Ultimately, these will be further closed out. But first consider how to prepare the initial closing entries in the following example.

Application 3.3 shows a final balance of $12,368. This is because the revenues for the accounting period exceeded the expenses and thus created a net profit. This also must be closed out, and a decision must be made as to how the profit should be used.

APPLICATION 3.3

Date	Account	Debit	Credit
12/31	Fees and Revenues	105,824	
	Income Summary		105,824
12/31	Income Summary	93,456	
	Expenses		93,456

If some of the money is to be held back for future expenditures such as unexpected expenses, a period in which revenue is less than expenses, or perhaps saving for expansion of some element of the business, it can be moved into the retained earnings account. If some or all of the profit is paid out to the owners of the business, it is recorded appropriately as a dividend, an owner bonus, or some other designation that clearly states that profits were distributed. This type of closing entry is shown in Application 3.4.

Once the entries have been made and all temporary account balances have been returned to zero, the final documentation for the accounting period can be prepared. These documents are referred to as **financial statements** and are discussed in Section G. However, it should be kept in mind that once the accounting period is officially concluded, it is necessary to prepare the books for the opening of the next accounting period by reestablishing the temporary accounts. This is done through what are known as reversing entries. The process is quite simple. For each adjusting entry to close out a balance of a temporary account, a mirror image reversing entry is prepared to restore any balance that is carried over into another accounting period. For example, if one week of a two-week payroll period is included in the first accounting period and the second week is in the following accounting period, it is necessary to restore the one week of accrued payroll back into the accounting journal and ledgers in order to have the proper payroll amount at the time it is paid out. Permanent accounts need no reversing entries as their balances carry through the end of the period, into the financial statements, and on to the next accounting period. An example of such an account would be the asset—cash account.

FINANCIAL STATEMENTS

Documents that reflect the overall health and activity of a business, prepared for the end of an accounting period.

APPLICATION 3.4

Date	Account	Debit	Credit
12/3	Retained Earnings	6,368	
	Income Summary		6,368
12/31	Dividends		
	Partner A	2,000	
	Partner B	2,000	
	Partner C	2,000	
	Income Summary		6,000

G. FINANCIAL STATEMENTS

The financial statements prepared for the end of an accounting period are those documents that reflect the overall health and activity of a business. Many of these statements have already been discussed as the information to support them has been explained. The purpose of each different type of financial statement is to consider the business from a different perspective. As discussed in Chapter 2, different documents provide different types of information.

The Balance Sheet is used to track trends among different accounting periods and over time. It demonstrates ebbs and flows in income and expenses. The information in the balance sheet supports the general accounting equation of Assets = Equity + Liabilities. The data included is that of the various permanent accounts under each primary category (Asset, Equity, Liability) and their balances at the end of the accounting period.

The Income statement, by contrast, is not focused on the general financial status of the business but, rather, on its income producing activity and whether the activity is trending toward profit or loss. The income statement is also commonly referred to as a Profit and Loss Statement. The information contained within the income statement supports a different type of equation, specifically, Income = Revenue – Expenses. This document concerns itself much less with the balances in the accounts but instead with the final outcome of whether the business operated at a profit or a loss during the accounting period.

In addition to the Balance Sheet and Income Statement, a **Statement of Capital** often is prepared. This is used to show changes in the owner's capital accounts over time. For a business owner such as a partner in a law firm, the capital account for that individual represents how much of the company owned by them. At the close of the accounting cycle, any net income becomes the owner's income. Whether all or part is reinvested in the business or taken out as a dividend or as personal income is the decision of the owners. The owner's statement of capital will reflect any changes to the capital account.

Finally, owners of a business typically are interested in the source of the income used to pay expenses and generate profit. This information is contained in the **Cash-Flow Statement**. The cash-flow statement shows every source of income and the way in which a company's money is expended during the accounting period. Sources of cash listed on the statement include all types of revenues, long-term financing, an increase in any current liability account, or a decrease in any current asset account through depletion, depreciation, or sale. Uses of cash include expenses, operating losses, debt repayment, equipment purchases, and increases in any current asset account. Because it shows whether a business's cash flow is increasing or decreasing, a cash-flow statement is useful to ward off cash-flow problems in the future through budgeting and expense reduction when necessary.

■ **STATEMENT OF CAPITAL**

Used to show changes in the owner's capital accounts over time.

■ **CASH-FLOW STATEMENT**

Shows every source of income and the way in which a company's money is expended during the accounting period.

Once the various financial statements have been prepared, the owners of the business can review them and make informed decisions about the future of a business. If one does not review these statements, this can cause a failure to plan and budget accordingly for future accounting periods.

As can be seen from the example in Application 3.5, even a single failure to properly review financial statements before taking any steps out of the ordinary with the business can create substantial difficulties for a business. In this case, the company would likely have to take out a loan to cover immediate costs, and more than likely expenses would either need to be cut or an additional capital contribution from the partners would be necessary.

APPLICATION **3.5**

The partners in the A, B, &C law firm have worked hard this year. There have been a lot of evenings and weekends dedicated to promoting the firm and drawing in new clients. And it has worked. The number of active files in the firm has doubled since the end of the previous year. It is December and Christmas is around the corner. The partners will not receive the financial statements for the year-end and the current quarter until after the New Year. Confident in their success, they award each of the 12 employee a $1,000 bonus. They also grant themselves each a $10,000 bonus. On January 15, they receive the financial statements. The partners had not taken into account a $50,000 balloon note on their building due December 20 of the preceding year. This note did not appear on the quarterly statement. They also failed to take into account the large number of clients that fail to make monthly payments during December and revenues were down significantly over the prior months. As a result, they are starting out the year with a significant deficit and are unable to meet the January 15 payroll.

ETHICAL QUESTION

Maria previously was a bookkeeping assistant for the partners of a small law firm. Recently, the bookkeeper died unexpectedly. The partners have asked Maria to step in and assume the duties of the bookkeeper. Maria knows for a fact that the previous bookkeeper paid an outside accountant to prepare financial statements and then passed them off as her own work. She covered the payments to the accountant by padding expenses in some of the client files. The bookkeeper rationalized the action by stating that if it were not for the clients, there would be no need for all the financial statements. According to her, the clients were just paying for the work that they generated in the office. Maria also does not have the skills to prepare financial statements. Her dilemma is whether to tell the attorneys of the conduct by the prior bookkeeper and Maria's own inability to do the work as well.

(continues)

ETHICAL QUESTION **?** *(continued)*

This would undoubtedly cost her the promotion to bookkeeper, as she is unable to do the work required. What is the ethical issue with the past practice of spreading the accounting costs among clients?

A client pays fees to an attorney in exchange for legal representation. That representation includes both the legal skill and advocacy of the attorney as well as the basic administrative costs associated with it. To continue the practice of padding client bills to cover costs that should have already been covered by the fees would be effectively billing the client twice. Although clients typically are asked to pay expenses, that is a different matter. Expenses are outside costs associated with the particular client's case. An example would be paying for copies of medical records for a particular client in a personal injury suit. General office expenses are not unique to any one client. Second, the bookkeeper was hired, among other things, to prepare the financial statements. The failure to do so and pass off the work of the accountant as her own indicates her knowledge that the action was improper and effectively cheating and defrauding her employer. Finally, financial statements are a necessary part of any active business. It is not purely the result of the client other than the fact that the clients are the customers of the business and result in the generation of income.

SUMMARY

In this chapter, the actual mechanics of accounting was explored more thoroughly. Specifically, it was noted how the entries are made, posted, and eventually converted into financial statements. The various types of financial statements such as Trial Balance, Balance Sheet, Income Statement, and Cash-Flow Statement each serve a distinct purpose in the evaluation of the current health of a business, trends, and planning for the future of the business. Although the Balance Sheet gives a snapshot view of the business at a particular moment in time, the Income Statement demonstrates how the business is faring in terms of financial activity and expenses. More specific, the Cash-Flow Statement allows the owners and other interested parties to examine exactly where the income is being generated. This in turn allows action to be taken to maximize and encourage those areas of growth.

▇ KEY TERMS

Periodic Accounting	worksheets or working papers	Statement of Capital
year-end	financial statements	Cash-Flow Statement

For additional resources, visit our Web site at www.westlegalstudies.com

4

Accounting in the Law Office

▣ OBJECTIVES

After completing this chapter, you will be able to:

❑ Explain the basic accounting procedures for incoming and outgoing funds

❑ Discuss the proper procedures for recordkeeping of transactions affecting escrow accounts

❑ Explain the basic accounting procedure to record and disburse settlements and associated expenses

❑ Distinguish the compensation of an employee from the independent contractor

❑ Discuss the effects of timekeeping and overtime pay for salaried versus hourly employees

❑ Describe the proper procedures for calculating periodic withholding for taxes on employee compensation

A. TRANSACTIONS

On any given day, there are multiple financial transactions that occur within the law office. There are those accrual transactions such as wages earned, continuous expenses such as utilities, and so on. These types of transactions are dealt with on a regular and periodic basis. However, there also are a number of transactions that occur intermittently and that must be tracked precisely in order to have accurate accounting not only for the business but for clients as well. Of these transactions, perhaps the most important are those related to the charges for professional service that the clients are obliged to pay and that keep the law firm in business.

1. Billing

The billing process for any law office is absolutely crucial to the firm's success and continued operation. If billing is inaccurate in its generation, distribution, or collection, the business operations can run into any number of difficulties that range from a cash-flow shortage to ethical violations resulting in attorney discipline, to a damaged reputation for the firm that in turn affects future business. Everyone associated with billing, from the legal professionals to those in accounting positions, has the responsibility to be very careful about their task to ensure that it is accurately performed. Unlike many other types of business in which charges are uniform, the law office often has different legal professionals who charge varying hourly rates as well as several totally distinct types of billing that are charged and collected in an entirely different way. The independent law practice, meaning those other than corporate or dependent on a single client, typically will engage in various types of billing. Two of these methods can produce large sums of revenue periodically. The other provides the regular income needed by most practices to keep the business afloat on a day to day basis.

a. Contingent Fee Billing.

Contingent fee billing typically is used for the types of cases that have an uncertain outcome associated with a monetary result. The opposite would be something such as a divorce in which both parties seek to dissolve a marriage and the outcome is relatively predictable. The contingent fee case often is used when one party seeks a financial outcome that the opposing party to the case seeks to avoid entirely. An example would be a personal injury lawsuit. In that type of case, one party claims the other party is legally responsible for the damages caused by an injury that is allegedly the fault of the opposing party. The injured party usually seeks monetary recourse. The party allegedly at fault takes the position that either no injury was caused or that they are not legally responsible. In this type of case, there may be a monetary award or there may be no liability imposed whatsoever.

CONTINGENT FEE BILLING

Typically used for the types of cases that have an uncertain outcome associated with a monetary result.

In a case in which initially the outcome is somewhat unpredictable, it is difficult to estimate the costs that would be associated with such a case. Additionally, the injured party very often is not in a position to finance such a case on an hourly basis. However, if the injured party prevails, there would likely be adequate funds to compensate the legal professionals for their services. As a result, many firms take cases on a contingent basis. What this means is that the attorney is only compensated for the work performed if the injured party receives some sort of monetary award or settlement. The injured party enters a contract agreeing to split a certain percentage of any net financial gain in the case with the attorney. In exchange, the attorney agrees not to charge for professional services if there is no settlement or award for the client. This type of case requires fairly astute judgment by the attorney as to the likelihood of winning such a case. Too many lost contingent fee cases and a firm could find itself in deep financial difficulty. In addition to the agreement regarding professional services, the client is obligated to pay for expenses of the case regardless of whether the case is won or lost. This would include things such as monies paid by the law firm to outside parties for deposition transcripts, records, expert witnesses, and so on. If the case ends successfully for the injured party, such expenses are also usually taken out of the settlement or award in addition to the attorney's fees. If the case is not successful, the firm has the right to collect the cost of expenses from the client, although in reality many firms do not attempt to collect such fees in the event of a lost case for several reasons. The client may simply not have the funds to pay expenses, which can be substantial. Consequently, attempts to collect may be futile. Also, for simple public relations reasons, many firms do not attempt to collect from contingent fee clients who received an unsuccessful result.

APPLICATION **4.1**

Sara was a senior in college when she was in a car accident. Her vehicle was hit by a drunk driver. Sara suffered serious injuries and had hospital bills in excess of $100,000. She will also be scarred and disfigured for the rest of her life, and she anticipates several future surgeries. She was delayed in graduating from college for a full semester and as result lost several months of potential income. The insurance company for the driver who caused the accident offered Sara a settlement of the cost of her current medical bills and claims that Sara was partially at fault in the accident, and as a result is not entitled to more. The Stiffler law firm accepts Sara's case on a contingent fee basis. If they prevail, the firm will be entitled to the expenses incurred as well as 33 percent of the monies collected. If they do not prevail, they will still be entitled to the cost of expenses.

Ultimately, Sara's case is settled for $400,000. The expenses incurred in the case amount to $19,000. The attorney's fees are one-third of $400,000, or $132,000. Sara receives the balance of $249,000. If the outcome were different and it was shown that Sara was substantially at fault for the accident for some reason, and there was no settlement or

(continues)

APPLICATION **4.1** *(continued)*

award in her favor, Sara would still be legally responsible for the $19,000 in fees. However, given her financial status, it is unlikely she would ever be able to pay them and the firm may well write the fees off as a bad debt.

When a contingent fee contract has been executed with a client, the client is not billed for professional services during the progression of the case. Historically, firms often did not even keep track of the time spent by the legal professionals, as there was only payment for these services in the event of a successful outcome and the amount paid was a percentage. There was no real connection with the amount of time spent to obtain the outcome. However, more and more as law firms attempt to maximize profit and remain competitive, it has become important to track the amount of time spent on a case and the professionals expending that time. This information can be used to evaluate not only the profit margin for time investment of particular types of cases but also the efficiency of the various legal professionals in a firm.

b. Flat Fee Billing.

The other kind of periodic payment for professional services is known as the flat fee. Unlike the contingency case, these cases require payment for professional services regardless of the outcome of the case. However, to remain competitive with other legal professionals, it is important to have established fees for certain types of cases that have a fairly predictable investment of time for the professional. Such types of cases often involve things such as routine traffic violations, uncontested divorces, drafting of legal documents such as wills, and so on.

In a **flat fee billing** situation, the client enters into a contract with the legal professional for representation on a specific matter for a set fee. The client pays a single amount, either in full or in installment payments as agreed, and representation is provided in whole for that fee. The fee paid does not usually guarantee the ultimate outcome, but it does ensure representation throughout the legal process. Often, there are conditions set out that convert the fee to an hourly charge if circumstances change the representation from one that is routine to a more complicated situation.

> **FLAT FEE BILLING**
>
> An established fee for certain types of cases that have a fairly predictable investment of time.

c. Hourly Billing.

The other type of billing is much like any other professional service. The legal professional tracks the work performed and the time expended. Often, standard units are used for certain types of work such as phone calls and correspondence. Although it may take only a moment or two to dictate a letter, considerations must include items such as reading incoming correspondence that might require a response, time spent formulating the content, labor associated with clerical work that is included in the professional's hourly rate, and so on. As a result, it is not uncommon for general

APPLICATION **4.2**

On March 1, 2006, Adam is charged with speeding and reckless driving. On March 3, 2006, he contracts with a local attorney to represent him on the charges filed against him. The contract states that Adam will be represented on all charges related to the March 1, 2006, incident for a fee of $350. It further states that any non-traffic-related criminal charges or civil claims arising from an occurrence on March 1, 2006, will be represented on an hourly basis at the rate of $185.00 per hour. On March 5, Adam is charged with leaving the scene of an accident and vehicular homicide all occurring as a direct result of the same incident on March 1, 2006. It seems that Adam neglected to inform his attorney that before he was picked up for speeding and reckless driving, he had run over a pedestrian and killed her while Adam was drag racing with another driver. All of Adam's charges for the speeding and reckless driving would be covered by the $350 flat fee. The other charges would be handled on an hourly basis.

correspondence or brief phone calls to be billed at a standard incremental rate such as one-fifth or one-quarter of an hour. Each legal professional tracks the time he or she spends in this way and attributes that time to the client for whom the time is expended.

When a client enters into an hourly contract with a law firm, they agree on an hourly amount to be billed by the attorney. Additionally, some firms also may bill the work of a nonattorney professional, such as a paralegal or legal investigator, at a lesser rate. This saves the client money for having some of the work done that traditionally might have been done by an attorney. Most of the work historically performed by attorneys, with the general exceptions of advocating with third parties on behalf of the client and giving legal advice, can be performed effectively by a properly trained paralegal.

The manner in which billing occurs varies dramatically from firm to firm. Some firms may still use the paper method, in which the attorney or paralegal tracks the time spent during the day on a time sheet, which is then turned over to accounting personnel. The individual in charge of handling billing then records the amounts charged to the various clients. Other firms utilize software that allow the legal professional to input the information directly into a computer program that the individual that handles billing can then access. In either event, the time spent must be apportioned to the particular client for billing and tracking purposes. Obviously, the software method is going to be more efficient. However, it can be expensive. Regardless of the method used, it is still important to check for errors such as duplication of charges, incorrect charges, assigning charges to the wrong client file or specific client case as some clients have more than one case pending at a time. In addition to billing, it is useful to know the time spent by legal professionals to determine whether the time spent on particular tasks is comparable to others in the firm, and whether the professional can work to improve on certain skills or possibly assist other legal professionals in maximizing the use of their own time. Many firms with a large percentage of **hourly billing** type clients employ standards or quotas of billing that the legal professionals must meet in order to advance in their careers. However, this must be balanced against the danger of fraudulently overbilling clients in order to present a more positive job performance. And, again, the performance of individuals can be compared to that of others in the group as a means to identify unusual trends.

One particular issue that has arisen with respect to client billing is multiple billings for the same time period. This can occur in two ways. In the event that more than one legal professional within the firm takes part in client representation, there can be more than one billing charge for the same time period. The other situation occurs when an attorney makes an appearance on the same day at the same court for more than one client. There may be billing of more than one client for items such as travel expenses. Such billing must be done with great care to avoid duplicity in billing for the same work or expense. Billing by legal professionals is a substantial issue and is governed by ethical rules and often state-legislated rules of practice. The attorney is considered a fiduciary in a legal position of trust with a client. This position of trust places the client at a disadvantage to the attorney and requires honor of that trust as part of the client representation. Unlike many other businesses in which billing discrepancies are considered nothing more than a danger of doing business that must be corrected, for the legal professional, billing discrepancies can threaten the very life of the practice. Rules are in place and conduct that is found to be unethical can result in discipline ranging from reprimand to disbarment along with restitution. As a result, failure to bill properly and truthfully can result in severe discipline and even suspension of the privilege to practice law.

> ### ■ HOURLY BILLING
>
> Billing based on tracking the time spent and attributed to the client for whom the time is expended.

APPLICATION 4.3

Clarissa is an attorney who has been out of law school for about two years. She takes on a very complicated case involving an entire subdivision that has been contaminated when a local manufacturer attempted to secretly discharge hazardous waste into an area waterway that ran through the subdivision. Clarissa represents the manufacturer. She has no experience in this type of case and meets numerous times with a senior partner for guidance on how to handle the matter. Clarissa bills her hourly rate for the meetings, which are categorized as research. However, the senior attorney also bills the client for the time he spends mentoring Clarissa. In a case such as this, the client would likely not be obligated to pay for the work of the senior attorney. If the attorney were performing legitimate work such as taking depositions, the billing may be considered appropriate. But billing a client for the purpose of educating another attorney would not.

ASSIGNMENT **4.1**

Consider the following situations and explain whether contingent, hourly, or flat fee billing would be most appropriate.

    a. Emilio has been charged with speeding.

    b. Danielle was injured at work and lost her right thumb.

    c. Kevin is seeking a divorce from his wife.

    d. Amelia needs to have a purchase agreement drawn up to use when selling her home.

    e. Amelia needs to have all the necessary documents prepared and steps taken to complete the sale of her home.

    f. Mark and James want to enter a partnership. They need a partnership agreement prepared. They have already provided all of the necessary information.

    g. Jim is a professional baseball player. A local store needs a contract drawn up between itself and Jim for a series of four personal appearances.

    h. Maxine hired a local contractor to put an addition on her home. The workmanship was terrible and the addition collapsed on the first story of Maxine's home. She wants to sue the contractor.

    i. Bond had a successful chocolate store built over a 40-year period. A few blocks away, some former **employees** have opened a competing store that is virtually identical to Bond's. The employees had a contract to not compete within 50 miles. Bond wants to sue them for a percentage of their profits.

    j. Jill received a ticket for not wearing a seatbelt.

2. Receipts

At first glance, it would appear that handling incoming funds to a law practice is a simple process with little room for complication. However, there are a number of considerations that must be addressed when money comes in. Perhaps most important is whether the funds are coming into the firm or whether it is money to be held for an outside party until it is either earned by the firm or redistributed. In some instances, the money comes in and is placed in one type of account for the firm and is subsequently transferred into another account once an event has occurred such as billing for services performed. The key ingredient to any of these transactions is that the funds must be properly recorded and deposited into the appropriate bank accounts. The proper accounting entries also must be made to reflect the other side of the accounting equation. For example, a payment from a client on an outstanding bill would be debited to cash and credited to the client's bill. However, even this can require close attention to the purpose of the receipt and accurate reflection of that purpose in the accounting records.

a. Payments.

Frequently, the monies coming into a law practice consist of payments on account. These are monies paid to the firm in exchange for the professional services offered by the firm and any expenses that may have been incurred on behalf of the client. It is important to ensure that incoming funds are appropriately credited to the proper client. In some instances, the funds also must be properly credited to the proper item within the client's account. For example, some firms require the client to pay items such as court filing fees to initiate a case. As a result, when money comes in, it is important to understand the type of fee agreement a particular client has, as well as any conditions such as payment of filing fees. Otherwise, the monies may be applied against the client's general account and used for things such as payment for professional services rather than as payment to the court. As can be seen, it is important to be familiar with fee arrangements of the various clients of the firm, which can be numerous. Also, it is essential that these transactions be recorded in detail to ensure a proper accounting for the firm and for the client as to how incoming funds represent items such as expenses or delivery of professional services. Software assists in the ease of recording funds. But it is still the job of the person recording the transaction to determine how the funds are to be applied. In Application 4.4, a simple daily entry for incoming funds is illustrated.

APPLICATION 4.4

On March 15, the daily receipts total $4,752. The accounting entries in the general ledger might appear something like the following:

Date	Entry		Debit	Credit
3/15	Cash		4752	
	Accounts Receivable			4752
		Client 4016 fees	$600	
		Client 4016 expenses	$152	
		Client 4583 fees	$250	
		Client 4941 fees	$3750	

(continues)

APPLICATION　4.4 *(continued)*

The journal for one of the individual clients above over the course of a month might look like this:

Client 4016 –hourly		Debit	Credit	Balance
2/21	fees - court appearance		350	350
2/22	expenses - court fees	152		502
2/26	fees - client interview	250		752
3/15	payment fees		600	152
3/15	payment expenses		152	0

b. Escrow.

Unlike many other types of business, not all incoming funds belong to the firm. One such type of income that is not debited to the general coffers of the firm would be money held in **escrow**. When a firm accepts escrow funds, it agrees to act as an independent third party and hold the funds until the proper owner receives distribution of the money. An example of the use of escrow might be a sale of real property or a business interest. Such transactions typically take a period of time to complete preliminary items such as evaluations, inspections, appraisals, contracts, and so on. It is common in these situations for the buyer to initially offer a portion of the purchase price as a down payment to represent a commitment to follow through with the purchase. The seller is not technically entitled to use of the funds as the sale is incomplete. As a result, the third-party escrow is an important element to promote the completion of the transaction. With an escrow account, both parties can proceed with the necessary steps to finalize the transaction safe in the knowledge that the down payment is protected until the sale is consummated. A party who holds money in escrow agrees to oversee the funds of the third parties until such time as distribution is appropriate. This task often falls to the law firm who is responsible for preparation of contracts and generally overseeing the transaction. Strict ethical rules prohibit mixing firm monies with escrowed funds. Depending on the circumstances, a sale may not be completed. In that case, the down payment may be returned to the buyer or paid to the seller according to the terms of the agreement. If the sale is completed, the down payment is typically turned over to the seller along with the rest of the purchase price.

ESCROW

A financial instrument (Securities, funds and other assets) held by a third party on behalf of the other two parties in a transaction. The funds are held by the escrow service until it receives the appropriate written or oral instructions confirming the obligations concerning the transaction have been fulfilled.

APPLICATION   4.5

A, B, & C law firm is contacted by Monroe James. Monroe intends to purchase a restaurant from a family that has owned and operated the business for more than 30 years. Monroe has signed a purchase agreement to buy the restaurant for $250,000 contingent on appraisals that support this value from three different independent accounting firms. He has offered the current owners $25,000 as a down payment. A,B, & C law firm will hold the $25,000 in escrow and will prepare the final documents to complete the transaction. In the event that the appraisals reveal that the business was highly overvalued and has a much lower fair market value, Monroe may have the opportunity to avoid the purchase and receive all or part of his down payment back. In the event that the appraisals are supportive but Monroe fails to complete the purchase for other reasons, the sellers may be entitled to the down payment. Finally, in the event that the sale is completed, only at that time would the sellers be entitled to receive the money.

c. Retainers.

Many clients, but specifically those who enter into an hourly or flat fee contract often make an advance payment to get the representation underway. Other clients such as businesses may pay an amount that ensures representation by a particular firm whenever legal services are needed. All of these payments are considered **retainers**. When this occurs, the client pays an amount of money to the firm that is held in an account separate from the funds of the firm. As the representation progresses and time is expended, the charges for that time are applied against the retainer and the funds are transferred into the firm's general accounts. Transfer of these funds before that can be considered an ethical violation in many jurisdictions. Once the retainer has been depleted, the client may deposit more advance funds, may be billed periodically (such as monthly), or may pay the total sum due at the conclusion of the case. This depends on the agreement between the attorney and the client. However, in most cases, regular payment is expected in response to the periodic billing once the retainer is exhausted.

RETAINER

An advance payment made to get representation underway.

APPLICATION   4.6

Marcus and Deshondra have decided to end their 14-year marriage. They are a relatively wealthy couple with substantial assets. Marcus hires an attorney to represent him in the legal proceedings. Marcus and the attorney enter into an hourly rate contract in which the attorney provides Marcus with representation for an agreed-on rate of $250.00 per hour. Marcus pays a $5,000 retainer fee to the attorney. This money will be used to pay any expenses as well as the hourly fee of the attorney until the amount has been depleted. At that time, Marcus's contract requires him to pay the attorney in response to periodic billing until the matter is concluded.

3. Expenses

In addition to daily incoming funds, there are also charges incurred and often paid out on a daily basis. In many cases, these charges are part of the cost of doing business. Such expenses are typically referred to in accounting terminology as "accounts payable." Other charges are those attributed to a particular client or case. It is essential that all expenditures be accurately recorded for a number of reasons. Many of the costs for the business are tax-deductible, but only if they are properly documented. This includes proper accounting records that detail the expenditure and maintaining supporting documents such as invoices and receipts. In the event of an audit, the government requires more than a canceled check to prove that a payment was made. In addition, invoices or receipts to support the basis for the payment made are typically required. Similarly, costs associated with a client or a client's case often are billable items, but again, only if properly documented. In the event that a client challenges a bill or expense item, it is necessary to prove the validity of the charge and the amount through external documentation.

a. Business Expenses—Accounts Payable.

When expenses for the business are incurred, there should be a system in place to document and properly account for the expense. For centuries, law offices often were operated completely by the attorneys with little or no support staff. Also, firms frequently consisted of no more than one or two individuals. The result was often haphazardly kept records or nothing more than notes to files. The practice of law was very much hands-on, and little or no technology or outside help was involved. But, as the practice of law developed a number of outside elements influenced the profession. Consequently, the number of attorneys and support staff grew dramatically. In direct proportion to this growth was the complexity of accounts, and it became increasingly important to properly track outgoing funds while properly attributing them to clients or cases. In a retail operation, an item that is not producing a sufficient profit will likely be discontinued. Similarly, in the practice of law, an expense or person generating expenses out of proportion to the profit generated must be identified and dealt with.

Today, most law practices document all expenses either through a paper invoice/purchase order system or on software that performs this function on computer. The key element in either system is the same. Any time that funds are distributed from the firm, there should be a record of the amount, the date, the reason for the expenditure, whether it was properly spent or approved if necessary, and any corresponding documentation. A purchase order is an internal document used within the firm to record an expenditure and when to appropriate, document approval. Typically, certain individuals have authority to incur various expenses. However, it is also common to require approval to spend money on behalf of the firm or for certain types of expenses, or amounts exceeding an established limit. The purchase order can be used for all of these purposes. It should detail the purpose of the expense, the date, the amount, and any necessary approval. Once this information is prepared, the item can be purchased and paid for with funds from the appropriate account.

An invoice is a document received from a third party that documents items already charged to the firm. It typically represents a charge that has been incurred before payment. Invoices are used for regular and systematic expenses such as utilities, phone, and so on, or for periodic expenses such as supplies, furniture, postage, and even reimbursements to employees. Often, the regular expenses that produce invoices have a standing approval and are paid automatically. Other invoices may require approval for specific items or amounts. In some instances invoices represent such significant amounts it is necessary to accrue or save money each month to enable timely payment of the expense when the invoice arrives. This also allows the expense to be distributed over the period of time when it is used rather than being applied against a single period. Examples of such items might be property taxes or malpractice insurance. Exhibit 5–5 demonstrates a purchase order. Application 4.7 illustrates an accounting entry to record the transactions.

APPLICATION 4.7

4/10	Office Supplies (Invoice 102345)		1,253	
		Cash (Check # 6789)		1,253
4/10	Office Equipment (PO 6984)		562	
		Cash (Check #6790)		562

APPLICATION 4.8

On the 25th of the month, the bookkeeper for a small law firm evaluates the expenses due by the end of the month excluding payroll and related taxes. These are items that must be paid or funds transferred to the proper accounts for accumulation of an upcoming payment.

Electric invoice	$352
Phone invoice	$752
Cellular phone invoice	$454
Office Supplies invoice	$255
Fed parcel Delivery invoice	$75

(continues)

APPLICATION 4.8 (continued)

(see purchase order 3412)	
Water invoice	$111
Mortgage	$2,000
Insurance - Accrued Property	$125
Insurance - Accrued Malpractice	$5,500
Accrued Property Tax	$460
Professional Dues	$675
Purchase Order #3412	
(new laptop Attorney 05)	$2,245
Purchase Order #3413	
(postage meter)	$500

b. Case/Client Expenses.

Unlike many other types of business, it is very common for a law practice to expend money on behalf of the clients. According to most fee agreements, the expenses outside of the law practice are typically the responsibility of the client and not the firm. However, to facilitate forward movement of the case, it is often necessary for the law firm to pay for such items and ultimately seek reimbursement from the client. This may be referred to as **Costs Advanced**. For example, a contingent fee case based on personal injury may have thousands of dollars in expenses that a disabled client may not be able to pay as the case progresses. As a result, the firm may pay these amounts and then deduct the expenses, along with fees, from any settlement or judgment received in the case. In a flat or hourly fee agreement, a firm may elect to pay the expenses up front and seek reimbursement from the client at a periodic billing interval. Regardless of the type of fee agreement, the expenses of a client case must be followed with proper accounting procedures for many reasons, some of which include:

- client expenses are not part of the general accounting for the firm and should not directly impact financial statements
- client expenses should be attributed to the particular client and type of case for purposes of evaluation of the business practices and trends
- client expenses are items that are collected separately from fees for professional services

■ **COST ADVANCE**

Costs paid by a law firm for items deemed necessary to facilitate forward movement of a case. The firm will ultimately seek reimbursement of these costs from the client.

Because of the items mentioned here, any time that an expense is incurred on behalf of a client, it is important that the time, date, detailed explanation, and purpose of the expense be documented. This should be done along with the amount and the client for whom the funds are spent. Documentation of this sort is useful not only in the operation of the business but also for purposes of collection of the expense. Consider the client who did not anticipate expenses to be as substantial as they were; much of the concern can be diffused if there is a thorough explanation of the expense, its necessity, and how it helped the case.

Accounting for payment of expenses on behalf of a client is performed in much the same way as when fees for professional services are recorded. It is important to indicate the account from which money is outgoing such as cash. Additionally, a corresponding entry is made to for the client to demonstrate that an amount has been debited (charged) to that client's account. For example, if a client's medical records are copied and sent to the law firm for use in a case, the entry might be as follows:

| 8/21 | Client Account 3654 (medical records) | | 318 | |
| | | Cash (Check #6792) | | 318 |

Then, depending on the terms of the client's fee agreement, the amount expended on behalf of the client can be recovered by the firm through direct payment or by subtracting it from an award or settlement at the conclusion of the case. However, not all items paid on behalf of a client are expenses directly related to the process of litigation. Some are fees paid to third parties on behalf of a client. These expenses are considered loans to the client and should be documented as such. Because of the cost and ethical considerations, often these debts are not paid but, rather, they are protected.

c. Protected Accounts (Lien Letters).

In some instances, the firm acts as an intermediary for the client on what are commonly known as protected accounts through the use of **lien letters**, otherwise referred to as **letters of protection**. In the event that the client is represented in a case in which a monetary award or judgment is sought, a firm may offer to protect the bills of a client's creditors. What this means is that the law firm advises a client's creditor that the lawsuit is pending and a monetary judgment is expected. The firm offers to pay the creditor directly from the judgment when it is received in exchange for stopping attempts to collect the amount due from the client while the case is pending.

When a firm protects a creditor's account, it is typically accomplished through a lien letter. This is a written document that acknowledges the debt and guarantees that the debt of the client will be paid directly by the firm on behalf of the client at the time a monetary award or settlement is received. Creditors may include a wide range of entities. Essentially anyone to whom the client owes a debt may be offered a lien letter. However, most firms will confine the use of these to those creditors who

LETTER OF PROTECTION/LIEN LETTER

A written document that acknowledges a debt and guarantees that the debt of the client will be paid directly by the firm on behalf of the client at the time a monetary award or settlement is received.

have a direct connection the client's case. For example, a client in a personal injury suit may have outstanding medical bills related to the injury. Part of the case would be to recover the cost of these medical expenses. If the case has been evaluated properly before litigation, the chances of recovering these expenses are probably quite high. Thus, the creditor and the firm are reasonable in the expectation that the amounts will be recovered in time.

When a lien letter is issued, there is typically no accounting entry necessary. At this point, no funds have been expended. It is possible that an entry will be made for the time spent by the legal professional in generating the agreement with the creditor. Otherwise, there is no change of assets or liabilities on behalf of the firm. The client file should be clearly noted with a copy of the lien letter or letter of protection. However, when the client receives an award or settlement, the outgoing funds would be recorded as an expense of the client's account. It is extremely important that the letter be maintained in the client file and be properly accounted for when the lien is ultimately satisfied.

APPLICATION 4.9

Samantha has hired a law firm to represent her against a manufacturer of a prescription drug that made Samantha very ill. The company defends that it had no knowledge of the ill effects of the product. However, through investigation, the law firm has located a former employer of the manufacturer who says that the company had full knowledge but covered it up. This turns out to be a very damaging piece of evidence in the case. The jury awards Samantha $1 million on her claim of fraudulent concealment. They award nothing on the negligence claim against the manufacturer. The award is distributed as follows:

$1,000,000

Less:		
	$333,000	Attorney's Fees
	$ 17,000	Expenses
	$ 75,000	Letters of Protection
To Client:	$575,000	

Samantha was distressed at the fact she ultimately received little more than half of the judgment. Because of accurate recordkeeping practices, it was a simple matter to provide her with the following breakdown of legal expenses:

(continues)

APPLICATION **4.9** *(continued)*

Deposition Expert Witness Dr. Raskiner (Samantha's physician)	$2,400
Court Transcriptionist for Raskiner Deposition	$600
Deposition ACM Manufacturing Former Employee Smith	$300
Travel to Smith Deposition	
Airfare	$700
Hotel	$300
Meals	$210
Rental Car	$240
Transcriptionist	$750
Deposition Independent Medical Expert	$3,000
Medical Expert Case Evaluation Fee	$1,500
Transcriptionist	$500
Deposition Independent Manufacturing Expert	$2,000
Manufacturing Expert Case Evaluation Fee	$2,600
Transcriptionist	$400
Deposition Defendant Employees	$300
Transcriptionist	$400
Medical Records Copies	$500
Misc. (Postage, Shipping, copies, long distance)	$300
Mercy Me Hospital	$43,000
Dr. Smith	$18,000
Dr. Wesson	$14,000

(continues)

APPLICATION **4.9** *(continued)*

While the case was on a contingent fee agreement, a record was kept to demonstrate the amount of time spent on the case. The professional services expended over the two and a half years that the case was pending were recorded as follows:

Attorneys

	Pretrial Court Appearances	66 hours
	Trial Preparation	36 hours
	Trial	72 hours
	Travel	68 hours
	Depositions	38 hours
	Client Meetings	48 hours
	Phone Conferences	8.5 hours
	Correspondence	11.5 hours
	Document Drafting	26 hours
	Meetings/Case Evaluation	28 hours

Paralegal

	Research	63 hours
	Client Meeting/Phone	22 hours
	Discovery Documents	42 hours

Investigation

	Witness Statements	28 hours
	Interviews	22 hours
	Note Preparations for file	16 hours
	Meetings with Attorney	8 hours
	Trial Preparation/Assistance	42 hours

Clerical Support		83 hours

B. SETTLEMENTS

Despite all of the media attention focused on jury awards in recent years, the reality is that the vast majority of lawsuits are settled between the parties. When a case is settled, the accounting occurs in much the same way as it would with a court judgment or jury award. A payment is typically issued to the law firm and client jointly in the form of a draft/check. The payment is deposited into the accounts of the firm. Typically, the amount will be held in escrow until it is certain that the draft has cleared the bank on which it was drawn. Following this, the funds are properly transferred in accounting records and only then is the money actually distributed to the firm, client, and any protected parties. As a result of the need to wait for the draft to clear the bank, there are multiple accounting entries required. When the check is first received, the money is placed in escrow accounts for the firm and client. Subsequently, when the check has cleared, the money is transferred into the cash account and the client account. Ultimately, the client's and any other third-party payments are issued by debiting the client account and crediting cash. Although the process for closing out a settled claim is essentially the same for a jury award, there is one additional and distinct requirement. Typically, no funds will be issued on a settlement until such time as the settlement documents have been drafted and signed by all concerned parties. These documents vary in some respects, but generally they will contain a contractual agreement to settle the dispute among the parties for an agreed-on sum. Although a settlement may occur, it may be a significant period of time before the documents are drafted and the money transferred, cleared, and finally distributed. This has significance for the accounting personnel when the items take place over the course of more than one accounting period. When that occurs, it may be necessary to make special entries in the accounting books to close the accounts for one period and reestablish the accounts in the next as is done with other types of accounts, such as those that accumulate funds over more than one accounting period.

ASSIGNMENT **4.2**

Describe each of the accounting entries necessary for the following situation.

Duane Skiff is a client whose case has just been settled for $100,000. The settlement occurs on November 10. The settlement documents are signed on December 6. The $100,000 draft is issued on December 13, and received on December 19 by the attorneys representing Duane. The money is deposited in escrow and clears the bank on December 30. The office is closed for the New Year's holiday and reopens on January 2. The firm receives one-third of the settlement. Duane owes $17,666 in costs advanced. The balance is paid to him directly on January 3. The fiscal year of the firm ended on December 31. The new year for the firm began on January 1.

C. PAYROLL

A fundamental part of most business' accounting includes payroll. This is the process of calculation, recording, and disbursement of money owed to individuals who work for the business. Some businesses have the payroll function performed by an outside company and merely record how the transactions affect the assets of the business such as a credit to cash accounts and debit to payroll accounts. However, a large percentage of businesses, including many law firms, complete their own payroll process. Although the concept of payroll is straightforward, there a number of variables that can make payroll for even a small operation fairly complex. First, there are a variety of forms by which individuals can be characterized for the purpose of payment in exchange for work performed. These in turn affect how pay, benefits, and taxes are calculated. Second, the manner in which the payment is calculated may vary based on how the individual is compensated. And, finally, there are government required documents to report payments made, and, in many cases, periodic taxes that must be withheld and subsequently turned over to the federal, state, and even local governments. All of these factors require strict attention to payroll issues and proper accounting procedures in the delivery of payroll.

1. Employee versus Independent Contractor

INDEPENDENT CONTRACTOR

Usually employed on a project-by-project basis and is responsible for completing the task assigned independently.

As stated earlier, individuals who perform work for a business may be characterized in different ways. An employee is the most common. This is a person who works for the business on a regular basis and who is generally subject to the direct supervision and control of the employer. By contrast, an **independent contractor** is usually employed on a project-by-project basis and is responsible for completing the task assigned independently. The independent contractor is not entitled to benefits such as overtime or holiday pay. The employer has no obligation to provide one-half of the contribution for social security or medicare tax, or any worker's compensation or unemployment tax. There are a number of circumstances when the line between employee and independent contractor becomes blurred. Whether an individual is an independent contractor or employee affects a number of things that range from some legal liability for an employee's conduct toward third parties to a lack of responsibility for tax withholding and payment on behalf of the independent contractor. For this reason, the courts have developed a number of factors to consider when making the distinction:

- right to control manner in which work is done
- method of payment; right to discharge
- skill required in the work to be done; who provides tools, materials, or equipment
- whether worker's occupation is related to that of alleged employer
- whether alleged employer deducted for withholding tax

For employers with staff whose duties and compensation fall into a gray area, the Internal Revenue Service provides a valuable tool. The form **SS-8 Determination of Worker Status for Purposes of Federal Employment Taxes and Income Tax Withholding** is a document that can be completed and filed with the Internal Revenue Service. The document is evaluated and a determination is made as to the status of worker as an employee or independent contractor. This can also be a valuable instrument in the event a dispute arises between employer and employee as to status for any number of reasons.

In the law office setting, it is very common to have both regular employees and independent contractors. Regular employees often serve in the role of office personnel such as clerical, accounting, reception and scheduling, and so on. Attorneys may be present as owners, employees, or a combination. Paralegals may be employed on a regular basis or hired as free lance independent contractors for a specific case. Similarly, legal investigators may work for one firm as an employee or may serve as independent contractors on a case by case basis. It is extremely important for tax withholding and reporting purposes that the distinction of whether an individual is an independent contractor or employee be clearly established.

SS-8 DETERMINATION OF WORKER STATUS FOR PURPOSES OF FEDERAL EMPLOYMENT TAXES AND INCOME TAX WITHHOLDING

An IRS form used to determine whether a person is considered an employee or independent contractor.

APPLICATION **4.10**

Suzanne is a recent law school graduate. As she prepares to take the bar exam for licensure a few months after graduation, she is hired for the summer by a local attorney in a private practice. Suzanne works 40 hours per week for the attorney performing legal research, client and witness interviews, and drafting legal documents. All work is reviewed by the attorney and corrected or updated as suggestions are made to Suzanne. She is paid on a biweekly basis. She receives a net check with no description of withholdings. However, the check is in fact for an amount that is about 80 percent of the $20 per hour she agreed to for wages when she hired on. This is Susan's first job other than as a student worker. So she is unfamiliar with private employer paychecks and how they typically appear. After passing the bar, Suzanne accepts a position with a large firm just at the end of the calendar year. In late January, she receives a Form 1099 from the attorney she worked for during the summer. To her dismay, the attorney has declared Suzanne as an independent contractor, paid no taxes despite her claim he withheld them, and she now has a federal and state tax liability of more than two thousand dollars. Suzanne sues the attorney and, much to his surprise, presents at trial copies of the time sheets kept in 15-minute increments of all the work that she performed, notes from the attorney about corrections to her work that he desired, and a letter from the attorney extending an offer to her to work for him at a rate of $20 per hour. With this information, Suzanne was able to establish that she was in fact an employee and the attorney is held accountable for the taxes due as well as the employer's contribution.

Form **SS-8**
(Rev. November 2006)
Department of the Treasury
Internal Revenue Service

Determination of Worker Status
for Purposes of Federal Employment Taxes
and Income Tax Withholding

OMB No. 1545-0004

Name of firm (or person) for whom the worker performed services	Worker's name

Firm's address (include street address, apt. or suite no., city, state, and ZIP code)	Worker's address (include street address, apt. or suite no., city, state, and ZIP code)

Trade name	Daytime telephone number ( )	Worker's social security number

Telephone number (include area code) ( )	Firm's employer identification number	Worker's employer identification number (if any)

Note. If the worker is paid by a firm other than the one listed on this form for these services, enter the name, address, and employer identification number of the payer. ▶

Disclosure of Information

The information provided on Form SS-8 may be disclosed to the firm, worker, or payer named above to assist the IRS in the determination process. For example, if you are a worker, we may disclose the information you provide on Form SS-8 to the firm or payer named above. The information can only be disclosed to assist with the determination process. If you provide incomplete information, we may not be able to process your request. See *Privacy Act and Paperwork Reduction Act Notice* on page 5 for more information. **If you do not want this information disclosed to other parties, do not file Form SS-8.**

Parts I–V. All filers of Form SS-8 must complete all questions in Parts I–IV. Part V must be completed if the worker provides a service directly to customers or is a salesperson. If you cannot answer a question, enter "Unknown" or "Does not apply." If you need more space for a question, attach another sheet with the part and question number clearly identified.

Part I   General Information

1 This form is being completed by: ☐ Firm ☐ Worker; for services performed _____ to _____ .
   (beginning date)   (ending date)

2 Explain your reason(s) for filing this form (for example, you received a bill from the IRS, you believe you erroneously received a Form 1099 or Form W-2, you are unable to get worker's compensation benefits, or you were audited or are being audited by the IRS). ....
   ....
   ....

3 Total number of workers who performed or are performing the same or similar services _____ .

4 How did the worker obtain the job? ☐ Application   ☐ Bid   ☐ Employment Agency   ☐ Other (specify) _____

5 Attach copies of all supporting documentation (contracts, invoices, memos, Forms W-2 or Forms 1099-MISC issued or received, IRS closing agreements, IRS rulings, etc.). In addition, please inform us of any current or past litigation concerning the worker's status. If no income reporting forms (Form 1099-MISC or W-2) were furnished to the worker, enter the amount of income earned for the year(s) at issue $ _____ .
   If both Form W-2 and Form 1099-MISC were issued or received, explain why. ....

6 Describe the firm's business. ....
   ....

7 Describe the work done by the worker and provide the worker's job title. ....
   ....
   ....

8 Explain why you believe the worker is an employee or an independent contractor. ....
   ....
   ....

9 Did the worker perform services for the firm in any capacity before providing the services that are the subject of this determination request?
   ☐ Yes   ☐ No   ☐ N/A
   If "Yes," what were the dates of the prior service? ....
   If "Yes," explain the differences, if any, between the current and prior service. ....
   ....
   ....

10 If the work is done under a written agreement between the firm and the worker, attach a copy (preferably signed by both parties). Describe the terms and conditions of the work arrangement. ....
   ....

For Privacy Act and Paperwork Reduction Act Notice, see page 5.   Cat. No. 16106T   Form **SS-8** (Rev. 11-2006)

EXHIBIT 4–1   SS-8 *(continues)*

Form SS-8 (Rev. 11-2006)   Page **2**

Part II   Behavioral Control

1   What specific training and/or instruction is the worker given by the firm? ....

2   How does the worker receive work assignments? ....

3   Who determines the methods by which the assignments are performed? ....
4   Who is the worker required to contact if problems or complaints arise and who is responsible for their resolution? ......

5   What types of reports are required from the worker? Attach examples. ....

6   Describe the worker's daily routine such as, schedule, hours, etc. ....

7   At what location(s) does the worker perform services (e.g., firm's premises, own shop or office, home, customer's location, etc.)? Indicate
     the appropriate percentage of time the worker spends in each location, if more than one. ....

8   Describe any meetings the worker is required to attend and any penalties for not attending (e.g., sales meetings, monthly meetings, staff
     meetings, etc.). ....
9   Is the worker required to provide the services personally? . . . . ☐ Yes   ☐ No
10   If substitutes or helpers are needed, who hires them? ....
11   If the worker hires the substitutes or helpers, is approval required? . . . . ☐ Yes   ☐ No
     If "Yes," by whom? ....
12   Who pays the substitutes or helpers? ....
13   Is the worker reimbursed if the worker pays the substitutes or helpers? . . . . ☐ Yes   ☐ No
     If "Yes," by whom? ....

Part III   Financial Control

1   List the supplies, equipment, materials, and property provided by each party:
     The firm   ....
     The worker   ....
     Other party   ....
2   Does the worker lease equipment? . . . . ☐ Yes   ☐ No
     If "Yes," what are the terms of the lease? (Attach a copy or explanatory statement.) ....

3   What expenses are incurred by the worker in the performance of services for the firm? ....

4   Specify which, if any, expenses are reimbursed by:
     The firm   ....
     Other party   ....
5   Type of pay the worker receives: ☐ Salary   ☐ Commission   ☐ Hourly Wage   ☐ Piece Work
     ☐ Lump Sum   ☐ Other (specify) ....
     If type of pay is commission, and the firm guarantees a minimum amount of pay, specify amount $ _____ .
6   Is the worker allowed a drawing account for advances? . . . . ☐ Yes   ☐ No
     If "Yes," how often? ....
     Specify any restrictions. ....

7   Whom does the customer pay? . . . . ☐ Firm   ☐ Worker
     If worker, does the worker pay the total amount to the firm? ☐ Yes   ☐ No   If "No," explain. ....

8   Does the firm carry worker's compensation insurance on the worker? . . . . ☐ Yes   ☐ No
9   What economic loss or financial risk, if any, can the worker incur beyond the normal loss of salary (e.g., loss or damage of equipment,
     material, etc.)? ....

Form **SS-8** (Rev. 11-2006)

EXHIBIT 4–1   SS-8 *(continued)*

Form SS-8 (Rev. 11-2006)   Page **3**

Part IV   Relationship of the Worker and Firm

1   List the benefits available to the worker (e.g., paid vacations, sick pay, pensions, bonuses, paid holidays, personal days, insurance benefits). ....

2   Can the relationship be terminated by either party without incurring liability or penalty? . . . . ☐ **Yes** ☐ **No**
     If "No," explain your answer. ....

3   Did the worker perform similar services for others during the same time period? . . . . ☐ **Yes** ☐ **No**
     If "Yes," is the worker required to get approval from the firm? . . . . ☐ **Yes** ☐ **No**

4   Describe any agreements prohibiting competition between the worker and the firm while the worker is performing services or during any later period. Attach any available documentation. ....

5   Is the worker a member of a union? . . . . ☐ **Yes** ☐ **No**

6   What type of advertising, if any, does the worker do (e.g., a business listing in a directory, business cards, etc.)? Provide copies, if applicable.

7   If the worker assembles or processes a product at home, who provides the materials and instructions or pattern? ....

8   What does the worker do with the finished product (e.g., return it to the firm, provide it to another party, or sell it)? ....

9   How does the firm represent the worker to its customers (e.g., employee, partner, representative, or contractor)? ....

10   If the worker no longer performs services for the firm, how did the relationship end (e.g., worker quit or was fired, job completed, contract ended, firm or worker went out of business)? ....

Part V   **For Service Providers or Salespersons.** Complete this part if the worker provided a service directly to customers or is a salesperson.

1   What are the worker's responsibilities in soliciting new customers? ....

2   Who provides the worker with leads to prospective customers? ....

3   Describe any reporting requirements pertaining to the leads. ....

4   What terms and conditions of sale, if any, are required by the firm? ....

5   Are orders submitted to and subject to approval by the firm? . . . . ☐ **Yes** ☐ **No**

6   Who determines the worker's territory? ....

7   Did the worker pay for the privilege of serving customers on the route or in the territory? . . . . ☐ **Yes** ☐ **No**
     If "Yes," whom did the worker pay? ....
     If "Yes," how much did the worker pay? . . . . $ ....

8   Where does the worker sell the product (e.g., in a home, retail establishment, etc.)? ....

9   List the product and/or services distributed by the worker (e.g., meat, vegetables, fruit, bakery products, beverages, or laundry or dry cleaning services). If more than one type of product and/or service is distributed, specify the principal one. ....

10   Does the worker sell life insurance full time? . . . . ☐ **Yes** ☐ **No**

11   Does the worker sell other types of insurance for the firm? . . . . ☐ **Yes** ☐ **No**
     If "Yes," enter the percentage of the worker's total working time spent in selling other types of insurance . . . .%

12   If the worker solicits orders from wholesalers, retailers, contractors, or operators of hotels, restaurants, or other similar establishments, enter the percentage of the worker's time spent in the solicitation . . . .%

13   Is the merchandise purchased by the customers for resale or use in their business operations? . . . . ☐ **Yes** ☐ **No**
     Describe the merchandise and state whether it is equipment installed on the customers' premises. ....

Sign Here   ▶   Under penalties of perjury, I declare that I have examined this request, including accompanying documents, and to the best of my knowledge and belief, the facts presented are true, correct, and complete.

_____   Title ▶ _____   Date ▶ _____
Type or print name below signature.

Form **SS-8** (Rev. 11-2006)

EXHIBIT 4–1   SS-8 *(continued)*

ASSIGNMENT **4.3**

Consider the following individuals and determine if they would likely be an employee or independent contractor. Explain your answer.

a. Connie is a paralegal who has been hired to perform the discovery in a large class action suit. The case is expected to take two to three years to complete. Connie does not receive any job benefits.

b. Michelle has been hired as an attorney to work on a large class action suit. The case is expected to take one year to complete. Michelle is allowed to participate in the law firm's 401K retirement plan.

c. Claire has been hired to fill in for a secretary who is on three months' leave of absence due to maternity. Claire receives a paycheck with Social Security taxes and income taxes withheld.

d. Scott is a legal investigator with an office in a large law firm. He works on a variety of cases as assigned and is paid a set salary per week. Scott, however, is in complete control of how he performs the investigations.

e. Scott's brother Drake is also a legal investigator with the same firm. Drake, however, is paid on an hourly basis for the cases he actually investigates. Drake works from his home. Drake is also in complete control of how he performs the investigations.

2. Timekeeping—Salaried versus Hourly, Overtime

In earlier chapters, the discussion was focused on timekeeping by legal professionals for purposes client billing. Additionally, timekeeping is, for most businesses (including law firms), a payroll function. Under a variety of state and federal laws, a minimum wage is established along with rules for the number of hours an individual can be required to work, breaks during the work period, overtime pay, and even the frequency of wage payment. Very often, employees who perform tasks that are considered routine, repetitive, or that require limited independent judgment/skill are paid on an hourly basis. By contrast, individuals who exercise personal judgment or skill in order to complete a task are compensated for the work performed rather than the amount of time taken to accomplish the task. These employees are typically paid a flat salary regardless of the amount of time involved in performing the work. Although parties may agree to either form of compensation, the issue arises with respect to overtime. Historically, salaried employees were not entitled to additional payment for hours worked beyond the standardized units established by law for full-time employment. As a result, a large number of employers began making all employees salaried in an attempt to save money for the business. In response, legislation was passed that places general definitions on who is entitled to overtime pay regardless of whether they are ordinarily paid as salaried or hourly employees.

From an accounting and payroll perspective, it is important to track the hours worked by all personnel who may be entitled to overtime pay. Additionally, laws require employers to maintain such records for hourly employees. Even if the firm deems the individual salaried and professional or management level (not usually entitled to overtime pay), it is still advisable to track the time of these individuals in the event a dispute should ever arise. In that event, if the person were declared entitled, at least there would be proper records by which to calculate any additional payments due. The methods of timekeeping by employees, varies dramatically. Some firms still use handwritten documentation, others use time clocks, and yet others employ a computerized system. Regardless of the method, it is important to note when an employee's work exceeds the statutory limit for regular pay and triggers payment at a higher rate for overtime. Once the amount of time that an employee has worked is established, the calculation for payment due is relatively straightforward. However, it is at this point that the issue of tax and withholding comes into play.

APPLICATION **4.11**

Nick is hired to do the bookkeeping for a local law firm. The firm is relatively small with just five employees. At the end of the pay period, he has the following payroll to prepare:

Employee #	Hours	Hourly Rate	(H)/Salaried (S)	Entitled to Overtime
10618	42	10.00	H	Y
10619	46	11.050	S	Y
10620	50	18.00	S	N
10621	38	9.00	H	Y

Employee #10618 would be entitled to 40 hours worth of pay at 10.00 per hour and 2 hours of pay at the overtime rate.

Employee #10619 would be entitled to the salary rate of 40 hours worth of pay at 11.50 per hour and 6 hours pay at the overtime rate. If the employee's salary is a set amount per month or year, that amount may need to be divided by 40 hours per week for 52 weeks to obtain the hourly rate to use in calculating overtime.

Employee #10620 would be entitled to 40 hours worth of pay at 18.00 per hour, and no additional compensation would be due for the additional 10 hours worked.

Employee #10621 would be entitled to 38 hours worth of pay at 9.00 per hour. No more than 40 hours was worked, so overtime is not an issue.

3. Withholding and Form W-4

Once a worker has been classified as an employee and the rate of pay is established, the process of creating the pay document and associated records is much more complicated than one might realize. The federal and state governments have mandatory requirements with respect to the frequency and manner of payment of monies due to employees. Additionally, both state and federal tax withholding requirements apply. The amount withheld may be a mandatory amount or may be affected by factors unique to the individual employee.

When an individual is hired by an employer, it is necessary for that person to complete a **Form W-4**. This document is used by the Internal Revenue Service (IRS) to assist individuals in having the proper amount of pay withheld for income tax purposes. On an individual's tax return, there is a portion of income allowed to each person in a household that is exempt from being taxed. On the individual return, this is known as a **personal exemption**. Form W-4 is used to assist individuals in having the right amount of tax withheld from their pay by taking into account the amount of income over the course of a year that will be taxed after the personal exemption amount for the household is excluded.

Form W-4 asks a series of questions and provides a formula to complete. The result is the number of exemptions that an individual can claim. However, this is based on a variety of general considerations and an individual may need to adjust the number of exemptions claimed in order to have an adequate amount of tax withheld. There is a general assumption in the W-4 calculation that a person will hold one job during the year. Furthermore, the assumption is made that the larger the family, the larger number of deductible expenses that also can be taken against income along with the personal exemptions. After these two amounts are subtracted, the remaining income is subject to tax. Additionally, once the tax is determined, there may be applicable credits that lower the tax. Most of these credits are also attributed to families. However, if a person does not fit into this mold of general assumptions, more income may be subject to tax and as a result the tax due may be higher. Thus, an individual may need to change their W-4 exemptions claimed in order to have sufficient tax withheld. Similarly, if an individual claims less than the allowed number of exemptions and has more than adequate deductions to apply as well, that person may end up having more than enough tax withheld resulting in a tax refund. This also can be converted to more income throughout the year by increasing the number of exemptions claimed.

FORM W-4

An IRS document that helps determine the proper amount of an individual's pay to withhold for income tax

PERSONAL EXEMPTION

Portion of income allowed to each person in a household that is exempt from being taxed.

Form W-4 (2007)

Purpose. Complete Form W-4 so that your employer can withhold the correct federal income tax from your pay. Because your tax situation may change, you may want to refigure your withholding each year.

Exemption from withholding. If you are exempt, complete **only** lines 1, 2, 3, 4, and 7 and sign the form to validate it. Your exemption for 2007 expires February 16, 2008. See Pub. 505, Tax Withholding and Estimated Tax.

Note. You cannot claim exemption from withholding if (a) your income exceeds $850 and includes more than $300 of unearned income (for example, interest and dividends) and (b) another person can claim you as a dependent on their tax return.

Basic instructions. If you are not exempt, complete the **Personal Allowances Worksheet** below. The worksheets on page 2 adjust your withholding allowances based on

itemized deductions, certain credits, adjustments to income, or two-earner/multiple job situations. Complete all worksheets that apply. However, you may claim fewer (or zero) allowances.

Head of household. Generally, you may claim head of household filing status on your tax return only if you are unmarried and pay more than 50% of the costs of keeping up a home for yourself and your dependent(s) or other qualifying individuals.

Tax credits. You can take projected tax credits into account in figuring your allowable number of withholding allowances. Credits for child or dependent care expenses and the child tax credit may be claimed using the **Personal Allowances Worksheet** below. See Pub. 919, How Do I Adjust My Tax Withholding, for information on converting your other credits into withholding allowances.

Nonwage income. If you have a large amount of nonwage income, such as interest or dividends, consider making estimated tax payments using Form 1040-ES, Estimated Tax

for Individuals. Otherwise, you may owe additional tax. If you have pension or annuity income, see Pub. 919 to find out if you should adjust your withholding on Form W-4 or W-4P.

Two earners/Multiple jobs. If you have a working spouse or more than one job, figure the total number of allowances you are entitled to claim on all jobs using worksheets from only one Form W-4. Your withholding usually will be most accurate when all allowances are claimed on the Form W-4 for the highest paying job and zero allowances are claimed on the others.

Nonresident alien. If you are a nonresident alien, see the Instructions for Form 8233 before completing this Form W-4.

Check your withholding. After your Form W-4 takes effect, use Pub. 919 to see how the dollar amount you are having withheld compares to your projected total tax for 2007. See Pub. 919, especially if your earnings exceed $130,000 (Single) or $180,000 (Married).

Personal Allowances Worksheet (Keep for your records.)

A Enter "1" for **yourself** if no one else can claim you as a dependent . . . . **A** _____

B Enter "1" if: { • You are single and have only one job; or
• You are married, have only one job, and your spouse does not work; or
• Your wages from a second job or your spouse's wages (or the total of both) are $1,000 or less. } . . **B** _____

C Enter "1" for your **spouse.** But, you may choose to enter "-0-" if you are married and have either a working spouse or more than one job. (Entering "-0-" may help you avoid having too little tax withheld.) . . . . **C** _____

D Enter number of **dependents** (other than your spouse or yourself) you will claim on your tax return . . . . . . **D** _____

E Enter "1" if you will file as **head of household** on your tax return (see conditions under **Head of household** above) . **E** _____

F Enter "1" if you have at least $1,500 of **child or dependent care expenses** for which you plan to claim a credit . . **F** _____
(**Note.** Do **not** include child support payments. See Pub. 503, Child and Dependent Care Expenses, for details.)

G **Child Tax Credit** (including additional child tax credit). See Pub 972, Child Tax Credit, for more information.
• If your total income will be less than $57,000 ($85,000 if married), enter "2" for each eligible child.
• If your total income will be between $57,000 and $84,000 ($85,000 and $119,000 if married), enter "1" for each eligible child plus "1" **additional** if you have 4 or more eligible children. . . . . **G** _____

H Add lines A through G and enter total here. (**Note.** This may be different from the number of exemptions you claim on your tax return.) ▶ **H** _____

For accuracy, complete all worksheets that apply. { • If you plan to **itemize or claim adjustments to income** and want to reduce your withholding, see the **Deductions and Adjustments Worksheet** on page 2.
• If you have **more than one job** or are **married and you and your spouse both work** and the combined earnings from all jobs exceed $40,000 ($25,000 if married) see the **Two-Earners/Multiple Jobs Worksheet** on page 2 to avoid having too little tax withheld.
• If **neither** of the above situations applies, **stop here** and enter the number from line H on line 5 of Form W-4 below. }

Cut here and give Form W-4 to your employer. Keep the top part for your records.

Form **W-4**	**Employee's Withholding Allowance Certificate**	OMB No. 1545-0074
Department of the Treasury Internal Revenue Service	▶ Whether you are entitled to claim a certain number of allowances or exemption from withholding is subject to review by the IRS. Your employer may be required to send a copy of this form to the IRS.	20**07**

1 Type or print your first name and middle initial.	Last name		2 Your social security number
Home address (number and street or rural route)		**3** ☐ Single ☐ Married ☐ Married, but withhold at higher Single rate. Note. If married, but legally separated, or spouse is a nonresident alien, check the "Single" box.	
City or town, state, and ZIP code		**4** If your last name differs from that shown on your social security card, check here. You must call 1-800-772-1213 for a replacement card. ▶ ☐	

5 Total number of allowances you are claiming (from line **H** above **or** from the applicable worksheet on page 2)   **5** _____

6 Additional amount, if any, you want withheld from each paycheck . . . .   **6** $ _____

7 I claim exemption from withholding for 2007, and I certify that I meet **both** of the following conditions for exemption.
• Last year I had a right to a refund of **all** federal income tax withheld because I had **no** tax liability **and**
• This year I expect a refund of **all** federal income tax withheld because I expect to have **no** tax liability.
If you meet both conditions, write "Exempt" here . . . . ▶ **7** _____

Under penalties of perjury, I declare that I have examined this certificate and to the best of my knowledge and belief, it is true, correct, and complete.

Employee's signature
(Form is not valid unless you sign it.) ▶ _____   **Date ▶** _____

8 Employer's name and address (Employer: Complete lines 8 and 10 only if sending to the IRS.)	9 Office code (optional)	10 Employer identification number (EIN)

For Privacy Act and Paperwork Reduction Act Notice, see page 2.   Cat. No. 10220Q   Form **W-4** (2007)

EXHIBIT 4–2 Form W-4 (*continues*)

Form W-4 (2007)   Page **2**

Deductions and Adjustments Worksheet

Note. Use this worksheet *only* if you plan to itemize deductions, claim certain credits, or claim adjustments to income on your 2007 tax return.

1. Enter an estimate of your 2007 itemized deductions. These include qualifying home mortgage interest, charitable contributions, state and local taxes, medical expenses in excess of 7.5% of your income, and miscellaneous deductions. (For 2007, you may have to reduce your itemized deductions if your income is over $156,400 ($78,200 if married filing separately). See *Worksheet 2* in Pub. 919 for details.) . . **1** $ _____

2. Enter: { $10,700 if married filing jointly or qualifying widow(er)
   $ 7,850 if head of household
   $ 5,350 if single or married filing separately } . . . . **2** $ _____

3. **Subtract** line 2 from line 1. If zero or less, enter "-0-" . . . . **3** $ _____
4. Enter an estimate of your 2007 adjustments to income, including alimony, deductible IRA contributions, and student loan interest **4** $ _____
5. **Add** lines 3 and 4 and enter the total. (Include any amount for credits from *Worksheet 8* in Pub. 919) . **5** $ _____
6. Enter an estimate of your 2007 nonwage income (such as dividends or interest) . . . . **6** $ _____
7. **Subtract** line 6 from line 5. If zero or less, enter "-0-" . . . . **7** $ _____
8. **Divide** the amount on line 7 by $3,400 and enter the result here. Drop any fraction . . . . **8** _____
9. Enter the number from the **Personal Allowances Worksheet**, line H, page 1 . . . . **9** _____
10. **Add** lines 8 and 9 and enter the total here. If you plan to use the **Two-Earners/Multiple Jobs Worksheet**, also enter this total on line 1 below. Otherwise, **stop here** and enter this total on Form W-4, line 5, page 1 **10** _____

Two-Earners/Multiple Jobs Worksheet (See *Two earners/multiple jobs* on page 1.)

Note. Use this worksheet *only* if the instructions under line H on page 1 direct you here.

1. Enter the number from line H, page 1 (or from line 10 above if you used the **Deductions and Adjustments Worksheet**) **1** _____
2. Find the number in **Table 1** below that applies to the **LOWEST** paying job and enter it here. **However,** if you are married filing jointly and wages from the highest paying job are $50,000 or less, do not enter more than "3." . . . . **2** _____
3. If line 1 is **more than or equal to** line 2, subtract line 2 from line 1. Enter the result here (if zero, enter "-0-") and on Form W-4, line 5, page 1. **Do not** use the rest of this worksheet . . . . **3** _____

Note. If line 1 is *less than* line 2, enter "-0-" on Form W-4, line 5, page 1. Complete lines 4–9 below to calculate the additional withholding amount necessary to avoid a year-end tax bill.

4. Enter the number from line 2 of this worksheet . . . . **4** _____
5. Enter the number from line 1 of this worksheet . . . . **5** _____
6. **Subtract** line 5 from line 4 . . . . **6** _____
7. Find the amount in **Table 2** below that applies to the **HIGHEST** paying job and enter it here . . . . **7** $ _____
8. **Multiply** line 7 by line 6 and enter the result here. This is the additional annual withholding needed . . **8** $ _____
9. Divide line 8 by the number of pay periods remaining in 2007. For example, divide by 26 if you are paid every two weeks and you complete this form in December 2006. Enter the result here and on Form W-4, line 6, page 1. This is the additional amount to be withheld from each paycheck . . . . **9** $ _____

Table 1				Table 2			
Married Filing Jointly		**All Others**		**Married Filing Jointly**		**All Others**	
If wages from **LOWEST** paying job are—	Enter on line 2 above	If wages from **LOWEST** paying job are—	Enter on line 2 above	If wages from **HIGHEST** paying job are—	Enter on line 7 above	If wages from **HIGHEST** paying job are—	Enter on line 7 above
$0 - $4,500	0	$0 - $6,000	0	$0 - $65,000	$510	$0 - $35,000	$510
4,501 - 9,000	1	6,001 - 12,000	1	65,001 - 120,000	850	35,001 - 80,000	850
9,001 - 18,000	2	12,001 - 19,000	2	120,001 - 170,000	950	80,001 - 150,000	950
18,001 - 22,000	3	19,001 - 26,000	3	170,001 - 300,000	1,120	150,001 - 340,000	1,120
22,001 - 26,000	4	26,001 - 35,000	4	300,001 and over	1,190	340,001 and over	1,190
26,001 - 32,000	5	35,001 - 50,000	5				
32,001 - 38,000	6	50,001 - 65,000	6				
38,001 - 46,000	7	65,001 - 80,000	7				
46,001 - 55,000	8	80,001 - 90,000	8				
55,001 - 60,000	9	90,001 - 120,000	9				
60,001 - 65,000	10	120,001 and over	10				
65,001 - 75,000	11						
75,001 - 95,000	12						
95,001 - 105,000	13						
105,001 - 120,000	14						
120,001 and over	15						

EXHIBIT 4–2 Form W-4 *(continued)*

Once each employee has a completed W-4 form for the employer, federal and state income tax tables can be used to calculate the proper amount of income tax withholding. The federal tax tables are located in the Internal Revenue Service publication **Circular E Employer's Tax Guide**. The tables in the guide are divided by the frequency of the pay period such as weekly, biweekly, semimonthly, and monthly. Then they are subdivided by individuals who are claiming as married or single. After that, a chart is used that combines the number of exemptions claimed with the amount of earnings (see Exhibit 4–8). For example, consider someone paid every other Friday claiming married and three exemptions earns $250 in the two-week period. By going to the chart for married individuals paid biweekly, locate the line for three exemptions and follow it to the point in the chart that corresponds to wages of $250. The amount listed will be the amount of tax properly to be withheld. This calculation must be done each pay period, for each individual's gross amount of pay, for federal income tax. In states that have a state income tax, the same calculation must be done to determine the proper amount of state income tax to withhold. Fortunately, there are now readily available computer software programs that perform the calculations. They may be as simple as those that require someone to input certain values for each employee such as the number of exemptions and wages earned, or so sophisticated that the entire payroll is calculated and checks printed in response to the employee inputting time worked by way of a computerized time clock system.

APPLICATION **4.12**

Alex is married and the father of two children. Alex works two part-time jobs as a laborer. His wife Jackie has one full-time job as a teacher. Both Alex and Jackie claimed four exemptions on their W-4 forms with their employers. Alex and Jackie have just taken out a mortgage and bought a home, they contribute regularly to retirement plan accounts, their children are both in full-time day care, a full 10 percent of their income is given to charity/ church, they pay for their own health insurance, and one of the children requires expensive monthly prescriptions and frequent doctor visits. Under these circumstances, it is likely that Alex and Jackie's tax deductions in addition to their personal exemptions would eliminate any tax liability. In fact, they may well be entitled to a substantial refund. However, consider the following change in circumstances:

Alex and Jackie have two children both out of high school and attending college on full scholarships. Alex and Jackie rent their home, do not contribute to charity, and have no substantial medical expenses. Neither contribute to retirement plans. Under these circumstances, they have virtually no deductions and only their exemptions to offset their income. As a result, it is very possible that they are not having enough tax withheld to cover the tax liability on their income. To increase the tax withheld, they would need to reduce the number of exemptions (and thus the amount of tax-exempt income) claimed.

(For Wages Paid in 2007)

Alternative 1.—Tables for Percentage Method Withholding Computations

Table A(1)—WEEKLY PAYROLL PERIOD (Amount for each allowance claimed is $65.38)

	Single Person				Married Person		
If the wage in excess of allowance amount is:		The income tax to be withheld is:		If the wage in excess of allowance amount is:		The income tax to be withheld is:	
		Of such wage—	From product			Of such wage—	From product
Over—	But not over—			Over—	But not over—		
$0	—$51	0%	$0	$0	—$154	0%	$0
$51	—$195	10% less	$5.10	$154	—$449	10% less	$15.40
$195	—$645	15% less	$14.85	$449	—$1,360	15% less	$37.85
$645	—$1,482	25% less	$79.35	$1,360	—$2,573	25% less	$173.85
$1,482	—$3,131	28% less	$123.81	$2,573	—$3,907	28% less	$251.04
$3,131	—$6,763	33% less	$280.36	$3,907	—$6,865	33% less	$446.39
$6,763	—	35% less	$415.62	$6,865	—	35% less	$583.69

Table B(1)—BIWEEKLY PAYROLL PERIOD (Amount for each allowance claimed is $130.77)

	Single Person				Married Person		
If the wage in excess of allowance amount is:		The income tax to be withheld is:		If the wage in excess of allowance amount is:		The income tax to be withheld is:	
		Of such wage—	From product			Of such wage—	From product
Over—	But not over—			Over—	But not over—		
$0	—$102	0%	$0	$0	—$308	0%	$0
$102	—$392	10% less	$10.20	$308	—$898	10% less	$30.80
$392	—$1,289	15% less	$29.65	$898	—$2,719	15% less	$75.70
$1,289	—$2,964	25% less	$158.55	$2,719	—$5,146	25% less	$347.60
$2,964	—$6,262	28% less	$247.47	$5,146	—$7,813	28% less	$501.98
$6,262	—$13,525	33% less	$560.57	$7,813	—$13,731	33% less	$892.63
$13,525	—	35% less	$831.07	$13,731	—	35% less	$1,167.25

Table C(1)—SEMIMONTHLY PAYROLL PERIOD (Amount for each allowance claimed is $141.67)

	Single Person				Married Person		
If the wage in excess of allowance amount is:		The income tax to be withheld is:		If the wage in excess of allowance amount is:		The income tax to be withheld is:	
		Of such wage—	From product			Of such wage—	From product
Over—	But not over—			Over—	But not over—		
$0	—$110	0%	$0	$0	—$333	0%	$0
$110	—$422	10% less	$11.00	$333	—$973	10% less	$33.30
$422	—$1,397	15% less	$32.10	$973	—$2,946	15% less	$81.95
$1,397	—$3,211	25% less	$171.80	$2,946	—$5,575	25% less	$376.55
$3,211	—$6,783	28% less	$268.13	$5,575	—$8,465	28% less	$543.80
$6,783	—$14,652	33% less	$607.28	$8,465	—$14,875	33% less	$967.05
$14,652	—	35% less	$900.32	$14,875	—	35% less	$1,264.55

Table D(1)—MONTHLY PAYROLL PERIOD (Amount for each allowance claimed is $283.33)

	Single Person				Married Person		
If the wage in excess of allowance amount is:		The income tax to be withheld is:		If the wage in excess of allowance amount is:		The income tax to be withheld is:	
		Of such wage—	From product			Of such wage—	From product
Over—	But not over—			Over—	But not over—		
$0	—$221	0%	$0	$0	—$667	0%	$0
$221	—$843	10% less	$22.10	$667	—$1,946	10% less	$66.70
$843	—$2,793	15% less	$64.25	$1,946	—$5,892	15% less	$164.00
$2,793	—$6,423	25% less	$343.55	$5,892	—$11,150	25% less	$753.20
$6,423	—$13,567	28% less	$536.24	$11,150	—$16,929	28% less	$1,087.70
$13,567	—$29,304	33% less	$1,214.59	$16,929	—$29,750	33% less	$1,934.15
$29,304	—	35% less	$1,800.67	$29,750	—	35% less	$2,529.15

Table E(1)—DAILY OR MISCELLANEOUS PAYROLL PERIOD
(Amount for each allowance claimed per day for such period is $13.08)

	Single Person				Married Person		
If the wage in excess of allowance amount divided by the number of days in the pay period is:		The income tax to be withheld multiplied by the number of days in such period is:		If the wage in excess of allowance amount divided by the number of days in the pay period is:		The income tax to be withheld multiplied by the number of days in such period is:	
		Of such wage—	From product			Of such wage—	From product
Over—	But not over—			Over—	But not over—		
$0.00	—$10.20	0%	$0	$0.00	—$30.80	0%	$0
$10.20	—$38.90	10% less	$1.02	$30.80	—$89.80	10% less	$3.08
$38.90	—$128.90	15% less	$2.97	$89.80	—$271.90	15% less	$7.57
$128.90	—$296.40	25% less	$15.86	$271.90	—$514.60	25% less	$34.76
$296.40	—$626.20	28% less	$24.74	$514.60	—$781.30	28% less	$50.19
$626.20	—$1,352.50	33% less	$56.06	$781.30	—$1,373.10	33% less	$89.25
$1,352.50	—	35% less	$83.11	$1,373.10	—	35% less	$116.72

Note.—The adjustment factors may be reduced by one-half cent (e.g., 7.50 to 7.495; 69.38 to 69.375) to eliminate separate half rounding operations.

The first two brackets of these tables may be combined, provided zero withholding is used to credit withholding amounts computed by the combined bracket rates, e.g., $0 to $51 and $51 to $192 combined to read, Over $0, But not over $192.

The employee's excess wage (gross wage less amount for allowances claimed) is used with the applicable percentage rates and subtraction factors to calculate the amount of income tax withheld.

EXHIBIT 4–3   Sample Page from Circular E Federal Tax table for biweekly pay of $250

In addition to income tax, it is also necessary to consider what are commonly referred to as Social Security and Medicare taxes. These also may be called FICA (Federal Insurance Contributions Act). At the time of publication, employers are required to withhold 1.45 percent and contribute a matching 1.45 percent of each employee's wages for Medicare coverage to be made available to the employee on the occurrence of a specified age or disability (this is subject to definition and change by federal law). In addition, private (nongovernment) employers must withhold 6.2 percent along with an employer-matching contribution on wages earned up to a specific amount. That amount has changed periodically over the years. However, all employees must contribute on at least part of their earnings during the year until they have earned an amount sufficient to reach the statutory limit. Once the threshold has been reached, only Medicare is withheld and matched. Government employees, state and federal, are often in different types of retirement plans and do not contribute to Social Security, or only the Medicare portion.

For each employee, typically there are deductions from the gross pay for federal and sometimes state and/or local income tax, Social Security, Medicare, and unemployment taxes. In addition, many employers offer a variety of benefits at some cost to the employee. These also are typically paid for by withholding an established amount. Such benefits range from 401K retirement plans to health insurance, and also to federally approved plans known as 125 Plans that allow an employer to withhold money before taxes are withheld and then permit the employee to use such money for certain approved expenses. This has the effect of making that income withheld and used for the itemized expenses tax free.

Once the withholding amounts are determined for each employee, the payroll can be completed. A net check is prepared and distributed to the employee along with a statement that describes the amounts withheld. The records of time worked, wages earned, withholdings, and payroll generated is used to accomplish the payment of wages and support the accounting records that detail how the payroll affects the income of the business. Exhibit 4–4 illustrates a payroll flowchart to demonstrate how the payroll function is accomplished.

However, when payroll is calculated, the process has really just begun for the employer. Once the money has been withheld, what happens to it? The amount of tax withheld in a business determines how frequently the various taxes that have been withheld must be paid to the proper government agency. As the overall payroll increases, so do the taxes. As the amount of payroll tax increases, so does the frequency with which it must be paid.

In general, a business must report all of the wages paid and federal taxes withheld along with employer contributions on Form 941. The employer must then actually deposit the income tax withheld as well as both the employer and employee Social Security, and Medicare taxes. Deposits can be made either electronically, using the Electronic Federal Tax Payment System– Electronic Funds Transfer Authorization (EFTA), or by taking the deposit and Form 8109-B, Federal Tax Deposit Coupon along with federal Form 941 to an authorized financial institution or a Federal Reserve Bank. To encourage prompt payment of withheld income and

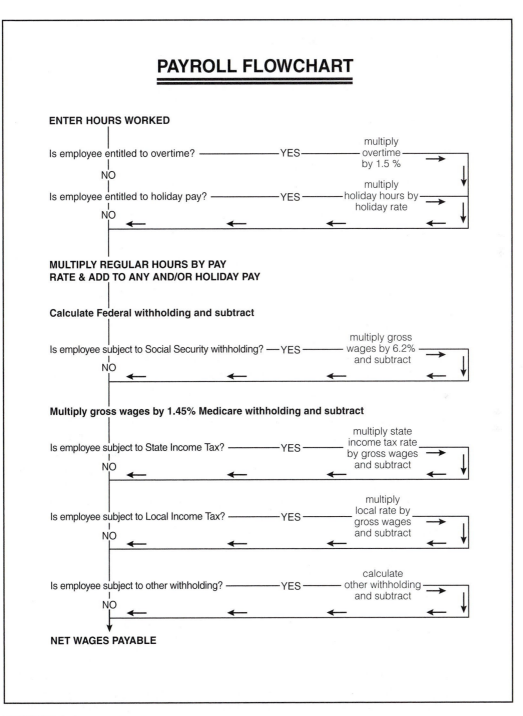

PAYROLL FLOWCHART

ENTER HOURS WORKED

Is employee entitled to overtime? ——————YES————— multiply overtime by 1.5 % →

NO

Is employee entitled to holiday pay? ——————YES————— multiply holiday hours by holiday rate →

NO   ←   ←   ←   ←

MULTIPLY REGULAR HOURS BY PAY
RATE & ADD TO ANY AND/OR HOLIDAY PAY

Calculate Federal withholding and subtract

Is employee subject to Social Security withholding? — YES ————— multiply gross wages by 6.2% and subtract →

NO   ←   ←   ←

Multiply gross wages by 1.45% Medicare withholding and subtract

Is employee subject to State Income Tax? —————— YES ————— multiply state income tax rate by gross wages and subtract →

NO   ←   ←   ←

Is employee subject to Local Income Tax? —————— YES ————— multiply local rate by gross wages and subtract →

NO   ←   ←   ←

Is employee subject to other withholding? —————— YES ————— calculate other withholding and subtract →

NO   ←   ←   ←

NET WAGES PAYABLE

EXHIBIT 4–4   Payroll Flowchart

employment taxes, including Social Security taxes, railroad retirement taxes, or collected excise taxes. Beginning in 2006, some small businesses may only need to file and pay withholding taxes annually instead of quarterly. These employers use Form 944 rather than the quarterly Form 941. The IRS notifies individuals eligible to file the annual Form 944 and also informs them of any change that would require them to switch to the quarterly Form 941. However, the responsibility for determination of the proper form and time period to file ultimately rests with the employer. If a business is required to deposit according to Form 941, the deposit should be made before the due date.

New employers who have never filed 941 forms are considered to be a monthly schedule depositor for the first calendar year of business unless you are subject to a special exception to the rule. Monthly Schedule Depositors should deposit taxes from all of their paydays in a month by the 15th of the next month, even if they pay wages every week. Employers with prior payrolls and taxes of $2,500 or more per quarter must determine if they make either monthly schedule deposits or semiweekly schedule deposits. This determination is based on Form 941 taxes during a four-quarter Lookback Period. The lookback period will determine if deposits should be made monthly or semiweekly based on whether the total taxes paid during the entire period were more or less than a specified amount. At the time of this publication, the reference amount is $50,000.00. In addition to paying quarterly taxes, the records of taxes paid must be maintained by the employer for at least four years.

Employers may have two separate employment tax deposits that must be made periodically. In addition to the Social Security, Medicare, and income tax, which are generally paid together on one form, the Federal Unemployment Tax Act (FUTA) may require payment to be made periodically as well. Like the other taxes, which are the product of withholding and/or employer contributions, an employer may have an obligation to pay the FUTA tax on behalf of the business that is providing employment. Generally there also will be a state unemployment tax that requires payment. The amount due under these funds is determined by applying a formula provided by the government for each business. The funds are then used to pay unemployment to compensate former employees who meet the state requirements. The FUTA tax is made using federal Form 940. If a business is required to deposit according to Form 940, the deposit should be made by the last day of the first month after the quarter ends. Many small businesses fill their FUTA return annually because the liability is an amount low enough to only require a yearly payment.

In addition to the federal taxes and funds, as mentioned, typically there also are required state withholdings and/or employer contributions that need to be properly reported and paid. Each state has its own system and forms to complete this step. By contacting the state department of revenue, the appropriate instructions and forms can be obtained. Additionally, many local jurisdictions such as cities may require payment of employment-related taxes. It is important that the proper forms and schedules for these be adhered to for two reasons. First, the business has a legal obligation to the state or local jurisdiction. Second, the individual employee's income tax liability may be affected by this withholding and thus it must be reported properly to the state and federal government.

Form **941 for 2006:** Employer's QUARTERLY Federal Tax Return
(Rev. January 2006)

Department of the Treasury — Internal Revenue Service

990106

OMB No. 1545-0029

(EIN)
Employer identification number ☐☐ — ☐☐☐☐☐☐☐

Name (not your trade name)

Trade name (if any)

Address

Number   Street   Suite or room number

City   State   ZIP code

Report for this Quarter ...
(Check one.)

☐ 1: January, February, March

☐ 2: April, May, June

☐ 3: July, August, September

☐ 4: October, November, December

Read the separate instructions before you fill out this form. Please type or print within the boxes.

Part 1: Answer these questions for this quarter.

1 Number of employees who received wages, tips, or other compensation for the pay period including: *Mar. 12* (Quarter 1), *June 12* (Quarter 2), *Sept. 12* (Quarter 3), *Dec. 12* (Quarter 4)   1

2 Wages, tips, and other compensation   2

3 Total income tax withheld from wages, tips, and other compensation   3

4 If no wages, tips, and other compensation are subject to social security or Medicare tax . .   ☐ Check and go to line 6.

5 Taxable social security and Medicare wages and tips:

	Column 1		Column 2
5a Taxable social security wages		× .124 =	
5b Taxable social security tips		× .124 =	
5c Taxable Medicare wages & tips		× .029 =	

5d Total social security and Medicare taxes (*Column 2*, lines 5a + 5b + 5c = line 5d) . .   5d

6 Total taxes before adjustments (lines 3 + 5d = line 6)   6

7 **TAX ADJUSTMENTS** (Read the instructions for line 7 before completing lines 7a through 7h.):

7a Current quarter's fractions of cents . . . .

7b Current quarter's sick pay . . . .

7c Current quarter's adjustments for tips and group-term life insurance

7d Current year's income tax withholding (attach Form 941c) . . .

7e Prior quarters' social security and Medicare taxes (attach Form 941c)

7f Special additions to federal income tax (attach Form 941c) . . .

7g Special additions to social security and Medicare (attach Form 941c)

7h **TOTAL ADJUSTMENTS** (Combine all amounts: lines 7a through 7g.) 7h

8 Total taxes after adjustments (Combine lines 6 and 7h.)   8

9 Advance earned income credit (EIC) payments made to employees   9

10 Total taxes after adjustment for advance EIC (line 8 – line 9 = line 10)   10

11 Total deposits for this quarter, including overpayment applied from a prior quarter . . .   11

12 Balance due (If line 10 is more than line 11, write the difference here.)   12
Make checks payable to *United States Treasury.*

13 Overpayment (If line 11 is more than line 10, write the difference here.)   Check one ☐ Apply to next return.
☐ Send a refund.

▶ You **MUST** fill out both pages of this form and **SIGN** it.

Next ➡

For Privacy Act and Paperwork Reduction Act Notice, see the back of the Payment Voucher.   Cat. No. 17001Z   Form **941** (Rev. 1-2006)

EXHIBIT 4–5 Forms 941 and 944 (continues)

990206

Name *(not your trade name)*	Employer identification number (EIN)

Part 2: Tell us about your deposit schedule and tax liability for this quarter.

If you are unsure about whether you are a monthly schedule depositor or a semiweekly schedule depositor, see *Pub. 15 (Circular E), section 11.*

14 [ ][ ]   Write the state abbreviation for the state where you made your deposits OR write "MU" if you made your deposits in *multiple* states.

15   Check one: [ ]   Line 10 is less than $2,500. Go to Part 3.

[ ]   You were a monthly schedule depositor for the entire quarter. Fill out your tax liability for each month. Then go to Part 3.

Tax liability: Month 1 [   ]   .

Month 2 [   ]   .

Month 3 [   ]   .

Total liability for quarter [   ]   .   Total must equal line 10.

[ ]   You were a semiweekly schedule depositor for any part of this quarter. Fill out *Schedule B (Form 941): Report of Tax Liability for Semiweekly Schedule Depositors*, and attach it to this form.

Part 3: Tell us about your business. If a question does NOT apply to your business, leave it blank.

16   If your business has closed or you stopped paying wages . . . . [ ] Check here, and

enter the final date you paid wages [/   /   ]   .

17   If you are a seasonal employer and you do not have to file a return for every quarter of the year . . [ ] Check here.

Part 4: May we speak with your third-party designee?

Do you want to allow an employee, a paid tax preparer, or another person to discuss this return with the IRS? See the instructions for details.

[ ] Yes. Designee's name [   ]

Phone ([   ])   [   ] – [   ]   Personal Identification Number (PIN) [ ][ ][ ][ ][ ]

[ ] No.

Part 5: Sign here. You MUST fill out both sides of this form and SIGN it.

Under penalties of perjury, I declare that I have examined this return, including accompanying schedules and statements, and to the best of my knowledge and belief, it is true, correct, and complete.

X   Sign your name here [   ]

Print name and title [   ]

Date [/   /   ]   Phone ([   ])   [   ] – [   ]

Part 6: For PAID preparers only *(optional)*

Paid Preparer's Signature		
Firm's name		
Address		EIN
		ZIP code
Date / / Phone ( ) –		SSN/PTIN
[ ] Check if you are self-employed.		

EXHIBIT 4–5   Forms 941 and 944 *(continued)*

Form **944 for 2006:** **Employer's ANNUAL Federal Tax Return**   790106

Department of the Treasury — Internal Revenue Service

OMB No. 1545-2007

Employer identification number (EIN)

Name (not your trade name)

Trade name (if any)

Address

Number   Street   Suite or room number

City   State   ZIP code

Who Must File Form 944

You must file annual Form 944 instead of filing quarterly Forms 941 **only if the IRS notified you in writing.**

Read the separate instructions before you fill out this form. Please type or print within the boxes.

Part 1: Answer these questions for 2006.

1 Wages, tips, and other compensation 1

2 Total income tax withheld from wages, tips, and other compensation 2

3 If no wages, tips, and other compensation are subject to social security or Medicare tax . 3 ☐ Check and go to line 5.

4 Taxable social security and Medicare wages and tips:

	Column 1		Column 2
4a Taxable social security wages		× .124 =	
4b Taxable social security tips		× .124 =	
4c Taxable Medicare wages & tips		× .029 =	

4d **Total social security and Medicare taxes** (Column 2, lines 4a + 4b + 4c = line 4d) . . . 4d

5 Total taxes before adjustments (lines 2 + 4d = line 5) 5

6 TAX ADJUSTMENTS (Read the instructions for line 6 before completing lines 6a through 6f.):

6a **Current year's adjustments** (See instructions) 6a

6b **Prior years' income tax withholding adjustments** (See instructions. Attach Form 941c.) 6b

6c **Prior years' social security and Medicare tax adjustments** (See instructions. Attach Form 941c.) 6c

6d **Special additions to federal income tax** (reserved use). Attach Form 941c 6d

6e **Special additions to social security and Medicare taxes** (reserved use). Attach Form 941c 6e

6f **TOTAL ADJUSTMENTS** (Combine all amounts: lines 6a through 6e.) 6f

7 **Total taxes after adjustments** (Combine lines 5 and 6f.) 7

8 Advance earned income credit (EIC) payments made to employees 8

9 Total taxes after adjustment for advance EIC (line 7 – line 8 = line 9) 9

10 Total deposits for this year, including overpayment applied from a prior year 10

11 **Balance due** (If line 9 is more than line 10, write the difference here.) Make your check payable to the *United States Treasury* and write your EIN, *Form 944*, and *2006* on the check 11

12 **Overpayment** (If line 10 is more than line 9, write the difference here.)   12

Check one ☐ Apply to next return.
☐ Send a refund.

▶ **You MUST fill out both pages of this form and SIGN it.**

Next ➡

For Privacy Act and Paperwork Reduction Act Notice, see the back of the Payment Voucher.   Cat. No. 39316N   Form **944** (2006)

EXHIBIT 4–5   Forms 941 and 944 *(continued)*

790206

Name *(not your trade name)*	Employer identification number (EIN)

Part 2: Tell us about your tax liability for 2006.

13   Check one: ☐ Line 9 is less than $2,500. Go to Part 3.

☐ Line 9 is $2,500 or more, fill out your tax liability for each month.

	Jan.		Apr.		Jul.		Oct.
13a	.	13d	.	13g	.	13j	.
	Feb.		May		Aug.		Nov.
13b	.	13e	.	13h	.	13k	.
	Mar.		Jun.		Sep.		Dec.
13c	.	13f	.	13i	.	13l	.

Total liability for year (Add lines 13a through 13l). Total must equal line 9.   13m ☐ .

14 ☐☐ If you made deposits of taxes reported on this form, write the state abbreviation for the state where you made your deposits OR write *MU* if you made your deposits in *multiple* states.

Part 3: Tell us about your business. If question 15 does NOT apply to your business, leave it blank.

15   If your business has closed or you stopped paying wages...

☐ Check here and enter the final date you paid wages.   /   /

Part 4: May we speak with your third-party designee?

Do you want to allow an employee, a paid tax preparer, or another person to discuss this return with the IRS? (See the instructions for details.)

☐ Yes. Designee's name

Select a 5-digit Personal Identification Number (PIN) to use when talking to IRS.   ☐ ☐ ☐ ☐ ☐

☐ No.

Part 5: Sign here. You MUST fill out both pages of this form and SIGN it.

Under penalties of perjury, I declare that I have examined this return, including accompanying schedules and statements, and to the best of my knowledge and belief, it is true, correct, and complete.

✗ **Sign your name here**

Print your name here

Print your title here

Date   /   /

Best daytime phone (   )   –

Part 6: For paid preparers only *(optional)*

If you were PAID to prepare this return and are not an employee of the business that is filing this return, you may choose to fill out Part 6.

Paid Preparer's name		Preparer's SSN/PTIN	
Paid Preparer's signature		Date	/ /
☐ Check if you are self employed.			
Firm's name		Firm's EIN	
Address			
City		State	ZIP code

Form **944** (2006)

EXHIBIT 4–5   Forms 941 and 944 *(continued)*

AMOUNT OF DEPOSIT (Do NOT type, please print.)

DOLLARS | CENTS

Darken only one
TYPE OF TAX

Darken only one
TAX PERIOD

MONTH TAX
YEAR ENDS →

EMPLOYER IDENTIFICATION NUMBER →

BANK NAME/
DATE STAMP

Name _____

Address _____

City _____

State _____ ZIP _____

Telephone number (____) _____

○ ◄ 941   ○ ◄ 945   ○ ◄ 1st Quarter

○ ◄ 1120   ○ ◄ 1042   ○ ◄ 2nd Quarter

○ ◄ 943   ○ ◄ 990-T   ○ ◄ 3rd Quarter

○ ◄ 720   ○ ◄ 990-PF   ○ ◄ 4th Quarter

○ ◄ CT-1   ○ ◄ 944

○ ◄ 940   Bb

IRS USE ONLY

FOR BANK USE IN MICR ENCODING

Federal Tax Deposit Coupon
Form 8109-B (Rev. 12-2006)

⬆ SEPARATE ALONG THIS LINE AND SUBMIT TO DEPOSITARY WITH PAYMENT ⬆   OMB NO. 1545-0257

What's new. The oval for Form 990-C has been deleted. Form 990-C has been replaced by Form 1120-C, U.S. Income Tax Return for Cooperative Associations. Filers of Form 1120-C must use the 1120 oval when completing Form 8109-B.

The type of tax ovals for the 1120, 1042, and 944 have been moved on the coupon. Read the type of tax to the right of the oval before you darken the oval.

Note. Except for the name, address, and telephone number, entries must be made in pencil. Use soft lead (for example, a #2 pencil) so that the entries can be read more accurately by optical scanning equipment. The name, address, and telephone number may be completed other than by hand. You cannot use photocopies of the coupons to make your deposits. Do not staple, tape, or fold the coupons.

The IRS encourages you to make federal tax deposits using the Electronic Federal Tax Payment System (EFTPS). For more information on EFTPS, go to www.eftps.gov or call 1-800-555-4477.

Purpose of form. Use Form 8109-B to make a tax deposit only in the following two situations.

1. You have not yet received your resupply of preprinted deposit coupons (Form 8109).

2. You are a new entity and have already been assigned an employer identification number (EIN), but you have not received your initial supply of preprinted deposit coupons (Form 8109). If you have not received your EIN, see Exceptions below.

Note. If you do not receive your resupply of deposit coupons and a deposit is due or you do not receive your initial supply within 5–6 weeks of receipt of your EIN, call 1-800-829-4933.

How to complete the form. Enter your name as shown on your return or other IRS correspondence, address, and EIN in the spaces provided. Do not make a name or address change on this form (see Form 8822, Change of Address). If you are required to file a Form 1120, 1120-C, 990-PF (with net investment income), 990-T, or 2438, enter the month in which your tax year ends in the MONTH TAX YEAR ENDS boxes. For example, if your tax year ends in January, enter 01; if it ends in December, enter 12. Make your entries for EIN and MONTH TAX YEAR ENDS (if applicable) as shown in Amount of deposit below.

Exceptions. If you have applied for an EIN, have not received it, and a deposit must be made, do not use Form 8109-B. Instead, send your payment to the IRS address where you file your return. Make your check or money order payable to the United States Treasury and show on it your name (as shown on Form SS-4, Application for Employer Identification Number), address, kind of tax, period covered, and date you applied for an EIN. Do not use Form 8109-B to deposit delinquent taxes assessed by the IRS. Pay those taxes directly to the IRS. See Pub. 15 (Circular E), Employer's Tax Guide, for information.

Amount of deposit. Enter the amount of the deposit in the space provided. Enter the amount legibly, forming the characters as shown below:

1 2 3 4 5 6 7 8 9 0

Hand print money amounts without using dollar signs, commas, a decimal point, or leading zeros. If the deposit is for whole dollars only, enter "00" in the CENTS boxes. For example, a deposit of $7,635.22 would be entered like this:

DOLLARS | CENTS

7 6 3 5 | 2 2

Caution. Darken only one space for TYPE OF TAX and only one space for TAX PERIOD. Darken the space to the left of the applicable form and tax period. Darkening the wrong space or multiple spaces may delay proper crediting to your account. See below for an explanation of Types of Tax and Marking the Proper Tax Period.

Types of Tax

Form 941 Employer's QUARTERLY Federal Tax Return (includes Forms 941-M, 941-PR, and 941-SS)

Form 943 Employer's Annual Tax Return for Agricultural Employees

Form 944 Employer's ANNUAL Federal Tax Return (includes Forms 944-PR, 944(SP), and 944-SS)

Form 945 Annual Return of Withheld Federal Income Tax

Form 720 Quarterly Federal Excise Tax Return

Form CT-1 Employer's Annual Railroad Retirement Tax Return

Form 940 Employer's Annual Federal Unemployment (FUTA) Tax Return (includes Form 940-PR)

Form 1120 U.S. Corporation Income Tax Return (includes Form 1120 series of returns, such as new Form 1120-C, and Form 2438)

Form 990-T Exempt Organization Business Income Tax Return

Form 990-PF Return of Private Foundation or Section 4947(a)(1) Nonexempt Charitable Trust Treated as a Private Foundation

Form 1042 Annual Withholding Tax Return for U.S. Source Income of Foreign Persons

Marking the Proper Tax Period

Payroll taxes and withholding. For Forms 941, 940, 943, 944, 945, CT-1, and 1042, if your liability was incurred during:

• January 1 through March 31, darken the 1st quarter space;
• April 1 through June 30, darken the 2nd quarter space;
• July 1 through September 30, darken the 3rd quarter space; and
• October 1 through December 31, darken the 4th quarter space.

Note. If the liability was incurred during one quarter and deposited in another quarter, darken the space for the quarter in which the tax liability was incurred. For example, if the liability was incurred in March and deposited in April, darken the 1st quarter space.

Excise taxes. For Form 720, follow the instructions above for Forms 941, 940, etc. For Form 990-PF, with net investment income, follow the instructions on page 2 for Form 1120, 990-T, and 2438.

Department of the Treasury
Internal Revenue Service

Form **8109-B** (Rev. 12-2006)
Cat. No. 61042S

EXHIBIT 4–6   Form 8109B

Form **940 for 2006:** Employer's Annual Federal Unemployment (FUTA) Tax Return

Department of the Treasury — Internal Revenue Service

850106

OMB No. 1545-0028

(EIN)
Employer identification number ☐☐ – ☐☐☐☐☐☐☐

Name *(not your trade name)*

Trade name *(if any)*

Address
Number   Street   Suite or room number
City   State   ZIP code

Type of Return
(Check all that apply.)

☐ a. Amended
☐ b. Successor employer
☐ c. No payments to employees in 2006
☐ d. Final: Business closed or stopped paying wages

Read the separate instructions before you fill out this form. Please type or print within the boxes.

Part 1: Tell us about your return. If any line does NOT apply, leave it blank.

1   If you were required to pay your state unemployment tax in ...

    1a One state only, write the state abbreviation . . . . . 1a ☐☐
    - OR -
    1b More than one state (You are a multi-state employer) . . . . 1b ☐ Check here. Fill out Schedule A.

2

Part 2: Determine your FUTA tax before adjustments for 2006. If any line does NOT apply, leave it blank.

3   Total payments to all employees . . . . 3 [   ].

4   Payments exempt from FUTA tax . . . . 4 [   ].

    Check all that apply: **4a** ☐ Fringe benefits   **4c** ☐ Retirement/Pension **4e** ☐ Other
    4b ☐ Group term life insurance **4d** ☐ Dependent care

5   Total of payments made to each employee in excess of $7,000 . . . . 5 [   ].

6   **Subtotal** (line 4 + line 5 = line 6) . . . . 6 [   ].

7   Total taxable FUTA wages (line 3 – line 6 = line 7) . . . . 7 [   ].

8   FUTA tax before adjustments (line 7 × .008 = line 8) . . . . 8 [   ].

Part 3: Determine your adjustments. If any line does NOT apply, leave it blank.

9   If ALL of the taxable FUTA wages you paid were excluded from state unemployment tax, multiply line 7 by .054 (line 7 × .054 = line 9). Then go to line 12 . . . . . . 9 [   ].

10   If SOME of the taxable FUTA wages you paid were excluded from state unemployment tax, OR you paid ANY state unemployment tax late (after the due date for filing Form 940), fill out the worksheet in the instructions. Enter the amount from line 7 of the worksheet onto line 10 . . 10 [   ].

11

Part 4: Determine your FUTA tax and balance due or overpayment for 2006. If any line does NOT apply, leave it blank.

12   Total FUTA tax after adjustments (lines 8 + 9 + 10 = line 12) . . . . 12 [   ].

13   FUTA tax deposited for the year, including any payment applied from a prior year . . . . 13 [   ].

14   Balance due (If line 12 is more than line 13, enter the difference on line 14.)
    ● If line 14 is more than $500, you must deposit your tax.
    ● If line 14 is $500 or less and you pay by check, make your check payable to the United States Treasury and write your EIN, *Form 940*, and *2006* on the check . . . . 14 [   ].

15   Overpayment (If line 13 is more than line 12, enter the difference on line 15 and check a box below.) . . . . 15 [   ].

Check one ☐ Apply to next return.
☐ Send a refund.

▶ You **MUST** fill out both pages of this form and **SIGN** it.

Next ➡

For Privacy Act and Paperwork Reduction Act Notice, see the back of Form 940-V, Payment Voucher.   Cat. No. 11234O   Form **940** (2006)

EXHIBIT 4–7   Federal Form 940 *(continues)*

850206

Name *(not your trade name)*	Employer identification number (EIN)

Part 5: Report your FUTA tax liability by quarter only if line 12 is more than $500. If not, go to Part 6.

16 Report the amount of your FUTA tax liability for each quarter; do NOT enter the amount you deposited. If you had no liability for a quarter, leave the line blank.

16a **1st quarter** (January 1 – March 31) . . . . 16a [.   ]

16b **2nd quarter** (April 1 – June 30) . . . . 16b [.   ]

16c **3rd quarter** (July 1 – September 30) . . . . 16c [.   ]

16d **4th quarter** (October 1 – December 31) . . . . . . 16d [.   ]

17 **Total tax liability for the year** (lines 16a + 16b + 16c + 16d = line 17) 17 [.   ] Total must equal line 12.

Part 6: May we speak with your third-party designee?

Do you want to allow an employee, a paid tax preparer, or another person to discuss this return with the IRS? See the instructions for details.

☐ **Yes.** Designee's name [   ]

Select a 5-digit Personal Identification Number (PIN) to use when talking to IRS [ ][ ][ ][ ][ ]

☐ **No.**

Part 7: Sign here.

You MUST fill out both pages of this form and SIGN it.

Under penalties of perjury, I declare that I have examined this return, including accompanying schedules and statements, and to the best of my knowledge and belief, it is true, correct, and complete, and that no part of any payment made to a state unemployment fund claimed as a credit was, or is to be, deducted from the payments made to employees.

✗ **Sign your name here** [   ]

Print your name here [   ]

Print your title here [   ]

Date [/   /   ]

Best daytime phone (   )   –

Part 8: For PAID preparers only (optional)

If you were paid to prepare this return and are not an employee of the business that is filing this return, you may choose to fill out Part 8.

Paid Preparer's name [   ]   Preparer's SSN/PTIN [   ]

Paid Preparer's signature [   ]   Date [/   /   ]

☐ Check if you are self-employed.

Firm's name [   ]   Firm's EIN [   ]

Street address [   ]

City [   ] State [   ] ZIP code [   ]

Page **2**   Form **940** (2006)

EXHIBIT 4–7   Federal Form 940 *(continued)*

At the end of each year, every employee and the government is provided with a summary of the employee's wages paid. This is done by using Form W-2. When an individual files their personal income tax return, the amounts reported for wages earned (taken from the W-2s received from employers during the year, are compared with the W-2s sent for that individual to the IRS from employers. If the amounts reported by employers do not correspond to the amounts reported by the employee, it is typically the responsibility of the employee to resolve the matter by obtaining a corrected W-2 from the employer and/or working with the IRS.

When a payroll is completed, it is necessary to withdraw money from the appropriate cash accounts and distribute it to the appropriate payroll related accounts. This requires payroll accounting by recording the transaction in the appropriate ledger and journal accounts. As with most accounting procedures, the amounts are first recorded in the journal. Then each element is recorded in its appropriate ledger account. The following would be an example of the corresponding entries. Either in a separate file or as part of the general accounting system, the amounts withheld or contribute by employee must be outlined in order to properly prepare the periodic and annual reporting for income tax purposes.

	Journal	Debit	Credit
3/15	Payroll Expense		
	Federal Withholding Tax Payable		
	Medicare Tax Payable		
	Social Security Tax (FICA) Payable		
	State Withholding Tax Payable		
	Local Withholding Tax Payable		
	Cash		
3/15	Payroll Tax Expense		
	Employer Contribution FICA Tax Payable		
	Employer Contribution Medicare Tax Payable		
	FUTA (Federal Unemployment Tax) Payable		
	SUTA (State Unemployment Tax) Payable		
4/15	Federal Withholding Tax Payable		
	Medicare Tax Payable		

(continues)

(continued)

	Journal	Debit	Credit
	Social Security Tax (FICA) Payable		
	State Withholding Tax Payable		
	Local Withholding Tax Payable		
	Employer Contribution FICA Tax Payable		
	Employer Contribution Medicare Tax Payable		
	FUTA (Federal Unemployment Tax) Payable		
	SUTA (State Unemployment Tax) Payable		
	Cash		

ASSIGNMENT 4.4

For purposes of this assignment, assume the following:

Each employee is subject to:

> federal income tax rate withholding of .07
>
> state income tax rate withholding rate of .015
>
> local withholding tax rate is .01
>
> FICA rate is .075 for employer and employee
>
> Medicare rate is .0145 for employer and employee

The employer FUTA rate is .0025 of the total payroll.

The employer SUTA rate is .001 of the total payroll.

There are no additional withholdings (other than those listed above). Using this information, calculate the withholding and net payroll for each employee. Assume that no employee has passed the FICA earnings threshold. Also calculate the employer tax contributions.

> Caesar: 42 hours at $12.00 per hour (eligible for overtime compensation)
>
> Angel: 31 hours at $11.00 per hour (eligible for overtime compensation)
>
> Stella: 46 hours at $15.00 per hour (not eligible for overtime compensation)

ETHICAL QUESTION

What is the consequence when an attorney is involved in improper billing practices?

JUDICIAL OPINION
MATTER OF LASSEN 672 A2D 988 (DE 1996).

I. FACTS

On January 21, 1992, partners of a Delaware law firm (the "firm", pursuant to their duty under DLRPC 8.3(a), reported several ethical violations by Respondent, a Firm partner, to the Office of Disciplinary Counsel ("DC". The circumstances surrounding these violations resulted in Respondent's voluntary resignation from the Firm.

On December 30, 1992, the ODC filed with the Board a petition for discipline (the "petition", which included allegations that Respondent violated the following rules of the DLRPC: 1.5(a) , 3.3(a)(1) , 3.3(a)(4) , 3.4(b) , 4.1(a) , 5.3(c)(1) , 8.4(b) , 8.4(c) , and 8.4(d). The Board held a hearing on May 25, 1995. At the hearing, the ODC relied exclusively on certain stipulated facts (the "stipulated facts") to form its case. In addition to Respondent, three witnesses-a Firm partner, a partner from another firm (the "prior Firm") of which Respondent had previously been a member, and Respondent's treating psychologist-testified on Respondent's behalf. The relevant stipulated facts before the Board and this Court are as follows:

1. The Respondent is a member of the Bar of the Supreme Court of the State of Delaware, having been admitted to practice in 1971.

2. At all times relevant to the Petition, Respondent was engaged in the private practice of law in the State of Delaware as one of the partners of a law firm (the "firm".)

3. Respondent withdrew as a member of the Firm effective December 31, 1991.

4. On several occasions between October 13, 1990 and February 14, 1991, Respondent used the Firm's credit card at various restaurants to charge meals totaling $262.18 that were not related to the business of the Firm nor properly chargeable to any of the Firm's clients (the "personal Restaurant Charges".

5. On several occasions between October 13, 1990, and February 14, 1991, Respondent directed the Firm's accounting and bookkeeping personnel to designate the Personal Restaurant Charges as billable to certain of the Firm's clients.

(continues)

JUDICIAL OPINION
MATTER OF LASSEN 672 A2D 988 (DE 1996). *(continued)*

6. On some occasions between October 13, 1990, and February 14, 1991, Respondent directed the Firm's accounting and bookkeeping personnel to combine the Personal Restaurant Charges with various other legitimate costs typically billed to the firm's clients (e.g. "photocopies", such that the Personal Restaurant Charges would then be re-designated on the clients' bills as "delivery charges" "photocopies" "telephone charges" or "travel expenses".)

7. In December 1990, Respondent approved $1,354.93 of false charges (which includes the $262.18 of Personal Restaurant Charges) to be billed to at least three of the Firm's clients.

8. In April of 1991, Respondent sent bills for a portion of the $1,354.93 of false charges (i.e., the $262.18 of Personal Restaurant Charges) to at least one of the Firm's clients.

9. In April of 1991, after the Firm's partners had discussed with Respondent the impropriety of some of the false charges in three client matters in which the client had not yet been sent a bill, Respondent agreed not to send a bill to those clients for such amounts, but to have the amounts charged instead against his capital account at the firm.

10. In October of 1991, Respondent signed, under oath, a pleading entitled "point Application by Attorneys for Equity Security Holders Committee for Interim Compensation and Reimbursement of Expenses"(the "Fee Application"), attached to which was an itemization of the Firm's fee and expense charges containing a false charge of $131.75 for personal restaurant meals.

11. The Fee Application was filed with the United States Bankruptcy Court for the District of Arizona in November of 1991 in the case of In re: Reddington/El Conquistador Limited Partnership, Case No. 87-0917-TUC-RTB, and was approved by the order of the Court on December 23, 1991.

12. In at least four client matters (the "our Client Matters") in which Respondent was the "filing attorney"at the firm, and which were being billed on an hourly-rate basis, Respondent reported in his time records for the Firm that he had spent substantial amounts of his professional time working on such matters when in fact the Respondent had not performed the work so recorded.

(continues)

JUDICIAL OPINION
MATTER OF LASSEN 672 A2D 988 (DE 1996). *(continued)*

13. With respect to the Four Client Matters, Respondent billed clients in those matters for the following amounts of his professional time purportedly worked on such matters when in fact the Respondent had not performed such work . . .

14. The voluminous records of the Firm reflecting the time charges in paragraphs 12 and 13 also contain at least 90 instances where other members of the Firm show conferences with Respondent, while his records show no corresponding time entry. In addition, there are at least 65 instances in those time records where one lawyer or paralegal other than Respondent reported a conference with another Firm employee whose time record does not show a corresponding entry to corroborate these conferences.

15. Except for Respondent, none of the Firm's partners has ever been asked to resign from the Firm because of matters pertaining to the billing of clients or the keeping of time records.

In summary, the facts before this Court show that Respondent: (a) submitted to clients and to the bankruptcy court as disbursements personal charges totaling $1,486.68; (b) attempted to disguise those charges; (c) improperly attempted to charge to clients in "at least" four matters fictitious hourly billings totaling $38,184; and (d) entered other questionable billable hours on firm records. The facts also show that neither the Firm nor any client suffered any financial loss as a result of Respondent's misconduct.

In addition, Respondent resigned in 1982 from the Prior Firm and received a private censure from the Board, due to unethical billing practices...The Preliminary Report of the member of the Board assigned to that matter, upon which report the private censure appears to have been based, concluded as follows:

Mr. Laser's own account shows that he was in violation of DR1-102(A)(4) and (6). These provisions provide respectively that:

"A) A lawyer shall not:

(4) Engage in conduct involving dishonesty, fraud, deceit, or misrepresentation; and

(6) Engage in any other conduct that adversely reflects on his fitness to practice law."

Also, I find that Mr. Lassen was in violation of DR2-106(B) in that he did charge an excessive fee, i.e., one for which there was no basis in fact.

On the other hand, it is my belief that while Mr. Lassen knew his conduct to be wrongful, he had no intention of defrauding the firm's client on a long-term basis and did intend to make up the time to the client when his personal situation had cleared up. I also

(continues)

JUDICIAL OPINION
MATTER OF LASSEN 672 A2D 988 (DE 1996). *(continued)*

find that once confronted with his wrongful conduct, Mr. Lassen has accepted full responsibility for that conduct, has expressed his shame and embarrassment, voluntarily resigned from his firm at considerable financial sacrifice and has brought the matter to the attention of the Board on Professional Responsibility himself. In addition, I find that no member of the public has actually been injured by his conduct; that the member of the public affected by his conduct "as no further interest in the matter" . . .

Though stipulating to the above facts, Respondent denied violating the DLRPC, arguing that the conduct currently before the Court was not "one knowingly or intentionally to obtain any improper or unreasonable fee, to obtain any personal benefit at the expense of any other person, or with any fraudulent or illegal intent." Alternatively, Respondent urged the Board to recommend a sanction consisting of a private admonition conditioned on the Permanent Retirement Sanction, which prohibits Respondent from ever again engaging in the practice of law in Delaware and elsewhere.

II. THE BOARD'S REPORT

In its Report, the Board concluded as follows:

. . . The Board finds that there is clear and convincing evidence that the Respondent violated the Rules set forth in Counts One to Nine of the Petition, except for Count Seven . . .

The Respondent argues that the Disciplinary Counsel has not adduced clear and convincing evidence of intent necessary to establish a violation of any of the Rules set forth in the Counts of the Petition. Disciplinary Counsel argues that a person intends the natural and probable consequences of his acts and, therefore, the requisite intent is presumed from the Respondent's conduct. The Respondent, however, points out that the presumption is refutable. The Respondent argues the evidence shows that the Respondent did not intend knowingly or intentionally to make false statements or intend to defraud or to deceive anyone, nor did he act with any motive of personal monetary gain, and, accordingly, the Respondent concludes there is not the requisite clear and convincing evidence of the specific mental state that is a required element for a violation of each of the Rules.

The Board disagrees with the Respondent's position. The evidence adduced at the hearing explains the reason for Respondent's conduct, but does not excuse or justify it. The Board finds that the stipulated and admitted facts are sufficient affirmative evidence of the state of mind requisite for the violations of the Rules charged, other than Rule 8.4(b).

(continues)

JUDICIAL OPINION
MATTER OF LASSEN 672 A2D 988 (DE 1996). *(continued)*

3. A majority of the Board concludes that the Respondent should be disciplined publicly for his conduct and that the imposition of a private admonition, coupled with voluntary permanent retirement is not an appropriate sanction . . .

A majority of the Board concludes that it is appropriate for the Respondent to be sanctioned publicly and recommends a suspension equal to the time that the Respondent has already voluntarily absented himself from the practice of law. . . . A majority of the panel has so concluded for the following reasons:

a. The Board has no authority under the rules to recommend a retirement sanction. . . . If it is to be imposed in this case, then a majority of the Board feels that it is for the Court to do so.

b. A majority of the Board doubts whether or not the permanent retirement sanction is enforceable because of its permanent nature. . . . We have substantial questions whether or not a permanent retirement sanction could pass substantive due process muster. . .

c. The Respondent's conduct does not consist of a single occasion of improper charges for meals, a single occasion of directing personnel to hide restaurant charges by disguising them as other office expenses, or a single occasion of over billing. If the Respondent's repeated conduct resulted from negligence, then it must be considered gross negligence . . .

d. A majority of the panel is also concerned that the Respondent is not [remorseful]. . . . Throughout the original proceedings and at the remand hearing, the Respondent has continued to deny any wrongful intention on his part . . .

e. It was also admitted at the hearing that the only reason there was no injury to Respondent's clients, when these restaurant charges were renamed and billed to clients, is because of the intervention of his partners . . .

f. The majority of the panel has inferred the necessary intent from the Respondent's conduct to find a violation of the Rules. Even if the panel were unwilling to so infer, we believe that in the Matter ofFigliola,I.Supr., 652 A.2d 1071 (1995) is more on point with this case on the matter of sanctions than is [In re: A Member of the Bar, Del.Supr., No. 186, 1994, Walt, J. (Aug. 15, 1994) . . .

(continues)

JUDICIAL OPINION
MATTER OF LASSEN 672 A2D 988 (DE 1996). *(continued)*

With respect to misappropriation of clients' property, the Court found that suspension is appropriate in cases of knowing misappropriation, which is what a majority of the panel has inferred here, and that a public reprimand and/or fine is appropriate in instances of negligence. Here, a majority of the panel has concluded that Respondent's conduct constitutes at least gross negligence, and a majority of the panel is willing to infer a wrongful intention.

. . . The panel is sympathetic to the Respondent's family, however, we believe that one risk of public life that all public officials face is being brought into Court embarrassed and having their privacy invaded. No evidence has been adduced before us that makes the Respondent's case any different than any other such public official or lawyer facing discipline . . .

For the foregoing reasons, a majority of the panel recommends that the Respondent be suspended effective December 31, 1991 for a period of three years, and that upon a showing by clear and convincing evidence of professional rehabilitation and fitness to practice law and competence, as well as a showing that the resumption of the practice of law will not be detrimental to the administration of justice, then the suspension should be lifted and the Respondent should be reinstated.

III. FINDINGS AND CONCLUSIONS OF THIS COURT

Respondent argues that the Board failed to find the mental state necessary to prove the eight violations. Alternatively, Respondent contends that, if the Board made such a finding, it is unsupported by the evidence contained in the record. The ODC replies that the Board inferred that Respondent acted purposefully and knowingly, and that the Board's finding is supported by the record. We agree with the ODC.

We infer from this record that Respondent's conduct was consistent only with a wrongful intention and is inconsistent with concepts of negligence, even gross negligence. We therefore disagree with that portion of the Board's findings set forth at p. 995, supra, which introduced the concept of gross negligence. Nevertheless, we do not disturb the Board's finding that there was insufficient evidence to establish the requisite intent to constitute a violation of Rule 8.4(b), which relates to professional misconduct by committing a criminal act. Supra p. 994.

In cases charging violations of the DLRPC, this Court independently reviews the Board's findings of fact and conclusions of law. In ReAgostiniDel.Supr., 632 A.2d 80, 81 (1993). The scope of review is whether the record below contains substantial evidence to

(continues)

JUDICIAL OPINION
MATTER OF LASSEN 672 A2D 988 (DE 1996). *(continued)*

support the Board's findings. Id.; In re Browser,Del.Supr.,587 A.2d 1067, 1069 (1991). The Court reviews questions of law de novo. In re BarrettDel.Supr., 630 A.2d 652, 656 (1993). This case requires the Court to consider Respondent's contention that the Board erred in finding that Respondent violated the pertinent eight rules. We conclude that the Board's determinations are sufficiently supported by the record.

We conclude from this record that Respondent knowingly and improperly: (a) made personal restaurant charges to clients' accounts; (b) disguised these charges; (c) made misrepresentations to the bankruptcy court in connection with the misallocation of personal charges to a client's account; and (d) charged fictitious billable hours to clients' accounts.

The rules define "knowingly" as denoting "actual knowledge of the fact in question." DLRPC Terminology. It is well settled that a person is presumed to have intended the natural consequences of his or her acts, see, e.g., In reFrabizzioDel.Supr., 498 A.2d 1076, 1081 (1985) ; In reMorfordDel.Supr., 80 A.2d 429, 432 (1951), thus, "knowledge may be inferred from the circumstances," DLRPC Terminology; cf. 11Del.C.§ 307(a) (jury may infer accused's knowledge from his or her conduct); Whalen v. State,Del.Supr., 492 A.2d 552, 564 (1985) ("Under Delaware law . . . a person is presumed to intend the natural and probable consequences of his [or her] act".

Accordingly, we agree with the ODC that Respondent violated the following provisions of the DLRPC: 1.5(a) ("a] lawyer's fee shall be reasonable"; 3.3(a)(1) ("a] lawyer shall not knowingly . . . make a false statement of material fact or law to a tribunal"; 3.3(a)(4) ("a] lawyer shall not knowingly . . . offer evidence that the lawyer knows to be false"; 3.4(b) ("a] lawyer shall not falsify evidence"; 4.1(a) ("i]n the course of representing a client a lawyer shall not knowingly . . . make a false statement of material fact or law to a third person"; 5.3(c)(1) (" lawyer shall be responsible for conduct of [a nonlawyer employed or retained by or associated with the lawyer] that would be a violation of the [DLRPC] if engaged in by a lawyer[,] if . . . the lawyer orders . . . the conduct involved"; 8.4(c) ("i]t is professional misconduct for a lawyer to . . . engage in conduct involving dishonesty, fraud, deceit or misrepresentation"; and 8.4(d) ("i]t is professional misconduct for a lawyer to . . . engage in conduct that is prejudicial to the administration of justice".

The alleged violations of DLRPC 3.3(a)(1) & (4) , 3.4(b) and 8.4(d) stem from Respondent's submission of the fee application to the bankruptcy court. The stipulated facts were the only evidence the ODC presented in support of its allegations. These facts indicate that Respondent improperly submitted personal restaurant expenses totaling $131.75 to the

(continues)

JUDICIAL OPINION
MATTER OF LASSEN 672 A2D 988 (DE 1996). *(continued)*

bankruptcy court under oath. Contrary to Respondent's contention, this fact is sufficiently supportive of the Board's conclusion that Respondent violated DLRPC 3.3(a)(1) & (4) , 3.4(b) and 8.4(d). . .

The charged violation of DLRPC 8.4(c) is grounded upon Respondent's general misrepresentations to clients regarding the bills and the fee application, as outlined above. Respondent stipulated to the underlying facts relating to the improper billing and the fee application. The Court determines that, based on those stipulations and the other evidence in the record, the Board's finding that Respondent violated DLRPC 8.4(c) is supported by the record . . .

IV. THE APPROPRIATE SANCTION UNDER THE UNIQUE CIRCUMSTANCES OF THIS CASE

Respondent contends that application of pertinent guidelines, as delineated in the ABA Standards, with or without consideration of the mitigating factors present in this case, would authorize a sanction no greater than a public reprimand. Because the Permanent Retirement Sanction is more severe than a public reprimand, Respondent argues that it must logically suffice as an appropriate sanction. The Board rejected the proffered Permanent Retirement Sanction, concluding that a private admonition would be inappropriate in this case.

ABA Standards for Imposing Lawyer Sanctions (1991) (hereinafter "ABA Standards".) This Court often relies on the American Bar Association's standards for imposing sanctions to provide guidance in cases involving lawyer discipline. See, e.g., In reAgostini,Del.Supr., 632 A.2d 80, 81 (1993).

This Court has exclusive authority and wide latitude in determining disciplinary sanctions over lawyers. Agostini,632A.2d at 81. While the Board is empowered to recommend a sanction to the Court, it is the ultimate responsibility of this Court to impose sanctions. In the Final Report, a majority of the Board recommended a public, three-year suspension to run concurrently with the Respondent's voluntary withdrawal from practice.

In deciding to accept or reject the Board's recommendation, we recognize that each case is fact-sensitive. "In determining an appropriate sanction, this Court must 'protect the interests of the public and the [B]ar while giving due consideration to the interests of the individual involved.'" In reTos,Del.Supr., 610 A.2d 1370, 1372 (1992) (citation omitted); see also ABA Standards Preface (listing such relevant policy considerations as "protecting the public, ensuring the administration of justice, and maintaining the integrity of the profession".

(continues)

JUDICIAL OPINION
MATTER OF LASSEN 672 A2D 988 (DE 1996). *(continued)*

The primary purpose of the disciplinary system is "to protect the public." ABA Standard 1.1 cmt. As we stated in In re Tos, however, "although protection of the [public] . . . is a primary purpose of disciplinary action, there are other important purposes to be served by lawyer discipline. Disciplinary proceedings also serve to foster public confidence in the Bar, to preserve the integrity of the profession, and to deter other lawyers from similar misconduct." Tos,610A.2dat1373 (citing In re Sullivan,Del.Supr., 530 A.2d 1115, 1119 (1987)). The United States Supreme Court has recently recognized that preservation of the integrity of the bar and maintenance of the public's perception of the bar are valid objectives of state regulation of attorneys. FloridaBar v. Went For It, Inc.,515U.S.618, ——, 115S.Ct. 2371, 2380, 132 L.Ed.2d 541 (1995). Though the Court may consider the deterrent effect of the various proposed sanctions, Agostini,632 A.2d at 81, and ABA Standard 1.2 cmt, the lawyer disciplinary system is not penal or punitive in nature, see, e.g., In re Rich,Del.Supr., 559 A.2d 1251, 1257 (1989) ; In reBennethumDel.Supr., 161 A.2d 229, 236 (1960). Of significant weight in determining the appropriate sanction, however, is the impact the chosen sanction will have on the preservation of the integrity of the Bar and the public's perception of the Bar.

The general framework for determining an appropriate sanction for a violation of the DLRPC includes consideration of the following four factors: (i) the nature of the duty violated; (ii) the attorney's mental state; (iii) the actual or potential injury caused by the misconduct; and (iv) the existence of aggravating and mitigating circumstances. see Agostini632 A.2d at 81 n. 2 (citing ABA Standard 3.0). The available sanctions vary in degrees of severity. Suspensions may be imposed for a period of up to three years. Bd.Prof.Resp.R. 8(a)(2) ; Barrett630 A.2d at 657 (suspending lawyer for a period of three years). At the end of a suspension period exceeding six months, a lawyer may apply for reinstatement. Bd.Prof.Resp.R. 23(a). Similarly, a disbarred lawyer may apply for reinstatement after five years. Bd.Prof.Resp.R. 23(d). Under either scenario, reinstatement will be allowed only upon a "production[of] clear and convincing evidence of professional rehabilitation, fitness to practice, and competence," InreReedDel.Supr., 584 A.2d 1207, 1209 (1990) (interpreting Rule 23 of the Rules of the Board on Professional Responsibility) (emphasis omitted), and "hat the resumption of the practice of law within Delaware will not be detrimental to the administration of justice…"Bd.Prof.Resp.R.23(f). Lawyers, not originally successful, may reapply for reinstatement. See In reClark,Del.Supr., 406 A.2d 28 (1979) (denying disbarred lawyer's first petition for reinstatement); In reClark,Del.Supr., 430 A.2d 1082 (1981) (denying second petition); In re Clark, Del.Supr., No. 170, 1984,

(continues)

JUDICIAL OPINION
MATTER OF LASSEN 672 A2D 988 (DE 1996). *(continued)*

McNeilly, J. (Sept. 24, 1984) (ORDER) (denying third petition); In reClarkDel.Supr., 607 A.2d 1230, 1236-37 (1992) (granting fourth petition, but only upon satisfaction of enumerated conditions); see also Bennethum, 278 A.2d at 832-834 (granting third reinstatement petition by disbarred lawyer).

We conclude that Respondent's conduct, in light of the 1982 private censure, warrants a suspension of three years. Respondent has already voluntarily withdrawn from the practice of law and has not practiced since December 31, 1991, although he has not resigned from the Delaware Bar. Accordingly, the effect of the suspension will be mitigated so that Respondent may apply for reinstatement upon compliance with the conditions of the Judgment of the Court set forth at the end of this Opinion. It would not advance the public's perception and acceptance of the disciplinary system to permit immediate and unconditional reinstatement, and it would not be fair to Respondent to give him no credit for his voluntary withdrawal from the practice of law. . . . We agree with the recommendation of the Board that, as a condition of reinstatement, Respondent must show "by clear and convincing evidence . . . professional rehabilitation and fitness to practice law and competence, as well as a showing that the resumption of the practice of law will not be detrimental to the administration of justice." That showing must include a recognition by Respondent of the wrongfulness of his conduct and appropriate remorse.

Factors tending toward mitigation in this case include: Respondent's timely, good faith effort to rectify the consequences of the misconduct and make restitution; the absence of client harm or loss; full cooperation with the disciplinary authorities and other relevant parties; reputation for good character and professional skill in the legal community; voluntary effort to seek rehabilitation to overcome the awaiting personal challenge; voluntary withdrawal from the practice of law since December 31, 1991; and the impact of a public reprimand on his wife and young children.

The Court is not unmoved by considerations of Respondent's family. The record indicates that Respondent has several children from two separate marriages. It is Respondent, however, who is responsible for the public scrutiny this sanction will bring upon his family. As the Board suggested in its Final Report, public sanction is one of the risks attendant to public life. The Court may not temper its treatment of Respondent to protect the interests of those peripherally affected if to do so would undermine the interests of the lawyer discipline system.

(continues)

JUDICIAL OPINION
MATTER OF LASSEN 672 A2D 988 (DE 1996). *(continued)*

In light of the above considerations and prior case law, the Court determines that the appropriate sanction is a three-year suspension. The Court approaches the specific issue in this case-whether or not to accept the proffered Permanent Retirement Sanction in lieu of the public, three-year suspension-against the backdrop of the policy considerations discussed above.

Whether or not to accept a tendered resignation, as part of or in lieu of a sanction, is solely within this Court's discretion. Reed, 429 A.2d at 994. Whether a resignation is accepted "s dependent on the [C]ourt's assessment of the impact that the resignation will have on public policy interests such as the integrity of the legal profession, the administration of justice, and the protection of the public." Lori J. Henkel, Annotation, Propriety of Attorney's ResignationFromBar in Light of Pending or Potential Disciplinary Action54 A.L.R.4th 264, 278 (1987).

Under the Permanent Retirement Sanction, Respondent would never again be permitted to practice law or to reapply for admission to this Bar or the bar of any other state. That is a significant distinction which differentiates this case from Clark or Bennethum. The Permanent Retirement Sanction offered here is a sanction that can be imposed only if voluntarily offered. It is not an available involuntary sanction under Board on Professional Responsibility Rule 8 ("Rule 8". Theoretically, it is more severe than suspension or disbarment. The question is whether this sanction should be substituted for a public sanction consisting of a three-year suspension, on condition of anonymity. This question involves important policy considerations and careful balancing.

Rule 8 sets forth the types of sanctions available in a disciplinary action. For purposes of this case, the pertinent ones include disbarment, suspension for a fixed period up to three years, a public reprimand, private admonition, assessment of costs, and limitation on future practice. It is understandable that the Board feels constrained to reject Respondent's proffer of the Permanent Retirement Sanction in exchange for a private admonition. First, the Rules fail to provide specific authorization for such a result. Second, a private "admonition" is not appropriate for one entering permanent retirement. An "admonition" is "form of non-public discipline which declares the conduct of the lawyer improper, but does not limit the lawyer's right to practice." ABA Standard 2.6. Admonition implies advice to correct. This concept does not fit the instant case because it makes no sense to instruct a permanently retired lawyer to correct a fault in his or her practice. Moreover, the serious misconduct here should not receive any sanction which this Court considers a mild rebuke. Respondent contends that he is reluctant to give up the practice of law. He believes that he is a good lawyer and wants to continue practicing law. We assume these facts, arguendo, but we infer from this record that the Respondent's offer to retire from the Bar "voluntarily" is a

(continues)

JUDICIAL OPINION
MATTER OF LASSEN 672 A2D 988 (DE 1996). *(continued)*

rationalization emanating from the inevitability of a severe sanction, the difficulty of rehabilitating a credible practice and the hope of successfully convincing the Court to grant anonymity in exchange for permanent retirement.

The following definitions serve as examples of the common use of that term:

admonish-1. to caution, advise, or counsel against something. 2. to reprove or scold, esp. in a mild and good-willed manner: The teacher admonished him about excessive noise. 3. to urge to a duty; remind: to admonish them about their obligations . .

admonition-1. an act of admonishing. 2. counsel, advice, or caution. 3. a gentle reproof.

Random House Unabridged Dictionary 26 (2d ed. 1993).

An overarching issue here, however, is the impact a private sanction will have on the integrity of the profession, the public's perception of the profession and the credibility of the regulators of the Bar as instruments to control and sanction unethical conduct-and in this case, repeated unethical conduct.

The Permanent Retirement Sanction is a certain way of preventing further wrongdoing by the permanent removal from the practice of law of this apparently healthy, relatively young (53), skilled miscreant. The alternative, a public suspension with Respondent being eligible to seek reinstatement to the Bar of this Court, does not provide the same tenured insulation of the public from Respondent's availability to perform legal services. Nevertheless, the public sanction imposed here will better advance the interests of the lawyer disciplinary system as a whole than anonymity even with permanent retirement. As we stated in In re Figliola, "hen deciding upon the appropriate sanction the Court must consider that 't]he primary purpose of disciplinary proceedings is to protect the public; to foster public confidence in the Bar; to preserve the integrity of the profession; and to deter other lawyers from similar misconduct.'" In re Figliola652 A.2d 1071, 1076 (1995) (quoting Agostini632 A.2d at 81). Moreover, the public's perception of the legal profession and its ability to regulate itself is essential to the proper functioning of the Bar as a whole, and is quite distinct from the impermissible objective of "punishment." As the United States Supreme Court recently held, "t]he Bar has [a] substantial interest both in protecting injured [members of the public] . . . from invasive conduct by lawyers and in preventing erosion of confidence in the profession that such repeated invasions have engendered." Went For It, Inc.,515U.S.at ——,115S.Ct. at 2380.

The ABA Standards discuss extensively the propriety of publicly disciplining lawyers who breach ethical obligations. Private admonitions are generally reserved for cases of minor misconduct, when there is little chance of repetition. Cf. In reClyne,Del.Supr., 581 A.2d 1118, 1126 (1990); ABA Standard 1.2. In severe instances, as here, public censure is

(continues)

JUDICIAL OPINION
MATTER OF LASSEN 672 A2D 988 (DE 1996). *(continued)*

appropriate. The guiding principle in determining whether a sanction should be public or private remains the protection of the public. See ABA Standard 1.2. Lawyers naturally want to avoid the public stigma and embarrassment associated with a public sanction, both for their families and themselves. The public at large and the profession as a whole benefit from making public the sanctions imposed in serious cases such as this one. The public benefits because other lawyers are deterred from engaging in misconduct in the future. The profession benefits because such censure fosters the public's knowledge of, and confidence in, the profession's ability to police itself. Id. 1.2 cmt. Moreover, anonymity under the circumstances of this case would not be fair to other lawyers who have been publicly sanctioned and suspended. The Court agrees with these general principles and has determined that they are well served by the disposition in this case.

The ABA Standards recognize the common practice of private admonitions in certain minor cases. The misconduct here certainly is not "minor," and involves a repetition of similar, prior misconduct. A private admonition is inappropriate in this case. Its equivalent, anonymity, is likewise inappropriate, even if the anonymity is coupled with the Permanent Retirement Sanction.

The ABA Standards state in relevant part:

In cases of minor misconduct, when there is little or no injury to a client, the public, the legal system, or the profession, and when there is little or no likelihood of repetition, the court or disciplinary counsel should consider imposing an admonition. A private sanction in such cases informs the lawyer that his or her actions are unethical, but does not unnecessarily stigmatize a lawyer from whom the public needs no protection. To deter other lawyers, the court can still issue a public report describing the facts in cases where admonitions are imposed, but omitting the names of the disciplined lawyer . . .

ABA Standard 1.2 cmt. (emphasis added).

Recently the ABA retained this approach. A 1992 ABA Report urged full disclosure, triggered by the complainant's initial communication with a disciplinary agency, in all cases of lawyer disciplinary proceedings. The ABA House of Delegates rejected this report, instead opting to preserve existing ABA policy regarding disclosure and confidentiality of disciplinary proceedings. See ABA's New Discipline Goals Resist Greater Openness, 8 Laws. Man. on Prof.Conduct (ABA/BNA) 14, 15 (Feb. 12, 1992).

. . . The egregiousness of Respondent's misconduct in light of his earlier offense is inexcusable and very disturbing to this Court. To shelter such conduct from the light of public scrutiny does violence to the policies underlying the lawyer disciplinary system and undermines public confidence in the profession which traditionally has been built on trust and self-regulation. Dispensing a non-public sanction in this case runs a substantial risk of

(continues)

JUDICIAL OPINION
MATTER OF LASSEN 672 A2D 988 (DE 1996). *(continued)*

damaging the reputation of the Bar and the Court with the community at large, and provides an improper message to practitioners that egregious misdeeds may be engaged in without fear of public opprobrium. Moreover, Respondent's proposed result here may result in a dangerous and sometimes unworkable precedent, and would be unfair to other publicly sanctioned lawyers.

Imposition of the Permanent Retirement Sanction may create the appearance that Respondent has been allowed to choose his own sanction, even though it would not be Respondent's unilateral choice because the Court would have to accept the offer. This Court alone is vested with discretion to determine the appropriate sanction to be dispensed in a particular case of attorney misconduct. In this case, a public reprimand is the sanction prescribed by the ABA Standards. See ABA Standard 1.2. This is the sanction this Court has prescribed in cases of similar misconduct. See, e.g., Barrett, 630 A.2d 652. To deviate now from the pattern of past cases would be wrong.

In choosing to impose a public sanction in this case, the Court takes cognizance of Respondent's argument that there may be a chilling effect on the reporting of misconduct in the future. It is, of course, the duty of professional colleagues to correct and report unethical practices of another. DLRPC 8.3(a). The Court commends the Respondent's partners in both the Firm and the Prior Firm for honoring their ethical obligations and reporting the Respondent's unethical conduct. By highlighting the professionalism and integrity of Respondent's partners, the Court hopes to foster the fulfillment of the ethical duty of prompt and voluntary reporting of ethical breaches by those in positions to know of their occurrence. See ABA Standards Preface (noting that one of the most significant problems in the disciplinary system is the overall reluctance of lawyers and judges to report misconduct). In the instant case, Respondent's own partners dutifully and promptly reported the misconduct to the ODC, at the risk of the Firm incurring additional liability and reduced credibility in the eyes of present clients, potential clients, and the public. Their conduct was in the highest tradition of the professionalism for which the Delaware Bar has a notable and honorable national reputation.

VI. CONCLUSION

The circumstances of this case are unique. The Court has not heretofore been presented with the precise choice here. On the facts presented, however, we hold that anonymity coupled with the Permanent Retirement Sanction will not adequately advance the interests of the lawyer disciplinary system. We have therefore determined that the Respondent should publicly be suspended from the practice of law for a period of three years, ameliorated as noted in the Judgment because of Respondent's voluntary withdrawal from practice since December 31, 1991. (1) Respondent shall be prohibited and suspended from engaging in the practice of law for an aggregate period of three years.

SUMMARY

Much like other types of business, the law office has financial transactions that are recorded as funds that come in and out of the firm. However, unlike most other types of business, the law office handles money not only for its own business, but also for the business of others such as clients and third parties. It is important not only that the funds be kept separate but also that they be recorded properly to avoid any opportunity for confusion as to who is the rightful owner. Additionally, the law office may sell its product, professional services, in a variety of ways. Services may be contracted for a flat one-time fee, an hourly rate, or on a contingency. Each affects tracking, billing, and collection for professional services differently. As a result, the accounting is affected. Also, unlike many other types of business, the law office may advance funds on behalf of clients and seek reimbursement at a later time, or not at all. This is in addition to the funds spent by the business for legitimate expenses related to supporting the law practice. When a firm accepts funds on behalf of a client, that money must be properly accounted for and distributed according to the agreement between the client and attorney.

Finally, as a business, the law office must address the issue of paying those individuals who work for the firm. The compensation may be to owners of the practice, employees, or independent contractors. Each is paid in a different manner and, as a result, the payments are recorded differently. In addition to regular pay, issues such as timekeeping and eligibility for overtime must be calculated and recorded. As part of payroll to regular employees, the issue of tax payments at the federal, state, and sometimes local level must be addressed in terms of withholdings and employer contributions. And, finally, the year end information statements must be provided to the various types of individuals who have rendered services to the firm in exchange for compensation. As a result of the increasing complexity of payroll issues, some firms now contract out to businesses that specialize in administration of payroll and benefits. However, the majority continue to include it as part of the accounting functions performed within the firm.

▓ KEY TERMS

contingent fee billing

flat fee billing

hourly billing

employee

escrow

retainer

Cost Advance

letter of protection/lien letter

independent contractor

SS-8 Determination of Worker Status for Purposes of Federal Employment Taxes and Income Tax Withholding

Form W-4

personal exemption

CHAPTER 5

Business Organizations

■ OBJECTIVES

After completing this chapter, you will be able to:

❑ Distinguish service and retail profit-based business

❑ Identify the characteristics of the sole proprietorship

❑ Discuss traits of partnership

❑ Distinguish the general and limited partnership

❑ Describe the various types of corporate status

A. SERVICE VERSUS RETAIL

When considering a business organization from the perspective of tax and accounting, the type of business has an enormous impact on the documentation and manner in which tax and accounting functions are performed. Although both of these are necessary elements for all types of business, the way that records are kept and reported may vary dramatically from one type of business to another. Recall in earlier chapters when items such as the Chart of Accounts were discussed. It was pointed out that a service-oriented business would document different types of information than a retail-oriented business. This will be explored in further detail in this chapter. Additionally, there are differences in the manner in which a corporation's accounting and tax issues and those of a sole proprietorship are addressed. Both are approached differently than a partnership. As a result, it is important to have an understanding of the distinctive characteristics of the various types of business.

The fundamental difference in a business that is service-oriented from one that is considered retail or merchandising, is the manner in which revenue is generated. In a retail or merchandising business, the owners prepare a product for sale to customers. If the business actually creates the product, there may be numerous presale expenditures for raw materials, labor, and costs associated with manufacture, shipping, and so on. Even if the business does not create the product but rather prepares it for sale, there are also presale expenditures such as acquisition of inventory, advertising, display, packaging, and so on. For accounting and tax purposes, all of this information needs to be maintained and organized in a manner that allows the calculation of an item known as **cost of goods sold**. The cost of goods sold calculation actually figures the amount that the business expended to prepare the item for the sale transaction. This may be quite different from the cost of the inventory or raw materials. The cost of goods sold not only provides important accounting information for the business but also is a key element in the preparation of tax documents and determination of tax liability.

The cost of goods sold calculation apportions the associated costs with inventory in a particular accounting period. It is unlikely that a business will start and end each accounting period with a zero inventory balance. Thus, it is necessary to calculate how much of the costs associated with inventory preparation is related to the inventory actually sold within the period. This allows an objective view of the trends of the business, seasonal fluctuations, costs of storing inventory, and so on. For purposes of preparing the accounting financial statements and tax returns for a small business, detailed and complete records of the relevant costs associated with production is absolutely necessary.

COST OF GOODS SOLD

Presale expenditures for a product in the retail or merchandising business.

APPLICATION 5.1

The Dreyer SO and SEW Shop specializes in customized clothing. They imprint and embroider company logos, names, and novelty items on clothing. They started the year with items of clothing valued at $25,000. They also have $1,375 in logo transfers, $1,215 in embroidery threads, and $1,250 in necessary supplies related directly to the preparation of inventory. During the year, they purchased $2,300 in additional clothing items, $220 in logo transfers, and $480 in embroidery threads. The shop has one part-time employee and the labor cost for this employee was $7,000. At the end of the year, the inventory of clothing and necessary supplies totaled $6,530. This would indicate a cost of goods sold of $32,310.

(continues)

APPLICATION **5.1** *(continued)*

When calculating income or profit, this figure would be subtracted from the Gross Profit to establish the Gross Income. Further calculations would be necessary to identify the actual or net profit for the owner that would be subject to income tax.

Jan 1. Clothing 25,000

Supplies 1,250

Thread 1,215

Logos 1,375

Subtotal Inventory +28,840

December 31

Jan–Dec Purchases

Clothing 2,300

Thread 480

Logos 220

Labor 7,000

Subtotal Expenses +10,000

Inventory & Supplies

on 12/31 −6,530

Cost of Goods Sold 32,310

Application 5.1 is a very simplified illustration. Obviously, most businesses would require a much more detailed calculation, with a number of additional variables to be considered. This is true for both the accounting and tax preparation functions. With respect to tax document preparation, the tax forms used by businesses provide a detailed method for the calculation of the cost of goods sold. Typically, it is necessary to have the periodic accounting complete before the necessary figures can be supplied as required on the tax documents used in the cost of goods sold calculation. Much more attention will be given to the tax documentation in subsequent chapters. The point at this stage is to distinguish the retail or merchandising business from one that is service-oriented.

In the service business, there is little, if any inventory prepared in advance for a client's purchase. Rather, in most cases, the client determines what the "product" will be based on the needs of the client. For example, a client will contact a law firm about a particular type of representation. The nature, extent, and duration of the representation will drive the amount of revenue produced, as opposed to the retail business, in which the tangible product drives the income of the business. Additionally, in the service business, such as the practice of law, there are relatively few costs in terms of tangible items associated with generation of revenue. More often, the significant costs are those associated with labor and day-to-day operations. Generally, any extraordinary costs or external expenditures associated with a particular client are charged to the client in addition to fees for service. Examples include the cost of obtaining an expert witness, court costs, depositions, and so on. Otherwise, basic costs of delivery of service, for example, day-to-day operations, are built into the revenue and are applied in the general accounting equation as a liability against the revenue asset. Thus, for accounting and tax purposes, there is no real need for a cost of goods sold statement related to items of inventory in a service business. Whether a business is founded in generating income from service or sales, however, the type of business also impacts the accounting and tax principles applied.

B. THE SOLE PROPRIETORSHIP

The simplest and most common form of business organization in the United States is the **sole proprietorship**. This was one of the first types of business to be established in the United States and, despite the many changes and developments in society, law, technology, and general culture, it remains the most popular. In fact, after a trend of nearly 100 years away from small, independent businesses and toward partnerships and then large corporate conglomerates, recent trends have shown an increasing desire by the American population to regain some sense of control over its career and employment through entrepreneurship. Many times these businesses are operated by a single individual out of the home or at a nearby location.

To qualify as a sole proprietorship, the entire ownership interest of the business must be vested in a single individual. There is no need for legal documents to establish the business, define its structure, purpose, or delegate ownership responsibilities. There is no need to set forth in writing how the business is to be funded, how profits and losses are to be handled, or how liability for debts or judgments is to be distributed. These are all the domain and responsibility of the individual who owns the business. Even so, although there are no legal requirements on separate account maintenance for purposes of financial activity, it is extremely important to track business transactions for the purposes of tax reporting. This includes all transactions that are purely business and apportioning percentage to those items that are part business and part personal.

It is possible for sole proprietorships to employ other persons. In fact, there is no limit to the number of persons a sole proprietor may employ. As a practical matter, however, when a business grows to a size in which there are multiple employees, other forms of business such as incorporation may be a more desirable alternative from the standpoint of legal liability, tax liability, and so on. The key element with employees in a sole proprietorship is not the number but, rather, whether they are

SOLE PROPRIETORSHIP

The entire ownership interest of the business is vested in a single individual.

APPLICATION   5.2

Ben operates his own law practice as a sole proprietorship. Although Ben is not accountable to any other owners and need not maintain proper accounting records for the purpose of stating profit and loss, they are helpful to identify the aspects of the business that are the least cost-effective or the most profitable. These records are absolutely necessary for tax purposes. Ben uses his personal car to travel to and from work. This is not an ordinarily deductible expense for the business. However, the miles driven for the business such as trips to court, client and witness interviews, depositions, and so on are entirely deductible on the business portion of Ben's personal tax return. The same is true for all expenditures that are completely for the business or some that are even partially business-related.

allowed to take part in ownership decisions, the right or obligation to share in profits and losses, and responsibility for the debts of the business regardless of how those debts were generated, and any role the employee may have played with the possible exception of criminal activity in some circumstances. The business must remain individually owned to retain its status as a sole proprietorship.

Similarly, if ownership changes, the sole proprietorship ends and a new business entity begins. This may occur without much notice to casual observers. The name and manner of doing business may remain essentially the same. However, the change in owners signals a legal change in the form of the business. It is essentially an entirely new business that simply has purchased or taken control of the assets of the previous business. It is not, for legal or tax purposes, a continuing venture. The prior owner was the party in control of and responsible for all legal matters associated with his or her sole proprietorship. When a new owner takes over, an entirely new business begins and with it new control and responsibilities. A key concern of sole proprietors when selling their business is whether the new owner accepts as part of the purchase all known and unknown liabilities of the business. For example, someone may have been injured on the premises, but at the time of the sale neither the original owner nor the new owner were aware of this. It should be made clear who will be responsible for dealing with issues if something as a subsequent lawsuit is filed for damages. There also may be liability to consider for certain tax issues. Although the income of the business is considered personal and would follow the business owner at the time the income was generated, payments for taxes such as Social Security and unemployment are not as clear, and the liability for any such obligations should be clearly spelled out.

The reasons that many sole proprietorships ultimately convert to some other form of business entity, such as a corporation, is twofold. In some instances, a sole proprietorship has fewer tax advantages than a corporation. The rules for what deductions may be used to offset income and what income must be declared as an individual may make the corporate form more appealing. This is especially true when an individual has several sources of income. An especially high profit year in the sole proprietorship added to the other sources of personal and/or spousal income might increase the individual's income to a level that is taxed at a much higher rate or cause the individual to be phased out of certain tax benefits that are tied to income. This may be true even though the income is left within the business to promote growth.

Another reason for the decline of some sole proprietorships is judgment liability. When an outside party sues a sole proprietorship and wins, the judgment can be enforced against the individual owner, including many of the owner's personal assets and those owned with others. However, some forms of corporations and partnership may provide a shield of liability for the owners and limit any recovery against a corporation to the assets of the company and not to the individual assets of owners. Many sole proprietors who are engaged in businesses in which the risk of litigation is high may opt for the protection of a more formalized business entity.

Still, sole proprietorships remain a popular form of business. Much of the appeal lies in the simplicity of this form of business. This is especially true for the single entrepreneur just starting out in a business with a low risk of litigation resulting from personal or financial injuries to third parties. Many home-based businesses are begun as sole proprietorships to determine whether the business is viable. The business can be started informally and ended just as easily. The only record often is a Schedule C attached to the owner's tax returns showing the activity of the business, including deductions against income of the business for tax purposes. This informality appeals to the business owner who is more properly trained to conduct the nature of the business than to act in an administrative role. It is important that anyone who undertakes to establish a sole proprietorship seeks competent advice from professionals in these matters, such as a lawyer and/or accountant, to ensure that proper records are maintained and all applicable laws and regulations are complied with. This becomes especially important when employees are added to the business operation.

APPLICATION 5.3

Macey is an attorney. He decides to go into private practice. To save money, Macey does most of his own clerical work and accounting. The rest is contracted out to independent contractors. This eliminates the costs associated with paying Social Security, Medicare, federal and state unemployment tax, as well as any benefits for employees. Macey considers this financial benefit to outweigh the higher cost of an independent contractor at this point. At the end of each quarter, Macey prepares his own financial statements for the practice. In the third quarter, the practice is beginning to build. By the end of the first year, the costs for part-time outside help have exceeded the cost for a full-time employee, including the salary and associated taxes and benefits.

(continues)

APPLICATION 5.3 (continued)

	1st Quarter	4th Quarter
Independent Contractor 40 hours at $25.00	$1,000	
Independent Contractor 120 hours at $25.00		$3,000
TOTAL	$1,000	$3,000
vs.		
Clerical Employee 40 hours at $12.00	$480.00	
Clerical Employee 120 hours at $12.00	$1,440.00	
Accounting fees to prepare payroll/tax reports	$125.00	$125.00
Social Security and Medicare Employer Contrib.	$36.72	$110.16
Federal Unemployment Tax	$4.35	$13.04
State Unemployment Tax	$.50	$7.15
TOTAL	$646.57	$1,695.35

As shown, the trend as the business grows is that the gap in the expenses between an independent contractor and an employee is changing. The cost per month for an employee in the first quarter was $646.57 versus $1,000 for an independent contractor. Although the cost initially of an independent contract was about 35 percent more expensive, there was no need to provide any benefits, work space, and so on. Additionally, the business was not as busy (demonstrated by the lack of work) that in turn made the use of a full-time employee less important. However, by the end of the same year, the cost of an independent contractor jumped to more than 43 percent over that of an employee. Although there are a number of associated costs with bringing on an employee, those items would be quickly absorbed and the business would have the added benefit of another individual to assist with answering phones, meeting clients, scheduling, and so on. This is especially important in something like a law firm, in which the nature of the business requires the attorney/owner to be absent a fair percentage of the time.

As the business grows and develops into an operation involving the owner, employees, and a widening client/customer base, the legal requirements concerning compliance with government regulations and laws increase. Tax laws and rate structures for business income and deductions become more relevant and complicated. The greater the number of employees and their interaction with customers, the greater the number of potential litigation. All of these factors cause an increasing complexity that is often more than the original concept of sole proprietorship was envisioned to accommodate. Consequently, there is a trend for growing businesses to start or convert to a more formal mode of business entity such as a corporation.

As mentioned earlier, the federal tax reporting for a sole proprietorship without employees is very simple. There is no need for a separate tax return or even quarterly reports. All that is necessary is an attachment to the individual's return. This is done on a Schedule C. There are provisions on Schedule C to report income, cost of goods sold calculations, and appropriate deductions. Thus, it is important to have accurate accounting practices in place in order to have the proper documentation to support the information reported to the IRS. In addition to the Schedule C, it is often necessary to file a Schedule SE. Because the sole proprietor is his or her own employer, any required contributions to Social Security and Medicare are doubled representing both the employer and matching employee share. It will be discussed later how a portion of this payment is deductible. For now, it is necessary to understand that the person who is both his or her own employer and employee may be required to pay both portions of the mandatory tax. In this instance, it is referred to as self-employment tax.

C. THE PARTNERSHIP

Partnerships are the counterpart to sole proprietorships. Although the sole proprietorship is an entity owned by an individual, the partnership is an entity shared in ownership by more than one individual. Partnerships have been recognized as forms of business from the very beginning of the American legal system.

A **partnership** requires an interaction of individuals who then act on behalf of the common goals of the business owners. This establishes partners as agents of the collective partnership that is, in turn, the principal or party responsible for actions of its agents. Because the partnership itself is the product of a contractual agreement, legal issues that arise among partners are usually resolved by the application of the legal standards of contract and agency law. Within these areas, and in the law of business organizations generally, a number of legal standards peculiar to the issues of partnerships have been developed. With respect to the creation, operation, and end of partnerships, common issues are addressed specifically by state statutes. In an effort to promote consistency for partnerships doing interstate business, and with interstate members, a majority of states have enacted legislation that adopts all or part of two standardized sets of rules for partnerships. These are known as the Uniform Partnership Act and the Revised Uniform Limited Partnership Act. However, as with any uniform law, the adoption by each state legislature is voluntary and the state has the option to substitute its own law or statutory language for any part of a uniform code. As a result, never assume that a state has complete adherence

PARTNERSHIP

An entity shared in ownership by more than one individual.

to a uniform act. It is always important to consider each of the applicable state and federal laws and regulations used to govern a form of business, and its accounting and tax practices.

Partners have a fiduciary relationship with one another. Each partner is trusted to place the interest of the partnership above personal gain or interest when it comes to competing interests. Therefore, any partner who makes a profit in a business venture of the type the partnership would ordinarily be involved in owes that profit to the partnership. Additionally, unless otherwise agreed, partners are not entitled to payment for services rendered as a regular employee would be. A partner is only entitled by law to a share of the net profits, if any. The exception is when a partner or partners are winding up the partnership business after the death of another partner. In that case, surviving partners typically are entitled to reasonable compensation for their services in closing the partnership accounts.

When things go badly for a joint venture, it is not uncommon for a party to claim no partnership existed. If the parties did not have a formalized partnership agreement, the dispute may result in litigation. At this point, a court will employ a number of tests to determine if a partnership was in place and functioning. Some of the factors considered include the following:

1. Do the alleged partners have some type of joint title to real or personal property?

2. Do the alleged partners operate under a single name?

3. Do the alleged partners share in the profits and losses of the business?

4. How much money and time does each alleged partner invest in the business?

5. Was there ever a documented agreement that would indicate an intent to create a partnership?

APPLICATION **5.4**

Steve wanted Lisa to assist him in developing a business. Steve persuaded Lisa to invest approximately $100,000. He would, in turn, contribute his knowledge and expertise to the business. They agreed to share profits. The two opened a joint bank account. However, Steve never got around to signing the partnership agreement that Lisa had prepared for him. All administrative and business decisions were his. Steve worked part time in the business and hired an employee with income from the business to work and supervise Lisa as she learned the business. Lisa worked in the business part time and under Steve's express direction. Lisa asked to have her name or at the very least the partnership name put on the title to the one piece of real estate used to house the business. Steve owned the property in his name alone. Also, because Steve had made the initial startup of the business as a sole

(continues)

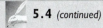
proprietorship before his agreement with Lisa, the business was in his name. Steve never got around to getting that done, either. Within less than two years, the business had failed and all of the money was gone. Canceled checks showed that the vast majority had gone to Steve in the form of a personal cellular phone, gasoline and repairs for his personal vehicle, improvements to his property, travel, and various cash payments. Lisa also had kept Steve's property out of foreclosure by making personal payments for the property when the business did not generate enough income to cover them. Lisa filed suit, claiming that no partnership had ever really been created and that, instead, the money had been treated by Steve like a personal loan. Lisa sought repayment of her money. Steve claimed that there was a partnership and that, as a result, it was a lost investment and he owed Lisa nothing.

Generally, every partner in a partnership has authority to act as an agent or representative of the partnership. The partnership entity is consequently liable for the acts of its partners. A partner may transfer title to property held in the partnership name or obligate the partnership in business agreements or purchases that relate to the business of the partnership. If, however, the transaction is one that would not ordinarily be encountered in the business of the partnership, a partner must have actual authority from the partnership before he or she can make a binding agreement with third parties.

In addition to having joint and several liability for contract obligations, in some instances a partnership also may be held responsible to third parties for wrongful acts of the partners or partnership employees. For example, if a partner carelessly causes an accident injuring a third party, the partnership may be held liable.

The liability of partners in such a situation can be claimed in one of two ways. Some jurisdictions take the position that the liability is joint and that each partner must be sued for the injuries. However, the majority of jurisdictions have adopted the position that the liability of a partnership for the acts of each individual partner is joint and several. In this instance, that would mean that all of the partners are individual and or jointly responsible for the acts of any of the partners in the partnership as if the act were their own. This, as in the contractual situation, could require payment of the entire debt. The partner could then seek reimbursement by the other partners if they had sufficient assets to contribute.

ASSIGNMENT **5.1**

Consider the scenario in Application 5.4. Apply the factors to determine the existence of a partnership and explain why a partnership did or did not exist.

Any change in the identity of the partners will result in the dissolution of the original partnership. Similar to a change in ownership of a sole proprietorship, when a partner dies, declares bankruptcy, sells his or her interest in the partnership, or withdraws, the partnership is dissolved. A new partnership may be created and there may be an apparently seamless transition. But it is still a different organization and requires all the necessities of ending the previous partnership, including a final accounting, closing of the books, and final tax return and related tax documents. Notice also must be given to partnership creditors and debtors as well as how the new partnership intends to handle the accounts.

In the event that a partnership elects to dissolve and cease doing business, there is a distinct pattern of events that needs to occur. First, all regular business previously used to generate income must be stopped. The partners must then wind up pending business, collect all viable accounts receivable, liquidate assets by converting them to cash, pay all debts of the partnership and prepare a final accounting, as well as appropriate final tax documents. These are varied based on the size of the partnership, whether there were employees, and so on. Only when all of the steps to convert assets to cash and payment of all debts can the partners consider a distribution to repay themselves for their capital investment and any leftover profits. These are distributed according to the partnership agreement. In the event that there is no agreement, the laws of each state provide how partnership assets are to be divided.

1. The General Partnership

GENERAL PARTNERSHIP

Consists of two or more general partners and personal liability is unlimited.

LIMITED PARTNERSHIP

Protects the personal assets of the limited partner from liability.

There are two basic forms of partnership. They are commonly referred to as the **general partnership** and the **limited partnership**. Each has distinct characteristics. A general partnership consists of two or more general partners and personal liability is unlimited. This means that in the event of a judgment against the partnership for a debt or other type of civil liability, the assets of the partnership as well as many of the personal assets of each of the individual partners may be reached and, if necessary, seized or sold to satisfy the judgment. In addition, the rule of law in a majority of jurisdictions regarding a general partner's liability is that the partners are jointly and severally liable for the acts of one another. This means that in the event of a judgment of debt for the partnership, that debt can be collected from any or all of the partners rather than as an equal share from each partner. In the event that there is a determination that the partnership owes a debt that exceeds the worth of the partnership assets, any individual partner or all partners together may be forced to pay the debt. An obligation does not have to be divided among the partners equally. Thus, a partner with greater personal wealth could be required to pay a greater portion of the debt. Any reimbursement to that partner from other partners would be determined by the partnership agreement between the parties and the financial ability of those partners to satisfy the terms of the agreement. As a result, great care should be taken when making the decision to enter a partnership with others.

Unlike the sole proprietorship, in which all assets of the business are considered personally owned by the sole proprietor, a partnership may own assets as a separate entity. This includes both real and personal property. It is legal to title property in the name of the partnership for the purpose of government license and taxes. However, financing for the purchase of real or personal property may still be required to be signed for and secured by the individual partners as an additional protection for the party providing the financing. The debt as paid for partnership property is balanced against revenue when determining the profit or loss of the business in an accounting period. Partnership property is not reported or attributed separately to the partners.

If a dispute arises in regard to whether property belongs to the partnership or an individual partner(s), there are a number of tests employed by the courts to determine the rightful owners. They are typically applied in the following questions:

1. Was the property acquired with partnership funds?

2. Has the partnership made primary use of the property?

3. Does the partnership have legal title to the property?

4. Is the property of a type that would be used in the business of the partnership?

5. Has the partnership taken any steps to maintain or improve the condition of the property?

6. Is the property recorded in the accounting books of the partnership as an asset?

APPLICATION **5.5**

Max is in partnership with his friend Moe. The men do small moving jobs that range from moving furniture within a house to moving the entire contents of a small house or apartment to another location. In addition to his personal vehicle, Max owns a small van. Since the beginning of the business four years ago, the van has been kept at the business location of the partnership. It has been used exclusively for partnership business. The partnership has paid for oil changes and gas. However, Max has kept the vehicle titled in his name and has paid the insurance. The men keep rudimentary books and have never made an actual list of assets because there were none of significant value. Now the van needs significant repairs. The cost estimate is between $2,000 and $3,000. Max wants the repairs to be paid for by the partnership. Moe takes the position that because the van is titled and insured in Max's name, repairs are not the responsibility of the partnership. It is important to make a determination of whether the property is that of the partnership not only for repairs but also for tax reporting purposes in the decision of what items are expenses of the business and what are private (and likely nondeductible) expenses.

INFORMATION RETURN

A separate return is also filed for the partnership.

For tax purposes, the partnership is somewhat unique. The profits or loss shared by the partners is reported on their personal tax return as a personal item of income or loss. However, a separate return is also filed for the partnership. This return is called an **Information Return**. No income tax is assessed directly against the business. Rather, the information return reports the profit or loss of the business and how it was attributed to the various partners. Then, that information can be compared against the personal returns of partners to ensure the profit or loss of the business is properly reported. Each partner also receives a tax information document referred to as a K-1 Partnership form. This document contains the information for the partnership as well as the personal share of profits received by the partner receiving it. The information on the K-1 is reported on the individual return and should match that reported by the partnership on its information return.

2. The Limited Partnership

A limited partnership protects the personal assets of the limited partner from liability. The Revised Uniform Limited Partnership Act is model law adopted by a majority of the states as statute and sets forth the specific rights, liabilities, and means of creating and dissolving a limited partnership. Generally, in a limited partnership, a limited partner is held liable only for the amount of his or her investment or promised investment in the partnership. In this sense, a limited partner is similar to a corporate shareholder. The cost to a limited partner for this protection is the loss of all control or influence in the operation of the partnership.

A limited partner can have no input into the operation of the business of the partnership. A limited partner cannot work for the partnership. Finally, the limited partner's name cannot be used in the partnership name. If any of these rules are broken, a limited partner may be treated as a general partner and be subject to joint and several liability. Because limited partners cannot contribute services to the partnership, as a practical necessity, the partnership must also have general partners who operate the business of the partnership. Although these general partners manage the continuing business of the partnership, their personal assets are at risk as well.

With respect to the general operations of a limited partnership, it functions much the same as a general partnership. The same accounting practices are employed. The same tax forms are required. The primary differences are in how the profits and losses are distributed and how the information on the tax documents are reported. As long as the limited partner refrains from delving into the management decisions or working within the partnership, the limited status and its protections will stay in place. If, however, a limited partner is found to have become involved in the operations of the partnership, the limited status and its protections may be abandoned by the courts. As a result, the decision to enter any partnership, including a limited partnership, should not be one based on emotion, relationship, or any other factor except business acumen and sound indications of the likelihood of success of the business as well as the abilities of the general partners to run the business.

D. CORPORATIONS

A **corporation** is recognized by the law as a person or entity in and of itself. It can be taxed and held responsible for its acts for the purposes of lawsuits. In the past, however, a corporation was not considered to be capable of committing crimes. When criminal conduct occurred, the individuals who actually committed the crime were held responsible. This outlook has been changing in recent times. More and

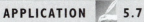 **CORPORATION**

Recognized by the law as a person or entity in and of itself.

more state and federal laws permit corporations and those acting on their behalf to be convicted of criminal acts. Although a corporation cannot be imprisoned, it can be fined or dissolved as a penalty for illegal conduct. In addition, the acting individual can be held criminally responsible.

Once initiated, a corporation generally continues indefinitely as long as the requirements of the statutes that permitted its creation are met. The statutes that set forth the ways in which a corporation must be created often establish annual obligations that must be met for the corporation to continue to exist. Often these obligations include such things as payment of an annual governmental fee, continued registration with the state where the business is incorporated (and in some instances does business), and annual reports describing the activities of the corporation during the preceding year. Unlike sole proprietorships and partnerships, a change in ownership does not cause an end to the corporation in existence.

Perhaps the greatest advantage of a corporation is that individuals who invest in it have limited exposure for losses. Ordinarily, a person who invests in a corporation is called a shareholder to represent his or her percentage or share of ownership. The greater the investment, the greater the percentage of ownership. If the corporation does well, the shareholder's ownership becomes more valuable in terms of the price of the shares or the distribution of profits. If the corporation does badly or a large monetary judgment is rendered against it as the result of a lawsuit, the shareholders usually stand to lose no more than the amount of their original investment. Thus, the corporation differs from most other types of business entities in which the owners are responsible for the entire judgment regardless of whether it exceeds their investment.

Why, then, would someone enter into a different type of business such as a sole proprietorship or partnership and place personal assets at risk? The question is often answered by the tax impact. Generally speaking, all of the net income of a sole proprietorship or partnership passes through the business and directly to the owner who claims it as personal income for tax purposes. The corporation, however, pays taxes as an entity in and of itself on the net income it generates. Typically, corporations periodically distribute part of net profits to the owner stockholders in the form of dividends. In the event that any of the profits are distributed to the owners as dividends, that income is then determined to be personal and is taxed for the individual. Just as it appears, some corporate income results in taxation twice. In a smaller business with one or only a few owners, this double taxation may outweigh the risk to personal assets in the event of litigation or if the business fails. After all, most individuals do not go into business with the idea they will be sued or that the business is going to fail and fail badly. Conversely, a very large corporation may keep a large percentage of profits in reserve for further business development. If this income is not distributed as dividends to the owners, those owners incur no personal tax liability. Additionally, ownership in a sole proprietorship or general partnership has an essential element of control over the business. This is not necessarily true of the general corporation.

APPLICATION   5.8

Max is married and owns a sole proprietorship. In the preceding year, his business had a net profit of $40,000. After the personal deductions on Max's tax return, his taxable income was $22,000. The tax rate on his taxable income was 10 percent, or $2,200. Not including other taxes, Max was left with $37,800. The following year, Max incorporated his business. The business again had a net profit of $40,000. The tax on the corporation was 28 percent, or $11,200. Max took home the remaining $28,800. After his personal deductions, his taxable income was $10,800. The tax was 10 percent, or $1,080. After this was paid from the $28,800, and not including other taxes, Max was left with $27,720, or $10,080 less than the previous year. Depending on the nature of the business and its financial health, Max may have been better off to risk the loss of investment rather than accept a greater than $10,000 pay cut.

1. The General Corporation

Initially, there was only the general corporation. This type of business was initially created for common business purposes such as manufacture or retail sales. Statutes allowing the creation of a business owned by multiple parties encouraged economic growth with some basic protections for the investors. Typically, the general corporation has owners, also known as shareholders, stock issued to represent the percentage of ownership held by the stockholders, a board of directors, officers, and all of the other characteristics of the traditional corporation. Other types of corporations developed in more recent years will be discussed later in this chapter. But for now, consider the general corporation.

The general corporation may be openly or closely held. The openly or publicly held corporation is one in which shares of stock or ownership are available to the general public. Anyone can purchase available shares of stock and become a partial owner in the business. Periodic meetings, often held annually, allow the stockholders to vote on major issues of business for the corporation. These issues typically affect

ASSIGNMENT   5.3

Determine whether general corporation or sole proprietorship would be in Maureen's best interest. Explain your answer.

a. Maureen is involved in an online auction and retail business. She purchases clothing items at a discount and then sells them online for a profit.

b. Maureen is involved in an online auction and retail business. She purchases guns and sells them online for a profit. She has a notice posted online that purchasers must be 18 but uses no method to confirm the identity of the purchasers or their age.

the general direction of the business and such major items as whether to sell all or part of the business to another business, or to acquire other businesses and bring them in as part of the existing corporation. Less significant decisions are made by the board of directors, which meets periodically. Day-to-day operations are handled by the officers of the corporation, who typically are selected and appointed by the board of directors.

All states have some type of statutory law to govern the creation, operation, and dissolution of corporate entities. A majority of the states have enacted the Model Business Corporation Act. This is a series of laws that addresses the legal aspects of corporate existence. The act includes provisions for everything from establishing a corporate name to the proper procedures for dissolution. By establishing the same basic statutory provisions in most states, the process of handling legal disputes over corporate statutes is much easier to accomplish in a time when business is often conducted across state lines.

In some instances, a corporation will be treated as one for legal and tax purposes even if the corporation is not one with "de jure" status. A de jure corporation is one that meets each requirement of relevant statutes that provide for forming and maintaining the corporation. On occasion, incorporators attempt to satisfy the statutes but are not successful. In some cases, the law will recognize the organization as a de facto corporation (corporation by fact or actions). The shareholders of a business are protected in liability the same as de jure corporation shareholders would be. For example, an annual registration fee is often required to maintain the status of an existing corporation. If the person responsible for paying the fee neglected to do so, the corporation would not necessarily be considered dissolved or inactive. Rather, if all other formalities are met, it would likely be considered a de facto corporation in the event of a challenge to corporate status by a third party. Generally, there must be evidence that the incorporators, board of directors, and officers made a good faith attempt to comply with the state laws as a whole regarding incorporation and continuance of the corporation, and that the business has been conducted as if it were a corporation. It also must be shown that the corporation was represented as such and not as another type of business entity and that outside persons dealt with the business as if it were a corporation. When all such evidence exists, the court often recognizes the entity as a de facto corporation and allows it to claim all of the privileges of a de facto corporation.

Another issue with respect to corporate status occurs when an attempt to avoid corporate status is denied. This is known as a corporation "by estoppel" (preclusion from denial of corporate existence). This comes into play in one of two ways. In the first, a person or persons hold a business out as a corporation to the public and deal with the public as a corporation but later attempt to deny that the corporation ever existed. The second occurs when outsiders deal with a business as a corporation with knowledge that it is not a proper corporation. When a dispute arises between the two, the outsiders attempt to deny that a corporation exists and claim that the owners should be personally liable. In either instance, the courts may treat the business as a

APPLICATION **5.9**

Jose and Juan are the adult children of a very wealthy family. The net worth of Jose and Juan is estimated to exceed $150 million. Jose and Juan want to go into business for themselves and incorporate. They have patented a product and begin production and retail sales. About two years after beginning their enterprise, a lawsuit is filed claiming serious injury from the product. At the time of the suit, the corporation has yet to show a net profit and has no substantial assets. Jose and Juan are sued personally rather than a suit filed against the corporation. When they attempt to have the suit dismissed, the plaintiff alleges that there is no corporation and that Jose and Juan are personally liable. The plaintiff claims there is no registered agent for the corporation (the publicly designated party to accept legal documents on behalf of the corporation) and no registration of the corporate name. Jose and Juan present evidence that they hired an attorney at the time of incorporation to make sure all requirements were met, and the same attorney was retained to take care of any annual corporate requirements. The brothers introduce evidence that the law firm also prepared the annual and quarterly tax returns and that both state and federal returns were filed as a general corporation. They also present evidence that all annual fees and required annual corporate reports were filed, all business was conducted as a corporation, and they were personally unaware of the deficiencies until the suit was filed.

On hearing the evidence, the court finds that there is no evidence to support a finding that the brothers were aware of the deficiencies or ever benefited in any way from the failure to observe the technical requirements. Significant attempts were made to function as a corporation and the failure to register the name or appoint a registered agent did not directly impact the plaintiff's case in the lawsuit. As a result, the judge orders the suit to be dismissed with permission for the plaintiff to refile against the business as a de facto corporation.

corporation by estoppel and apply the law as if it were a real corporation. The rationale is that people should not be able to derive all of the benefits from acting as or dealing with a corporation while avoiding the obligations of one.

The IRS designates the common general corporation as a "C-corporation." The corporation files a Form C to report taxable activity. This is the document used to file the tax return for the corporation. This is to be distinguished from the sole proprietor who files one of the types of Form 1040 with a supporting Schedule C to report the business activity of the sole proprietorship. There are also subtypes of corporations that have become popular in recent years that are essentially hybrid combinations of sole proprietorship, partnership, and general corporations. The type of form used for the tax return is guided by the type of corporate or business status. These businesses have a combination of traits and taxable status that are more desirable to many smaller businesses.

APPLICATION   5.10

Consider the case described in Application 5.9. Now change the facts to introduce evidence that for the last two years Juan and Jose filed tax returns as a partnership rather than a corporation. On their returns, both Jose and Juan each claimed one-half of the losses of the business as deductions against their personal income and in the process lowered their personal tax liability. In such a situation, the court would be much more likely to stop them from claiming corporate status for the purposes of the lawsuit.

2. Close Corporations, Professional Corporations, and Limited Liability Companies

Many small corporations are hybrid forms of the general or C-corporations. They are often known as "S-corporations," close corporations, professional corporations, and limited liability companies. These businesses file informational tax returns like partnerships. They are not subject to the C-corporation tax on corporate income. Each of these types of corporations provides some degree of limitation on personal liability for corporate acts, but each allows the income of the corporation to flow through directly to the owners for tax purposes. As noted earlier, with a general corporation, profits are taxed at a corporate rate and separate from the owners. Any distribution of profits to the owner shareholders is in the form of dividends. A document known as a 1099-DIV is issued annually to the shareholder and reported to the government stating the amount of dividends issued. This is then considered personal income of the recipient for the purpose of income taxes. The closely held S-corporations, professional corporations, and limited liability companies issue a form K-1 that describes in basic terms the activity of the business and indicates the amount of profit or loss for the business attributable to each of the owners. Similar to partnerships, the information return filed by the business provides the government with a check and balance against the amount of income or loss claimed by the individual owners, and it allows the government to use the information as one of its tools to determine the activity and progress or decline of the various forms of business for use in evaluating the health and direction of economic growth.

The more personal and closely held corporations are totally created and overseen through statutory law just as the general corporation. Specific statutes prescribe the necessary steps to create, maintain, and dissolve such corporations. Historically, S-corporations were used for small operations of several individuals in virtually any type of legal business who sought to limit the exposure to liability they might have in a partnership. However, unlike the C-corporation, there may still be some personal liability in specific circumstances. The **professional corporation** also known as the **professional service corporation** was created for licensed professionals whose business was to provide services rather than ordinary types of commercial business. This corporate form continues to be common among licensed professionals such as

PROFESSIONAL CORPORATION/ PROFESSIONAL SERVICE CORPORATION

Created for licensed professionals whose business was to provide services rather than ordinary types of commercial business.

APPLICATION 5.11

Mckenna and Mason create a professional service corporation for their physical therapy business. As a corporation, the liability for acts unrelated to the delivery of professional services is limited to the assets of the corporation. This might include something along the lines of someone falling in the parking lot and subsequently suing the corporation. However, McKenna and Mason would not be free from personal liability reaching beyond the assets of the corporation for something such as negligently inflicting injury on a patient during physical therapy.

physicians, attorneys, accountants, and other similarly situated independent service providers. However, the limitation of liability will not protect the professional for his or her own personal malfeasance in the delivery of professional services. In this way, the public is protected from those who might seek to act less than prudently in the delivery of professional services.

The newest corporate form, the **limited liability company**, or LLC, is rapidly growing in acceptance and has been recognized by statute in a majority of jurisdictions as well as by the IRS. Typically, the professional corporation statutes require all shareholders to be members of a common profession. Under the LLC, individuals who are not members of the profession that is the basis for the business may be owners. For example, a physician may enter into an LLC with an attorney in which the physician provides medical services as the primary business of the corporation, and the attorney is responsible for other issues such as the management of the business. In this type of company, most often the shareholders are subject to the personal liability only for their own personal conduct. Thus, in this example, the attorney would not ordinarily be held accountable for the medical malpractice of the physician. Therefore, if an action were brought against the LLC for matters related to property ownership or business dealings, any judgment could only be recovered from assets of the business and not the owners. However, if a judgment for malfeasance were obtained against the business for the professional actions of an owner engaged in the primary focus of the business, the professional found culpable also would be subject to personal liability.

LIMITED LIABILITY COMPANY

Individuals who are not members of the profession that is the basis for the business may be owners of an LLC.

APPLICATION 5.12

Consider the facts in Application 5.11. Assume that McKenna is the accountant and administrator of the business and Mason is the physical therapist. They have formed a limited liability company. On one occasion, Mason is very busy with several clients, including a client who has lost much of the use of her right leg as a result of an injury. Anxious to make up time, Mason instructs the patient to go to the hydrotherapy room after physical therapy rather than his usual escorting her there and providing some support while she

(continues)

APPLICATION **5.12** *(continued)*

walks. The patient attempts to comply but falls and breaks her hip. An action against Mason for his allegedly negligent handling of the patient would not likely result in personal liability for McKenna.

ASSIGNMENT **5.4**

You work for a law firm that specializes in representing small businesses. At the end of the year, you are asked to assist in preparation of the various tax documents for several clients. For each type of client, using the list given here, indicate the various tax documents that would need to be issued or filed for the business and for the owners (if different from those of the business).

Tax Documents

       Partnership Informational Return

       C Return

       1040 Return

       K-1

       1099-DIV

       Schedule C

       S Return

  a. Sole Proprietorship

  b. Partnership

  c. General Corporation

  d. S-Corporation

  e. Limited Liability Company

  f. Professional Service Corporation

ETHICAL QUESTION

Jonas and Laura are in business together. They operate the local sandwich shop in a small rural community. The sandwich shop is known as "Carnes Sandwich Stop." Their shop is not part of the national and well-known Carne's chain. But no attempt is made to distinguish the shop from the national corporation of sandwich shops. The menu and even the decor is

(continues)

ETHICAL QUESTION *(continued)*

strikingly similar to that of the national chain. Jonas and Laura each filed individual tax returns last year claiming all of the expenses of the business as expenses against a sole proprietorship. Each also claimed that the money paid to the other partner was a labor cost for the business. In actuality, the business is being run as a partnership. This is despite the public perception that it is part of a corporation and the personal knowledge that it is a partnership. As the business has grown, accounting and tax issues have become more complicated. This year, the two brought the information for preparation of tax returns to the law office that handles other matters for them as individuals. The attorney in the office also assists clients with tax matters. He has suspected for some time that his clients have been less than forthright about their business status. When records are reviewed, it is clear that returns filed in the past have not only been in error; the information provided to the government is untrue with respect to the business status and expenses of the business. What would be the ethical obligation of the attorney with respect to these two?

SUMMARY

The goal of this chapter was to orient the student to the various types of business organizations from a general and an accounting perspective. These forms of business included the individually owned sole proprietorship, multiple owner partnership, limited partnership, and various forms of corporate status. The benefits as well as restrictions on each type of business demonstrate why there are several necessary business organization formats to meet the needs of various types of objectives. Service-oriented businesses have different requirements for tax and accounting than those that are based in retail or manufacturing. In addition to issues of control over the business and limitation of personal asset liability, each form of business has distinct tax implications. Some forms of business income can be taxed twice, whereas others may tax income that is not removed from the business. There are many considerations that need to be applied when determining the best type of business form for a particular enterprise.

■ KEY TERMS

cost of goods sold	limited partnership	professional corporation/ professional service corporation
sole proprietorship	Information Return	
partnership	corporation	limited liability company
general partnership		

For additional resources, visit our Web site at www.westlegalstudies.com

6

Basic Principles and Terminology of Tax

◼ OBJECTIVES_____

After completing this chapter, you will be able to:

❑ Define the various types of taxation

❑ Discuss the basic elements of federal income tax income, status, and filing requirements

❑ Distinguish the types of tax preparers

❑ Distinguish Gross, Adjusted Gross, and Taxable Income

"Our new Constitution is now established, and has an appearance that promises permanency; but in the world nothing can be said to be certain except death and taxes."

Benjamin Franklin - Letter to Jean-Baptiste Leroy [Nov. 13, 1789]

A. TAX CLASSIFICATIONS

The federal, state, and local governments typically raise revenues to pay for government programs and benefits through the process of taxing the members of the public who are intended to receive the greatest advantage of those programs and benefits. These range from items as broad as road construction/repair to law enforcement to public health and safety to things as specific as hot lunch programs in schools and individual medical care. Quite often, funding for public programs is derived from a combination of federal and state money. As a result, individuals are generally taxed in some form by both entities. By assisting states with funding programs, the public receives direct benefits and it is a tool by which the federal government can influence the state governments in the legislation they pass.

The ways in which revenues are raised through taxes covers a broad range. Some taxes are raised by taxing the individuals most likely to utilize the corresponding government benefits. Other taxes are imposed on all individuals as a result of transactions in which they engage. The federal and state governments vary on the types and amount of tax imposed. However, most derive revenues from a combination of different types of taxes. Although this is not an exhaustive discussion, it does explain some of the more common tax concepts employed by the federal and or state governments.

1. Income Tax

The notion of a tax on **income** was conceived and included as part of Article I of the original U.S. Constitution and it made periodic appearances thereafter. However, it was not until the 1900s, specifically 1913, that income tax became a permanent fixture in the generation of government revenues. The circumstances and amounts of income that trigger the need to pay income taxes have continued to change over time. However, the original concept remains the same. That is the idea that if an individual or business generates what the government considers to be income, a percentage of that income may be owed to the government to support government

■ INCOME

Money received by a person or organization because of effort (work) or from return on investments.

APPLICATION 6.1

During the latter 1960s and early 1970s, there was a large push to lower the legal age for consumption of alcohol. Much of the argument was that if young people were considered old enough to vote and to serve in the armed forces (this was also at the height of the Vietnam conflict), at age 18, they also should be considered old enough to drink responsibly. A large number of states subsequently lowered the legal drinking age to below 21. In direct correlation to this, the number of highway fatalities involving alcohol use increased dramatically. By the late 1970s, the federal government wanted the states to raise the drinking age back to 21. To further encourage the states to do so, the federal government linked funding for highway construction in the states to the age for consumption of alcohol. Essentially, to maintain or increase this funding, the state was required to raise its legal age for alcohol. As a result, in a matter of just a few years, every state re-established the legal drinking age at 21.

programs that benefit citizens and the overall economy. This is justified by the ability to work and earn freely in the American capitalist economy and take advantage of government benefits.

Income tax may be required of individuals, business entities such as sole proprietorships, partnerships, corporations, and even the estate of those who have died. In the next section and in the following chapters, more detailed information as well as commonly encountered tax forms and methods of filing income tax will be discussed. At this juncture, the point is to recognize that the federal and state government may in fact tax individuals, businesses, and estates on income generated.

2. Property Tax

A type of state and local tax frequently imposed is the property tax. This tax can take more than one form. Generally, real property taxes are applied to the owners of land and any permanent improvements on the land. The amount of tax due often is tied to a calculation based on the value of the property and its permanent improvements. Frequently, the real property tax will have a number of components, which are calculated at different rates to fund different programs such as state and local roads or schools. The various calculations are computed and then added together to reach the property tax due each year on the property. The sometimes difficult concept for people to understand is how the taxes are paid. In most jurisdictions, real property taxes are paid in the year after they are incurred. Thus, if a property is sold mid-year, the seller must usually pay the unpaid taxes for the entire previous year and the portion of the year the seller held the property to the buyer because it will not be due until the current and following year. This affects federal, and sometimes state, income taxes because real property taxes are often used as a deduction. However, if the taxes are paid as much as a year in advance of when they are due, the question becomes when should the deduction be claimed on income taxes? This is something that varies from state to state and should be considered at the time that taxes are filed. For federal purposes, it is usually considered paid at the time the taxes are paid rather than when actually due. Often this is handled at the closing of a real property transaction. However, some states require that the taxes be claimed as a deduction in the actual year they were paid.

In addition to real property tax, many state and local jurisdictions also place a tax on certain items of personal property. Often, these are items registered with the government such as automobiles, boats, and recreational vehicles. When one of these items is obtained, registration is often mandatory. When registration occurs, it triggers a process to establish a value for the vehicle and generate a personal property tax based on the value. Each year, for as long as the item is owned, the value is reassessed and a corresponding tax is due.

APPLICATION **6.2**

Cassie owned a house but intended to move to a new home. The property tax on the original house was $1,200 annually and was due October 1 for the preceding year. On March 31, 2006, Cassie sold the home. When she received her purchase money, $1,500 was withheld from the purchase price for property taxes that had been incurred by Cassie but not yet paid. This would cover the $1,200 in taxes that would be due in October 2006 for the 2005 tax year and the $300 taxes due for the first three months of 2006 when Cassie owned the property and that would be due in October 2007. Cassie would be entitled to the tax deduction of $1,500 when she filed her federal income tax return.

3. Sales Tax

It is probably safe to say that virtually every consumer has been affected by a sales tax. State and local jurisdictions levy sales tax on the purchase of goods and sometimes services. Although the amount of tax and the type of items subject to tax vary by jurisdiction and locale, the concept is the same. Each time a transaction subject to tax occurs, the appropriate percentage of the purchase price representing the tax rate is collected. Periodically, the sales tax is paid into the state and/or local government along with a report of the amount of sales transactions for the period reported. Some jurisdictions exclude certain goods or services from tax. Additionally, it is not uncommon to have a different rate of tax for high value items that are bought for an amount above a certain threshold purchase price.

Sales tax became a very relevant topic in 2004 when the federal government included it as an option when considering itemized deductions applied against income before determining the amount of income tax due. The new tax law allows individual tax payers who elect to itemize their deductions the option of deducting the amount of state income tax paid or the amount of sales tax paid as part of the calculation of federal income tax due. This change in the law attempts to put all taxpayers on a more equal footing regardless of where they live. A number of states do not have a state income tax. By allowing the state income tax paid as a deduction

APPLICATION **6.3**

Remo buys a new car in a state that imposes a 2 percent personal property tax. The car is purchased for a price of $20,000. In the year of purchase, the tax is $400. The next year, the state assesses the value of the car as $18,000. The annual tax would be $360 and so on. The issue that often arises is whether the assessment is accurate and whether the property has appreciated (increased in value) or depreciated. This is something that may be challenged by taxpayers. However, there must be convincing evidence to establish a value different than that determined by the taxing jurisdiction in order to cause an alteration in the tax.

APPLICATION **6.4**

In 2006, George lived and worked in the state of Illinois. He filed federal tax form 1040A, in which he itemized the deductions for which he was eligible. During that year, he paid $1,378 in state income tax. In the same year, he paid $1,200 in sales tax. For George, the best election under these circumstances would be to deduct his state income tax on his personal tax return. However, if George had lived in Florida, Texas, or in any other state that does not have a state income tax, the best option would be for him to deduct the $1,200 sales tax since he would have paid $0 in state income tax.

against the federal income tax owed, people in states with a state income tax stood to receive a better result on their federal income tax liability as the result of greater itemized deductions. However, by adding in the alternative of a sales tax deduction, taxpayers in states without a state income tax were given a method of calculating a similar deduction. Those who do live in a state with a state income tax were allowed to choose the option of deducting state income tax or sales tax paid so that all have the same advantage regardless of their state of residence. Finally, in an effort to avoid what could be a recordkeeping nightmare for taxpayers, tax preparers, and accountants, a calculation has been provided by the federal government to allow an estimation of the amount of sales tax paid based on the amount of income available to the taxpayer during the year.

4. Excise Tax

Excise taxes are taxes paid when purchases are made on specific goods, such as gasoline. Excise taxes are often included in the price of the product and may be charged by any or all of federal, state, and local governments. There also may be excise taxes on activities, such as on gambling or on highway usage by heavy vehicles. One of the major components of the federal excise program is motor fuel as a means to fund road construction and repair. The rationale is that those who utilize products that affect the environment, public benefits, individuals, and the economy, are in the best position to bear the brunt of the costs generated by such use. Typically, the price of fuel includes a percentage for an excise tax. In recent years, a number of jurisdictions have imposed a heavy excise tax on tobacco products in response to the greatly increased demand for government services as the result of tobacco related illnesses.

APPLICATION   6.5

Josephine was a heavy smoker for 40 years. She has now developed emphysema to the point that she is no longer able to care for herself. Josephine has insufficient assets and insurance to address the costs of her care. As a result, she receives supplemental government assistance. This and similar scenarios have become so prevalent that the states had to come up with another source of income to fund the type of services provided to Josephine and other similarly situated persons. A popular method has been to increase the tax on tobacco-related products based on the rationale that those who voluntarily use the product that produces the illness should bear a larger percentage of the ultimate cost.

5. Estate Taxes

The estate tax is a tax on the right to transfer property at death. Taxes imposed on death provide incentive to transfer assets before death and thereby promote maximum use of those assets. However, gift tax laws are generally designed to prevent complete tax avoidance by this route. The federal estate tax is integrated with the federal gift tax so that large estates cannot be shielded from taxation by lifetime giving. Many states also impose an estate tax. An estate tax is based on an accounting of everything owned or in which the individual had a financial interest in at the date of death. The fair market value of these items is used, as opposed to what was paid for them or what their values were when they were obtained. The total of all of these items is known as the Gross Estate. The property included in the Gross Estate may consist of cash and securities, real estate, insurance, trusts, annuities, business interests, personal property, and other assets. Once the total value is determined, certain deductions (and, in special circumstances, reductions to value) are allowed when arriving at the amount of the estate that may be subject to tax. These deductions may include mortgages and other debts, estate administration expenses, and property that passes to surviving spouses and qualified charities. The value of some operating business interests or farms may even be reduced for estates that qualify. Although the amount changes periodically, at the time of publication, the amount of deductions and credits typically reduce the computed tax so that only total taxable estates and lifetime gifts that exceed $1,000,000 will actually have to pay tax. As a result, the federal estate tax only affects the wealthiest 2 percent of all Americans.

"Death Taxes" is a term that may be used to describe either estate taxes or another form of tax related to the death of an individual but that affects the heir. These are inheritance taxes. At this time, the federal government and a minority of states have estate taxes that tax the estate before it is distributed. But a small number of states impose a tax on an inheritance from an estate. A majority of states and the District of Columbia also have what is often called a "pickup" estate tax. Although there are variations, it is generally designed to tax state residents in an amount that equals the credit that the federal estate tax allows for state death taxes paid. So, if a state resident does not have a federal estate tax liability, she should not have a liability under a state pickup tax. Essentially, the pickup tax takes a portion of the federal estate tax and shifts it to the states.

State death taxes can include any combination of the following three areas:

- pickup taxes
- inheritance taxes
- estate taxes

An inheritance tax is levied on the right to property received through inheritance. The recipients, known as beneficiaries are divided into classes according to the closeness or remoteness of their relationship to the decedent, with different exemptions and tax rates applied to each class. Generally, the closer the relationship, the greater the exemption and the lower the tax. As the federal government takes steps to modify its estate tax laws, it is very likely there will be many corresponding changes in state laws. As a result, it is important to always stay current on the laws affecting death estates in your jurisdiction.

6. Gift Tax

The gift tax is a tax on the change of ownership of property by one individual to another when the donor (the party making the gift) receives nothing, or less than full value, in return. The tax applies whether the donor intends the transfer to be a gift or not. The gift tax applies to the transfer by gift of any property whether it is real (land or improvements to land) or personal (tangible items). A gift is made if property (including money), is given or the use of or income from the property is given, without expecting to receive something of at least equal value in return. If you sell something at less than its full value or if you make an interest-free or reduced-interest loan, you may be making a gift. The general rule is that any gift is a taxable gift. However, there are many exceptions to this rule. Gifts made to qualifying charities may be claimed by the donor who itemizes the gift on the tax return as a tax deduction. Much greater discussion of this topic is provided in the subsequent chapter that details the Gift Tax Return. However, for the limited purpose of this discussion, the following gifts are not generally considered exempt from federal tax:

- Gifts that are not more than the annual exclusion for the calendar year. Currently, this amount is $11,000 per recipient from any single donor. For married donors, the amount that can be given tax free is doubled. Each is entitled to the annual exclusion amount on the gift. Together, a married couple can give $22,000 to each donee.

- Tuition or medical expenses paid on behalf of someone (the educational and medical exclusions).

- Gifts to one's spouse.

- Gifts to a political organization for its use.

APPLICATION 6.6

Joe and Marguerite are married and have a married daughter. Joe and Marguerite give their daughter and her husband a gift of $44,000. This entire gift is not taxable because each recipient was given $11,000 from each of the donors.

ASSIGNMENT 6.1

Calculate how much of each gift below would be taxable based on the information provided in the text:

a. Misty, a single mom, received a gift from her parents to fund a return to college. Her parents gave her $40,000 in cash.

b. Misty, a single mom, received a gift from her parents to fund a return to college. Her parents paid the university $40,000 to cover all tuition and expenses necessary to finish her degree.

c. Sara, Bill, and their four children received a gift from Bill's parents in the form of an investment portfolio with a value of $132,000 on the date of the gift.

d. Sara, Bill, and their four children received a gift from Bill's mother in the form of an investment portfolio with a value of $132,000 on the date of the gift.

e. As an engagement present, Mark presented his future wife with a gift certificate for a shopping spree in the amount of $20,000 to purchase items for their new home.

f. As a wedding present, Mark presented his wife with a gift certificate for a shopping spree in the amount of $20,000 to purchase items for their new home.

g. Caroline gave each of her three children from her prior marriage $11,000. Caroline's new husband also gave each of Caroline's children $11,000.

h. Caroline gave each of her three children from her prior marriage $11,000. Caroline's ex-husband also gave each of the three children $11,000.

i. Maxwell donated $50,000 to the "Save the World from Wild Animals" registered charity.

j. Maxwell gave his son $50,000 that was to be used for travel expenses on the son's trips to Africa to volunteer with various relief organizations.

7. Social Security and Medicare

At the very least, most people are vaguely aware of the concept of Social Security. Individuals pay in a percentage of their earnings and, on attainment of a specific age or event, they are entitled to certain monetary benefits from the government. Social Security is far different today than its origins. The laws providing for Social Security as a form of retirement income to supplement other retirement income for individuals was enacted in 1935. Initially, it was a one-time lump-sum payment. The first person to collect received a payment in 1935 for 17¢. Shortly thereafter, the laws were amended to provide for regular monthly retirement benefits. In 1939, the handling of Social Security collections was put under the general supervision of the Internal Revenue Service (IRS), which also collected other types of taxes. At this time, the Social Security tax name was changed and since then has been collected as the Federal Insurance Contributions Act (FICA). Throughout the years, a variety of additional benefits of have been made for individuals, including survivor's children and widows in 1939, and disability in 1956. The ages and conditions on which Social Security can be collected by the individual, children, or survivors have changed over time as well. However, the requirement to make contributions has stayed essentially the same other than adjustments in amounts designed to keep pace with inflation. As discussed in the earlier chapter addressing issues of payroll, employees and their employers contribute matching amounts to Social Security up to a threshold level of pay. Those who are self-employed must contribute both portions of the tax. However, they are entitled to a tax deduction on their federal income tax for the one-half paid that would otherwise be paid by the employer if the individual were an employee. Some individuals who are employed by government entities do not pay into Social Security via the FICA tax. Rather, they pay into a governmentally sponsored retirement plan that operates under similar principles.

Although it is often grouped together in discussion with Social Security tax, Medicare is a totally separate entity. Passed in 1965 and first available in 1966, Medicare's design is to provide supplemental health care insurance for those receiving Social Security benefits. Unlike FICA tax withholdings, there is no upper limit on which contributions are required. Generally speaking, all workers who earn income whether as employees or self-employed individuals must contribute a percentage of their earnings to the Medicare program. The percentage collected may change over time but it is a regular required contribution. Like FICA, it may be paid through payroll deductions, or with income tax contributions including with the annual tax return.

B. INCOME TAX

Some discussion already has been given to the topic of income tax in this and in earlier chapters. However, at this point, a more detailed examination is necessary to fully understand the application of the income tax system, which has become increasingly complex over the last century. Although the first actual income tax took effect in 1862, it was ended in 1872 as the costs of the Civil War and Reconstruction era had largely abated. It was reenacted in 1894, but in 1895, was held unconstitutional in the way it was implemented. Finally, in 1913, the passage of the 16th Amendment laid the framework for an income tax system that has been in place ever since. Income tax is a vehicle used to pay for a large percentage of government programs. However, it is constantly undergoing change as the government attempts to make it more fair to the seemingly infinite number of individual circumstances that are affected or created by the income tax system. Changes occurred periodically in the early years. However, in 1986, President Reagan signed into effect the most sweeping tax reforms ever with the Tax Reform Act of 1986. Since that time, there have been major amendments to the tax system almost every year. The Legislative Branch, or Congress, is responsible for the major laws that are applied to all taxpayers. However, it is up to the Internal Revenue Service, under the supervision of the Executive Branch of government, that is, the president, to define these laws as they apply to individual persons and businesses. The Internal Revenue Service also processes the tax returns, collects the taxes, and follows up on disputed taxes as well as those who simply elect not to file or pay when required. Ultimately, some disputes end up in the Judicial Branch as cases between the Internal Revenue Service and taxpayers are resolved. As a result, all three branches of government play an active role in the income tax process that is used to fuel the machinery of the U.S. government.

APPLICATION 6.7

Nancy works as a nurse at a local hospital. She also works part time as a nurse for an elderly neighbor. Nancy's regular payroll check includes withholdings for FICA and Medicare totaling 7.65 percent of her gross wages. Her employer, the hospital, also contributes a similar amount on Nancy's behalf. Additionally, each quarter, Nancy makes quarterly estimated deposits with the Internal Revenue Service to cover her self employment tax for FICA and Medicare and income tax. At the end of the year, when Nancy's tax return is prepared, she receives various adjustments to her **taxable income** including one-half of the amount paid for self-employment tax as well as expenses she incurs related to her job as a self-employed individual. She completes a tax form that calculates the FICA and Medicare due as the result of self employment. If there is a balance due, it is to be paid with her tax return. If there is a refund due, it can be applied as a credit to items such as income tax that may be due for the current or upcoming year.

TAXABLE INCOME

The amount of net income used in calculating income tax.

1. Federal versus State

The federal government and a large majority of the states impose a tax on the income generated within the states. The tax may be on the individual or an entity such as a general corporation. Typically, there is a detailed computation that is required to determine the amount of tax that is due. The purpose of state income tax is similar to that of the federal income tax. It is used to fund a variety of programs and benefits provided by the state to its citizens and visitors. There are a few states that do not impose an income tax. This is not due to a lack of a need for revenue. Rather, these are typically states that have adequate resources through other types of tax to cover the costs of the government. For example, Texas has a strong oil production industry that generates a great deal of associated tax revenue. States such as Nevada and Florida raise significant revenues through taxes connected to their large tourism industry. Unfortunately, most states do not have these types of large revenue resources and must supplement with income tax. Each state has its own calculation based on the types of income earned by citizens, businesses, and other relevant factors. Because the manner in which states impose tax is so diverse, and the fact that several states do not have an income tax, the discussion from this point forward will be confined to the federal income tax that is administered by the IRS.

The federal income tax is a very complicated system and varies dramatically in how it is applied both for individuals and businesses. In addition to the frequent legislative changes to the tax code, the IRS has the ability to define the code through its interpretations of the various provisions in the tax laws. This is something that occurs continually throughout the year. As a result, it is extremely important to keep up with changes in the tax code as they occur frequently, and sometimes with very little notice to the taxpayer. Each year, the IRS issues a publication known as Pub. 17, which summarizes the changes in the individual taxpayer tax code for the preceding tax year. This booklet also provides references to other IRS publications that may assist in answering more specific and complicated questions about income tax. However, because it is a paper document and changes occur after its publication, it still may be necessary to check with the IRS for the most current changes. This can be done most easily by accessing the IRS Web site http://www.IRS.gov, at which specific questions can be input for the most current information.

TAX EVASION

Occurs when efforts are made by individuals and other entities to dodge the payment of taxes by breaking the law.

TAX AVOIDANCE

Legal use of the terms of the tax code to one's own advantage.

2. Who Must File—Evasion versus Avoidance

One of the first things individuals affected by the income tax laws must be aware of is the distinction between tax evasion and tax avoidance. It is probably safe to say that no one is anxious to pay more tax than they are required to pay by law. As a result, individuals and businesses alike look to identify methods to minimize the tax liability. However, such reductions must be done in a legal fashion to avoid criminal penalties. This leads to the distinctions between **tax evasion** and **tax avoidance**. Tax evasion occurs when efforts are made by individuals and other entities to dodge the

APPLICATION 6.8

Tamara is a client of the Trident Law Firm. She comes into the office and seeks assistance with preparation of her tax return. A paralegal is assigned to help Tamara. Tamara's question is this: She has a personal injury case against another motorist arising from an automobile accident the previous year. Tamara took out a loan to cover some of her expenses while she was off work due to her injuries. She does not know if the loan would be considered income for the purposes of her tax return. After all, she did use the proceeds of the loan as she would have normally used her paycheck, which is taxable. The paralegal consults the most current Pub. 17 for a definition of income and informs Tamara that the loan itself does not constitute income as it is money she is obligated to return (with

payment of taxes by breaking the law. Tax evasion often involves taxpayers who deliberately misrepresent or conceal the true state of their affairs to the tax authorities in order to reduce their tax liability, and includes, in particular, dishonest tax reporting (such as underdeclaring income, profits, or gains; and/or overstating deductions). However, tax avoidance is the legal use of the terms of the tax code to one's own advantage. This can be done to reduce the amount of tax that is payable by means that are within the law, while making a full disclosure of the relevant and material information to the tax authorities. Tax avoidance occurs through taking full advantage of the exclusions, deductions, and credits available under the circumstances.

APPLICATION 6.9

Consider Tamara in Application 6.8. Because she could not work at her regular job as a result of her injuries, she took out a loan to cover expenses. In order to make the loan payments, Tamara baby-sat for her sister's children. Tamara was paid in cash and neither she nor her sister reported the transaction on their taxes. By failing to report earned income, Tamara was engaged in tax evasion. However, consider the following change in circumstances.

Tamara reported the income. But she also reported the expenses of transporting the children to and from school, activities, food provided to the children, and the use of her home as a location to watch the children. When these legal deductions were applied against the amounts she received, the result was minimal actual income for Tamara. In fact, the amount was so low as to relieve Tamara of any tax liability at all. This would be considered legal tax avoidance.

ASSIGNMENT 6.2

Consider the following situations and determine if they constitute income tax evasion or income tax avoidance or neither.

a. Duane sold a number of items on an Internet auction site. His income from the site was $4,325. He had expenses from the sales in the form of auction fees and shipping in an amount of $1,323. Duane reported miscellaneous income of $4,325.

b. Consider Duane. However, change the facts to reflect that he reported $4,002 in miscellaneous income.

c. Assume that Duane did not report the money from the auction because he did not consider it earned and thus subject to income tax.

d. Mary Ann purchased $250 of merchandise at an estate auction and donated it to a homeless shelter. She then deducted $250 from the income she earned. This reduced her tax liability by $37.50.

e. Mary Ann purchased $250 of merchandise at an estate auction and donated it to a homeless shelter. She then adjusted her reported income to result in a $250 reduction of tax liability.

f. Suzanne, a single woman without children, but with 12 dogs whom she considered her children, paid out $3,622 in veterinary bills this year. She has claimed them as a medical expense for a dependent. The tax definition of a dependent does not include animals.

g. James works as a delivery driver in his own business. His route includes a number of daily stops including his children's school. James arranges his delivery schedule in order to drop his kids off for school while on his route. He claims all of his mileage for his deliveries as a deduction.

h. Jennifer holds yard sales one weekend a month. The other three weekends she spends attending garage sales and acquiring items she plans to resell at a profit. Jennifer does not report her garage sale income as earnings. She has no other job.

i. Austin bought two new computers for a package price of $2,000. He keeps one at home and uses it for personal business. The other is used at his office. Austin deducted $2,000 as a business expense.

j. Alexa started a Senior Citizen's Center in her small town. She works for a set hourly wage for 25 hours per week. Alexa's husband works full time. But he frequently helps out by donating 5 to 10 hours per week to the Senior Citizen's Center. At the end of the year, Alexa deducted the number of hours donated by her husband from her own income that would then be reported on her tax return.

a. Individuals.

The general rule is that all individuals, regardless of age, with income either earned or through investment may be subject to income tax. This even includes minors with income. The income does not have to be earned in the form of wages or profit from a business; it can be from basically any type of effort to produce money through sale of property, investments, and so on. Each year, individuals with a threshold level of income are required to report that income on an individual tax return. In some situations, members of the same household may file income information on the same return. Whether individuals can report together and how the income is reported depends largely on the construction of the family and how assets of the family are received and distributed. For example, a married couple may elect to file their income tax return jointly; however, a brother and sister sharing a home and expenses may not file a joint return. Yet, in certain circumstances, one who is supporting another individual may elect to include that person as a dependent on the return. This has tax effects for the reporting individual and the dependent. Yet, the dependent also may elect to file her own tax return and exclude herself from the personal exemption element of tax. This is a deduction allowed each person that in turn reduces the amount of income subject to the income tax. At this stage, the details of these situations are not as relevant as the concept that how individual income is reported can be a complicated process and requires careful evaluation and knowledge of the method that provides the best, yet legal, outcome. More discussion of actual return preparation is provided in subsequent chapters.

b. Businesses.

In Chapter 4, the various types of business entities were discussed. At that time, it was mentioned that some businesses, such as C corporations, are required to report and pay tax on income. Other businesses are what may be commonly referred to as **pass-through** entities. These are businesses that report income; however, the income itself is passed through the business and to the individual owner(s) for purposes of determining taxation.

> **PASS-THROUGH**
>
> Businesses that report income; however, the income itself is passed through the business and to the individual owner(s) for purposes of determining taxation.

APPLICATION **6.10**

Katrina is a single working mother of two. Her sons are 8 and 12. Katrina lives with her longtime boyfriend and they share household expenses equally. Although Katrina may claim her children as dependents, her nonrelative boyfriend must file his own individual return. Katrina's sister Kristin is also a single working mother of two. Her daughters are 16 and 25. Kristin's eldest daughter is employed and pays rent to Kristin as well as most of her own living/personal expenses. Kristin's disabled mother also lives with the family and Kristin is responsible for all of the mother's expenses. In this case, Kristin may include her youngest daughter and her mother on her return. However, the oldest daughter must file her own individual return.

Recall that a general or "C" corporation generates income and is taxed on that income as an entity just as if the corporation were a person (although different tax rates, forms, and rules may apply). The individual holder of stock (ownership) in the corporation is only affected if a share of the income remaining after taxes is distributed. In that event, the corporation pays tax on its income and then the individual must pay tax as well on any distribution of net (after tax and expenses) profit is received from the corporation. For example, the Brandeis Corporation has income of $1.2 million. The tax is computed and paid. Afterward, there is $850,000 of profit remaining. Of that profit, $50,000 is distributed to the five owners as a dividend. Each of the owners would be responsible for declaring and pay tax on their share or $10,000. This double taxation is one thing that should be considered when determining the proper business form.

However, in a partnership, a return is filed with the government that indicates the income of the partnership and how it was distributed among the partners. Each of the partners must then file a corresponding return that reflects the amount of income received from the partnership. However, no income tax is paid by the partnership itself. At first glance, this may seem more appealing that the double taxation of some corporate income. However, other factors such as limited personal liability for debts of the business, and in some cases special tax benefits for corporations, and so on, are also significant factors to consider.

Finally, in the sole proprietorship, all income is reported by the individual her personal return. However, a specific form for the type of business that produced the income is attached and allows various deductions before the tax is computed. The tax percentage will be at the same rate as the other ordinary income the individual or other persons on the return may have had. As stated earlier, this will be examined in much greater detail in discussions that follow.

APPLICATION **6.11**

Two brothers were entrepreneurs. Adam was the major stockholder in a corporation. In 2006, Adam's corporation generated substantial income. The corporation paid substantial tax. Adam received a return on his investment in the form of a dividend (percentage of profits). Adam was then liable for the tax on the dividend. However, because it was investment income (passive and not earned), no Social Security or Medicare tax was due on the dividend. The corporation filed an income tax return with the IRS. In addition, it provided the IRS with a statement detailing the amount of dividend paid to each shareholder and the shareholder's identity.

Bill, Adam's next youngest brother, was a sole proprietor. His business, too, did very well. However, Bill had to declare all of the net profits (profit less business expense deductions) on his personal tax return. The profits were considered self-employment

(continues)

APPLICATION   6.11 *(continued)*

income. As a result, in addition to the income tax, Bill had to also pay the employer and employee share of Social Security and Medicare taxes calculated on all the net profits of the business.

3. Filing Status for Individuals

Individuals, as opposed to various types of businesses, are required to report all income above a certain level. Typically, employers file quarterly reports as well as one at the end of the calendar year that detail the income paid to each employee. For amounts paid to independent contractors over an amount set by the IRS, a similar report is filed on form 1099. The amounts received during the year in wages or 1099-type income for each person are recorded with the IRS by individual Social Security number. Additionally, at the end of each calendar year the employer is obligated to provide all persons to whom it paid some sort of compensation for services performed, a record of the amount paid either on a form W-2 or 1099.

When an individual has income, either through wages, self-employment, investment, retirement, Social Security, or in some instances sale of property, she may be required to file an individual income tax return. Even minors may be required to report income and possibly pay taxes if the amount of income is sufficient to meet the minimum threshold. Whether a person files a tax return as an individual or with someone else depends on the circumstances of the household in which the individual resides. The status a person uses when filing a tax return may have an enormous impact on the amount of tax paid or refunded. As a result, selecting the legal status available that will provide the most tax benefit is a crucial step in the tax preparation process.

The options for filing status are **Head of Household**, **Qualifying Widow**, **Single**, **Married Filing Jointly**, and **Married Filing Separate** With Dependent Child. Although at first glance these seem relatively simple and straightforward, the definition of a family in the United States has become so complex that there are a wide variety of rules that have affected how a person is categorized for the purposes of filing taxes. The discussion here will examine each filing status and the most commonly employed rules and exceptions.

a. Single.

Single is generally the most straightforward filing status. The rule for filing under single status is that the person must be unmarried, or legally separated under a divorce or separate maintenance decree. The time for the determination is the last day of the year. It does not matter that someone was married for the first 364 days of the year. If she became divorced on December 31, she is considered single. However, there are exceptions to this rule. For example, individuals are not considered single if they divorced with the intent to file under **single status** and also

HEAD OF HOUSEHOLD

An individual who is responsible for the support of certain other individuals.

QUALIFYING WIDOW(ER)

A tax status available to widows and widowers for up to two years following their spouse's death provided they have at least one dependent and meet certain IRS criteria concerning their previous filing status.

■ MARRIED FILING JOINTLY

A filing status for married couples that have wed before the end of the tax year. Both spouses record their respective incomes, exemptions, and deductions on the same tax return. Best if only one spouse has a significant income. In most cases, "married filing jointly" offers the most tax savings, especially when the spouses have different income levels.

■ MARRIED FILING SEPARATE

A filing status for married couples who choose to record their respective incomes, exemptions, and deductions on separate tax returns. Best when both spouses work and the income and itemized deductions are large and very unequal.

■ SINGLE STATUS

The filing status used by a taxpayer who is unmarried and does not qualify for any other filing status.

had the intent to remarry each other after the first of the year to achieve a better tax consequence. Also, if the taxpayer becomes widowed before the start of the tax year, does not remarry within the year, and does not have dependent children single status must be used for that year. One who is widowed during the tax year may continue to file a joint return (an exception to the rule about being married on December 31). Finally, a marriage that has been legally annulled by an order of court is considered never have to actually existed. In that case, single filing status would be appropriate for any year of the marriage in which a joint return was or would have been filed. If a return has already been filed, the individuals may go back and amend their returns.

b. Married Filing Jointly and Married Filing Separate.

Although a couple may be married, the tax effects may be different based on whether they file under joint or separate status. The first determination is whether the parties are entitled to either of the married status' for filing. Under the tax code, a couple is considered married if they meet any one of the following:

- legally married and living together as husband and wife;
- living together by a common law marriage that is recognized in the state where residing or the state where the common law marriage began;
- married and living apart but not legally separated under a decree of divorce or separate maintenance;
- separated under a temporary decree of divorce.
- married and one member of the couple is widowed from the other at any point during the year. However, if the surviving member remarried during the year, the deceased's return is filed married filing separate and the surviving member is filed as joint with the new spouse.

In some instances, a married person may desire to file her tax return as an individual head of household rather than part of a married couple. This is allowed in a very limited situation. When this occurs, the other spouse uses Married Filing Separate Status. To be married and legally file as Head of Household is discussed here.

The vast majority of people who are married file under the Married Filing Jointly status. This is because it usually provides the greatest tax benefits. This type of filing status combines the income, deductions, and credits of the parties. It is available even if one spouse had no income during the year. Married Filing Jointly often results in a lower tax liability than if the returns were filed as Married Filing Separate. One drawback, however, is that both parties are considered jointly responsible for the tax regardless of whether one of the parties incurred the tax.

In some instances, it may be beneficial for a married couple to file their return as Married Filing Separate. Although the tax result for filing under this status is often higher, there are circumstances when it is more beneficial to use this method. Some of the disadvantages are the following special rules that are imposed on returns filed as Married Filing Separate:

- the exemption amount used to figure the alternative minimum tax is one-half that of a return filed under Married Filing Jointly status;

- there are strong limitations on the ability to claim child and dependent care and related expenses, job benefits;

- no earned income credit is allowed;

- generally no exclusion credit for adoption expenses is allowed; no education credits, student loan interest, tuition/fees deduction, and education-related interest income exclusions are allowed;

- if the parties resided together at any time during the year there are limitations relating to deductions, exemptions, or credits associated with conditions such as elderly, disabled, Social Security benefits, IRAs;

- the following deductions and credits may be reduced by one-half that allowed on a joint return:

  Child Tax Credit
  Retirement Savings Contributions Credit
  Itemized Deductions
  Personal Exemptions

Additionally, if one spouse itemizes deductions (discussed in greater detail later), the other spouse must itemize as well. If the standard deduction is used instead of itemizing, the parties are each only entitled to one-half of the deduction allowed a couple who is Married Filing Jointly. There are additional restrictions that apply to the Married Filing Separate that result in it being beneficial only in very limited

APPLICATION **6.12**

John and Cindy have recently separated and have filed for divorce. They were married for the entire year previously and now are preparing their tax returns. John has no interest in having anything to do with Cindy and wants to file Married Filing Separate. Cindy's tax preparer, however, has advised her that by filing Married Filing Jointly, the parties are entitled to an earned income credit that will generate a refund of more than $2,000. However, by filing Married Filing Separate, the earned income credit is not allowed and there will be no refund. In this instance, it would be more beneficial and entirely legal for John and Cindy to file their return for the previous year as Married Filing Jointly and receive the benefit of the earned income credit that could be shared or distributed as they saw fit.

situations. Thus, even if parties are contemplating divorce, as long as they are still legally married on the last day of the year, it may be beneficial to agree to file the return jointly.

c. Head of Household.

A commonly used status is Head of Household. This is available to those who are single, or unmarried for tax purposes, and responsible for the support of certain other individuals. Head of Household provides tax benefits to encourage individuals to assist in the financial care and support of others. It is available to those persons who meet the following qualifications:

- Single or Unmarried for tax purposes on the last day of the year, and

- Have paid more than half the cost of keeping up a home for the year, and

- Provided a home for more than half the year for a **qualifying person**, the full year for a foster child, or more than half the support for a dependent parent who may or may not live with the taxpayer.

To qualify for Head of Household status, a married taxpayer must be considered unmarried for tax purposes. The only married individuals entitled to do this are those who:

- did not file a joint return, and

- paid more than half the cost of keeping up their home for the tax year, and

- have a spouse that did not live in the home for the last 6 months of the year, and

- provided the home as the main home of a dependent child, adopted child, or stepchild for more than half of the year, and the entire year for foster children (special rules apply to children who were born, died, or temporarily absent during the year), and

- are eligible to claim the personal exemption for the child unless the only reason not to claim the exemption is that it is legally provided to the other spouse, or

- the spouse is a nonresident alien for any part of the year and the spouse is not claimed as a resident alien, or a dependent for head of household purposes.

Under Head of Household status, the key issue is often what constitutes a "qualifying person," which in turn qualifies the taxpayer for the filing status. Exhibit 6–1, taken from the IRS Pub. 17, provides a valuable tool to determine if an individual is a qualifying person for determination of whether a taxpayer is entitled to file under Head of Household Status.

QUALIFYING PERSON

A dependent or other individual who is eligible for a given tax credit or deduction through the fulfillment of certain IRS criteria.

Table 2-1. **Who Is a Qualifying Person Qualifying You To File as Head of Household?**[1]

> **Caution.** *See the text of this publication for the other requirements you must meet to claim head of household filing status.*

IF the person is your . . .	AND . . .	THEN that person is . . .
qualifying child (such as a son, daughter, or grandchild who lived with you more than half the year and meets certain other tests)[2]	he or she is single	a qualifying person, whether or not you can claim an exemption for the person.
	he or she is married <u>and</u> you can claim an exemption for him or her	a qualifying person.
	he or she is married <u>and</u> you cannot claim an exemption for him or her	not a qualifying person. [3]
qualifying relative [4] who is your father or mother	you can claim an exemption for him or her[5]	a qualifying person.[6]
	you cannot claim an exemption for him or her	not a qualifying person.
qualifying relative [4] other than your father or mother (such as a grandparent, brother, or sister who meets certain tests)[7]	he or she lived with you more than half the year, <u>and</u> you can claim an exemption for him or her [5]	a qualifying person.
	he or she did not live with you more than half the year	not a qualifying person.
	you cannot claim an exemption for him or her	not a qualifying person.

[1]A person cannot qualify more than one taxpayer to use the head of household filing status for the year.
[2]The term "qualifying child" is defined in chapter 3. **Note.** If you are a noncustodial parent, the term "qualifying child" for head of household filing status does not include a child who is your qualifying child for exemption purposes only because of the rules described under *Children of divorced or separated parents* under *Qualifying Child* in chapter 3. If you are the custodial parent and those rules apply, the child generally is your qualifying child for head of household filing status even though the child is not a qualifying child for whom you can claim an exemption.
[3] This person is a qualifying person if the only reason you cannot claim the exemption is that you can be claimed as a dependent on someone else's return.
[4]The term "qualifying relative" is defined in chapter 3.
[5]If you can claim an exemption for a person only because of a multiple support agreement, that person is not a qualifying person. See *Multiple Support Agreement* in chapter 3.
[6]See *Special rule for parent* for an additional requirement.
[7]A person who is your qualifying relative only because he or she lived with you all year as a member of your household is not a qualifying person.

EXHIBIT 6–1   Table 2.1 IRS Pub. 17

d. Qualifying Widow(er) With Dependent Child.

Finally, a narrowly defined status is available to those who are recently widowed and left with dependent children. This status essentially allows the benefits of Married Filing Jointly status during a time of financial transition for the widow from two adults to one. For the year in which the spouse died, the widow(er) may continue to file using Married Filing Jointly status. Following that, if the conditions are satisfied, the return can be filed using the status of a Qualifying Widower With Dependent Child for up to an additional 2 years. The conditions for using this status are relatively straightforward:

- The widow(er) was eligible to file Married Filing Jointly at the time of the spouse's death.

- The widow(er) has not remarried between the end of the year of the spouse's death and two full calendar years following (remarriage ends the eligibility for this status in the year the remarriage occurred).

- The widow(er) has a child, stepchild, adopted child, or foster child for whom the widow(er) is eligible to claim as an exemption.

- The widow(er) was paid for more than one-half of keeping up the main home for her or himself and the child for the entire year (temporary absences such as school are not considered a failure to provide a home for the entire year).

If the parties had begun divorce proceedings at the time of one spouse's death, and the divorce was not final, then the surviving spouse would still be permitted to file Married Filing Jointly, and consequently Qualifying Widow(er), assuming the other conditions were met. As mentioned earlier, the status of Qualifying Widow(er) is available for a full 2 years following the year of the death of the spouse unless it is extinguished by the remarriage of the surviving spouse.

APPLICATION **6.13**

Marvin was married to Jennifer. Jennifer died on January 1, 2005. In 2006, when Marvin filed his tax return for the 2005 tax year, he was eligible to file the return as married filing jointly. This is even though the parties were in the process of getting a divorce, which was due to be finalized January 2, 2005. Furthermore, as the surviving parent of their 8-year-old child, Marvin would be entitled to file his 2006 and 2007 return as a Qualifying Widower With Dependent Child. However, if Marvin remarried at any time before January 1, 2008, he would not have the Qualifying Widower status available to him for the year of remarriage and any year thereafter.

ASSIGNMENT **6.3**

Based on the information provided in the text, what status would be used for the each of the following adult individuals if they were required to file a federal income tax return for the tax year 2006?

(continues)

ASSIGNMENT **6.3** *(continued)*

a. Maya is an 18-year-old mother of one. She lived all of 2006 with Mose, the father of her child, in a state that does not recognized common law marriage. The child is 2 years old.

b. Davonne is a 24-year-old man. He was married to Sue until their divorce on February 10, 2006. On December 31, 2006, Davonne married Coleen. Sue has not remarried.

c. Cecil and Joann are married. However, they have not lived in the same household for 12 years including all of 2006. They have a daughter age 14. They worked things out themselves and never obtained a court order regarding their separation.

d. Caroline is raising her four grandchildren all of whom are under age 10 and have no income of their own. She does not have legal custody, but they live with her full time and have for the past 3 years. Their mother is deceased and the father has been unemployed and homeless for more than 2 years. His whereabouts are unknown.

e. Jim and Joann married at 12:01 a.m. on January 1. Both had never been married before.

f. Caesar and Stella were married on January 1, 2006. On June 25, 2006, Caesar moved out of the house and filed for divorce. Stella remained with her daughter from a former marriage. Stella's daughter is aged 12. The divorce was final on December 20, 2006.

g. Same as "f," except the divorce was not final until January 1, 2007.

h. Cornell's wife Amanda passed away on January 1, 2006. Cornell continued to provide a home to Amanda's adopted daughter Lisa, age 8, for the entire year.

i. Same as "h," except for the additional fact that Cornell married Rose on December 31, 2006.

j. Cornell's wife Amanda passed away on January 1, 2004. Cornell continued to provide a home to Amanda's adopted daughter Lisa, age 8 (10 years in 2006). On December 31, 2006, Cornell married Rose.

4. Dependent Status.

A fascinating occurrence took place in the United States in 1987 when an estimated 7.5 million children disappeared, never to be seen or heard from again. Missing persons reports for these children were not filed. No searches were launched for them by family, friends, or law enforcement. The only clue appeared to have been the enactment of a new income tax requirement under the Tax Reform Act of 1986, which mandated that all dependents over the age of 5, claimed on a tax return for the purpose of reducing taxes and tax benefits, must have a recognized Social Security number listed with the child's name on the return. In 1996, the requirement was expanded to require inclusion of a Social Security number for all dependents regardless of age. Once again, children previously claimed on tax returns began to disappear. Regardless of the mass disappearances, for those remaining, there are still tens of millions of individuals claimed each year as dependents on tax returns. The question of whether someone qualifies to be claimed as a dependent by another is answered by the application of a five-prong test.

In order for one person to claim another as a dependent on a tax return, the person claimed must be considered a qualifying child or qualifying relative. The distinction between these two has to do with what additional tax deductions/credits may be claimed for each.

A dependent exemption for a qualifying child or qualifying relative is only allowed if these three tests are met:

- Dependent taxpayer test. A dependent cannot be claimed if the taxpayer or spouse, if filing jointly, could be claimed as a dependent by another taxpayer.

- Joint return test. A married person who files a joint return cannot be claimed as a dependent unless that joint return is only a claim for refund and there would be no tax liability for either spouse on separate returns.

- Citizen or resident test. A dependent cannot be claimed unless that person is a U.S. citizen, U.S. resident, U.S. national, or a resident of Canada or Mexico, for some part of the year.

In order to be considered a "Qualifying Child" which allows not only the personal exemption but also various deductions and credits:

- The child must be related to the taxpayer as the son, daughter, stepchild, eligible foster child, brother, sister, half brother, half sister, stepbrother, stepsister, or a descendant of any of them.

- The child must be (a) under age 19 at the end of the year, (b) under age 24 at the end of the year and a full-time student, or (c) any age if permanently and totally disabled.

- The child must have lived with the taxpayer for more than half of the year.

- The child must not have provided more than half of her own support for the year.

- If the child meets the rules to be a qualifying child of more than one person, the taxpayer must be the person entitled to claim the child as a qualifying child.

In order to be considered a "Qualifying Relative," which entitles the personal exemption but not additional deductions and credits:

That person must:

- Live with or be related to the taxpayer,
- Not have more than the IRS-stated amount of gross (total) income ($3,300 for the year 2006),
- Be supported (generally more than 50%) by the taxpayer for the whole year, and
- Be neither the taxpayer's qualifying child nor the qualifying child of anyone else.

There are some exceptions, and these should be consulted if an individual does not fall squarely within the definition.

Exhibits 6–2 and 6–3 provide a flowchart to follow in the determination of whether an individual is eligible to be claimed as a dependent on another person's tax return. The second chart demonstrates how dependency is determined for a child of divorced or separated parents. However, these are general tests, and should be considered in conjunction with rules for special situations as described in the IRS Pub. 17.

Table 3-1. **Overview of the Rules for Claiming an Exemption for a Dependent**

Caution. This table is only an overview of the rules. For details, see the rest of this chapter.

- You cannot claim any dependents if you, or your spouse if filing jointly, could be claimed as a dependent by another taxpayer.
- You cannot claim a married person who files a joint return as a dependent unless that joint return is only a claim for refund and there would be no tax liability for either spouse on separate returns.
- You cannot claim a person as a dependent unless that person is a U.S. citizen, U.S. resident alien, U.S. national, or a resident of Canada or Mexico, for some part of the year. [1]
- You cannot claim a person as a dependent unless that person is your **qualifying child** or **qualifying relative.**

Tests To Be a Qualifying Child	Tests To Be a Qualifying Relative
1. The child must be your son, daughter, stepchild, eligible foster child, brother, sister, half brother, half sister, stepbrother, stepsister, or a descendant of any of them.	1. The person cannot be your qualifying child or the qualifying child of anyone else.
2. The child must be (a) under age 19 at the end of the year, (b) under age 24 at the end of the year and a full-time student, or (c) any age if permanently and totally disabled.	2. The person either (a) must be related to you in one of the ways listed under *Relatives who do not have to live with you,* or (b) must live with you all year as a member of your household (and your relationship must not violate local law). [2]
3. The child must have lived with you for more than half of the year. [2]	3. The person's gross income for the year must be less than $3,300. [3]
4. The child must not have provided more than half of his or her own support for the year.	4. You must provide more than half of the person's total support for the year. [4]
5. If the child meets the rules to be a qualifying child of more than one person, you must be the person entitled to claim the child as a qualifying child.	

[1]There is an exception for certain adopted children.
[2]There are exceptions for temporary absences, children who were born or died during the year, children of divorced or separated parents, and kidnapped children.
[3]There is an exception if the person is disabled and has income from a sheltered workshop.
[4]There are exceptions for multiple support agreements, children of divorced or separated parents, and kidnapped children.

EXHIBIT 6–2   "Can You Claim an Exemption for a Dependent?"

Children of divorced or separated parents. In most cases, because of the residency test, a child of divorced or separated parents is the qualifying child of the custodial parent. However, the child will be treated as the qualifying child of the noncustodial parent if all four of the following statements are true.

1. The parents:

   a. Are divorced or legally separated under a decree of divorce or separate maintenance,

   b. Are separated under a written separation agreement, or

   c. Lived apart at all times during the last 6 months of the year.

2. The child received over half of his or her support for the year from the parents.

3. The child is in the custody of one or both parents for more than half of the year.

4. Either of the following statements is true.

   a. The custodial parent signs a written declaration, discussed later, that he or she will not claim the child as a dependent for the year, and the noncustodial parent attaches this written declaration to his or her return. (If the decree or agreement went into effect after 1984, see *Divorce decree or separation agreement made after 1984*, later.)

   b. A pre-1985 decree of divorce or separate maintenance or written separation agreement that applies to 2006 states that the noncustodial parent can claim the child as a dependent, the decree or agreement was not changed after 1984 to say the noncustodial parent cannot claim the child as a dependent, and the noncustodial parent provides at least $600 for the child's support during the year.

Custodial parent and noncustodial parent. The custodial parent is the parent with whom the child lived for the greater part of the year. The other parent is the noncustodial parent.

If the parents divorced or separated during the year and the child lived with both parents before the separation, the custodial parent is the one with whom the child lived for the greater part of the rest of the year.

Example. Your child lived with you for 10 months of the year. The child lived with your former spouse for the other 2 months. You are considered the custodial parent.

Written declaration. The custodial parent may use either Form 8332 or a similar statement (containing the same information required by the form) to make the written declaration to release the exemption to the noncustodial parent. The noncustodial parent must attach the form or statement to his or her tax return.

The exemption can be released for 1 year, for a number of specified years (for example, alternate years), or for all future years, as specified in the declaration. If the exemption is released for more than 1 year, the original release must be attached to the return of the noncustodial parent for the first year, and a copy must be attached for each later year.

Divorce decree or separation agreement made after 1984. If the divorce decree or separation agreement went into effect after 1984, the noncustodial parent can attach certain pages from the decree or agreement instead of Form 8332. To be able to do this, the decree or agreement must state all three of the following.

1. The noncustodial parent can claim the child as a dependent without regard to any condition, such as payment of support.

2. The custodial parent will not claim the child as a dependent for the year.

3. The years for which the noncustodial parent, rather than the custodial parent, can claim the child as a dependent.

The noncustodial parent must attach all of the following pages of the decree or agreement to his or her tax return.

- The cover page (write the other parent's social security number on this page).

- The pages that include all of the information identified in items (1) through (3) above.

- The signature page with the other parent's signature and the date of the agreement.

 The noncustodial parent must attach the required information even if it was filed with a return in an earlier year.

Remarried parent. If you remarry, the support provided by your new spouse is treated as provided by you.

Parents who never married. This special rule for divorced or separated parents also applies to parents who never married.

Table 3-2. When More Than One Person Files a Return Claiming the Same Qualifying Child (Tie-Breaker Rule)

Caution. If a child is treated as the qualifying child of the noncustodial parent under the rules for children of divorced or separated parents, see *Applying this special test to divorced or separated parents.*

IF more than one person files a return claiming the same qualifying child and . . .	THEN the child will be treated as the qualifying child of the. . .
only one of the persons is the child's parent,	parent.
two of the persons are parents of the child and they do not file a joint return together,	parent with whom the child lived for the longer period of time during the year.
two of the persons are parents of the child, they do not file a joint return together, and the child lived with each parent the same amount of time during the year,	parent with the higher adjusted gross income (AGI).
none of the persons are the child's parent,	person with the highest AGI.

EXHIBIT 6–3
"Support Test for Children of Divorced or Separated Parents"

> **APPLICATION** **6.14**
>
> All persons in the example were born in the United States. Rick and Debbie are a married couple. They have one child of their own, Amanda, aged 2. They also are the foster parents for a 9-year-old child, Sam, placed with them by the state 2 years ago. Rick has legal custody of a daughter, Leigh, from a former marriage, who is 17 years old. Leigh married Connelly in July of the past year. Connelly is also 17. Both Leigh and Connelly worked part time. But their income is less than $3,300. Leigh and Connelly had a child together, Savannah, in May of the past year. Leigh, Connelly, and Savannah lived with Rick and Debbie for the entire year and do not pay rent or contribute to household bills. Rick and Debbie may claim Amanda, Sam, Leigh, and Savannah as dependents on their tax return. They may not claim Connelly because he does not satisfy the relationship test.

5. Income

A common misconception among those beginning to pay income tax for the first time is that the only income subject to income tax is that earned through wages such as received from employment. In fact, there are a variety of types of income. Some are subject to income tax but not Social Security and Medicare tax. Some are subject to both. And yet other types of income may be subject to neither. In this section, income is explored as it is defined by the IRS.

a. Earned.

One of the primary sources of income in the United States is that which is considered to have been earned. At first, the definition might seem to be very simple. **Earned income** would consist of the money paid to a person who is employed. However, it is much more complicated than that. The IRS defines earned income as any wages, salaries, tips, and other employee compensation that are includible in gross income for the taxable year, plus the amount of the taxpayer's net earnings from self-employment for the taxable year (within the meaning of IRC section 1402(a)). These net earnings are determined with regard to the deduction allowed to the taxpayer by IRC section 164(f), which is the allowable deduction for self-employment tax.

Although not exhaustive or inclusive for every type of employee such as governmental, the following list contains items that might not constitute traditional wages, but that are usually considered earned income for income tax purposes:

- Advance payments such as a draw on sales commissions
- A court-ordered judgment or legal settlement for back pay
- Safety or longevity awards of personal property totaling value over 1 year at more than statutory amount (there are some exclusions)

EARNED INCOME

Consists of the money paid to a person who is employed.

- Severance pay

- Property of value in exchange for services

- Some fringe benefits including, but not limited to, retirement contributions, health plan, transportation provided for personal use, educational, adoptive, child care benefits, and so on

- Certain Social Security benefits (if additional wages are earned above the threshold amount)

- Tips

There are a number of exceptions to earned income, which is considered taxable. Thus, any type of income other than traditional wages or self-employment income should first be identified as taxable through the IRS publications. Many items have conditions that affect whether the item is taxable in part or in total. Some of those items that are typically considered nontaxable are discussed later in this chapter.

b. Investment and Passive Income.

It is not necessary that income be received in exchange for work or services in order for it to be considered taxable income. Indeed, a variety of sources of income to individuals and businesses can generate income tax liability. Investments that generate tax liability can consist of anything held by a taxpayer with the purpose of generating income. This might be something as basic as raw land or as sophisticated as a work of art. The object is not the issue in investment property. Rather, it is the intent for which the object is owned, and whether a gain or loss is generated when ownership of the object ends. Because it is impossible to discern the intent of every taxpayer who acquires property, the rules for taxability of items acquired and then resold (other than business inventory—which constitute earned income) are subject to the rules applied to capital gain or loss on sales of real and personal property. Also, the issue of tax liability is not always limited to the final disposition of the asset. Commonly owned items that produce investment income while owned include financial instruments such as stocks, bonds, notes, and funds. These items often produce income during ownership without the requirement of actual labor or services by the taxpayer. This income may be subject to tax as interest or dividends on property held. The income generated by investments is subject to a variety of rules and computations based on the type of income, whether it produced income or the asset was disposed of in some way, and any intervening factors such as whether the item had been subject to previous tax rules such as depreciation. These rules and calculations are discussed in somewhat more detail in a subsequent chapter.

In addition to investment income, another type of income that may be subject to income tax is known as **passive income**. Similar to investment income, passive income is generated by income producing property held by the tax payer. The distinction lies in the nature of the property. For example, investment property typically consists of an object such as artwork, a collection, or a financial instrument such as stock. Property that produces passive income is typically something that

PASSIVE INCOME

Typically something that regularly produces income for the owner with minimal involvement such as a rental property, a businesses ownership interest in which the taxpayer does not materially participate in the business operations, or authorship by the taxpayer of a creative work that produces royalties.

regularly produces income for the owner with minimal involvement such as a rental property, a businesses ownership interest in which the taxpayer does not materially participate in the business operations, or authorship by the taxpayer of a creative work that produces royalties (unless this is the usual type of employment for the taxpayer). Material participation occurs when the taxpayer is involved in the daily or regular decisions with respect to the business. Typically, one who is involved in more than 5 percent of the business operations is considered to be a material participant. The key to passive income activities is that it does not require the payment of Social Security and Medicare tax imposed on earned income. But qualification for passive income status demands that the taxpayer have no significant involvement with the business.

APPLICATION **6.15**

Claire and Nate are a married couple. Nate is employed as a machinist. The couple owns one rental house to generate additional income. In 2006, Nate inherited 1,000 shares of stock in a well known beverage company. He received $600 in stock dividends in 2005 and $850 in dividends in 2007. Claire works as a teacher at a preschool that she owns and operates. In 2006, Claire was published as an author for the first time. Her book was quite successful. In 2007, Claire took up writing as her primary career. She sold the preschool business to a partner who gave Claire a promissory note to buy Claire out over time. However, she immediately gave up 98 percent of her control over the business.

In 2006, Nate and Claire would have the following items considered for income tax purposes:

Wages and other earned income (subject to income tax, Social Security, Medicare)

Nate's wages as a machinist.

Claire's income from her partnership in which she materially participated.

Investment and Passive Income (not subject to Social Security and Medicare).

Rental property net income.

Royalties from Claire's book.

Dividends from Nate's stock.

In 2007, the changes in circumstances would affect the consideration of taxable income as follows:

Wages and other earned income (subject to income tax, Social Security, Medicare)

Nate's wages as a machinist.

Royalties from Claire's writing.

(continues)

APPLICATION 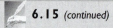 **6.15** *(continued)*

Investment and Passive Income (not subject to Social Security and Medicare)

   Rental property net income.

   Dividends from Nate's stock.

   Claire's income from her partnership in which she did not materially participate. Because Claire gave up material participation in the partnership, her income from the business/sale was no longer considered earned income. However, because she took up writing as her primary income endeavor, it took on the characteristics of employment including taxes associated with employment.

c. Tax Exempt/Nontaxable.

Not all income received is subject to income tax. There are certain types of income that are considered tax exempt or nontaxable. These have the effect of avoiding the impact of income tax on the receipts by the taxpayer. Tax exempt or nontaxable income is that which is free from income tax liability in whole or in part, depending on the circumstances. Tax exempt and nontaxable income should be distinguished from the outset from tax deferred income. When income is tax deferred, it has the effect of delaying the income tax calculation. This is typically done when the taxpayer anticipates a point in time when her taxable rate will be lower and thus the tax would be less. One common example is money put into a retirement account that is tax deferred. In this instance, the taxpayer anticipates having less income when retired than during working years. By placing the money into an account for retirement, when it is drawn out, the taxpayer foresees the lower income resulting in a lower tax rate (tax rates generally increase with increases in income). IRS Pub. 525 is dedicated entirely to the determination of whether income is taxable or tax exempt. This regularly updated publication discusses in detail those items not subject to tax and any conditions that may apply to render the income nontaxable.

The most common types of tax-exempt income that is not subject to federal (not necessarily state) income tax are:

- Federal tax refunds
- Interest from municipal bonds
- Most gifts
- Most inheritance and bequests
- Workers compensation
- Welfare benefits and some Social Security benefits
- Some scholarships/fellowships
- Veteran's benefits

Additional IRS publications address more specific questions about income that may or may not be taxable, depending on the circumstances. The following are some of the more commonly encountered situations and the corresponding IRS publication:

- Sale of a Home: Pub. 523

- Residential Rental Property (Including Rental of Vacation Homes) Pub. 527

- Investment Income and Expenses (Including Capital Gains and Losses) Pub. 550

- Survivors, Executors, and Administrators Pub. 559

- Mutual Fund Distributions Pub. 564

- Pension and Annuity Income Pub. 575

- Social Security and Equivalent Railroad Retirement Benefits Pub. 915

- Tax Benefits for Education Pub. 970

In the case of scholarships, some are considered taxable and others are not. For example, scholarships for tuition and fees are generally considered tax exempt, whereas scholarship funds that are used for living expenses may be subject to tax. A good indicator is whether or not the taxpayer receives a W2 form for scholarship income. If so, then the scholarship is taxable and should be entered with wages and salaries. However, not getting a W2 form for scholarship income does not mean it is tax exempt. If a W2 form for scholarship income is not received but the student is not pursuing a degree, the full amount is still taxable and should be included with the wages and salary amount. If the student is a degree candidate and does not receive a W2 form for a scholarship or fellowship, the amount applied to tuition, fees, or school-related supplies is fully excludable from taxation. Any scholarship designated for room and board is taxable and should be added to any wage or salary amount.

Another consideration with regard to tax-exempt or nontaxable income is thresholds. For some types of income, the tax-exempt status applies only to amounts above or below an established threshold. For example, individuals who have taxable income from other sources and receive Social Security retirement or disability benefits may receive a set dollar amount of these benefits tax free. However, once the other income reaches a threshold amount (that is changed periodically to reflect cost of living increases), a part of the federal benefits may be subject to Social Security tax. Similar types of threshold amounts apply to the profits from the sale of the taxpayer's primary residence, and other sources of otherwise nontaxable income.

6. Adjusted Gross Income/Taxable Income

Key elements in any income tax calculation is the **Adjusted Gross Income** and the Taxable Income of the individual. The adjusted gross income allows certain deductions against income before the determination for certain tax benefits is made.

ADJUSTED GROSS INCOME

Allows certain deductions against income before the determination for certain tax benefits is made.

APPLICATION 6.16

Constantine was seriously injured in an accident in March and left totally disabled. Before the accident, he had worked full time and had earned a substantial income. He began receiving Social Security disability benefits in October. As a result of the accident, Constantine was forced to sell his two-story residence of 10 years and move into a single-story dwelling. He made a considerable profit on the residence. When it comes time to complete Constantine's annual tax return, his income from January 1 until the date of the accident will be compared against the threshold for earned income by someone receiving Social Security benefits. If the income is more than the threshold, Constantine will be required to apply a calculation to his income and benefits to determine if any of the Social Security benefits are subject to income tax. Additionally, the net profit from the sale of his home will be measured against the threshold amount and a calculation will be applied to determine if Constantine is subject to a capital gain income tax on any part of the profit from the sale.

MODIFIED ADJUSTED GROSS INCOME

Allows even more deductions against income before the determination for certain tax benefits is made.

STANDARD DEDUCTION

The amount that each taxpayer(s) is eligible to claim on the return.

For example, someone who is self-employed will pay both the employer and the employee component of Social Security tax. This in turn reduces the amount of income that the self-employed individual actually receives (as more of the income is used to pay the tax). The adjusted gross income calculation allows the taxpayer to remove the amount of money paid for the employer's portion of social security tax from the equation to place the self-employed taxpayer on equal footing with the regularly employed individual. There are several factors such as this that are applied in an attempt to equalize the position of taxpayers. Additionally, for some special credits that allow taxpayers extra tax benefits such as the Earned Income Credit (discussed later) a **Modified Adjusted Gross Income** makes even more adjustments to the overall income of the taxpayer before the credit is calculated. In addition to the Adjusted and/or Modified Adjusted Gross Income, the amount of income tax due by every taxpayer is ultimately considered based on the taxpayer's taxable income. Each taxpayer is allowed a certain amount of income that is excluded from tax. This amount varies with the filing status. For example, an individual filing as a single person is allowed an amount less than that of a couple filing Married Filing Jointly or one with dependents and filing under Head of Household status. The amount each taxpayer(s) is eligible to claim on the return is known as the **Standard Deduction** and it corresponds to filing status. As an alternative, the taxpayer can attach "Schedule A," which allows a specified group of expenses to be listed item by item with the amount. If the Schedule A amount is greater than the Standard Deduction, then the taxpayer may elect to claim the larger itemized Schedule A amount instead of the Standard Deduction. Next, the taxpayer applies the appropriate personal exemptions. For every individual listed on a tax return as a taxpayer or a dependent, a specific amount is allowed to be exempt from income tax. This amount may be increased for conditions such as blindness, disability, and

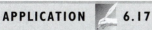

APPLICATION   6.17

Danny has an Adjusted Gross Income of $75,000. He is a single employed person who has few deductions that can be itemized and no dependents. The Standard Deduction and 1 Personal Exemption are subtracted from his Adjusted Gross Income. The result is his Taxable Income. The IRS Tax Table indicates the tax on this amount of income by a single person with no dependents is $13,488. During the year, Danny had $9,000 withheld in taxes from his employment. In addition, he made estimated tax payments of $3,000 to the IRS. Finally, he received a tax credit for education expenses known as the Hope Credit in the amount of $2,000. His total payments and credits equaled $14,000. As a result, Danny overpaid his tax of $13,488 by $512, which he can receive as a refund or apply toward the upcoming year's taxes.

advanced age. Once the proper amount for the individuals listed on the return are added together, the Standard Deduction/Schedule A amount and the amount for personal exemptions is subtracted from the Adjusted Gross Income. This final amount is the taxpayer's Taxable Income and the amount on which income tax is calculated. After the tax is determined, various credits, tax withholdings, tax payments, self-employment taxes, and possible penalties are applied to reach the final amount of any additional tax due or refund for the taxpayer. In following chapters, many of the forms and schedules used to figure tax deductions from the determination of taxable income and credits applied to calculate the tax or refund due will be discussed.

7. Tax Preparers

The previous discussion was a small glimpse into the complexities of the income tax system. Additionally, the lives of the average taxpayers continue to increase in complexity. As a result, the business of commercial companies offering tax preparation services has become a substantial industry in the United States. Indeed, the business of individual (excluding corporate returns) tax return preparation is estimated to be one that generates several billion dollars per year. As with any popular product or service, the number of individuals who offer the service continues to grow. Although a large percentage of individuals do not necessarily have contact with a private accountant, many do have contact with an attorney. Not only do these individuals have contact with an attorney for matters such as estates, domestic relations issues, business matters, and so on, but their tax status is affected by these very same issues. As a result, the law office may become a logical place to turn for many individuals needing assistance with tax preparation.

a. Third Party Preparers.

The tax preparation industry consists of a variety of businesses and individuals with a range of skill that spans from highly trained and licensed professionals to those who may be incompetent by any definition. Third party tax preparers come in a wide variety including, but not limited to, Certified Public Accountants, Tax Preparation Companies, Individual sole proprietorships, and tax preparation offered as an added benefit to customers of other businesses. Virtually anyone can set up business as a tax preparer. As a result, the public at large has the responsibility to investigate the qualifications of someone entrusted with something as significant as a personal tax return. At this point in time, the only substantial safeguards for the public are criminal and civil penalties imposed on individuals who have previously violated the individual trust and laws with respect to the IRS rules and regulations for income tax preparation. Unfortunately, even those individuals associated with some well-known companies may have limited education and training. It is incumbent on the taxpayer, whose signature verifies the validity of the information on the return, to question the information in the return and the qualifications of the third party preparer. The IRS does require any person who prepares a tax return on behalf of another individual to identify herself as a third party preparer on the return. Additionally, there are methods to file complaints with the IRS by taxpayers against the various types of preparers. But these are after the fact and do not prevent the injury to the taxpayer. Despite the number of individuals who are not well qualified to act as third party preparers, there are many thousands of preparers who take their responsibility quite seriously as well as a number of safeguards for the individual taxpayers. First, as mentioned, is the required disclosure of third party preparers to the IRS. Second, more and more tax returns are prepared using commercial computer software that is designed to properly compute taxes and credits if complete and accurate information is put into the system as information is requested. Finally, as the IRS system of checking returns becomes more sophisticated, errors in electronically submitted returns are frequently caught within a matter of hours of submission of the return and sent back for correction. This then gives the tax preparer the opportunity to meet with the taxpayer and correct any obvious errors before the return is actually due and penalties may apply.

As the tax system and personal circumstances become increasingly complicated, the law office is an obvious choice for many taxpayers that require assistance with preparation of their personal returns. Historically, it was not uncommon for some law offices to specialize in the representation of taxpayers who were facing legal disputes with the IRS. However, this representation often developed as a result of problems in the tax preparation that had already occurred. In more recent years, it has not been uncommon for offices to offer tax preparation to clients as part of the legal services offered by the office. Nevertheless, because of the volatility of the tax regulations and laws, it is necessary for anyone acting as a third party preparer, whether it be in a law office or private business setting, to maintain a thorough and current knowledge of the applicable tax principles.

b. Enrolled Agents

Individuals who spend much time involved with tax preparation soon encounter the term **Enrolled Agent**. Enrolled Agents are also frequently referred to as EAs. An Enrolled Agent is an individual who has demonstrated proficiency and advanced technical competence in the areas of taxation. Enrolled Agents also are legally permitted to represent taxpayers before all administrative levels of the IRS.

Enrolled Agents are licensed by the federal government. Because of this, they are authorized to appear in place of the taxpayer when dealing with the IRS. Only Enrolled Agents, licensed attorneys, and certified public accounts may represent taxpayers before the IRS. The Enrolled Agent profession first came about in 1884 when, after questionable claims had been presented for Civil War losses, Congress acted to regulate persons who represented citizens in their dealings with the Treasury Department.

Enrolled Agents can advise, represent, and prepare tax returns for individuals, partnerships, corporations, estates, trusts, and any entities with tax-reporting requirements. Throughout the country, Enrolled Agents prepare millions of tax returns each year. Their expertise in the continually changing field of tax law enables them to effectively represent taxpayers audited by the IRS.

Licensed attorneys and certified professional accountants (CPAs) demonstrate their expertise in matters of law and accounting when they pass the state requirements for licensure where they practice. Enrolled Agents are required to demonstrate their competence in matters of taxation by exam with the IRS before they may represent a taxpayer before the IRS. EAs are limited to representation before the IRS and are not licensed to represent taxpayers in other legal forums.

Unlike attorneys and certified public accounts who must demonstrate several years of successful and specific postsecondary education before eligibility for licensure occurs, the Enrolled Agent designate requires no particular educational background or degree. However, the test to become an enrolled agent is a rigorous one and requires an advanced knowledge of tax principles. The candidate also must pass an extensive background check. An alternative method to become an enrolled agent is through experience working for the IRS. With this method, an individual may become an EA based on at least 5 years of employment at the IRS in a job that required regular application and interpretation of the provisions of the Internal Revenue Code and regulations. Once licensed, an EA is required to complete 72 hours of continuing professional education, reported every 3 years, to maintain licensure. Currently, there are approximately 35,000 active EAs in the United States.

■ **ENROLLED AGENT**

An individual who has demonstrated proficiency and advanced technical competence in the areas of taxation.

APPLICATION 6.18

Carson is a licensed attorney in private practice. He also employs a paralegal. Both of them prepare taxes for clients of the firm using a tax preparation software program. Next door is a franchise office for a nationwide tax preparation services. In the office, John has successfully completed the tax preparation course offered by the company and John prepares taxes for individuals on behalf of the company. Also in John's office is Racine, who is an Enrolled Agent. Racine prepares taxes and assists individuals who are audited by the IRS. Racine has represented individuals who have prepared their own returns, had their returns prepared by herself or John, and is available for hire to represent individuals whose returns have been prepared by attorneys and CPAs.

ETHICAL QUESTION

Mary Joe has opened her own local business as a tax preparer. She uses a commercially available software program to prepare tax returns for members of the public. Dominic comes into Mary Joe's office for the first time to have his taxes prepared. Dominic is the sole source of support for his former girlfriend's son. The girlfriend left more than a year ago and Dominic has been afraid to let authorities know because he thinks the child, who has lived with Dominic since his birth 5 years ago, will be taken away and placed in foster care. Dominic has always claimed the boy as dependent on his return in the past. He does not think the boy's biological father even knows that the child exists and the mother is an unemployed drug addict living on the streets. By claiming the boy as a dependent, Dominic would be entitled to a great deal more tax refund and he could really use the money to help support the child. However, the tests for dependency are not met. Mary Joe has a legal obligation to inform Dominic that he does not meet the legal standards to claim the boy as a dependent. Ethically, even though she understands Dominic's dilemma, she is obligated to prepare the return in accordance with the rules of the IRS.

Janet comes into Mary Joe's office on the same day as Dominic to have her taxes done as well. Janet routinely claims her unemployed sister's children as her own. In reality, Janet has no children. But after eavesdropping on Dominic's meeting with Mary Joe, Janet decides not to be fully honest with Mary Joe. Janet informs Mary Joe that she is a single working mother with two children. As part of the interview, Mary Joe asks for the birthdates and Social Security cards for the children. Janet does not know their birth dates and has the Social Security numbers for the children written on a piece of paper. Mary Joe has an ethical obligation under questionable circumstances to ask further questions of Janet to determine whether the children are properly claimed as dependents. Mary Joe also should make a note of the questions asked. In the event of an audit of the return, Mary Joe would then be able to show due diligence in the preparation of a factual return. If she could not do so, she could be

(continues)

ETHICAL QUESTION *(continued)*

legally penalized for aiding and abetting in the submission of false information to the IRS and subject to heavy fines. What should Mary Joe do in the event Janet makes a follow-up appointment and returns with the necessary information, even though it was clear earlier that she did not know the birthdates of the children nor the whereabouts of their Social Security cards?

SUMMARY

This chapter explored the myriad of taxes faced by the general population of the United States on a regular basis. Tax may be tied to income, occurrences such as death, specific types of transactions or activities, consumption of goods, and even ownership of real and personal property. The goal of taxes is to apply them fairly and to the individuals who most benefit from the event or item tied to the tax. Taxes are used for a variety of purposes. However, generally speaking, they support the state and federal government programs and services made available to the residents of the United States. Because all individuals who generate income, regardless of the source, may be subject to income tax, the IRS has attempted to develop a complex set of rules used to levy and collect the taxes in a somewhat fair and consistent manner. This includes various types of filing status, special deductions and credits for individuals who provide financial support to others, and a variety of deductions and credits to place taxpayers on a more equal footing. Because the circumstances of individuals vary so greatly, the complex tax code is difficult to navigate. As a result, many turn to professionals for assistance with preparation of required tax returns. These range from the basic third party tax professional who prepares even the most basic return, to the Enrolled Agent, Certified Public Accountants, and Attorneys who not only prepare taxes but also provide professional and expert representation before governmental entities such as the IRS on matters involving tax.

◼ KEY TERMS

income	Qualifying Widow	passive income
taxable income	Married Filing Jointly	Adjusted Gross Income
tax evasion	Married Filing Separate	Modified Adjusted Gross Income
tax avoidance	single status	Standard Deduction
pass-through	qualifying person	Enrolled Agent
Head of Household	earned income	

For additional resources, visit our Web site at www.westlegalstudies.com

Commonly Encountered Information Documents

■ OBJECTIVES_____

After completing this chapter, you will be able to:

❑ Explain the purpose of federal income information documents

❑ Discuss the types of data included on federal income information documents

❑ Distinguish the various types of federal business income information documents

A. INFORMATION/RETURN SUPPORTING DOCUMENTS PREPARED AND FILED BY BUSINESSES AND EMPLOYERS

The primary method used by the government to track and assess taxes due by individuals and businesses alike is through the use of **information forms**. Although these documents may or may not be required to be submitted along with business or individual tax returns, the information contained in them is reported to the government at the same time it is reported to the person or business to whom the information pertains. Additionally, much of the information, if not the entire form, may be included with the actual return. This enables the IRS to cross-check the information reported to substantiate the amount of tax a business or individual claims to owe. The immediate discussion introduces the nature and purpose of some of the more commonly used forms it is by no means exhaustive for the business or the individual. Rather, the discussion introduces many of the forms most commonly encountered. Section B of this chapter contains a more thorough discussion of these forms and how they are used by the recipient taxpayer.

Although the actual appearance of information forms may change, the data required by the IRS is constant. Typically, the forms will consist of numbered boxes. The IRS designates what information is to be included in each box. As a result, although the location of a particular numbered box may change with the format of the document, the type of information contained within that box will remain the same.

1. Quarterly Reports

In Chapter 5, there was a fair amount of discussion with regard to payroll in the law office, or for that matter, any business that has employees. Part of processing payroll is the reporting and payment of taxes associated with payroll. For most small businesses, this is done on a quarterly basis. Also, the taxes for small businesses subject to retail sales and excise taxes will also often report and pay these taxes on a quarterly basis. Those taxes are discussed in further detail in Section 2.

As explained in Chapter 5, quarterly reports related to payroll serve the function of paying the employer and/or employee portions of income tax, Social Security, Medicare, and unemployment taxes. They also allow the IRS to track the wages and number of persons employed in various businesses in the United States. This information is typically reported on the Forms 940 and 941 described in Chapter 5. Similar forms are typically required in the states. Even if a state does not have an income tax, there is still the need to account for the state unemployment tax, which, along with the federal FUTA tax, provides the basis for unemployment payments to eligible individuals.

2. State and Local Retail and Excise Tax

Currently, there is no federal sales tax for individual transactions. However, businesses engaged in any type of retail transactions typically must collect, report, and pay various types of state and/or federal tax. The tax may be on sale of goods or services. Additionally, areas that have a high amount of tourism also may impose a similar tax on tourism activities such as hotel, rental car, and so on, often known as an entertainment tax. These taxes are usually imposed at the state, and frequently local levels. In the majority of jurisdictions, sales tax is paid at least quarterly. Depending on the size of the business entity and the amount of sales tax collected, the frequency with which reports and tax are due may increase. The report for sales tax typically

INFORMATION FORM

The primary method used by the government to track and assess taxes due by individuals and businesses.

includes a summary of the transactions completed, along with a calculation that computes tax that should have been collected, less refunds. That amount is then payable to the proper governmental entity. As mentioned, this form of reporting may be necessary not only to the state, but also to local governments as well. Exhibit 7–1 is a sample form used for reporting a state sales tax.

Similar to sales tax, an excise tax also may be imposed. As discussed in Chapter 6, the excise tax tends to occur on particular products or transactions in an attempt to place more of the cost associated with of these transactions on the parties most significantly affected. A common example is an excise tax on something such as tobacco sales. Typically, an excise tax will be in addition to a sales tax if one is applicable to the transaction. Also, an excise tax may be imposed by the federal, state, and local governments. Exhibit 7–2 is a sample reporting form for an excise tax. Those who incur an excise tax as part of their business may need to report this on their tax return.

3. Annual Reports

Every business is required to file certain information documents on an annual basis. Very small businesses may only be required to file these documents and no others. However, even large businesses that file information reports and tax payments on a frequent basis must still file certain cumulative annual reports at the end of each calendar year in addition to the tax returns that may be due at the end of the fiscal year.

At the end of each year, the IRS sends form 940 to businesses to report on gross wages and unemployment tax paid/due for the year. An adjustment must be made for the amount paid to employees over a statutorily set amount or those exempt from the FUTA tax. The difference in the two figures is the FUTA taxable wages. The gross wages are then multiplied by the current applicable rate to determine the FUTA tax liability. The total payments made for the year is recorded. Subtracting the two figures will determine if additional money is owed or if the business is entitled to a refund. This form reconciles any discrepancies in the quarterly 940 reports if any were filed. Form 940 is discussed in Chapter 5. The forms 941 and 944 are prepared for the end of the fourth quarter of the calendar year. However, certain portions of the form 941 include calculations involving cumulative amounts for the year and thus create annual totals.

The form W-3 is used by employers to summarize the annual wages paid to all of the employees for the year. The form contains no personal information for individual employees but, rather, general information about totals for the business in terms of the number of employees through the year, wages, certain benefits, and taxes paid to federal, state, and local governments. The information on the W-3 must correspond to the information on the employee's W-2s as well as the tax return for the business. For specialized forms of business such as agricultural, or those who employ nonresident aliens, additional federal and state tax forms may be required.

Reset Form

Ohio Department of
TAXATION
Please do not use staples.

07030103

UST 1 Long Rev. 10/06
Universal Ohio State, County
and Transit Sales Tax Return

Vendor's license number

Reporting period (mm dd yy)
to

For State Use Only

FEIN or Social Security number

Must be received by (mm dd yy)

Please mark here
if paid through EFT.

Please mark here
if **amended** return.

Name	Address	City	State	ZIP

1. Gross sales .... 1.

2. Exempt sales (including exempt motor vehicle sales) .... 2.

3. Net taxable sales (subtract line 2 from line 1) .... 3.

4. Sales upon which tax was paid to clerks of courts (motor vehicles, trailers, etc.) . 4.

5. Reportable taxable sales (subtract line 4 from line 3) .... 5.

6. Tax liability on sales reported on line 5 .... 6.

7. Minus discount (see instructions) .... 7.

8. Plus additional charge (see instructions) .... 8.

9. Net amount due .... 9.

STOP **Use the following lines *only* if you made**
accelerated sales tax payments!

10. Accelerated payments and carryover from previous period .... 10.

11. Balance due (if line 10 is less than line 9, subtract line 10 from line 9) .... 11.

12. Overpayment* (if line 10 is greater than line 9, subtract line 9 from line 10) .... 12.
    *Overpayment will be credited to the next period.

To Cancel Vendor's License Enter
Last Day of Business (mm dd yy)

Do **not** staple check to form or attach check stub.
Do **not** send cash. Make remittance payable to the
Ohio Treasurer of State and mail all four pages of this form to:
Ohio Department of Taxation
P.O. Box 16560
Columbus, OH 43216-6560

Go paperless!
File your return through
Ohio Business Gateway.

www.obg.ohio.gov

I declare under penalties of perjury that this return, including any accompanying
schedules and statements, has been examined by me and, to the best of my
knowledge and belief, is a true, correct and complete return and report.

For State Use Only

Signature   Title   Date

UST 1 – pg. 1 of 4

EXHIBIT 7–1   State Sales Tax

Form **720**	**Quarterly Federal Excise Tax Return**			OMB No. 1545-0023	
(Rev. January 2007) Department of the Treasury Internal Revenue Service	▶ See the Instructions for Form 720.				

If you are not using the preaddressed Form 720, enter your name, address, employer identification number, and calendar quarter of return. See the instructions. ▶

Name		Quarter ending	
Number, street, and room or suite no. (If you have a P.O. box, see the instructions.)		Employer identification number	
City, state, and ZIP code. (If you have a foreign address, see the instructions.)			

FOR IRS USE ONLY

T	
FF	
FD	
FP	
I	
T	

Check here if:

☐ Final return

☐ Address change

Part I

IRS No.	**Environmental Taxes** (attach Form 6627)		Tax	IRS No.
18	Domestic petroleum oil spill tax			18
21	Imported petroleum products oil spill tax			21
98	Ozone-depleting chemicals (ODCs)			98
19	ODC tax on imported products			19

	Communications and Air Transportation Taxes (see instructions)		Tax	
22	Local telephone service and teletypewriter exchange service			22
26	Transportation of persons by air			26
28	Transportation of property by air			28
27	Use of international air travel facilities			27

IRS No.	**Fuel Taxes**	Number of gallons	Rate	Tax	IRS No.
	(a) Diesel fuel, tax on removal at terminal rack		$.244		
60	(b) Diesel fuel, tax on taxable events other than removal at terminal rack		.244		60
	(c) Diesel fuel, tax on sale or removal of biodiesel mixture other than removal at terminal rack		.244		
104	Diesel-water fuel emulsion		.198		104
71	Dyed diesel fuel used in trains		.001		71
105	Dyed diesel fuel, LUST tax		.001		105
107	Dyed kerosene, LUST tax		.001		107
119	LUST tax, other exempt removals (see instructions)		.001		119
35	(a) Kerosene, tax on removal at terminal rack (see instructions)		.244		
	(b) Kerosene, tax on taxable events other than removal at terminal rack		.244		35
69	Kerosene for use in aviation (see instructions)		.219		69
77	Kerosene for use in commercial aviation (other than foreign trade) (see instructions)		.044		77
111	Kerosene for use in aviation, LUST tax on nontaxable uses, including foreign trade		.001		111
79	Other fuels (see instructions)				79
	(a) Gasoline, tax on removal at terminal rack		.184		
62	(b) Gasoline, tax on taxable events other than removal at terminal rack		.184		62
	(c) Gasoline, tax on sale or removal of alcohol fuel mixture other than removal at terminal rack		.184		
14	Aviation gasoline		.194		14
112	Liquefied petroleum gas (LPG)		.183		112
118	"P Series" fuels		.184		118
120	Compressed natural gas (CNG) (GGE = 126.67 cu. ft.)		.183		120
121	Liquefied hydrogen		.184		121
122	Any liquid fuel derived from coal (including peat) through the Fischer-Tropsch process		.244		122
123	Liquid hydrocarbons derived from biomass		.244		123
124	Liquefied natural gas (LNG)		.243		124

	Retail Tax		Rate	Tax	
33	Truck, trailer, and semitrailer chassis and bodies, and tractors		12% of sales price		33

For Privacy Act and Paperwork Reduction Act Notice, see the instructions.   Cat. No. 10175Y   Form **720** (Rev. 1-2007)

EXHIBIT 7–2   Excise Tax *(continues)*

Form 720 (Rev. 1-2007)   Page **2**

IRS No.	Ship Passenger Tax	Number of persons	Rate	Tax	IRS No.
29	Transportation by water		$3 per person		29
	Other Excise Tax	Amount of obligations	Rate	Tax	
31	Obligations not in registered form		$ .01		31

IRS No.	Manufacturers Taxes	Number of tons	Sales price	Rate	Tax	IRS No.
36	Coal—Underground mined			$1.10 per ton		36
37				4.4% of sales price		37
38	Coal—Surface mined			$ .55 per ton		38
39				4.4% of sales price		39
108	Taxable tires other than biasply or super single tires (see instructions)					108
109	Taxable biasply or super single tires (other than super single tires designed for steering) (see instructions)					109
113	Taxable tires, super single tires designed for steering (see instructions)					113
40	Gas guzzler tax. Attach Form 6197. Check if one-time filing. ☐					40
97	Vaccines (see instructions)					97

IRS No.	Foreign Insurance Taxes	Premiums paid	Rate	Tax	IRS No.
30	Policies issued by foreign insurers (see instructions) Casualty insurance and indemnity bonds		$ .04		30
	Life insurance, sickness and accident policies, and annuity contracts		.01		
	Reinsurance		.01		

1 Total. Add all amounts in Part I. Complete Schedule A unless one-time filing.   ▶ $

Part II

IRS No.		Rate	Tax	IRS No.
41	Sport fishing equipment (other than fishing rods and fishing poles)	10% of sales price		41
110	Fishing rods and fishing poles (limits apply, see instructions)	10% of sales price		110
42	Electric outboard motors	3% of sales price		42
114	Fishing tackle boxes	3% of sales price		114
44	Bows, quivers, broadheads, and points	11% of sales price		44
106	Arrow shafts	$ .42 per shaft		106

IRS No.		Number of gallons	Rate	Tax	IRS No.
64	Inland waterways fuel use tax		$ .201		64
51	Alcohol sold as but not used as fuel (see instructions)				51
117	Biodiesel sold as but not used as fuel (see instructions)				117

IRS No.	Floor Stocks Tax	Tax	IRS No.
20	Ozone-depleting chemicals (floor stocks). Attach Form 6627.		20

2 Total. Add all amounts in Part II.   ▶ $

Part III

3 Total tax. Add line 1, Part I, and line 2, Part II . . . .   ▶ **3**

4 Claims (see instructions; complete Schedule C) . . . . . . ▶ **4**

5 Deposits made for the quarter . . . . ▶ **5**
   ☑ Check here if you used the safe harbor rule to make your deposits.

6 Overpayment from previous quarters . ▶ **6**

7 Enter the amount from Form 720X included on line 6, if any . . . . . ▶ **7**

8 Total of lines 5 and 6 . . . . ▶ **8**

9 Add lines 4 and 8 . . . .   ▶ **9**

10 **Balance Due.** If line 3 is greater than line 9, enter the difference. Pay the full amount with the return. Enclose Form 720-V with your check or money order for full amount payable to the "United States Treasury." Write your EIN, "Form 720," and the quarter on it ▶ **10**

11 **Overpayment.** If line 9 is greater than line 3, enter the difference. Check if you want the overpayment: ☐ Applied to your next return, or ☑ Refunded to you.   **11**

Third Party Designee	Do you want to allow another person to discuss this return with the IRS (see the instructions)? ☐ **Yes.** Complete the following. ☐ **No.**
	Designee name ▶ Phone no. ▶ ( ) Personal identification number (PIN) ▶ ☐☐☐☐☐

Under penalties of perjury, I declare that I have examined this return, including accompanying schedules and statements, and to the best of my knowledge and belief, it is true, correct, and complete.

Sign Here

▶ Signature _____   Date _____   ▶ Title _____

Type or print name below signature. _____   Telephone number (   )

Form **720** (Rev. 1-2007)

EXHIBIT 7–2 Excise Tax *(continued)*

DO NOT STAPLE

33333	a Control number	For Official Use Only ▶ OMB No. 1545-0008

b Kind of Payer	941 ☐ Military ☐ 943 ☐ 944 ☐ CT-1 ☐ Hshld. emp. ☐ Medicare govt. emp. ☐ Third-party sick pay ☐	1 Wages, tips, other compensation	2 Federal income tax withheld
		3 Social security wages	4 Social security tax withheld
c Total number of Forms W-2	d Establishment number	5 Medicare wages and tips	6 Medicare tax withheld
e Employer identification number (EIN)		7 Social security tips	8 Allocated tips
f Employer's name		9 Advance EIC payments	10 Dependent care benefits
		11 Nonqualified plans	12 Deferred compensation
		13 For third-party sick pay use only	
		14 Income tax withheld by payer of third-party sick pay	
g Employer's address and ZIP code			
h Other EIN used this year			
15 State Employer's state ID number		16 State wages, tips, etc.	17 State income tax
		18 Local wages, tips, etc	19 Local income tax
Contact person		Telephone number ( )	For Official Use Only
Email address		Fax number ( )	

Under penalties of perjury, I declare that I have examined this return and accompanying documents, and, to the best of my knowledge and belief, they are true, correct, and complete.

Signature ▶   Title ▶   Date ▶

Form **W-3** Transmittal of Wage and Tax Statements   **2007**   Department of the Treasury Internal Revenue Service

Send this entire page with the entire Copy A page of Form(s) W-2 to the Social Security Administration. Photocopies are not acceptable.

Do not send any payment (cash, checks, money orders, etc.) with Forms W-2 and W-3.

What's New

Relocation of form ID on Form W-3. For consistency with the revisions to Form W-2, we relocated the form ID number ("33333") to the top left corner of Form W-3.

Reminder

Separate instructions. See the 2007 Instructions for Forms W-2 and W-3 for information on completing this form.

Purpose of Form

Use Form W-3 to transmit Copy A of Form(s) W-2, Wage and Tax Statement. Make a copy of Form W-3 and keep it with Copy D (For Employer) of Form(s) W-2 for your records. Use Form W-3 for the correct year. **File Form W-3 even if only one Form W-2 is being filed.** If you are filing Form(s) W-2 electronically, **do not** file Form W-3.

When To File

File Form W-3 with Copy A of Form(s) W-2 by February 29, 2008.

Where To File

Send this entire page with the entire Copy A page of Form(s) W-2 to:

Social Security Administration Data Operations Center Wilkes-Barre, PA 18769-0001

Note. If you use "Certified Mail" to file, change the ZIP code to "18769-0002." If you use an IRS-approved private delivery service, add "ATTN: W-2 Process, 1150 E. Mountain Dr." to the address and change the ZIP code to "18702-7997." See Publication 15 (Circular E), Employer's Tax Guide, for a list of IRS-approved private delivery services.

For Privacy Act and Paperwork Reduction Act Notice, see the back of Copy D of Form W-2.

Cat. No. 10159Y

EXHIBIT 7–3   Form W-3

As a general rule anyone who works as an employee receives a form W-2. This is a document that taxpayers use to calculate income taxes based on their personal circumstances. However, what a surprisingly large percentage of the population does not seem to realize is that a copy of the form W-2 is transmitted to the IRS at the same time as it is provided to employees. At first glance, this may seem to be a duplication of efforts because employees are required to attach a copy of their W-2 to their tax returns. However, by having copies of W-2 on file the IRS not only can double-check the amount of income reported by the taxpayer, it also has a permanent record of wages paid and reported by employers in the event the individual needs this information at a future date and cannot obtain it from the employer, or if the taxpayer contradicts the amount employer has reported. The W-2 is used to report wages paid, taxes withheld, and benefits paid that may have tax consequences. More detail about the form W-2 is discussed later in this chapter.

In the event that a business hires an independent contractor to perform services, the income paid is reported on the form 1099-MISC. The 1099-MISC is a widely used form to report a variety of types of income paid to other persons. Some of the examples for use of the 1099-MISC include, but are not limited to, the following (amounts are effective as of 2006):

- At least $10 in royalties or broker payments in lieu of dividends or tax-exempt interest;

- Payments to independent contractors of amounts greater than $600 (lesser amounts may be but are not required to be reported by the payer). This includes all nonemployee compensation of $600 or more. Including fees, commissions, prizes and awards for services performed as a nonemployee, other forms of compensation for services performed for the payer's trade or business by an individual who is not an employee. It also includes expenses incurred for the use of an entertainment facility that treated as compensation to a nonemployee;

- Transit passes and parking for independent contractors. Although the payor cannot provide qualified transportation fringe benefits to independent contractors, the working condition and de minimus fringe rules for transit passes and parking apply to independent contractors.

- Tokens or farecards that enable an independent contractor to commute on a public transit system (not including privately operated van pools) are excludable from the independent contractor's gross income and are not reportable on Form 1099-MISC if their value in any month is $21 or less.

- Board of Directors' fees and all other remuneration;

- When an escrow agent maintains owner-provided funds in an escrow account for a construction project, performs management and oversight functions relating to the construction project, and makes payments for the owner and the general contractor, the escrow agent must file Form 1099-MISC for reportable payments of $600 or more.

- Also enter in box 3 prizes and awards that are not for services performed. Include the fair market value (FMV) of merchandise won on game shows. Also include amounts paid to a winner of a sweepstakes not involving a wager. If a wager is made, report the winnings on Form W-2G, Certain Gambling Winnings.

- Amounts of $600 or more for all types of rents include real and personal property. If the machine rental is part of a contract that includes both the use of the machine and the operator, the rental should be prorated between the rent of the machine (reported in box 1) and the operator's charge (reported as nonemployee compensation in box 7).

How the income reported in the 1099-MISC is treated for tax computation purposes varies based on which portion of the form the amount is located. For this reason, it is very important that the income reported in a 1099-MISC be properly placed within the form. How the individual deals with the receipt of a form 1099-MISC is addressed later in this chapter. For the purposes of this discussion, it is important to recognize that there are circumstances when the business is required to issue the form, and as a result, pertinent information such as the legal name, address, and tax identification number of the independent contractor or other payee be determined when payment is made and then maintained for the preparation of the 1099-MISC at the end of the calendar year.

4. Business Returns

Earlier discussions in previous chapters made reference to the tax returns that are prepared and submitted by business entities. Recall that the sole proprietor does not file an independent return for the business but, rather, includes business return information as part of the individual taxpayer return. However, this is the only type of business that is not required to file either a separate tax return, or an informational return. Additionally, as with the wage and labor reports above, there are a variety of other informational reporting forms that a business may be required to submit. Anyone, including a corporation, partnership, individual, estate, and trust, who makes reportable transactions during the calendar year must file information returns to report those transactions to the IRS. Persons required to file Information Returns to the IRS must also furnish statements to the recipients of the income such as the W-2, 1099, and so on.

a. Corporations.

General corporations vary from other types of business in that they are considered to be a "legal fiction." Even though the corporation is an intangible object with no physical form, the law recognizes it as a real entity. Simply put, this means that for most purposes, the law treats the corporation as if it were a person. The corporation can be held accountable for illegal conduct in civil or criminal court, and in the element of taxability, the corporation is responsible to pay tax on its own income. Corporations file their returns on either Form 1120 or 1120-A (short form). "S" corporations file their returns using the 1120-S. At this time the LLC is not formally recognized by the IRS as a separate legal entity and must file returns using partnership forms that designate the business as an LLC in the identification portion. The key element to remember is that for any business entity other than the general or "C" corporation, the income or loss of the business flows through to the individual owner(s) tax returns. The difference lies in how it is reported based on the nature of the business.

If a general corporation distributes part of its income as discussed earlier, it is given in the form of a dividend, which in the simplest terms is essentially a share of profits. This is done via the 1099-DIV, which is discussed in much greater detail later in this chapter. However, at this point, it is important to know that the corporation must also file the information for the 1099-DIV issued to all shareholders with the IRS. In turn, this enables the IRS to monitor income received by taxpayers from their investments.

b. Partnerships.

When a partnership that engages in a trade, business, or in some manner generates income (regardless of whether it exceeds costs), it is required to file an information return. This is done on Form 1065 showing its income, deductions, and other required information. The partnership return must show the names and addresses of each partner and each partner's share of taxable income or net loss. Additionally, the return must be signed by a general partner. If a limited liability company is treated as a partnership, it must file Form 1065 and one of its members must sign the return. Note that the partnership is not required to pay tax on income. Rather, each partner will report their respective share of any net income on their personal return and account for any tax there. If a partnership does not receive income or generate or pay any expenses treated as deductions or credits for federal income tax purposes the partnership is not considered to engage in a trade or business, and is not required to file a Form 1065.

The partnership must furnish copies of Schedule K–1-P (Form 1065) to the partners by the date Form 1065 is required to be filed, including extensions. A partner's income or loss from a partnership is reported to the partner on Schedule K–1-P (Form 1065). This is discussed in much greater detail in Section B.

ASSIGNMENT   7.1

In each of the three situations, identify the documents that should be filed by the business.

a. Matt, Jerome, and Ben own and operate a full-service gas station and convenience store. They employ three part-time clerks in addition to their own labor that is provided. The business is a partnership. They share all net profits equally. They have

(continues)

ASSIGNMENT **7.1** *(continued)*

a contract with a woman to come in once per week and thoroughly clean the facility when it is closed and no one else is present. They sell a variety of food, auto, and travel-related products in the convenience store.

b. The same as in a, with the following change: The business is a corporation owned by a large number of shareholders. Matt, Jerome, and Ben, although also shareholders, are considered to be employed by the business.

c. The same as in a, with the following change: Matt and Ben sold their interest to Jerome, who has operated it as a sole proprietorship for the past two years.

B. INFORMATION DOCUMENTS RECEIVED BY TAXPAYERS

The majority of tax returns filed in the United States are filed by individuals. A great deal of the information contained in a tax return comes from those documents received by the taxpayer that report taxable income, deductions and credits. All of these affect the amount of tax imposed, and in some cases as well as the amount of refund a taxpayer may receive for overpayment of that tax such as through overwithholding.

1. W-2 Wages

With a population of several hundred million people in the United States, the W-2 is easily the most commonly used IRS information form. The W-2 is used to report the annual taxable and nontaxable compensation received as wages and related benefits, as well as certain other items such as taxes withheld including federal income, state income, and FICA. Those persons in the employment of another and who receive compensation are entitled to receive a W-2 form at the end of the tax year. The W-2 is a multipurpose document. It not only is used in the calculation of the compensation that may be taxable; it also can be used to affect tax benefits such as the Earned Income Credit, IRA Contributions, and various other available deductions and credits. As a result, the W-2 is one of the most influential documents a taxpayer will receive. Unlike other information documents, the W-2 is actually attached to the federal individual tax return. If the return is filed electronically, a copy must be kept available for the IRS, and all of the information contained on the W-2 is submitted electronically.

Every W-2 will contain identifying information for the employer and the employee. This includes name, address, and federal identification number such as an employer identification number or a Social Security number of the business owner.

As with other information documents, numbered boxes are used to consistently report the various types of monetary and descriptive information included, regardless of the actual format of the report. Because the format of W-2 forms used by various employers varies dramatically, it is important to focus on the numbered boxes when locating relevant information. The location of the boxes on the page may change but the types of information designated for each box does not. For example, wages that may be subject to tax will always be reported in box 1. The box that reports wages subject to social security are listed in box 3. Wages subject to Medicare are reported in box 5. Boxes 2, 4, and 6 are used to report the amounts actually withheld for those taxes respectively. The amounts in boxes 1, 3, and 5 may vary because not all compensation is always subject to all three types of tax. Consider the examples in Application 7.1.

The remaining boxes address special job circumstances and tax related fringe benefits. With regard to job circumstances, those who work in the service industries frequently receive a lower wage because a portion of their compensation is received in the form of tips. Before 1982, the IRS estimated that only 16% of tip income was reported for income tax purposes. Along with a number of tax reform measures, in 1982 employers were given the added responsibility of tracking tips of their employees and reporting them to the IRS and the employees. The IRS holds that anyone receiving tips for service must report it. A large number of these professions have been identified and employers in these areas are required to "allocate" tips. Under the allocated tips requirement, each employee who receives tips is presumed to receive at least 8% of the amount of revenue generated for the business in the form of tips. For example, a food server who generates $100 in sales of food in a

APPLICATION   7.1

Marinda is employed during the year and earned $75,000. However, she had $5,000 deducted for contributions to be made with pretax earnings according to her company retirement plan and in accordance with IRS regulations. This money was withdrawn from her pay before any taxes were calculated or withheld by her employer. Thus, $5,000 was not subject to income tax and not considered in box 1 or 2. The amount reported in box 1 of taxable wages would be $5,000 less than the amount subject to Social Security and Medicare taxes reported in boxes 3 and 5.

Jasmine worked for the same company and earned $100,000. She did not contribute to the retirement plan. But the amounts reported in boxes 1, 3, and 5 were still not the same. The year of the employment, Social Security imposed a ceiling for withholding of $90,000. Earnings above this amount were not subject to Social Security but were subject to Medicare tax. For Jasmine, the amounts reported in boxes 1 (taxable wages) and 5 (wages subject to Medicare) were the same. But only $90,000 of wages (the amount below the Social Security ceiling) were reported as taxable for Social Security purposes in box 3. Social Security adjusts the ceiling amounts periodically and employers must keep abreast of these changes to ensure proper withholding.

restaurant is presumed to have generated $8.00 in tip income. Employers usually require employees to report tips earned regularly and this amount, or 8%, whichever is higher, is reported on the form W-2. Amounts reported are included in box 1 of the W-2 as wages. If an employee reports less than 8%, the difference is reported as allocated tips in box 8. Employers also report an annual form 8027 to the IRS, which includes allocated tip income for all employees. It is up to the employee to report the difference on the actual tax return and be able to provide adequate substantiation that the tips were different from the allocated amount of 8%. For example, a drink server in a buffet style restaurant would typically not generate as much in tips as a server in a full-service restaurant. Also, if either server shared tips with other staff such as the bartender or busperson (as is common in the food service industry and referred to as "tipping out"), the amount could fall below 8%. But, as stated, this must be addressed by the taxpayer on the tax return.

Other boxes on the W-2 include boxes that report cash value benefits that may or may not be taxable depending on employee circumstances. They also may affect a taxpayer's deductions/credits. Also included is the information about the availability of a retirement plan and state as well as local wages and taxes. The latter information can be used by the taxpayers who itemize their deductions and on state income tax returns for those who work or live in states and/or cities with income tax.

a Employee's social security number		
22222	OMB No. 1545-0008	
b Employer identification number (EIN)	1 Wages, tips, other compensation	2 Federal income tax withheld
c Employer's name, address, and ZIP code	3 Social security wages	4 Social security tax withheld
	5 Medicare wages and tips	6 Medicare tax withheld
	7 Social security tips	8 Allocated tips
d Control number	9 Advance EIC payment	10 Dependent care benefits
e Employee's first name and initial Last name Suff.	11 Nonqualified plans	12a
	13 Statutory employee Retirement plan Third-party sick pay	12b
	14 Other	12c
		12d
f Employee's address and ZIP code		

15 State Employer's state ID number	16 State wages, tips, etc.	17 State income tax	18 Local wages, tips, etc.	19 Local income tax	20 Locality name

Form **W-2** Wage and Tax Statement   **2007**   Department of the Treasury—Internal Revenue Service
Copy 1—For State, City, or Local Tax Department

EXHIBIT 7–4 W-2

2. W-2G Gambling Winnings

Years ago, gambling earnings and losses were something that was not widely considered by the public as a tax-related transaction. However, in more recent years, the dramatic increase in gaming through casinos, lotteries, and so on, drew attention to the large amount of revenues not being subjected to tax. As a result, the IRS imposed regulations that required licensed gaming establishments to report customers who won over a certain dollar amount. Additionally, the customer receives a form W2-G stating the amount won as well as details of the circumstances of the win. Gambling that results in a one-time event or accumulated net income (wins greater than losses) may be reported to the IRS. Regulations do allow a limited amount of gambling losses to be deducted. However, the losses can only be deducted to the extent there were winnings and only if the taxpayer itemizes deductions rather than using the Standard Deduction. For example, if a taxpayer wins $10,000 over the course of the year and loses $30,000, only $10,000 in losses may be deducted on an itemized return. As a general rule, itemization is the most advantageous only if the total of the itemized deductions is greater than the optional standard deduction. But, if a taxpayer can establish as much in losses as winnings, and files an itemized tax return, then tax on that amount of winnings can be legally avoided. To this end, many gaming establishments offer customers a method to track their gambling including winning and losses and provide them with an annual report for use in tax preparation.

3232	☐ CORRECTED		OMB No. 1545-0238
PAYER'S name	**1** Gross winnings	**2** Federal income tax withheld	2007
Street address	**3** Type of wager	**4** Date won	**Form W-2G**
City, state, and ZIP code	**5** Transaction	**6** Race	**Certain Gambling Winnings**
Federal identification number Telephone number	**7** Winnings from identical wagers	**8** Cashier	
WINNER'S name	**9** Winner's taxpayer identification no.	**10** Window	For Privacy Act and Paperwork Reduction Act Notice, see the **2007 General Instructions for Forms 1099, 1098, 5498, and W-2G.**
Street address (including apt. no.)	**11** First I.D.	**12** Second I.D.	
City, state, and ZIP code	**13** State/Payer's state identification no.	**14** State income tax withheld	File with Form 1096.
Under penalties of perjury, I declare that, to the best of my knowledge and belief, the name, address, and taxpayer identification number that I have furnished correctly identify me as the recipient of this payment and any payments from identical wagers, and that no other person is entitled to any part of these payments.			**Copy A For Internal Revenue Service Center**
Signature ▶ Date ▶			
Form **W-2G**	Cat. No. 10138V	Department of the Treasury—Internal Revenue Service	

EXHIBIT 7–5 W-2G

3. 1098E—Student Loan Payments

Because the government wants to encourage education, certain tax benefits have been created to assist taxpayers who have pursued higher education (beyond high school). The first is a deduction for interest paid on student loans. This deduction was disallowed along with all other personal interest in the latter 1980s. However, in the later 1990s, the student loaned interest deduction was reintroduced to allow those who were paying off student loans to avoid being taxed on those dollars of income used for interest on the loans. The effects of this encourage students who may not otherwise be able to afford the expenses of college or vocational training to seek out loans, and to assist those who have recently ended their college/training in paying off these loans. There are some conditions for eligibility for the student loan interest deduction. These will be discussed further in the portion of the text dedicated to tax return preparation. However, for the purposes of this discussion, keep in mind that anytime student loan interest is received by a financial institution, that interest should be reported to the IRS, and the party to whom the loan was issued in the form of a 1098E.

	☐ CORRECTED (if checked)				
RECIPIENT'S/LENDER'S name, address, and telephone number			OMB No. 1545-1576		**Student Loan Interest Statement**
			2007		
			Form **1098-E**		
RECIPIENT'S federal identification no.	BORROWER'S social security number	1 Student loan interest received by lender $			**Copy B** **For Borrower**
BORROWER'S name					This is important tax information and is being furnished to the Internal Revenue Service. If you are required to file a return, a negligence penalty or other sanction may be imposed on you if the IRS determines that an underpayment of tax results because you overstated a deduction for student loan interest.
Street address (including apt. no.)					
City, state, and ZIP code					
Account number (see instructions)		2 Box 1 includes loan origination fees and/or capitalized interest (if checked) . . . . . ☐			
Form **1098-E**		(keep for your records)	Department of the Treasury - Internal Revenue Service		

EXHIBIT 7–6   1098E

4. 1098 T Tuition Payments

Another education tax benefit is the deduction for all or part of the amounts paid for tuition and related education expenses. There are several different types of deductions or credits to choose. The individual circumstances with respect to the type of education (full time, part time, periodic, freshman, sophomore, junior-graduate, nondegree, etc.) and other tax-related information will provide an indication of which is the most applicable and beneficial for the taxpayer. However, the amount used to calculate the deduction is always reported in the same way.

Any postsecondary (after high school) institution that is considered an eligible institution by the Department of Education, and that charges and receives tuition, is required to document receipts. Furthermore, the educational institution is required to distinguish the amounts paid for tuition and fees from room and board. Any amounts paid through scholarship at no cost to the student for tuition and fees must be reported as well. This is done on form 1098T. Once received, the student can proceed to determine the best option for claiming the deduction. Typically, a student is not allowed to deduct expenses that have been paid through scholarship. This does not include loans because the student has an obligation to repay them. Similarly, if a student receives a scholarship or waiver in exchange for some future performance such as work in a particular area on graduation, the student would not be required to pay the expenses and thus could not deduct them. However, if the student failed to live up to the terms of the agreement and was then charged for the educational expenses, they may become eligible for a deduction/credit.

☐ CORRECTED		
FILER'S name, street address, city, state, ZIP code, and telephone number	**1** Payments received for qualified tuition and related expenses $ **2** Amounts billed for qualified tuition and related expenses $	OMB No. 1545-1574 2007 Form **1098-T** **Tuition Statement**
FILER'S federal identification no. STUDENT'S social security number	**3** If this box is checked, your educational institution has changed its reporting method for 2007 ☐	**Copy B** **For Student**
STUDENT'S name	**4** Adjustments made for a prior year $ **5** Scholarships or grants $	This is important tax information and is being furnished to the Internal Revenue Service.
Street address (including apt. no.) City, state, and ZIP code	**6** Adjustments to scholarships or grants for a prior year $ **7** Checked if the amount in box 1 or 2 includes amounts for an academic period beginning January - March 2008 ▶ ☐	
Service Provider/Acct. No. (see instr.)	**8** Checked if at least half-time student ☐ **9** Checked if a graduate student ☐ **10** Ins. contract reimb./refund $	
Form **1098-T**	(keep for your records)	Department of the Treasury - Internal Revenue Servicee

EXHIBIT 7–7   1098T

5. 1099-B—Reportable Capital Transactions

This form is seen much less frequently than the 1099-DIV, which is used when dividends are paid or stock is sold. Rather, the 1099-B is a document used when a capital investment changes form. For example, if a taxpayer holds stock in Corporation A and that corporation is sold to Corporation B, the taxpayer's stock may be exchanged for Corporation B stock. In that event, a 1099-B is issued. The form 1099-B is filed by the broker who represents the stockholder and oversees the transaction on behalf of the stockholder. Some transactions are exempt and need not be reported to the IRS or the taxpayer on a form 1099-B. Thus, it is important to clarify the status of the stockholder and the transaction before reporting a 1099-B on Schedule D of the individual tax return.

EXHIBIT 7–8   1099-B

6. 1099-C. Cancellation of Debt

One of the most confusing forms that a taxpayer may receive is a 1099-C. It is not that the form is confusing. Rather, the purpose and use of the form is very often something the taxpayer does not anticipate or fully understand. When a taxpayer incurs a debt such as an installment loan, the benefit associated with that debt goes to the taxpayer, for example, clothes bought by using a credit card. However, in some instances, the taxpayer is unable to pay the debt. Rather than go through a bankruptcy proceeding, the party who provided the financing for the purchase, such as a bank or credit card company, on occasion releases the taxpayer from paying part or all of the debt. An example might be if a credit card company cancels a large sum of interest due in exchange for a commitment from the debtor to pay the principal amount. For many taxpayers, the perception is that this is the end of the obligation. However, the IRS looks at this not as a gift from the creditor but, rather, as income to the debtor. Technically speaking, this is money that the taxpayer owed, should have paid, and was ultimately not required to pay. As a result, the taxpayer is the beneficiary of that amount. The taxpayer is obligated to report the amount of debt that was canceled as income. If the amount canceled was more than $600, the creditor should issue a form 1099-C to the taxpayer detailing the transaction. This is then reported as income to the taxpayer and potentially subject to tax. An important note is that there are a number of exceptions to the taxability of a debt that is canceled. As a result, before a taxpayer reports 1099-C income and subjects it to the possibility of tax, it is imperative that any possible exceptions be explored. Failure to do so may result in substantial additional tax for the taxpayer, which could have been legally avoided.

☐ CORRECTED (if checked)			
CREDITOR'S name, street address, city, state, and ZIP code		OMB No. 1545-1424 2007 Form **1099-C**	**Cancellation of Debt**
CREDITOR'S federal identification number DEBTOR'S identification number	1 Date canceled	2 Amount of debt canceled $	**Copy B For Debtor**
DEBTOR'S name	3 Interest if included in box 2 $	4	This is important tax information and is being furnished to the Internal Revenue Service. If you are required to file a return, a negligence penalty or other sanction may be imposed on you if taxable income results from this transaction and the IRS determines that it has not been reported.
Street address (including apt. no.) City, state, and ZIP code	5 Debt description		
Account number (see instructions)	6 Bankruptcy (if checked) ☐	7 Fair market value of property $	
Form **1099-C**	(keep for your records)	Department of the Treasury - Internal Revenue Service	

EXHIBIT 7–9 1099-C

7. 1099-DIV—Dividends and Capital Gain Distributions

As mentioned previously in the text, a corporation may issue a share of profits to the shareholders (owners) in the form of a dividend. Because this is a return on investment, it is treated as income and may be taxable. Because dividends represent income from property held for investment and not wages or other earnings, they are not subject to Social Security and Medicare taxes. Additionally, they may be subject to different tax rates depending on how long the investment has been owned, and how it was owned such as through a retirement plan, as an individual investment, and certain types of companies such as small businesses.

CAPITAL TRANSACTION

Occurs when ownership of stock in a corporation changes.

An additional purpose of the form 1099-DIV is to report what are known as **capital transactions**. This occurs when ownership of stock in a corporation changes. For example, when a taxpayer purchases stock and later sells the stock, a capital transaction has occurred. If the stock was sold at a gain or loss over the original purchase price, the taxpayer may incur tax on the gain, or a tax deduction due to a

☐ CORRECTED (if checked)		

| PAYER'S name, street address, city, state, ZIP code, and telephone no. | **1a** Total ordinary dividends

$ | OMB No. 1545-0110 |
| | **1b** Qualified dividends

$ | **2007**
Form **1099-DIV** | **Dividends and Distributions** |

| PAYER'S federal identification number | RECIPIENT'S identification number | **2a** Total capital gain distr.

$ | **2b** Unrecap. Sec. 1250 gain

$ | **Copy B
For Recipient** |

RECIPIENT'S name	**2c** Section 1202 gain $	**2d** Collectibles (28%) gain $
	3 Nondividend distributions $	**4** Federal income tax withheld $
Street address (including apt. no.)		**5** Investment expenses $
City, state, and ZIP code	**6** Foreign tax paid $	**7** Foreign country or U.S. possession
Account number (see instructions)	**8** Cash liquidation distributions $	**9** Noncash liquidation distributions $

This is important tax information and is being furnished to the Internal Revenue Service. If you are required to file a return, a negligence penalty or other sanction may be imposed on you if this income is taxable and the IRS determines that it has not been reported.

| Form **1099-DIV** | (keep for your records) | Department of the Treasury - Internal Revenue Service |

EXHIBIT 7–10   1099-DIV

APPLICATION **7.2**

Franco owned 500 shares of stock in a well-known soft drink company. He purchased the stock for $50 per share at a total cost of $25,000. During the year, he received dividends each quarter in the amount of $.83 per share. This came to $415.00 per quarter or $1,660 for the year. Additionally, the stock increased in value by $2.00 per share. Because he continued to own the stock, he has no income tax effect on the increased value. This will occur at the time he sells the stock if the value has increased or decreased over the original purchase price. However, he did receive the immediate cash benefit of the dividends and thus is required to report the income of $1,660 on his tax return.

loss on the investment. A number of factors must be considered to determine whether, and to what extent, the transaction has tax effects such as how long the stock was owned, the type of stock, and even the nature of the business of the company from whom the stock was purchased (some may not be taxable).

On the form 1099-DIV, the format may change but the same numbered boxes are used to consistently report the type of transaction, whether it is dividend or capital, whether the transaction is taxable, whether income taxes were withheld for the taxpayer on the transactions, and in some instances, the type of investment that may be subject to tax exemption or a particular tax rate. The important thing to remember about the 1099-DIV is that it does not always contain all of the information necessary to compute the tax effect of the transaction. For example, if someone sells stock at a profit or gain over the original purchase price, the rate of tax on the gain is influenced by whether the stock was held for a short term (less than one year) or a long term (one year or more). Very often, the date of purchase is not included and must be obtained separately before the 1099-DIV can be processed and the appropriate information included on the return.

8. 1099-G Government Payments

One of the more frequently encountered tax forms is the 1099-G. This form serves to report a variety of different types of income. A common misconception among taxpayers is that unemployment is not considered taxable income. In fact, unemployment is used as a means to substitute earnings for the taxpayer while he or she searches for new employment. Consequently, unemployment income is treated by the government as taxable. A person receiving unemployment benefits will receive a form 1099-G that indicates the amount collected. This in turn is reported on the individual tax return. If the individual elected to have a percentage of the unemployment withheld for federal taxes, this is also reported on the 1099-G and is applied toward the tax liability/refund of the individual.

☐ CORRECTED (if checked)			
PAYER'S name, street address, city, state, ZIP code, and telephone no.	**1** Unemployment compensation $	OMB No. 1545-0120 20**07** Form **1099-G**	**Certain Government Payments**
	2 State or local income tax refunds, credits, or offsets $		
PAYER'S federal identification number RECIPIENT'S identification number	**3** Box 2 amount is for tax year	**4** Federal income tax withheld $	**Copy B For Recipient**
RECIPIENT'S name	**5** ATAA payments $	**6** Taxable grants $	This is important tax information and is being furnished to the Internal Revenue Service. If you are required to file a return, a negligence penalty or other sanction may be imposed on you if this income is taxable and the IRS determines that it has not been reported.
Street address (including apt. no.)	**7** Agriculture payments $	**8** Box 2 is trade or business income ▶ ☐	
City, state, and ZIP code			
Account number (see instructions)			
Form **1099-G**	(keep for your records)	Department of the Treasury - Internal Revenue Service	

EXHIBIT 7–11   1099-G

Another purpose of the 1099-G is the reporting of state and local tax refunds. When taxes are filed, if the taxpayer itemizes their deductions, they are allowed to deduct on the federal return the amount of taxes paid to state and local government that year. This in turn often reduces the amount of taxes owed to the federal government. However, if any of the money that was claimed as a federal deduction of taxes paid to the state in a previous year is given back to the taxpayer in the form of a state or local tax refund, then the year following the refund, that amount must be reported as income on the federal return (because it was not in fact paid to the state as previously reported) and subjected to the tax calculation for the federal tax return.

Finally, the 1099-G is used for farmers with agricultural subsidies and taxable government grants. These are payments not typically received by the majority of the population and are subject to specific rules for determining taxability and how they should be reported. However, if someone is a recipient, the information needs to be properly processed on the tax return just as the taxable refunds and unemployment are reported.

9. 1099-INT. Interest Income

The 1099-INT is a multipurpose information document. It is used to report both interest paid out and interest received. Individuals who place money with a bank or other financial institution for investment are typically entitled to interest. At the end of the calendar year, a 1099-INT is sent to the taxpayer to report the total amount of interest paid during the year. The form reports not only the interest paid but also any

☐ CORRECTED (if checked)

PAYER'S name, street address, city, state, ZIP code, and telephone no.	Payer's RTN (optional)	OMB No. 1545-0112	
	1 Interest income $	20**07**	**Interest Income**
	2 Early withdrawal penalty $	Form **1099-INT**	

PAYER'S federal identification number	RECIPIENT'S identification number	3 Interest on U.S. Savings Bonds and Treas. obligations $	**Copy B** **For Recipient**
RECIPIENT'S name		4 Federal income tax withheld $	5 Investment expenses $
Street address (including apt. no.)		6 Foreign tax paid $	7 Foreign country or U.S. possession
City, state, and ZIP code		8 Tax-exempt interest	9 Specified private activity bond interest
Account number (see instructions)		$	$

This is important tax information and is being furnished to the Internal Revenue Service. If you are required to file a return, a negligence penalty or other sanction may be imposed on you if this income is taxable and the IRS determines that it has not been reported.

Form **1099-INT**   (keep for your records)   Department of the Treasury - Internal Revenue Service

EXHIBIT 7–12 1099-INT

amounts that are withheld and paid to the IRS toward the taxpayer's income tax liability. Interest such as this is not earned or exchanged for labor or services. Consequently, it is not subject to Social Security and Medicare tax.

The other function of the 1099-INT is to report interest paid by the taxpayer on a mortgage. Because the government encourages home ownership, a deduction is allowed for mortgage interest and real estate taxes incurred by taxpayers. When a party purchases a property, it is often subject to a mortgage. In reality, the financing party such as a loan company or bank, purchases the property with the buyer. A mortgage is then issued, which is a contract that allows the buyer to purchase the ownership rights of the financing party (lender) over time. These payments are typically made to repay the principal or amount of money advanced as well as interest on the outstanding debt. During the life of the mortgage, the mortgagor (financing party) reports annually, the amount of interest paid. This is done on a form 1099-INT. Additionally, if the mortgagee (debtor) pays property taxes through the mortgagor as part of the installment payment, that amount is also included on the 1099-INT. The 1099-INT can be used to increase and decrease tax liability for the taxpayer depending on the type of information reported.

10. 1099-LTC—Long-Term Care Benefits

If an individual collects under an insurance policy that provides for long-term care benefits in the event of chronic or terminal illness, the company who issues the policy and makes the payments must issue a form 1099-LTC to the taxpayer.

☐ CORRECTED (if checked)			
PAYER'S name, street address, city, state, ZIP code, and telephone no.	**1** Gross long-term care benefits paid $	OMB No. 1545-1519 20**07** Form **1099-LTC**	**Long-Term Care and Accelerated Death Benefits**
	2 Accelerated death benefits paid $		
PAYER'S federal identification number	POLICYHOLDER'S identification number	**3** ☐ Per diem ☐ Reimbursed amount	INSURED'S social security no.	**Copy B** **For Policyholder**
POLICYHOLDER'S name		INSURED'S name		This is important tax information and is being furnished to the Internal Revenue Service. If you are required to file a return, a negligence penalty or other sanction may be imposed on you if this item is required to be reported and the IRS determines that it has not been reported.
Street address (including apt. no.)		Street address (including apt. no.)		
City, state, and ZIP code		City, state, and ZIP code		
Account number (see instructions)	**4** Qualified contract ☐ (optional)	**5** (optional)	☐ Chronically ill Date certified ☐ Terminally ill	
Form **1099-LTC**		(keep for your records)	Department of the Treasury—Internal Revenue Service	

EXHIBIT 7–13   1099-LTC

Typically, these payments are not taxable. However, in certain situations such as per diem payments (specific amounts made based on the number of days ill, but not associated costs), a portion of the payment may be taxable. Also, if a patient is terminally ill, a policy may provide for accelerated death benefits. This allows the taxpayer to receive the benefit of a life insurance policy before they die. These payments are also reported on a form 1099-LTC.

It is important to consider the 1099-LTC in tax preparation in the event that a portion of the payments received by the taxpayer may be taxable.

11. 1099-MISC—Miscellaneous Income

Perhaps the most versatile information document in terms of content is the 1099-MISC. The government establishes a baseline amount of income. Any amount above this that is paid by one party to another in exchange for services that is not covered by a more specific document such as a W-2 or other 1099 generally is reported on a 1099-MISC. This includes regular, periodic, and even one-time payments. Independent contractors are probably the most common recipients of the 1099-MISC.

Some of the payments for which the 1099-MISC is used include the following:

- Royalties
- Broker payments
- Rents greater than $600
- Payments for independent services greater than $600

- Prizes and awards
- Wages paid after an individual is deceased (Social Security and Medicare is reportable on W-2)
- Medical and health care payments
- Damages received in litigation that are not compensation for physical injury

Because many of the circumstances in which a 1099-MISC is not a regular occurrence for the taxpayer, it is important to fully read the IRS regulations that pertain to a specific type of payment to ensure that the amount is properly reported and to determine whether it should be reported on the individual tax return, and, if so, where.

□ VOID □ CORRECTED			
PAYER'S name, street address, city, state, ZIP code, and telephone no.	**1** Rents $	OMB No. 1545-0115 20**07** Form **1099-MISC**	**Miscellaneous Income**
	2 Royalties $		
	3 Other income $	**4** Federal income tax withheld $	**Copy 1 For State Tax Department**
PAYER'S federal identification number	RECIPIENT'S identification number	**5** Fishing boat proceeds $	**6** Medical and health care payments $	
RECIPIENT'S name		**7** Nonemployee compensation $	**8** Substitute payments in lieu of dividends or interest $	
Street address (including apt. no.)		**9** Payer made direct sales of $5,000 or more of consumer products to a buyer (recipient) for resale ▶ □	**10** Crop insurance proceeds $	
City, state, and ZIP code		**11**	**12**	
Account number (see instructions)		**13** Excess golden parachute payments $	**14** Gross proceeds paid to an attorney $	
15a Section 409A deferrals $	**15b** Section 409A income $	**16** State tax withheld $ .... $	**17** State/Payer's state no.	**18** State income $ .... $

Form **1099-MISC**   Department of the Treasury - Internal Revenue Service

EXHIBIT 7–14 1099-MISC

12. 1099-SA

A great deal of media attention in recent years has focused on the skyrocketing costs of health care including prescriptions. As a result, a number of measures have been taken by Congress to assist taxpayers. One of the more popular methods has been to allow individuals in certain circumstances to create special types of savings accounts to cover medical expenses the taxpayers anticipate over the coming year. This money is placed in the account and is not subject to income tax if it is withdrawn for use in the payment of health care-related expenses. If the money is used for other purposes, it becomes taxable and any distributions, and in some cases money not distributed at all, is included as part of the taxpayer's income and subjected to income tax. As a result, when a taxpayer withdraws from such an account, the financial institution issues a 1099-SA to the taxpayer and the IRS. The taxpayer must be able to document that the money was spent for health care expenses or include it as income.

13. 1099-Q—Qualified Tuition

This form is one that will probably see increased use in the years to come. Although there have been education fund programs for many years, such as the Coverdell program, in more recent years a majority of states have instituted savings programs that encourage taxpayers through tax benefits to put money away for future education expenses. Programs such as the 529 Education Savings Plan and others allow taxpayers to avoid tax on the income tax on earnings generated by investing their money if they put it into an education plan. Then, if the money removed is used for tuition and educational expenses that are qualified within the plan and under any

□ CORRECTED (if checked)				
TRUSTEE'S/PAYER'S name, street address, city, state, and ZIP code		OMB No. 1545-1517 **2007** Form **1099-SA**		**Distributions From an HSA, Archer MSA, or Medicare Advantage MSA**
PAYER'S federal identification number	RECIPIENT'S identification number	**1** Gross distribution $	**2** Earnings on excess cont. $	**Copy B For Recipient**
RECIPIENT'S name		**3** Distribution code	**4** FMV on date of death $	
Street address (including apt. no.) City, state, and ZIP code		**5** HSA □ Archer MSA □ MA MSA □		This information is being furnished to the Internal Revenue Service.
Account number (see instructions)				
Form **1099-SA**	(keep for your records)			Department of the Treasury - Internal Revenue Service

EXHIBIT 7–15   1099-SA

government regulations, the money can be withdrawn tax-free. If it is not used for a qualified purpose, then tax may be due on the earnings the investment has generated over time. These plans allow the taxpayer to invest money and allow the investment to grow with the potential of that growth being tax-free. As a result, the plans have become popular in recent times. Any time that money is withdrawn from such an investment, it is reported by the financial institution that holds the money. The taxpayer must include the earnings from the investment in income unless they can document an exception such as proof of tuition paid. As discussed previously, this is done by producing a 1098-T, which documents amounts paid for postsecondary education. If less than the full amount withdrawn is used for qualified education expenses, the difference is the only amount that will be taxable. Different rules apply to different types of education savings plans. As a result, it is important to consult state and federal tax regulations applicable to a particular plan when including the information on a tax return.

14. 1099-R—Retirement Fund Distribution

A fairly common 1099 information document received by taxpayers is generated when the taxpayer receives money from a retirement fund. This not only occurs on retirement but also at any time that someone withdraws funds from a retirement plan and does not have the money reinvested directly into another plan. As a result, any time someone cashes out their interest in a 401K plan, IRA, or other type of retirement plan, a 1099-R is used to report that transaction to the IRS. Additionally, individuals who are of appropriate retirement age (usually 591/2) and begin making withdrawals from a retirement plan should receive a 1099-R. To the taxpayer, the 1099-R may be somewhat confusing. This is because premature withdrawals from a tax-deferred retirement plan may generate additional tax and penalties. However, in most cases, the distribution will be made either without any tax withheld, or with an amount withheld for application toward income tax. Because any distribution may be treated as income and there fore generate income tax, often taxpayers think that the withholding is sufficient. However, generally, these withholdings do not address or cover the additional tax and penalties that may be associated with an early withdrawal. Consequently, it is not unusual for a taxpayer who received a distribution from a retirement plan and received a 1099-R to have a much greater than anticipated tax liability.

One important feature of the 1099-R is box 2a. Even if an amount is included, or the box is left blank, very often the taxability of any or all of the distribution cannot be accurately determined at the time the money is paid out to the taxpayer. Thus, this information cannot be relied on as the sole source for determining whether the distribution is taxable, and if so to what extent, or subject to penalty. It is important to calculate the taxability of any distribution reported on form 1099-R, taking into consideration the specific circumstances of the distribution, and within the context of the rest of the taxpayer's financial information.

☐ VOID ☐ CORRECTED				
PAYER'S name, street address, city, state, and ZIP code	**1** Gross distribution $	OMB No. 1545-0119 2007 Form **1099-R**		**Distributions From Pensions, Annuities, Retirement or Profit-Sharing Plans, IRAs, Insurance Contracts, etc.**
	2a Taxable amount $			
	2b Taxable amount not determined ☐	Total distribution ☐		**Copy 1** **For** **State, City,** **or Local** **Tax Department**
PAYER'S federal identification number	RECIPIENT'S identification number	**3** Capital gain (included in box 2a) $	**4** Federal income tax withheld $	
RECIPIENT'S name		**5** Employee contributions /Designated Roth contributions or insurance premiums $	**6** Net unrealized appreciation in employer's securities $	
Street address (including apt. no.)		**7** Distribution code(s) | IRA/ SEP/ SIMPLE ☐	**8** Other $ %	
City, state, and ZIP code		**9a** Your percentage of total distribution %	**9b** Total employee contributions $	
	1st year of desig. Roth contrib.	**10** State tax withheld $ $	**11** State/Payer's state no.	**12** State distribution $ $
Account number (see instructions)		**13** Local tax withheld $ $	**14** Name of locality	**15** Local distribution $ $

Form **1099-R**   Department of the Treasury — Internal Revenue Service

EXHIBIT 7–16   1099-R

15. RRB-1099—Distribution of Funds from Railroad Retirement Board

Form RRB-1099 reports the benefits paid to certain railroad workers in lieu of Social Security benefits. For tax purposes, the RRB payments are similar to Social Security payments. At least a portion of them may be subject to income tax depending on the other income of the recipient. The same calculation is used as for Social Security retirement benefits. Railroad retirement benefits are not subject to state income tax. Depending on the time in which the benefits were generated in terms of employment and the nature of the benefits such as retirement, worker's compensation, and so on, a portion may be nontaxable. Any nontaxable amounts are not reported on the standard RRB-1099. However, a supplemental RRB-1099-R may be issued in addition to the 1099-R. This may contain payments treated for tax purposes as private pension retirement and are subject to taxes in the same manner

UNFOLD TO SEE ALL TAX STATEMENT FORMS - SEE REVERSE SIDE FOR GENERAL INFORMATION

PAYER'S NAME, STREET ADDRESS, CITY, STATE, AND ZIP CODE		
UNITED STATES RAILROAD RETIREMENT BOARD	**2006**	PAYMENTS BY THE RAILROAD RETIREMENT BOARD
844 N RUSH ST CHICAGO IL 60611-2092	3. Gross Social Security Equivalent Benefit Portion of Tier 1 Paid in 2006	
PAYER'S FEDERAL IDENTIFYING NO. 36-3314600		
1. Claim Number and Payee Code	4. Social Security Equivalent Benefit Portion of Tier 1 Repaid to RRB in 2006	COPY C -
2. Recipient's Identification Number	5. Net Social Security Equivalent Benefit Portion of Tier 1 Paid in 2006	FOR RECIPIENT'S RECORDS
Recipient's Name, Street Address, City, State, and Zip Code	6. Workers' Compensation Offset in 2006	
	7. Social Security Equivalent Benefit Portion of Tier 1 Paid for 2005	THIS INFORMATION IS BEING FURNISHED TO THE INTERNAL REVENUE SERVICE.
	8. Social Security Equivalent Benefit Portion of Tier 1 Paid for 2004	
	9. Social Security Equivalent Benefit Portion of Tier 1 Paid for Years Prior to 2004	
	10. Federal Income Tax Withheld	11. Medicare Premium Total

FORM RRB-1099   DO NOT ATTACH TO YOUR INCOME TAX RETURN

EXHIBIT 7–17 RRB-1099

as any other employee pension plan. Various IRS publications, including Pub. 575 and Pub. 939, can be consulted to determine the taxability of any RRB payments reported on the RRB-1099.

16. SSA-1099—Social Security Benefit Statement (Retirement, Survivors, Disability)

Because Social Security was never intended to become a sole source of income for citizens, there is the assumption that most individuals will have other types of income as well. Consequently, it is possible that in some instances where the individual has substantial other income, Social Security may be subject to income tax. Each year, a form SSA-1099 is issued to those who receive Social Security benefits of any kind, whether it is retirement, disability, or survivor's benefits. The form SSA-1099 contains the individual's identity, the amount of benefits issued, whether any benefits were repaid to Social Security, and whether any amounts were withheld for taxes or other items such as Medicare insurance premiums.

Although Social Security benefits are not automatically subject to income tax, if an individual has earned wages above a threshold amount established by the IRS, then a percentage of the benefits may be taxable. The more income one earns, the greater the percentage of Social Security benefits may be taxable. There is a limit on how much of Social Security benefits are taxable and this is established, along with the threshold amount of earnings, by the IRS. As a result, if someone anticipates having a significant amount of earned income in addition to Social Security benefits, it may be wise to have a portion of the benefits voluntarily withheld for taxes.

FORM SSA-1042S – SOCIAL SECURITY BENEFIT STATEMENT

2006

• THIS FORM IS FOR USE IN FILING A UNITED STATES FEDERAL INCOME TAX RETURN.
• DO NOT RETURN IT TO SOCIAL SECURITY. READ THE INFORMATION ON THE REVERSE.

Box 1. Name	Box 2. Beneficiary's Social Security Number

Box 3. Benefits Paid in 2006	Box 4. Benefits Repaid to SSA in 2006	Box 5. Net Benefits for 2006 *(Box 3 minus Box 4)*

DESCRIPTION OF AMOUNT IN BOX 3	DESCRIPTION OF AMOUNT IN BOX 4

Box 10. Address

Box 6. Rate of Tax

Box 7. Amount of Tax Withheld

Box 8. Amount of Tax Refunded

Box 11. Claim Number *(Use this number if you need to contact SSA.)*

Box 9. Net Tax Withheld During 2006 *(Box 7 minus Box 8)*

Form SSA-1042S-SM (1-2007)

EXHIBIT 7–18 I099-SSA

17. Schedule K-1-E (Form 1041)

The K-1-E (Form 1041) is the schedule used to report income paid to the beneficiary of an estate. It also includes an accounting of the pro rata share of the deductions or credits for the estate that are attributable to the beneficiary.

APPLICATION **7.3**

Molly receives Social Security retirement benefits. She is 63 years old. She also continues her employment part time as a substitute teacher. In 2004, Molly worked full time until she started receiving Social Security in June. Her earnings for the first five months of the year were $22,000. The rest of the year, she earned an additional $12,000 for a total of $34,000 in earned income. Her Social Security benefits were $1,000 per month for 7 months ($7,000). Because Molly earned an amount over the threshold, a computation had to be performed on her 2004 tax return to determine how much of her Social Security benefits were taxable.

Change the facts as follows: Assume Molly started receiving Social Security benefits in January. She earned $4,000 in wages throughout the year. Because this would fall behold the established threshold for 2004, none of Molly's $12,000 in Social Security benefits would be subject to income tax.

The Schedule K-1-E is not attached to the personal income tax return. However, the information may be required to be included. The fiduciary in charge of administering an estate is required to prepare a Schedule K-1-E (Form 1041) for each beneficiary. Copies are also sent to the IRS enabling a cross-check to be performed in the event any of the income given over to the beneficiary is taxable.

It is important to determine if the income is taxable, and, if so, whether any deductions or credits of the estate are applicable to the income of the beneficiary to reduce the amount that is taxable. As mentioned, even though the estate K-1 is contained on a tax form, it is not included with the return. Only certain elements of the information on the K-1 may be necessary to report on the return.

18. K-1 Partnership Report

As discussed in earlier chapters and above, a partnership is generally not subject to income tax as a business. Rather, each partner is accountable for his or her share of the net income of the business. This is true regardless of whether the partner actually takes the money out of the business. Income from a partnership is reported annually to each partner on IRS Form 1065, Schedule K-1-P. This document is not filed with the personal tax return of the partner. However, the information included is filed on a separate schedule that is included with the return. There are general limitations that may cause the credits and deductions a partner may claim to be different than those that appear on the K–P1. However, there are some exceptions that apply to small partnerships under IRS regulations. The circumstances of the partnership, as well as the activity of the partner, determine whether particular deductions, credits, or limitations apply. One of the questions that must be answered on the tax return with respect to a partnership is whether the partner materially participated in the partnership as defined by the IRS. This in turn affects the tax treatment of the partnership income as either nonpassive or passive income. Earlier discussions demonstrated how passive income is not subject to certain taxes such as Social Security and Medicare. However, even if a partner generates passive income, if money is paid to the partner in the form of a "guaranteed payment" as defined by IRS regulations, then that money is considered nonpassive.

19. Form 1120-S K-1 Corporation

Finally, although ordinary corporate shareholders receive documents that are used to report capital transactions such as sales or purchases of stock and dividend payments, owners of small corporations are treated differently for tax purposes. These smaller closely held corporations such as limited liability companies, S corporations, and professional corporations do not function exactly the same way as a publicly held corporation. As discussed in earlier chapters, the closely held corporation is a pass-through entity for tax purposes. The corporation itself does not pay taxes like a general corporation. Rather, all net income is divided according to percentage of ownership or an owner agreement and is included on each owner's personal return. Although the form is relatively short, it allows for a great deal of variety in the types of information included. Often information documents have standardized boxes that include very specific information. The 1120-S K-1 uses

APPLICATION **7.4**

Diane, her husband Dwayne, and Dave were equal partners in a thriving business. Each year, all three contributed to the operations of the business and shared profits equally. Diane died unexpectedly. The following year, Dave agreed to buy out Dwayne and Diane's interest over time. Dave gave up all participation in the business. Dave agreed to pay Dwayne $10,000 per year for 10 years with interest to repay his original investment. Dwayne would also receive 2% of any net profits. Additionally, until the purchase was completed, Dwayne would pay $350 per month to Dwayne for health insurance costs. In this scenario, the partners started out as three materially participating partners. Any profits received would be considered personal nonpassive income and subject to possible income, Social Security, and Medicare taxes. After Diane's death and the buyout began, Dwayne's situation changed. The interest on the loan would be taxable as passive income in the form of interest on an investment. The return of investment would be a return of his own funds and not taxable. The annual 2% profit share would be considered passive income and only subject to income tax as Dwayne would no longer meet any of the tests of material participation. However, the $350 monthly payment would constitute a guaranteed payment and would be considered nonpassive income and subject to income tax, Social Security, and Medicare. See Exhibit 10–2

standardized boxes as well. However, room is included for descriptions about the more specific type of information reported in boxes that represent general categories rather than distinct items. The back of the form provides a very detailed listing of what information should be included and where it should be located on the form. In turn, when the owner transfers relevant information to Schedule E which is attached to the tax return, the two can be cross-referenced by looking to the various lines numbers or boxes on each. (see Exhibit 10–2).

ASSIGNMENT 7.2

Give an example of a situation that would generate each of the following documents:

a. W-2

b. W-2G

c. 1098-E

d. 1098-T

e. 1099-Q

f. 1099-DIV

g. RRB-1099

h. 1099-SA

i. 1065 K-1

j. 1120-S K-1

k. 1041 K-1

l. 1099-B

m. 1099-R

n. 1099-C

o. 1099-G

p. 1099-LTC

q. 1099-MISC

r. 1099-SSA

s. 1099-INT

ETHICAL QUESTION ?

Historically, and before the advent of computers, it was very easy for the business owner and/or taxpayer to take a more lax approach toward reporting information to the IRS for the purpose of calculating taxes. Today, with increased reporting requirements for both parties, and the ability to cross-reference information by computer, the income tax system has become much more comprehensive and accurate. However, issues can still arise. Consider the following scenario. Stella owns her own business. In the past, she has done her own taxes. She simply calculated the net profits of her business by adding up all of her bank deposits for the year. Then she deducted as business expenses those items for which checks were written. The result would be the amount on which she paid tax. For 30 years, Stella drew her own pay, as well as that of her sister-in-law employee, directly from the cash register. No taxes were ever withheld or even reported for this income. If this process was acceptable to Stella and her sister-in-law, what is the problem that could arise for the sister-in-law now aged 66 and single?

SUMMARY

It should be apparent by the end of this chapter that there is an enormous amount of information that has the potential to affect the tax return for both the business and the individual, and, consequently, the tax liability of both. The various information forms are used to report income that may or may not be taxable, items that may affect deductions or credits, and taxes that have already been withheld. Businesses may not only be required to file their own return but also must provide relevant information to interested parties such as owners, shareholders, employees, and independent contractors for use in preparation of personal returns.

Information documents may vary in format but are consistent in the information reported. The documents use standardized boxes that each have specific instructions with regard to what items are reported. Some parties who prepare information documents will expand them to contain additional items, but only those required by the IRS must be included for consideration in the preparation of the tax return.

Although, typically, information documents are not attached to the tax return, the items included are placed all or in part on the return. Additionally, copies of information documents are provided to the IRS and/or the Social Security Administration. One notable exception to the attachment rule is the form W-2. The information on a W-2 is included on the tax return and the information document is attached as well. If the return is filed electronically, the document must be available if requested by the IRS.

KEY TERMS

information form   capital transaction

For additional resources, visit our Web site at www.westlegalstudies.com

Common Federal Income Tax Individual Forms

▉ OBJECTIVES

After completing this chapter, you will be able to:

❏ Distinguish the different types of individual federal income tax returns

❏ Distinguish federal forms, schedules, supporting statements

❏ Discuss the most common federal schedules

A. REPORTING DOCUMENTS

In the previous chapter, various information documents provided to taxpayers were explored. Most information documents, with the notable exception of the W-2, are not included with the individual tax return submitted to the IRS. The tax return is the document used to report financial information, and used in calculating any tax liability or refund due. Some discussion was given in previous chapters to the type and form of return filed by businesses. In this chapter, the reporting forms, commonly called returns, for the individual are considered. For most individuals, the tax return is completed using one of four forms: the 1040-EZ, 1040-A, 1040, or the 1040-X. Each of these will be discussed in this chapter.

1. Form 1040-EZ

The simplest and shortest tax return form that can be used is the 1040-EZ. This is a limited-use document. It is only appropriate when an individual has potentially taxable income and there are no required supporting documents, such as schedules, attached to the return other than the W-2. Examples of supporting documents may be for deductions, or credits other than the Earned Income Credit. The 1040-EZ is designed to allow taxpayers with very simple returns to prepare the returns themselves or with minimal assistance thereby reducing the expense of a more detailed and complicated return.

The 1040-EZ is not appropriate for all taxpayers. This return can only be used by those with a filing status of single or married filing jointly. It is not appropriate for those claiming qualifying widow, head of household, married filing separate, or individuals aged 65 or above at the end of the tax year. To use the 1040-EZ, income can only be from limited sources, including wages reported on a W-2, taxable interest received of less than $1,500, unemployment, taxable scholarships, grants, or income from the Alaska Permanent Fund. The form does not apply if the taxpayer has any dependents, income from self-employment, a partnership, estate, corporation, or capital transactions such as stock sales. There is no provision with the 1040-EZ to claim a variety of deductions and credits that may be available to taxpayers. Frequently, the 1040-EZ is used by taxpayers who have little or no tax liability, no deductions or credits (except earned income credit) and who simply want to retrieve the taxes withheld from their wages that are not due. The IRS proves the following guidelines of when to use the form 1040-EZ:

- Taxable income below $100,000
- Single or Married Filing Jointly
- Under age 65
- No dependents
- Interest income of $1,500 or less

APPLICATION **8.1**

Michie is 19 years old and single. She does not live with her parents and they do not claim her as a dependent. In the previous year, Michie worked part time. She earned $7,850. She had federal taxes withheld in the amount of $610. According to the IRS regulations applicable to that year, Michie owed no federal tax. In her circumstances, she is not entitled to the earned income credit, but she is entitled to a refund of her taxes withheld in the amount of $610. Because no other deductions or credits apply to her situation, she can complete the 1040-EZ and obtain her refund.

Department of the Treasury—Internal Revenue Service

Form 1040EZ

Income Tax Return for Single and Joint Filers With No Dependents (99) **2006**

OMB No. 1545-0074

Label
(See page 11.)
Use the IRS label.
Otherwise, please print or type.

L A B E L   H E R E

Your first name and initial	Last name		Your social security number
If a joint return, spouse's first name and initial	Last name		Spouse's social security number
Home address (number and street). If you have a P.O. box, see page 11.		Apt. no.	▲ You **must** enter your SSN(s) above. ▲
City, town or post office, state, and ZIP code. If you have a foreign address, see page 11.			Checking a box below will not change your tax or refund.

Presidential Election Campaign (page 11) ▶

Check here if you, or your spouse if a joint return, want $3 to go to this fund . . . . ▶ ☐ You   ☐ Spouse

Income

Attach Form(s) W-2 here.

Enclose, but do not attach, any payment.

1	Wages, salaries, and tips. This should be shown in box 1 of your Form(s) W-2. Attach your Form(s) W-2.	1	
2	Taxable interest. If the total is over $1,500, you cannot use Form 1040EZ.	2	
3	Unemployment compensation and Alaska Permanent Fund dividends (see page 13).	3	
4	Add lines 1, 2, and 3. This is your **adjusted gross income.**	4	
5	If someone can claim you (or your spouse if a joint return) as a dependent, check the applicable box(es) below and enter the amount from the worksheet on back. ☐ You ☐ Spouse If no one can claim you (or your spouse if a joint return), enter $8,450 if **single;** $16,900 if **married filing jointly.** See back for explanation.	5	
6	Subtract line 5 from line 4. If line 5 is larger than line 4, enter -0-. This is your **taxable income.** ▶	6	

Payments and tax

7	Federal income tax withheld from box 2 of your Form(s) W-2.	7	
8a	**Earned income credit (EIC).**	8a	
b	Nontaxable combat pay election.	8b	
9	Credit for federal telephone excise tax paid. Attach Form 8913 if required.	9	
10	Add lines 7, 8a, and 9. These are your **total payments.** ▶	10	
11	**Tax.** Use the amount on **line 6 above** to find your tax in the tax table on pages 24–32 of the booklet. Then, enter the tax from the table on this line.	11	

Refund

Have it directly deposited! See page 18 and fill in 12b, 12c, and 12d or Form 8888.

12a	If line 10 is larger than line 11, subtract line 11 from line 10. This is your **refund.** If Form 8888 is attached, check here ▶ ☐	12a	
▶ b	Routing number		▶ c Type: ☐ Checking ☐ Savings
▶ d	Account number		

Amount you owe

| 13 | If line 11 is larger than line 10, subtract line 10 from line 11. This is the **amount you owe.** For details on how to pay, see page 19. ▶ | 13 | |

Third party designee

Do you want to allow another person to discuss this return with the IRS (see page 20)? ☐ **Yes.** Complete the following. ☐ **No**

Designee's name ▶   Phone no. ▶ (   )   Personal identification number (PIN) ▶

Sign here

Joint return? See page 11.

Keep a copy for your records.

Under penalties of perjury, I declare that I have examined this return, and to the best of my knowledge and belief, it is true, correct, and accurately lists all amounts and sources of income I received during the tax year. Declaration of preparer (other than the taxpayer) is based on all information of which the preparer has any knowledge.

| Your signature | Date | Your occupation | Daytime phone number (   ) |
| Spouse's signature. If a joint return, **both** must sign. | Date | Spouse's occupation | |

Paid preparer's use only

Preparer's signature ▶	Date		Check if self-employed ☐	Preparer's SSN or PTIN
Firm's name (or yours if self-employed), address, and ZIP code ▶			EIN	
			Phone no. ( )	

For Disclosure, Privacy Act, and Paperwork Reduction Act Notice, see page 22.   Cat. No. 11329W   Form **1040EZ** (2006)

EXHIBIT 8–1   1040-EZ

2. Form 1040-A

The slightly broader use for form 1040-A is used by taxpayers who do not itemize their deductions and have only limited types of income and financial transactions. Unlike the 1040-EZ, any filing status can be used on the 1040-A. Additionally, it accounts for more types of income and credits. Recall the earlier discussion that distinguished the standard deduction from the itemized deduction return. Essentially, a certain portion of income is free from tax. This amount is a set figure for each type of filing status. For example, the amount allotted a couple with the status of married filing joint receives exactly double the amount of standard deduction allotted a person filing under single status. However, in some instances one's life expenses that are assumed to be covered by the standard deduction consist of items whose amounts are greater than the amount allowed under the standard deduction for that filing status deduction. In that case the taxpayer can file an itemized return using IRS Form 1040. Those not itemizing use 1040-A. The following are IRS guidelines of when to use the form 1040-A:

- Taxable income below $100,000
- Capital gain distributions, but no other capital gains or losses
- Only tax credits for child, education, earned income, child and dependent care expenses, adoption, elderly and retirement savings contributions
- Only deductions for IRA contributions, student loan interest, educator expenses or higher education tuition and fees
- No itemized deductions

3. Form 1040

Form 1040 is the most comprehensive return that can be filed by an individual taxpayer. This form encompasses all types of income, deductions, and credits. However, it is significant to note that although totals are included on the 1040, supporting schedules and in some cases worksheets with calculations are often required to be attached. Because the 1040 is used for more complicated returns, it is important to provide the necessary information to explain the content of the return and prevent any misinterpretation or incorrect conclusions by the IRS. The 1040 can be used for any filing status. It can be used for any individual. However, it requires additional computation and documentation than the 1040-EZ and 1040-A.

Form
1040A

Department of the Treasury—Internal Revenue Service

U.S. Individual Income Tax Return (99) **2006**   IRS Use Only—Do not write or staple in this space.

OMB No. 1545-0074

Label
(See page 18.)

L
A
B
E
L

H
E
R
E

Your first name and initial   Last name

Your social security number

If a joint return, spouse's first name and initial   Last name

Spouse's social security number

Home address (number and street). If you have a P.O. box, see page 18.   Apt. no.

Use the IRS label.
Otherwise, please print or type.

City, town or post office, state, and ZIP code. If you have a foreign address, see page 18.

▲ You **must** enter your SSN(s) above. ▲

Checking a box below will not change your tax or refund.

Presidential Election Campaign ▶ Check here if you, or your spouse if filing jointly, want $3 to go to this fund (see page 18) ▶ ☐ You ☐ Spouse

Filing status
Check only one box.

1 ☐ Single
2 ☐ Married filing jointly (even if only one had income)
3 ☐ Married filing separately. Enter spouse's SSN above and full name here. ▶
4 ☐ Head of household (with qualifying person). (See page 19.) If the qualifying person is a child but not your dependent, enter this child's name here. ▶
5 ☐ Qualifying widow(er) with dependent child (see page 20)

Exemptions

6a ☐ **Yourself.** If someone can claim you as a dependent, **do not** check box 6a.
b ☐ **Spouse**
c **Dependents:**

If more than six dependents, see page 21.

(1) First name Last name	(2) Dependent's social security number	(3) Dependent's relationship to you	(4) ✓ if qualifying child for child tax credit (see page 21)
			☐
			☐
			☐
			☐
			☐
			☐

Boxes checked on 6a and 6b ___
No. of children on 6c who:
• lived with you ___
• did not live with you due to divorce or separation (see page 22) ___
Dependents on 6c not entered above ___
Add numbers on lines above ▶ ☐

d Total number of exemptions claimed.

Income

Attach Form(s) W-2 here. Also attach Form(s) 1099-R if tax was withheld.

If you did not get a W-2, see page 24.

Enclose, but do not attach, any payment.

7 Wages, salaries, tips, etc. Attach Form(s) W-2. 7
8a **Taxable** interest. Attach Schedule 1 if required. 8a
b **Tax-exempt** interest. **Do not** include on line 8a. 8b
9a Ordinary dividends. Attach Schedule 1 if required. 9a
b Qualified dividends (see page 25). 9b
10 Capital gain distributions (see page 25). 10
11a IRA distributions. 11a   11b Taxable amount (see page 25). 11b
12a Pensions and annuities. 12a   12b Taxable amount (see page 26). 12b
13 Unemployment compensation, Alaska Permanent Fund dividends, and jury duty pay. 13
14a Social security benefits. 14a   14b Taxable amount (see page 28). 14b
15 Add lines 7 through 14b (far right column). This is your **total income.** ▶ 15

Adjusted gross income

16 Penalty on early withdrawal of savings (see page 28). 16
17 IRA deduction (see page 28). 17
18 Student loan interest deduction (see page 31). 18
19 Jury duty pay you gave your employer (see page 31). 19
20 Add lines 16 through 19. These are your **total adjustments.** 20
21 Subtract line 20 from line 15. This is your **adjusted gross income.** ▶ 21

For Disclosure, Privacy Act, and Paperwork Reduction Act Notice, see page 58.   Cat. No. 11327A   Form **1040A** (2006)

EXHIBIT 8–2 1040-A (continues)

Form 1040A (2006) Page **2**

Tax, credits, and payments	**22**	Enter the amount from line 21 (adjusted gross income).		22	
	23a	Check if: ☐ **You** were born before January 2, 1942, ☐ Blind ☐ **Spouse** was born before January 2, 1942, ☐ Blind } **Total boxes checked ▶** 23a			
Standard Deduction for—	**b**	If you are married filing separately and your spouse itemizes deductions, see page 32 and check here ▶ 23b ☐			
• People who checked any box on line 23a or 23b **or** who can be claimed as a dependent, see page 32.	**24**	Enter your **standard deduction** (see left margin).		24	
	25	Subtract line 24 from line 22. If line 24 is more than line 22, enter -0-.		25	
	26	If line 22 is over $112,875, or you provided housing to a person displaced by Hurricane Katrina, see page 32. Otherwise, multiply $3,300 by the total number of exemptions claimed on line 6d.	26		
	27	Subtract line 26 from line 25. If line 26 is more than line 25, enter -0-. This is your **taxable income.**	▶	27	
• All others: Single or Married filing separately, $5,150	**28**	**Tax,** including any alternative minimum tax (see page 32).		28	
	29	Credit for child and dependent care expenses. Attach Schedule 2.	29		
Married filing jointly or Qualifying widow(er), $10,300	**30**	Credit for the elderly or the disabled. Attach Schedule 3.	30		
	31	Education credits. Attach Form 8863.	31		
	32	Retirement savings contributions credit. Attach Form 8880.	32		
Head of household, $7,550	**33**	Child tax credit (see page 37). Attach Form 8901 if required.	33		
	34	Add lines 29 through 33. These are your **total credits.**		34	
	35	Subtract line 34 from line 28. If line 34 is more than line 28, enter -0-.		35	
	36	Advance earned income credit payments from Form(s) W-2, box 9.		36	
	37	Add lines 35 and 36. This is your **total tax.**	▶	37	
	38	Federal income tax withheld from Forms W-2 and 1099.	38		
	39	2006 estimated tax payments and amount applied from 2005 return.	39		
If you have a qualifying child, attach Schedule EIC.	**40a**	**Earned income credit (EIC).**	40a		
	b	Nontaxable combat pay election. 40b			
	41	Additional child tax credit. Attach Form 8812.	41		
	42	Credit for federal telephone excise tax paid. Attach Form 8913 if required.	42		
	43	Add lines 38, 39, 40a, 41, and 42. These are your **total payments.**	▶	43	
Refund	**44**	If line 43 is more than line 37, subtract line 37 from line 43. This is the amount you **overpaid.**		44	
Direct deposit? See page 53 and fill in 45b, 45c, and 45d or Form 8888.	**45a**	Amount of line 44 you want **refunded to you.** If Form 8888 is attached, check here ▶ ☐		45a	
	▶ b	Routing number ⬚⬚⬚⬚⬚⬚⬚⬚⬚ ▶ **c** Type: ☐ Checking ☐ Savings			
	▶ d	Account number ⬚⬚⬚⬚⬚⬚⬚⬚⬚⬚⬚⬚⬚⬚⬚⬚⬚			
	46	Amount of line 44 you want **applied to your 2007 estimated tax.**	46		
Amount you owe	**47**	**Amount you owe.** Subtract line 43 from line 37. For details on how to pay, see page 54.	▶	47	
	48	Estimated tax penalty (see page 54).	48		

Third party designee	Do you want to allow another person to discuss this return with the IRS (see page 55)? ☐ **Yes.** Complete the following. ☐ **No**
	Designee's name ▶ Phone no. ▶ ( ) Personal identification number (PIN) ▶ ⬚⬚⬚⬚⬚

Sign here

Joint return? See page 18. Keep a copy for your records.

Under penalties of perjury, I declare that I have examined this return and accompanying schedules and statements, and to the best of my knowledge and belief, they are true, correct, and accurately list all amounts and sources of income I received during the tax year. Declaration of preparer (other than the taxpayer) is based on all information of which the preparer has any knowledge.

Your signature	Date	Your occupation	Daytime phone number ( )
Spouse's signature. If a joint return, **both** must sign.	Date	Spouse's occupation	

Paid preparer's use only

Preparer's signature ▶	Date	Check if self-employed ☐	Preparer's SSN or PTIN
Firm's name (or yours if self-employed), address, and ZIP code ▶		EIN	
		Phone no. ( )	

Form **1040A** (2006)

EXHIBIT 8–2 1040-A (continued)

As a result, to use the 1040 when not necessary would only result in additional work rather than any recognizable tax benefit. The IRS has identified any one of the following situations as appropriate for use of the 1040 to file an individual tax return:

- Total taxable income of $100,000 or more
- Itemized deductions
- Self-employment income
- Income from sale of property

4. Form 1040-X

For a variety of reasons, it is necessary for some taxpayers to change the information originally reported on an individual tax return. If the return should be filed electronically and is rejected by the IRS before the filing deadline as the result of a discrepancy, then the return can simply be corrected and resubmitted. However, if the return has been accepted by the IRS or the need for change is discovered after the return has been filed by mail and the filing deadline is passed, then an amended return is filed. When this occurs, a special form is used to amend the information originally reported. An amended return can be filed at any time. However, each year, amended returns for the previous tax year are typically not considered by the IRS until after a specific date. With regard to individual taxpayers, this is generally around mid-March. If no original return was filed previously, or an amended return is submitted that would result in a refund for the taxpayer, it needs to be filed within three years of when the original return was due in order to collect the refund. In very specific situations, there are special circumstances identified by the IRS that may be applied to alter this deadline. The form used to amend a return is the IRS Form 1040-X. This return can be used to change items such as filing status or dependents. It also can be used to change amounts reported, claim, or give up deductions or credits and recalculate the tax liability. When preparing a 1040-X, it is essential to have the information from the original return available, as the 1040 requires the original information to be included as well as any changes. A federal 1040-X does not correct issues with a state return. Whenever a 1040-X is filed, an evaluation of the state return(s) should be conducted to determine if an amended state return should be filed as well.

A federal 1040-X is appropriate in any of the following circumstances:

- Income was not reported
- Deductions and/or credits were improperly claimed or omitted
- The wrong filing status was claimed (after the original due date of the return, status cannot be changed from Married Filing Jointly to Married Filing Separate unless by the executor of the estate of a deceased person who was party to the marriage).

Form **1040**

Department of the Treasury—Internal Revenue Service

U.S. Individual Income Tax Return 2006 (99) IRS Use Only—Do not write or staple in this space.

Label (See instructions on page 16.) **Use the IRS label.** Otherwise, please print or type.	For the year Jan. 1–Dec. 31, 2006, or other tax year beginning , 2006, ending , 20 OMB No. 1545-0074

L A B E L   H E R E

Your first name and initial — Last name — Your social security number

If a joint return, spouse's first name and initial — Last name — Spouse's social security number

Home address (number and street). If you have a P.O. box, see page 16. — Apt. no.

City, town or post office, state, and ZIP code. If you have a foreign address, see page 16.

You must enter your SSN(s) above. ▲

Checking a box below will not change your tax or refund.

Presidential Election Campaign ▶ Check here if you, or your spouse if filing jointly, want $3 to go to this fund (see page 16) ▶ ☐ You ☐ Spouse

Filing Status

Check only one box.

1 ☐ Single
2 ☐ Married filing jointly (even if only one had income)
3 ☐ Married filing separately. Enter spouse's SSN above and full name here. ▶
4 ☐ Head of household (with qualifying person). (See page 17.) If the qualifying person is a child but not your dependent, enter this child's name here. ▶
5 ☐ Qualifying widow(er) with dependent child (see page 17)

Exemptions

6a ☐ **Yourself.** If someone can claim you as a dependent, **do not** check box 6a
b ☐ **Spouse**
c **Dependents:**

(1) First name Last name	(2) Dependent's social security number	(3) Dependent's relationship to you	(4) ✓ if qualifying child for child tax credit (see page 19)
			☐
			☐
			☐
			☐

If more than four dependents, see page 19.

d Total number of exemptions claimed

Boxes checked on 6a and 6b
No. of children on 6c who:
• lived with you
• did not live with you due to divorce or separation (see page 20)
Dependents on 6c not entered above
Add numbers on lines above ▶

Income

Attach Form(s) W-2 here. Also attach Forms W-2G and 1099-R if tax was withheld.

If you did not get a W-2, see page 23.

Enclose, but do not attach, any payment. Also, please use Form 1040-V.

7	Wages, salaries, tips, etc. Attach Form(s) W-2	7	
8a	**Taxable** interest. Attach Schedule B if required	8a	
b	Tax-exempt interest. **Do not** include on line 8a	8b	
9a	Ordinary dividends. Attach Schedule B if required	9a	
b	Qualified dividends (see page 23)	9b	
10	Taxable refunds, credits, or offsets of state and local income taxes (see page 24)	10	
11	Alimony received	11	
12	Business income or (loss). Attach Schedule C or C-EZ	12	
13	Capital gain or (loss). Attach Schedule D if required. If not required, check here ▶ ☐	13	
14	Other gains or (losses). Attach Form 4797	14	
15a	IRA distributions 15a	b Taxable amount (see page 25)	15b	
16a	Pensions and annuities 16a	b Taxable amount (see page 26)	16b	
17	Rental real estate, royalties, partnerships, S corporations, trusts, etc. Attach Schedule E	17	
18	Farm income or (loss). Attach Schedule F	18	
19	Unemployment compensation	19	
20a	Social security benefits 20a	b Taxable amount (see page 27)	20b	
21	Other income. List type and amount (see page 29)	21	
22	Add the amounts in the far right column for lines 7 through 21. This is your **total income** ▶	22	

Adjusted Gross Income

23	Archer MSA deduction. Attach Form 8853	23	
24	Certain business expenses of reservists, performing artists, and fee-basis government officials. Attach Form 2106 or 2106-EZ	24	
25	Health savings account deduction. Attach Form 8889	25	
26	Moving expenses. Attach Form 3903	26	
27	One-half of self-employment tax. Attach Schedule SE	27	
28	Self-employed SEP, SIMPLE, and qualified plans	28	
29	Self-employed health insurance deduction (see page 29)	29	
30	Penalty on early withdrawal of savings	30	
31a	Alimony paid b Recipient's SSN ▶	31a	
32	IRA deduction (see page 31)	32	
33	Student loan interest deduction (see page 33)	33	
34	Jury duty pay you gave to your employer	34	
35	Domestic production activities deduction. Attach Form 8903	35	
36	Add lines 23 through 31a and 32 through 35	36	
37	Subtract line 36 from line 22. This is your **adjusted gross income** ▶	37	

For Disclosure, Privacy Act, and Paperwork Reduction Act Notice, see page 80.   Cat. No. 11320B   Form **1040** (2006)

EXHIBIT 8–3   1040 (continues)

Form 1040 (2006)   Page **2**

Tax and Credits	38	Amount from line 37 (adjusted gross income)		**38**	
	39a	Check if: ☐ **You** were born before January 2, 1942, ☐ Blind. ☐ **Spouse** was born before January 2, 1942, ☐ Blind. } Total boxes checked ▶ 39a			
Standard Deduction for—	b	If your spouse itemizes on a separate return or you were a dual-status alien, see page 34 and check here ▶39b ☐			
	40	**Itemized deductions** (from Schedule A) **or** your **standard deduction** (see left margin) . .		**40**	
	41	Subtract line 40 from line 38		**41**	
• People who checked any box on line 39a or 39b **or** who can be claimed as a dependent, see page 34.	42	If line 38 is over $112,875, or you provided housing to a person displaced by Hurricane Katrina, see page 36. Otherwise, multiply $3,300 by the total number of exemptions claimed on line 6d		**42**	
	43	**Taxable income.** Subtract line 42 from line 41. If line 42 is more than line 41, enter -0-		**43**	
	44	**Tax** (see page 36). Check if any tax is from: **a** ☐ Form(s) 8814 **b** ☐ Form 4972 . . .		**44**	
• All others:	45	**Alternative minimum tax** (see page 39). Attach Form 6251		**45**	
Single or Married filing separately, $5,150	46	Add lines 44 and 45 . . . . ▶		**46**	
	47	Foreign tax credit. Attach Form 1116 if required . . .	47		
Married filing jointly or Qualifying widow(er), $10,300	48	Credit for child and dependent care expenses. Attach Form 2441	48		
	49	Credit for the elderly or the disabled. Attach Schedule R .	49		
	50	Education credits. Attach Form 8863	50		
	51	Retirement savings contributions credit. Attach Form 8880 .	51		
Head of household, $7,550	52	Residential energy credits. Attach Form 5695	52		
	53	Child tax credit (see page 42). Attach Form 8901 if required	53		
	54	Credits from: **a** ☐ Form 8396 **b** ☐ Form 8839 **c** ☐ Form 8859	54		
	55	Other credits: **a** ☐ Form 3800 **b** ☐ Form 8801 **c** ☐ Form _____	55		
	56	Add lines 47 through 55. These are your **total credits**		**56**	
	57	Subtract line 56 from line 46. If line 56 is more than line 46, enter -0- . . . . . . ▶		**57**	
Other Taxes	58	Self-employment tax. Attach Schedule SE		**58**	
	59	Social security and Medicare tax on tip income not reported to employer. Attach Form 4137 .		**59**	
	60	Additional tax on IRAs, other qualified retirement plans, etc. Attach Form 5329 if required .		**60**	
	61	Advance earned income credit payments from Form(s) W-2, box 9		**61**	
	62	Household employment taxes. Attach Schedule H		**62**	
	63	Add lines 57 through 62. This is your **total tax** . . . . ▶		**63**	
Payments	64	Federal income tax withheld from Forms W-2 and 1099 .	64		
	65	2006 estimated tax payments and amount applied from 2005 return	65		
If you have a qualifying child, attach Schedule EIC.	66a	**Earned income credit (EIC)**	66a		
	b	Nontaxable combat pay election ▶ 66b			
	67	Excess social security and tier 1 RRTA tax withheld (see page 60)	67		
	68	Additional child tax credit. Attach Form 8812	68		
	69	Amount paid with request for extension to file (see page 60)	69		
	70	Payments from: **a** ☐ Form 2439 **b** ☐ Form 4136 **c** ☐ Form 8885	70		
	71	Credit for federal telephone excise tax paid. Attach Form 8913 if required	71		
	72	Add lines 64, 65, 66a, and 67 through 71. These are your **total payments** . . . ▶		**72**	
Refund Direct deposit? See page 61 and fill in 74b, 74c, and 74d, or Form 8888.	73	If line 72 is more than line 63, subtract line 63 from line 72. This is the amount you **overpaid**		**73**	
	74a	Amount of line 73 you want **refunded to you.** If Form 8888 is attached, check here ▶ ☐		**74a**	
	▶ b	Routing number |_|_|_|_|_|_|_|_|_| ▶ c Type: ☐ Checking ☐ Savings			
	▶ d	Account number |_|_|_|_|_|_|_|_|_|_|_|_|_|_|_|_|			
	75	Amount of line 73 you want **applied to your 2007 estimated tax** ▶ 75			
Amount You Owe	76	**Amount you owe.** Subtract line 72 from line 63. For details on how to pay, see page 62 ▶		**76**	
	77	Estimated tax penalty (see page 62) 77			

Third Party Designee

Do you want to allow another person to discuss this return with the IRS (see page 63)? ☐ **Yes.** Complete the following. ☐ **No**

Designee's name ▶	Phone no. ▶ ( )	Personal identification number (PIN) ▶ |_|_|_|_|_|

Sign Here
Joint return? See page 17.
Keep a copy for your records.

Under penalties of perjury, I declare that I have examined this return and accompanying schedules and statements, and to the best of my knowledge and belief, they are true, correct, and complete. Declaration of preparer (other than taxpayer) is based on all information of which preparer has any knowledge.

Your signature	Date	Your occupation	Daytime phone number ( )
Spouse's signature. If a joint return, **both** must sign.	Date	Spouse's occupation	

Paid Preparer's Use Only

Preparer's signature ▶	Date	Check if self-employed ☐	Preparer's SSN or PTIN
Firm's name (or yours if self-employed), address, and ZIP code ▶		EIN	
		Phone no. ( )	

Form **1040** (2006)

EXHIBIT 8–3 1040 *(continued)*

APPLICATION **8.2**

Joe and Josie are a married couple with two young children. During the tax year 2005, Josie was in the military and stationed in Iraq. Joe worked out of a labor hall on various construction sites. Joe prepared and filed the tax return for the couple. Although all of Josie's income was combat pay and excludable from income tax, Joe did not know this and reported it as taxable income. Additionally, after the return had been filed, Joe received a W-2 for a job he had done during the same tax year. He did not think it would be that important to report the additional income because the W-2 showed that taxes had been withheld.

About a year after the return was filed, Joe and Josie received a letter form the IRS stating that according to IRS calculations (including the additional W-2) they would not only owe additional tax but also interest and penalties for underpayment of tax because not enough had been withheld. Joe and Josie sought professional tax advice. They filed a 1040-X excluding the combat pay and including the additional W-2. By excluding the combat pay from taxable income, their tax was substantially reduced. Not only were the tax, penalties, and interest abated, but they received a sizable refund.

ASSIGNMENT

Consider the following situations and determine which would be the most appropriate type of return for the taxpayer to file:

1. Cassandra is a 25-year-old single mother with income less than the standard deduction amount. As a result, all of her federally withheld tax is refundable to her.

2. Thomas is married to Kim. Together they have taxable earnings of $101,000. They have no substantial deductions.

3. In June 2006, Jeff decided to file a tax return for the 2005 tax year. The filing deadline was April 15, 2006. Jeff did not obtain an extension or file any tax related documents. Jeff had numerous deductions, including substantial mortgage interest and state tax withholding.

4. In February 2007, Elaine filed her 2006 tax return. In March 2007, she received a substantial refund from the IRS for her 2006 tax return. In April 2007, Elaine received a W-2 from a business where she had worked in January of the previous year. The business had closed and Elaine had forgotten about the W-2 from more than a year before the time that she filed her return.

5. Paisley and Zachary are married with no children. They rent their home. Their combined income for the year was $28,000.

Form **1040X**
(Rev. February 2007)

Department of the Treasury—Internal Revenue Service

Amended U.S. Individual Income Tax Return

▶ See separate instructions.

OMB No. 1545-0074

This return is for calendar year ▶ _____ , or fiscal year ended ▶ _____ , _____ .

Please print or type

Your first name and initial	Last name	Your social security number
If a joint return, spouse's first name and initial	Last name	Spouse's social security number
Home address (no. and street) or P.O. box if mail is not delivered to your home	Apt. no.	Phone number ( )
City, town or post office, state, and ZIP code. If you have a foreign address, see page 3 of the instructions.		

A If the address shown above is different from that shown on your last return filed with the IRS, would you like us to change it in our records? . . . . ▶ ☐ Yes   ☐ No

B Filing status. Be sure to complete this line. **Note.** You cannot change from joint to separate returns after the due date.

On original return ▶ ☐ Single ☐ Married filing jointly ☐ Married filing separately ☐ Head of household ☐ Qualifying widow(er)

On this return ▶ ☐ Single ☐ Married filing jointly ☐ Married filing separately ☐ Head of household* ☐ Qualifying widow(er)

* If the qualifying person is a child but not your dependent, see page 3 of the instructions.

Use Part II on the back to explain any changes		**A. Original amount** or as previously adjusted (see page 3)	**B. Net change—** amount of increase or (decrease)— explain in Part II	**C. Correct amount**
Income and Deductions (see instructions)				
1 Adjusted gross income (see page 3)	**1**			
2 Itemized deductions or standard deduction (see page 3) .	**2**			
3 Subtract line 2 from line 1	**3**			
4 Exemptions. If changing, fill in Parts I and II on the back (see page 4)	**4**			
5 Taxable income. Subtract line 4 from line 3	**5**			
6 Tax (see page 5). Method used in col. C_____	**6**			
7 Credits (see page 5)	**7**			
8 Subtract line 7 from line 6. Enter the result but not less than zero	**8**			
9 Other taxes (see page 5)	**9**			
10 Total tax. Add lines 8 and 9	**10**			
11 Federal income tax withheld and excess social security and tier 1 RRTA tax withheld. If changing, see page 5 . . .	**11**			
12 Estimated tax payments, including amount applied from prior year's return	**12**			
13 Earned income credit (EIC)	**13**			
14 Additional child tax credit from Form 8812	**14**			
15 Credits: Federal telephone excise tax or from Forms 2439, 4136, or 8885	**15**			
16 Amount paid with request for extension of time to file (see page 5)	**16**			
17 Amount of tax paid with original return plus additional tax paid after it was filed	**17**			
18 Total payments. Add lines 11 through 17 in column C	**18**			
Refund or Amount You Owe				
19 Overpayment, if any, as shown on original return or as previously adjusted by the IRS . . .	**19**			
20 Subtract line 19 from line 18 (see page 6)	**20**			
21 **Amount you owe.** If line 10, column C, is more than line 20, enter the difference and see page 6 .	**21**			
22 If line 10, column C, is less than line 20, enter the difference	**22**			
23 Amount of line 22 you want **refunded to you**	**23**			
24 Amount of line 22 you want **applied to your** _____ estimated tax	**24**			

Sign Here
Joint return?
See page 2.
Keep a copy for your records.

Under penalties of perjury, I declare that I have filed an original return and that I have examined this amended return, including accompanying schedules and statements, and to the best of my knowledge and belief, this amended return is true, correct, and complete. Declaration of preparer (other than taxpayer) is based on all information of which the preparer has any knowledge.

▶ Your signature	Date	▶ Spouse's signature. If a joint return, **both** must sign.	Date

Paid Preparer's Use Only

Preparer's signature ▶	Date	Check if self-employed ☐	Preparer's SSN or PTIN
Firm's name (or yours if self-employed), address, and ZIP code ▶		EIN	
		Phone no. ( )	

For Paperwork Reduction Act Notice, see page 6 of instructions.   Cat. No. 11360L   Form **1040X** (Rev. 2-2007)

EXHIBIT 8–4 1040-X *(continues)*

Form 1040X (Rev. 2-2007)   Page **2**

Part I **Exemptions.** See Form 1040 or 1040A instructions.

Complete this part **only** if you are:

- Increasing or decreasing the number of exemptions claimed on line 6d of the return you are amending, or
- Increasing or decreasing the exemption amount for housing individuals displaced by Hurricane Katrina.

		A. Original number of exemptions reported or as previously adjusted	B. Net change	C. Correct number of exemptions
25	Yourself and spouse	25		
	Caution. If someone can claim you as a dependent, you cannot claim an exemption for yourself.			
26	Your dependent children who lived with you	26		
27	Your dependent children who did not live with you due to divorce or separation	27		
28	Other dependents	28		
29	Total number of exemptions. Add lines 25 through 28	29		
30	Multiply the number of exemptions claimed on line 29 by the amount listed below for the tax year you are amending. Enter the result here and on line 4.			

Tax year	Exemption amount	But see the instructions for line 4 on page 3 if the amount on line 1 is over:
2006	$3,300	$112,875
2005	3,200	109,475
2004	3,100	107,025
2003	3,050	104,625

		30
31	If you are claiming an exemption amount for housing individuals displaced by Hurricane Katrina, enter the amount from Form 8914, line 2 for 2005 or line 6 for 2006 (see instructions for line 4)	31
32	Add lines 30 and 31. Enter the result here and on line 4	32

33 Dependents (children and other) not claimed on original (or adjusted) return:

(a) First name Last name	(b) Dependent's social security number	(c) Dependent's relationship to you	(d) ✓ if qualifying child for child tax credit (see page 6)	No. of children on 33 who:
			☐	• lived with you . . ► ☐
			☐	• **did not** live with you due to divorce or separation (see page 6) . ► ☐
			☐	
			☐	Dependents on 33 not entered above ► ☐
			☐	

Part II **Explanation of Changes**

Enter the line number from the front of the form for each item you are changing and give the reason for each change. Attach only the supporting forms and schedules for the items changed. If you do not attach the required information, your Form 1040X may be returned. Be sure to include your name and social security number on any attachments.

If the change relates to a net operating loss carryback or a general business credit carryback, attach the schedule or form that shows the year in which the loss or credit occurred. See page 2 of the instructions. Also, check here . . . . . . ► ☐

_____

_____

_____

_____

_____

Part III **Presidential Election Campaign Fund.** Checking below will not increase your tax or reduce your refund.

If you did not previously want $3 to go to the fund but now want to, check here . . . . ► ☐
If a joint return and your spouse did not previously want $3 to go to the fund but now wants to, check here . . . ► ☐

Form **1040X** (Rev. 2-2007)

EXHIBIT 8–4 1040-X *(continued)*

B. SUPPORTING SCHEDULES

A supporting schedule generally is attached to the return. This is contrary to most information forms, worksheets, and forms used in computation of a tax, deduction, or credit. Although the return contains the total amounts of various sources of income, deductions, and credits, the supporting schedule contains the information that is not generally included on the return but is used to reach these totals. And, in the event of an audit, the information documents are used to explain the information in the supporting documents. Consider the example shown in Application 8.3.

1. Schedule A—Itemized Deductions

This schedule is one of the most commonly employed. As discussed previously, the IRS provides two options with regard to the amount of deduction taken to allow for generalized living expenses. First is the standard deduction. All taxpayers are entitled to reduce their income by this amount and exclude it from federal tax liability. However, many taxpayers expend much more than this on the categories of expenditures covered by the deduction. For them, it may make more sense to itemize their deductions specifically. This is the second option and is accomplished by completing Schedule A.

The categories that can be used to sustain the deduction claimed on Schedule A are fairly limited and succinct. They include the following:

- Medical Expenses that exceed a stated amount of the adjusted gross income
- State Income Tax or, as an alternative, State Sales Tax paid
- Personal Property Tax
- Real Property Tax
- Mortgage Interest, Investment Interest, Points
- Charitable Contributions (subject to rules of substantiation)

APPLICATION **8.3**

Sheila is retired. Throughout her life, she made numerous investments. Annually, she receives 1099-INT forms from 10 different bank accounts. She also receives 1099-DIV from three separate corporations and a brokerage firm that handles some of her money. She uses the information documents to enter the proper information on the supporting form Schedule B. The amounts on Schedule B are then computed to determine the amount that is treated as taxable income and/or a deduction. Those final amounts are then transferred onto Sheila's individual tax return.

- Miscellaneous expenses such as unreimbursed employee expenses in amounts exceeding 2 percent of the adjusted gross income, tax preparation fees, gambling losses (to the extent of winnings), and casualty and theft losses.

Each of these is subject to rules and limitations that must be satisfied in order to lawfully claim the deduction. However, if the total amount exceeds the standard deduction, it can result in a lesser tax liability for the taxpayer.

2. Schedule B—Interest and Dividend Income

This schedule is used to report interest and dividend income that has been received by the taxpayer (as opposed to amounts paid out) through the year. Typically, most of these items will be reported to the taxpayer on information documents 1099-DIV and 1099-INT. Although the information documents are not filed with the return, the content is placed on Schedule B and submitted with the return. The failure to receive information documents does not relieve the taxpayer of the responsibility to report the income and pay any tax that might be due. Because individuals often receive multiple forms 1099-DIV and 1099-INT from different investments, Schedule B allows for the reporting of all of them on a single document. Schedule B supports and provides additional information about the total amount reported.

Schedule B is not necessary if the only interest and dividends reported are less than a specified amount. Most recently, the amount used by the IRS has been $400. In this instance, the interest and dividends are reported as miscellaneous income along with other similar small income items. If the total amount received exceeds the IRS stated amount for this type of income, then Schedule B is used. The schedule is divided into separate parts for interest and dividends. The interest section requires the source, the amount, whether any of it is tax exempt, and the type of interest such as ordinary interest received on bank accounts, and so on. The taxable amounts from all sources are then combined for a total that is reported on the return.

The dividend portion of the schedule is used only to report amounts received as dividends for shares owned by the taxpayer. It is not the appropriate place to report the tax effects of stock transactions such as sales of shares of stocks reported on a separate schedule. As discussed earlier in the text, corporations often distribute a percentage of the profits by declaring a dividend in a stated amount for each share of stock. That amount is then multiplied by the number of shares a taxpayer owns and the result is then paid to the taxpayer. It is not necessary for the dividend to actually be paid out in order for it to become taxable. For example, many stockholders have their dividends automatically applied toward the purchase of additional shares. Even though the taxpayer does not see the actual money from the dividend, the benefit of that is received in the form of additional stock. Consequently, it may be treated as taxable income. The exception is if the investment is in something that has tax exempt status in which case it is not taxable.

SCHEDULES A&B		**Schedule A—Itemized Deductions**		OMB No. 1545-0074
(Form 1040)		(Schedule B is on back)		20**06**
Department of the Treasury Internal Revenue Service (99)		► Attach to Form 1040. ► See Instructions for Schedules A&B (Form 1040).		Attachment Sequence No. 07
Name(s) shown on Form 1040				Your social security number

Medical and Dental Expenses		Caution. Do not include expenses reimbursed or paid by others.		
	1	Medical and dental expenses (see page A-1) . . .	1	
	2	Enter amount from Form 1040, line 38 __2__		
	3	Multiply line 2 by 7.5% (.075).	3	
	4	Subtract line 3 from line 1. If line 3 is more than line 1, enter -0-		4
Taxes You Paid (See page A-3.)	5	State and local income taxes	5	
	6	Real estate taxes (see page A-3)	6	
	7	Personal property taxes	7	
	8	Other taxes. List type and amount ►....................	8	
	9	Add lines 5 through 8		9
Interest You Paid (See page A-3.)	10	Home mortgage interest and points reported to you on Form 1098	10	
	11	Home mortgage interest not reported to you on Form 1098. If paid to the person from whom you bought the home, see page A-3 and show that person's name, identifying no., and address ►		
Note. Personal interest is not deductible.			11	
	12	Points not reported to you on Form 1098. See page A-4 for special rules	12	
	13	Investment interest. Attach Form 4952 if required. (See page A-4.)	13	
	14	Add lines 10 through 13		14
Gifts to Charity If you made a gift and got a benefit for it, see page A-4.	15	Gifts by cash or check. If you made any gift of $250 or more, see page A-5	15	
	16	Other than by cash or check. If any gift of $250 or more, see page A-5. You **must** attach Form 8283 if over $500	16	
	17	Carryover from prior year	17	
	18	Add lines 15 through 17		18
Casualty and Theft Losses	19	Casualty or theft loss(es). Attach Form 4684. (See page A-6.)		19
Job Expenses and Certain Miscellaneous Deductions (See page A-6.)	20	Unreimbursed employee expenses—job travel, union dues, job education, etc. Attach Form 2106 or 2106-EZ if required. (See page A-6.) ►.............................	20	
	21	Tax preparation fees.	21	
	22	Other expenses—investment, safe deposit box, etc. List type and amount ►.............................	22	
	23	Add lines 20 through 22	23	
	24	Enter amount from Form 1040, line 38 __24__		
	25	Multiply line 24 by 2% (.02)	25	
	26	Subtract line 25 from line 23. If line 25 is more than line 23, enter -0-		26
Other Miscellaneous Deductions	27	Other—from list on page A-7. List type and amount ►.............................		27
Total Itemized Deductions	28	Is Form 1040, line 38, over $150,500 (over $75,250 if married filing separately)?		
		☐ **No.** Your deduction is not limited. Add the amounts in the far right column for lines 4 through 27. Also, enter this amount on Form 1040, line 40. ►		28
		☐ **Yes.** Your deduction may be limited. See page A-7 for the amount to enter.		
	29	If you elect to itemize deductions even though they are less than your standard deduction, check here ► ☐		

For Paperwork Reduction Act Notice, see Form 1040 instructions.   Cat. No. 11330X   Schedule A (Form 1040) 2006

EXHIBIT 8–5   Schedule A

Schedules A&B (Form 1040) 2006   OMB No. 1545-0074   Page **2**

Name(s) shown on Form 1040. Do not enter name and social security number if shown on other side.   **Your social security number**

Schedule B—Interest and Ordinary Dividends   Attachment Sequence No. **08**

			Amount
Part I **Interest** (See page B-1 and the instructions for Form 1040, line 8a.)	**1**	List name of payer. If any interest is from a seller-financed mortgage and the buyer used the property as a personal residence, see page B-1 and list this interest first. Also, show that buyer's social security number and address ▶	
			1
Note. If you received a Form 1099-INT, Form 1099-OID, or substitute statement from a brokerage firm, list the firm's name as the payer and enter the total interest shown on that form.			
	2	Add the amounts on line 1	**2**
	3	Excludable interest on series EE and I U.S. savings bonds issued after 1989. Attach Form 8815	**3**
	4	Subtract line 3 from line 2. Enter the result here and on Form 1040, line 8a ▶	**4**

Note. If line 4 is over $1,500, you must complete Part III.

			Amount
Part II **Ordinary Dividends** (See page B-1 and the instructions for Form 1040, line 9a.)	**5**	List name of payer ▶	
			5
Note. If you received a Form 1099-DIV or substitute statement from a brokerage firm, list the firm's name as the payer and enter the ordinary dividends shown on that form.			
	6	Add the amounts on line 5. Enter the total here and on Form 1040, line 9a . ▶	**6**

Note. If line 6 is over $1,500, you must complete Part III.

Part III **Foreign Accounts and Trusts** (See page B-2.)	You must complete this part if you **(a)** had over $1,500 of taxable interest or ordinary dividends; or **(b)** had a foreign account; or **(c)** received a distribution from, or were a grantor of, or a transferor to, a foreign trust.	Yes	No
	7a At any time during 2006, did you have an interest in or a signature or other authority over a financial account in a foreign country, such as a bank account, securities account, or other financial account? See page B-2 for exceptions and filing requirements for Form TD F 90-22.1.		
	b If "Yes," enter the name of the foreign country ▶		
	8 During 2006, did you receive a distribution from, or were you the grantor of, or transferor to, a foreign trust? If "Yes," you may have to file Form 3520. See page B-2		

For Paperwork Reduction Act Notice, see Form 1040 instructions.   Schedule B (Form 1040) 2006

EXHIBIT 8–6   Schedule B

Dividends are reported in a similar fashion as interest. Each dividend source is identified along with the amount and type of transaction. Some dividends known as "qualified" dividends may be subject to a different tax rate. Typically, the 1099-DIV will identify whether any or all of the dividends are qualified. Then, like interest, the taxable amounts on the dividend portion are computed and the total is transferred to the return.

3. Schedule C—Self-Employment Income

Unlike corporations that file separate returns to report the activities of the business, the sole proprietor includes all business activity on the individual tax return. However, in order to properly determine the amount of tax due or deduction on a personal business endeavor, it is necessary to account for the various expenses of the business that affect the net profits. Not all expenses are deductible. However, most ordinary and common business expenses ranging from rent to the costs of inventory are applied against the income of the business to reach the net taxable profit, or in some cases a loss. However, it should be noted that if a sole proprietorship results in a loss for several years, the IRS may consider the endeavor a hobby rather than a business in which case the taxable computation changes dramatically. This prevents individuals from claiming deductions year after year for money they have paid out toward what is more a hobby than a genuine attempt to produce income. A good rule of thumb is that a business may not suffer a net loss for more than three years of a five-year period without coming under scrutiny.

When an individual works as an independent contractor, he or she may receive a form 1099-MISC. That income is then reported on a Schedule C. However, even if no 1099-MISC is reported, the individual is still obligated to report any income received from a sole proprietorship on a Schedule C. The amounts on Schedule C are different from other schedules because they represent what is considered earned income by a sole proprietor. In many ways, this income is similar to wages reported on a W-2. The significant difference though lies in the payment of Social Security and Medicare taxes. Although an employed individual contributes a share equal to that paid by the employer for these taxes, the sole proprietor as both employer and employee pays both portions of this tax. There is a deduction on the individual tax return for one-half of the amount paid. But this only reduces the amount of income subject to tax; it does not totally eliminate the amount paid for both taxes.

Even though for many the cost of self-employment with regard to taxable income results in fewer dollars, the benefits of owning one's own business outweigh the greater amount of tax that might be paid. And, in some situations, a business may result in a positive tax effect, although this is much less common.

The financial status of a sole proprietorship is reported on the personal return. Schedule C allows the sole proprietor to record the various costs associated with doing business on all aspects. Typical items include a calculation for the cost of goods sold, advertising, rents, professional fees, utilities, and so on. This schedule and

APPLICATION **8.4**

Rose was employed by Acme Manufacturing. She earned $20,000. From this, $1,530 of Rose's income was withheld and paid toward Social Security and Medicare taxes, resulting in a net reduction of take-home pay of $1,530. Her employer was required to match that contribution and also paid $1,530 into Rose's Social Security and Medicare accounts. Now assume that Rose was a sole proprietor. Her net profit that she generated and took out of the business was $20,000. As a sole proprietor, Rose paid $3,060 to Social Security (both the employer and employee portion).

Assume further that Rose was single, with no dependents or other credits. Her taxable income would be calculated like this:

	As an employee	As a sole proprietor
Wages	$20,000	Income $20,000
less personal exemption	3,100	3,100
less social security deduction		1,550
less itemized deduction	4,900	4,900
taxable income	12,000	10,450
tax owed	1,200	1,045

Rose owed more tax as an employed person than a sole proprietor. However, take into account the following facts: Through the year as an employee, Rose paid $1,530 out of her $20,000 income toward Social Security and Medicare. This left her with income of $18,470 to pay tax of $1,200, resulting in a net income of $17,270. As a sole proprietor, Rose paid $3,060 toward Social Security and Medicare. This left her with income of $16,940 to pay tax of $1,045, resulting in a net income of $15,895. This was a full $1,375 less in disposable income.

supporting forms can even be used to calculate a deduction for the business use of a portion of one's primary residence. Once all of the expenses are applied to the gross profit, a net taxable income can be determined. This amount is used to calculate the Social Security and Medicare tax due. It is also transferred onto the personal return. Additionally, once the Social Security and Medicare amounts are determined, the total can be entered on the return as well as the deduction for one-half of that amount used in determining taxable income as demonstrated in Application 8.4. Very small or simple sole proprietorships can file the relatively new, and much less complicated, Schedule C-EZ.

SCHEDULE C
(Form 1040)

Department of the Treasury
Internal Revenue Service   (99)

Profit or Loss From Business
(Sole Proprietorship)

▶ **Partnerships, joint ventures, etc., must file Form 1065 or 1065-B.**
▶ **Attach to Form 1040, 1040NR, or 1041.** ▶ **See Instructions for Schedule C (Form 1040).**

OMB No. 1545-0074

2006

Attachment
Sequence No. **09**

Name of proprietor

Social security number (SSN)

A	Principal business or profession, including product or service (see page C-2 of the instructions)	B Enter code from pages C-8, 9, & 10 ▶

C	Business name. If no separate business name, leave blank.	D Employer ID number (EIN), if any

E   Business address (including suite or room no.) ▶
     City, town or post office, state, and ZIP code

F   Accounting method: **(1)** ☐ Cash   **(2)** ☐ Accrual   **(3)** ☐ Other (specify) ▶

G   Did you "materially participate" in the operation of this business during 2006? If "No," see page C-3 for limit on losses   ☐ Yes   ☐ No

H   If you started or acquired this business during 2006, check here   .   .   .   .   ▶ ☐

Part I   Income

1	Gross receipts or sales. **Caution.** If this income was reported to you on Form W-2 and the "Statutory employee" box on that form was checked, see page C-3 and check here . . . . . ▶ ☐	1	
2	Returns and allowances	2	
3	Subtract line 2 from line 1	3	
4	Cost of goods sold (from line 42 on page 2)	4	
5	**Gross profit.** Subtract line 4 from line 3	5	
6	Other income, including federal and state gasoline or fuel tax credit or refund (see page C-3) . . .	6	
7	**Gross income.** Add lines 5 and 6 . . . . ▶	7	

Part II   Expenses. Enter expenses for business use of your home **only** on line 30.

8	Advertising	8		18	Office expense	18	
9	Car and truck expenses (see page C-4)	9		19	Pension and profit-sharing plans	19	
10	Commissions and fees . .	10		20	Rent or lease (see page C-5):		
11	Contract labor (see page C-4)	11			**a** Vehicles, machinery, and equipment .	20a	
12	Depletion	12			**b** Other business property . .	20b	
13	Depreciation and section 179 expense deduction (not included in Part III) (see page C-4)	13		21	Repairs and maintenance . .	21	
				22	Supplies (not included in Part III) .	22	
				23	Taxes and licenses	23	
				24	Travel, meals, and entertainment:		
14	Employee benefit programs (other than on line 19). .	14			**a** Travel	24a	
15	Insurance (other than health) .	15			**b** Deductible meals and entertainment (see page C-6)	24b	
16	Interest:			25	Utilities	25	
a	Mortgage (paid to banks, etc.) .	16a		26	Wages (less employment credits) .	26	
b	Other	16b		27	Other expenses (from line 48 on page 2)	27	
17	Legal and professional services	17					

28	**Total expenses** before expenses for business use of home. Add lines 8 through 27 in columns . ▶	28	

29	Tentative profit (loss). Subtract line 28 from line 7	29	
30	Expenses for business use of your home. Attach **Form 8829**	30	
31	**Net profit or (loss).** Subtract line 30 from line 29.		

• If a profit, enter on both **Form 1040, line 12,** and **Schedule SE, line 2,** or on **Form 1040NR, line 13** (statutory employees, see page C-6). Estates and trusts, enter on Form 1041, line 3.

• If a loss, you **must** go to line 32.

31	

32   If you have a loss, check the box that describes your investment in this activity (see page C-6).

• If you checked 32a, enter the loss on both **Form 1040, line 12,** and **Schedule SE, line 2,** or on **Form 1040NR, line 13** (statutory employees, see page C-6). Estates and trusts, enter on Form 1041, line 3.

• If you checked 32b, you **must** attach **Form 6198.** Your loss may be limited.

32a ☐ All investment is at risk.
32b ☐ Some investment is not at risk.

For Paperwork Reduction Act Notice, see page C-8 of the instructions.   Cat. No. 11334P   Schedule C (Form 1040) 2006

EXHIBIT 8–7   Schedule C and Schedule C-EZ *(continues)*

Schedule C (Form 1040) 2006   Page **2**

Part III   **Cost of Goods Sold** (see page C-7)

33   Method(s) used to value closing inventory: **a** ☐ Cost   **b** ☐ Lower of cost or market   **c** ☐ Other (attach explanation)

34   Was there any change in determining quantities, costs, or valuations between opening and closing inventory? If "Yes," attach explanation   . . . .   ☐ **Yes**   ☐ **No**

35	Inventory at beginning of year. If different from last year's closing inventory, attach explanation . .	**35**	
36	Purchases less cost of items withdrawn for personal use	**36**	
37	Cost of labor. Do not include any amounts paid to yourself	**37**	
38	Materials and supplies	**38**	
39	Other costs	**39**	
40	Add lines 35 through 39	**40**	
41	Inventory at end of year	**41**	
42	**Cost of goods sold.** Subtract line 41 from line 40. Enter the result here and on page 1, line 4 . .	**42**	

Part IV   **Information on Your Vehicle.** Complete this part **only** if you are claiming car or truck expenses on line 9 and are not required to file Form 4562 for this business. See the instructions for line 13 on page C-4 to find out if you must file Form 4562.

43   When did you place your vehicle in service for business purposes? (month, day, year) ▶ . . . . /. . . . . . . /. . . . . .

44   Of the total number of miles you drove your vehicle during 2006, enter the number of miles you used your vehicle for:

a   Business . . . .   **b** Commuting (see instructions) . . . .   **c** Other . . . .

45   Do you (or your spouse) have another vehicle available for personal use? . . . . ☐ **Yes**   ☐ **No**

46   Was your vehicle available for personal use during off-duty hours? . . . . ☐ **Yes**   ☐ **No**

47a   Do you have evidence to support your deduction? . . . . ☐ **Yes**   ☐ **No**

    b   If "Yes," is the evidence written? . . . . ☐ **Yes**   ☐ **No**

Part V   **Other Expenses.** List below business expenses not included on lines 8–26 or line 30.

48	**Total other expenses.** Enter here and on page 1, line 27	**48**

Schedule C (Form 1040) 2006

EXHIBIT 8–7   Schedule C and Schedule C-EZ *(continued)*

SCHEDULE C-EZ (Form 1040)	**Net Profit From Business** (Sole Proprietorship) ▶ Partnerships, joint ventures, etc., must file Form 1065 or 1065-B.	OMB No. 1545-0074 **2006**
Department of the Treasury Internal Revenue Service	▶ Attach to Form 1040, 1040NR, or 1041. ▶ See instructions on back.	Attachment Sequence No. **09A**
Name of proprietor		Social security number (SSN)

Part I General Information

You May Use Schedule C-EZ Instead of Schedule C Only If You:
- Had business expenses of $5,000 or less.
- Use the cash method of accounting.
- Did not have an inventory at any time during the year.
- Did not have a net loss from your business.
- Had only one business as either a sole proprietor or statutory employee.

And You:
- Had no employees during the year.
- Are not required to file **Form 4562**, Depreciation and Amortization, for this business. See the instructions for Schedule C, line 13, on page C-4 to find out if you must file.
- Do not deduct expenses for business use of your home.
- Do not have prior year unallowed passive activity losses from this business.

A Principal business or profession, including product or service

B Enter code from pages C-8, 9, & 10 ▶

C Business name. If no separate business name, leave blank.

D Employer ID number (EIN), if any

E Business address (including suite or room no.). Address not required if same as on page 1 of your tax return.

City, town or post office, state, and ZIP code

Part II Figure Your Net Profit

1 Gross receipts. Caution. If this income was reported to you on Form W-2 and the "Statutory employee" box on that form was checked, see **Statutory Employees** in the instructions for Schedule C, line 1, on page C-3 and check here . . . . ▶ ☐ | **1** |

2 Total expenses (see instructions). If more than $5,000, you **must** use Schedule C . . . . . | **2** |

3 Net profit. Subtract line 2 from line 1. If less than zero, you **must** use Schedule C. Enter on both **Form 1040, line 12,** and **Schedule SE, line 2,** or on **Form 1040NR, line 13.** (Statutory employees **do not** report this amount on Schedule SE, line 2. Estates and trusts, enter on Form 1041, line 3.) . . . . | **3** |

Part III Information on Your Vehicle. Complete this part **only** if you are claiming car or truck expenses on line 2.

4 When did you place your vehicle in service for business purposes? (month, day, year) ▶ .... / .... / ....

5 Of the total number of miles you drove your vehicle during 2006, enter the number of miles you used your vehicle for:

a Business .... **b** Commuting (see instructions) .... **c** Other ....

6 Do you (or your spouse) have another vehicle available for personal use? . . . . ☐ Yes ☐ No

7 Was your vehicle available for personal use during off-duty hours? . . . . ☐ Yes ☐ No

8a Do you have evidence to support your deduction? . . . . ☐ Yes ☐ No

b If "Yes," is the evidence written? . . . . ☐ Yes ☐ No

For Paperwork Reduction Act Notice, see page 2.   Cat. No. 14374D   Schedule C-EZ (Form 1040) 2006

EXHIBIT 8–7 Schedule C and Schedule C-EZ *(continued)*

Instructions

You can use Schedule C-EZ instead of Schedule C if you operated a business or practiced a profession as a sole proprietorship or you were a statutory employee and you have met all the requirements listed in Schedule C-EZ, Part I.

Line A

Describe the business or professional activity that provided your principal source of income reported on line 1. Give the general field or activity and the type of product or service.

Line B

Enter the six-digit code that identifies your principal business or professional activity. See pages C-8 through C-10 of the Instructions for Schedule C for the list of codes.

Line D

You need an employer identification number (EIN) only if you had a qualified retirement plan or were required to file an employment, excise, estate, trust, or alcohol, tobacco, and firearms tax return. If you need an EIN, see the Instructions for Form SS-4. If you do not have an EIN, leave line D blank. Do not enter your SSN.

Line E

Enter your business address. Show a street address instead of a box number. Include the suite or room number, if any.

Line 1

Enter gross receipts from your trade or business. Include amounts you received in your trade or business that were properly shown on Forms 1099-MISC. If the total amounts that were reported in box 7 of Forms 1099-MISC are more than the total you are reporting on line 1, attach a statement explaining the difference. You must show all items of taxable income actually or constructively received during the year (in cash, property, or services). Income is constructively received when it is credited to your account or set aside for you to use. Do not offset this amount by any losses.

Line 2

Enter the total amount of all deductible business expenses you actually paid during the year. Examples of these expenses include advertising, car and truck expenses, commissions and fees, insurance, interest, legal and professional services, office expenses, rent or lease expenses, repairs and maintenance, supplies, taxes, travel, the allowable percentage of business meals and

entertainment, and utilities (including telephone). For details, see the Instructions for Schedule C, Parts II and V, on pages C-3 through C-8. If you wish, you can use the optional worksheet below to record your expenses. Enter on lines **b** through **g** the type and amount of expenses not included on line **a**.

If you claim car or truck expenses, be sure to complete Schedule C-EZ, Part III.

Line 5b

Generally, commuting is travel between your home and a work location. If you converted your vehicle during the year from personal to business use (or vice versa), enter your commuting miles only for the period you drove your vehicle for business. For information on certain travel that is considered a business expense rather than commuting, see the Instructions for Form 2106.

Paperwork Reduction Act Notice. We ask for the information on this form to carry out the Internal Revenue laws of the United States. You are required to give us the information. We need it to ensure that you are complying with these laws and to allow us to figure and collect the right amount of tax.

You are not required to provide the information requested on a form that is subject to the Paperwork Reduction Act unless the form displays a valid OMB control number. Books or records relating to a form or its instructions must be retained as long as their contents may become material in the administration of any Internal Revenue law. Generally, tax returns and return information are confidential, as required by Internal Revenue Code section 6103.

The time needed to complete and file this form will vary depending on individual circumstances. The estimated burden for individual taxpayers filing this form is included in the estimates shown in the instructions for their individual income tax return. The estimated burden for all other taxpayers who file this form is approved under OMB control number 1545-1973 and is shown below.

Recordkeeping . . . . 45 min.
Learning about the law or the form . . . . 4 min.
Preparing the form . . . . 35 min.
Copying, assembling, and sending the form to the IRS . . . . . . 20 min.

If you have comments concerning the accuracy of these time estimates or suggestions for making this form simpler, we would be happy to hear from you. See the instructions for the tax return with which this form is filed.

Optional Worksheet for Line 2 (keep a copy for your records)

a Deductible business meals and entertainment (see pages C-5 and C-6)	a	
b	b	
c	c	
d	d	
e	e	
f	f	
g	g	
h **Total.** Add lines **a** through **g.** Enter here and on line 2	h	

EXHIBIT 8–7   Schedule C and Schedule C-EZ *(continued)*

4. Capital Gains Transactions

Schedule D is used to report transactions that relate to the sale or change in ownership of capital assets. Most property, real or personal, that is held for personal use, pleasure, or investment is considered a capital asset. Typically, this includes things such as stocks, mutual funds, real estate, and so on. When the ownership of property held for investment changes, the transaction may be subject to tax or reduction of tax if the transfer results in financial loss. Depending on the circumstances of the transaction, there may be no tax, capital gains tax, a deduction for a capital loss, or tax on the transaction for which the gain is treated as ordinary income. Factors that affect and determine the type and amount of tax or deduction include things such as the length of time the investment was owned; the reason for the investment such as income, primary residence, and so on; the costs associated with the acquisition, maintenance, and sale of the investment; and the net profit or loss realized on the transaction. Certain types of transactions are also detailed on other forms submitted to the IRS. But Schedule D is the form to be used for the summary and net tax effect for most capital asset transactions conducted during the year by the taxpayer with regard to personally owned property or interests. Information that is necessary to complete the supplemental forms and Schedule D includes the following:

- Date of acquisition
- Date of sale or transfer of ownership
- Cost/basis (amount invested) in the property
- Amount realized from the transaction
- Net profit or loss (sale price/basis)
- Whether depreciation or other tax-related deductions were taken during ownership of the property, and, if so, the amounts.

As mentioned, some capital transactions result in a loss for the taxpayer. There are limitations on some capital transactions in terms of the amount that may be deducted as a loss in a given year; some transactions may require that the remaining portion of the loss be carried over for a limited amount year to year until the entire loss has been deducted. However, such losses can only be taken for certain types of property and thus each transaction should be analyzed.

APPLICATION **8.5**

Randy bought a classic automobile as an investment. He paid $10,000 for the vehicle. He spent an additional $4,000 on restoration. He subsequently sold the vehicle for $24,000. Randy's net gain of $6,000 would be reported on Schedule D. How it would be reported and the potential tax effects would be impacted by whether Randy was regularly engaged in this type of transaction as a business, the length of time he owned the vehicle, and so on?

SCHEDULE D (Form 1040)	Capital Gains and Losses	OMB No. 1545-0074

SCHEDULE D (Form 1040)

Department of the Treasury
Internal Revenue Service   (99)

Capital Gains and Losses

▶ Attach to Form 1040 or Form 1040NR.   ▶ See Instructions for Schedule D (Form 1040).
▶ Use Schedule D-1 to list additional transactions for lines 1 and 8.

OMB No. 1545-0074

2006

Attachment
Sequence No. **12**

Name(s) shown on return

Your social security number

Part I Short-Term Capital Gains and Losses—Assets Held One Year or Less

	(a) Description of property (Example: 100 sh. XYZ Co.)	**(b)** Date acquired (Mo., day, yr.)	**(c)** Date sold (Mo., day, yr.)	**(d)** Sales price (see page D-6 of the instructions)	**(e)** Cost or other basis (see page D-7 of the instructions)	**(f)** Gain or (loss) Subtract (e) from (d)
1						

2	Enter your short-term totals, if any, from Schedule D-1, line 2	**2**		
3	**Total short-term sales price amounts.** Add lines 1 and 2 in column (d)	**3**		
4	Short-term gain from Form 6252 and short-term gain or (loss) from Forms 4684, 6781, and 8824	**4**	
5	Net short-term gain or (loss) from partnerships, S corporations, estates, and trusts from Schedule(s) K-1	**5**	
6	Short-term capital loss carryover. Enter the amount, if any, from line 10 of your **Capital Loss Carryover Worksheet** on page D-7 of the instructions	**6**	( )
7	**Net short-term capital gain or (loss).** Combine lines 1 through 6 in column (f)	**7**	

Part II Long-Term Capital Gains and Losses—Assets Held More Than One Year

	(a) Description of property (Example: 100 sh. XYZ Co.)	**(b)** Date acquired (Mo., day, yr.)	**(c)** Date sold (Mo., day, yr.)	**(d)** Sales price (see page D-6 of the instructions)	**(e)** Cost or other basis (see page D-7 of the instructions)	**(f)** Gain or (loss) Subtract (e) from (d)
8						

9	Enter your long-term totals, if any, from Schedule D-1, line 9	**9**		
10	**Total long-term sales price amounts.** Add lines 8 and 9 in column (d)	**10**		
11	Gain from Form 4797, Part I; long-term gain from Forms 2439 and 6252; and long-term gain or (loss) from Forms 4684, 6781, and 8824	**11**	
12	Net long-term gain or (loss) from partnerships, S corporations, estates, and trusts from Schedule(s) K-1	**12**	
13	Capital gain distributions. See page D-2 of the instructions	**13**	
14	Long-term capital loss carryover. Enter the amount, if any, from line 15 of your **Capital Loss Carryover Worksheet** on page D-7 of the instructions	**14**	( )
15	**Net long-term capital gain or (loss).** Combine lines 8 through 14 in column (f). Then go to Part III on the back	**15**	

For Paperwork Reduction Act Notice, see Form 1040 or Form 1040NR instructions.   Cat. No. 11338H   **Schedule D (Form 1040) 2006**

EXHIBIT 8–8 Schedule D *(continues)*

Schedule D (Form 1040) 2006   Page **2**

Part III   **Summary**

16   Combine lines 7 and 15 and enter the result. If line 16 is a loss, skip lines 17 through 20, and
      go to line 21. If a gain, enter the gain on Form 1040, line 13, or Form 1040NR, line 14. Then go
      to line 17 below   .   .   .   . | **16**

17   Are lines 15 and 16 **both** gains?
      ☐ **Yes.** Go to line 18.
      ☐ **No.** Skip lines 18 through 21, and go to line 22.

18   Enter the amount, if any, from line 7 of the **28% Rate Gain Worksheet** on page D-8 of the
      instructions .   .   .   .   ▶ | **18**

19   Enter the amount, if any, from line 18 of the **Unrecaptured Section 1250 Gain Worksheet** on
      page D-9 of the instructions   .   .   .   .   ▶ | **19**

20   Are lines 18 and 19 **both** zero or blank?
      ☐ **Yes.** Complete Form 1040 through line 43, or Form 1040NR through line 40. Then complete
         the **Qualified Dividends and Capital Gain Tax Worksheet** on page 38 of the Instructions for
         Form 1040 (or in the Instructions for Form 1040NR). **Do not** complete lines 21 and 22 below.

      ☐ **No.** Complete Form 1040 through line 43, or Form 1040NR through line 40. Then complete the
         Schedule D Tax Worksheet on page D-10 of the instructions. **Do not** complete lines 21 and
         22 below.

21   If line 16 is a loss, enter here and on Form 1040, line 13, or Form 1040NR, line 14, the **smaller**
      of:

      • The loss on line 16 or   ⎫
                                         ⎬   .   .   .   . | **21** | (⟩
      • ($3,000), or if married filing separately, ($1,500) ⎭

      Note. When figuring which amount is smaller, treat both amounts as positive numbers.

22   Do you have qualified dividends on Form 1040, line 9b, or Form 1040NR, line 10b?
      ☐ **Yes.** Complete Form 1040 through line 43, or Form 1040NR through line 40. Then complete
         the **Qualified Dividends and Capital Gain Tax Worksheet** on page 38 of the Instructions for
         Form 1040 (or in the Instructions for Form 1040NR).
      ☐ **No.** Complete the rest of Form 1040 or Form 1040NR.

                                                                                   Schedule D (Form 1040) 2006

EXHIBIT 8–8   Schedule D *(continued)*

5. Schedule E—Supplemental Income (Rent/Royalty/Partnership/S-Corporations, Estate, etc.)

A great deal of discussion has already been given throughout the text on the various business entities, the income they generate, and the consequent information forms used to report individual income from these businesses. Because an individual may well have more than one source of income from endeavors such as rental property, creative or productive assets, small businesses, and even estates, a single form has been developed to report these items. Much like all of the taxable wages on multiple W-2 forms for an individual are calculated and reported as a single amount on the tax return, Schedule E allows for a similar compilation of income items from varying sources. Items on Schedule E may or may not be subject to income, Social Security, or Medicare tax. To deal with this, each type of income is calculated separately for these issues. Then, totals are determined and carried from Schedule E to the appropriate locations on the individual tax return.

6. Schedule F—Profit/Loss from Farming

The farm return is often quite distinct from the individual tax return. Unlike Schedule C, which has relatively simple deductions for the self-employed, the deductible expenses and credits associated with farming are often affected by various federal regulations and programs designed to assist those who derive much or all of their income from farming. Farming can include crop or livestock production. The proper preparation of these returns requires a detailed knowledge of all of the applicable legal standards from the IRS and the federal government.

Schedule F summarizes the profits, deductible expenses, and credits associated with a farming operation. The schedule then directs the computations to be used with those figures and results in an amount that is taxable or deductible from the individual return. In some instances, additional forms are used with Schedule F to create the return for the farmer.

7. Schedule H—Household Employment Taxes

Schedule H is one of the few IRS documents whose first task is to identify whether it even needs to be filed. Most forms deal with this issue in the instructions. But the applicability of Schedule H is addressed on the form itself. This document is used not only to support an individual tax return but also may cause the taxpayer to generate other forms. For example, a taxpayer who answers the questions at the beginning of Schedule H in the affirmative also may be required to prepare forms such as a W-2, W-4, 940, 941, and so on. All of these are forms associated with an established employee.

SCHEDULE E
(Form 1040)

Department of the Treasury
Internal Revenue Service (99)

Supplemental Income and Loss

(From rental real estate, royalties, partnerships,
S corporations, estates, trusts, REMICs, etc.)

▶ Attach to Form 1040, 1040NR, or Form 1041. ▶ See Instructions for Schedule E (Form 1040).

OMB No. 1545-0074

2006

Attachment
Sequence No. **13**

Name(s) shown on return

Your social security number

Part I	Income or Loss From Rental Real Estate and Royalties **Note.** If you are in the business of renting personal property, use **Schedule C** or **C-EZ** (see page E-3). Report farm rental income or loss from **Form 4835** on page 2, line 40.

1	List the type and location of each **rental real estate property:**	2	For each rental real estate property listed on line 1, did you or your family use it during the tax year for personal purposes for more than the greater of:	Yes	No
A			• 14 days **or**	A	
B			• 10% of the total days rented at fair rental value?	B	
C			(See page E-3.)	C	

Income:

			Properties			Totals (Add columns A, B, and C.)
			A	B	C	
3	Rents received	3				3
4	Royalties received	4				4

Expenses:

5	Advertising	5				
6	Auto and travel (see page E-4)	6				
7	Cleaning and maintenance	7				
8	Commissions	8				
9	Insurance	9				
10	Legal and other professional fees	10				
11	Management fees	11				
12	Mortgage interest paid to banks, etc. (see page E-4)	12				12
13	Other interest	13				
14	Repairs	14				
15	Supplies	15				
16	Taxes	16				
17	Utilities	17				
18	Other (list) ▶	18				
19	Add lines 5 through 18	19				19
20	Depreciation expense or depletion (see page E-4)	20				20
21	Total expenses. Add lines 19 and 20	21				
22	Income or (loss) from rental real estate or royalty properties. Subtract line 21 from line 3 (rents) or line 4 (royalties). If the result is a (loss), see page E-5 to find out if you must file **Form 6198**	22				
23	Deductible rental real estate loss. **Caution.** Your rental real estate loss on line 22 may be limited. See page E-5 to find out if you must file **Form 8582.** Real estate professionals must complete line 43 on page 2	23	( )	( )	( )	
24	**Income.** Add positive amounts shown on line 22. **Do not** include any losses					24
25	**Losses.** Add royalty losses from line 22 and rental real estate losses from line 23. Enter total losses here					25 ( )
26	**Total rental real estate and royalty income or (loss).** Combine lines 24 and 25. Enter the result here. If Parts II, III, IV, and line 40 on page 2 do not apply to you, also enter this amount on Form 1040, line 17, or Form 1040NR, line 18. Otherwise, include this amount in the total on line 41 on page 2					26

For Paperwork Reduction Act Notice, see page E-7 of the instructions.   Cat. No. 11344L   Schedule E (Form 1040) 2006

EXHIBIT 8–9 Schedule E *(continues)*

Schedule E (Form 1040) 2006   Attachment Sequence No. **13**   Page **2**

Name(s) shown on return. Do not enter name and social security number if shown on other side. | Your social security number

Caution. The IRS compares amounts reported on your tax return with amounts shown on Schedule(s) K-1.

| **Part II** | **Income or Loss From Partnerships and S Corporations**   **Note.** If you report a loss from an at-risk activity for which **any** amount is **not** at risk, you **must** check the box in column **(e)** on line 28 and attach **Form 6198**. See page E-1. |

27   Are you reporting any loss not allowed in a prior year due to the at-risk or basis limitations, a prior year unallowed loss from a passive activity (if that loss was not reported on Form 8582), or unreimbursed partnership expenses?   ☐ Yes   ☐ No
If you answered "Yes," see page E-6 before completing this section.

28	(a) Name	(b) Enter P for partnership; S for S corporation	(c) Check if foreign partnership	(d) Employer identification number	(e) Check if any amount is not at risk
A			☐		☐
B			☐		☐
C			☐		☐
D			☐		☐

	Passive Income and Loss		Nonpassive Income and Loss		
	(f) Passive loss allowed (attach **Form 8582** if required)	(g) Passive income from **Schedule K-1**	(h) Nonpassive loss from **Schedule K-1**	(i) Section 179 expense deduction from **Form 4562**	(j) Nonpassive income from **Schedule K-1**
A					
B					
C					
D					
29a Totals					
b Totals					

30   Add columns (g) and (j) of line 29a   . . . . | **30** |
31   Add columns (f), (h), and (i) of line 29b   . . . . | **31** (   )
32   **Total partnership and S corporation income or (loss).** Combine lines 30 and 31. Enter the result here and include in the total on line 41 below   . . . . | **32** |

| **Part III** | **Income or Loss From Estates and Trusts** |

33	(a) Name	(b) Employer identification number
A		
B		

	Passive Income and Loss		Nonpassive Income and Loss	
	(c) Passive deduction or loss allowed (attach **Form 8582** if required)	(d) Passive income from **Schedule K-1**	(e) Deduction or loss from **Schedule K-1**	(f) Other income from **Schedule K-1**
A				
B				
34a Totals				
b Totals				

35   Add columns (d) and (f) of line 34a   . . . . | **35** |
36   Add columns (c) and (e) of line 34b   . . . . | **36** (   )
37   **Total estate and trust income or (loss).** Combine lines 35 and 36. Enter the result here and include in the total on line 41 below   . . . . | **37** |

| **Part IV** | **Income or Loss From Real Estate Mortgage Investment Conduits (REMICs)—Residual Holder** |

38	(a) Name	(b) Employer identification number	(c) Excess inclusion from Schedules Q, line 2c (see page E-7)	(d) Taxable income (net loss) from **Schedules Q**, line 1b	(e) Income from **Schedules Q**, line 3b

39   Combine columns (d) and (e) only. Enter the result here and include in the total on line 41 below | **39** |

| **Part V** | **Summary** |

40   Net farm rental income or (loss) from **Form 4835.** Also, complete line 42 below   . . . . . | **40** |
41   **Total income or (loss).** Combine lines 26, 32, 37, 39, and 40. Enter the result here and on Form 1040, line 17, or Form 1040NR, line 18 ▶ | **41** |

42   **Reconciliation of farming and fishing income.** Enter your **gross** farming and fishing income reported on Form 4835, line 7; Schedule K-1 (Form 1065), box 14, code B; Schedule K-1 (Form 1120S), box 17, code T; and Schedule K-1 (Form 1041), line 14, code F (see page E-7)   . . . . | **42** |

43   **Reconciliation for real estate professionals.** If you were a real estate professional (see page E-1), enter the net income or (loss) you reported anywhere on Form 1040 or Form 1040NR from all rental real estate activities in which you materially participated under the passive activity loss rules   . | **43** |

Schedule E (Form 1040) 2006

EXHIBIT 8–9   Schedule E *(continued)*

SCHEDULE F
(Form 1040)

Department of the Treasury
Internal Revenue Service   (99)

Profit or Loss From Farming

▶ Attach to Form 1040, Form 1040NR, Form 1041, Form 1065, or Form 1065-B.

▶ See Instructions for Schedule F (Form 1040).

OMB No. 1545-0074

2006

Attachment
Sequence No. **14**

Name of proprietor

Social security number (SSN)

A Principal product. Describe in one or two words your principal crop or activity for the current tax year.

B Enter code from Part IV
▶

C Accounting method: **(1)** ☐ Cash   **(2)** ☐ Accrual

D Employer ID number (EIN), if any

E Did you "materially participate" in the operation of this business during 2006? If "No," see page F-2 for limit on passive losses. ☐ Yes ☐ No

Part I **Farm Income—Cash Method.** Complete Parts I and II (Accrual method. Complete Parts II and III, and Part I, line 11.)
Do not include sales of livestock held for draft, breeding, sport, or dairy purposes. Report these sales on Form 4797.

1	Sales of livestock and other items you bought for resale	1	
2	Cost or other basis of livestock and other items reported on line 1 . . .	2	
3	Subtract line 2 from line 1	**3**	
4	Sales of livestock, produce, grains, and other products you raised	**4**	
5a	Cooperative distributions (Form(s) 1099-PATR)	5a		**5b** Taxable amount	**5b**	
6a	Agricultural program payments (see page F-3) .	6a		**6b** Taxable amount	**6b**	
7	Commodity Credit Corporation (CCC) loans (see page F-3):		
a	CCC loans reported under election	**7a**	
b	CCC loans forfeited	7b		**7c** Taxable amount	**7c**	
8	Crop insurance proceeds and federal crop disaster payments (see page F-3):		
a	Amount received in 2006	8a		**8b** Taxable amount	**8b**	
c	If election to defer to 2007 is attached, check here ▶ ☐	**8d** Amount deferred from 2005		**8d**	
9	Custom hire (machine work) income	**9**	
10	Other income, including federal and state gasoline or fuel tax credit or refund (see page F-3)	**10**	
11	**Gross income.** Add amounts in the right column for lines 3 through 10. If you use the accrual method, enter the amount from Part III, line 51 . . . . ▶	**11**	

Part II **Farm Expenses—Cash and Accrual Method.**
Do not include personal or living expenses such as taxes, insurance, or repairs on your home.

12	Car and truck expenses (see page F-4). Also attach **Form 4562** . .	**12**		25	Pension and profit-sharing plans	**25**	
13	Chemicals	**13**		26	Rent or lease (see page F-5):		
14	Conservation expenses (see page F-4)	**14**		a	Vehicles, machinery, and equipment	**26a**	
15	Custom hire (machine work) .	**15**		b	Other (land, animals, etc.) . .	**26b**	
16	Depreciation and section 179 expense deduction not claimed elsewhere (see page F-4) . .	**16**		27	Repairs and maintenance . .	**27**	
				28	Seeds and plants	**28**	
				29	Storage and warehousing . .	**29**	
17	Employee benefit programs other than on line 25	**17**		30	Supplies	**30**	
18	Feed	**18**		31	Taxes	**31**	
19	Fertilizers and lime	**19**		32	Utilities	**32**	
20	Freight and trucking. . . .	**20**		33	Veterinary, breeding, and medicine	**33**	
21	Gasoline, fuel, and oil . . .	**21**		34	Other expenses (specify):		
22	Insurance (other than health) .	**22**		a	....	**34a**	
23	Interest:			b	....	**34b**	
a	Mortgage (paid to banks, etc.)	**23a**		c	....	**34c**	
b	Other	**23b**		d	....	**34d**	
24	Labor hired (less employment credits)	**24**		e	....	**34e**	
				f	....	**34f**	

35	**Total expenses.** Add lines 12 through 34f. If line 34f is negative, see instructions . . . . ▶	**35**	
36	**Net farm profit or (loss).** Subtract line 35 from line 11.		
	• If a profit, enter the profit on **Form 1040, line 18,** and also on **Schedule SE, line 1.** } If you file Form 1040NR, enter the profit on **Form 1040NR, line 19.** • If a loss, you **must** go to line 37. Estates, trusts, and partnerships, see page F-6.	**36**	
37	If you have a loss, you **must** check the box that describes your investment in this activity (see page F-6).		
	• If you checked 37a, enter the loss on **Form 1040, line 18,** and also on **Schedule SE, line 1.** If you file Form 1040NR, enter the loss on **Form 1040NR, line 19.** • If you checked 37b, you **must** attach **Form 6198.** Your loss may be limited. }	**37a** ☐ All investment is at risk. **37b** ☐ Some investment is not at risk.

For Paperwork Reduction Act Notice, see page F-7 of the instructions.   Cat. No. 11346H   Schedule F (Form 1040) 2006

EXHIBIT 8–10 Schedule F *(continues)*

Schedule F (Form 1040) 2006   Page **2**

Part III   **Farm Income—Accrual Method** (see page F-7).
      Do not include sales of livestock held for draft, breeding, sport, or dairy purposes. Report these sales on Form 4797 and do not include this livestock on line 46 below.

38	Sales of livestock, produce, grains, and other products	38	
39a	Cooperative distributions (Form(s) 1099-PATR) 39a	39b Taxable amount	39b
40a	Agricultural program payments 40a	40b Taxable amount	40b
41	Commodity Credit Corporation (CCC) loans:		
a	CCC loans reported under election		41a
b	CCC loans forfeited 41b	41c Taxable amount	41c
42	Crop insurance proceeds		42
43	Custom hire (machine work) income		43
44	Other income, including federal and state gasoline or fuel tax credit or refund		44
45	Add amounts in the right column for lines 38 through 44		45
46	Inventory of livestock, produce, grains, and other products at beginning of the year	46	
47	Cost of livestock, produce, grains, and other products purchased during the year	47	
48	Add lines 46 and 47	48	
49	Inventory of livestock, produce, grains, and other products at end of year	49	
50	Cost of livestock, produce, grains, and other products sold. Subtract line 49 from line 48*		50
51	**Gross income.** Subtract line 50 from line 45. Enter the result here and on Part I, line 11 ▶		51

*If you use the unit-livestock-price method or the farm-price method of valuing inventory and the amount on line 49 is larger than the amount on line 48, subtract line 48 from line 49. Enter the result on line 50. Add lines 45 and 50. Enter the total on line 51 and on Part I, line 11.

Part IV   **Principal Agricultural Activity Codes**

⚠ CAUTION   *File Schedule C (Form 1040) or Schedule C-EZ (Form 1040) instead of Schedule F if (a) your principal source of income is from providing agricultural services such as soil preparation, veterinary, farm labor, horticultural, or management for a fee or on a contract basis, or (b) you are engaged in the business of breeding, raising, and caring for dogs, cats, or other pet animals.*

These codes for the Principal Agricultural Activity classify farms by their primary activity to facilitate the administration of the Internal Revenue Code. These six-digit codes are based on the North American Industry Classification System (NAICS).

Select the code that best identifies your primary farming activity and enter the six digit number on page 1, line B.

Crop Production

111100	Oilseed and grain farming
111210	Vegetable and melon farming
111300	Fruit and tree nut farming
111400	Greenhouse, nursery, and floriculture production
111900	Other crop farming

Animal Production

112111	Beef cattle ranching and farming
112112	Cattle feedlots
112120	Dairy cattle and milk production
112210	Hog and pig farming
112300	Poultry and egg production
112400	Sheep and goat farming
112510	Animal aquaculture
112900	Other animal production

Forestry and Logging

113000	Forestry and logging (including forest nurseries and timber tracts)

Schedule F (Form 1040) 2006

EXHIBIT 8–10   Schedule F *(continued)*

Someone working within the household may not be considered by many as an employee in the traditional sense. But, for tax purposes, the IRS may consider a household employee in no different light than someone in a commercial workplace.

The following questions on Schedule H are used to identify whether this or other forms should be generated by the taxpayer:

a. Was any one household employee paid cash wages of $1,400 or more during the calendar year?

b. Was any household employee a spouse, child under age 21, parent, or individual under age 18?

c. Were federal income taxes withheld during the calendar year for any employee?

d. Were cash wages of $1,000 or more in any calendar quart of the preceding two years paid to all household employees combined (excluding payments to spouses, the taxpayer's children under age 21, or the taxpayer's parents)?

Based on the answers to these questions, the taxpayer is guided as to whether Schedule H is necessary. If so, then the appropriate sections should be completed as well as any other indicated tax documents such as a W-2, and so on.

ASSIGNMENT

Consider the following situation. Identify which facts would require use of a particular schedule and identify the appropriate schedule for those facts.

Richard and Peggy were married. Both worked as busy physicians. They employed a full-time nanny to care for their children during the day in their home. They also employed a housekeeper who worked two mornings per week for four hours each morning. The nanny was a cousin of Peggy and turned age 19 on December 31 of the tax year. The housekeeper was not related and aged 66. As part of a plan for their future, Richard and Peggy each contributed money to tax-exempt education funds for their children. They also had investments in the stock market. They buy and sell stocks several times every year. Last year, Richard's parents were killed in an accident. Richard received a large sum of cash as part of the estate. In addition, he and his brother became partners and continued the operations of their deceased parents' dairy farm. As a creative outlet, Peggy writes short stories in her spare time. During the last year, she has had four stories published. She was paid a fee of $500 for one of her stories. Richard and Peggy own their own home, although it is subject to a large mortgage. They are active in their church and contribute 10 percent of their income as a tithe. Richard operates a small orchard from their property and sells the produce to a local market.

SCHEDULE H
(Form 1040)

Department of the Treasury
Internal Revenue Service (99)

Household Employment Taxes

(For Social Security, Medicare, Withheld Income, and Federal Unemployment (FUTA) Taxes)

▶ **Attach to Form 1040, 1040NR, 1040-SS, or 1041.**

▶ **See separate instructions.**

OMB No. 1545-1971

2006

Attachment
Sequence No. **44**

Name of employer

Social security number

Employer identification number

A Did you pay **any one** household employee cash wages of $1,500 or more in 2006? (If any household employee was your spouse, your child under age 21, your parent, or anyone under age 18, see the line A instructions on page H-3 before you answer this question.)

☐ **Yes.** Skip lines B and C and go to line 1.
☐ **No.** Go to line B.

B Did you withhold federal income tax during 2006 for any household employee?

☐ **Yes.** Skip line C and go to line 5.
☐ **No.** Go to line C.

C Did you pay **total** cash wages of $1,000 or more in **any** calendar **quarter** of 2005 or 2006 to **all** household employees? (**Do not** count cash wages paid in 2005 or 2006 to your spouse, your child under age 21, or your parent.)

☐ **No.** **Stop.** Do not file this schedule.
☐ **Yes.** Skip lines 1-9 and go to line 10 on the back. (Calendar year taxpayers having no household employees in 2006 **do not** have to complete this form for 2006.)

Part I   Social Security, Medicare, and Income Taxes

1	Total cash wages subject to social security taxes (see page H-4)	**1**	
2	Social security taxes. Multiply line 1 by 12.4% (.124)	**2**	
3	Total cash wages subject to Medicare taxes (see page H-4) . .	**3**	
4	Medicare taxes. Multiply line 3 by 2.9% (.029)	**4**	
5	Federal income tax withheld, if any	**5**	
6	**Total social security, Medicare, and income taxes.** Add lines 2, 4, and 5	**6**	
7	Advance earned income credit (EIC) payments, if any	**7**	
8	**Net taxes** (subtract line 7 from line 6)	**8**	

9 Did you pay **total** cash wages of $1,000 or more in **any** calendar **quarter** of 2005 or 2006 to household employees? (**Do not** count cash wages paid in 2005 or 2006 to your spouse, your child under age 21, or your parent.)

☐ **No.** **Stop.** Enter the amount from line 8 above on Form 1040, line 62. If you are not required to file Form 1040, see the line 9 instructions on page H-4.

☐ **Yes.** Go to line 10 on the back.

For Privacy Act and Paperwork Reduction Act Notice, see page 7 of the separate instructions.   Cat. No. 12187K   **Schedule H (Form 1040) 2006**

EXHIBIT 8–11   Schedule H *(continues)*

Schedule H (Form 1040) 2006   Page **2**

Part II   **Federal Unemployment (FUTA) Tax**

			Yes	No
10	Are you required to pay unemployment contributions to only one state?	10		
11	Did you pay all state unemployment contributions for 2006 by April 16, 2007? Fiscal year filers, see page H-4.	11		
12	Were all wages that are taxable for FUTA tax also taxable for your state's unemployment tax?	12		

Next: If you checked the **"Yes"** box on **all** the lines above, complete Section A.
If you checked the **"No"** box on **any** of the lines above, skip Section A and complete Section B.

Section A

13   Name of the state where you paid unemployment contributions ▶ ....

14   State reporting number as shown on state unemployment tax return ▶ ....

15   Contributions paid to your state unemployment fund (see page H-4)   **15**

16   Total cash wages subject to FUTA tax (see page H-4)   **16**

17   **FUTA tax.** Multiply line 16 by .008. Enter the result here, skip Section B, and go to line 26   **17**

Section B

18   Complete all columns below that apply (if you need more space, see page H-5):

(a) Name of state	(b) State reporting number as shown on state unemployment tax return	(c) Taxable wages (as defined in state act)	(d) State experience rate period		(e) State experience rate	(f) Multiply col. (c) by .054	(g) Multiply col. (c) by col. (e)	(h) Subtract col. (g) from col. (f). If zero or less, enter -0-.	(i) Contributions paid to state unemployment fund
			From	To					

19   Totals   **19**

20   Add columns (h) and (i) of line 19   **20**

21   Total cash wages subject to FUTA tax (see the line 16 instructions on page H-4)   **21**

22   Multiply line 21 by 6.2% (.062)   **22**

23   Multiply line 21 by 5.4% (.054)   **23**

24   Enter the **smaller** of line 20 or line 23   **24**

25   **FUTA tax.** Subtract line 24 from line 22. Enter the result here and go to line 26   **25**

Part III   **Total Household Employment Taxes**

26   Enter the amount from line 8. If you checked the "Yes" box on line C of page 1, enter -0-   **26**

27   Add line 17 (or line 25) and line 26   **27**

28   Are you required to file Form 1040?
   ☐ **Yes. Stop.** Enter the amount from line 27 above on Form 1040, line 62. **Do not** complete Part IV below.
   ☐ **No.** You may have to complete Part IV. See page H-5 for details.

Part IV   **Address and Signature**—Complete this part **only** if required. See the line 28 instructions on page H-5.

Address (number and street) or P.O. box if mail is not delivered to street address   Apt., room, or suite no.

City, town or post office, state, and ZIP code

Under penalties of perjury, I declare that I have examined this schedule, including accompanying statements, and to the best of my knowledge and belief, it is true, correct, and complete. No part of any payment made to a state unemployment fund claimed as a credit was, or is to be, deducted from the payments to employees.

▶ _____   ▶ _____
Employer's signature   Date

                                                 Schedule H (Form 1040) 2006

EXHIBIT 8–11   Schedule H *(continued)*

C. FREQUENTLY USED SUPPORTING FORMS

The focus of the discussion so far has been on those documents that are required as part of the tax return for the individual taxpayer. The following discussion considers the documents that are necessary to determine what forms will ultimately be required and the amounts to be included on those documents. Many of these forms are referred to as "worksheets." This is because all of the information relevant to the calculations of the taxable amount, gain, loss, deduction, or credit is entered on the form and the appropriate calculations are performed to reach the answer. In this discussion, the actual computations will not be applied. Rather, a brief description of each worksheet will be provided along with applicable exhibits.

1. Capital Transaction Involving Real Estate

In 1997, the method for determining the tax effects of selling real estate changed dramatically. Under the present code, the proceeds from real estate that is occupied as a residence is subject to a substantial exclusion from taxable income. This is almost a total reversal of the previous policy. What this means is that today if the taxpayer sells the primary residence at a profit, a large percentage of that profit may be exempted from income tax. Unfortunately, if the personal residence is sold at a loss, the loss cannot be taken against taxable income on the return. If the property is not the taxpayer's residence but is held for investment, then an entirely different computation is applied to determine gain or loss from investment property.

Someone who transfers an interest in real estate may or may not receive information form 1099-S. If this is received, the taxpayer should make sure that a copy also has been provided to the IRS. Even if one is not received, the taxpayer is not relieved of the obligation to address the sale of property. Most tax software programs and qualified tax professionals use the basic IRS calculations to determine if any of the proceeds of the transactions are taxable. Essentially, if residency requirements are satisfied in terms of occupation and use of the property, a taxpayer is entitled to exclude $250,000 (as of 2006) of profit and double that amount for married couples who meet the requirements. Real estate transactions are a matter of public record and there is no statute of limitations on tax evasion. As a result, if at any point, the IRS would determine that tax on the sale of property was evaded, then all tax, penalties, interest, and possibly criminal sanctions could apply.

For property held as an investment, IRS Form 4797 is used to calculate the tax effects of the transaction. This also may require the use of additional forms that consider such items as whether the property was depreciated, how long it was held, if it was held for personal or business use, and so on. If depreciation is taken on property, then a portion of the value of the property is deducted on the return. If that property is then sold, depreciation is recaptured or added back to determine the actual profit on the transaction.

2. IRS Form 4562—Depreciation

One of the more complicated issues in tax is that of depreciation. In simple terms, depreciation is a concept used to spread the cost of an item over time. It is an allowance for the wear and tear, deterioration, and/or obsolescence of the property. For example, if a computer is purchased for business use, the cost of that computer is not necessarily reported in the year of purchase as a business expense. Because the computer is used over time, the cost can be spread out during that time. In the case of a computer, the cost has been assigned a five-year period by the IRS for depreciation. Various tables indicate the useful life of all sorts of items and real estate. Each year, a computation is done using the tables to determine how much of the cost of the computer can be taken as a depreciation expense on the tax return. As mentioned earlier, if the asset, such as real estate, is sold at a profit, then the depreciation (used up portion of the property) is recaptured or added back to the value of the asset to make a true assessment of its value.

One widely used and special deduction that allows an expense to be taken entirely in one year, in lieu of the depreciation expense, is the Section 179 expense. Both Section 179 expenses and depreciation/amortization of property is calculated on IRS Form 4562. Because of the vast diversity of assets, a number of special rules may apply to specific types of property. As a result, there are numerous IRS publications generated and periodically updated to address more specific questions in terms of property ownership, acquisition, transfer, and so on. For the purposes of this discussion, it is important to note that property used for business purposes may be subject to depreciation and a resulting positive effect on one's taxable income.

When depreciating property, it is important to have all of the necessary information that includes, but may not be limited to, the following:

- Method of acquisition (gift, purchase, inheritance, etc.)
- Cost of acquisition
- Value of improvements to the property
- Date of acquisition
- Date of transfer of ownership to another (if any)
- Value of improvements to the asset
- Type of property
- IRS classification of the property
- Percentage of business use of the property
- Fair market value of the property at the time ownership is transferred from the taxpayer (if any)
- Any applicable special allowances by the IRS
- If a vehicle, miles driven during the year as well as miles driven for business use

Form **4562**	**Depreciation and Amortization**	OMB No. 1545-0172
Department of the Treasury Internal Revenue Service	**(Including Information on Listed Property)** ▶ See separate instructions. ▶ Attach to your tax return.	20**06** Attachment Sequence No. **67**

Name(s) shown on return	Business or activity to which this form relates	Identifying number

Part I   **Election To Expense Certain Property Under Section 179**
Note: *If you have any listed property, complete Part V before you complete Part I.*

1	Maximum amount. See the instructions for a higher limit for certain businesses	**1**	$108,000
2	Total cost of section 179 property placed in service (see instructions)	**2**	
3	Threshold cost of section 179 property before reduction in limitation	**3**	$430,000
4	Reduction in limitation. Subtract line 3 from line 2. If zero or less, enter -0-	**4**	
5	Dollar limitation for tax year. Subtract line 4 from line 1. If zero or less, enter -0-. If married filing separately, see instructions	**5**	

	(a) Description of property	(b) Cost (business use only)	(c) Elected cost
6			

7	Listed property. Enter the amount from line 29	**7**	
8	Total elected cost of section 179 property. Add amounts in column (c), lines 6 and 7	**8**	
9	Tentative deduction. Enter the **smaller** of line 5 or line 8	**9**	
10	Carryover of disallowed deduction from line 13 of your 2005 Form 4562	**10**	
11	Business income limitation. Enter the smaller of business income (not less than zero) or line 5 (see instructions)	**11**	
12	Section 179 expense deduction. Add lines 9 and 10, but do not enter more than line 11 . . .	**12**	
13	Carryover of disallowed deduction to 2007. Add lines 9 and 10, less line 12 ▶	**13**	

Note: *Do not use Part II or Part III below for listed property. Instead, use Part V.*

Part II   **Special Depreciation Allowance and Other Depreciation (Do not** include listed property.) (See instructions.)

14	Special allowance for qualified New York Liberty or Gulf Opportunity Zone property (other than listed property) placed in service during the tax year (see instructions)	**14**	
15	Property subject to section 168(f)(1) election	**15**	
16	Other depreciation (including ACRS)	**16**	

Part III   **MACRS Depreciation (Do not** include listed property.) (See instructions.)

Section A

17	MACRS deductions for assets placed in service in tax years beginning before 2006	**17**	
18	If you are electing to group any assets placed in service during the tax year into one or more general asset accounts, check here . . . . ▶ ☐		

Section B—Assets Placed in Service During 2006 Tax Year Using the General Depreciation System

(a) Classification of property	(b) Month and year placed in service	(c) Basis for depreciation (business/investment use only—see instructions)	(d) Recovery period	(e) Convention	(f) Method	(g) Depreciation deduction
19a 3-year property						
b 5-year property						
c 7-year property						
d 10-year property						
e 15-year property						
f 20-year property						
g 25-year property			25 yrs.		S/L	
h Residential rental property			27.5 yrs.	MM	S/L	
			27.5 yrs.	MM	S/L	
i Nonresidential real property			39 yrs.	MM	S/L	
				MM	S/L	

Section C—Assets Placed in Service During 2006 Tax Year Using the Alternative Depreciation System

20a Class life					S/L	
b 12-year			12 yrs.		S/L	
c 40-year			40 yrs.	MM	S/L	

Part IV   **Summary** (see instructions)

21	Listed property. Enter amount from line 28	**21**	
22	**Total.** Add amounts from line 12, lines 14 through 17, lines 19 and 20 in column (g), and line 21. Enter here and on the appropriate lines of your return. Partnerships and S corporations—see instr.	**22**	
23	For assets shown above and placed in service during the current year, enter the portion of the basis attributable to section 263A costs . . .	**23**	

For Paperwork Reduction Act Notice, see separate instructions.   Cat. No. 12906N   Form **4562** (2006)

EXHIBIT 8–12   Form 4562 *(continues)*

Form 4562 (2006)   Page **2**

Part V   **Listed Property** (Include automobiles, certain other vehicles, cellular telephones, certain computers, and property used for entertainment, recreation, or amusement.)

Note: *For any vehicle for which you are using the standard mileage rate or deducting lease expense, complete **only** 24a, 24b, columns (a) through (c) of Section A, all of Section B, and Section C if applicable.*

Section A—Depreciation and Other Information (Caution: *See the instructions for limits for passenger automobiles.***)**

24a   Do you have evidence to support the business/investment use claimed? ☐ Yes ☐ No   24b If "Yes," is the evidence written? ☐ Yes ☐ No

(a) Type of property (list vehicles first)	(b) Date placed in service	(c) Business/ investment use percentage	(d) Cost or other basis	(e) Basis for depreciation (business/investment use only)	(f) Recovery period	(g) Method/ Convention	(h) Depreciation deduction	(i) Elected section 179 cost
25 Special allowance for qualified New York Liberty or Gulf Opportunity Zone property placed in service during the tax year and used more than 50% in a qualified business use (see instructions)					25			
26 Property used more than 50% in a qualified business use:								
		%						
		%						
		%						
27 Property used 50% or less in a qualified business use:								
		%			S/L –			
		%			S/L –			
		%			S/L –			
28 Add amounts in column (h), lines 25 through 27. Enter here and on line 21, page 1. . .					28			
29 Add amounts in column (i), line 26. Enter here and on line 7, page 1.							29	

Section B—Information on Use of Vehicles

Complete this section for vehicles used by a sole proprietor, partner, or other "more than 5% owner," or related person.
If you provided vehicles to your employees, first answer the questions in Section C to see if you meet an exception to completing this section for those vehicles.

		(a) Vehicle 1		(b) Vehicle 2		(c) Vehicle 3		(d) Vehicle 4		(e) Vehicle 5		(f) Vehicle 6	
30	Total business/investment miles driven during the year (**do not** include commuting miles)												
31	Total commuting miles driven during the year												
32	Total other personal (noncommuting) miles driven												
33	Total miles driven during the year. Add lines 30 through 32												
		Yes	No	Yes	No	Yes	No	Yes	No	Yes	No	Yes	No
34	Was the vehicle available for personal use during off-duty hours?												
35	Was the vehicle used primarily by a more than 5% owner or related person?												
36	Is another vehicle available for personal use?												

Section C—Questions for Employers Who Provide Vehicles for Use by Their Employees

Answer these questions to determine if you meet an exception to completing Section B for vehicles used by employees who **are not** more than 5% owners or related persons (see instructions).

		Yes	No
37	Do you maintain a written policy statement that prohibits all personal use of vehicles, including commuting, by your employees?		
38	Do you maintain a written policy statement that prohibits personal use of vehicles, except commuting, by your employees? See the instructions for vehicles used by corporate officers, directors, or 1% or more owners		
39	Do you treat all use of vehicles by employees as personal use?		
40	Do you provide more than five vehicles to your employees, obtain information from your employees about the use of the vehicles, and retain the information received?		
41	Do you meet the requirements concerning qualified automobile demonstration use? (See instructions.)		
	Note: *If your answer to 37, 38, 39, 40, or 41 is "Yes," do not complete Section B for the covered vehicles.*		

Part VI   **Amortization**

(a) Description of costs	(b) Date amortization begins	(c) Amortizable amount	(d) Code section	(e) Amortization period or percentage	(f) Amortization for this year
42 Amortization of costs that begins during your 2006 tax year (see instructions):					
43 Amortization of costs that began before your 2006 tax year			43		
44 **Total.** Add amounts in column (f). See the instructions for where to report			44		

Form **4562** (2006)

EXHIBIT 8-12   Form 4562 *(continued)*

3. Earned Income Credit (EIC) Worksheet

The earned income credit is an incentive for low-income taxpayers to work. Based on the marital status and whether the taxpayer has dependent children, the credit may produce additional income for the taxpayer. The credit works on an arc-type scale. For those earning the least amount of income, the amount of the credit is lower. As the earned income rises, so does the credit to a certain point. After that point, as the taxpayer begins to earn income that would raise him or her above the government established poverty level, the amount of the credit begins to decline. For those without dependent qualifying children, the credit is only available for workers from age 25 to age 65. For those with dependent qualifying children, the lower age limit is lifted. The credit is not available to those with married-filing-separate status. The credit is not available to those who did not reside legally in the United States for at least one-half of the year and for those who can be claimed as a dependent of another. There are a number of other additional factors to consider, such as whether the taxpayer was in the military and had combat pay, or whether the dependent is a child by adoption or birth or a qualifying relative or foster child.

The earned income credit is also a credit that can be claimed in advance through an employer if the employee qualifies. However, this advance payment is calculated on a number of assumptions. If any of these change during the year, it could result in the required return of advance payments. IRS individual tax return instructions as well as IRS Pub. 596 contain a worksheet that can be used to calculate whether a taxpayer is eligible for the earned income credit and if so, how much credit can be received. More detailed discussion is provided for this credit in subsequent chapters.

4. IRS Form 2106 and Other Employee Business Expenses

It is not at all uncommon for an employee to incur expenses associated with employment. In some instances, if these expenses are not reimbursed, they may be deductible against income on the taxpayer's return when calculating taxable income. Ordinary out-of-pocket and unreimbursed expenses may be included on Schedule A as an itemized deduction. However, these are generally subject to a subtraction of 2 percent of the amount of adjusted gross income in order to calculate the deductible amount. Additional deductions may be entered on form 2106 for use of a vehicle, travel, meals, and entertainment related to business. The 2106 totals are also included on Schedule A. There are a number of variables that must be considered when determining if an employee should file a 2106. Because of this, the IRS has developed a flowchart for use by employees. On the 2106 flowchart, a series of questions is asked. Based on the answers, the employee will be able to decide if a 2106 is appropriate.

IF the type of reimbursement (or other expense allowance) arrangement is under:	THEN the employer reports on Form W-2:	AND the employee reports on Form 2106: *
An accountable plan with:		
Actual expense reimbursement: Adequate accounting made and excess returned.	No amount.	No amount.
Actual expense reimbursement: Adequate accounting and return of excess both required but excess not returned.	The excess amount as wages in box 1.	No amount.
Per diem or mileage allowance up to the federal rate: Adequate accounting made and excess returned.	No amount.	All expenses and reimbursements only if excess expenses are claimed. Otherwise, form is not filed.
Per diem or mileage allowance up to the federal rate: Adequate accounting and return of excess both required but excess not returned.	The excess amount as wages in box 1. The amount up to the federal rate is reported only in box 12—it is not reported in box 1.	No amount.
Per diem or mileage allowance exceeds the federal rate: Adequate accounting up to the federal rate only and excess not returned.	The excess amount as wages in box 1. The amount up to the federal rate is reported only in box 12—it is not reported in box 1.	All expenses (and reimbursement reported on Form W-2, box 12) only if expenses in excess of the federal rate are claimed. Otherwise, form is not required.
A nonaccountable plan with:		
Either adequate accounting or return of excess, or both, not required by plan	The entire amount as wages in box 1.	All expenses.
No reimbursement plan:	The entire amount as wages in box 1.	All expenses.
* You may be able to use Form 2106-EZ. See *Completing Forms 2106 and 2106-EZ.*		

EXHIBIT 8–13   Form 2106 Flowchart

Form 2106

Department of the Treasury
Internal Revenue Service (99)

Employee Business Expenses

▶ See separate instructions.

▶ Attach to Form 1040 or Form 1040NR.

OMB No. 1545-0074

2006

Attachment
Sequence No. **54**

Your name	Occupation in which you incurred expenses	Social security number

Part I   Employee Business Expenses and Reimbursements

Step 1 Enter Your Expenses		Column A Other Than Meals and Entertainment	Column B Meals and Entertainment
1	Vehicle expense from line 22 or line 29. (Rural mail carriers: See instructions.)	1	
2	Parking fees, tolls, and transportation, including train, bus, etc., that **did not** involve overnight travel or commuting to and from work . .	2	
3	Travel expense while away from home overnight, including lodging, airplane, car rental, etc. **Do not** include meals and entertainment .	3	
4	Business expenses not included on lines 1 through 3. **Do not** include meals and entertainment.	4	
5	Meals and entertainment expenses (see instructions)	5	
6	**Total expenses.** In Column A, add lines 1 through 4 and enter the result. In Column B, enter the amount from line 5	6	

Note: *If you were not reimbursed for any expenses in Step 1, skip line 7 and enter the amount from line 6 on line 8.*

Step 2   Enter Reimbursements Received From Your Employer for Expenses Listed in Step 1

7	Enter reimbursements received from your employer that were **not** reported to you in box 1 of Form W-2. Include any reimbursements reported under code "L" in box 12 of your Form W-2 (see instructions)	7	

Step 3   Figure Expenses To Deduct on Schedule A (Form 1040)

8	Subtract line 7 from line 6. If zero or less, enter -0-. However, if line 7 is greater than line 6 in Column A, report the excess as income on Form 1040, line 7 (or on Form 1040NR, line 8) . . .	8	
	Note: *If **both columns** of line 8 are zero, you cannot deduct employee business expenses. Stop here and attach Form 2106 to your return.*		
9	In Column A, enter the amount from line 8. In Column B, multiply line 8 by 50% (.50). (Employees subject to Department of Transportation (DOT) hours of service limits: Multiply meal expenses incurred while away from home on business by 75% (.75) instead of 50%. For details, see instructions.)	9	
10	Add the amounts on line 9 of both columns and enter the total here. **Also, enter the total on Schedule A (Form 1040), line 20** (or on Schedule A (Form 1040NR), line 9). (Reservists, qualified performing artists, fee-basis state or local government officials, and individuals with disabilities: See the instructions for special rules on where to enter the total.) . . . . ▶	10	

For Paperwork Reduction Act Notice, see instructions.   Cat. No. 11700N   Form **2106** (2006)

EXHIBIT 8–14   Form 2106 *(continues)*

Form 2106 (2006)   Page **2**

Part II	**Vehicle Expenses**		

Section A—General Information (You must complete this section if you are claiming vehicle expenses.)

			(a) Vehicle 1	**(b)** Vehicle 2
11	Enter the date the vehicle was placed in service	11	/ /	/ /
12	Total miles the vehicle was driven during 2006	12	miles	miles
13	Business miles included on line 12	13	miles	miles
14	Percent of business use. Divide line 13 by line 12	14	%	%
15	Average daily roundtrip commuting distance.	15	miles	miles
16	Commuting miles included on line 12	16	miles	miles
17	Other miles. Add lines 13 and 16 and subtract the total from line 12. . .	17	miles	miles
18	Do you (or your spouse) have another vehicle available for personal use?		☐ Yes ☐ No
19	Was your vehicle available for personal use during off-duty hours?		☐ Yes ☐ No
20	Do you have evidence to support your deduction?.		☐ Yes ☐ No
21	If "Yes," is the evidence written?.		☐ Yes ☐ No

Section B—Standard Mileage Rate (See the instructions for Part II to find out whether to complete this section or Section C.)

22	Multiply line 13 by 44.5¢ (.445)	22	

Section C—Actual Expenses		**(a)** Vehicle 1		**(b)** Vehicle 2	
23	Gasoline, oil, repairs, vehicle insurance, etc.	23			
24a	Vehicle rentals	24a			
b	Inclusion amount (see instructions) .	24b			
c	Subtract line 24b from line 24a .	24c			
25	Value of employer-provided vehicle (applies only if 100% of annual lease value was included on Form W-2—see instructions)	25			
26	Add lines 23, 24c, and 25 . .	26			
27	Multiply line 26 by the percentage on line 14 . . .	27			
28	Depreciation (see instructions) .	28			
29	Add lines 27 and 28. Enter total here and on line 1	29			

Section D—Depreciation of Vehicles (Use this section only if you owned the vehicle and are completing Section C for the vehicle.)

			(a) Vehicle 1		**(b)** Vehicle 2	
30	Enter cost or other basis (see instructions)	30				
31	Enter section 179 deduction (see instructions)	31				
32	Multiply line 30 by line 14 (see instructions if you claimed the section 179 deduction or special allowance)	32				
33	Enter depreciation method and percentage (see instructions) .	33				
34	Multiply line 32 by the percentage on line 33 (see instructions) . .	34				
35	Add lines 31 and 34	35				
36	Enter the applicable limit explained in the line 36 instructions	36				
37	Multiply line 36 by the percentage on line 14 . . .	37				
38	Enter the **smaller** of line 35 or line 37. If you skipped lines 36 and 37, enter the amount from line 35. Also enter this amount on line 28 above .	38				

Form **2106** (2006)

EXHIBIT 8–14 Form 2106 *(continued)*

5. IRS Form 2441—Child and Dependent Care Expenses

The credit for child and dependent care expenses is used to encourage individuals to work or look for work. It allows a credit against actual tax liability (rather than a deduction) for a portion of the money spent on items such as day care for children, and care for other dependents such as disabled children or adults. As the income increases, the amount of the credit decreases. Although it is not a dollar credit per dollar spent, it does provide some financial relief. The credit is fairly broad in its definition. Expenses subject to credit may be incurred not only for very young children but also for children under age 13, as well as for disabled individuals, including children, spouses, parents, and others for whom the taxpayer is responsible. Although the credit cannot be applied to items such as clothing or entertainment, it can be used to offset the expenses of items such as primary care, cooking, and cleaning that are necessary for the well being and protection of the child or dependent.

One item that is important to understand is that anyone who claims the credit in turn implies income to the party who provided the care. For example, a grandmother who provides care for a grandchild while parents work is entirely acceptable. However, if the grandmother accepts payment for the care and those payments are reported for the Child and Dependent Care Expense credit, the grandmother, in turn, would be accountable for the amounts received as income on her own tax return. To avoid abuse of the credit, it is required that the tax identification or Social Security number of the care provider along with other identifying information be included on the form.

The Child and Dependent Care Expense is claimed on IRS Form 2441. The form requires identifying information for the taxpayer, qualifying child or dependent, and care provider. Additionally, the form allows for a calculation of the credit. It is important to note that money received specifically for this expense from an employer or other entity, such as a government agency that provides dependent care benefits, cannot be used in the calculation unless those amounts have been reported as income to the taxpayer. For example, if a working mother receives a dependent care benefit allowance of $1,000 per year from her employer, she cannot claim $1,000 of the money spent on child care unless she added that $1,000 to her gross income subject to tax.

Form **2441**

Department of the Treasury
Internal Revenue Service (99)

Child and Dependent Care Expenses

▶ Attach to Form 1040 or Form 1040NR.

▶ See separate instructions.

OMB No. 1545-0074

20**06**

Attachment
Sequence No. **21**

Name(s) shown on return	Your social security number

Before you begin: You need to understand the following terms. See **Definitions** on page 1 of the instructions.

- **Dependent Care Benefits**
- **Qualifying Person(s)**
- **Qualified Expenses**

Part I **Persons or Organizations Who Provided the Care**—You **must** complete this part.
(If you need more space, use the bottom of page 2.)

1	(a) Care provider's name	(b) Address (number, street, apt. no., city, state, and ZIP code)	(c) Identifying number (SSN or EIN)	(d) Amount paid (see instructions)

Did you receive **dependent care benefits?**

— No ──────▶ Complete only Part II below.

— Yes ──────▶ Complete Part III on the back next.

Caution. If the care was provided in your home, you may owe employment taxes. See the instructions for Form 1040, line 62, or Form 1040NR, line 57.

Part II Credit for Child and Dependent Care Expenses

2   Information about your **qualifying person(s).** If you have more than two qualifying persons, see the instructions.

(a) Qualifying person's name		(b) Qualifying person's social security number	(c) Qualified expenses you incurred and paid in 2006 for the person listed in column (a)
First	Last		

3   Add the amounts in column (c) of line 2. **Do not** enter more than $3,000 for one qualifying person or $6,000 for two or more persons. If you completed Part III, enter the amount from line 33 . . . .   **3**

4   Enter your **earned income.** See instructions **4**

5   If married filing jointly, enter your spouse's earned income (if your spouse was a student or was disabled, see the instructions); **all others,** enter the amount from line 4 . . .   **5**

6   Enter the **smallest** of line 3, 4, or 5 . . . .   **6**

7   Enter the amount from Form 1040, line 38, or Form 1040NR, line 36 . . . .   **7**

8   Enter on line 8 the decimal amount shown below that applies to the amount on line 7

If line 7 is:				If line 7 is:			
Over	But not over	Decimal amount is		Over	But not over	Decimal amount is	
$0—15,000		.35		$29,000—31,000		.27	
15,000—17,000		.34		31,000—33,000		.26	
17,000—19,000		.33		33,000—35,000		.25	
19,000—21,000		.32		35,000—37,000		.24	
21,000—23,000		.31		37,000—39,000		.23	
23,000—25,000		.30		39,000—41,000		.22	
25,000—27,000		.29		41,000—43,000		.21	
27,000—29,000		.28		43,000—No limit		.20	

8   × .

9   Multiply line 6 by the decimal amount on line 8. If you paid 2005 expenses in 2006, see the instructions **9**

10   Enter the amount from Form 1040, line 46, minus any amount on Form 1040, line 47, or Form 1040NR, line 43, minus any amount on Form 1040NR, line 44 . . . .   **10**

11   **Credit for child and dependent care expenses.** Enter the **smaller** of line 9 or line 10 here and on Form 1040, line 48, or Form 1040NR, line 45 . . . .   **11**

For Paperwork Reduction Act Notice, see page 4 of the instructions.   Cat. No. 11862M   Form **2441** (2006)

EXHIBIT 8–15 Form 2441 (continues)

Form 2441 (2006)   Page **2**

Part III Dependent Care Benefits

12	Enter the total amount of **dependent care benefits** you received in 2006. Amounts you received as an employee should be shown in box 10 of your Form(s) W-2. **Do not** include amounts reported as wages in box 1 of Form(s) W-2. If you were self-employed or a partner, include amounts you received under a dependent care assistance program from your sole proprietorship or partnership **12**	
13	Enter the amount, if any, you carried over from 2005 and used in 2006 during the grace period. See instructions **13**	
14	Enter the amount, if any, you forfeited or carried forward to 2007. See instructions . . **14**	( )
15	Combine lines 12 through 14. See instructions **15**	
16	Enter the total amount of **qualified expenses** incurred in 2006 for the care of the **qualifying person(s)** . . **16**	
17	Enter the **smaller** of line 15 or 16 . . . . **17**	
18	Enter your **earned income.** See instructions . . . **18**	
19	Enter the amount shown below that applies to you. • If married filing jointly, enter your spouse's earned income (if your spouse was a student or was disabled, see the instructions for line 5). • If married filing separately, see the instructions for the amount to enter. • All others, enter the amount from line 18. **19**	
20	Enter the **smallest** of line 17, 18, or 19 . . . . . **20**	
21	Enter the amount from line 12 that you received from your sole proprietorship or partnership. If you did not receive any such amounts, enter -0- **21**	
22	Subtract line 21 from line 15 . . . . **22**	
23	Enter $5,000 ($2,500 if married filing separately **and** you were required to enter your spouse's earned income on line 19) **23**	
24	**Deductible benefits.** Enter the **smallest** of line 20, 21, or 23. Also, include this amount on the appropriate line(s) of your return. See instructions **24**	
25	Enter the **smaller** of line 20 or 23 . . . . **25**	
26	Enter the amount from line 24 . . . . **26**	
27	**Excluded benefits.** Subtract line 26 from line 25. If zero or less, enter -0- **27**	
28	**Taxable benefits.** Subtract line 27 from line 22. If zero or less, enter -0-. Also, include this amount on Form 1040, line 7, or Form 1040NR, line 8. On the dotted line next to Form 1040, line 7, or Form 1040NR, line 8, enter "DCB". **28**	

To claim the child and dependent care
credit, complete lines 29–33 below.

29	Enter $3,000 ($6,000 if two or more qualifying persons) **29**	
30	Add lines 24 and 27 . . . . **30**	
31	Subtract line 30 from line 29. If zero or less, **stop.** You cannot take the credit. **Exception.** If you paid 2005 expenses in 2006, see the instructions for line 9 . . . **31**	
32	Complete line 2 on the front of this form. **Do not** include in column (c) any benefits shown on line 30 above. Then, add the amounts in column (c) and enter the total here . . . **32**	
33	Enter the **smaller** of line 31 or 32. Also, enter this amount on line 3 on the front of this form and complete lines 4–11 . . . . **33**	

Form **2441** (2006)

EXHIBIT 8–15   Form 2441 (continued)

6. Form 3903—Moving Expenses

There is a deduction allowed for individuals who move a substantial distance for reasons related to employment. Before the deduction is made available, however, the taxpayer must meet certain tests. First, the new workplace must be a sufficient distance from the old residence. The test requires the taxpayer to enter the distance from the old home and the new home to the workplace. The difference must be greater than 50 miles. For example, Bart lived in City A and drove 85 miles each way to his new job. Bart then moved to City B where he only had to drive 15 miles to his new job. The difference between the two commutes was 60 miles (greater than the required 50). As a result, Bart met the first test to qualify for the moving expense deduction.

The second test involves the amount of time spent working in the new community. The taxpayer is not required to stay at the same job. However, he or she must be employed in the general vicinity of the new job for at least 39 weeks for the 12 months after the move. If the taxpayer is self-employed, he or she must be employed for at least 78 weeks of the first 24 months. The moving expense deduction can be claimed in the year the expense is incurred. However, if the return claiming the deduction is filed and then the taxpayer subsequently fails to meet the employment/time test, it is necessary to account for the deduction. This can be done by amending the return for the year in which the deduction was claimed, or the taxpayer can claim the amount of the deduction as income in the year in which the test was not met. If the taxpayer does not take the deduction, even though eligible, in the year of the move, the return for that year can be amended to include the deduction.

7. Form 4797—Business Gain/Loss

One of the more complicated forms that is used in tax preparation is form 4797. This form is used to document various types of transactions that result in the disposal of business property and the net tax effects. Form 4797 details the transaction, recapture of any depreciation previously claimed, and calculation of whether a gain or loss resulted. At first, it might be simple to assume that if you purchase an item for use in your business at one price and sell it for another, the math would be quite easy to deduce a gain or loss. However, consider the possibilities. What if the item were land, and the taxpayer added a permanent building, and the building was depreciated over time as a separate item. Various improvements were added as well. A portion of the property was for personal use and another portion for business. Some of the improvements were held less than one year before the sale. A natural disaster struck and destroyed 20 percent of the original building. Then the land, building, and improvements were sold for a substantial profit. How is that amount to be calculated and reported for tax purposes? That is where form 4797 comes into play.

Form **3903**	Moving Expenses	OMB No. 1545-0074
Department of the Treasury Internal Revenue Service	▶ Attach to Form 1040 or Form 1040NR.	**20** **06** Attachment Sequence No. **62**

Name(s) shown on return	Your social security number

Before you begin: √ See the **Distance Test** and **Time Test** in the instructions to find out if you can deduct your moving expenses.

√ See **Members of the Armed Forces** on the back, if applicable.

1	Transportation and storage of household goods and personal effects (see instructions) . .	**1**	
2	Travel (including lodging) from your old home to your new home (see instructions). **Do not** include the cost of meals	**2**	
3	Add lines 1 and 2	**3**	
4	Enter the total amount your employer paid you for the expenses listed on lines 1 and 2 that is **not** included in box 1 of your Form W-2 (wages). This amount should be shown in box 12 of your Form W-2 with code **P**	**4**	
5	Is line 3 **more than** line 4?		

☐ **No.** You **cannot** deduct your moving expenses. If line 3 is less than line 4, subtract line 3 from line 4 and include the result on Form 1040, line 7, or Form 1040NR, line 8.

☐ **Yes.** Subtract line 4 from line 3. Enter the result here and on Form 1040, line 26, or Form 1040NR, line 26. This is your **moving expense deduction** . . . . | **5** |

General Instructions

What's New

For 2006, the standard mileage rate for using your vehicle to move to a new home is 18 cents a mile.

Purpose of Form

Use Form 3903 to figure your moving expense deduction for a move related to the start of work at a new principal place of work (workplace). If the new workplace is outside the United States or its possessions, you must be a U.S. citizen or resident alien to deduct your expenses.

If you qualify to deduct expenses for more than one move, use a separate Form 3903 for each move.

For more details, see Pub. 521, Moving Expenses.

Moving Expenses You Can Deduct

You can deduct the reasonable expenses of moving your household goods and personal effects and of traveling from your old home to your new home. Reasonable expenses can include the cost of lodging (but not meals) while traveling to your new home. You cannot deduct the cost of sightseeing trips.

Who Can Deduct Moving Expenses

If you move to a new home because of a new principal workplace, you may be able to deduct your moving expenses whether you are self-employed or an employee. But you must meet both the distance test and time test that follow.

TIP *Members of the Armed Forces may not have to meet the distance test and time test. See instructions on the back.*

Distance Test

Your new principal workplace must be at least 50 miles farther from your old home than your old workplace was. For example, if your old workplace was 3 miles from your old home, your new workplace must be at least 53 miles from that home. If you did not have an old workplace, your new workplace must be at least 50 miles from your old home. The distance between the two points is the shortest of the more commonly traveled routes between them.

TIP *To see if you meet the distance test, you can use the worksheet below.*

Distance Test Worksheet

Keep a Copy for Your Records

1.	Number of miles from your **old home** to your **new workplace**	**1.**	_____	miles
2.	Number of miles from your **old home** to your **old workplace**	**2.**	_____	miles
3.	Subtract line 2 from line 1. If zero or less, enter -0-.	**3.**	_____	miles

Is line 3 at least 50 miles?

☐ **Yes.** You meet this test.

☐ **No.** You do not meet this test. You **cannot** deduct your moving expenses. **Do not** complete Form 3903.

For Paperwork Reduction Act Notice, see back of form.   Cat. No. 12490K   Form **3903** (2006)

EXHIBIT 8–16 Form 3903

Form **4797**

Department of the Treasury
Internal Revenue Service   (99)

Sales of Business Property
(Also Involuntary Conversions and Recapture Amounts
Under Sections 179 and 280F(b)(2))
►Attach to your tax return. ►See separate instructions.

OMB No. 1545-0184

2006

Attachment
Sequence No. **27**

Name(s) shown on return

Identifying number

1   Enter the gross proceeds from sales or exchanges reported to you for 2006 on Form(s) 1099-B or 1099-S (or substitute statement) that you are including on line 2, 10, or 20 (see instructions) **1**

Part I   **Sales or Exchanges of Property Used in a Trade or Business and Involuntary Conversions From Other Than Casualty or Theft—Most Property Held More Than 1 Year** (see instructions)

(a) Description of property	(b) Date acquired (mo., day, yr.)	(c) Date sold (mo., day, yr.)	(d) Gross sales price	(e) Depreciation allowed or allowable since acquisition	(f) Cost or other basis, plus improvements and expense of sale	(g) Gain or (loss) Subtract (f) from the sum of (d) and (e)
2						

3   Gain, if any, from Form 4684, line 42   . . . .   **3**

4   Section 1231 gain from installment sales from Form 6252, line 26 or 37   . . . .   **4**

5   Section 1231 gain or (loss) from like-kind exchanges from Form 8824 .   . . .   **5**

6   Gain, if any, from line 32, from other than casualty or theft **6**

7   Combine lines 2 through 6. Enter the gain or (loss) here and on the appropriate line as follows: **7**

   Partnerships (except electing large partnerships) and S corporations. Report the gain or (loss) following the instructions for Form 1065, Schedule K, line 10, or Form 1120S, Schedule K, line 9. Skip lines 8, 9, 11, and 12 below.

   Individuals, partners, S corporation shareholders, and all others. If line 7 is zero or a loss, enter the amount from line 7 on line 11 below and skip lines 8 and 9. If line 7 is a gain and you did not have any prior year section 1231 losses, or they were recaptured in an earlier year, enter the gain from line 7 as a long-term capital gain on the Schedule D filed with your return and skip lines 8, 9, 11, and 12 below.

8   Nonrecaptured net section 1231 losses from prior years (see instructions) **8**

9   Subtract line 8 from line 7. If zero or less, enter -0-. If line 9 is zero, enter the gain from line 7 on line 12 below. If line 9 is more than zero, enter the amount from line 8 on line 12 below and enter the gain from line 9 as a long-term capital gain on the Schedule D filed with your return (see instructions). **9**

Part II   **Ordinary Gains and Losses** (see instructions)

10   Ordinary gains and losses not included on lines 11 through 16 (include property held 1 year or less):

11   Loss, if any, from line 7 .   . . .   **11** (   )

12   Gain, if any, from line 7 or amount from line 8, if applicable **12**

13   Gain, if any, from line 31   . . . .   **13**

14   Net gain or (loss) from Form 4684, lines 34 and 41a **14**

15   Ordinary gain from installment sales from Form 6252, line 25 or 36   . . . .   **15**

16   Ordinary gain or (loss) from like-kind exchanges from Form 8824   . . . .   **16**

17   Combine lines 10 through 16   . . . .   **17**

18   For all except individual returns, enter the amount from line 17 on the appropriate line of your return and skip lines a and b below. For individual returns, complete lines a and b below:

a   If the loss on line 11 includes a loss from Form 4684, line 38, column (b)(ii), enter that part of the loss here. Enter the part of the loss from income-producing property on Schedule A (Form 1040), line 27, and the part of the loss from property used as an employee on Schedule A (Form 1040), line 22. Identify as from "Form 4797, line 18a." See instructions **18a**

b   Redetermine the gain or (loss) on line 17 excluding the loss, if any, on line 18a. Enter here and on Form 1040, line 14 .   . . .   **18b**

For Paperwork Reduction Act Notice, see separate instructions.   Cat. No. 13086I   Form **4797** (2006)

EXHIBIT 8–17   Form 4797 (continues)

Form 4797 (2006)   Page **2**

Part III   Gain From Disposition of Property Under Sections 1245, 1250, 1252, 1254, and 1255
               (see instructions)

19	**(a)** Description of section 1245, 1250, 1252, 1254, or 1255 property:	**(b)** Date acquired (mo., day, yr.)	**(c)** Date sold (mo., day, yr.)
A			
B			
C			
D			

	These columns relate to the properties on lines 19A through 19D. ▶		**Property A**	**Property B**	**Property C**	**Property D**
20	Gross sales price (**Note:** *See line 1 before completing.*) . .	20				
21	Cost or other basis plus expense of sale	21				
22	Depreciation (or depletion) allowed or allowable	22				
23	Adjusted basis. Subtract line 22 from line 21	23				
24	Total gain. Subtract line 23 from line 20	24				
25	**If section 1245 property:**					
a	Depreciation allowed or allowable from line 22	25a				
b	Enter the **smaller** of line 24 or 25a	25b				
26	**If section 1250 property:** If straight line depreciation was used, enter -0- on line 26g, except for a corporation subject to section 291.					
a	Additional depreciation after 1975 (see instructions) . .	26a				
b	Applicable percentage multiplied by the **smaller** of line 24 or line 26a (see instructions)	26b				
c	Subtract line 26a from line 24. If residential rental property **or** line 24 is not more than line 26a, skip lines 26d and 26e	26c				
d	Additional depreciation after 1969 and before 1976 . . .	26d				
e	Enter the **smaller** of line 26c or 26d	26e				
f	Section 291 amount (corporations only)	26f				
g	Add lines 26b, 26e, and 26f	26g				
27	**If section 1252 property:** Skip this section if you did not dispose of farmland or if this form is being completed for a partnership (other than an electing large partnership).					
a	Soil, water, and land clearing expenses	27a				
b	Line 27a multiplied by applicable percentage (see instructions)	27b				
c	Enter the **smaller** of line 24 or 27b	27c				
28	**If section 1254 property:**					
a	Intangible drilling and development costs, expenditures for development of mines and other natural deposits, and mining exploration costs (see instructions)	28a				
b	Enter the **smaller** of line 24 or 28a	28b				
29	**If section 1255 property:**					
a	Applicable percentage of payments excluded from income under section 126 (see instructions)	29a				
b	Enter the **smaller** of line 24 or 29a (see instructions) . .	29b				

Summary of Part III Gains. Complete property columns A through D through line 29b before going to line 30.

30	Total gains for all properties. Add property columns A through D, line 24	30	
31	Add property columns A through D, lines 25b, 26g, 27c, 28b, and 29b. Enter here and on line 13	31	
32	Subtract line 31 from line 30. Enter the portion from casualty or theft on Form 4684, line 36. Enter the portion from other than casualty or theft on Form 4797, line 6	32	

Part IV   Recapture Amounts Under Sections 179 and 280F(b)(2) When Business Use Drops to 50% or Less
               (see instructions)

			(a) Section 179	**(b)** Section 280F(b)(2)
33	Section 179 expense deduction or depreciation allowable in prior years	33		
34	Recomputed depreciation (see instructions)	34		
35	Recapture amount. Subtract line 34 from line 33. See the instructions for where to report . . .	35		

Form **4797** (2006)

EXHIBIT 8–17   Form 4797 *(continued)*

The first portion of form 4797, Part I, is used to report disposition of business property, other than by casualty or theft, that was held for more than one year. Part II is used to report the disposition of property held less than one year. Part III reports the disposition of very specific types of property. Specifically, it applies to property disposed of under the following IRS regulations:

> Section 1245—Depreciable property held more than one year and sold/exchanged at a gain. (Losses are reported in Part I.)

> Section 1250—Depreciable residential rental property held more than one year and sold/exchanged at a gain. (Losses are reported in Part I.)

> Section 1252—Farmland held less than 10 years (but greater than 1) on which water or land clearing expenses were deducted and for whom the sale/exchange resulted in a gain (Losses are reported in Part I.)

> Section 1255—Disposition of cost-sharing payment property as defined in IRS Section 126.

Other more specific rules apply to the reporting of livestock transactions, and much depends on how the livestock was used and whether it had been raised. Additionally, there are reporting requirements for passive activities such as items not used in a trade or business but held for investment.

Part IV of form 4797 allows the taxpayer to add in the recapture of depreciation previously claimed on property that had been expensed under Section 179. It is also used to recapture depreciation of an asset that is not sold or exchanged but for which the business use drops to less than 50 percent. The key to reporting transactions on form 4797 is to have adequate information about the transaction and to properly place it on the form. The instructions for this form are some of the most detailed for any IRS document and should be consulted thoroughly.

8. Form 5329—Additional Tax on Qualified Plans and Other Tax Favored Accounts

A common misconception among the general public is that retirement funds withdrawn prematurely are only subject to income tax. In an attempt to discourage taxpayers from dipping into their retirement accounts, either through self-funded plans such as Individual Retirement Arrangements (IRAs) or employer plans, there are significant penalties and tax associated with early withdrawals. Even if a withdrawal is made for reasons included within the exceptions to the tax and penalties, these reasons must be properly documented on the return for the year in which the withdrawal was made. This is done via form 5329. This form is used to report additional tax and penalties with regard to distributions from IRAs, other qualified retirement plans such as employment sponsored plans, and self-employment plans, modified endowment contracts, Covered Educational Savings Accounts, Qualified Tuition Plans, Archer Medical Savings Accounts, and Health Savings Accounts.

Generally, form 5329 must be filed with the tax return in the following instances:

- An early distribution was taken from a Roth IRA and the amount reported on form 8606, line 23 is greater than zero, and the amount on form 5329 is greater than zero.

- An early distribution from a qualified retirement plan (other than a Roth IRA) was taken and the 1099-R distribution code in box 7 is not "1" (if "1" is shown and only tax is owed, it can be reported directly on the return).

- Form 1099R box 7 shows code "1," but the taxpayer meets an exception to the tax and penalties on early withdrawal.

- A taxable distribution was made from a Covered Education Savings Account or Qualified Tuition Plan (e.g., 529 plan).

- A distribution was made to withdraw contributions made that exceeded the limit for retirement and educational plans.

- A distribution was made to establish the minimum required distribution based on IRS regulations and plan requirements.

The rules for distributions from the various types of accounts and from one type of account to another are very specific. Any time that such a transfer takes place, it should be properly documented and conveyed in accordance with the time and other requirements imposed to avoid additional tax and penalties. If the distribution is subject to one of the recognized exceptions, such as financial hardship, this too must be properly documented on form 5329 and supported with any necessary additional documentation.

9. Form 6251—Alternative Minimum Tax

Just when the tax code got complicated, it got more complicated. Several years ago, the IRS discovered that some high-income taxpayers with certain types of income and multiple deductions were legally avoiding tax altogether. Enter the Alternative Minimum Tax (AMT). This tax was designed to prevent high-income taxpayers from avoidance in paying their fair share of taxes. Although the objective was originally one of fairness, as income of the general population has risen, along with the cost of living and inflation, the AMT now applies to a record number of taxpayers. Moreover, as various tax programs expire and incomes continue to rise, the number of individuals subjected to the AMT is projected to affect more and more of the public at large.

What is the AMT? Essentially, after each taxpayer calculates his or her taxable income and tax liability, an additional AMT calculation should be performed. This calculation refigures some of the exemptions and deductions and assesses a minimum tax that the taxpayer is presumed to owe. The taxpayer is responsible to pay the higher of the two tax calculations. Obviously, the AMT is not a popular item with most taxpayers. However, as more and more taxpayers are affected, it is something that must be considered for virtually all income levels.

Form **5329**

Department of the Treasury
Internal Revenue Service (99)

**Additional Taxes on Qualified Plans
(Including IRAs) and Other Tax-Favored Accounts**

▶ Attach to Form 1040 or Form 1040NR.
▶ See separate instructions.

OMB No. 1545-0074

20**06**

Attachment
Sequence No. **29**

Name of individual subject to additional tax. If married filing jointly, see instructions.

Your social security number

**Fill in Your Address Only
If You Are Filing This
Form by Itself and Not
With Your Tax Return**

Home address (number and street), or P.O. box if mail is not delivered to your home	Apt. no.
City, town or post office, state, and ZIP code	If this is an amended return, check here ▶ ☐

If you **only** owe the additional 10% tax on early distributions, you may be able to report this tax directly on Form 1040, line 60, or on Form 1040NR, line 55, without filing Form 5329. See the instructions for Form 1040, line 60, or for Form 1040NR, line 55.

Part I   **Additional Tax on Early Distributions**

Complete this part if you took a taxable distribution (other than a qualified hurricane distribution), before you reached age 59½, from a qualified retirement plan (including an IRA) or modified endowment contract (unless you are reporting this tax directly on Form 1040—see above). You may also have to complete this part to indicate that you qualify for an exception to the additional tax on early distributions or for certain Roth IRA distributions (see instructions).

1	Early distributions included in income. For Roth IRA distributions, see instructions	1	
2	Early distributions included on line 1 that are not subject to the additional tax (see instructions). Enter the appropriate exception number from the instructions: _____	2	
3	Amount subject to additional tax. Subtract line 2 from line 1	3	
4	**Additional tax.** Enter 10% (.10) of line 3. Include this amount on Form 1040, line 60, or Form 1040NR, line 55	4	

Caution: *If any part of the amount on line 3 was a distribution from a SIMPLE IRA, you may have to include 25% of that amount on line 4 instead of 10% (see instructions).*

Part II   **Additional Tax on Certain Distributions From Education Accounts**

Complete this part if you included an amount in income, on Form 1040 or Form 1040NR, line 21, from a Coverdell education savings account (ESA) or a qualified tuition program (QTP).

5	Distributions included in income from Coverdell ESAs and QTPs	5	
6	Distributions included on line 5 that are not subject to the additional tax (see instructions) . .	6	
7	Amount subject to additional tax. Subtract line 6 from line 5	7	
8	**Additional tax.** Enter 10% (.10) of line 7. Include this amount on Form 1040, line 60, or Form 1040NR, line 55	8	

Part III   **Additional Tax on Excess Contributions to Traditional IRAs**

Complete this part if you contributed more to your traditional IRAs for 2006 than is allowable or you had an amount on line 17 of your 2005 Form 5329.

9	Enter your excess contributions from line 16 of your 2005 Form 5329 (see instructions). If zero, go to line 15		9	
10	If your traditional IRA contributions for 2006 are less than your maximum allowable contribution, see instructions. Otherwise, enter -0-	10		
11	2006 traditional IRA distributions included in income (see instructions)	11		
12	2006 distributions of prior year excess contributions (see instructions)	12		
13	Add lines 10, 11, and 12		13	
14	Prior year excess contributions. Subtract line 13 from line 9. If zero or less, enter -0-		14	
15	Excess contributions for 2006 (see instructions)		15	
16	Total excess contributions. Add lines 14 and 15		16	
17	**Additional tax.** Enter 6% (.06) of the **smaller** of line 16 **or** the value of your traditional IRAs on December 31, 2006 (including 2006 contributions made in 2007). Include this amount on Form 1040, line 60, or Form 1040NR, line 55		17	

Part IV   **Additional Tax on Excess Contributions to Roth IRAs**

Complete this part if you contributed more to your Roth IRAs for 2006 than is allowable or you had an amount on line 25 of your 2005 Form 5329.

18	Enter your excess contributions from line 24 of your 2005 Form 5329 (see instructions). If zero, go to line 23		18	
19	If your Roth IRA contributions for 2006 are less than your maximum allowable contribution, see instructions. Otherwise, enter -0- . . .	19		
20	2006 distributions from your Roth IRAs (see instructions)	20		
21	Add lines 19 and 20		21	
22	Prior year excess contributions. Subtract line 21 from line 18. If zero or less, enter -0-		22	
23	Excess contributions for 2006 (see instructions)		23	
24	Total excess contributions. Add lines 22 and 23		24	
25	**Additional tax.** Enter 6% (.06) of the **smaller** of line 24 **or** the value of your Roth IRAs on December 31, 2006 (including 2006 contributions made in 2007). Include this amount on Form 1040, line 60, or Form 1040NR, line 55		25	

For Privacy Act and Paperwork Reduction Act Notice, see page 6 of the instructions.   Cat. No. 13329Q   Form **5329** (2006)

EXHIBIT 8–18   Form 5329 *(continues)*

Form 5329 (2006)   Page **2**

Part V   Additional Tax on Excess Contributions to Coverdell ESAs
Complete this part if the contributions to your Coverdell ESAs for 2006 were more than is allowable or you had an amount on line 33 of your 2005 Form 5329.

26	Enter the excess contributions from line 32 of your 2005 Form 5329 (see instructions). If zero, go to line 31	26	
27	If the contributions to your Coverdell ESAs for 2006 were less than the maximum allowable contribution, see instructions. Otherwise, enter -0- **27**		
28	2006 distributions from your Coverdell ESAs (see instructions) **28**		
29	Add lines 27 and 28	29	
30	Prior year excess contributions. Subtract line 29 from line 26. If zero or less, enter -0-	30	
31	Excess contributions for 2006 (see instructions)	31	
32	Total excess contributions. Add lines 30 and 31	32	
33	**Additional tax.** Enter 6% (.06) of the **smaller** of line 32 **or** the value of your Coverdell ESAs on December 31, 2006 (including 2006 contributions made in 2007). Include this amount on Form 1040, line 60, or Form 1040NR, line 55	33	

Part VI   Additional Tax on Excess Contributions to Archer MSAs
Complete this part if you or your employer contributed more to your Archer MSAs for 2006 than is allowable or you had an amount on line 41 of your 2005 Form 5329.

34	Enter the excess contributions from line 40 of your 2005 Form 5329 (see instructions). If zero, go to line 39	34	
35	If the contributions to your Archer MSAs for 2006 are less than the maximum allowable contribution, see instructions. Otherwise, enter -0- **35**		
36	2006 distributions from your Archer MSAs from Form 8853, line 10 . **36**		
37	Add lines 35 and 36	37	
38	Prior year excess contributions. Subtract line 37 from line 34. If zero or less, enter -0-	38	
39	Excess contributions for 2006 (see instructions)	39	
40	Total excess contributions. Add lines 38 and 39	40	
41	**Additional tax.** Enter 6% (.06) of the **smaller** of line 40 **or** the value of your Archer MSAs on December 31, 2006 (including 2006 contributions made in 2007). Include this amount on Form 1040, line 60, or Form 1040NR, line 55	41	

Part VII   Additional Tax on Excess Contributions to Health Savings Accounts (HSAs)
Complete this part if you, someone on your behalf, or your employer contributed more to your HSAs for 2006 than is allowable or you had an amount on line 49 of your 2005 Form 5329.

42	Enter the excess contributions from line 48 of your 2005 Form 5329. If zero, go to line 47 . .	42	
43	If the contributions to your HSAs for 2006 are less than the maximum allowable contribution, see instructions. Otherwise, enter -0- **43**		
44	2006 distributions from your HSAs from Form 8889, line 14 **44**		
45	Add lines 43 and 44	45	
46	Prior year excess contributions. Subtract line 45 from line 42. If zero or less, enter -0-	46	
47	Excess contributions for 2006 (see instructions)	47	
48	Total excess contributions. Add lines 46 and 47	48	
49	**Additional tax.** Enter 6% (.06) of the **smaller** of line 48 **or** the value of your HSAs on December 31, 2006 (including 2006 contributions made in 2007). Include this amount on Form 1040, line 60, or Form 1040NR, line 55	49	

Part VIII   Additional Tax on Excess Accumulation in Qualified Retirement Plans (Including IRAs)
Complete this part if you did not receive the minimum required distribution from your qualified retirement plan.

50	Minimum required distribution for 2006 (see instructions)	50	
51	Amount actually distributed to you in 2006	51	
52	Subtract line 51 from line 50. If zero or less, enter -0-	52	
53	**Additional tax.** Enter 50% (.50) of line 52. Include this amount on Form 1040, line 60, or Form 1040NR, line 55	53	

Signature. Complete **only** if you are filing this form by itself and not with your tax return.

Please Sign Here

Under penalties of perjury, I declare that I have examined this form, including accompanying schedules and statements, and to the best of my knowledge and belief, it is true, correct, and complete. Declaration of preparer (other than taxpayer) is based on all information of which preparer has any knowledge.

▶ Your signature _____   ▶ Date _____

Paid Preparer's Use Only

Preparer's signature ▶	Date	Check if self-employed ☐	Preparer's SSN or PTIN
Firm's name (or yours if self-employed), address, and ZIP code ▶		EIN	
		Phone no. ( )	

Form **5329** (2006)

EXHIBIT 8-18   Form 5329 *(continued)*

Form **6251**

Department of the Treasury
Internal Revenue Service (99)

Alternative Minimum Tax—Individuals

▶ See separate instructions.

▶ Attach to Form 1040 or Form 1040NR.

OMB No. 1545-0074

20**06**

Attachment
Sequence No. **32**

Name(s) shown on Form 1040 or Form 1040NR

Your social security number

Part I   **Alternative Minimum Taxable Income** (See instructions for how to complete each line.)

1	If filing Schedule A (Form 1040), enter the amount from Form 1040, line 41 (minus any amount on Form 8914, line 6), and go to line 2. Otherwise, enter the amount from Form 1040, line 38 (minus any amount on Form 8914, line 6), and go to line 7. (If less than zero, enter as a negative amount.)	1
2	Medical and dental. Enter the **smaller** of Schedule A (Form 1040), line 4, **or** 2½% of Form 1040, line 38	2
3	Taxes from Schedule A (Form 1040), line 9	3
4	Enter the home mortgage interest adjustment, if any, from line 6 of the worksheet on page 2 of the instructions	4
5	Miscellaneous deductions from Schedule A (Form 1040), line 26	5
6	If Form 1040, line 38, is over $150,500 (over $75,250 if married filing separately), enter the amount from line 11 of the **Itemized Deductions Worksheet** on page A-7 of the instructions for Schedule A (Form 1040)	6 ( )
7	Tax refund from Form 1040, line 10 or line 21	7 ( )
8	Investment interest expense (difference between regular tax and AMT)	8
9	Depletion (difference between regular tax and AMT)	9
10	Net operating loss deduction from Form 1040, line 21. Enter as a positive amount	10
11	Interest from specified private activity bonds exempt from the regular tax	11
12	Qualified small business stock (7% of gain excluded under section 1202)	12
13	Exercise of incentive stock options (excess of AMT income over regular tax income)	13
14	Estates and trusts (amount from Schedule K-1 (Form 1041), box 12, code A)	14
15	Electing large partnerships (amount from Schedule K-1 (Form 1065-B), box 6)	15
16	Disposition of property (difference between AMT and regular tax gain or loss)	16
17	Depreciation on assets placed in service after 1986 (difference between regular tax and AMT)	17
18	Passive activities (difference between AMT and regular tax income or loss)	18
19	Loss limitations (difference between AMT and regular tax income or loss)	19
20	Circulation costs (difference between regular tax and AMT)	20
21	Long-term contracts (difference between AMT and regular tax income)	21
22	Mining costs (difference between regular tax and AMT)	22
23	Research and experimental costs (difference between regular tax and AMT)	23
24	Income from certain installment sales before January 1, 1987	24 ( )
25	Intangible drilling costs preference	25
26	Other adjustments, including income-based related adjustments	26
27	Alternative tax net operating loss deduction	27 ( )
28	**Alternative minimum taxable income.** Combine lines 1 through 27. (If married filing separately and line 28 is more than $200,100, see page 7 of the instructions.)	28

Part II   **Alternative Minimum Tax**

29   Exemption. (If this form is for a child under age 18, see page 7 of the instructions.)

IF your filing status is . . .	**AND line 28 is not over . . .**	**THEN enter on line 29 . . .**	
Single or head of household	$112,500	$42,500	
Married filing jointly or qualifying widow(er)	150,000	62,550	29
Married filing separately	75,000	31,275	

If line 28 is **over** the amount shown above for your filing status, see page 7 of the instructions.

30	Subtract line 29 from line 28. If more than zero **or** you are filing Form 2555 or 2555-EZ, go to line 31. If zero or less and you are not filing Form 2555 or 2555-EZ, enter -0- on lines 33 and 35 and skip the rest of Part II	30
31	• If you are filing Form 2555 or 2555-EZ, see page 8 of the instructions for the amount to enter. • If you reported capital gain distributions directly on Form 1040, line 13; you reported qualified dividends on Form 1040, line 9b; **or** you had a gain on both lines 15 and 16 of Schedule D (Form 1040) (as refigured for the AMT, if necessary), complete Part III on the back and enter the amount from line 55 here. • **All others:** If line 30 is $175,000 or less ($87,500 or less if married filing separately), multiply line 30 by 26% (.26). Otherwise, multiply line 30 by 28% (.28) and subtract $3,500 ($1,750 if married filing separately) from the result.	31
32	Alternative minimum tax foreign tax credit (see page 8 of the instructions)	32
33	Tentative minimum tax. Subtract line 32 from line 31	33
34	Tax from Form 1040, line 44 (minus any tax from Form 4972 and any foreign tax credit from Form 1040, line 47). If you used Schedule J to figure your tax, the amount for line 44 of Form 1040 must be refigured without using Schedule J (see page 9 of the instructions)	34
35	**Alternative minimum tax.** Subtract line 34 from line 33. If zero or less, enter -0-. Enter here and on Form 1040, line 45	35

For Paperwork Reduction Act Notice, see page 10 of the instructions.   Cat. No. 13600G   Form **6251** (2006)

EXHIBIT 8–19   Form 6251 (continues)

Form 6251 (2006)   Page **2**

Part III   Tax Computation Using Maximum Capital Gains Rates

36   Enter the amount from Form 6251, line 30 . . . .   **36**

37   Enter the amount from line 6 of the Qualified Dividends and Capital Gain Tax
      Worksheet in the instructions for Form 1040, line 44, or the amount from line
      13 of the Schedule D Tax Worksheet on page D-10 of the instructions for
      Schedule D (Form 1040), whichever applies (as refigured for the AMT, if
      necessary) (see page 10 of the instructions) **37**

38   Enter the amount from Schedule D (Form 1040), line 19 (as refigured for the
      AMT, if necessary) (see page 10 of the instructions) **38**

39   If you did not complete a Schedule D Tax Worksheet for the regular tax or
      the AMT, enter the amount from line 37. Otherwise, add lines 37 and 38, and
      enter the **smaller** of that result or the amount from line 10 of the Schedule
      D Tax Worksheet (as refigured for the AMT, if necessary) **39**

40   Enter the **smaller** of line 36 or line 39 . . . .   **40**

41   Subtract line 40 from line 36 . . . .   **41**

42   If line 41 is $175,000 or less ($87,500 or less if married filing separately), multiply line 41 by 26% (.26).
      Otherwise, multiply line 41 by 28% (.28) and subtract $3,500 ($1,750 if married filing separately) from the
      result . . . . ▶   **42**

43   Enter:
      • $61,300 if married filing jointly or qualifying widow(er),
      • $30,650 if single or married filing separately, or   } - - - - -   **43**
      • $41,050 if head of household.

44   Enter the amount from line 7 of the Qualified Dividends and Capital Gain Tax
      Worksheet in the instructions for Form 1040, line 44, or the amount from line
      14 of the Schedule D Tax Worksheet on page D-10 of the instructions for
      Schedule D (Form 1040), whichever applies (as figured for the regular tax). If
      you did not complete either worksheet for the regular tax, enter -0- . . .   **44**

45   Subtract line 44 from line 43. If zero or less, enter -0- **45**

46   Enter the **smaller** of line 36 or line 37 . . . .   **46**

47   Enter the **smaller** of line 45 or line 46 . . . .   **47**

48   Multiply line 47 by 5% (.05) . . . . ▶   **48**

49   Subtract line 47 from line 46 . . . .   **49**

50   Multiply line 49 by 15% (.15) . . . . ▶   **50**

      If line 38 is zero or blank, skip lines 51 and 52 and go to line 53. Otherwise, go to line 51.

51   Subtract line 46 from line 40 . . . .   **51**

52   Multiply line 51 by 25% (.25) . . . . ▶   **52**

53   Add lines 42, 48, 50, and 52 . . . .   **53**

54   If line 36 is $175,000 or less ($87,500 or less if married filing separately), multiply line 36 by 26% (.26).
      Otherwise, multiply line 36 by 28% (.28) and subtract $3,500 ($1,750 if married filing separately) from the
      result **54**

55   Enter the **smaller** of line 53 or line 54 here and on line 31 . . . .   **55**

Form **6251** (2006)

EXHIBIT 8–19   Form 6251 (continued)

The first part of the AMT calculation is to identify the alternative minimum taxable income. This is done by adjusting various figures in the determination of the ordinary taxable income. For example, the amounts used in the preparation of Schedule A are considered as well as dispositions of property, estate and trust income, net operating losses, and so on. Part II of the form uses different amounts for personal exemptions and then refigures the AMT. Finally, Part III refigures the tax rate imposed on capital gains. As can be seen, the tax most affects items such as mortgage interest, dispositions of property, and investment transactions. These were once items almost exclusively engaged in by the wealthier sector of the population. However, today a large portion of the population is affected by at least some of the items through self-employment, investments, inheritances, and so on. As a result, the AMT is an appropriate calculation to consider for all taxpayers.

10. Form 8283—Non-Cash Charitable Contributions

Schedule A for itemized deductions allows for reducing the amount of taxable income for charitable contributions. Although this does not reduce the tax dollar for dollar, it does reduce the amount of income that is subject to be taxed. Ordinarily, limited monetary contributions can be claimed without proof. Beyond that amount, receipts are necessary to substantiate the contribution. However, many individuals make non-cash contributions. These consist of tangible items and out-of-pocket expenses directly related to the charity such as donations of personal property. Similarly, some perform volunteer work for charities and incur expenses that are never charged to the charity. For example, consider those who, at their own expense, deliver meals through a nonprofit organization to homebound individuals. Although the volunteer work itself is not deductible, the associated expenses such as mileage may well be.

For non-cash contributions and out-of-pocket expenses associated with volunteer work, a limited amount may be included on the return without submitting further detail. Of course, the taxpayer should always maintain adequate records and receipts to support the claim in the event of an audit. Amounts valued more than $500 must be detailed and supported with information included on IRS form 8283. This form requires a great deal of detail to substantiate the deduction. It includes the date the item was acquired, date donated, cost, and **fair market value** at the time of donation, and the method used to reach this amount. Also necessary is the identity of the receiving charity and some documentation by that charity that the contribution was received. As of August 17, 2006, all donations of personal property must be in good or better condition.

■ FAIR MARKET VALUE

The price that a given property or asset would fetch in the marketplace, assuming prospective buyers and sellers are reasonably knowledgeable about the asset; they are behaving in their own best interests and are free of undue pressure to trade.

Many taxpayers do not trouble themselves to identify charitable contributions with a receipt. The thought is that the amount could not be that significant. However, consider the following true illustration:

APPLICATION   8.6

Demitri regularly gave items to a charity that accepted used clothing and household items. His tax preparer asked for a receipt to substantiate the deduction and Demitri had never obtained one. He had no way to prove the donation and thus was unable to claim a deduction. He was advised to do so and maintain a list of his donations. The following year, Demitri came to his tax preparer with receipts and lists in hand for each donation he had made. The amounts were similar to donations he made most years and consisted primarily of used clothing and small household items. When the items on the list were valued based on an IRS-approved tax valuation guide for donated property, the amount came to more than $800. Demitri was in a 15 percent tax bracket. This reduced his taxable income by $800 and his tax owed by $120.

INNOCENT SPOUSE

A co-signer of a joint tax return who is deemed to have been unaware of the understatement of tax made by his or her spouse and thus should not be held liable.

INJURED SPOUSE

A co-signer of a joint tax return whose tax refund is used to pay one spouse's past-due child and/or spousal support, a past-due federal debt, or past-due state income tax. The injured spouse can claim his or her share of the refund using form 8379.

More significant donated items, such as vehicles, artwork, collections, and so on, may require appraisal. Additionally, the appraiser must sign form 8283. Also, the organization is required to acknowledge the donation on form 8283. However, most charitable organizations that regularly receive items of significant value will produce and form 8283 and provide it to the donor who can then attach the form to his or her personal return.

11. Form 8379—Injured Spouse

Unlike the **Innocent Spouse** rule, which allows a spouse to claim exemption from liability for a tax-related debt that was incurred during a period in which a married-filing-joint return was filed, the **Injured Spouse** return seeks relief from other types of debt associated with the spouse and that may or may not have been incurred during the marriage. In recent years, the IRS has accommodated a number of programs by allowing them to attach tax refunds of taxpayers in an attempt to collect overdue payments on things such as child support and student loans. When a lien such as this is placed against a tax return, the refund is paid directly by the IRS to the creditor with the lien at the time the return is filed and the taxpayer never sees the check. Although this has been an effective tool to collect otherwise delinquent accounts, it can have the effect of penalizing a spouse unfairly. Consider the example in Application 8.7.

Form **8283**

(Rev. December 2006)

Department of the Treasury
Internal Revenue Service

Noncash Charitable Contributions

▶ Attach to your tax return if you claimed a total deduction
of over $500 for all contributed property.

▶ See separate instructions.

OMB No. 1545-0908

Attachment
Sequence No. **155**

Name(s) shown on your income tax return

Identifying number

Note. Figure the amount of your contribution deduction before completing this form. See your tax return instructions.

Section A. **Donated Property of $5,000 or Less and Certain Publicly Traded Securities**—List in this section **only** items (or groups of similar items) for which you claimed a deduction of $5,000 or less. Also, list certain publicly traded securities even if the deduction is more than $5,000 (see instructions).

Part I   **Information on Donated Property**—If you need more space, attach a statement.

1	(a) Name and address of the donee organization	(b) Description of donated property (For a donated vehicle, enter the year, make, model, condition, and mileage, and attach Form 1098-C if required.)
A		
B		
C		
D		
E		

Note. If the amount you claimed as a deduction for an item is $500 or less, you do not have to complete columns (d), (e), and (f).

	(c) Date of the contribution	(d) Date acquired by donor (mo., yr.)	(e) How acquired by donor	(f) Donor's cost or adjusted basis	(g) Fair market value (see instructions)	(h) Method used to determine the fair market value
A						
B						
C						
D						
E						

Part II   **Partial Interests and Restricted Use Property**—Complete lines 2a through 2e if you gave less than an entire interest in a property listed in Part I. Complete lines 3a through 3c if conditions were placed on a contribution listed in Part I; also attach the required statement (see instructions).

2a Enter the letter from Part I that identifies the property for which you gave less than an entire interest ▶ _____ .
If Part II applies to more than one property, attach a separate statement.

  b Total amount claimed as a deduction for the property listed in Part I: **(1)** For this tax year   ▶ _____ .
                                                 (2) For any prior tax years   ▶ _____ .

  c Name and address of each organization to which any such contribution was made in a prior year (complete only if different from the donee organization above):

Name of charitable organization (donee)

Address (number, street, and room or suite no.)

City or town, state, and ZIP code

  d For tangible property, enter the place where the property is located or kept ▶ _____
  e Name of any person, other than the donee organization, having actual possession of the property ▶ _____

		Yes	No
3a	Is there a restriction, either temporary or permanent, on the donee's right to use or dispose of the donated property?		
b	Did you give to anyone (other than the donee organization or another organization participating with the donee organization in cooperative fundraising) the right to the income from the donated property or to the possession of the property, including the right to vote donated securities, to acquire the property by purchase or otherwise, or to designate the person having such income, possession, or right to acquire?		
c	Is there a restriction limiting the donated property for a particular use?		

For Paperwork Reduction Act Notice, see separate instructions.   Cat. No. 62299J   Form **8283** (Rev. 12-2006)

EXHIBIT 8–20   Form 8283 *(continues)*

Form 8283 (Rev. 12-2006)　　　　　　　　　　　　　　　　　　　　　　　　　　　　　　Page **2**

Name(s) shown on your income tax return	Identifying number

Section B. Donated Property Over $5,000 (Except Certain Publicly Traded Securities)—List in this section only items (or groups of similar items) for which you claimed a deduction of more than $5,000 per item or group (except contributions of certain publicly traded securities reported in Section A). An appraisal is generally required for property listed in Section B (see instructions).

Part I　Information on Donated Property—To be completed by the taxpayer and/or the appraiser.

4 Check the box that describes the type of property donated:

- ☐ Art* (contribution of $20,000 or more)
- ☐ Art* (contribution of less than $20,000)
- ☐ Collectibles**
- ☐ Qualified Conservation Contribution
- ☐ Other Real Estate
- ☐ Intellectual Property
- ☐ Equipment
- ☐ Securities
- ☐ Other

*Art includes paintings, sculptures, watercolors, prints, drawings, ceramics, antiques, decorative arts, textiles, carpets, silver, rare manuscripts, historical memorabilia, and other similar objects.

**Collectibles include coins, stamps, books, gems, jewelry, sports memorabilia, dolls, etc., but not art as defined above.

Note. In certain cases, you must attach a qualified appraisal of the property. See instructions.

5	(a) Description of donated property (if you need more space, attach a separate statement)	(b) If tangible property was donated, give a brief summary of the overall physical condition of the property at the time of the gift	(c) Appraised fair market value
A			
B			
C			
D			

	(d) Date acquired by donor (mo., yr.)	(e) How acquired by donor	(f) Donor's cost or adjusted basis	(g) For bargain sales, enter amount received	(h) Amount claimed as a deduction	(i) Average trading price of securities
A						
B						
C						
D						

Part II　Taxpayer (Donor) Statement—List each item included in Part I above that the appraisal identifies as having a value of $500 or less. See instructions.

I declare that the following item(s) included in Part I above has to the best of my knowledge and belief an appraised value of not more than $500 (per item). Enter identifying letter from Part I and describe the specific item. See instructions. ▶

Signature of taxpayer (donor) ▶　　　　　　　　　　　　Date ▶

Part III　Declaration of Appraiser

I declare that I am not the donor, the donee, a party to the transaction in which the donor acquired the property, employed by, or related to any of the foregoing persons, or married to any person who is related to any of the foregoing persons. And, if regularly used by the donor, donee, or party to the transaction, I performed the majority of my appraisals during my tax year for other persons.

Also, I declare that I hold myself out to the public as an appraiser or perform appraisals on a regular basis; and that because of my qualifications as described in the appraisal, I am qualified to make appraisals of the type of property being valued. I certify that the appraisal fees were not based on a percentage of the appraised property value. Furthermore, I understand that a false or fraudulent overstatement of the property value as described in the qualified appraisal or this Form 8283 may subject me to the penalty under section 6701(a) (aiding and abetting the understatement of tax liability). In addition, I understand that a substantial or gross valuation misstatement resulting from the appraisal of the value of the property that I know, or reasonably should know, would be used in connection with a return or claim for refund, may subject me to the penalty under section 6695A. I affirm that I have not been barred from presenting evidence or testimony by the Office of Professional Responsibility.

Sign Here　Signature ▶　　　Title ▶　　　Date ▶

Business address (including room or suite no.)　　　Identifying number

City or town, state, and ZIP code

Part IV　Donee Acknowledgment—To be completed by the charitable organization.

This charitable organization acknowledges that it is a qualified organization under section 170(c) and that it received the donated property as described in Section B, Part I, above on the following date ▶

Furthermore, this organization affirms that in the event it sells, exchanges, or otherwise disposes of the property described in Section B, Part I (or any portion thereof) within 3 years after the date of receipt, it will file **Form 8282**, Donee Information Return, with the IRS and give the donor a copy of that form. This acknowledgment does not represent agreement with the claimed fair market value.

Does the organization intend to use the property for an unrelated use? . . . . ▶ ☐ Yes ☐ No

Name of charitable organization (donee)	Employer identification number
Address (number, street, and room or suite no.)	City or town, state, and ZIP code
Authorized signature	Title	Date

Printed on Recycled Paper　　　Form **8283** (Rev. 12-2006)

EXHIBIT 8–20　Form 8283 (continued)

APPLICATION **8.7**

Bob and Barbara are a married couple. Barbara is a homemaker and does not work outside the home. Bob is employed and produces all of the income for the couple. Before their marriage, Barbara attended a two-year community college and borrowed $4,500 in student loans to assist with the expense. After one year, she dropped out. She later married Bob, and took over the care of their home and Bob's two children from a former marriage. She has never worked and never made a single payment on her student loan. This year, the couple anticipated a sizable tax refund. Bob deliberately overwithheld from his wages to ensure a sizable refund because he and Barbara are not very good at saving money on their own. They do not live in a community property state (which has different rules regarding spousal debt). They filed their tax return and were notified that their anticipated refund of $3,500 had been seized to pay Barbara's student loans. Furthermore, they were informed that an additional $3,000 was owed in remaining principal plus interest and would be withheld from future refunds. By filing form 8379 for the current year and future returns, Bob may well be able to avoid seizure of his refunds to satisfy Barbara's debt. This does not remove the item from their credit report and the negative effects associated with it. But Bob should be allowed to recapture his refund.

Form 8379 is very specific in its instructions and provides detailed information about who may be eligible for the relief. Additionally, much of the information used in preparation of the tax return is also necessary to be reported on form 8379, such as income of each party, entitlement to exemptions, taxes withheld, and so on. Once this information is submitted, the IRS will perform the calculations and determine whether any of the refund was that of the Injured Spouse and ineligible for the offset that would otherwise be used to pay the debt.

12. Form 8606—Nondeductible IRAs

With regard to the **Saver's Credit**, some contributions to a retirement plan, including an IRA, can result in additional tax savings for the taxpayer. There is also an additional form of IRA contribution that does not directly result in a taxable income reduction. This is the nontraditional IRA, commonly referred to as a Roth IRA. Also, some contributions to traditional IRAs are not deductible. An example might be someone who contributed a deductible amount to an IRA but who also converted his or her interest in a 401K plan to an IRA. The latter amount would not be a deductible contribution. This occurs fairly frequently as individuals leave an employer in which the taxpayer had been involved in a 401K plan. They are entitled to transfer their interest in the plan to an IRA.

SAVER'S CREDIT

Some contributions to a retirement plan, including an IRA, which can result in additional tax savings for the taxpayer.

Form **8379**

(Rev. January 2006)

Department of the Treasury
Internal Revenue Service

Injured Spouse Allocation

▶ See instructions.

OMB No. 1545-0074

Attachment
Sequence No. **104**

Part I   Information About the Joint Tax Return for Which This Form Is Filed

1   Enter the following information exactly as it is shown on the tax return for which you are filing this form.
The spouse's name and social security number shown first on that tax return must also be shown first below.

First name, initial, and last name shown first on the return	Social security number shown first	If Injured Spouse, check here ▶ ☐
First name, initial, and last name shown second on the return	Social security number shown second	If Injured Spouse, check here ▶ ☐

Note. If you are filing Form 8379 with your tax return, skip to line 5.

2   Enter the tax year for which you are filing this form (for example, 2004) ▶ _____

3   _____
Current home address   City   State   ZIP code

4   Is the address on your joint return different from the address shown above? . . . . ☐ Yes ☐ No

5   Check this box only if you are divorced or separated from the spouse with whom you filed the joint return
and you want your refund issued in your name only . . . . ☐

6   Was your main home in a community property state (Arizona, California, Idaho, Louisiana, Nevada, New
Mexico, Texas, Washington, or Wisconsin) at any time during the year entered on line 2? . . . . . ☐ Yes ☐ No
If "Yes," which community property state(s)? _____
Note. Overpayments affected by state community property laws will be allocated by the IRS according to those laws.

Part II   Allocation Between Spouses of Items on the Joint Tax Return (see instructions)

Allocated Items	(a) Amount shown on joint return	(b) Allocated to injured spouse	(c) Allocated to other spouse
7 Income: **a.** Wages			
b. All other income			
8 Adjustments to income			
9 Standard deduction or Itemized deductions			
10 Number of exemptions			
11 Credits (**do not** include any earned income credit)			
12 Other taxes			
13 Federal income tax withheld			
14 Payments			

Part III   Signature. Complete this part only if you are filing Form 8379 by itself and not with your tax return.

Under penalties of perjury, I declare that I have examined this form and any accompanying schedules or statements and to the best of my knowledge and belief, they are true, correct, and complete. Declaration of preparer (other than taxpayer) is based on all information of which preparer has any knowledge.

Keep a copy of this form for your records	Injured spouse's signature		Date	Phone number (optional) ( )

Paid Preparer's Use Only	Preparer's signature ▶	Date	Check if self-employed ☐	Preparer's SSN or PTIN
	Firm's name (or yours if self-employed), address, and ZIP code ▶		EIN	
			Phone no. ( )	

For Privacy Act and Paperwork Reduction Act Notice, see page 3.   Cat. No. 62474Q   Form **8379** (Rev. 1-2006)

EXHIBIT 8–21   Form 8379

Form **8606**

Department of the Treasury
Internal Revenue Service (99)

Nondeductible IRAs

▶ See separate instructions.

▶ Attach to Form 1040, Form 1040A, or Form 1040NR.

OMB No. 1545-0074

2006

Attachment
Sequence No. **48**

Name. If married, file a separate form for each spouse required to file Form 8606. See page 5 of the instructions.

Your social security number

**Fill in Your Address Only
If You Are Filing This
Form by Itself and Not
With Your Tax Return**

Home address (number and street, or P.O. box if mail is not delivered to your home)

Apt. no.

City, town or post office, state, and ZIP code

Part I   **Nondeductible Contributions to Traditional IRAs and Distributions From Traditional, SEP, and SIMPLE IRAs**

Complete this part only if one or more of the following apply.

- You made nondeductible contributions to a traditional IRA for 2006.
- You took distributions from a traditional, SEP, or SIMPLE IRA in 2006 **and** you made nondeductible contributions to a traditional IRA in 2006 or an earlier year. For this purpose, a distribution does not include a rollover (other than a repayment of a qualified hurricane distribution), qualified charitable distribution, conversion, recharacterization, or return of certain contributions.
- You converted part, but not all, of your traditional, SEP, and SIMPLE IRAs to Roth IRAs in 2006 (excluding any portion you recharacterized) **and** you made nondeductible contributions to a traditional IRA in 2006 or an earlier year.

1	Enter your nondeductible contributions to traditional IRAs for 2006, including those made for 2006 from January 1, 2007, through April 16, 2007 (see page 5 of the instructions)	**1**
2	Enter your total basis in traditional IRAs (see page 5 of the instructions)	**2**
3	Add lines 1 and 2	**3**

In 2006, did you take a distribution from traditional, SEP, or SIMPLE IRAs, or make a Roth IRA conversion?

— No ——▶ Enter the amount from line 3 on line 14. Do not complete the rest of Part I.

— Yes ——▶ Go to line 4.

4	Enter those contributions included on line 1 that were made from January 1, 2007, through April 16, 2007	**4**
5	Subtract line 4 from line 3	**5**
6	Enter the value of **all** your traditional, SEP, and SIMPLE IRAs as of December 31, 2006, plus any outstanding rollovers. Subtract any repayments of qualified hurricane distributions. If the result is zero or less, enter -0- (see page 5 of the instructions)	**6**
7	Enter your distributions from traditional, SEP, and SIMPLE IRAs in 2006. **Do not** include rollovers (other than repayments of qualified hurricane distributions), qualified charitable distributions, conversions to a Roth IRA, certain returned contributions, or recharacterizations of traditional IRA contributions (see page 6 of the instructions). . .	**7**
8	Enter the net amount you converted from traditional, SEP, and SIMPLE IRAs to Roth IRAs in 2006. **Do not** include amounts converted that you later recharacterized (see page 6 of the instructions). Also enter this amount on line 16	**8**
9	Add lines 6, 7, and 8 . . . . **9**	
10	Divide line 5 by line 9. Enter the result as a decimal rounded to at least 3 places. If the result is 1.000 or more, enter "1.000" . . .	**10** ✕ .
11	Multiply line 8 by line 10. This is the nontaxable portion of the amount you converted to Roth IRAs. Also enter this amount on line 17 . . .	**11**
12	Multiply line 7 by line 10. This is the nontaxable portion of your distributions that you did not convert to a Roth IRA	**12**
13	Add lines 11 and 12. This is the nontaxable portion of all your distributions	**13**
14	Subtract line 13 from line 3. This is **your total basis in traditional IRAs for 2006 and earlier years**	**14**
15a	Subtract line 12 from line 7	**15a**
b	Amount on line 15a attributable to qualified hurricane distributions (see page 6 of the instructions). Also enter this amount on Form 8915, line 22	**15b**
c	**Taxable amount.** Subtract line 15b from line 15a. If more than zero, also include this amount on Form 1040, line 15b; Form 1040A, line 11b; or Form 1040NR, line 16b	**15c**

Note: *You may be subject to an additional 10% tax on the amount on line 15c if you were under age 59½ at the time of the distribution (see page 6 of the instructions).*

For Privacy Act and Paperwork Reduction Act Notice, see page 8 of the instructions.   Cat. No. 63966F   Form **8606** (2006)

EXHIBIT 8–22   Form 8606

The form is also used to report certain types of distributions from IRAs after previously making nondeductible contributions. The key to form 8606 is to report transactions that affect the potential tax effects of retirement accounts that typically receive favorable tax treatment at the time of the contribution (traditional) or at the time of distribution (Roth). This includes reporting those accounts that are converted from one type of retirement plan to another. Any of these transactions can have a net effect on taxable income. Form 8606 is used to calculate this and determine if there is any tax or penalty associated with the transactions. Although the government wants to encourage retirement savings, there are very strict rules with respect to retirement account contributions, distributions, and conversions. These are to prevent tax evasion but permit tax avoidance by those taxpayers in the income ranges that are least likely to otherwise contribute to retirement funds and leave the contributions intact until the time of their retirement.

13. Form 8829—Business Use of Home

This form is of limited and specific use. Form 8829 is only for use in conjunctions with the Schedule C filed by individuals who were self-employed during part or all of the year. For individuals who have a home office or who use a part of their home for activities related to employment, the deduction is calculated in association with Schedule A. Form 8829 is used exclusively to support Schedule C for self-employment income. If someone is eligible to use form 8829, the form can be used to claim deductions for a percentage of all of the expenses of maintaining the property, just as those expenses would be deductible from the income of the business if a separate business address were maintained. This includes rent or mortgage interest, utilities, taxes, insurance, maintenance, and so on. For example, if the home office occupies 10 percent of the square footage of the home, then 10 percent of the expenses can be claimed. However, if the home is owned and subject to a mortgage, the amount of mortgage interest claimed on Schedule A—Itemized Deductions cannot include the amount claimed on form 8829, as this would be double-dipping. Another requirement is that the area, whether it is the floor space occupied by a desk or an actual office, must be regularly and exclusively used for business-related activities such as storage of inventory, samples, work space, and so on.

Form 8829 allows the calculation of the business use of home to be done in either of two methods. First, those expenses that are exclusive to the business are reported on the form as "**Direct Expenses.**" Second, those expenses that are included with the rest of the home, such as real property taxes, are reported as "**Indirect Expenses.**" The indirect expenses are then apportioned according to the percentage of the home occupied by business use. Some of the nonbusiness portion of expenses may be deducted on another part of the return such as mortgage interest on Schedule A.

DIRECT EXPENSES

Expenses that are exclusive to the business.

INDIRECT EXPENSES

Expenses that are included with the rest of the home such as real property taxes.

Form **8829**

Department of the Treasury
Internal Revenue Service   (99)

Expenses for Business Use of Your Home

▶ **File only with Schedule C (Form 1040). Use a separate Form 8829 for each home you used for business during the year.**

▶ **See separate instructions.**

OMB No. 1545-0074

20**06**

Attachment
Sequence No. **66**

Name(s) of proprietor(s)

Your social security number

Part I	Part of Your Home Used for Business		
1	Area used regularly and exclusively for business, regularly for daycare, or for storage of inventory or product samples (see instructions)	1	
2	Total area of home	2	
3	Divide line 1 by line 2. Enter the result as a percentage	3	%
	For daycare facilities not used exclusively for business go to line 4. All others go to line 7.		
4	Multiply days used for daycare during year by hours used per day	4 hr.	
5	Total hours available for use during the year (365 days × 24 hours) (see instructions)	5 8,760 hr.	
6	Divide line 4 by line 5. Enter the result as a decimal amount	6 .	
7	Business percentage. For daycare facilities not used exclusively for business, multiply line 6 by line 3 (enter the result as a percentage). All others, enter the amount from line 3 ▶	7	%

Part II	Figure Your Allowable Deduction			
8	Enter the amount from Schedule C, line 29, **plus** any net gain or (loss) derived from the business use of your home and shown on Schedule D or Form 4797. If more than one place of business, see instructions		8	
	See instructions for columns (a) and (b) before completing lines 9–21.	**(a)** Direct expenses	**(b)** Indirect expenses	
9	Casualty losses (see instructions)	9		
10	Deductible mortgage interest (see instructions)	10		
11	Real estate taxes (see instructions)	11		
12	Add lines 9, 10, and 11	12		
13	Multiply line 12, column (b) by line 7		13	
14	Add line 12, column (a) and line 13			14
15	Subtract line 14 from line 8. If zero or less, enter -0-			15
16	Excess mortgage interest (see instructions)	16		
17	Insurance	17		
18	Rent	18		
19	Repairs and maintenance	19		
20	Utilities	20		
21	Other expenses (see instructions)	21		
22	Add lines 16 through 21	22		
23	Multiply line 22, column (b) by line 7		23	
24	Carryover of operating expenses from 2005 Form 8829, line 41		24	
25	Add line 22 in column (a), line 23, and line 24		25	
26	Allowable operating expenses. Enter the **smaller** of line 15 or line 25		26	
27	Limit on excess casualty losses and depreciation. Subtract line 26 from line 15		27	
28	Excess casualty losses (see instructions)	28		
29	Depreciation of your home from Part III below	29		
30	Carryover of excess casualty losses and depreciation from 2005 Form 8829, line 42	30		
31	Add lines 28 through 30		31	
32	Allowable excess casualty losses and depreciation. Enter the **smaller** of line 27 or line 31		32	
33	Add lines 14, 26, and 32		33	
34	Casualty loss portion, if any, from lines 14 and 32. Carry amount to **Form 4684,** Section B		34	
35	Allowable expenses for business use of your home. Subtract line 34 from line 33. Enter here and on Schedule C, line 30. If your home was used for more than one business, see instructions ▶		35	

Part III	Depreciation of Your Home		
36	Enter the **smaller** of your home's adjusted basis or its fair market value (see instructions)	36	
37	Value of land included on line 36	37	
38	Basis of building. Subtract line 37 from line 36	38	
39	Business basis of building. Multiply line 38 by line 7	39	
40	Depreciation percentage (see instructions)	40	%
41	Depreciation allowable (see instructions). Multiply line 39 by line 40. Enter here and on line 29 above	41	

Part IV	Carryover of Unallowed Expenses to 2007		
42	Operating expenses. Subtract line 26 from line 25. If less than zero, enter -0-	42	
43	Excess casualty losses and depreciation. Subtract line 32 from line 31. If less than zero, enter -0-	43	

For Paperwork Reduction Act Notice, see page 4 of separate instructions.   Cat. No. 13232M   Form **8829** (2006)

EXHIBIT 8–23   Form 8829

It is also possible to claim depreciation of the business use area by using Part III of form 8829. However, it is important to keep in mind that when the house is sold, the reporting of the sale to determine whether there is tax on any profit will require that the depreciation be added back in as a recapture of value. In some situations, it is possible that this could ultimately result in capital gains taxes on the sale of the property. As a result, before claiming depreciation, the potential effects of a sale of the property in the future should be considered.

14. Child Tax Credits

The child tax credits assist families with children who are generally too young to assist with personal or family finances. The child tax credit allows a dollar for dollar credit against tax owed by up to $1,000 for each qualifying child under age 17. However, in addition to the requirement that the child has been under age 17 on the last day of the year, a qualifying child for this credit also must be someone who

- is claimed as a dependent qualifying child.

- is the taxpayer's son, daughter, adopted child, grandchild, stepchild or eligible foster child, your sibling, stepsibling or their descendant (although this may change with the implementation of the uniform definition of a child for tax purposes).

- is a U.S. citizen or resident alien.

If the taxpayer's modified adjusted gross income (MAGI) is above a certain amount, a limit may be imposed on the amount of child tax credit received. The amount at which the phase-out begins varies depending on the filing status of the taxpayer.

In addition, the Child Tax Credit is limited by the amount of the income tax owed as well as any alternative minimum tax owed. For example, if the income tax owed is $450, under ordinary circumstances the Child Tax Credit will be limited to $450 regardless of the fact that other facts such as the MAGI would allow a credit of $1,000. If the amount of Child Tax Credit is greater than the amount of income tax owed, the taxpayer may be able to claim some or all of the difference under the provisions for Additional Child Tax Credit.

The first possibility to maximize a credit is affected by the amount of earned income. This method of claiming the Additional Child Tax Credit provides that a taxpayer may claim up to 15 percent of the amount by which earned income exceeds an amount established by the IRS (for members of the Armed Forces who served in a combat zone, nontaxable combat pay counts as earned income when figuring this credit limit). The second method occurs if the taxpayer has three or more qualifying children. In that event, the taxpayer may claim up to the amount of Social Security taxes paid during the year, minus any Earned Income Tax Credit received. If the taxpayer can qualify under both these methods, the one that provides the greater benefit is allowed up to the difference between tax liability and the regular Child Tax

Credit. For example, using 2006 figures, if a Child Tax Credit of $450 is allowed, and the Additional Child Tax Credit would be $3,000, in a family with three children, only $2,550 would be allowed as an Additional Child Tax Credit (under the original Child Tax Credit this would have been the maximum credit).

Form 8812 is used to figure both the Child Tax Credit and the Additional Child Tax Credit. Part I of the form calculates the Child Tax Credit and any limitations that apply. It also calculates any Additional Child Tax Credit based on the exception related to earnings. If the taxpayer has three or more qualifying children and there is a limitation of the credit and the additional credit, then he or she can complete Part II to determine if that method will provide any additional credit that might be greater than under the earnings exception.

15. Form 8839—Adoption Credit

The Adoption Credit is one of the most generous credits, but it is also one of the most complicated to apply. Because the adoption process frequently takes place over a period greater than a year, multiple tax years may be involved. Additionally, special rules apply with regard to special needs children, related children, children from foreign countries, and the income of the adoptive parents. All of these require a great deal of tax planning to obtain the maximum benefit of the credit.

The maximum Adoption Credit is $10,390 for tax year 2006 and before. As a credit, it reduces dollar for dollar tax owed (rather than a reduction of taxable income as with a deduction). The credit generally is allowed for the year following the year in which the expenses are paid. However, a taxpayer who paid qualifying expenses in a year for which an adoption that became final may be eligible to claim the credit on the same year. The Adoption Credit is not available for any reimbursed expense. Thus, if an employer assists with the expenses, these reimbursements will usually limit the Adoption Credit. However, the reimbursement from an employer may be excludable from gross (and in turn taxable) income.

Those expenses that are considered qualified include the following reasonable and necessary adoption fees: court costs, attorney fees, traveling expenses (including amounts spent for meals and lodging while away from home), and other expenses directly related to and for which the principal purpose is the legal adoption of an eligible child.

In addition, the adopted child must be eligible to support the claim of the credit. This includes children under 18 years old, or who are physically or mentally incapable of caring for themselves. If an adoption is of a non-U.S. citizen or legal resident, no expenses can be claimed unless the adoption is finalized. For example, if someone goes to a foreign country to adopt a child and for some reason the adoption does not complete, the Adoption Credit or exclusion cannot be taken. A special needs child is a child who is a U.S. citizen or resident, and a state determines that the child cannot or should not be returned to his or her parents' home and probably will not be adopted unless assistance is provided.

Form **8812**

Department of the Treasury
Internal Revenue Service (99)

Additional Child Tax Credit

Complete and attach to Form 1040, Form 1040A, or Form 1040NR.

1040
1040A
1040NR
8812

OMB No. 1545-0074

2006

Attachment
Sequence No. **47**

Name(s) shown on return

Your social security number

Part I   All Filers

1   Enter the amount from line 1 of your Child Tax Credit Worksheet on page 43 of the Form 1040 instructions,
    page 38 of the Form 1040A instructions, or page 20 of the Form 1040NR instructions. If you used Pub.
    972, enter the amount from line 8 of the worksheet on page 4 of the publication **1**

2   Enter the amount from Form 1040, line 53, Form 1040A, line 33, or Form 1040NR, line 48 . . . .   **2**

3   Subtract line 2 from line 1. If zero, **stop**; you cannot take this credit **3**

4a Enter your total earned income (see instructions on back) **4a**

 b Nontaxable combat pay (see instructions on
    back) **4b**

5   Is the amount on line 4a more than $11,300?
    ☐ **No.** Leave line 5 blank and enter -0- on line 6.
    ☐ **Yes.** Subtract $11,300 from the amount on line 4a. Enter the result   **5**

6   Multiply the amount on line 5 by 15% (.15) and enter the result **6**
    Next. Do you have three or more qualifying children?
    ☐ **No.** If line 6 is zero, stop; you cannot take this credit. Otherwise, skip Part II and enter the
              smaller of line 3 or line 6 on line 13.
    ☐ **Yes.** If line 6 is equal to or more than line 3, skip Part II and enter the amount from line 3 on
              line 13. Otherwise, go to line 7.

Part II   Certain Filers Who Have Three or More Qualifying Children

7   Withheld social security and Medicare taxes from Form(s) W-2, boxes 4 and
    6. If married filing jointly, include your spouse's amounts with yours. If you
    worked for a railroad, see instructions on back **7**

8   **1040 filers:**   Enter the total of the amounts from Form 1040, lines
                       27 and 59, plus any uncollected social security and
                       Medicare or tier 1 RRTA taxes included on line 63.
    1040A filers: Enter -0-.
    1040NR filers: Enter the total of the amounts from Form 1040NR, line
                       54, plus any uncollected social security and Medicare
                       or tier 1 RRTA taxes included on line 58.   **8**

9   Add lines 7 and 8 . . . .   **9**

10 **1040 filers:**   Enter the total of the amounts from Form 1040, lines
                       66a and 67.
    1040A filers: Enter the total of the amount from Form 1040A, line
                       40a, plus any excess social security and tier 1 RRTA
                       taxes withheld that you entered to the left of line 43
                       (see instructions on back).
    1040NR filers: Enter the amount from Form 1040NR, line 61.   **10**

11 Subtract line 10 from line 9. If zero or less, enter -0- **11**

12 Enter the **larger** of line 6 or line 11 . . . .   **12**

    Next, enter the **smaller** of line 3 or line 12 on line 13.

Part III   Additional Child Tax Credit

13 **This is your additional child tax credit** **13**

1040
1040A
1040NR

*Enter this amount on
Form 1040, line 68,
Form 1040A, line 41, or
Form 1040NR, line 62.*

For Paperwork Reduction Act Notice, see back of form.   Cat. No. 10644E   Form **8812** (2006)

EXHIBIT 8–24   Form 8812 *(continues)*

Form 8812 (2006)   Page **2**

Instructions

Purpose of Form

Use Form 8812 to figure your additional child tax credit. The additional child tax credit may give you a refund even if you do not owe any tax.

Who Should Use Form 8812

First, complete the Child Tax Credit Worksheet that applies to you. See the instructions for Form 1040, line 53, Form 1040A, line 33, or Form 1040NR, line 48. If you meet the condition given in the *TIP* at the end of your Child Tax Credit Worksheet, use Form 8812 to see if you can take the additional child tax credit.

Effect of Credit on Welfare Benefits

Any refund you receive as a result of taking the additional child tax credit will not be used to determine if you are eligible for the following programs, or how much you can receive from them. But if the refund you receive because of the additional child tax credit is not spent within a certain period of time, it may count as an asset (or resource) and affect your eligibility.

- Temporary Assistance for Needy Families (TANF).
- Medicaid and supplemental security income (SSI).
- Food stamps and low-income housing.

Nontaxable Combat Pay

Enter on line 4b the total amount of nontaxable combat pay that you, and your spouse if filing jointly, received in 2006. This amount should be shown in Form W-2, box 12, with code Q.

Railroad Employees

If you worked for a railroad, include the following taxes in the total on Form 8812, line 7.

- Tier 1 tax withheld from your pay. This tax should be shown in box 14 of your Form(s) W-2 and identified as "Tier 1 tax."
- If you were an employee representative, 50% of the total tier 1 tax and tier 1 Medicare tax you paid for 2006.

1040A Filers

If you, or your spouse if filing jointly, had more than one employer for 2006 and total wages of over $94,200, figure any excess social security and tier 1 railroad retirement (RRTA) taxes withheld. See Pub. 505. Include any excess on Form 8812, line 10.

Paperwork Reduction Act Notice. We ask for the information on this form to carry out the Internal Revenue laws of the United States. You are required to give us the information. We need it to ensure that you are complying with these laws and to allow us to figure and collect the right amount of tax.

You are not required to provide the information requested on a form that is subject to the Paperwork Reduction Act unless the form displays a valid OMB control number. Books or records relating to a form or its instructions must be retained as long as their contents may become material in the administration of any Internal Revenue law. Generally, tax returns and return information are confidential, as required by Internal Revenue Code section 6103.

The average time and expenses required to complete and file this form will vary depending on individual circumstances. For the estimated averages, see the instructions for your income tax return.

If you have suggestions for making this form simpler, we would be happy to hear from you. See the instructions for your income tax return.

Earned Income Chart—Line 4a

IF you...	AND you...	THEN enter on line 4a...
have net earnings from self-employment	use either optional method to figure those net earnings	the amount figured using Pub. 972.
are taking the EIC on Form 1040, line 66a, or Form 1040A, line 40a	completed Worksheet B on page 51 of your Form 1040 instructions	your earned income from Worksheet B, line 4b, plus all of your nontaxable combat pay if you did not elect to include it in earned income for the EIC. If you were a member of the clergy, subtract (a) the rental value of a home or the nontaxable portion of an allowance for a home furnished to you (including payments for utilities), and (b) the value of meals and lodging provided to you, your spouse, and your dependents for your employer's convenience.
	did not complete Worksheet B or filed Form 1040A	your earned income from Step 5 on page 48 of your 1040 instructions or page 42 of your 1040A instructions, plus all of your nontaxable combat pay if you did not elect to include it in earned income for the EIC.
are not taking the EIC	were self-employed, or you are filing Schedule SE because you were a member of the clergy or you had church employee income, or you are filing Schedule C or C-EZ as a statutory employee	the amount figured using Pub. 972.
	are not self-employed or filing Schedule SE, C, or C-EZ for the above reasons	your earned income figured as follows: Line 7 of Form 1040 or Form 1040A, or line 8 of Form 1040NR Subtract, if included on line 7 (line 8 for Form 1040NR), any: • Taxable scholarship or fellowship grant not reported on a Form W-2. • Amount received for work performed while an inmate in a penal institution (put "PRI" and the amount subtracted in the space next to line 7 of Form 1040 or 1040A (line 8 for Form 1040NR)). • Amount received as a pension or annuity from a nonqualified deferred compensation plan or a nongovernmental section 457 plan (put "DFC" and the amount subtracted in the space next to line 7 of Form 1040 or Form 1040A (line 8 for Form 1040NR)). This amount may be shown in box 11 of your Form W-2. If you received such an amount but box 11 is blank, contact your employer for the amount received as a pension or annuity. • Amount from Form 2555, line 43, or Form 2555-EZ, line 18. Add all your nontaxable combat pay from Form(s) W-2, box 12, with code Q <div align="right">Earned income =</div>

EXHIBIT 8–24   Form 8812 *(continued)*

Form **8839**	**Qualified Adoption Expenses**	OMB No. 1545-0074
Department of the Treasury Internal Revenue Service	▶ Attach to Form 1040 or 1040NR. ▶ See separate instructions.	2006 Attachment Sequence No. **38**

Name(s) shown on return | Your social security number

Before you begin: See **Definitions** on page 1 of the instructions.

Part I **Information About Your Eligible Child or Children—You must** complete this part. See page 2 of the instructions for details, including what to do if you need more space.

1	(a) Child's name		(b) Child's year of birth	Check if child was—			(f) Child's identifying number
	First	Last		(c) born **before 1989** and disabled	(d) a child with special needs	(e) a foreign child	
Child 1				☐	☐	☐	
Child 2				☐	☐	☐	

Caution. If the child was a foreign child, see **Special rules** in the instructions for line 1, column (e), that begin on page 2, before you complete Part II or Part III. If you received **employer-provided adoption benefits,** complete Part III on the back next.

Part II **Adoption Credit**

			Child 1		Child 2	
2	Maximum adoption credit per child . . .	2	$10,960	00	$10,960	00
3	Did you file Form 8839 for a prior year for the same child?					
	☐ **No.** Enter -0-.					
	☐ **Yes.** See page 4 of the instructions for the amount to enter.	3				
4	Subtract line 3 from line 2	4				
5	**Qualified adoption expenses** (see page 4 of the instructions)	5				
	Caution. Your qualified adoption expenses may not be equal to the adoption expenses you paid in 2006.					
6	Enter the **smaller** of line 4 or line 5 . . .	6				

7	Add the amounts on line 6. If zero, skip lines 8 through 11 and enter -0- on line 12 . . .	7	
8	Modified adjusted gross income (see page 4 of the instructions) . .	8	
9	Is line 8 more than $164,410?		
	☐ **No.** Skip lines 9 and 10, and enter -0- on line 11.		
	☐ **Yes.** Subtract $164,410 from line 8	9	
10	Divide line 9 by $40,000. Enter the result as a decimal (rounded to at least three places). Do not enter more than 1.000	10	✕ .
11	Multiply line 7 by line 10	11	
12	Subtract line 11 from line 7	12	
13	Credit carryforward from prior years (line 23 of your **Credit Carryforward Worksheet** on page 5 of the **2005** Form 8839 instructions)	13	
14	Add lines 12 and 13	14	
15	Enter the amount from Form 1040, line 46, or Form 1040NR, line 43 .	15			
16	**1040 filers:** Enter the total of any amounts from Form 1040, lines 47 through 51 and line 53; Form 8396, line 11; and Form 5695, line 12.	16			
	1040NR filers: Enter the total of any amounts from Form 1040NR, lines 44 through 46 and line 48; Form 8396, line 11; and Form 5695, line 12.				
17	Subtract line 16 from line 15	17	
18	**Adoption credit.** Enter the smaller of line 14 or line 17 here and include on Form 1040, line 54, or Form 1040NR, line 49. Check box **b** on that line. If line 17 is smaller than line 14, you may have a credit carryforward (see page 4 of the instructions)	18	

For Paperwork Reduction Act Notice, see page 6 of the instructions.   Cat. No. 22843L   Form **8839** (2006)

EXHIBIT 8–25 Form 8839 *(continues)*

Form 8839 (2006)   Page **2**

Part III Employer-Provided Adoption Benefits

		Child 1		Child 2	
19	Maximum exclusion per child . . .	**19**	$10,960	00	$10,960	00

20 Did you receive employer-provided adoption benefits for a prior year for the same child?
☐ **No.** Enter -0-.
☐ **Yes.** See page 4 of the instructions for the amount to enter.
20

21 Subtract line 20 from line 19 . . . .   **21**

22 Employer-provided adoption benefits you received in 2006. This amount should be shown in box 12 of your 2006 Form(s) W-2 with code **T** . . .   **22**

23 Add the amounts on line 22 . . . .   **23**

24 Enter the **smaller** of line 21 or line 22. But if the child was a child with special needs and the adoption became final in 2006, enter the amount from line 21 .   **24**

25 Add the amounts on line 24. If zero, skip lines 26 through 29, enter -0- on line 30, and go to line 31 . . . .   **25**

26 Modified adjusted gross income (from the worksheet on page 6 of the instructions) **26**

27 Is line 26 more than $164,410?
☐ **No.** Skip lines 27 and 28, and enter -0- on line 29.
☐ **Yes.** Subtract $164,410 from line 26 . . . .   **27**

28 Divide line 27 by $40,000. Enter the result as a decimal (rounded to at least three places). Do not enter more than 1.000 . . .   **28**   ✕   .

29 Multiply line 25 by line 28 . . . .   **29**

30 **Excluded benefits.** Subtract line 29 from line 25 . . . .   **30**

31 **Taxable benefits.** Is line 30 more than line 23?
☐ **No.** Subtract line 30 from line 23. Also, include this amount, if more than zero, on line 7 of Form 1040 or line 8 of Form 1040NR. On the dotted line next to line 7 of Form 1040 or line 8 of Form 1040NR, enter "AB."
☐ **Yes.** Subtract line 23 from line 30. Enter the result as a negative number. Reduce the total you would enter on line 7 of Form 1040 or line 8 of Form 1040NR by the amount on Form 8839, line 31. Enter the result on line 7 of Form 1040 or line 8 of Form 1040NR. Enter "SNE" on the dotted line next to the entry line.
31

TIP You may be able to claim the adoption credit in Part II on the front of this form if either of the following applies.
• The total adoption expenses you paid in 2006 were not fully reimbursed by your employer and the adoption became final in 2006 or earlier.
• You adopted a child with special needs and the adoption became final in 2006.

Form **8839** (2006)

EXHIBIT 8–25   Form 8839 *(continued)*

The Adoption Credit or exclusion is limited to $10,390 for each effort to adopt an eligible child. However, the adoption credit and income exclusion are mutually independent. What this means is that both are calculated without regard to the other. Recall the Child Tax and Additional Child Tax credits, which are interrelated. The Adoption Credit and income exclusion are not. But the $10,390 amount is the maximum amount of qualifying expenses taken into account over all taxable years. If part of the credit has already been claimed in a prior year, that amount must be reduced from the total credit before the current year credit can be calculated.

There are also limits on the credit as affected by the income of the taxpayer. If the MAGI is $155,860 or less, the income limit will not affect the credit or exclusion. If the MAGI is more than $155,860, the credit or exclusion will be reduced. If the MAGI is $195,860 or more, the credit or exclusion will be eliminated. These figures are schedule to increase for the 2007 tax year.

Another limiting factor is filing status. Generally, if the adoptive parents are married, a joint return must be filed to take the Adoption Credit or exclusion. If filing status is married filing separately, the credit or exclusion can be claimed only if certain requirements are met.

The Adoption Credit is calculated for each year affected on form 8839. This form assumes that the taxpayer has already determined that the child is eligible, that the expenses are qualified, and that the amounts and the amount of employer provided adoption benefits, if any, are known. Once these items are determined, the form itself is relatively straightforward.

16. Form 8857—Request for Innocent Spouse Relief

Unlike most of the other forms in this discussion, the Request for Innocent Spouse Relief is not used to alter tax liability as a deduction or credit. Rather, it is used to protect one spouse from the potential tax debt, penalties, and interest generated by the other spouse. This form is confined to use for issues relating directly to tax, penalties, and interest and not other types of debt. Consider Application 8.8.

APPLICATION **8.8**

Miriam was married to Hiram, a self-employed excavation contractor. She was also employed and had taxes withheld from her salary. Each year, Hiram prepared the tax return for the couple and the business. Hiram and Miriam would both sign the annual joint return. Miriam knew that Hiram typically made quarterly estimated tax payments for his business income. In 2006, the couple divorced. Not long after, Miriam received a notice from the IRS that she and Hiram were liable on their joint return for tax, penalties, and interest for underpayment of tax in the amount of $41,000. After some investigation, Miriam discovered that for the last two years of their marriage, Hiram had not paid the quarterly estimates. This is despite the fact that he reported them as paid on the joint return.

Form **8857**	**Request for Innocent Spouse Relief**	OMB No. 1545-1596

Form 8857
(Rev. June 2007)
Department of the Treasury
Internal Revenue Service (99)

▶ **Do not file with your tax return.**   ▶ **See separate instructions.**

Important things you should know

- Answer all the questions on this form that apply, attach any necessary documentation, and sign on page 4. Do not delay filing this form because of missing documentation. See instructions.
- By law, the IRS must contact the person who was your spouse for the years you want relief. There are no exceptions, even for victims of spousal abuse or domestic violence. Your personal information (such as your current name, address, and employer) will be protected. However, if you petition the Tax Court, your personal information may be released. See instructions for details.
- If you need help, see *How To Get Help* in the instructions.

Part I   **Should you file this form?** You **must** complete this part for each tax year.

		Tax Year 1	Tax Year 2	Tax Year 3*
1	Enter each tax year you want relief. It is important to enter the correct year. For example, if the IRS used your 2006 income tax refund to pay a 2004 tax amount you jointly owed, enter tax year 2004, not tax year 2006 . . . . ▶ **Caution.** The IRS generally cannot collect the amount you owe until your request for each year is resolved. However, the time the IRS has to collect is extended. See *Collection Statute of Limitations* on page 3 of the instructions.			

		Tax Year 1		Tax Year 2		Tax Year 3	
2	Check the box for each year you would like a refund if you qualify for relief. You may be required to provide proof of payment. See instructions . . . . ▶	☐		☐		☐	
		Yes	No	Yes	No	Yes	No
3	Did the IRS use your share of the joint refund to pay any of the following past-due debts of your spouse: federal tax, state income tax, child support, spousal support, or federal non-tax debt such as a student loan? • If "Yes," **stop here**; do not file this form for that tax year. Instead, file Form 8379. See instructions. • If "No," go to line 4	☐	☐	☐	☐	☐	☐
4	Did you file a joint return for the tax year listed on line 1? • If "Yes," skip line 5 and go to line 6. • If "No," go to line 5	☐	☐	☐	☐	☐	☐
5	If you did not file a joint return for that tax year, were you a resident of Arizona, California, Idaho, Louisiana, Nevada, New Mexico, Texas, Washington, or Wisconsin? • If "Yes," see *Community Property Laws* on page 2 of the instructions. • If "No" on both lines 4 and 5, **stop here.** Do not file this form for that tax year . .	☐	☐	☐	☐	☐	☐

*If you want relief for more than 3 years, fill out an additional form.

Part II   **Tell us about yourself**

6	Your current name (see instructions)	**Your social security number**
	Your current home address (number and street). If a P.O. box, see instructions.	Apt. no. **County**
	City, town or post office, state, and ZIP code. If a foreign address, see instructions.	Best daytime phone number ( )

Part III   **Tell us about you and your spouse for the tax years you want relief**

7   **Who was your spouse for the tax years you want relief?** File a separate Form 8857 for tax years involving different spouses or former spouses.

That person's current name	**Social security number** (if known)
Current home address (number and street) (if known). If a P.O. box, see instructions.	Apt. no.
City, town or post office, state, and ZIP code. If a foreign address, see instructions.	Best daytime phone number ( )

For Privacy Act and Paperwork Reduction Act Notice, see instructions.   Cat. No. 24647V   Form **8857** (Rev. 6-2007)

EXHIBIT 8–26 Form 8857 *(continues)*

Form 8857 (Rev. 6-2007)   Page **2**

Note. If you need more room to write your answer for any question, attach more pages. Be sure to write your name and social security number on the top of all pages you attach.

Part III   *(Continued)*

8   What is the current marital status between you and the person on line 7?

☐ Married and still living together

☐ Married and living apart since ___/___/___
                              MM DD YYYY

☐ Widowed since ___/___/___   Attach a photocopy of the death certificate and will (if one exists).
                   MM DD YYYY

☐ Legally separated since ___/___/___   Attach a photocopy of your entire separation agreement.
                        MM DD YYYY

☐ Divorced since ___/___/___   Attach a photocopy of your entire divorce decree.
               MM DD YYYY

Note. A divorce decree stating that your former spouse must pay all taxes does not necessarily mean you qualify for relief.

9   What was the highest level of education you had completed when the return(s) were filed? If the answers are **not** the same for all tax years, explain.

☐   High school diploma, equivalent, or less
☐   Some college
☐   College degree or higher. List any degrees you have ▶ _____

List any college-level business or tax-related courses you completed ▶ _____

Explain ▶ _____

10   Were you a victim of spousal abuse or domestic violence during any of the tax years you want relief? If the answers are **not** the same for all tax years, explain.

☐ Yes. **Attach a statement** to explain the situation and **when** it started. Provide photocopies of any documentation, such as police reports, a restraining order, a doctor's report or letter, or a notarized statement from someone who was aware of the situation.

☐ No.

11   Did you sign the return(s)? If the answers are **not** the same for all tax years, explain.

☐ Yes. If you were forced to sign under duress (threat of harm or other form of coercion), check here ▶ ☐ . See instructions.

☐ No. Your signature was forged. See instructions.

12   When any of the returns were signed, did you have a mental or physical health problem or do you have a mental or physical health problem now? If the answers are **not** the same for all tax years, explain.

☐ Yes. **Attach a statement** to explain the problem and **when** it started. Provide photocopies of any documentation, such as medical bills or a doctor's report or letter.

☐ No.

Part IV   Tell us how you were involved with finances and preparing returns for those tax years

13   How were you involved with preparing the returns? Check all that apply and explain, if necessary. If the answers are **not** the same for all tax years, explain.

☐ You filled out or helped fill out the returns.
☐ You gathered receipts and cancelled checks.
☐ You gave tax documents (such as Forms W-2, 1099, etc.) to the person who prepared the returns.
☐ You reviewed the returns before they were signed.
☐ You did not review the returns before they were signed. Explain below.
☐ You were not involved in preparing the returns.
☐ Other ▶ _____

Explain how you were involved ▶ _____

_____

_____

_____

Form **8857** (Rev. 6-2007)

EXHIBIT 8–26   Form 8857 *(continued)*

Form 8857 (Rev. 6-2007)   Page **3**

Note. If you need more room to write your answer for any question, attach more pages. Be sure to write your name and social security number on the top of all pages you attach.

Part IV *(Continued)*

14 **When the returns were signed, were you concerned that any of the returns were incorrect or missing information?** Check all that apply and explain, if necessary. If the answers are **not** the same for all tax years, explain.

☐ You knew something was incorrect or missing, but you said nothing.
☐ You knew something was incorrect or missing and asked about it.
☐ You did not know anything was incorrect or missing.
Explain ▶ ....

15 **When any of the returns were signed, what did you know about the income of the person on line 7?** If the answers are **not** the same for all tax years, explain.

☐ You knew that person had income.
List each type of income on a separate line. (Examples are wages, social security, gambling winnings, or self-employment business income.) Enter each tax year and the amount of income for each type you listed. If you do not know any details, enter "I don't know."

Type of income	Who paid it to that person	Tax Year 1	Tax Year 2	Tax Year 3
		$	$	$
		$	$	$
		$	$	$

☐ You knew that person was self-employed and you helped with the books and records.
☐ You knew that person was self-employed and you did not help with the books and records.
☐ You knew that person had no income.
☐ You did not know if that person had income.
Explain ▶ ....

16 **When the returns were signed, did you know any amount was owed to the IRS for those tax years?** If the answers are **not** the same for all tax years, explain.

☐ Yes. Explain when and how you thought the amount of tax reported on the return would be paid ▶ ....
....
☐ No.
Explain ▶ ....

17 **When any of the returns were signed, were you having financial problems** (for example, bankruptcy or bills you could not pay)? If the answers are **not** the same for all tax years, explain.

☐ Yes. Explain ▶ ....
....
☐ No.
☐ Did not know.
Explain ▶ ....

18 **For the years you want relief, how were you involved in the household finances?** Check all that apply. If the answers are **not** the same for all tax years, explain.

☐ You knew the person on line 7 had separate accounts.
☐ You had joint accounts but you had limited use of them or did not use them. Explain below.
☐ You used joint accounts. You made deposits, paid bills, balanced the checkbook, or reviewed the monthly bank statements.
☐ You made decisions about how money was spent. For example, you paid bills or made decisions about household purchases.
☐ You were not involved in handling money for the household.
☐ Other ▶ ....
Explain anything else you want to tell us about your household finances ▶ ....

19 **Has the person on line 7 ever transferred assets (money or property) to you?** (Property includes real estate, stocks, bonds, or other property to which you have title.) See instructions.

☐ Yes. List the assets and the dates they were transferred. Explain why the assets were transferred ▶ ....
....
....
☐ No.

Form **8857** (Rev. 6-2007)

EXHIBIT 8–26 Form 8857 *(continued)*

Form 8857 (Rev. 6-2007)   Page **4**

Part V   **Tell us about your current financial situation**

20   **Tell us the number of people currently in your household.**   Adults _____   Children _____

21   **Tell us your current average monthly income and expenses for your entire household.** If family or friends are helping to support you, include the amount of support as gifts under **Monthly income.** Under **Monthly expenses,** enter all expenses, including expenses paid with income from gifts.

Monthly income	Amount	Monthly expenses	Amount
		Federal, state, and local taxes deducted from your paycheck	
Gifts		Rent or mortgage	
Wages (Gross pay)		Utilities	
Pensions		Telephone	
Unemployment			
Social security			
Government assistance, such as housing, food stamps, grants		Food	
		Car expenses, payments, insurance, etc.	
Alimony		Medical expenses, including medical insurance	
Child support		Life insurance	
Self-employment business income . .		Clothing	
Rental income		Child care	
Interest and dividends		Public transportation	
Other income, such as disability payments, gambling winnings, etc. List the type below:		Other expenses, such as real estate taxes, child support, etc. List the type below:	
Type		Type	
Type		Type	
Type		Type	
Total . . . . ▶		Total . . . . ▶	

22   **Please provide any other information you want us to consider in determining whether it would be unfair to hold you liable for the tax.** If you need more room, attach more pages. Be sure to write your name and social security number on the top of all pages you attach.

Caution
By signing this form, you understand that, by law, we must contact the person on line 7. See instructions for details.

Sign Here   Under penalties of perjury, I declare that I have examined this form and any accompanying schedules and statements, and to the best of my knowledge and belief, they are true, correct, and complete. Declaration of preparer (other than taxpayer) is based on all information of which preparer has any knowledge.

Keep a copy for your records.

Your signature		Date

Paid Preparer's Use Only	Preparer's signature ▶	Date	Check if self-employed ☐	Preparer's SSN or PTIN
	Firm's name (or yours if self-employed), address, and ZIP code ▶		EIN	
			Phone no. ( )	

Form **8857** (Rev. 6-2007)

EXHIBIT 8–26   Form 8857 *(continued)*

Essentially, when spouses file a joint return and it comes to the attention of one that the other has incurred tax, penalties, and interest without his or her knowledge or consent, he or she may seek relief from the tax liability. However, it is not relief that is automatically granted. The innocent spouse must establish that he or she was reasonably unaware of the facts leading to the tax liability and must file form 8857 as soon as possible after becoming aware. Typically, form 8857 will not be accepted more than two years following the first attempt by the IRS to seek payment from the innocent spouse for the taxes incurred during the tax year(s) in which a joint return was filed. For example, if a spouse had two jobs and only reported the wages from one job on the tax return, it would be difficult to establish a lack of knowledge on the part of the other spouse who also signed the return.

17. Form 8863—Education Credits

Because there is a direct correlation between education and increased job opportunities and income, the education credits provided to taxpayers are an incentive to pursue education beyond the secondary (high school) level. The credits are not available for individuals who are enrolled in preschool, elementary, or secondary programs. The credits can be fairly generous. They encompass tuition, fees, and some associated costs of attending qualified educational institutions. They are available as credits. Unlike a deduction, recall that a tax credit reduces the amount of tax owed dollar for dollar rather than the amount of income that is taxed. The education credits are available even if the educational expenses were paid with student loans. Although the loans came at no initial cost, they will in fact have to be repaid and thus eventually will result in the payment for the education against whom the credit is claimed. An additional benefit of student loans is that in many cases the interest is deductible, which is yet another benefit to those pursuing education.

The education credits have two distinct paths. In addition, there is a general tuition and fees deduction (note that this is not a credit) available if the student does not qualify for one of the education credits, or if it would provide a better tax effect. The tuition and fees expense will be discussed later in this book. It is important to note here that both cannot be taken simultaneously. The education credits are known as the "Hope" and the "Lifetime" credits. Both are available only if the education expense was associated with an eligible education institution. The IRS will determine whether a specific institution is eligible. However, most traditional colleges, universities, and vocational schools qualify. Nevertheless, this would be an important question to ask of any educational institution before making the decision to attend, especially if it is a nontraditional school such as an online learning course.

One limitation on the Hope and Lifetime credits is that they are not available if any of the expenses were not ultimately the responsibility of the taxpayer and/or the student. For example, if a student receives a $1,000 scholarship, that student cannot then turn and claim that same $1,000 spent on education as a credit. The same applies for any other sources of financial aid for which there is no obligation to repay the amount of assistance.

Form **8863**	**Education Credits**	OMB No. 1545-0074
Department of the Treasury Internal Revenue Service (99)	**(Hope and Lifetime Learning Credits)** ▶ See instructions. ▶ Attach to Form 1040 or Form 1040A.	20**06** Attachment Sequence No. **50**

Name(s) shown on return | Your social security number

Caution: You **cannot** take the Hope credit and the lifetime learning credit for the **same student** in the same year.

Part I   **Hope Credit.** Caution: You **cannot** take the Hope credit for more than **2** tax years for the **same student.**

1	**(a)** Student's name (as shown on page 1 of your tax return) First name _____ Last name	**(b)** Student's social security number (as shown on page 1 of your tax return)	**(c)** Qualified expenses (see instructions). **Do not** enter more than $2,200* for each student.	**(d)** Enter the **smaller** of the amount in column (c) or $1,100**	**(e)** Add column (c) and column (d)	**(f)** Enter one-half of the amount in column (e)

* For each student who attended an eligible educational institution in the Gulf Opportunity Zone, **do not** enter more than $4,400.
** For each student who attended an eligible educational institution in the Gulf Opportunity Zone, enter the **smaller** of the amount in column (c) or $2,200.

2   **Tentative Hope credit.** Add the amounts on line 1, column (f). If you are taking the lifetime learning credit for another student, go to Part II; otherwise, go to Part III . . . . ▶ | **2** |

Part II   **Lifetime Learning Credit**

3	**(a)** Student's name (as shown on page 1 of your tax return) First name _____ Last name	**(b)** Student's social security number (as shown on page 1 of your tax return)	**(c)** Qualified expenses (see instructions)

4	Add the amounts on line 3, column (c), and enter the total	**4**	
5a	Enter the **smaller** of line 4 or $10,000	**5a**	
b	For students who attended an eligible educational institution in the Gulf Opportunity Zone, enter the smaller of $10,000 or their qualified expenses included on line 4 (see special rules on page 3)	**5b**	
c	Subtract line 5b from line 5a	**5c**	
6a	Multiply line 5b by 40% (.40)	**6a**	
b	Multiply line 5c by 20% (.20)	**6b**	
c	**Tentative lifetime learning credit.** Add lines 6a and 6b and go to Part III	**6c**	

Part III   **Allowable Education Credits**

7	Tentative education credits. Add lines 2 and 6c		**7**	
8	Enter: $110,000 if married filing jointly; $55,000 if single, head of household, or qualifying widow(er)	**8**		
9	Enter the amount from Form 1040, line 38*, or Form 1040A, line 22 . .	**9**		
10	Subtract line 9 from line 8. If zero or less, **stop;** you cannot take any education credits	**10**		
11	Enter: $20,000 if married filing jointly; $10,000 if single, head of household, or qualifying widow(er)	**11**		
12	If line 10 is equal to or more than line 11, enter the amount from line 7 on line 13 and go to line 14. If line 10 is less than line 11, divide line 10 by line 11. Enter the result as a decimal (rounded to at least three places) . . . . ▶		**12**	✕ .
13	Multiply line 7 by line 12		**13**	
14	Enter the amount from Form 1040, line 46, or Form 1040A, line 28 . .	**14**		
15	Enter the total, if any, of your credits from Form 1040, lines 47 through 49, or Form 1040A, lines 29 and 30	**15**		
16	Subtract line 15 from line 14. If zero or less, **stop;** you cannot take any education credits	**16**		
17	**Education credits.** Enter the **smaller** of line 13 or line 16 here and on Form 1040, line 50, or Form 1040A, line 31		**17**	

* If you are filing Form 2555, 2555-EZ, or 4563, or you are excluding income from Puerto Rico, see Pub. 970 for the amount to enter.

For Paperwork Reduction Act Notice, see page 4.   Cat. No. 25379M   Form **8863** (2006)

EXHIBIT 8–27   Form 8863 (continues)

Form 8863 (2006)   Page **2**

General Instructions

What's New

Hope credit increased. For 2006, the maximum amount of the Hope credit has been increased to $1,650 ($3,300 for a Gulf Opportunity (GO) Zone student).

Reminder

Gulf Opportunity Zone students. For tax years beginning in 2006, the education credits continue to be expanded for students attending an eligible educational institution in the Gulf Opportunity (GO) Zone. See *Special Rules for Gulf Opportunity Zone Students* on page 3 and the instructions for Parts I and II.

Purpose of Form

Use Form 8863 to figure and claim your education credits. The education credits are:

● The Hope credit, and

● The lifetime learning credit.

These credits are based on qualified education expenses paid to an eligible postsecondary educational institution. See *Qualified Education Expenses* and *Eligible Educational Institution*, later, for more information.

Who Can Take the Credits

You may be able to take the credits if you, your spouse, or a dependent you claim on your tax return was a student enrolled at or attending an eligible educational institution. The credits are based on the amount of qualified education expenses paid for the student in 2006 for academic periods beginning in 2006 and the first 3 months of 2007.

  Qualified education expenses must be reduced by any expenses paid directly or indirectly using tax-free educational assistance. See Tax-Free Educational Assistance and Refunds of Qualified Education Expenses *on this page.*

Note. If a student is claimed as a dependent on another person's tax return, only the person who claims the student as a dependent can claim the credits for the student's qualified education expenses. If a student is not claimed as a dependent on another person's tax return, only the student can claim the credits.

Generally, qualified education expenses paid on behalf of the student by someone other than the student (such as a relative) are treated as paid by the student. Also, qualified education expenses paid (or treated as paid) by a student who is claimed as a dependent on your tax return are treated as paid by you. Therefore, you are treated as having paid expenses that were paid from your dependent student's earnings, gifts, inheritances, savings, etc.

You cannot take the education credits if any of the following apply.

● You are claimed as a dependent on another person's tax return, such as your parent's return (but see the *Note* above).

● Your filing status is married filing separately.

● Your adjusted gross income on Form 1040, line 38, or Form 1040A, line 22, is (a) $110,000 or more if married filing jointly, or (b) $55,000 or more if single, head of household, or qualifying widow(er).

● You (or your spouse) were a nonresident alien for any part of 2006 and the nonresident alien did not elect to be treated as a resident alien.

  At the time these instructions went to print, Congress was considering legislation that would extend the deduction for tuition and fees that expired at the end of 2005. In some cases, taking the tuition and fees deduction may be more

beneficial than taking an education credit, but you cannot take both an education credit and the tuition and fees deduction for the same student in the same year. To find out if this legislation was enacted, and for more details, go to www.irs.gov, *click on* More Forms and Publications, *and then on* What's Hot in forms and publications, *or see Pub. 553.*

Additional Information

See Pub. 970, Tax Benefits for Education, for more information about these credits.

Rules That Apply to Both Credits

Qualified Education Expenses

Generally, qualified education expenses are amounts paid in 2006 for tuition and fees required for the student's enrollment or attendance at an eligible educational institution. It does not matter whether the expenses were paid in cash, by check, by credit card, or with borrowed funds.

Qualified education expenses do not include amounts paid for:

● Room and board, insurance, medical expenses (including student health fees), transportation, or other similar personal, living, or family expenses.

● Course-related books, supplies, equipment, and nonacademic activities, except for fees required to be paid to the institution as a condition of enrollment or attendance.

● Any course or other education involving sports, games, or hobbies, or any noncredit course, unless such course or other education is part of the student's degree program or (for the lifetime learning credit only) helps the student to acquire or improve job skills.

You should receive Form 1098-T, Tuition Statement, from the college or university reporting either payments received in box 1 or amounts billed in box 2. However, the amounts in boxes 1 and 2 of Form 1098-T may be different than what you actually paid. On Form 8863, lines 1 and 3, enter only the amounts you paid in 2006 for qualified expenses. See chapters 2 and 3 of Pub. 970.

If you or the student take a deduction for higher education expenses, such as on Schedule A or Schedule C (Form 1040), you cannot use those expenses when figuring your education credits.

  Any qualified expenses used to figure the education credits cannot be taken into account in determining the amount of a distribution from a Coverdell ESA or a qualified tuition program that is excluded from gross income.

Tax-Free Educational Assistance and Refunds of Qualified Education Expenses

Tax-free educational assistance includes a tax-free scholarship or Pell grant or tax-free employer-provided educational assistance. See Pub. 970 for specific information.

You must reduce the total of your qualified education expenses by any tax-free educational assistance and by any refunds of your expenses. If the refund or tax-free assistance is received in the same year in which the expenses were paid or in the following year before you file your tax return, reduce your qualified education expenses by the amount received and figure your education credits using the reduced amount of qualified expenses. If the refund or tax-free assistance is received after you file your return for the year in which the expenses were paid, you must figure the amount by which your education credits would have been reduced if the refund or tax-free assistance had been received in the year for which you claimed the education credits. Include that amount as an additional tax for the year the refund or tax-free assistance was received.

EXHIBIT 8–27   Form 8863 *(continued)*

Form 8863 (2006)   Page **3**

Example. You paid $8,000 tuition and fees in December 2005, and your child began college in January 2006. You filed your 2005 tax return on February 2, 2006, and claimed a lifetime learning credit of $1,600. After you filed your return, your child dropped two courses and you received a refund of $1,400. You must refigure your 2005 lifetime learning credit using $6,600 of qualified expenses instead of $8,000. The refigured credit is $1,320. You must include the difference of $280 on your 2006 Form 1040, line 44, or Form 1040A, line 28.

Prepaid Expenses

Qualified education expenses paid in 2006 for an academic period that begins in the first 3 months of 2007 can be used in figuring your 2006 education credits. For example, if you pay $2,000 in December 2006 for qualified tuition for the 2007 winter quarter that begins in January 2007, you can use that $2,000 in figuring your 2006 education credits (if you meet all the other requirements).

You cannot use any amount paid in 2005 or 2007 to figure your 2006 education credits.

Eligible Educational Institution

An eligible educational institution is generally any accredited public, nonprofit, or proprietary (private) college, university, vocational school, or other postsecondary institution. Also, the institution must be eligible to participate in a student aid program administered by the Department of Education. Virtually all accredited postsecondary institutions meet this definition.

Special Rules for Gulf Opportunity Zone Students

The following rules apply only to students attending an eligible educational institution in the Gulf Opportunity (GO) Zone, which includes the following areas in three states.

Alabama. The counties of Baldwin, Choctaw, Clarke, Greene, Hale, Marengo, Mobile, Pickens, Sumter, Tuscaloosa, and Washington.

Louisiana. The parishes of Acadia, Ascension, Assumption, Calcasieu, Cameron, East Baton Rouge, East Feliciana, Iberia, Iberville, Jefferson, Jefferson Davis, Lafayette, Lafourche, Livingston, Orleans, Plaquemines, Pointe Coupee, St. Bernard, St. Charles, St. Helena, St. James, St. John the Baptist, St. Martin, St. Mary, St. Tammany, Tangipahoa, Terrebonne, Vermilion, Washington, West Baton Rouge, and West Feliciana.

Mississippi. The counties of Adams, Amite, Attala, Choctaw, Claiborne, Clarke, Copiah, Covington, Forrest, Franklin, George, Greene, Hancock, Harrison, Hinds, Holmes, Humphreys, Jackson, Jasper, Jefferson, Jefferson Davis, Jones, Kemper, Lamar, Lauderdale, Lawrence, Leake, Lincoln, Lowndes, Madison, Marion, Neshoba, Newton, Noxubee, Oktibbeha, Pearl River, Perry, Pike, Rankin, Scott, Simpson, Smith, Stone, Walthall, Warren, Wayne, Wilkinson, Winston, and Yazoo.

All of the other rules discussed on page 2 (as modified by these rules) must still be met. The Hope credit for a GO Zone student is 100% of the first $2,200 of qualified education expenses and 50% of the next $2,200 of qualified education expenses for a maximum credit of $3,300 per student. The lifetime learning credit rate for a GO Zone student is 40%.

The definition of qualified education expenses is expanded for GO Zone students. In addition to tuition and fees required for enrollment or attendance at an eligible educational institution, qualified education expenses for a GO Zone student include the following.

1. Books, supplies, and equipment required for enrollment or attendance at an eligible educational institution.

2. For a special needs student, expenses that are necessary for that person's enrollment or attendance at an eligible educational institution.

3. For a student who is at least a half-time student, the reasonable costs of room and board, but only to the extent that the costs are not more than the greater of the following two amounts.

a. The allowance for room and board, as determined by the eligible educational institution, that was included in the cost of attendance (for federal financial aid purposes) for a particular academic period and living arrangement of the student.

b. The actual amount charged if the student is residing in housing owned or operated by the eligible educational institution.

You will need to contact the eligible educational institution for qualified room and board costs.

Specific Instructions

Part I
Hope Credit

You may be able to take a credit of up to $1,650 ($3,300 if a GO Zone student) for qualified education expenses (defined earlier) paid for each student who qualifies for the Hope credit. The Hope credit equals 100% of the first $1,100 ($2,200 if a GO Zone student) and 50% of the next $1,100 ($2,200 if a GO Zone student) of qualified expenses paid for each eligible student. You can take the Hope credit for a student if all of the following apply.

● As of the beginning of 2006, the student had not completed the first 2 years of postsecondary education (generally, the freshman and sophomore years of college), as determined by the eligible educational institution. For this purpose, do not include academic credit awarded solely because of the student's performance on proficiency examinations.

● The student was enrolled in 2006 in a program that leads to a degree, certificate, or other recognized educational credential.

● The student was taking at least one-half the normal full-time workload for his or her course of study for at least one academic period beginning in 2006.

● The Hope credit was not claimed for that student's expenses in more than one prior tax year.

● The student has not been convicted of a felony for possessing or distributing a controlled substance.

If a student does not meet all of the above conditions, you may be able to take the lifetime learning credit for part or all of that student's qualified education expenses instead.

Line 1

Complete columns (a) through (f) on line 1 for each student who qualifies for and for whom you elect to take the Hope credit.

Note. If you have more than three students who qualify for the Hope credit, enter "See attached" next to line 1 and attach a statement with the required information for each additional student. Include the amounts from line 1, column (f), for all students in the total you enter on line 2.

Column (c)

For each student, enter the amount of qualified education expenses remaining after reduction by certain tax-free amounts and refunds, as explained earlier. The expenses must have been paid for the student in 2006 for academic periods beginning after 2005 but before April 1, 2007, as explained earlier under *Prepaid Expenses*. If the student's expenses are more than $2,200 ($4,400 if a GO Zone student), enter $2,200 ($4,400 if a GO Zone student). You may use the worksheet on the next page to figure the correct amount to enter in column (c).

EXHIBIT 8–27   Form 8863 *(continued)*

Form 8863 (2006)   Page **4**

Qualified Education Expenses Worksheet for Column (c)
(Do a separate worksheet for each student)

1. Total qualified education expenses _____

2. Less adjustments:

   a. Tax-free educational assistance . _____

   b. Refunds of qualified education
      expenses . . . . _____

   c. Other adjustments (see Pub. 970) . _____

3. Total adjustments (add lines 2a–2c) _____

4. Qualified education expenses (subtract
line 3 from line 1). Enter here and on Form
8863, Part I or II, column (c) . . . _____

Part II
Lifetime Learning Credit

The maximum lifetime learning credit is $4,000 for GO Zone students and $2,000 for all other students, regardless of the number of students. If you are claiming a lifetime learning credit for both GO Zone students and other students, the qualified education expenses taken into account in Part II for other students cannot exceed $10,000 reduced by the qualified education expenses of the GO Zone students.

 You cannot take the lifetime learning credit for any student for whom you are taking the Hope credit.

Line 3

Complete columns (a) through (c) for each student for whom you are taking the lifetime learning credit.

Note. If you are taking the lifetime learning credit for more than three students, enter "See attached" next to line 3 and attach a statement with the required information for each additional student. Include the amounts from line 3, column (c), for all students in the total you enter on line 4.

Column (c)

For each student, enter the amount of qualified education expenses remaining after reduction by certain tax-free amounts and refunds, as explained earlier. The expenses must have been paid for the student in 2006 for academic periods beginning after 2005 but before April 1, 2007, as explained under *Prepaid Expenses* on page 2. You may use the worksheet on this page to figure the correct amount to enter in column (c).

Paperwork Reduction Act Notice. We ask for the information on this form to carry out the Internal Revenue laws of the United States. You are required to give us the information. We need it to ensure that you are complying with these laws and to allow us to figure and collect the right amount of tax.

You are not required to provide the information requested on a form that is subject to the Paperwork Reduction Act unless the form displays a valid OMB control number. Books or records relating to a form or its instructions must be retained as long as their contents may become material in the administration of any Internal Revenue law. Generally, tax returns and return information are confidential, as required by Internal Revenue Code section 6103.

The average time and expenses required to complete and file this form will vary depending on individual circumstances. For the estimated averages, see the instructions for your income tax return.

If you have suggestions for making this form simpler, we would be happy to hear from you. See the instructions for your income tax return.

EXHIBIT 8–27 Form 8863 *(continued)*

The Hope credit is available for students in their first two years of postsecondary education. It does not include any credits awarded by proficiency exam and only applies to the first two academic years. The student must be enrolled and carrying at least one-half of a full-time workload for his or her course of study. The student is not required to be in school during the summer or breaks. However, the credit cannot have been claimed in more than one previous tax year. An additional limitation is that the student cannot have been convicted of a felony on a drug-related offense. Because Hope is an education credit and reduces tax, rather than taxable income, there are limitations both on the amount claimed and the amount of reported income on the tax return. At the time of calculation, the Hope credit was limited to $1,500 per student in the household. Additionally, it is required to be claimed on the same return in which the student is listed as either a taxpayer or a dependent. For example, parents cannot claim the education credit on their return and the student claim himself or herself as a personal exemption on a separate return. The calculations to determine the amount of the Hope credit is determined using Part I and Part III of form 8863.

The second educational credit is the Lifetime credit. This can be used for those who pursue education generally. Although this credit is somewhat more limited, it can be taken on the tax return year after year and does not require the individual to be enrolled in a degree or certificate course of study. With this exception, the Lifetime credit has similar restrictions in terms of who may claim it and the expenses for which it is applicable. The Lifetime credit has a household limit of $2,000. Although the $1,500 Hope credit can be taken for an unlimited number of eligible dependents, the maximum lifetime credit per return is $2,000. The lifetime credit is calculated using Part II and Part III of form 8863.

18. Form 8880—Credit for Qualified Retirement Savings Contributions

One of the more recent credits incorporated into the tax code is the "Credit for Qualified Retirement Savings Contributions," commonly referred to as the Saver's Credit. When Social Security was first put in place in the early 20th century, it was never intended to be the sole source of income for retirees. Nevertheless, the public became more and more dependent on Social Security funds, and over several decades people began to save less and less for those years beyond retirement. Coupled with the ever-increasing potential lifespan, a growing retired population, a shrinking working population, and an uncertain future for the solvency of the Social Security system, a recipe for disaster has been put in place. As one of many efforts to combat this looming problem for America's aging population, the Saver's Credit was developed as a test that has currently been extended through 2007. The IRS has provided a means for a tax credit, applying credit against dollars of tax owed as an incentive to middle- and lower-income taxpayers to start saving for their retirement.

Form **8880**	**Credit for Qualified Retirement Savings Contributions**	OMB No. 1545-0074

Form **8880**

Department of the Treasury
Internal Revenue Service

Credit for Qualified Retirement Savings Contributions

▶ Attach to Form 1040, Form 1040A, or Form 1040NR.
▶ See instructions on back.

OMB No. 1545-0074

2006

Attachment Sequence No. **129**

Name(s) shown on return   Your social security number

 CAUTION You **cannot** take this credit if **either** of the following applies.
● The amount on Form 1040, line 38; Form 1040A, line 22; or Form 1040NR, line 36 is more than $25,000 ($37,500 if head of household; $50,000 if married filing jointly).
● The person(s) who made the qualified contribution or elective deferral **(a)** was born after January 1, 1989, **(b)** is claimed as a dependent on someone else's 2006 tax return, or **(c)** was a **student** (see instructions).

		(a) You	(b) Your spouse
1	Traditional and Roth IRA contributions for 2006. **Do not** include rollover contributions		
2	Elective deferrals to a 401(k) or other qualified employer plan, voluntary employee contributions, and 501(c)(18)(D) plan contributions for 2006 (see instructions)		
3	Add lines 1 and 2		
4	Certain distributions received **after** 2003 and **before** the due date (including extensions) of your 2006 tax return (see instructions). If married filing jointly, include **both** spouses' amounts in **both** columns. See instructions for an exception		
5	Subtract line 4 from line 3. If zero or less, enter -0-		
6	In each column, enter the **smaller** of line 5 or $2,000		
7	Add the amounts on line 6. If zero, **stop**; you cannot take this credit	7	
8	Enter the amount from Form 1040, line 38*; Form 1040A, line 22; or Form 1040NR, line 36	8	
9	Enter the applicable decimal amount shown below:		

If line 8 is—		And your filing status is—		
Over—	But not over—	Married filing jointly	Head of household	Single, Married filing separately, or Qualifying widow(er)
		Enter on line 9—		
---	$15,000	.5	.5	.5
$15,000	$16,250	.5	.5	.2
$16,250	$22,500	.5	.5	.1
$22,500	$24,375	.5	.2	.1
$24,375	$25,000	.5	.1	.1
$25,000	$30,000	.5	.1	.0
$30,000	$32,500	.2	.1	.0
$32,500	$37,500	.1	.1	.0
$37,500	$50,000	.1	.0	.0
$50,000	---	.0	.0	.0

9   X .

Note: If line 9 is zero, **stop**; you cannot take this credit.

10	Multiply line 7 by line 9	10	
11	Enter the amount from Form 1040, line 46; Form 1040A, line 28; or Form 1040NR, line 43	11	
12	**1040 filers:** Enter the total of your credits from lines 47 through 50. **1040A filers:** Enter the total of your credits from lines 29 through 31. **1040NR filers:** Enter the total of your credits from lines 44 and 45.	12	
13	Subtract line 12 from line 11. If zero, **stop**; you cannot take this credit	13	
14	**Credit for qualified retirement savings contributions.** Enter the **smaller** of line 10 or line 13 here and on Form 1040, line 51; Form 1040A, line 32; or Form 1040NR, line 46	14	

*See Pub. 590 for the amount to enter if you are filing Form 2555, 2555-EZ, or 4563 or you are excluding income from Puerto Rico.

For Paperwork Reduction Act Notice, see back of form.   Cat. No. 33394D   Form **8880** (2006)

EXHIBIT 8–28 Form 8880 (continues)

Form 8880 (2006)   Page **2**

General Instructions

Section references are to the Internal Revenue Code.

Purpose of Form

Use Form 8880 to figure the amount, if any, of your retirement savings contributions credit.

This credit can be claimed in addition to any IRA deduction claimed on Form 1040, line 32; Form 1040A, line 17; or Form 1040NR, line 31.

Who Can Take This Credit

You may be able to take this credit if you, or your spouse if filing jointly, made (a) contributions (other than rollover contributions) to a traditional or Roth IRA, (b) elective deferrals to a 401(k), 403(b), governmental 457, SEP, or SIMPLE plan, (c) voluntary employee contributions to a qualified retirement plan as defined in section 4974(c) (including the federal Thrift Savings Plan), or (d) contributions to a 501(c)(18)(D) plan.

However, you cannot take the credit if either of the following applies:

● The amount on Form 1040, line 38; Form 1040A, line 22; or Form 1040NR, line 36, is more than $25,000 ($37,500 if head of household; $50,000 if married filing jointly).

● The person(s) who made the qualified contribution or elective deferral (a) was born after January 1, 1989, (b) is claimed as a dependent on someone else's 2006 tax return, or (c) was a student.

You were a student if during any part of 5 calendar months of 2006 you:

● Were enrolled as a full-time student at a school, or

● Took a full-time, on-farm training course given by a school or a state, county, or local government agency.

A school includes technical, trade, and mechanical schools. It does not include on-the-job training courses, correspondence schools, or schools offering courses only through the Internet.

Specific Instructions

Column (b)

Complete column (b) only if you are filing a joint return.

Line 2

Include on line 2 any of the following amounts.

● Elective deferrals to a 401(k) or 403(b) plan (including designated Roth contributions under section 402A), or to a governmental 457, SEP, or SIMPLE plan.

● Voluntary employee contributions to a qualified retirement plan as defined in section 4974(c) (including the federal Thrift Savings Plan).

● Contributions to a 501(c)(18)(D) plan.

These amounts may be shown in box 12 of your Form(s) W-2 for 2006.

Line 4

Enter the total amount of distributions you, and your spouse if filing jointly, received after 2003 and before the due date of your 2006 return (including extensions) from any of the following types of plans.

● Traditional or Roth IRAs.

● 401(k), 403(b), governmental 457, 501(c)(18)(D), SEP, or SIMPLE plans.

● Qualified retirement plans as defined in section 4974(c) (including the federal Thrift Savings Plan).

Do not include any:

● Distributions not taxable as the result of a rollover or a trustee-to-trustee transfer.

● Distributions from your IRA (other than a Roth IRA) rolled over to your Roth IRA.

● Loans from a qualified employer plan treated as a distribution.

● Distributions of excess contributions or deferrals (and income allocable to such contributions or deferrals).

● Distributions of contributions made during a tax year and returned (with any income allocable to such contributions) on or before the due date (including extensions) for that tax year.

● Distributions of dividends paid on stock held by an employee stock ownership plan under section 404(k).

● Distributions from a military retirement plan.

If you are filing a joint return, include both spouses' amounts in both columns.

Exception. Do not include your spouse's distributions with yours when entering an amount on line 4 if you and your spouse did not file a joint return for the year the distribution was received.

Example. You received a distribution of $5,000 from a qualified retirement plan in 2006. Your spouse received a distribution of $2,000 from a Roth IRA in 2004. You and your spouse file a joint return in 2006, but did not file a joint return in 2004. You would include $5,000 in column (a) and $7,000 in column (b).

Line 7

Add the amounts from line 6 columns (a) and (b), and enter the total.

Paperwork Reduction Act Notice. We ask for the information on this form to carry out the Internal Revenue laws of the United States. You are required to give us the information. We need it to ensure that you are complying with these laws and to allow us to figure and collect the right amount of tax.

You are not required to provide the information requested on a form that is subject to the Paperwork Reduction Act unless the form displays a valid OMB control number. Books or records relating to a form or its instructions must be retained as long as their contents may become material in the administration of any Internal Revenue law. Generally, tax returns and return information are confidential, as required by section 6103.

The average time and expenses required to complete and file this form will vary depending on individual circumstances. For the estimated averages, see the instructions for your income tax return.

If you have suggestions for making this form simpler, we would be happy to hear from you. See the instructions for your income tax return.

EXHIBIT 8–28   Form 8880 *(continued)*

The Saver's Credit is calculated on form 8880. It is only available to taxpayers whose income is at or below a level that the IRS has determined historically is below a reasonable level for retirement. For taxpayers whose income is below this ceiling amount, the percentage used to calculate the amount of credit received rises as income goes down. The net effect is that the lowest income contributors receive the greatest amount of credit and, consequently, the greatest incentive to save.

APPLICATION 8.9

Elena is a single taxpayer with an adjusted gross income of $23,000. For the 2006 tax year, she contributed $2,000 to an IRA account. She had no retirement plan through her job. Elena has no dependents. Her taxable income was $15,000. Her tax was $1,500. She received an education credit of $500. She also received a Saver's Credit of $1,000. This reduced her tax to $0. The net effect would be that by contributing $2,000 along with her education credit, Elena saved $1,500, or 75 percent of the cost of her IRA.

ASSIGNMENT

Identify which supporting forms could be used to address each of the following situations:

a. Mitch donated a car to the American Kidney Foundation.

b. Approximately 80 percent of the use of Sharondica's new car this year was for business purposes in her job as a pharmaceutical sales representative. She wants to know if she can use a portion of the cost of the car as a deduction.

c. Christian sold his vacation home and received a profit of $400,000. Christian is widowed.

d. Bridget is a single mother of two and finished her education as a dental hygienist in August. She accepted her first job and began working in September. But her earned income for the year was limited because she only worked for a few months.

e. Ashton, whose adjusted gross income was $22,000, made a contribution to a deductible IRA of $2,000.

f. Bob started his business as a golf instructor. He had business expenses of $13,000 but income of only $10,000. He did not incorporate.

g. Brenda and Jimmy are working parents with three children age 3 and under. Both parents work full time.

h. Sam adopted a son who had previously been his foster child. Sam paid all of the expenses of the adoption.

(continues)

ASSIGNMENT *(continued)*

   i. Marie does not want to use her refund to pay back child support owed by her new husband, Rich.

   j. Marie does not want to use her refund to pay back taxes owed by her ex-husband, Rich, for income that she never even knew he had.

   k. Kristin plans to put money into a Roth IRA.

   l. Tyrell has opened his own insurance agency. He has converted his garage into a fully finished office space.

  m. Kate changed jobs during the year. She used the distribution from her 401K to move to a new city where her boyfriend lives. She has not returned to work and at this point does not plan to work.

   n. Cindy has six children aged 12, 13, 14, 15, 16, and 17. She wants to know if there are any tax benefits for all six, other than claiming them as dependents.

   o. Jessica and Nate have a son who is about to graduate high school. If he attends college next year and Nate also takes some college courses, are there any tax benefits to help them?

   p. Marcus received a letter from the IRS stating that in addition to his income tax, he owed an additional $1,200 in taxes, not because of any errors or the timeliness in the preparation of his return or disallowed deductions.

   q. Carley accepted a new position in a city 1,000 miles from where she currently lives. The employer has offered no incentives to assist her in relocating.

   r. Alana has numerous unreimbursed expenses that she has incurred in her job.

ETHICAL QUESTION

Mark is employed by a local law firm to assist in the preparation of tax returns for clients of the firm. Mark is bound by the requirements imposed on the attorneys and staff of the firm with respect to confidentiality of the information developed during representation of clients. During the preparation of the return for a particular client, Mark sees that Michael Osborne is filing a return as the natural father of 6-year-old Jireh Smith. Michael is claiming head of household status, Jireh as a dependent, and is receiving various associated tax benefits, including great standard deduction, child tax, and earned income credits. Mark knows Michael through a personal acquaintance, namely Jireh's mother. Mark further knows that

(continues)

ETHICAL QUESTION *(continued)*

Michael only met Jireh's mother when he moved to the area a few months ago and the two have been dating. Under the ethical code of conduct, Michael is obligated to keep information confidential. However, in this circumstance, to do so would not only be assisting Michael in criminal conduct; as the tax return preparer, Mark would be involved in the criminal conduct as well. Consequently, the ethical code would not require Mark's silence on the matter. How should he handle the situation?

SUMMARY

The focus of this chapter was to identify the primary forms of filing the individual tax return. This included a simplified form, a form without itemized deductions, an itemized form, and an amended form. The circumstances of the individual dictate which form is the most appropriate. In addition to the actual return, it is often necessary to submit various schedules that detail one or more transactions or occurrences that contributed to the amount entered on a specific line of the tax return. Also, in some cases, supporting forms that show even more detail and various calculations are included to substantiate schedules and other entries on the tax return. The amount of information to be included depends largely on the type of item included on the return. For example, those items that include a reduction of tax liability or of the tax itself may require a great deal of information to support the claim. Finally, if an amended return is filed, it requires inclusion of not only the basis for the amendment and any resulting tax changes, but also a great deal of information from the original return.

▮ KEY TERMS

fair market value	Injured Spouse	Direct Expenses
Innocent Spouse	Saver's Credit	Indirect Expenses

For additional resources, visit our Web site at www.westlegalstudies.com

9

The Individual
Income Tax Return

▇ **OBJECTIVES**_____

After completing this chapter, you will be able to:

❑ Complete the primary components of an individual tax return

❑ Calculate necessary adjustments to achieve an adjusted gross income

❑ Calculate appropriate deductions and credits to determine taxable income

❑ Calculate tax on taxable income

❑ Apply appropriate nonrefundable and refundable credits and payments to achieve tax owed or overpayment

❑ Discuss the difference of a state and federal return and the concept of credits for tax paid in a nonresident state

A. COMPUTATION OF INDIVIDUAL INCOME TAX

Regardless of the source, all individuals with income may be subject to income tax. There are as many possible outcomes as there are taxpayers. In fact, there are probably more, given the variables that come into play for each of the taxpayers year to year. As a result, it is essential that all of the relevant information be gathered with respect to those variables and then combined in the appropriate way to best establish the true tax, if any, owed.

1. Income

Discussion in previous chapters focused on all the potential types of income. They included earned and unearned, wages and income from self-employment, investments, income from partnerships, corporations, sole proprietorships, property, and the list continues. Each of the types of income may be further divided into subcategories that may or may not be subject to income tax, Social Security taxes, Medicare, or any combination of the three.

The first step in preparation of an individual income tax return is to identify each form of income that the taxpayer received during the year. This should include income from all sources. Each source can then be properly evaluated as to its taxability. For example, someone who receives a cash gift may not consider that money income. However, depending on the size and nature of the gift, it may be subject to a gift tax. Also, if the gift was in any way compensation for acts of the recipient or a return on investment, it may be subject to income, capital gains, Social Security, Medicare, or other forms of tax. The fact that income is received from someone close to the taxpayer such as a family member does not negate the issue of tax. Also, even though income may not be subject to tax, it may still affect tax liability such as income that is not taxable but has an impact on deductions, adjusted gross income, filing status, and so on.

APPLICATION **9.1**

Oliver is a single parent who attends college full time. During the year, his parents provide him with $10,000 to help with expenses. Oliver also receives government benefits for food stamps and assistance with utilities in an amount of $6,000. Oliver works part time and through the year earned $4,000. Although the gift of $10,000 and the government assistance of $6,000 may not be subject to tax, they greatly impact the ability of Oliver to support his child. This information would likely affect his ability to file as head of household, as he did not provide more than one half of the support for his child.

In the initial interview with a taxpayer, a number of questions will glean most of the information needed to identify the income that is likely to play some part in the preparation of the return. Not all will directly result in taxable income, but still answers could affect the calculation. The following is a sample list of initial questions:

1. Is the taxpayer over 65, disabled, blind, or subject to being claimed by someone else as a dependent on their return?

2. Does the taxpayer have income from any of the following sources during the tax year:

   An employer

   Self-employment

   Scholarship money not used for tuition

   Gambling winnings or prizes

   A Partnership, S Corporation, or Estate

   Rents or Royalty income

   Gifts from one source exceeding $11,000 per taxpayer for the year

   Capital transactions (should have received a 1099-DIV)

   Interest and/or Dividends

   Sale of property

   Pension/Retirement Plan /Disability Income

   Social Security benefits

   Unemployment

   State or local tax refunds

   Income from farming

Once all of the income has been accounted for, it is necessary to identify the various types of income. This will in turn help determine filing status and guide the various forms, schedules, and worksheets that are necessary to determine any tax effects and properly report all income that should be included on the return. Often, different types of income affect one another in terms of tax liability and as such must be considered together. For example, income from Social Security generally is excluded from tax. However, if there are earnings above a certain amount, then a percentage of the Social Security benefits may become taxable for income tax but not for Social Security and Medicare taxes.

Once the source of income is determined, it must be addressed by type to remove those items that are not taxable, and/or to account for certain issues that affect the taxable amount. This requires calculation of the taxable amount of each of the types of income listed earlier. For this, appropriate worksheets and schedules must be completed. For example, before income can be reported on the return for self-employment income, Schedule C must be completed to reduce the gross amount of income by the amount of legally recognized expenses. The net amount is that which is reported as income.

2. Filing Status

The **filing status** of an individual greatly affects tax liability. Because each taxpayer and dependent is allowed an amount of income that is effectively excluded from tax, known as a personal exemption, this is a relatively straightforward calculation. Each taxpayer and dependent is allowed a specific amount per person, per year. But the standard deduction is affected by the type of household in which a person lives. For example, in addition to the personal exemptions, married individuals receive a standard deduction equal to twice the amount allowed a single individual. Single individuals who have one or more dependents receive a greater amount than an individual with no dependents. Qualified widows and widowers receive a higher amount for a period of 2 years following the year of the death of spouse to enable them to adjust to the change in income that may have resulted from the death of a spouse and the tax effects of no longer filing as married filing jointly. Individuals who are married but file separately receive yet another amount of standard deduction.

Households that do not fall into the stated categories are not entitled to claim the status regardless of the nature of the family unit. For example, at this point in time, a same sex couple may not file as Married Filing Jointly regardless of the level of personal commitment in the relationship. The logic used in this determination is that because the parties are not in a marriage recognized by law, they do not have the same legal commitment and in turn the tax status can more easily change throughout the year. The same logic is applied to individuals who house family members or friends on a temporary or even semipermanent basis without government sanctioned placement. For example, a single person may provide a home for friend's child. This does not create an opportunity for the individual to file under head of household status or even to claim the child as a dependent. However, if a state agency reviews the situation and declares it is an approved foster care placement, the filing and dependency status may be changed.

The filing status of each taxpayer must be determined before any other calculations because it affects the tax return as a whole in terms of exemptions, deductions, and **credits** that are available to the taxpayer. Marital status among living individuals is determined as of the end of the tax year December 31. It does not matter that a couple was married on December 31, if they were legally divorced before midnight. In that case, married filing jointly status is not available. Similarly, if a couple became married on December 31, their status is considered married for the entire year. The rule is not the same for dependents. For dependents who are not the children of the taxpayer, a determination must be made according to IRS rules as to whether the individual (child or adult) qualifies to be claimed as a dependent. If a dependent is the child of the taxpayer and meets the other requirements such as age, the dependency can be claimed for the entire year regardless of the date on which the child was born, or died. For unmarried taxpayers who share dependent children who do not themselves file married filing jointly, the right to claim a dependent child is generally provided to the custodial parent unless an exception

FILING STATUS

Can greatly affect tax liability.

CREDITS

A dollar-for-dollar reduction of taxes owed. Differs from a deduction, which reduces the amount of income subject to tax.

applies. Following determination of the proper filing status and reported amounts of taxable income, it is necessary to adjust the total income by certain tax preferred items known as **adjustments**.

3. Adjustments

ADJUSTMENTS

Allow the taxpayer to remove certain portions of gross income from the taxable income computation.

Adjustments allow the taxpayer to remove certain portions of gross income from the taxable income computation and result in what is known as the Adjusted Gross Income (AGI). The adjustments can be used to alter the amount of income subject to tax. However, most adjustments are also expenses the taxpayer incurred during the year that decreased the taxpayer's income. Once the adjustments are applied against the gross income of the taxpayer, a net amount results. This net amount is referred to as the AGI. It is used to then apply deductions and credits to reach the final result with regard to tax owed. Adjustments include amounts (subject to limitations for each type of item) paid for the following items:

- Educator expenses
- Certain specified business expenses reported on form 2106
- Contributions to deductible IRAs
- Student loan interest (if qualified)
- Tuition and fees deduction (not Hope and Lifetime credits)
- Health Savings Account deductions reported on form 8889
- Moving expenses reported on form 3903
- One half of self-employment tax reported on Schedule SE
- Self-employed health insurance premiums
- Self-employed qualified retirement plans
- Penalties on early withdrawals of savings (this is an addition rather than deduction)
- Alimony paid (this does not include child support)

4. Items That Affect Taxable Income and Tax Owed

Once the net income and any adjustments are calculated, the real process of determining tax liability begins. This takes into account more of the personal circumstances as they affect tax liability for each taxpayer. There are a variety of items that affect the ultimate determination. Throughout the text, reference has been made to items that affect the amount of taxable income and tax liability such as deductions,

APPLICATION 9.2

Marquette had income from her job as a teacher in the amount of $38,500. She spent $250 for supplies for her classroom that were not provided by the school. She also had earnings from her Web site, which netted $11,500 (after Schedule C was completed). She paid $1,685 in Social Security/Medicare taxes on her self-employment. During the year, she contributed $2,000 to a retirement fund. Marquette does not receive health insurance benefits through her job and pays $4,000 annually for health insurance on a private plan. Marquette is working on an advanced degree and incurred $2,000 in expenses for tuition and fees. She is also paying back the student loans used to finance her Bachelor's degree and paid $1,358 in interest on her student loans this year. The interest qualifies for the adjustment. Her Adjusted Gross Income would be calculated as follows:

Earnings	$38,500		
Self-Employment Income	$11,500		
Gross Income			$50,000
Less Adjustments:			
Educator Expenses		$ 250	
Self-Employment Tax		$ 842	
Tuition and Fees Expense		$ 2,000	
IRA Contribution		$ 2,000	
Student Loan Interest		$ 1,358	
Total Adjustments			-$ 6,450
Adjusted Gross Income			$43,550

exemptions, and credits. The purpose and manner in which each of these affect the tax situation for an individual is different. The discussion that follows defines and distinguishes the various items that most affect the ultimate tax imposed.

a. Deductions.

A deduction can be applied at various points in the tax preparation process. A deduction is an allowable reduction of the amount of income that will be subjected to tax that is commonly referred to as taxable income. For example, if an individual has self-employment income, certain expenses incurred in the production of income can be subtracted from payments received to reach the actual amount subject to tax. The same is true for various other types of income such as rental property, investments, and so on.

The most common deduction is the one that is available to all taxpayers. Every household represented on a tax return is allowed to reduce the taxable income in one of two ways. The first choice is the Standard Deduction. This amount is established each year by the IRS. However, if a household has certain types of expenses that exceed the designated standard deduction, the taxpayer may opt to file an itemized return instead using Schedule A amounts in lieu of the standard deduction. This is separate and in addition to the personal exemption amount introduced previously and discussed in detail in the following section.

Schedule A (see Chapter 8) is the alternative to using the standard deduction. It includes items such as certain types of other taxes that have been paid, mortgage interest, charitable contributions, some expenses related to employment that were not reimbursed, and limited medical expenses. For some of these items, the amount that can be claimed as a deduction is limited. Regardless of whether the taxpayer elects to use the standard deduction or to itemize, the net effect is the same: The amount of taxable income is reduced before the calculation of tax.

b. Personal Exemptions.

The concept behind personal exemptions is similar in purpose to the standard deduction. The standard deduction provides a specified of income per household that is not subject to tax. The personal exemption provides an additional amount per person within the household that is not subject to tax. Thus, the household with five members would have a greater amount of income exempt from tax than the household with only two members. Each year, the amount allowed for personal exemptions increases to adjust for inflation. Additionally, certain conditions such as those subject to disability, blindness, or age beyond 65 receive an additional allowance. The disability and blindness elements require the condition to have been documented by a physician.

APPLICATION **9.3**

Jackie is the single mother of 10-year-old Carrina. In 2006, Jackie's adjusted gross income was $27,000. Filing under head of household status, Jackie received a standard deduction of $7,550. In addition, she received a personal exemption of $3,300 for herself and also for her daughter. The total of $14,150 is deducted from $27,000. The amount of income subject to tax for Jackie is $12,850. The amount of tax on this amount of income is $1,390. However, before a refund or tax liability can be calculated, it is necessary to determine if Jackie has any applicable credits.

c. Credits—Refundable versus Nonrefundable Credits.

Unlike the deduction that reduces the amount of income subject to tax, the credit is used to reduce the amount of tax owed dollar for dollar. Whether a credit is **refundable** or **nonrefundable** is extremely important in terms of the impact on the taxpayer. Even though deductions and credits are all positive for the taxpayer, when available, the refundable credit offers the greatest potential tax advantage as will be explained in the discussion that follows.

The taxpayer's taxable income is established by first completing the following steps:

a. Determining the filing status and status of dependents

b. Determining the amount of Gross Income (some deductions are applied this point)

c. Determining the Adjusted Gross Income (certain subtractions/additions to the Gross Income are calculated)

d. Application of the Standard Deduction/Schedule A amounts

e. Application of the Personal Exemption amount (including any special amounts)

Once these steps are completed, the resulting amount is the taxable income. The annual tax tables provide for the calculation of the exact amount of tax due per taxpayer. The annual tables take into account the filing status and the amount of taxable income. By locating the corresponding amount from these two columns (top and left) on the table, the amount of tax due is established. Following this, any eligible credits are applied to the tax and the ultimate tax liability or refund can then be established. This of course does not include the calculation of penalties, which, if any, are determined after all tax and credits are established.

i. Foreign Tax Credit. As a general rule, taxpayers are allowed to receive a nonrefundable credit against tax liability for the income taxes paid or accrued during the year to foreign countries or countries that are considered U.S. possessions, for example, St. Thomas in the U.S. Virgin Islands. An alternative is to treat the credit as an itemized deduction. A deduction will not generally have as significant of an effect as a credit. This is because deductions reduce the amount subject to the tax computation. Credits actually reduce the tax. However, if there is not enough tax liability to benefit from that credit, a deduction, when available, may be the wiser choice. If the income that caused the tax was excluded from the income in the United States under a special exclusion such as a foreign housing exclusion, the tax then paid cannot be claimed as a credit or deduction. The credit is calculated by dividing the total foreign taxable income by the total U.S. and foreign taxable income. This fraction is then multiplied against the total U.S. tax liability. As a nonrefundable item, the foreign tax credit cannot exceed this amount. The calculation is done by completing form 1116.

REFUNDABLE

Tax credits that can reduce tax liability below $0, resulting in a tax refund.

NONREFUNDABLE

Tax credits that cannot reduce tax liability below $0.

Form **1116**

Department of the Treasury
Internal Revenue Service (99)

Foreign Tax Credit
(Individual, Estate, or Trust)

▶ Attach to Form 1040, 1040NR, 1041, or 990-T.
▶ See separate instructions.

OMB No. 1545-0121

2006

Attachment
Sequence No. **19**

Name

Identifying number as shown on page 1 of your tax return

Use a separate Form 1116 for each category of income listed below. See **Categories of Income** on page 3 of the instructions. Check only one box on each Form 1116. Report all amounts in U.S. dollars except where specified in Part II below.

a ☐ Passive income
b ☐ High withholding tax interest
c ☐ Financial services income

d ☐ Shipping income
e ☐ Dividends from a DISC or former DISC
f ☐ Certain distributions from a foreign sales corporation (FSC) or former FSC

g ☐ Lump-sum distributions
h ☐ Section 901(j) income
i ☐ Certain income re-sourced by treaty
j ☐ General limitation income

k Resident of (name of country) ▶

Note: *If you paid taxes to only one foreign country or U.S. possession, use column A in Part I and line A in Part II. If you paid taxes to* **more than one** *foreign country or U.S. possession, use a separate column and line for each country or possession.*

Part I   Taxable Income or Loss From Sources Outside the United States (for Category Checked Above)

		Foreign Country or U.S. Possession			Total
		A	B	C	(Add cols. A, B, and C.)
l	Enter the name of the foreign country or U.S. possession . . . . ▶				
1a	Gross income from sources within country shown above and of the type checked above (see page 13 of the instructions):				1a
b	Check if line 1a is compensation for personal services as an employee, your total compensation from all sources is $250,000 or more, and you used an alternative basis to determine its source (see instructions) ▶ ☐				
*Deductions and losses (**Caution:** See pages 13 and 14 of the instructions):*					
2	Expenses **definitely related** to the income on line 1a (attach statement)				
3	Pro rata share of other deductions **not definitely related:**				
a	Certain itemized deductions or standard deduction (see instructions)				
b	Other deductions (attach statement)				
c	Add lines 3a and 3b				
d	Gross foreign source income (see instructions) .				
e	Gross income from all sources (see instructions)				
f	Divide line 3d by line 3e (see instructions) . .				
g	Multiply line 3c by line 3f				
4	Pro rata share of interest expense (see instructions):				
a	Home mortgage interest (use worksheet on page 13 of the instructions)				
b	Other interest expense				
5	Losses from foreign sources				
6	Add lines 2, 3g, 4a, 4b, and 5				6
7	Subtract line 6 from line 1a. Enter the result here and on line 14, page 2 . . . . ▶				7

Part II   Foreign Taxes Paid or Accrued (see page 14 of the instructions)

Country	Credit is claimed for taxes (you must check one)		Foreign taxes paid or accrued								
	(m) ☐ Paid (n) ☐ Accrued		In foreign currency				In U.S. dollars				
	(o) Date paid or accrued		Taxes withheld at source on:			(s) Other foreign taxes paid or accrued	Taxes withheld at source on:			(w) Other foreign taxes paid or accrued	(x) Total foreign taxes paid or accrued (add cols. (t) through (w))
			(p) Dividends	(q) Rents and royalties	(r) Interest		(t) Dividends	(u) Rents and royalties	(v) Interest		
A											
B											
C											
8	Add lines A through C, column (x). Enter the total here and on line 9, page 2 . . . . ▶									8	

For Paperwork Reduction Act Notice, see page 18 of the instructions.   Cat. No. 11440U   Form **1116** (2006)

EXHIBIT 9–1 IRS Form 1116 *(continues)*

Form 1116 (2006)   Page **2**

Part III   **Figuring the Credit**

9   Enter the amount from line 8. These are your total foreign taxes paid
    or accrued for the category of income checked above Part I . . | **9** |

10 Carryback or carryover (attach detailed computation) . . . . . | **10** |

11 Add lines 9 and 10. . . . . | **11** |

12 Reduction in foreign taxes (see page 15 of the instructions). . . | **12** |

13 Subtract line 12 from line 11. This is the total amount of foreign taxes available for credit . . . | **13** |

14 Enter the amount from line 7. This is your taxable income or (loss) from
    sources outside the United States (before adjustments) for the category
    of income checked above Part I (see page 15 of the instructions) . | **14** |

15 Adjustments to line 14 (see pages 15 and 16 of the instructions) . | **15** |

16 Combine the amounts on lines 14 and 15. This is your net foreign
    source taxable income. (If the result is zero or less, you have no foreign
    tax credit for the category of income you checked above Part I. Skip
    lines 17 through 21. However, if you are filing more than one Form
    1116, you must complete line 19.) . . . . | **16** |

17 **Individuals:** Enter the amount from Form 1040, line 41 (minus any
    amount on Form 8914, line 6). If you are a nonresident alien, enter the
    amount from Form 1040NR, line 38 (minus any amount on Form 8914,
    line 6). **Estates and trusts:** Enter your taxable income without the
    deduction for your exemption . . . . | **17** |

    Caution: *If you figured your tax using the lower rates on qualified dividends or capital gains, see
    page 16 of the instructions.*

18 Divide line 16 by line 17. If line 16 is more than line 17, enter "1" . . . . | **18** |

19 **Individuals:** Enter the amount from Form 1040, line 44. If you are a nonresident alien, enter the amount
    from Form 1040NR, line 41.

    Estates and trusts: Enter the amount from Form 1041, Schedule G, line 1a, or the total of Form 990-T,
    lines 36 and 37 . . . . | **19** |

    Caution: *If you are completing line 19 for separate category **g** (lump-sum distributions), see page 18 of the instructions.*

20 Multiply line 19 by line 18 (maximum amount of credit) . . . . | **20** |

21 Enter the **smaller** of line 13 or line 20. If this is the only Form 1116 you are filing, skip lines 22 through
    30 and enter this amount on line 31. Otherwise, complete the appropriate line in Part IV (see
    page 18 of the instructions) . . . . ▶ | **21** |

Part IV   **Summary of Credits From Separate Parts III** (see page 18 of the instructions)

22 Credit for taxes on passive income . . . . | **22** |

23 Credit for taxes on high withholding tax interest . . . . . | **23** |

24 Credit for taxes on financial services income . . . . . . | **24** |

25 Credit for taxes on shipping income . . . . | **25** |

26 Credit for taxes on dividends from a DISC or former DISC and certain
    distributions from a FSC or former FSC . . . . | **26** |

27 Credit for taxes on lump-sum distributions . . . . | **27** |

28 Credit for taxes on certain income re-sourced by treaty . . . . | **28** |

29 Credit for taxes on general limitation income . . . . . . | **29** |

30 Add lines 22 through 29 . . . . | **30** |

31 Enter the **smaller** of line 19 or line 30 . . . . | **31** |

32 Reduction of credit for international boycott operations. See instructions for line 12 on page 15 . | **32** |

33 Subtract line 32 from line 31. This is your **foreign tax credit.** Enter here and on Form 1040, line 47;
    Form 1040NR, line 44; Form 1041, Schedule G, line 2a; or Form 990-T, line 40a . . . . . ▶ | **33** |

Form **1116** (2006)

EXHIBIT 9–1   IRS Form 1116 *(continued)*

APPLICATION   9.4

Form 1116 provides the basic computation for the foreign tax credit. This is an illustration of how the credit is calculated.

The taxpayer had taxable foreign income of $10,000 and U.S. taxable income of $90,000. The taxpayer's U.S. tax liability was $9,000. The taxpayer also paid $1,500 in foreign income taxes.

1. $10,000

2. .10 x $9000 = $900.

3. Total Foreign Tax Credit Limit
   $100,000 = .10 $900 (of the $1500 paid).

There is an exception to the limitation on the foreign tax credit. However, it requires the taxpayer to satisfy all five tests. If each one is met, then form 1116 to limit the tax credit need not be applied:

1. All foreign income was from interest and dividends and all were reported on form 1099-INT or a Schedule K-1.

2. Any dividend income was from stock that had been held at least 16 days.

3. Form 4563 is not being filed, nor is there an exclusion of income from sources within Puerto Rico.

4. The foreign tax total did not exceed $300 for individuals or $600 for those using married filing jointly status.

5. All foreign taxes were owed and not subject to refund and paid to countries recognized by the United States and who do not support terrorism.

ii. Child and Dependent Care Expense Credit. The credit for child and dependent care expenses is a limited use credit designed to assist individuals who are responsible for the care of either young children or disabled persons. A primary requirement of the credit is that the taxpayer must be employed, actively seeking employment, or a full-time student. Additionally, the individual must have expended money for one of the following:

- the care of a child under age 13

- a spouse unable to care for him or herself as the result of disability

- an individual who lived with the taxpayer more than half the year and who is unable to care for him or herself and could have been claimed as a dependent except for the fact that the individual received more than $3200 in gross income, filed a joint return, or the taxpayer could have been claimed a dependent on someone else's return.

In the case of a married couple filing jointly, each spouse must meet one of the requirements. There are limitations on the amount of expense that can be claimed as a credit. These limitations are connected to the tax liability of the taxpayer, amount of income received, dependent care benefits such as through an employer benefit plan, and the amount expended for dependent care.

To claim the credit for child and dependent care expenses, it is first necessary to determine if the taxpayer qualifies to claim the credit. The IRS has published a flowchart to assist in this determination. A copy of the chart is located in Exhibit 10–1. The person receiving the payment for care must be properly identified with a name, address, and tax identification number. If the care provider is an individual, they may have a federal tax identification number or may use their Social Security number. It should be noted that one effect of claiming this credit is that it reports the income for the care provider to the IRS. As a result, care providers should always report the amount received as income on their own tax return. After the care provider and amount is properly identified, the calculation can be done to determine the amount of child and dependent care expenses that can be claimed as a nonrefundable tax credit.

Some employers provide dependent care benefits as part of an employment benefit package. These plans typically allow the employee to have money taken from their wages before taxes are applied. The money is placed into an account that can be drawn on to pay the expenses of dependent care. However, if the expenses are not withdrawn in the time allotted by the IRS, the funds are forfeited. The taxpayer does not pay tax on the unused funds because they are never received as earnings. If the funds are withdrawn and used to pay dependent car expenses, those funds are not eligible for the dependent care expense credit (an offset against taxes) because they were never taxed initially. Recall that these funds are withdrawn from earned wages before taxes are applied. Additionally, in an IRS qualified plan, the amount received for dependent care benefits reduces the limit per dependent. For example, in 2006, the amount of dependent care expense used in the credit calculation was $3,000 for one dependent and $6,000 for two or more dependents with expenses. If an employee participated in a qualified plan and received $1,000 in dependent care expenses, the limit would have been reduced by $1,000 to $2,000 before the final calculation of the credit would be completed. To determine the exact amount of the credit after income and dollar limits have been applied, it is necessary to apply the applicable percentage. The IRS chart for this credit in the tax year should be consulted. The percentage is tied directly to the adjusted gross income of the taxpayer. The lowest percentage as of writing is 20 percent. The percentage is applied to the amount of qualified dependent care expenses to reach the amount of the credit available, however, this is not necessarily the amount of the credit that will be received. As a nonrefundable credit the amount is also limited to the tax liability of the taxpayer. If the taxpayer owes an amount equal to or greater than the amount of credit figured, then the entire credit can be applied. However, if the amount of tax liability is less than the credit, the credit is limited to the lesser amount. The Child and Dependent Care Credit is claimed on form 2441. See Exhibit 8–15.

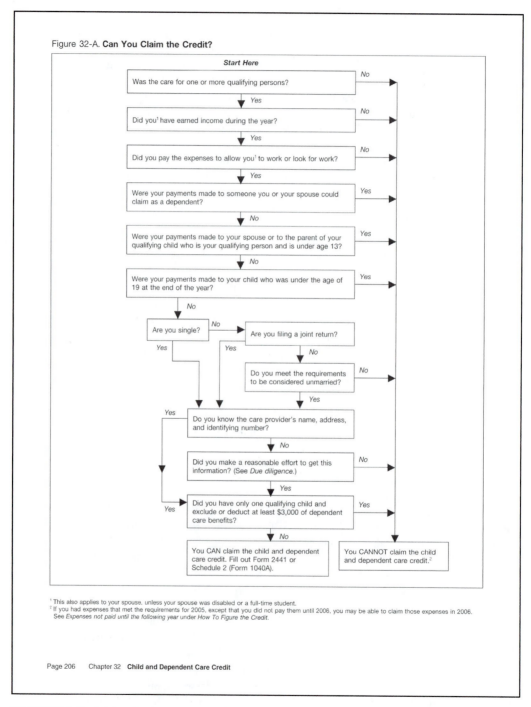

Figure 32-A. **Can You Claim the Credit?**

Start Here

Was the care for one or more qualifying persons? — No →

↓ Yes

Did you[1] have earned income during the year? — No →

↓ Yes

Did you pay the expenses to allow you[1] to work or look for work? — No →

↓ Yes

Were your payments made to someone you or your spouse could claim as a dependent? — Yes →

↓ No

Were your payments made to your spouse or to the parent of your qualifying child who is your qualifying person and is under age 13? — Yes →

↓ No

Were your payments made to your child who was under the age of 19 at the end of the year? — Yes →

↓ No

Are you single? — No → Are you filing a joint return?

Yes ↓   ↓ No / Yes

Do you meet the requirements to be considered unmarried? — No →

↓ Yes

Do you know the care provider's name, address, and identifying number? — Yes →

↓ No

Did you make a reasonable effort to get this information? (See *Due diligence*.) — No →

↓ Yes

Did you have only one qualifying child and exclude or deduct at least $3,000 of dependent care benefits? — Yes →

↓ No

You CAN claim the child and dependent care credit. Fill out Form 2441 or Schedule 2 (Form 1040A).

You CANNOT claim the child and dependent care credit.[2]

[1] This also applies to your spouse, unless your spouse was disabled or a full-time student.
[2] If you had expenses that met the requirements for 2005, except that you did not pay them until 2006, you may be able to claim those expenses in 2006. See *Expenses not paid until the following year* under *How To Figure the Credit*.

Page 206   Chapter 32   **Child and Dependent Care Credit**

EXHIBIT 9–2   IRS Pub. 17, Child Care Credit Flowchart

APPLICATION **9.5**

In 2005, a taxpayer with an adjusted gross income of $24,000 was entitled to claim 30 percent of the amount paid for qualified child and dependent care expenses as a tax credit. Carl, a single father, paid $100 per week for child care while he worked. Carl had two qualifying children, which provided a limit of $6,000 (regardless of how the expenses are split among the children). At the end of the year, Carl had paid $5,200 in child care expenses. Carl had an adjusted gross income of $24,000 and a tax liability of $1,100. Based on the income chart, his credit was 30 percent of $5,200, or $1,560. However, because the child and dependent care expense credit is nonrefundable (limited to the amount of tax liability), Carl could only reduce the tax liability to 0. This meant that he could claim a credit of $1,100.

iii. Credit for the Elderly or Disabled. The credit for the elderly or disabled is used to provide additional tax relief to certain individuals who are U.S. citizens, above age 65, and/or retired on permanent and total disability. This credit is nonrefundable and can only be used to reduce tax liability. Thus, if the taxpayer has no liability, it is not effective. To claim the credit, the qualified individual must meet the following tests:

- age 65 or older at the end of the tax year, OR

- under age 65 at the end of the tax year and meet all three of the following:

    a. retired on permanent disability, and

    b. received taxable disability income during the tax year, and

    c. as of January 1 of the tax year the individual had not reached mandatory retirement age. (This is the age set by the employer that the taxpayer would have been required to retire had there not been a disability.)

In order to qualify for the credit on the basis of disability, the individual also must be able to produce a physician's statement that certifies the taxpayer is disabled from substantial gainful activity for a period of more than 12 months. The document does not need to be attached to the return. However, it must be signed and dated before the filing of the return and kept on record in the event it is requested by the IRS. If the client is not government certified as disabled by the Veteran's Administration or Social Security, it may be necessary to obtain a physician's statement each year to support the claim of disability.

In addition to the requirements with respect to age and disability, there are some limitations on filing status and income. For example, in order for a married couple to claim the credit they must either file as married Filing Jointly, or have lived apart the entire year and file Married Filing Separately. Head of Household status can be used and the credit still be claimed if Head of Household filing tests are met. There are limits on the adjusted gross income and nontaxable pension and Social Security income. The limits vary based on the filing status. If the adjusted gross income and nontaxable pensions are each less than the income limits, the credit may be available. The adjusted gross income is modified for the calculation of the credit. The calculation allows the taxpayers to subtract the standard deduction amount for their filing status to determine the adjusted gross income for the purposes of the credit. The income limit of the AGI and nontaxable income also varies with filing status and the year of filing. Even if allowed, the credit may be limited. This limitation, if any, is calculated on Schedule R or Schedule 3, depending on the form being used by the taxpayer.

iv. Education Credits. These are credits available to all taxpayers who qualify and can reduce taxes by offsetting education expenses. There are two educational credits available, commonly known as Hope and Lifetime Learning credits. Unlike the less restrictive tuition and fees deduction and work-related expenses deductions that can be used to reduce the amount of income subject to tax, the educational credits actually reduce the amount of tax that is due. However, these are nonrefundable credits and thus cannot reduce the tax to an amount below $0. Whether an education credit or education related deduction is the most beneficial varies by taxpayer circumstances. However, unless there are expenses primarily consisting of tuition and fees, there is no tax liability, or the tax liability has already been eliminated by a credit, an educational credit that reduces tax dollar for dollar is generally preferable to a deduction.

APPLICATION 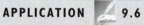 **9.6**

Consider the following scenario using 2006 tax rules: Joe and Jackie are married. Joe is 66 years old and retired from his job. He collects a taxable pension of $7,000. He also has nontaxable Social Security income of $2,000 per year. Jackie is 58 years old. She was injured at work and retired on disability. She received a disability pension of $8,000 per year. Her employer's retirement plan provided for retirement at age 59. They file their taxes using married filing jointly status. Both of them are eligible for the elderly and disabled credit. Their combined adjusted gross income is $15,000. They have no foreign tax credit or child and dependent care credit. By completing the calculations on Schedule R, the couple could be entitled to an elderly and dependent care credit of $450 against their tax liability. However, consider the fact that after the standard deduction of $10,300 for married filing jointly is applied, the taxable income is reduced to $3,700. They are also entitled to personal exemptions of $6,600. This is greater than the $3,700 and reduces the tax liability to 0. This does not even account for the additional allowance for Joe, who is older than 65. Because the elderly and disabled credit is nonrefundable, they would not benefit from the credit in this circumstance because there can be no subtraction form a tax liability of 0 for a nonrefundable credit.

Schedule R
(Form 1040)

Department of the Treasury
Internal Revenue Service   (99)

Name(s) shown on Form 1040

Credit for the Elderly or the Disabled

▶ Attach to Form 1040.   ▶ See Instructions for Schedule R (Form 1040).

OMB No. 1545-0074

2006

Attachment
Sequence No. **16**

Your social security number

You may be able to take this credit and reduce your tax if by the end of 2006:

- You were age 65 or older   **or**
- You were under age 65, you retired on **permanent and total** disability, and you received taxable disability income.

But you must also meet other tests. See page R-1.

TIP   In most cases, the IRS can figure the credit for you. See page R-1.

Part I   Check the Box for Your Filing Status and Age

If your filing status is:	And by the end of 2006:	Check only one box:

| Single, Head of household, or Qualifying widow(er) | **1** You were 65 or older . . . . **1** | ☐ |
| | **2** You were under 65 and you retired on permanent and total disability **2** | ☐ |

	3 Both spouses were 65 or older **3**	☐
	4 Both spouses were under 65, but only one spouse retired on permanent and total disability **4**	☐
Married filing jointly	**5** Both spouses were under 65, and both retired on permanent and total disability **5**	☐
	6 One spouse was 65 or older, and the other spouse was under 65 and retired on permanent and total disability **6**	☐
	7 One spouse was 65 or older, and the other spouse was under 65 and **not** retired on permanent and total disability **7**	☐

| Married filing separately | **8** You were 65 or older and you lived apart from your spouse for all of 2006 . . . . **8** | ☐ |
| | **9** You were under 65, you retired on permanent and total disability, and you lived apart from your spouse for all of 2006 . . . . **9** | ☐ |

| **Did you check box 1, 3, 7, or 8?** | — **Yes** ——▶ Skip Part II and complete Part III on back. |
| | — **No** ——▶ Complete Parts II and III. |

Part II   Statement of Permanent and Total Disability (Complete **only** if you checked box 2, 4, 5, 6, or 9 above.)

If: 1 You filed a physician's statement for this disability for 1983 or an earlier year, or you filed or got a statement for tax years after 1983 and your physician signed line B on the statement, **and**

    2 Due to your continued disabled condition, you were unable to engage in any substantial gainful activity in 2006, check this box . . . . ▶ ☐

- If you checked this box, you do not have to get another statement for 2006.

- If you **did not** check this box, have your physician complete the statement on page R-4. You **must** keep the statement for your records.

For Paperwork Reduction Act Notice, see Form 1040 instructions.   Cat. No. 11359K   Schedule R (Form 1040) 2006

EXHIBIT 9–3   Schedule R *(continues)*

Schedule R (Form 1040) 2006

Part III   Figure Your Credit

10 If you checked (in Part I):   Enter:

Box 1, 2, 4, or 7 . . . . $5,000

Box 3, 5, or 6 . . . . $7,500 . . . . **10**

Box 8 or 9 . . . . $3,750

Did you check box 2, 4, 5, 6, or 9 in Part I?	— Yes —▶	You **must** complete line 11.
	— No —▶	Enter the amount from line 10 on line 12 and go to line 13.

11 If you checked (in Part I):

● Box 6, add $5,000 to the taxable disability income of the spouse who was under age 65. Enter the total.

● Box 2, 4, or 9, enter your taxable disability income. **11**

● Box 5, add your taxable disability income to your spouse's taxable disability income. Enter the total.

TIP For more details on what to include on line 11, see page R-3.

12 If you completed line 11, enter the **smaller** of line 10 or line 11; **all others,** enter the amount from line 10 . . . . **12**

13 Enter the following pensions, annuities, or disability income that you (and your spouse if filing a joint return) received in 2006.

a Nontaxable part of social security benefits and
Nontaxable part of railroad retirement benefits treated as social security (see page R-3). . . **13a**

b Nontaxable veterans' pensions and
Any other pension, annuity, or disability benefit that is excluded from income under any other provision of law (see page R-3). . . **13b**

c Add lines 13a and 13b. (Even though these income items are not taxable, they **must** be included here to figure your credit.) If you did not receive any of the types of nontaxable income listed on line 13a or 13b, enter -0- on line 13c **13c**

14 Enter the amount from Form 1040, line 38 . . . . **14**

15 If you checked (in Part I):   Enter:
Box 1 or 2 . . . . . $7,500
Box 3, 4, 5, 6, or 7 . . . $10,000   **15**
Box 8 or 9 . . . . . $5,000

16 Subtract line 15 from line 14. If zero or less, enter -0- **16**

17 Enter one-half of line 16 . . . . **17**

18 Add lines 13c and 17 . . . . **18**

19 Subtract line 18 from line 12. If zero or less, **stop; you cannot** take the credit. Otherwise, go to line 20 . . . . **19**

20 Multiply line 19 by 15% (.15) **20**

21 Enter the amount from Form 1040, line 46 . . . . **21**

22 Add the amounts from Form 1040, lines 47 and 48, and enter the total **22**

23 Subtract line 22 from line 21 . . . . **23**

24 **Credit for the elderly or the disabled.** Enter the **smaller** of line 20 or line 23 here and on Form 1040, line 49 . . . . **24**

Schedule R (Form 1040) 2006

EXHIBIT 9–3   Schedule R *(continued)*

The Hope and Lifetime Learning credits are mutually exclusive and cannot be claimed for the same student in the same year. However, credits can be claimed for more than one person in the household subject to limitation. Other limitations apply as well. In order to claim either of the two credits, a number of conditions must be satisfied. Also, in certain situations, the neither the Hope or Lifetime Learning credits can be claimed and the only possible option is a deduction. Those who cannot claim the credits include the following:

- Taxpayers whose filing status is married filing separately
- Taxpayers whose modified adjusted gross income (as defined by the IRS) is greater than the amount established by the IRS for the taxpayer's respective filing status
- Anyone who is listed as a dependent on another person's return
- A taxpayer or spouse who is a nonresident alien for any part of the year and did not elect to be treated as a nonresident alien for tax purposes.

The amounts used for the Hope and Lifetime Learning credits also must have been applied to qualified education expenses (as defined by the IRS) and have been expended for education that commenced during the tax year or the first three months of the following year. This includes nonrefunded expenses for a student that withdraws from the educational course of study. In order to be a qualified educational expense, the monies must first be paid to an eligible educational institution. This is any postsecondary institution that is eligible to participate in student aid programs administered by the U.S. Department of Education. Qualified expenses include tuition and fees and other costs that must be paid to the institution as a condition of enrollment or attendance. Any other expenses that are not a condition of enrollment and thus not qualified may include things such as activity fees, books, equipment, supplies, and so on, unless they are required to be purchased at the school. Other expenses that do not qualify for the credits include insurance, medical expenses, room and board, transportation, and similar personal, living, or family expenses, and courses that involve sports, games, or hobbies (unless the course is part of the student's required degree program). The funds used to pay the expenses cannot be tax free or from the source of scholarships unless the scholarships reported to the student as income. The person who is entitled to claim the student as an exemption on the return is the party entitled to claim expenses. This is even if the student personally receives the money from a loan or third party. In that situation, it is considered as if the student received the payment and then in turn paid the qualified expenses. As the Modified Adjusted Gross Income of the taxpayer increases, the amount of the credit is phased out. Therefore, the proper form for the Hope or Lifetime Learning credit must be used to complete the calculation for the proper amount of credit.

So what is the difference between the Hope and Lifetime credits? The answer lies in the purpose. The Hope credit is designed to provide tax relief to individuals who are starting out on a path to obtain a college degree. The Lifetime credit is designed to encourage individuals to continue learning and attaining new skills throughout their lifetimes. The requirements for each are very distinct in terms of the amount that can be claimed. The limitations used to illustrate the credit calculations here are those used in 2006. However, these are adjusted periodically and should be checked before applying the calculation.

To claim the Hope credit:

- The student must not have had expenses that were used to claim a Hope credit in any two (one is acceptable) earlier tax years.

- The student has not completed the first 2 years of postsecondary education by the end of the tax year.

- For at least one academic period beginning in the tax year, the student was enrolled at least half time in a program leading to a degree, certificate, or other recognized educational credential.

- The student was free of any federal or state felony conviction for possession or distributing a controlled substance as of the end of the tax year.

The amount of Hope credit that can be claimed is figured in the following way: 100 percent of the first $1,000 of qualified expenses for an eligible student and 50 percent of the next $1,000 of qualified educational expenses for that same student. The maximum credit that can be claimed is $1,500 for each eligible student.

To claim the Lifetime credit:

The student had to be enrolled in one or more courses at an eligible educational institution. The lifetime credit is calculated by taking 20 percent of the first $10,000 of qualified education expenses for all eligible students on the tax return. However, as of 2006, no more than $2,000 can be taken as a lifetime learning credit on the entire return. This is distinguished form the Hope credit, which allows the maximum credit per eligible student. Both credits are claimed by completing IRS form 8863.

v. Child Tax Credit. The child tax credit is a nonrefundable credit that can reduce tax liability by as much as $1,000 per child. If a child qualifies the taxpayer for the credit, then certain additional tests must be applied to determine the amount of credit that can be claimed. To determine whether a child is a "qualifying child" is based on the several criteria.

In relationship to the taxpayer, the child must:

- be the son, daughter, stepchild, legally placed foster child, brother, sister, stepbrother, stepsister, or descendant of any of these;

- be under age 17 at the end of the tax year;

- not provide more than one half of his or her own support;

- live with the taxpayer for more than half of the tax year (this is considered to have been met if the child was born or died during the tax year and the taxpayer's home was the main home of the child during the time he/she was alive. Absences for school, camps, vacation, and so on count as time lived with the taxpayer).

APPLICATION **9.7**

Jack is a freshman attending a state community college vocational program. His tuition and fees amount to $2,450 per semester. He also took two physical education courses. His degree requires one course. But he was so interested in both sports of golf and bowling that he took a course in each. Each of the physical education courses included in his tuition represent $325 of the overall tuition. He lives in an apartment within walking distance of the campus. His living expenses amount to approximately $3,000 per semester. For the current semester, he purchased his books from a nearby bookstore that specializes in used textbooks. He did purchase a special-purpose calculator for $150 at the campus bookstore. The calculator was required for one of his degree courses. To pay for his education, Jack took out student loans of $3,000. His grandfather also paid $2,450 to the college toward Jack's tuition and fees. Jack's parents still claim him on their married filing jointly return. His parents have an adjusted gross income of $74,000.

Without calculating the Tuition and Fees deduction, the following would be available to Jack under the Hope credit:

- As a state college, the institution is more than likely an eligible one.

- His parents' adjusted gross income is within the limits to qualify.

- As a freshman, Jack initially qualifies for the credit.

- The living expenses and books do not qualify for the credit.

- One of the physical education courses do not qualify for the credit.

- Even though Jack is responsible for the loans and the other money came from his grandfather, the parents may still claim eligible expenses toward the credit.

- Of the $5,450 expended, approximately $2,275 would be eligible for the Hope credit calculation. However, because the credit is limited to $1,500, this is the amount that could be taken for Jack's educational expenses.

The credit can only be claimed by taxpayers who file form 1040 or form 1040-A (not 1040-EZ). The credit only reduces tax liability and thus cannot be used if the liability is $0. Additionally, the credit cannot be claimed when the Modified Adjusted Gross Income reaches certain thresholds based on filing status. For example in 2006, Married Filing Jointly, the threshold was $110,000. For Single, Head of Household, or qualifying widow(er), the threshold was $75,000. For Married Filing Separately, it was $55,000. The credit can only be claimed by one person. Thus, if more than one person is entitled to the credit, IRS tiebreaker rules are applied just as they would be for claiming the child as a dependent.

The MAGI is determined by adding the following amounts:

- Adjusted Gross Income;

- Income that may have been excluded from taxable income because it came from Puerto Rico;

- Foreign income on line 43 or 48 from form 2555;

- Income reported on line 18 from form 2555-EZ; and

- Amounts reported on line 15 of form 4563 (excluded income for residents of American Samoa).

One of the child tax credit worksheets is used to calculate the proper amount of child tax credit to be applied. The proper worksheet to use is determined by answering questions on the IRS Form 1040 Instructions. Essentially, if the AGI is above the threshold level or certain other credits or foreign income exclusions are claimed, then the worksheet in Pub. 972 must be used. Otherwise, the worksheet in the instructions to form 1040 can be applied to determine the amount of the credit. In the event that all or some of the child tax credit is excluded, a portion of the exclusion may be recaptured in the refundable Additional Child Tax Credit, which is discussed later in this chapter.

vi. Adoption Credit. One of the more generous nonrefundable credits is the Adoption credit. This is a credit available to adoptive parents in some circumstances for qualifying expenses paid to adopt an eligible child (including a child with special needs). A taxpayer who paid qualifying expenses in the same year for an adoption that became final may be eligible to claim the credit on the return for that year. As discussed in earlier chapters, the Adoption credit is not available for any reimbursed expense.

In the calculation of the credit, qualifying expenses include reasonable and necessary adoption fees, court costs, attorney fees, traveling expenses (including reasonable amounts spent for meals and lodging), and other expenses directly related to the legal adoption of an eligible child. An eligible child must be under 18 years old or be physically or mentally incapable of caring for himself or herself. The Adoption credit or exclusion cannot be taken for a child who is not a U.S. citizen or resident unless the adoption becomes final. In these cases, no credit can be taken until the year of, and following, the year the adoption was completed. A child with special needs may be eligible if he or she is a U.S. citizen or resident and a state determines that the child cannot or should not be returned to his or her parent's home and probably will not be adopted unless assistance is provided. Under certain circumstances, the amount of qualified adoption expenses may be increased if a special needs eligible child is adopted.

The credit and exclusion for qualifying adoption expenses both subject to a dollar limit and an income limit. The amount of the adoption credit or exclusion is limited to the dollar limit for the each year and each effort to adopt an eligible child. If the taxpayer is eligible to take both a credit and an exclusion, this dollar amount applies separately to each. For example, assume that the dollar limit for the year is $10,000.

Child Tax Credit Worksheet—Line 53   *Keep for Your Records*

⚠️ **CAUTION**
- To be a qualifying child for the child tax credit, the child must be **under age 17** at the end of 2006 and meet the other requirements listed on page 19.
- **Do not** use this worksheet if you answered "Yes" to question 1, 2, or 3 on page 42. Instead, use Pub. 972.

1. Number of qualifying children: ___2___ × $1,000. Enter the result.

   | 1 | 2,000 |

2. Enter the amount from Form 1040, line 46.

   | 2 | 1,334 |

3. Add the amounts from Form 1040:

   Line 47   _____

   Line 48   + ____225____

   Line 49   + _____

   Line 50   + _____

   Line 51   + _____

   Line 52*   + _____ Enter the total.

   | 3 | 225 |

   *Include only the amount, if any, from Form 5695, line 12.

4. Are the amounts on lines 2 and 3 the same?

   ☐ **Yes.** 🛑
   You cannot take this credit because there is no tax to reduce. However, you may be able to take the **additional child tax credit.** See the **TIP** below.

   ☑ **No.** Subtract line 3 from line 2.

   | 4 | 1,109 |

5. Is the amount on line 1 more than the amount on line 4?

   ☑ **Yes.** Enter the amount from line 4.
   Also, you may be able to take the **additional child tax credit.** See the **TIP** below.

   ☐ **No.** Enter the amount from line 1.

   This is your child tax credit.

   | 5 | 1,109 |

   Enter this amount on Form 1040, line 53. ⋯►

   TIP
   You may be able to take the **additional child tax credit** on Form 1040, line 68, if you answered "Yes" on line 4 **or** line 5 above.

   - First, complete your Form 1040 through line 67.
   - Then, use Form 8812 to figure any additional child tax credit.

1040 ◄⋯

Page 220   Chapter 34 **Child Tax Credit**

EXHIBIT 9–4 IRS Pub 17, Child Tax Credit Worksheet

The taxpayer paid $7,000 in qualifying adoption expenses for a final adoption, and received $4,000 of additional qualifying adoption expenses paid by an employer. The taxpayer may be able to claim a credit of up to $7,000 and also exclude up to $4,000 of income from the Gross Income calculation on the first page of form 1040. The dollar limit for a particular year must be reduced by the amount of qualifying expenses taken into account in previous years for the same adoption effort.

The income limit on the adoption credit or exclusion is determined by using the taxpayer's modified adjusted gross income (MAGI). The MAGI must be below the beginning phase-out amount for the year, or the income limit will fail to qualify for the fully eligible amount of credit or exclusion. If the MAGI is more than the beginning phase-out amount for the year, then the credit or exclusion is reduced according to the scale. If the MAGI is above the maximum phase-out amount for the year, then no credit or exclusion is allowed.

If the taxpayer is married, a joint return must generally be filed to qualify for the Adoption credit or exclusion. If married filing separately status is used, the credit or exclusion can be taken only if certain requirements are met.

Because the credit and exclusion are subject to so many limitations, it is important to complete form 8839 carefully. Additionally, the credit is refundable, which limits its use to the taxpayer's tax liability. However, unlike most other deductions, adjustments, and credits, the balance can be carried forward to future years until the eligible amount has been claimed. At the time of publication, the credit and phase-out amounts were scheduled to change for the tax year 2007.

vii. Mortgage Interest Credit. The Mortgage Interest credit is one of the tax incentives to assist lower-income families rise and stay above poverty level. If applied, it will reduce the amount of deduction claimed on Schedule A. However, in most instances, the tax benefit of a credit is greater than that of a deduction. Additionally, if the home for which the credit is received is sold within 9 years of the date that the mortgage is closed to purchase the home, part or all of the credit may have to be recaptured as income. The Mortgage Interest credit cannot be used unless the proper documentation is received from state or local government. As a result, lower-income taxpayers who purchase a home should contact their state or local government to determine if they qualify and ensure that they receive the Mortgage Credit Certificate (MCC), which entitles them to apply for the credit.

If an individual is issued an MCC from the state or local government, they may be entitled to the Mortgage Interest credit. The amount of the credit is calculated using form 8396. The credit is only allowed to the extent of the interest paid on the certified debt amount listed on the MCC. Once the credit is calculated, it can be applied against tax liability. Unlike most other nonrefundable credits, the unused part of the Mortgage Interest credit may be carried forward for up to 3 years or until the entire credit has been used, whichever occurs first.

Form **8396**	**Mortgage Interest Credit**	OMB No. 1545-0074

Form **8396**

Department of the Treasury
Internal Revenue Service

Mortgage Interest Credit

(For Holders of Qualified Mortgage Credit Certificates Issued by
State or Local Governmental Units or Agencies)

► Attach to Form 1040 or 1040NR.   ► See instructions on back.

OMB No. 1545-0074

2006

Attachment
Sequence No. **138**

Name(s) shown on your tax return

Your social security number

Enter the address of your main home to which the qualified mortgage certificate relates if it is different from the address shown on your tax return.

Name of Issuer of Mortgage Credit Certificate	Mortgage Credit Certificate Number	Issue Date

Part I   Current Year Mortgage Interest Credit

1 Interest paid on the certified indebtedness amount. If someone else (other than your spouse if filing jointly) also held an interest in the home, enter only your share of the interest paid . .   **1**

2 Enter the certificate credit rate shown on your **mortgage credit certificate. Do not** enter the interest rate on your home mortgage . . . .   **2**   %

3 If line 2 is 20% or less, multiply line 1 by line 2. If line 2 is more than 20%, or you refinanced your mortgage and received a reissued certificate, see the instructions for the amount to enter.   **3**
   You must reduce your deduction for home mortgage interest on Schedule A (Form 1040) by the amount on line 3.

4 Enter any 2003 credit carryforward from line 18 of your 2005 Form 8396 . . . .   **4**

5 Enter any 2004 credit carryforward from line 16 of your 2005 Form 8396 . . . .   **5**

6 Enter any 2005 credit carryforward from line 19 of your 2005 Form 8396 . . . .   **6**

7 Add lines 3 through 6 . . . .   **7**

8 Enter the amount from Form 1040, line 46, or Form 1040NR, line 43 . . . .   **8**

9 **1040 filers:**   Enter the total of the amounts from Form 1040, lines 47 through 51 and line 53 plus any credit from Form 5695, line 12

   1040NR filers: Enter the total of the amounts from Form 1040NR, lines 44 through 46 and line 48 plus any credit from Form 5695, line 12   **9**

10 Subtract line 9 from line 8. If zero or less, enter -0- here and on line 11 and go to Part II . .   **10**

11 **Current year mortgage interest credit.** Enter the **smaller** of line 7 or line 10. Also include this amount in the total on Form 1040, line 54, or Form 1040NR, line 49, and check box **a** on that line **11**

Part II   Mortgage Interest Credit Carryforward to 2007. (Complete only if line 11 is less than line 7.)

12 Add lines 3 and 4 . . . .   **12**

13 Enter the amount from line 7 . . . .   **13**

14 Enter the **larger** of line 11 or line 12 . . . .   **14**

15 Subtract line 14 from line 13 . . . .   **15**

16 2005 credit carryforward to 2007. Enter the **smaller** of line 6 or line 15 . . . .   **16**

17 Subtract line 16 from line 15 . . . .   **17**

18 2004 credit carryforward to 2007. Enter the **smaller** of line 5 or line 17 . . . .   **18**

19 2006 credit carryforward to 2007. Subtract line 11 from line 3. If zero or less, enter -0- .   **19**

For Paperwork Reduction Act Notice, see back of form.   Cat. No. 62502X   Form **8396** (2006)

EXHIBIT 9–5 IRS Form 8396

viii. Retirement Savings Contribution Credit. One nonrefundable credit is the credit used to encourage individuals to save for retirement. This credit was designed to provide an incentive to those who were the least likely to save but who would be the most likely to require supplemental income in addition to Social Security. Congress wanted to shift the focus from dependence on social security to individual retirement accounts. Changes in our culture and the costs of doing business have resulted in a reduction of retirement plans offered and funded by employers. This has resulted in fewer individuals with enough pension or retirement plan income to support themselves. Social Security was never intended as a primary source of retirement income. The current difficulties in the Social Security system and its inability to support an aging nation are widely known. As a result, citizens are going to be required to be more accountable for their own retirement. To help with this, the retirement savings contribution credit was initiated. This credit was scheduled to expire at the end of 2006 but has been permanently extended by Congress.

Those eligible to claim the credit are within a limited class. The taxpayer must have made voluntary contributions to a traditional/Roth IRA, a qualified employer retirement plan, 401(k), 403(b), governmental 457, SEP, or SIMPLE plan, or a 501 (c)(18)(D) plan. It cannot be claimed if any of the following apply:

a. the taxpayer must be over 18 and not claimed as a dependent on another's return;

b. if the taxpayer's adjusted gross income is more than $25,000 single, $37,500 head of household, or $50,000 married filing jointly;

c. if the taxpayer making the contribution or deferral was born after January 1, 1989 (this date changes annually),

d. if the taxpayer making the contribution is claimed as a dependent on someone else's return,

e. if the taxpayer was enrolled as a full-time student for any 5-month period during the tax year.

Using these criteria, if the taxpayer is eligible to claim the credit, it can be calculated using form 8880. The amount of the credit available is a percentage of the contribution. The percentage is phased out as the AGI approaches the threshold for the particular taxpayer's filing status. For example, in 2006 a couple with married filing jointly status can claim 50 percent of the contributions when their AGI is below $30,000. However, they can only claim 10 percent of their contributions when their AGI rises above $32,500. Once the percentage is determined and applied using form 8880, an additional limitation is applied. The amounts claimed on the return for Foreign Tax credit, Child and Dependent Care Expenses, and Education credits are subtracted from the Retirement Contribution Savings credit. The amount remaining is the amount that can be claimed.

APPLICATION **9.8**

Mackenna and Mason are married with two children. Their son Marcus is 18 and attends college. He is claimed on the return as a dependent. Their daughter Melissa is 10. They have an adjusted gross income of $30,000. They made contributions to an IRA of $4,000. They have a calculated Hope credit for $1,500. They also have a calculated Child Care Expense credit for $100. Their Retirement Savings Contribution credit initially is $2,000 (50 percent of $4,000). However, when the other credits are subtracted, the Retirement Savings Contribution credit is reduced to $400.

ix. 2006 Energy Credits. The Energy Policy Act of 2005 was put in place to encourage taxpayers to incorporate energy efficient systems into their homes, whether existing or new construction. It applies to improvements installed after December 1, 2005, and can be claimed on tax returns 2006 and later. There are particular requirements that must be met with regard to the type of improvement and the level of energy efficiency, however, if the criteria are met, then the credit can be claimed. At the time of publication, the IRS had not yet implemented the forms and specific calculations for the credit, yet consultation of the most current IRS Pub. 17 should provide appropriate guidance.

x. Other Credits. Some of the other less common credits should still be considered and applied if they are available to the taxpayer. They include the following:

a. Qualified Electric Vehicle—this is an incentive to taxpayers to take advantage of alternative fuel source vehicles and allows a credit for up to 10 percent of the cost of an electrically powered vehicle for use by the taxpayer on public streets and highways. There are a number of restrictions for the credit that must be considered when calculating the amount claimed.

b. Form 8859—District of Columbia First Time Homebuyer. This is a credit available only to first-time homebuyers in the District of Columbia. This limited credit should be considered for taxpayers who fall into this category.

c. Form 3800—General Business Credit. Employers who provide employment to particular classes of individuals may be eligible for this credit on the business portion of their return. This credit provides incentive to employ certain types of workers in particular circumstances. The purpose is to bring disadvantaged individuals into the workforce with the goal to eventually lead them out of poverty.

Other uncommon credits may be available for specific situations of taxpayers. The key is to consider all tax documents received by the taxpayer. If any do not fall into the general categories of reporting, then the proper IRS publications should be consulted both for how to treat the amounts on the documents and whether any credits may apply.

5. Additional Taxes

The annual tax return for individuals and business is used for more than one purpose. Although the primary function is the assessment and collection of income taxes, other taxes related to income are also collected through the same return. This includes the taxes paid to Social Security and Medicare on income generated by the individual rather than as an employee of another, taxes that are sometimes imposed on retirement plan distributions, repayment of Earned Income Credit that was paid in advance, taxes on domestic employees, and taxes for investment income of minor children in certain circumstances. Each of these is collected through the individual tax return in addition to any income tax that might be due.

After all income, adjustments, deductions, and credits are applied, the final figure for income tax liability/refund is established. Following this, the additional taxes that are identified on the return must be determined if any. An example would be self employment social security taxes. These are then applied toward the final income tax liability or refund to reach a net amount. Finally, any applicable penalties are determined and the resulting amount is that which the taxpayer must remit to the Department of Revenue, or that the Department of Revenue is obligated to refund to the taxpayer on confirmation of the amounts.

a. Self-Employment.

As discussed in earlier chapters, the sole proprietor is considered to be self-employed. Although this does not impact income tax in a particular way, it does have a significant impact in terms of self-employment taxes. Earlier chapters addressing issues of payroll first pointed out that the employer and employee make matching contributions to Social Security and Medicare. However, for the employee who works for his or herself, both halves of this equation must be satisfied by the same party. Form SE is used to calculate the amount of self-employment (Social Security and Medicare) tax that must be submitted by the taxpayer to the Department of Revenue in addition to any income tax that might become due. If the self-employment income is below a threshold amount (currently $400), form SE is not required.

In the event that form SE is required, the determination of whether to file SE short or long form is necessary. The long form is required for individuals from certain occupations or who received certain types of income. Form SE contains a flowchart and series of questions to assist the taxpayer in the decision of whether to file a long or short form SE to calculate the amount of self-employment tax due. This amount is then carried to the tax return. As discussed earlier, one-half of this amount can be used as a deduction in arriving at the AGI amount.

b. Social Security and Medicare Tax on Tip Income.

At first glance, this may appear to be a form of double taxation, when it is actually a method to protect the taxpayer. Employers are required to report and tax tip income of employees at a minimum rate of 8 percent. The amount of Social Security

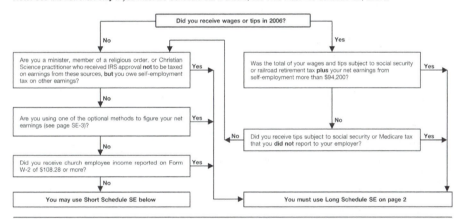

SCHEDULE SE
(Form 1040)

Department of the Treasury
Internal Revenue Service (99)

Self-Employment Tax

▶ Attach to Form 1040. ▶ See Instructions for Schedule SE (Form 1040).

OMB No. 1545-0074

2006

Attachment
Sequence No. **17**

Name of person with **self-employment** income (as shown on Form 1040)

Social security number of person
with **self-employment** income ▶

Who Must File Schedule SE

You must file Schedule SE if:

• You had net earnings from self-employment from **other than** church employee income (line 4 of Short Schedule SE or line 4c of Long Schedule SE) of $400 or more, **or**

• You had church employee income of $108.28 or more. Income from services you performed as a minister or a member of a religious order **is not** church employee income (see page SE-1).

Note. Even if you had a loss or a small amount of income from self-employment, it may be to your benefit to file Schedule SE and use either "optional method" in Part II of Long Schedule SE (see page SE-3).

Exception. If your only self-employment income was from earnings as a minister, member of a religious order, or Christian Science practitioner **and** you filed Form 4361 and received IRS approval not to be taxed on those earnings, **do not** file Schedule SE. Instead, write "Exempt–Form 4361" on Form 1040, line 58.

May I Use Short Schedule SE or Must I Use Long Schedule SE?

Note. Use this flowchart **only if** you must file Schedule SE. If unsure, see Who Must File Schedule SE, above.

Did you receive wages or tips in 2006?

No → Are you a minister, member of a religious order, or Christian Science practitioner who received IRS approval **not** to be taxed on earnings from these sources, **but** you owe self-employment tax on other earnings? — Yes →

No ↓

Are you using one of the optional methods to figure your net earnings (see page SE-3)? — Yes →

No ↓

Did you receive church employee income reported on Form W-2 of $108.28 or more? — Yes →

No ↓

You may use Short Schedule SE below

Yes → Was the total of your wages and tips subject to social security or railroad retirement tax **plus** your net earnings from self-employment more than $94,200? — Yes →

No ↓

Did you receive tips subject to social security or Medicare tax that you **did not** report to your employer? — No ← / Yes →

You must use Long Schedule SE on page 2

Section A—Short Schedule SE. Caution. Read above to see if you can use Short Schedule SE.

1	Net farm profit or (loss) from Schedule F, line 36, and farm partnerships, Schedule K-1 (Form 1065), box 14, code A	**1**	
2	Net profit or (loss) from Schedule C, line 31; Schedule C-EZ, line 3; Schedule K-1 (Form 1065), box 14, code A (other than farming); and Schedule K-1 (Form 1065-B), box 9, code J1. Ministers and members of religious orders, see page SE-1 for amounts to report on this line. See page SE-3 for other income to report	**2**	
3	Combine lines 1 and 2	**3**	
4	**Net earnings from self-employment.** Multiply line 3 by 92.35% (.9235). If less than $400, **do not** file this schedule; you do not owe self-employment tax . . . . ▶	**4**	
5	**Self-employment tax.** If the amount on line 4 is: • $94,200 or less, multiply line 4 by 15.3% (.153). Enter the result here and on **Form 1040, line 58.** • More than $94,200, multiply line 4 by 2.9% (.029). Then, add $11,680.80 to the result. Enter the total here and on **Form 1040, line 58.**	**5**	
6	**Deduction for one-half of self-employment tax.** Multiply line 5 by 50% (.5). Enter the result here and on **Form 1040, line 27** **6**		

For Paperwork Reduction Act Notice, see Form 1040 instructions.   Cat. No. 11358Z   Schedule SE (Form 1040) 2006

EXHIBIT 9–6   IRS Form SE *(continues)*

Schedule SE (Form 1040) 2006   Attachment Sequence No. **17**   Page **2**

Name of person with **self-employment** income (as shown on Form 1040) | Social security number of person with **self-employment** income ▶ |

Section B—Long Schedule SE

Part I Self-Employment Tax

Note. If your only income subject to self-employment tax is **church employee income**, skip lines 1 through 4b. Enter -0- on line 4c and go to line 5a. Income from services you performed as a minister or a member of a religious order **is not** church employee income. See page SE-1.

A If you are a minister, member of a religious order, or Christian Science practitioner **and** you filed Form 4361, but you had $400 or more of **other** net earnings from self-employment, check here and continue with Part I . . . . . . ▶ ☐

1	Net farm profit or (loss) from Schedule F, line 36, and farm partnerships, Schedule K-1 (Form 1065), box 14, code A. **Note.** Skip this line if you use the farm optional method (see page SE-4)	**1**	
2	Net profit or (loss) from Schedule C, line 31; Schedule C-EZ, line 3; Schedule K-1 (Form 1065), box 14, code A (other than farming); and Schedule K-1 (Form 1065-B), box 9, code J1. Ministers and members of religious orders, see page SE-1 for amounts to report on this line. See page SE-3 for other income to report. **Note.** Skip this line if you use the nonfarm optional method (see page SE-4)	**2**	
3	Combine lines 1 and 2	**3**	
4a	If line 3 is more than zero, multiply line 3 by 92.35% (.9235). Otherwise, enter amount from line 3	**4a**	
b	If you elect one or both of the optional methods, enter the total of lines 15 and 17 here . . .	**4b**	
c	Combine lines 4a and 4b. If less than $400, **stop**; you do not owe self-employment tax. **Exception.** If less than $400 and you had **church employee income**, enter -0- and continue. . . . . . ▶	**4c**	
5a	Enter your **church employee income** from Form W-2. See page SE-1 for definition of church employee income **5a**		
b	Multiply line 5a by 92.35% (.9235). If less than $100, enter -0-	**5b**	
6	**Net earnings from self-employment.** Add lines 4c and 5b	**6**	
7	Maximum amount of combined wages and self-employment earnings subject to social security tax or the 6.2% portion of the 7.65% railroad retirement (tier 1) tax for 2006	**7**	94,200 00
8a	Total social security wages and tips (total of boxes 3 and 7 on Form(s) W-2) and railroad retirement (tier 1) compensation. If $94,200 or more, skip lines 8b through 10, and go to line 11 . . . . **8a**		
b	Unreported tips subject to social security tax (from Form 4137, line 9) **8b**		
c	Add lines 8a and 8b	**8c**	
9	Subtract line 8c from line 7. If zero or less, enter -0- here and on line 10 and go to line 11 . ▶	**9**	
10	Multiply the **smaller** of line 6 or line 9 by 12.4% (.124)	**10**	
11	Multiply line 6 by 2.9% (.029)	**11**	
12	**Self-employment tax.** Add lines 10 and 11. Enter here and on **Form 1040, line 58**	**12**	
13	**Deduction for one-half of self-employment tax.** Multiply line 12 by 50% (.5). Enter the result here and on **Form 1040, line 27** **13**		

Part II Optional Methods To Figure Net Earnings (see page SE-3)

Farm Optional Method. You may use this method only if **(a)** your gross farm income[1] was not more than $2,400, **or (b)** your net farm profits[2] were less than $1,733.

14	Maximum income for optional methods	**14**	1,600 00
15	Enter the **smaller** of: two-thirds (⅔) of gross farm income[1] (not less than zero) **or** $1,600. Also include this amount on line 4b above	**15**	

Nonfarm Optional Method. You may use this method only if **(a)** your net nonfarm profits[3] were less than $1,733 and also less than 72.189% of your gross nonfarm income,[4] **and (b)** you had net earnings from self-employment of at least $400 in 2 of the prior 3 years.

Caution. You may use this method no more than five times.

16	Subtract line 15 from line 14	**16**	
17	Enter the **smaller** of: two-thirds (⅔) of gross nonfarm income[4] (not less than zero) **or** the amount on line 16. Also include this amount on line 4b above	**17**	

[1] From Sch. F, line 11, and Sch. K-1 (Form 1065), box 14, code B.

[2] From Sch. F, line 36, and Sch. K-1 (Form 1065), box 14, code A.

[3] From Sch. C, line 31; Sch. C-EZ, line 3; Sch. K-1 (Form 1065), box 14, code A; and Sch. K-1 (Form 1065-B), box 9, code J1.

[4] From Sch. C, line 7; Sch. C-EZ, line 1; Sch. K-1 (Form 1065), box 14, code C; and Sch. K-1 (Form 1065-B), box 9, code J2.

Schedule SE (Form 1040) 2006

EXHIBIT 9–6 IRS Form SE *(continued)*

taxes withheld over an employee's working life will have a direct impact on the amount of income that an employee can receive on retirement or a determination of disability. As a result, it is important to report all income accurately. If an employer does not report tip income for an employee accurately, and consequently does not tax that income, the employee can report the income on form 4137. This form enables the employee to claim the tip income and calculate the proper amount of tax. Additionally, the employee must add the amount of tip income to wages in order to properly calculate any income tax liability or refund. This is not always a negative outcome. If an individual is eligible for the Earned Income credit, additional income in some circumstances may increase the credit and ultimately the refund. Another scenario is if the wages and tips received were insufficient to pay the required employee contribution of the Social Security and Medicare tax. This will appear on the W-2, and the employee must account for and pay this amount with the return.

c. Tax on Qualified Plan Distributions.

Something that often comes as a shock to taxpayers is the common additional penalty tax on money that was removed from a qualified retirement plan during the year. Many taxpayers will respond, "They withheld tax already on my 401 K when I took the money out." That may well be true. But, most often, employers do not typically withhold an amount sufficient to cover the 10 percent penalty as well. After all, the employer does not know if the taxpayer will be eligible for one of several possible exceptions to the penalty. Consequently, the taxpayer very often is required to pay a hefty 10 percent of the distribution amount, before taxes were calculated or withheld, in addition to the income tax. Consider the true story in Application 9.9.

To determine if penalty is owed in the form of additional tax on a qualified plan distribution, form 5329 is used. The instructions that accompany the form provide discussion of the possible exceptions to the penalty. However, the 1099-R form reporting the distribution to the taxpayer and the IRS will have an assigned code in box 7. If this code is a 1, then the IRS will impose the penalty unless the taxpayer completes the appropriate steps as outlined in the instructions about establishing qualification for an exception to the penalty.

d. Advance Earned Income Credit Payments.

By completing form W-5, an employee may be eligible to receive at least part of the earned income credit before filing the annual tax return. If qualified, the employee will receive the credited amount from their employer along with wages. This allows the employee to spread the additional income out over the course of a year rather than receiving it in a lump sum as a tax refund. At the end of the year, the W-2 will indicate any amounts of advance earned income credit that was received. This in turn is reported on the tax return and subtracted from any earned income credit calculation.

Form **4137**	**Social Security and Medicare Tax on Unreported Tip Income**	OMB No. 1545-0074
Department of the Treasury Internal Revenue Service (99)	▶ See instructions on back. ▶ **Attach to Form 1040, Form 1040NR, Form 1040-SS, or Form 1040-PR.**	**20 06** Attachment Sequence No. **24**

Name of person who received tips. If married, complete a separate Form 4137 for each spouse with unreported tips.   **Social security number**

Name(s) of employer(s) to whom you were required to, but did not, report your tips:

....

....

....

1	Total cash and charge tips you **received** in 2006 (see instructions)	1	
2	Total cash and charge tips you **reported** to your employer in 2006	2	
3	Subtract line 2 from line 1. This amount is income you **must** include in the total on Form 1040, line 7 or Form 1040NR, line 8	3	
4	Cash and charge tips you received but did not report to your employer because the total was less than $20 in a calendar month (see instructions)	4	
5	Unreported tips subject to Medicare tax. Subtract line 4 from line 3. Enter here and on line 2 of Schedule U below	5	
6	Maximum amount of wages (including tips) subject to social security tax	6	94,200 00	
7	Total social security wages and social security tips (total of boxes 3 and 7 on Form(s) W-2) or railroad retirement (tier 1) compensation .	7		
8	Subtract line 7 from line 6. If line 7 is more than line 6, enter -0- here and on line 9 and go to line 11	8	
9	Unreported tips subject to social security tax. Enter the **smaller** of line 5 or line 8 here and on line 1 of Schedule U below. If you received tips as a federal, state, or local government employee, see instructions	9	
10	Multiply line 9 by .062	10	
11	Multiply line 5 by .0145	11	
12	Add lines 10 and 11. Enter the result here and on Form 1040, line 59, or Form 1040NR, line 54 ▶	12	

For Paperwork Reduction Act Notice, see instructions on back.   Form **4137** (2006)

- -

Do Not Detach

SCHEDULE U (Form 1040) Department of the Treasury Internal Revenue Service	**U.S. Schedule of Unreported Tip Income** For crediting to your social security record	**20 06**

Note: *The amounts you report below are for your social security record. This record is used to figure any benefits, based on your earnings, payable to you and your dependents or your survivors. Fill in each item accurately and completely.*

Print or type name of person who received tip income		**Social security number**
Address (number, street, and apt. no., or P.O. box if mail is not delivered to your home)	Occupation	
City, town or post office, state, and ZIP code		

1	Unreported tips subject to social security tax. Enter the amount from line 9 (Form 4137) above . ▶	1	
2	Unreported tips subject to Medicare tax. Enter the amount from line 5 (Form 4137) above . . ▶	2	

Please do not write in this space

DLN—

Cat. No. 12626C   Schedule U (Form 1040) 2006

EXHIBIT 9–7 IRS Form 4137

APPLICATION **9.9**

Dave was married with no children. He was employed and in 2006 had a taxable income of $37,000, which was very similar to his earlier two years' employment. However, during the previous year, his company was purchased by another corporation. At the time, he was given the option to cash out his 401K plan and reinvest it on his own, or transfer it directly into the new corporation's 401K plan. Dave had been employed for many years and was shocked to find out that his 401K plan account was worth $40,000. He accepted the cash-out. Rather than rolling it over immediately into another qualified plan and avoiding penalty, he thought the money would be better put to use in reducing personal debt. He had $6,000 withheld for taxes because he had been in the 15 percent marginal tax bracket for several years. He then used the remaining $34,000 to pay off his car, boat, credit card bills, and take a cruise with his family. He was thrilled to be debt-free, with the exception of his house. After all, he still had another 20 years to work and believed he could build the retirement back up. Why, he might even use some of the refund he always received in the range of $1500 to start one of those IRAs.

On April 10, 2007, Dave came to have his taxes prepared and was met with the following results:

Instead of the expected refund of $1500, the additional $40,000 brought him into a higher tax bracket for all of his taxable income ($37,000 + 40,000) and resulted in an amount due that was substantially more than he had withheld using his 15 percent bracket as a guide.

He also owed an additional $4,000 in penalties for premature withdrawal of the 401K plan.

Not only would there be no refund, his total tax bill after his withholding was applied was well over $10,000 and was due to the IRS in 2 weeks.

However, if a taxpayer's income from all sources disqualifies the taxpayer from receiving the credit, or an amount greater than the amount received in advance, then part or all of the credit may have to be repaid. Even though advance earned income credit received is reported on the form W-2, the amount received is reported separately from wages on the return. Any Advance Earned Income credit is reported on the second page of form 1040 or form 1040-A. It is then calculated against tax liability, payments, and credits to reach a final result as to a tax liability or refund.

d. Household Employment Taxes.

For some individuals, even though they are not self-employed or otherwise owners of a business, they have had employees during the year to whom wages were paid for domestic work. If there was no formal business, and the employees were not independent contractors or employed in an agency situation, then the taxpayer may be required to report the wages on Schedule H. The amount of wages paid will determine whether Schedule H should be filed. The IRS establishes threshold levels for this. If the threshold is met, the taxpayer may be required to pay federal unemployment tax (FUTA), the employer's portion of Social Security and Medicare Taxes (FICA), and possibly even the Advance Earned Income credit. Once the threshold is established and Schedule H has been completed, an amount will be indicated to transfer to the taxpayer's individual return on form 1040, line 62. (Form 1040-A cannot be used for someone with payments associated with Schedule H.) This amount is then added to any tax liability or applied against any refund.

e. Tax on Children under 18 Who Have Investment Income of More than $1700.

This is an option for anyone with taxable income to file an individual return. However, the majority of children under age 18 with income do not have a substantial amount. As a result, it may be easier to report the income on the parent's return. The report is done via form 8814. The method, either individual return or as part of the return of the taxpayer claiming the individual as a dependent, is elected by using form 8814. This election is available only if:

- the dependent was under age 18 on December 31,
- the dependent's income consists solely of interest and dividends,
- the dependent's gross income of interest and dividends are less than $8,500,
- there were no estimated tax payments under the dependent's Social Security number during the year, and
- there was no federal income tax withheld.

The child is permitted a standard deduction. Form 8814 considers the interest and dividend income of the child to the extent it exceeds $1,700, plus 15 percent of the lesser of $700 or the excess of the child's income over $700. The tax, if any, is calculated and then transferred from form 8814 to the taxpayer's 1040. Additionally, there are various requirements imposed on the parent filing the return as well. These vary with the filing status and should be carefully consulted as well as the monetary limits, which periodically are adjusted by the IRS.

6. Payments and Refundable Credits

The final stage of preparing the tax return is the calculation of any previously made tax payments from a variety of sources, the determination of refundable credits, if any, as well as applicable penalties. These figures are then applied to the tax liability to reach the final result. This provides the bottom line of the return in which taxpayers are most often interested. It is only with the completion of these steps that a taxpayer knows whether their obligations have been satisfied and whether any excess may be returned to them in the form of a refund. The calculation of these amounts is also a very important step for future tax planning. If a taxpayer's situation

Form **8814**

Department of the Treasury
Internal Revenue Service

**Parents' Election To Report
Child's Interest and Dividends**
▶ See instructions.
▶ **Attach to parents' Form 1040 or Form 1040NR.**

OMB No. 1545-0074

2006

Attachment
Sequence No. **40**

Name(s) shown on your return

Your social security number

Caution. The federal income tax on your child's income, including qualified dividends and capital gain distributions, may be less if you file a separate tax return for the child instead of making this election. This is because you cannot take certain tax benefits that your child could take on his or her own return. For details, see **Tax benefits you cannot take** on page 2.

A   Child's name (first, initial, and last)

B   Child's social security number

C   If more than one Form 8814 is attached, check here . . . . ▶

Part I   Child's Interest and Dividends To Report on Your Return

1a	Enter your child's **taxable** interest. If this amount is different from the amounts shown on the child's Forms 1099-INT and 1099-OID, see the instructions	**1a**
b	Enter your child's **tax-exempt** interest. **Do not** include this amount on line 1a **1b**	
2a	Enter your child's ordinary dividends, including any Alaska Permanent Fund dividends. If your child received any ordinary dividends as a nominee, see the instructions	**2a**
b	Enter your child's qualified dividends included on line 2a. See the instructions **2b**	
3	Enter your child's capital gain distributions. If your child received any capital gain distributions as a nominee, see the instructions	**3**
4	Add lines 1a, 2a, and 3. If the total is $1,700 or less, skip lines 5 through 12 and go to line 13. If the total is $8,500 or more, **do not** file this form. Your child **must** file his or her own return to report the income	**4**
5	Base amount	**5**	1,700 00
6	Subtract line 5 from line 4	**6**

If both lines 2b and 3 are zero or blank, skip lines 7 through 10, enter -0- on line 11, and go to line 12. Otherwise, go to line 7.

7	Divide line 2b by line 4. Enter the result as a decimal (rounded to at least three places) . . . . **7** .	
8	Divide line 3 by line 4. Enter the result as a decimal (rounded to at least three places) . . . . **8** .	
9	Multiply line 6 by line 7. Enter the result here. See the instructions for where to report this amount on your return **9**	
10	Multiply line 6 by line 8. Enter the result here. See the instructions for where to report this amount on your return **10**	
11	Add lines 9 and 10	**11**
12	Subtract line 11 from line 6. Include this amount in the total on Form 1040, line 21, or Form 1040NR, line 21. In the space next to line 21, enter "Form 8814" and show the amount. If you checked the box on line C above, see the instructions. Go to line 13 below	**12**

Part II   Tax on the First $1,700 of Child's Interest and Dividends

13	Amount not taxed	**13**	850 00
14	Subtract line 13 from line 4. If the result is zero or less, enter -0-.	**14**	
15	**Tax.** Is the amount on line 14 less than $850?		
	☐ **No.** Enter $85 here and see the **Note** below.	}	**15**
	☐ **Yes.** Multiply line 14 by 10% (.10). Enter the result here and see the **Note** below.		

Note. If you checked the box on line C above, see the instructions. Otherwise, include the amount from line 15 in the tax you enter on Form 1040, line 44, or Form 1040NR, line 41. Be sure to check box **a** on Form 1040, line 44, or Form 1040NR, line 41.

For Paperwork Reduction Act Notice, see page 3.   Cat. No. 10750J   Form **8814** (2006)

EXHIBIT 9–8   IRS Form 8814

is expected to remain relatively unchanged for the present year, the tax result for the previous year can be an excellent guide as to whether an appropriate amount of tax is being withheld/paid for the current year.

a. Withholding and Estimated Payments.

Individuals who are employees are required to complete a W-4 for their employer. This form provides a calculation used by the employer to withhold income tax from the employee's wages. In simple terms, the IRS operates under the assumption that the larger family will have lower tax liability than, say, a single individual because of the number of exemptions and size of standard deduction/ itemized expenses. Based on this theory, the more exemptions an individual claims on a tax return, the lower the amount of tax that is typically withheld.

b. Earned Income Credit.

Probably the most popular credit and certainly one of the most used is the Earned Income Credit (EIC). This credit is refundable so the taxpayer can receive the amount of the credit even if there is $0 tax liability. The goal of the EIC is a lofty one. It is designed to assist and provide incentive for indigent individuals to climb out of poverty through earned income such as wages received through employment. As the adjusted gross income of the taxpayer increases from $0, the amount of the credit goes up until the taxpayer reaches or exceeds a pivot point amount. Then as the income of the taxpayer continues to rise above this pivot point, the amount of the credit decreases until it is phased out. The logic is that once a base amount is achieved, the credit is needed less and less as the income of the taxpayer grows. The credit is only available in certain circumstances, is subject to numerous limitations, and has various pivot points and phase-outs. These limitations are based on source of income, filing status, and qualifying children as dependents.

In recent years, the EIC has come under fire as it was discovered that a large number of returns, estimated in the millions, contained fraudulently claimed dependents for the purpose of boosting the credit to the taxpayer. As a result, rules for claiming the credit were revised and a concentrated effort to audit this portion of tax returns was undertaken by the IRS. The goal is to reduce the fraudulent claims. An audit for EIC purposes typically requires the taxpayer to provide objective proof of the right to claim a dependent. For example, school records that demonstrate the child's address to be the same as that of the parents would be one type of document that might be submitted. Additionally, a birth certificate that lists the taxpayer as a parent might be another document to be submitted. These are a few of the types of proof that might be required by the IRS before an EIC would be allowed. In the event that the credit has already been paid out and the taxpayer fails the audit, the IRS may demand return of the amount paid. Because the EIC for families with dependents can reach well into the thousands, this can be a difficult situation for a low-income taxpayer. If unable to repay, the taxpayer may lose their eligibility for refunds for years to come. Although due diligence is always required on the part of a tax preparer, particular attention should be given to the return that contains a claim for the EIC. Failure to do so also can result in penalties for the tax preparer.

There are numerous additional requirements for the EIC. To determine if the taxpayer is even qualified to receive the EIC, the taxpayer should complete EIC Worksheet A, unless self-employed, a statutory employee that files Schedule C/C-EZ, a church employee, or a member of the clergy who files Schedule SE. These individuals should complete Worksheet B. Individuals with capital transactions and investment income are also subject to earned income limitations. It is assumed by the IRS that individuals with significant investment income have sufficient resources for financial assistance of their own and they are not the target audience that the EIC is designed to assist. If the taxpayer has capital transactions or investment income, they also must complete the worksheet for this to determine if they are limited in their eligibility. Once the worksheet is completed and there appears to be an eligible EIC, the information must be transferred. The amounts from the worksheet are moved to the return 1040 or 1040-A. If there are qualifying children to support the claim for the credit, Schedule EIC must be completed with identifying information and then attached to the tax return.

APPLICATION **9.10**

Carrie and Kenny are married. They are both employed full time. The got married in late December of the year for which they are preparing taxes. Carrie had been a single mom with two children and she earned approximately $15,000 per year. She claimed three exemptions on her W-4 and typically had less than enough tax withheld. She knew this but did it to maximize her take-home pay. She also knew that each year when the tax liability was offset against her earned income credit she still received an average refund of $3,000. By filing married filing jointly, Kenny's income of $25,000 was added to the equation. Neither Carrie nor Kenny had thought to ask a tax professional about how the marriage would affect their situation. Under married filing jointly status, and claiming $40,000 in income for the year, the couple was not entitled to the EIC. Furthermore, the tax bracket that applied to Carrie jumped from 10 to 15 percent. Both Carrie and Kenny had lived in separate apartments and maintained two separate living areas for 11.5 months of the tax year. Even combined, they did not have enough in deductible expenses to itemize because there were no property taxes, mortgage interest, and so on. They ended up not only losing the refund Carrie was used to, expected, and had already spent on the wedding, they owed a significant amount of tax to the IRS. By consulting a tax professional, they could have been advised to change their W-4 withholding before the marriage or been advised to delay the wedding until after the first of the year. This would have given them much more time to prepare for the tax changes. Also, Carrie would have still received her expected refund.

SCHEDULE EIC (Form 1040A or 1040) Department of the Treasury Internal Revenue Service (99)	**Earned Income Credit** Qualifying Child Information *Complete and attach to Form 1040A or 1040 only if you have a qualifying child.*		OMB No. 1545-0074 20**06** Attachment Sequence No. **43**

Name(s) shown on return | | | Your social security number

Before you begin: See the instructions for Form 1040A, lines 40a and 40b, or Form 1040, lines 66a and 66b, to make sure that **(a)** you can take the EIC, and **(b)** you have a qualifying child.

⚠️ CAUTION

- If you take the EIC even though you are not eligible, you may not be allowed to take the credit for up to 10 years. See back of schedule for details.
- It will take us longer to process your return and issue your refund if you do not fill in all lines that apply for each qualifying child.
- Be sure the child's name on line 1 and social security number (SSN) on line 2 agree with the child's social security card. Otherwise, at the time we process your return, we may reduce or disallow your EIC. If the name or SSN on the child's social security card is not correct, call the Social Security Administration at 1-800-772-1213.

Qualifying Child Information	Child 1	Child 2
	First name Last name	First name Last name
1 Child's name If you have more than two qualifying children, you only have to list two to get the maximum credit.		
2 Child's SSN The child must have an SSN as defined on page 43 of the Form 1040A instructions or page 49 of the Form 1040 instructions unless the child was born and died in 2006. If your child was born and died in 2006 and did not have an SSN, enter "Died" on this line and attach a copy of the child's birth certificate.		
3 Child's year of birth	Year ___ ___ ___ ___ *If born after 1987, skip lines 4a and 4b; go to line 5.*	Year ___ ___ ___ ___ *If born after 1987, skip lines 4a and 4b; go to line 5.*
4 If the child was born before 1988— **a** Was the child under age 24 at the end of 2006 and a student?	☐ **Yes.** ☐ **No.** *Go to line 5.* *Continue.*	☐ **Yes.** ☐ **No.** *Go to line 5.* *Continue.*
b Was the child permanently and totally disabled during any part of 2006?	☐ **Yes.** ☐ **No.** *Continue.* The child is not a qualifying child.	☐ **Yes.** ☐ **No.** *Continue.* The child is not a qualifying child.
5 Child's relationship to you (for example, son, daughter, grandchild, niece, nephew, foster child, etc.)		
6 Number of months child lived with you in the United States during 2006 • If the child lived with you for more than half of 2006 but less than 7 months, enter "7." • If the child was born or died in 2006 and your home was the child's home for the entire time he or she was alive during 2006, enter "12."	___ months *Do not enter more than 12 months.*	___ months *Do not enter more than 12 months.*

TIP You may also be able to take the additional child tax credit if your child **(a)** was under age 17 at the end of 2006, **and** **(b)** is a U.S. citizen or resident alien. For more details, see the instructions for line 41 of Form 1040A or line 68 of Form 1040.

For Paperwork Reduction Act Notice, see Form 1040A or 1040 instructions.   Cat. No. 13339M   Schedule EIC (Form 1040A or 1040) 2006

EXHIBIT 9–9 IRS Form EIC and EIC Worksheets *(continues)*

Schedule EIC (Form 1040A or 1040) 2006   Page **2**

Purpose of Schedule

After you have figured your earned income credit (EIC), use Schedule EIC to give the IRS information about your qualifying child(ren).

To figure the amount of your credit or to have the IRS figure it for you, see the instructions for Form 1040A, lines 40a and 40b, or Form 1040, lines 66a and 66b.

Taking the EIC when not eligible. If you take the EIC even though you are not eligible and it is determined that your error is due to reckless or intentional disregard of the EIC rules, you will not be allowed to take the credit for 2 years even if you are otherwise eligible to do so. If you fraudulently take the EIC, you will not be allowed to take the credit for 10 years. You may also have to pay penalties.

Qualifying Child

A qualifying child for the EIC is a child who is your . . .

Son, daughter, stepchild, foster child, brother, sister, stepbrother, stepsister, or a descendant of any of them (for example, your grandchild, niece, or nephew)

was . . .

Under age 19 at the end of 2006
or
Under age 24 at the end of 2006 and a student
or
Any age and permanently and totally disabled

who . . .

Lived with you in the United States for more than half of 2006. If the child did not live with you for the required time, see *Exception to time lived with you* beginning on page 42 of the Form 1040A instructions or page 49 of the Form 1040 instructions.

 If the child was married or meets the conditions to be a qualifying child of another person (other than your spouse if filing a joint return), special rules apply. For details, see page 43 of the Form 1040A instructions or page 49 of the Form 1040 instructions.

 Do you want part of the EIC added to your take-home pay in 2007? To see if you qualify, get Form W-5 from your employer, call the IRS at 1-800-TAX-FORM (1-800-829-3676), or go to *www.irs.gov.*

EXHIBIT 9–9 IRS Form EIC and EIC Worksheets *(continued)*

c. Additional Child Tax Credit.

The Child Tax credit is nonrefundable. However, if a family is eligible, they may receive the refundable additional Child Tax credit. To be eligible for a refund, the household must have earned income. If the family has qualifying children and owes less in tax than they would otherwise be entitled to, the additional child tax credit may be a way to recoup this credit. An additional requirement is that the family has above a threshold amount of taxable earned income. For 2006, the amount was $11,300. This is the level when other benefits such as the earned income credit are in the phase-out range. Taxable earned income is closely defined as follows:

- Wage/salary from your job(s)
- Tips
- Net earnings from self-employment (what you keep after your costs)
- Union strike benefits
- Long-term disability benefits received before minimum retirement age

The additional Child Tax credit requires the completion and attachment to the tax return of form 8812. This assists the taxpayer in establishing eligibility and the amount of the credit to be received. The form requires a number of figures from the earlier portions of form 1040 or 1040-A. As a result, form 8812 is one of the last that can be completed in preparation of the tax return.

d. Nontaxable Combat Pay Election.

Ordinarily, combat pay is not taxable, following a special enactment by Congress in 2004. However, if a taxpayer's household is funded by military service consisting of combat duty, this could eliminate the taxpayer from qualification for the EIC. As a result, military personnel on active combat duty are permitted to make a voluntary election to have the combat pay considered to be ordinary earned income for purposes of the EIC. Inclusion of the income could have the effect of increasing the amount of EIC. However, depending on the specific circumstances of the taxpayer, it is entirely possible that the election and consequent increase in earned income could cause a decrease in EIC. It is something that should be calculated with or without the election before a final determination is made. If the election is made to include the amount of nontaxable combat pay received by the taxpayer, this should be shown on form W-2, box 14, with a code of "Q." If the amount of combat pay is elected for inclusion in the EIC determination, that amount should be reported on form 1040, Line 65B. If made, the election must be complete. That is to say, that the combat pay cannot be split or apportioned. Either the entire amount is included or excluded in the EIC calculation. This election was scheduled to expire at the end of 2005. However, because of the continued military presence in conflict areas around the world at that time, this date has been extended by Congress. This is an item that is likely to expire in the relatively near future and should be tracked for congressional activity.

e. Excess Social Security and RRTA Withholding.

Employees are subject to Social Security withholding. Certain railroad employees are subject to a similar type of withholding, termed RRTA. However, both of these have an upper-limit ceiling for wages at which point the withholding is no longer required. If a taxpayer has more than one employer with an aggregate amount of wages exceeding the statutory ceiling for withholding, that employee may be entitled to receive a refund of the overwithholding. This does not include Medicare withholding, which has no ceiling. This amount is included on form 1040 or 1040-A. The ceiling amount is adjusted periodically. As a result, the proper amount should be established for the year of the return before a determination can be made as to whether an overpayment was made.

7. Alternative Minimum Tax

After all income, adjustments, deductions, tax liability, and credits are calculated, the taxpayer should have a final result right? Wrong. As discussed in Chapter 8, the Alternative Minimum Tax (AMT) computation was instituted to prevent wealthy taxpayers from avoiding tax through the overuse of deductions and credits. However, as income levels continue to rise, more and more taxpayers find themselves falling inside the boundaries of the AMT. Consequently, as a matter of course, an AMT calculation should be done for any taxpayer claiming deductions or credits, or for those with income that receives preferential tax treatment. By completing form 6251, the taxpayer can determine if the AMT applies. If it does, this is the amount that must be considered in the determination of the tax liability. The effect of the AMT is to limit the extent to which certain types of deductions can be used to avoid taxes.

APPLICATION **9.11**

Keith worked for ABC Corporation for 6 months in 2005. He received total wages of $48,000 and his share of Social Security (not Medicare) contributions amounted to $3,072. He also worked for XYZ Corporation for 5 months. During that time, he received wages of $63,000. His Social Security withholding was $3,906. In 2005, the ceiling for Social Security wages subject to withholding was $90,000. Keith earned $111,000. As a result, the Social Security withholdings for $21,000 of his income were in error. Neither employer made a mistake because each was withholding from wages below the $90,000 ceiling. However, when combined, the amount was exceeded, and as a result too much was withheld. Keith would be entitled to a refund of 6.2 percent (the individual contribution amount) of $21,000, or $1,302.

Form **6251**

Department of the Treasury
Internal Revenue Service (99)

Alternative Minimum Tax—Individuals

▶ See separate instructions.

▶ Attach to Form 1040 or Form 1040NR.

OMB No. 1545-0074

20**06**

Attachment
Sequence No. **32**

Name(s) shown on Form 1040 or Form 1040NR

Your social security number

Part I   Alternative Minimum Taxable Income (See instructions for how to complete each line.)

1	If filing Schedule A (Form 1040), enter the amount from Form 1040, line 41 (minus any amount on Form 8914, line 6), and go to line 2. Otherwise, enter the amount from Form 1040, line 38 (minus any amount on Form 8914, line 6), and go to line 7. (If less than zero, enter as a negative amount.)	1	
2	Medical and dental. Enter the **smaller** of Schedule A (Form 1040), line 4, **or** 2½ % of Form 1040, line 38	2	
3	Taxes from Schedule A (Form 1040), line 9	3	
4	Enter the home mortgage interest adjustment, if any, from line 6 of the worksheet on page 2 of the instructions	4	
5	Miscellaneous deductions from Schedule A (Form 1040), line 26	5	
6	If Form 1040, line 38, is over $150,500 (over $75,250 if married filing separately), enter the amount from line 11 of the **Itemized Deductions Worksheet** on page A-7 of the instructions for Schedule A (Form 1040)	6	( )
7	Tax refund from Form 1040, line 10 or line 21	7	( )
8	Investment interest expense (difference between regular tax and AMT)	8	
9	Depletion (difference between regular tax and AMT)	9	
10	Net operating loss deduction from Form 1040, line 21. Enter as a positive amount	10	
11	Interest from specified private activity bonds exempt from the regular tax	11	
12	Qualified small business stock (7% of gain excluded under section 1202)	12	
13	Exercise of incentive stock options (excess of AMT income over regular tax income)	13	
14	Estates and trusts (amount from Schedule K-1 (Form 1041), box 12, code A)	14	
15	Electing large partnerships (amount from Schedule K-1 (Form 1065-B), box 6)	15	
16	Disposition of property (difference between AMT and regular tax gain or loss)	16	
17	Depreciation on assets placed in service after 1986 (difference between regular tax and AMT)	17	
18	Passive activities (difference between AMT and regular tax income or loss)	18	
19	Loss limitations (difference between AMT and regular tax income or loss)	19	
20	Circulation costs (difference between regular tax and AMT)	20	
21	Long-term contracts (difference between AMT and regular tax income)	21	
22	Mining costs (difference between regular tax and AMT)	22	
23	Research and experimental costs (difference between regular tax and AMT)	23	
24	Income from certain installment sales before January 1, 1987	24	( )
25	Intangible drilling costs preference	25	
26	Other adjustments, including income-based related adjustments	26	
27	Alternative tax net operating loss deduction	27	( )
28	**Alternative minimum taxable income.** Combine lines 1 through 27. (If married filing separately and line 28 is more than $200,100, see page 7 of the instructions.)	28	

Part II   Alternative Minimum Tax

29   Exemption. (If this form is for a child under age 18, see page 7 of the instructions.)

IF your filing status is . . .	AND line 28 is not over . . .	THEN enter on line 29 . . .		
Single or head of household	$112,500	$42,500		
Married filing jointly or qualifying widow(er)	150,000	62,550		
Married filing separately	75,000	31,275	29	

If line 28 is **over** the amount shown above for your filing status, see page 7 of the instructions.

30	Subtract line 29 from line 28. If more than zero **or** you are filing Form 2555 or 2555-EZ, go to line 31. If zero or less and you are not filing Form 2555 or 2555-EZ, enter -0- on lines 33 and 35 and skip the rest of Part II	30	
31	• If you are filing Form 2555 or 2555-EZ, see page 8 of the instructions for the amount to enter. • If you reported capital gain distributions directly on Form 1040, line 13; you reported qualified dividends on Form 1040, line 9b; **or** you had a gain on both lines 15 and 16 of Schedule D (Form 1040) (as refigured for the AMT, if necessary), complete Part III on the back and enter the amount from line 55 here. • All others: If line 30 is $175,000 or less ($87,500 or less if married filing separately), multiply line 30 by 26% (.26). Otherwise, multiply line 30 by 28% (.28) and subtract $3,500 ($1,750 if married filing separately) from the result.	31	
32	Alternative minimum tax foreign tax credit (see page 8 of the instructions)	32	
33	Tentative minimum tax. Subtract line 32 from line 31	33	
34	Tax from Form 1040, line 44 (minus any tax from Form 4972 and any foreign tax credit from Form 1040, line 47). If you used Schedule J to figure your tax, the amount for line 44 of Form 1040 must be refigured without using Schedule J (see page 9 of the instructions)	34	
35	**Alternative minimum tax.** Subtract line 34 from line 33. If zero or less, enter -0-. Enter here and on Form 1040, line 45	35	

For Paperwork Reduction Act Notice, see page 10 of the instructions.   Cat. No. 13600G   Form **6251** (2006)

EXHIBIT 9–10   IRS Form 6251 (continues)

Form 6251 (2006)   Page **2**

Part III   **Tax Computation Using Maximum Capital Gains Rates**

36   Enter the amount from Form 6251, line 30 . . . . **36**

37   Enter the amount from line 6 of the Qualified Dividends and Capital Gain Tax Worksheet in the instructions for Form 1040, line 44, or the amount from line 13 of the Schedule D Tax Worksheet on page D-10 of the instructions for Schedule D (Form 1040), whichever applies (as refigured for the AMT, if necessary) (see page 10 of the instructions) **37**

38   Enter the amount from Schedule D (Form 1040), line 19 (as refigured for the AMT, if necessary) (see page 10 of the instructions) **38**

39   If you did not complete a Schedule D Tax Worksheet for the regular tax or the AMT, enter the amount from line 37. Otherwise, add lines 37 and 38, and enter the **smaller** of that result or the amount from line 10 of the Schedule D Tax Worksheet (as refigured for the AMT, if necessary) **39**

40   Enter the **smaller** of line 36 or line 39 . . . . **40**

41   Subtract line 40 from line 36 . . . . **41**

42   If line 41 is $175,000 or less ($87,500 or less if married filing separately), multiply line 41 by 26% (.26). Otherwise, multiply line 41 by 28% (.28) and subtract $3,500 ($1,750 if married filing separately) from the result . . . . ▶ **42**

43   Enter:
- $61,300 if married filing jointly or qualifying widow(er),
- $30,650 if single or married filing separately, or
- $41,050 if head of household.

             } **43**

44   Enter the amount from line 7 of the Qualified Dividends and Capital Gain Tax Worksheet in the instructions for Form 1040, line 44, or the amount from line 14 of the Schedule D Tax Worksheet on page D-10 of the instructions for Schedule D (Form 1040), whichever applies (as figured for the regular tax). If you did not complete either worksheet for the regular tax, enter -0- **44**

45   Subtract line 44 from line 43. If zero or less, enter -0- **45**

46   Enter the **smaller** of line 36 or line 37 . . . . **46**

47   Enter the **smaller** of line 45 or line 46 . . . . **47**

48   Multiply line 47 by 5% (.05) . . . . ▶ **48**

49   Subtract line 47 from line 46 . . . . **49**

50   Multiply line 49 by 15% (.15) . . . . ▶ **50**

     If line 38 is zero or blank, skip lines 51 and 52 and go to line 53. Otherwise, go to line 51.

51   Subtract line 46 from line 40 . . . . **51**

52   Multiply line 51 by 25% (.25) . . . . ▶ **52**

53   Add lines 42, 48, 50, and 52 . . . . **53**

54   If line 36 is $175,000 or less ($87,500 or less if married filing separately), multiply line 36 by 26% (.26). Otherwise, multiply line 36 by 28% (.28) and subtract $3,500 ($1,750 if married filing separately) from the result **54**

55   Enter the **smaller** of line 53 or line 54 here and on line 31 . . . . **55**

Form **6251** (2006)

EXHIBIT 9–10   IRS Form 6251 *(continued)*

8. Computation of Penalties

Many different types of penalties may be associated with tax returns. These include penalties for failing to properly file a timely return or extension, failure to pay taxes by the filing deadline of April 15 following the end of the tax year, and so on. However, if a taxpayer fails to properly withhold or make periodic estimated payments throughout the year, a penalty may be required to be paid with any tax due on or before the filing deadline of April 15. However, the failure to do this can generate additional interest on the penalty and any amounts of tax that remain unpaid.

If a taxpayer did not have withholding, make estimated payments, or the tax liability after withholding is more than 10 percent of the total tax owed, there may be penalties. This is determined by completion of form 2210. In most cases, form 2210 is not required. If 100 percent of the tax liability is paid and the return is filed on time, then the IRS will figure any penalty and send a bill. If the bill is paid timely, there will be no interest on the penalty. However, most sophisticated software programs can properly calculate the penalty and the taxpayer can pay it with the return or at least be prepared to pay it when the bill arrives from the IRS. The safe harbor rule is that an amount equal to 100 percent of the tax paid the previous year should be paid in or 90 percent of the current year liability. In calculating the penalty for underwithholding, not only is the amount of income required but also when it was generated during the year.

B. THE STATE RETURN

Although it would be impossible to prepare an accurate and up-to-date discussion of how to prepare returns for all states that impose income tax or other types of tax returns, there are a number of key elements common to most that will be addressed here. Keep in mind that every state has its own tax system and that every system is subject to change without notice. Consequently, it is important to check the most current applicable laws and regulations when preparing a federal or state return.

1. Filing Requirements

Filing requirements vary widely from state to state. These are the minimum levels of income that trigger the requirement to file a state return. In some states, this may be several thousand dollars per taxpayer. In other states, it might be as little as a single dollar. However, even if a tax return is not required, one may be filed anyway to secure the refund of taxes withheld that are not owed. Another factor in some jurisdictions for filing requirements is the source of the income. For example, if a retiree lives in a state that does not tax pension income and no other income was

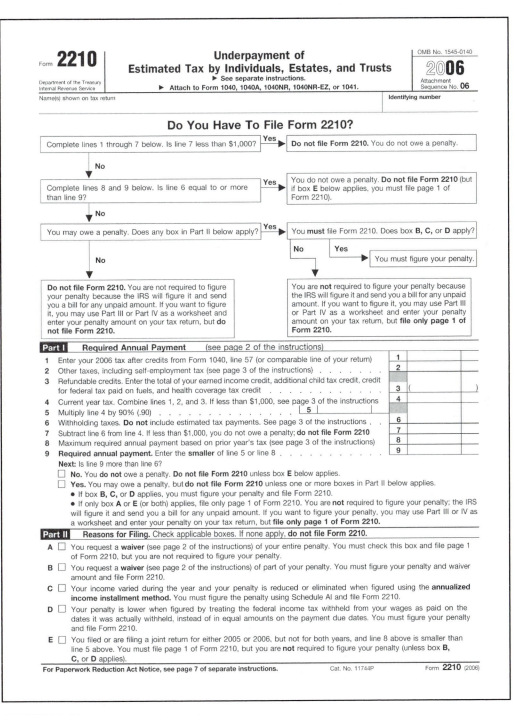

EXHIBIT 9–11   IRS Form 2210 *(continues)*

Form 2210 (2006)

Page **2**

Part III Short Method

You may use the short method if:

● You made no estimated tax payments (or your only payments were withheld federal income tax), **or**

● You paid estimated tax in **equal** amounts on your due dates.

You must use the regular method (Part IV) instead of the short method if:

● You made any estimated tax payments late.

● You checked box **C** or **D** in Part II, **or**

● You are filing Form 1040NR or 1040NR-EZ and you did not receive wages as an employee subject to U.S. income tax withholding.

TIP — You do not need to file Form 2210 unless you checked a box in Part II on page 1.

Note: *If any payment was made earlier than the due date, you may use the short method, but using it may cause you to pay a larger penalty than the regular method. If the payment was only a few days early, the difference is likely to be small.*

10	Enter the amount from Form 2210, line 9	**10**
11	Enter the amount, if any, from Form 2210, line 6	**11**
12	Enter the total amount, if any, of estimated tax payments you made	**12**
13	Add lines 11 and 12	**13**
14	**Total underpayment for year.** Subtract line 13 from line 10. If zero or less, stop here; you do not owe the penalty. **Do not file Form 2210 unless you checked box E on page 1** . . .	**14**
15	Multiply line 14 by .05258 (use the factor shown in the instructions if you are eligible for Hurricane Katrina relief)	**15**
16	● If the amount on line 14 was paid **on or after** 4/15/07, enter -0-. ● If the amount on line 14 was paid **before** 4/15/07, make the following computation to find the amount to enter on line 16. 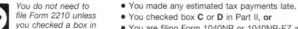 Amount on line 14 × Number of days paid before 4/15/07 × .00022	**16**
17	**Penalty.** Subtract line 16 from line 15. Enter the result here and on Form 1040, line 77; Form 1040A, line 48; Form 1040NR, line 75; Form 1040NR-EZ, line 27; or Form 1041, line 26 . . ▶	**17**

Form **2210** (2006)

EXHIBIT 9–11 IRS Form 2210 *(continued)*

received, that person may not need to file a return. However, if the retiree had a part-time job and earned wages, a return may be necessary to address that portion of income. Once it has been determined that a state return is necessary, other factors come into play that affect the tax liability.

2. Resident versus Nonresident Status

Typically, a state return will ask at the outset whether the taxpayer lived in the state for all or a portion of the year. If less than the full year, the taxpayer generally will have to provide dates and other states of residence. This allows the state to properly calculate the amount of tax generated by a resident versus a nonresident. This in turn may affect tax rate, tax adjustments, credits, deductions, and ultimately, tax liability. Additionally, some states have reciprocal agreements with other states where they provide credit automatically for earnings from the reciprocal jurisdiction. This most often happens when states have heavily populated areas along state lines where crossover of residency and employment is significant.

3. Credit for Tax Paid in Other States

When a taxpayer resides in one state and is employed in another, a dilemma may arise as to who is owed the state income tax. Unfortunately, the answer is often both states. The taxpayer receives the benefits of government programs in the state of residence as well as the state of employment. For example, a taxpayer's children may attend school in the state of residence. But, if laid off, the taxpayer would typically collect unemployment from the state where the employment was located. And the taxpayer receives the benefit of traveling on the roads in both states. The state of employment is generally obligated to withhold and pay state income tax to the state where the taxpayer works. When this occurs, the taxpayer is still likely to be required to file a state return in the state of residence. However, in these circumstances, the taxpayer can usually file a Schedule CR with the state of residence return. This identifies income earned in another jurisdiction and the final amount of state income tax paid there for the year. This is not to be confused with the amount of withholding, which may be more or less than that amount of tax that was ultimately determined to be due. The state of residence then applies a calculation that determines the amount of credit for tax paid in the other state against the tax due in the state of residence. This is typically not a dollar-for-dollar exchange, but it does provide some relief to the taxpayer.

ASSIGNMENT 9.1

Following is information for use in the preparation of the tax return for Margaret Smith, Social Security number 000-44-4444. Answer the following questions:

1. What is the most advantageous filing status available?

2. List all information necessary for each dependent she will claim.

3. What types of income does Margaret have? When would her income be reported on a form 1040? Is any of her Social Security income taxable?

4. Can Margaret deduct the child care expenses incurred while she attends school? If so, on what form is it claimed? And, if so, list the information necessary to claim the child care expense.

5. What is the total of Margaret's itemized deductions? Should she itemize?

6. Who, if anyone, of the children are eligible for the child care credits?

7. What information is necessary to claim adoption expenses? How much adoption expense can Margaret claim?

Margaret is a 40-year-old woman who retired on disability from her job. Her employer's minimum retirement age is 55. She is married. However, she has not seen or heard from her husband in 2 years. Margaret is the mother of three children. Tasha is Margaret's natural child and most recently turned 18 years old on December 31. Her Social Security number is 000-44-4441. She attends the local college and lives with Margaret. Miranda is 13 years old and is also Margaret's natural child. Miranda's Social Security number is 000-44-4442. In November, Margaret adopted Sanjay. Sanjay is a 4-year-old child with special needs.

Margaret's income during the year consisted of disability payments from her former employer of $8,500. She also received Social Security disability in the amount of $13,000. She also receives $6,000 per year in state benefits such as food stamps, reduction in property taxes, and so on, and constitutes less than half the income for the household. The benefits are not taxable.

Margaret emptied her savings and spent the entire $6,000 to accomplish the adoption of Sanjay, which began in January and concluded on November 30. Sanjay, an American citizen, was placed with Margaret by a local foster care agency 2 years before the adoption. Margaret spent $1,800 on child care in her home for Sanjay and Miranda while taking an educational course to retrain in a new career field that would enable her to work despite her disability. Margaret and Tash both received full scholarship for their tuition and books. The child care provider is Nancy Smith, 1111 Beetree Lane, Illinois City, Illinois. Nancy's Social Security number is 000-55-5555. Margaret is buying her home and paid $1,000 in mortgage interest. Her medical expenses were $750. She paid property taxes of $650. Charitable contributions totaled 10 percent of her cash income of $21,500.

ETHICAL QUESTION ❓

Christine has prepared the tax returns for the clients of A, B, & C Law Office for several years. She is also active in community activities and has a wide range of friends and acquaintances. Her close friend Sherry is a stay-at-home mom who lives on child support that she receives from her ex-husband and disability payments from Social Security. One day, Christine is preparing the taxes for a client and requests the Social Security cards of the client's dependents. One of the cards has the same name (and a rather unusual one) of Sherry's youngest child. When Christine asks what the relationship is, as part of the normal interview, the taxpayer claims the child is her niece and the daughter of the taxpayer's deceased sister. However, she provides the same birth date as Sherry's daughter. To further investigate, Christine asks in which hospital the child was born. The taxpayer does not realize this is an unusual question. But she says she cannot recall. Christine is in a position of confronting the taxpayer about whether she is claiming a child that she does not have the legal right to claim, or saying nothing. She does recall that Sherry recently said she was getting a cash prize and splitting it with another friend who helped her "win." Christine suspects that the two have conspired to get a large earned income credit refund. Sherry does not need to file a tax return and thus no one would be claiming the child as a dependent and the two would likely never be caught. What should Christine do?

SUMMARY

The process of preparing the individual tax return is a methodical process that must be completed in a particular order to obtain an accurate result. Before anything can be done, the filing status and dependents (both qualifying child and qualifying persons) must be decided. This will affect later aspects of the return with regard to credits allowed, amount of standard deduction, and so on. Then the various types of income must be identified and evaluated in terms of taxability. This may include the modification of some amounts that are subject to deductions and taxable income floors. Following this, adjustments are necessary to remove any expenses that are not considered as part of the taxpayer's income in terms of tax liability. This provides what is known as the Adjusted Gross Income.

Next, the standard deduction/ or itemized expenses are withdrawn from the amount of Adjusted Gross Income along with the allowance for the personal exemptions claimed. This results in the taxable income amount. The tax tables will establish the tax for the taxable income based upon the filing status. If the result is a positive number, nonrefundable credits are considered to reduce the taxable income dollar for dollar until either the credits or the tax liability is exhausted. After this, any payments and withholdings are credited against the tax liability. Nonrefundable credits that can surpass even a tax liability of $0 are applied to reach a final tax liability or refund result. Any penalties are added on and the final number is the amount the taxpayer must pay or can expect to receive assuming the IRS agrees with the calculation, filing status, reported income, deductions, credits, adjustments, withholding, payments, and penalty amounts.

KEY TERMS

filing status	adjustments	nonrefundable
credits	refundable	

For additional resources, visit our Web site at www.westlegalstudies.com

CHAPTER 10

Preparation of the Small Business Return

■ OBJECTIVES

After completing this chapter, you will be able to:

❑ Identify the necessary documents to report income/loss for a partnership and partners

❑ Identify the necessary documents to report income/loss for a close corporation

❑ Prepare a partnership return

❑ Prepare a return for a small business using Schedule C

A. NECESSARY DOCUMENTS FOR THE BUSINESS ENTITY

Corporations have their own legal existence as a taxpayer. Similarly, each individual is responsible to report certain financial information to the government. But the small business is somewhat of a hybrid. Some businesses may be required to file an informational document with the government. But, ultimately, the financial information, tax liability, deductions, credits, and refunds flow through to the individuals. This places the owners of small business in a position somewhere between the general corporation and the individual. The discussion that follows is a more practical approach to the end-of-year reporting and tax determination for the small business and its owners.

1. Partnership

Unlike the individual taxpayer who does not have to file a return if the filing requirements do not apply, a partnership established in the United States must file an income tax information form unless it generates no gross income, or pays or incurs no amount that would be treated as a deduction or credit for federal tax purposes. In essence, regardless of whether the business operates at a profit or a loss, if it operates and engages in any sort of financial transaction, the partnership should file an informational return.

The forms used to file partnership returns are twofold. The partnership is required to file form 1065, to report any income and expenses. The data received by the IRS is used for a number of purposes including matching the income and expenses reported to that reported by the individual partners. Just as an employer files a W-3 with the government to match against W-2 forms issued to and reported by employees, the 1065 is matched against information from the partners.

The partnership passes the information contained in the 1065 to the individual partners on Schedule K-1-P, associated with form 1065. Because partners are not employees of the partnership, no withholding is taken out of their distributions of profit or any other type of assets of the partnership. The specifics of the K-1-P are addressed later in this chapter. Because no taxes are withheld for partners, this means that the individuals must pay the taxes by including partnership profits in their individual return. This includes not only income tax associated with the income, but for actively participating partners, it also includes self employment tax. Generally speaking, partners are considered to be self-employed. If a taxpayer is a member of a partnership that carries on a trade or business, the share of income or loss from the partnership is treated in much the same way as net income from self-employment. Although the same reporting forms may not be used on the return, limited partners may be subject to self-employment tax on guaranteed payments, such as salary and professional fees for services rendered. And the self-employment tax includes the employer and employee portion of the tax. As a result, partners may need to pay quarterly estimated tax payments using form 1040-ES.

A partnership generally uses the same tax year of one or more partners who own (in total) more than a 50 percent interest in partnership profits and capital. If there is no majority interest during the tax year, the partnership is required to adopt the same tax year as that of the principal capital holder. In the event that neither condition is met, the partnership must use the calendar year. A Limited Liability Company (LLC) reporting as a partnership has the same tax year as a majority of its partners. Because individuals typically file their individual returns on a calendar year basis, most small partnerships are filed this way as well. One exception might be if a corporation owns a partnership interest in a business and the corporation operates on a fiscal year that does not follow a calendar year.

Even though any profit or loss from a partnership passes through as personal income or loss to the partners, the partnership still must have a separate federal tax identification number, most often referred to as an employer identification number (EIN). This is true even if the partnership does not have employees. The number is used by the government to identify the partnership entity on all government forms such as the annual form 1065. If there are significant changes in the ownership of the partnership, bankruptcy, and so on, the IRS has specific guidelines as to when a new EIN should be obtained. The EIN consists of a nine-digit number and cannot be substituted for a Social Security number (although sole proprietors may use their Social Security number as their EIN).

2. Close Corporation (S, LLC)

A Limited Liability Company (LLC) is an entity formed under state law by filing articles of organization as an LLC. The process is somewhat similar to that of a corporation. The function is more like that of a partnership or sole proprietorship in many respects. However, unlike a partnership, the members of an LLC are generally not personally liable for its business debts. An LLC may be classified for federal income tax purposes as if it were a sole proprietorship, a partnership, or a corporation. If the LLC is in a jurisdiction that allows formation with only one owner,

---

APPLICATION **10.1**

Carl, Henry, Bob, and Jenna May were partners. They each regularly took distributions from the partnership. Generally, on the first of the month, the four partners took a distribution of $4,000 each. This translated to a quarterly income of $12,000 per partner. However, no taxes were withheld for them because the partners were owners and not employees of the business for tax purposes. On one occasion, the four partners approached the firm that handled the accounting and end-of-year tax forms for the business. The partners asked that the business withhold a uniform amount for each of the partners and pay it in on their behalf as quarterly estimated payments. The partners could not be accommodated. Because the amount of income tax and self-employment tax is tied to the individual return and involves various calculations of deductions and credits, a standard amount would not necessarily satisfy the requirements for estimated payments and tax withholding for each individual. As a result, the estimated payments necessary may vary widely and one or more of the partners could end up subject to penalties. However, it would be important for each of the partners to consider their own personal tax situation and to pay quarterly estimated taxes in an amount sufficient to meet the requirements in order to avoid penalties.

it will automatically be treated as if it were a sole proprietorship unless the taxpayer makes an election to be treated as a corporation. If the LLC has two or more owners, the organization is treated for tax purposes as a partnership unless an election is made to be treated as a corporation. The election to be treated as a corporation is made by submitting form 8832. The LLC that is owned by a sole proprietor without any employees does not need a separate Federal Tax ID or EIN. If the LLC is a sole proprietorship and has employees, a separate Federal Tax ID is necessary. Additionally, if the LLC is owned and operated by more than one person, an EIN is required just as it would be for a partnership.

Some corporations elect to be treated as S-corporations for tax purposes. This election allows income to flow through the corporation without being taxed until it is claimed as income by the shareholders. This avoids double taxation of corporate profits. However, this election is not available in all circumstances such as with corporations with publicly traded stock. Overall, more corporate tax returns filed in the United States are filed as S-corporations than in any other form.

Unlike a partnership, pass-through income from an S-corporation is *not* subject to self-employment tax. In direct contrast, a partnership's pass-through ordinary income *is* generally subject to self-employment tax. At first glance, this might appear a clear tax advantage of an S-corporation versus a partnership. However, in terms of *"shareholder-employees"* of an S-corporation, the analysis does not end with the distribution of S-corporation income and filing of a return.

If a shareholder-employee of an S-corporation provides services to that S-corporation, then reasonable compensation subject to employment tax should be paid (and subject to withholding) before any nonwage distributions, such as profit sharing or return of capital, may be made to that shareholder-employee. Failure by S-corporations to do so in the past has resulted in a substantial number of lawsuits in which the IRS definition of who is an employee of the business has prevailed. As a result, those corporations were not only liable to pay withholding but also interest and penalties on previous years. If an S-corporation shareholder is an employee and has received an actual distribution, the only remaining area of question is what amount is considered "reasonable" compensation for the work of that particular shareholder-employee. This determination is made based on the relevant facts and circumstances of the particular situation. However, there are some established parameters.

Officers of corporations are treated as employees for employment tax (FUTA) purposes and their compensation is considered to be taxable wages. The IRS has identified that some S-corporations, in an effort to avoid employment taxes, improperly treat payments for services to officers as "corporate distributions" instead of salaries. Generally, an officer of a corporation is treated by the IRS as an employee of the corporation. However, an officer of a corporation who does not regularly perform any services or performs only minor or sporadic services and who neither receives nor is entitled to receive, directly or indirectly, any payment for those services is not usually considered to be an employee of the corporation.

In most cases, an S-corporation is exempt from federal income tax other than tax on certain capital gains and passive income. The S-corporation's shareholders include their share of the corporation's separately stated items of income, deduction, loss, and credit, and their share of collectively stated income or loss on their individual tax returns after the information has been reported to them as taxpayers on a form K-1(S). Similar to the K-1(P) for partnership, the details of this form are also discussed in subsequent sections.

B. PREPARATION OF THE RETURN

The preparation of tax forms for a small business consists of two parts. First, the business must account for its overall profit/loss. This is done by filing the appropriate information return with the IRS and, if necessary, the state(s) where business is conducted. Second, the proper documentation must be provided to the owners for inclusion in their own personal returns. Of course, these forms are in addition to the previously discussed forms that address taxes on wages paid to employees and, for some businesses, sales tax. As mentioned earlier, the forms to be filed vary according to the type of business organization.

1. Partnership.

The proper form to report for a partnership is *form 1065*. The partnership is not independently responsible for income tax. Rather, it is treated as a pass-through business organization in which profits or losses are passed on to the owners as individual taxpayers. However, the partnership is still required to file form 1065.

APPLICATION **10.2**

Terry, Brenda, and Marvin were the owners and officers of an S-corporation. After a few years, Brenda decided to open her own business and left the corporation. After that, Marvin decided to relocate to another part of the country. Because most of the corporate assets previously had been used by Terry and Marvin to buy out Brenda's interest, it was impossible for Terry to buy Marvin's interest immediately. As a result, Terry continued to work in the corporation. Marvin moved away and Terry paid him on an installment basis in the form of a loan against the ownership interest. To protect his interests, Marvin remained as an owner and officer of the corporation during the several-year buyout. Marvin did not actively participate in the business, and took no payments or profit-sharing other than the repurchase of his ownership interest in addition to a low rate of interest. Terry consulted with Marvin on major issues. Terry, however, continued to work regularly in the business that remained successful. For income tax purposes, Terry would likely be considered an employee, Marvin probably would not.

This provides the government with information about the status of partnerships in the nation as a whole. But, just as important, it allows the IRS to compare the information reported by the owner/taxpayers to the information reported by the partnership. This reduces the potential for fraudulent claims of deductions, credits, losses, and so on. Consequently, this improves the accuracy of the tax calculations. In the preparation of the partnership return, the business must disclose the names and addresses of each partner, the name and address of the partnership, as well as each partner's distributive share of taxable income. The return must be signed by a general partner. It is not necessary that all partners sign the return.

Part I of form 1065 requires the reporting of income related items including gross sales/receipts (less returns and allowances), other sources of income and profit as well as the Cost of Goods Sold. These figures are then calculated to reach the figure for the Total Income/Loss for the partnership. The Cost of Goods Sold calculation is based on the number determined in Schedule A on page two of the form 1065. It is calculated much the same as that discussed previously for a retail operation. If the partnership received any farm income, that profit or loss is carried over from a completed Schedule F (normally used to support form 1040). Additionally, if the partnership sold any business property through the year, whether at a gain or loss, form 4797 should be completed, and that final figure transferred to Part I of form 1065. If used, these forms also should be submitted with the return as supporting statements.

The next section for form 1065 is that of deductions. These are amounts that the partnership is allowed to deduct in the determination, for tax purposes, of whether the partnership, and in turn the partners, ended the tax period with a net ordinary income or a loss. The types of things allowed as deductions are very different from deductions on an individual tax return. Tax return deductions are used to determine the amount of taxable income. Deductions on a partnership information return are used to evaluate whether the business operated with a profit or at a loss.

The types of deductions have to do with the expenses and liabilities of the partnership. They include the following:

- Salaries and wages that are labor expenses subject to tax withholding
- Guaranteed payments to partners
- Repairs and maintenance to partnership property and equipment
- Uncollectable debts owed to the partnership
- Rent
- State and local taxes and license fees
- Depreciation (supported by form 4562)
- Depletion of assets
- Employee benefits and retirement plans
- Other miscellaneous deductions allowed by IRS rules.

In addition to the primary form 1065, there are several additional schedules for the form that assist in calculating the figures necessary to complete form 1065 and provide the required information to the government. Schedule A of form 1065 calculates the Cost of Goods Sold (COG). Various figures that have to do with the manufacture and merchandising of inventory are required and, through a series of instructions, the COG figure is determined.

Schedule B of form 1065 is used to provide information about the nature of the partnership and its owners. Although this section requires no calculations, it contains information vital to the determination of whether the partnership is in compliance with various regulations that may apply. For example, one of the questions asks if the partners received their own statement of partnership interests, Schedule K(P), in a timely manner. Based on how they are answered, some questions may generate the requirement for the completion of additional forms. Schedule B requires that a general partner be designated as the "Tax Matters Partner" with whom the IRS communicates on issues relating the tax year for which form 1065 and schedules are filed.

The final portion of the form 1065 for all partnerships is Schedule K. This is used to prepare a K-1 for each partner by carrying appropriate figures from Schedule K. Schedule K is a detailed statement of the business activity for the partnership throughout the tax year. It includes the following sections that must be completed:

- Income and/or Losses
- Deductions
- Self-employment, farming, fishing, nonfarm income/earnings
- Credits and credits previously claimed that must be recaptured as income due to ineligibility of part or all of the credit
- Foreign transactions
- Items that affect Alternative Minimum Tax
- Tax-exempt income (specified by type)

Once these sections are completed, the final portion of Schedule K-1 involves an examination of the sources of income and/or loss for the partnership. This section is known as the Analysis of Net Income (Loss). In this section, each type of partner (cumulative and not by individual partner) is assigned a portion of the income or loss allocated to that type of partner. This provides an overall examination of how the partnership distributes its profit or loss.

In addition to Schedules A, B, and K, the answers to questions in Schedule B may lead to Schedules L, M-1, and M-2. These are for use by partnerships that have significant income and/or assets. Schedule L is a reflection of the balance sheet for the partnership. Schedule M-1 reconciles the income/loss on the accounting books with that identified on the return. Schedule M-2 is an analysis of the Partner's Capital Accounts. It includes the amount contributed, distributions, and net increase or decrease in the partnership interests. The IRS regulations determine the income levels that will trigger the need for these forms. Other forms that may be necessary to provide information required on the return include depreciation schedules, forms for 179 election to expense rather than depreciate, and so on.

Once form 1065 has been completed, Schedule K-1-P can be prepared for each of the partners. Schedule K-1 is used for pass-through business organizations and different forms of K-1 are available for partnerships, S-corporations and limited liability companies, trusts, and estates. Form K-1(P) for partnerships is titled "Partner's Share of Income, Deductions, Credits, Etc."

The form is divided into three separate parts. Part I gives general information about the partnership such as name, address, EIN, and so on. Part II provides information about the specific partner receiving the form including name, identifying number (EIN or Social Security), type of partners, and the allocated share of profit or loss. Part III is used to report the specific partner's financial activity in the partnership by share of ownership rather than form 1065 that reports these items for the partnership as a whole. Schedule K-1 can be confusing because of the substantial number of codes to specifically identify the various amounts reported in each section. There are dozens of different codes for different types of information reported on the various forms of K-1. Although the forms have been updated recently, there is still a substantial opportunity for confusion and/or error. These codes are in addition to some items that are reported in response to specific questions on the form. Because the manner in which information is coded can have a significant impact on the taxpayer's tax liability, it is essential that the K-1 be properly filled in. Equally important is the reporting of this amount on the individual return.

As a general rule, the ordinary net business income or loss from the partnership is reported on Schedule E and attached to the individual return. However, some income items are reported in the other parts of the 1040 tax return. One example, interest and dividends passed-through by an LLC or partnership are reported on Schedule B. Capital gains are reported on Schedule D. Recall the example in Application 10.1. In the buyout, if the partner received his payments by installment, it is likely the amount was paid out with interest. The interest amount would be reported on Schedule B. The principal would be reported on Schedule E. Form K-1-P is not required to be submitted with the return. This information has already been reported to the IRS.

Form **1065** Department of the Treasury Internal Revenue Service		**U.S. Return of Partnership Income** For calendar year 2006, or tax year beginning .... , 2006, ending .... , 20 ...... ▶ See separate instructions.		OMB No. 1545-0099 **2006**
A Principal business activity	Use the IRS label. Other- wise, print or type.	Name of partnership		**D** Employer identification number
B Principal product or service		Number, street, and room or suite no. If a P.O. box, see the instructions.		**E** Date business started
C Business code number		City or town, state, and ZIP code		**F** Total assets (see the instructions) $

G Check applicable boxes: **(1)** ☐ Initial return   **(2)** ☐ Final return   **(3)** ☐ Name change   **(4)** ☐ Address change   **(5)** ☐ Amended return
H Check accounting method: **(1)** ☐ Cash   **(2)** ☐ Accrual   **(3)** ☐ Other (specify) ▶ ....
I Number of Schedules K-1. Attach one for each person who was a partner at any time during the tax year ▶ ....
J Check if Schedule M-3 required (attach Schedule M-3) . . . . ☐

Caution. Include **only** trade or business income and expenses on lines 1a through 22 below. See the instructions for more information.

Income	**1a** Gross receipts or sales	**1a**		
	b Less returns and allowances	**1b**	**1c**	
	2 Cost of goods sold (Schedule A, line 8)		**2**	
	3 Gross profit. Subtract line 2 from line 1c		**3**	
	4 Ordinary income (loss) from other partnerships, estates, and trusts *(attach statement)*. . .		**4**	
	5 Net farm profit (loss) *(attach Schedule F (Form 1040))*		**5**	
	6 Net gain (loss) from Form 4797, Part II, line 17 (attach Form 4797)		**6**	
	7 Other income (loss) *(attach statement)*		**7**	
	8 **Total income (loss).** Combine lines 3 through 7		**8**	
Deductions (see the instructions for limitations)	**9** Salaries and wages (other than to partners) (less employment credits)		**9**	
	10 Guaranteed payments to partners		**10**	
	11 Repairs and maintenance		**11**	
	12 Bad debts		**12**	
	13 Rent		**13**	
	14 Taxes and licenses		**14**	
	15 Interest		**15**	
	16a Depreciation *(if required, attach Form 4562)*	**16a**		
	b Less depreciation reported on Schedule A and elsewhere on return	**16b**	**16c**	
	17 Depletion **(Do not deduct oil and gas depletion.)**		**17**	
	18 Retirement plans, etc.		**18**	
	19 Employee benefit programs		**19**	
	20 Other deductions *(attach statement)*		**20**	
	21 **Total deductions.** Add the amounts shown in the far right column for lines 9 through 20 .		**21**	
	22 **Ordinary business income (loss).** Subtract line 21 from line 8		**22**	
	23 Credit for federal telephone excise tax paid (attach Form 8913)		**23**	

Sign Here

Under penalties of perjury, I declare that I have examined this return, including accompanying schedules and statements, and to the best of my knowledge and belief, it is true, correct, and complete. Declaration of preparer (other than general partner or limited liability company member manager) is based on all information of which preparer has any knowledge.

▶ ....
Signature of general partner or limited liability company member manager

▶ ....
Date

May the IRS discuss this return with the preparer shown below (see instructions)?   ☐ Yes   ☐ No

Paid Preparer's Use Only	Preparer's signature		Date	Check if self-employed ▶ ☐	Preparer's SSN or PTIN
	Firm's name (or yours if self-employed), address, and ZIP code	▶		EIN ▶	
				Phone no. ( )	

For Privacy Act and Paperwork Reduction Act Notice, see separate instructions.   Cat. No. 11390Z   Form **1065** (2006)

EXHIBIT 10–1   Form 1065 *(continues)*

Form 1065 (2006)   Page **2**

Schedule A   **Cost of Goods Sold** (see the instructions)

1	Inventory at beginning of year	**1**
2	Purchases less cost of items withdrawn for personal use	**2**
3	Cost of labor	**3**
4	Additional section 263A costs *(attach statement)*	**4**
5	Other costs *(attach statement)*	**5**
6	**Total.** Add lines 1 through 5	**6**
7	Inventory at end of year	**7**
8	**Cost of goods sold.** Subtract line 7 from line 6. Enter here and on page 1, line 2	**8**

9a Check all methods used for valuing closing inventory:
   (i) ☐ Cost as described in Regulations section 1.471-3
   (ii) ☐ Lower of cost or market as described in Regulations section 1.471-4
   (iii) ☐ Other (specify method used and attach explanation) ▶ ....
  b Check this box if there was a writedown of "subnormal" goods as described in Regulations section 1.471-2(c) . . . ▶ ☐
  c Check this box if the LIFO inventory method was adopted this tax year for any goods *(if checked, attach Form 970)* . ▶ ☐
  d Do the rules of section 263A (for property produced or acquired for resale) apply to the partnership? . . ☐ **Yes** ☐ **No**
  e Was there any change in determining quantities, cost, or valuations between opening and closing inventory? ☐ **Yes** ☐ **No**
     If "Yes," attach explanation.

Schedule B   **Other Information**

		Yes	No
1	What type of entity is filing this return? Check the applicable box:		

   a ☐ Domestic general partnership   **b** ☐ Domestic limited partnership
   c ☐ Domestic limited liability company   **d** ☐ Domestic limited liability partnership
   e ☐ Foreign partnership   **f** ☐ Other ▶ ....

2   Are any partners in this partnership also partnerships?

3   During the partnership's tax year, did the partnership own any interest in another partnership or in any foreign entity that was disregarded as an entity separate from its owner under Regulations sections 301.7701-2 and 301.7701-3? If yes, see instructions for required attachment

4   Did the partnership file Form 8893, Election of Partnership Level Tax Treatment, or an election statement under section 6231(a)(1)(B)(ii) for partnership-level tax treatment, that is in effect for this tax year? See Form 8893 for more details

5   Does this partnership meet all three of the following requirements?
  a The partnership's total receipts for the tax year were less than $250,000;
  b The partnership's total assets at the end of the tax year were less than $600,000; and
  c Schedules K-1 are filed with the return and furnished to the partners on or before the due date (including extensions) for the partnership return.
     If "Yes," the partnership is not required to complete Schedules L, M-1, and M-2; Item F on page 1 of Form 1065; or Item N on Schedule K-1.

6   Does this partnership have any foreign partners? If "Yes," the partnership may have to file Forms 8804, 8805 and 8813. See the instructions

7   Is this partnership a publicly traded partnership as defined in section 469(k)(2)?

8   Has this partnership filed, or is it required to file, a return under section 6111 to provide information on any reportable transaction?

9   At any time during calendar year 2006, did the partnership have an interest in or a signature or other authority over a financial account in a foreign country (such as a bank account, securities account, or other financial account)? See the instructions for exceptions and filing requirements for Form TD F 90-22.1. If "Yes," enter the name of the foreign country. ▶ ....

10 During the tax year, did the partnership receive a distribution from, or was it the grantor of, or transferor to, a foreign trust? If "Yes," the partnership may have to file Form 3520. See the instructions

11 Was there a distribution of property or a transfer (for example, by sale or death) of a partnership interest during the tax year? If "Yes," you may elect to adjust the basis of the partnership's assets under section 754 by attaching the statement described under *Elections Made By the Partnership* in the instructions

12 Enter the number of Forms 8865, Return of U.S. Persons With Respect to Certain Foreign Partnerships, attached to this return . . . . ▶

Designation of Tax Matters Partner (see the instructions)
Enter below the general partner designated as the tax matters partner (TMP) for the tax year of this return:

Name of designated TMP ▶ _____   Identifying number of TMP ▶ _____

Address of designated TMP ▶ _____

Form **1065** (2006)

EXHIBIT 10-1   Form 1065 *(continued)*

Form 1065 (2006)   Page **3**

Schedule K	Partners' Distributive Share Items		Total amount	

Income (Loss)

1	Ordinary business income (loss) (page 1, line 22)	**1**		
2	Net rental real estate income (loss) (attach Form 8825)	**2**		
3a	Other gross rental income (loss)	**3a**		
b	Expenses from other rental activities (attach statement). . . .	**3b**		
c	Other net rental income (loss). Subtract line 3b from line 3a . . .	**3c**		
4	Guaranteed payments	**4**		
5	Interest income	**5**		
6	Dividends: a Ordinary dividends	**6a**		
	b Qualified dividends	**6b**		
7	Royalties	**7**		
8	Net short-term capital gain (loss) (attach Schedule D (Form 1065))	**8**		
9a	Net long-term capital gain (loss) (attach Schedule D (Form 1065)) . . .	**9a**		
b	Collectibles (28%) gain (loss)	**9b**		
c	Unrecaptured section 1250 gain (attach statement)	**9c**		
10	Net section 1231 gain (loss) (attach Form 4797)	**10**		
11	Other income (loss) (see instructions) Type ▶	**11**		

Deductions

12	Section 179 deduction (attach Form 4562)	**12**		
13a	Contributions	**13a**		
b	Investment interest expense	**13b**		
c	Section 59(e)(2) expenditures: **(1)** Type ▶ .... **(2)** Amount ▶	**13c(2)**		
d	Other deductions (see instructions) Type ▶	**13d**		

Self-Employ-ment

14a	Net earnings (loss) from self-employment	**14a**		
b	Gross farming or fishing income	**14b**		
c	Gross nonfarm income	**14c**		

Credits

15a	Low-income housing credit (section 42(j)(5))	**15a**		
b	Low-income housing credit (other)	**15b**		
c	Qualified rehabilitation expenditures (rental real estate) (attach Form 3468).	**15c**		
d	Other rental real estate credits (see instructions) Type ▶	**15d**		
e	Other rental credits (see instructions) Type ▶	**15e**		
f	Other credits (see instructions) Type ▶	**15f**		

Foreign Transactions

16a	Name of country or U.S. possession ▶			
b	Gross income from all sources	**16b**		
c	Gross income sourced at partner level	**16c**		
	Foreign gross income sourced at partnership level			
d	Passive ▶ .... e Listed categories (attach statement) ▶ .... f General limitation ▶	**16f**		
	Deductions allocated and apportioned at partner level			
g	Interest expense ▶ .... h Other ▶	**16h**		
	Deductions allocated and apportioned at partnership level to foreign source income			
i	Passive ▶ .... j Listed categories (attach statement) ▶ .... k General limitation ▶	**16k**		
l	Total foreign taxes (check one): ▶ Paid ☐ Accrued ☐	**16l**		
m	Reduction in taxes available for credit (attach statement)	**16m**		
n	Other foreign tax information (attach statement)			

Alternative Minimum Tax (AMT) Items

17a	Post-1986 depreciation adjustment	**17a**		
b	Adjusted gain or loss	**17b**		
c	Depletion (other than oil and gas)	**17c**		
d	Oil, gas, and geothermal properties—gross income	**17d**		
e	Oil, gas, and geothermal properties—deductions	**17e**		
f	Other AMT items (attach statement)	**17f**		

Other Information

18a	Tax-exempt interest income	**18a**		
b	Other tax-exempt income	**18b**		
c	Nondeductible expenses	**18c**		
19a	Distributions of cash and marketable securities	**19a**		
b	Distributions of other property	**19b**		
20a	Investment income	**20a**		
b	Investment expenses	**20b**		
c	Other items and amounts (attach statement)			

Form **1065** (2006)

EXHIBIT 10–1   Form 1065 (continued)

Form 1065 (2006)   Page **4**

Analysis of Net Income (Loss)

1 Net income (loss). Combine Schedule K, lines 1 through 11. From the result, subtract the sum of
   Schedule K, lines 12 through 13d, and 16l **1**

2 Analysis by partner type:	(i) Corporate	(ii) Individual (active)	(iii) Individual (passive)	(iv) Partnership	(v) Exempt organization	(vi) Nominee/Other
a General partners						
b Limited partners						

Schedule L Balance Sheets per Books		Beginning of tax year		End of tax year	
Assets		(a)	(b)	(c)	(d)
1 Cash					
2a Trade notes and accounts receivable					
b Less allowance for bad debts					
3 Inventories					
4 U.S. government obligations					
5 Tax-exempt securities					
6 Other current assets (attach statement) . . .					
7 Mortgage and real estate loans					
8 Other investments (attach statement) . . .					
9a Buildings and other depreciable assets. . . .					
b Less accumulated depreciation					
10a Depletable assets					
b Less accumulated depletion					
11 Land (net of any amortization).					
12a Intangible assets (amortizable only)					
b Less accumulated amortization					
13 Other assets (attach statement)					
14 Total assets					
Liabilities and Capital					
15 Accounts payable					
16 Mortgages, notes, bonds payable in less than 1 year .					
17 Other current liabilities (attach statement) . . .					
18 All nonrecourse loans					
19 Mortgages, notes, bonds payable in 1 year or more .					
20 Other liabilities (attach statement)					
21 Partners' capital accounts					
22 Total liabilities and capital					

Schedule M-1 Reconciliation of Income (Loss) per Books With Income (Loss) per Return

Note. Schedule M-3 may be required instead of Schedule M-1 (see instructions).

1	Net income (loss) per books		6	Income recorded on books this year not included on Schedule K, lines 1 through 11 (itemize):	
2	Income included on Schedule K, lines 1, 2, 3c, 5, 6a, 7, 8, 9a, 10, and 11, not recorded on books this year (itemize):		a	Tax-exempt interest $	
3	Guaranteed payments (other than health insurance)		7	Deductions included on Schedule K, lines 1 through 13d, and 16l, not charged against book income this year (itemize):	
4	Expenses recorded on books this year not included on Schedule K, lines 1 through 13d, and 16l (itemize):		a	Depreciation $	
a	Depreciation $			....	
b	Travel and entertainment $		8	Add lines 6 and 7	
			9	Income (loss) (Analysis of Net Income (Loss), line 1). Subtract line 8 from line 5	
5	Add lines 1 through 4				

Schedule M-2 Analysis of Partners' Capital Accounts

1	Balance at beginning of year		6	Distributions: a Cash	
2	Capital contributed: a Cash			b Property	
	b Property . . .		7	Other decreases (itemize):	
3	Net income (loss) per books			....	
4	Other increases (itemize):				
	....		8	Add lines 6 and 7	
5	Add lines 1 through 4		9	Balance at end of year. Subtract line 8 from line 5	

Form **1065** (2006)

EXHIBIT 10–1 Form 1065 (continued)

651106

| | Final K-1 | | Amended K-1 | OMB No. 1545-0099 |

Schedule K-1
(Form 1065)

20**06**

Department of the Treasury
Internal Revenue Service

For calendar year 2006, or tax
year beginning _____ , 2006
ending _____ , 20____

Partner's Share of Income, Deductions,
Credits, etc. ▶ See back of form and separate instructions.

| **Part III** | **Partner's Share of Current Year Income, Deductions, Credits, and Other Items** |

1	Ordinary business income (loss)	15	Credits
2	Net rental real estate income (loss)		
3	Other net rental income (loss)	16	Foreign transactions
4	Guaranteed payments		
5	Interest income		
6a	Ordinary dividends		
6b	Qualified dividends		
7	Royalties		
8	Net short-term capital gain (loss)		
9a	Net long-term capital gain (loss)	17	Alternative minimum tax (AMT) items
9b	Collectibles (28%) gain (loss)		
9c	Unrecaptured section 1250 gain		
10	Net section 1231 gain (loss)	18	Tax-exempt income and nondeductible expenses
11	Other income (loss)		
		19	Distributions
12	Section 179 deduction		
13	Other deductions		
		20	Other information
14	Self-employment earnings (loss)		

*See attached statement for additional information.

Part I   **Information About the Partnership**

A   Partnership's employer identification number

B   Partnership's name, address, city, state, and ZIP code

C   IRS Center where partnership filed return

D   ☐ Check if this is a publicly traded partnership (PTP)
E   ☐ Tax shelter registration number, if any _____
F   ☐ Check if Form 8271 is attached

Part II   **Information About the Partner**

G   Partner's identifying number

H   Partner's name, address, city, state, and ZIP code

I   ☐ General partner or LLC member-manager   ☐ Limited partner or other LLC member

J   ☐ Domestic partner   ☐ Foreign partner

K   What type of entity is this partner? _____

L   Partner's share of profit, loss, and capital:

	Beginning	Ending
Profit	_____ %	_____ %
Loss	_____ %	_____ %
Capital	_____ %	_____ %

M   Partner's share of liabilities at year end:

Nonrecourse . . . . $ _____
Qualified nonrecourse financing . . $ _____
Recourse . . . . $ _____

N   Partner's capital account analysis:

Beginning capital account . . . . $ _____
Capital contributed during the year . $ _____
Current year increase (decrease) . . $ _____
Withdrawals & distributions . . . $ (_____)
Ending capital account . . . . $ _____

☐ Tax basis   ☐ GAAP   ☐ Section 704(b) book
☐ Other (explain)

For IRS Use Only

For Privacy Act and Paperwork Reduction Act Notice, see Instructions for Form 1065.   Cat. No. 11394R   **Schedule K-1 (Form 1065) 2006**

EXHIBIT 10–2   Form 1065—K-1 Partnership

ASSIGNMENT **10.1**

Consider the following items and determine whether the information should be reported on forms 1065, K-1, 1040 Schedule B, E. Partnership owned by Nikki and Ned Nolte.

1. A section 179 deduction was taken in the amount of $100,000 for the partnership.

2. Wages of $94,000 were paid to employees.

3. The partners each owned 50 percent and the partnership had a net profit of $150,000 in ordinary income.

4. In addition to the partnership interest, Ned made a loan to the partnership and received back $4,400 in principal and $600 in interest.

5. Rent was paid in the amount of $12,000.

6. Inventory was purchased in the amount of $39,000.

7. The partnership often sold products on an installment plan and received payments for products in the amount of $52,000 in addition to interest on the installment plans of $3,200.

8. The business owned some tax-free municipal bonds and received interest on these in the amount of $3,150.

9. The balance sheet showed a cash balance of $58,000 on January 1, and $64,000 on December 31.

10. The partnership has an EIN of 33-3333333.

2. The LLC and S-Corporation

Tax return preparation for the LLC can be somewhat precarious because the federal government does not recognize an LLC as a classification for federal tax purposes. As a result, these entities must figure out the proper form to report information for their return. With respect to tax returns, an LLC must file either as a corporation, a partnership, or a sole proprietorship. Certain types of LLC are automatically classified as corporations and must file their returns as such. These types of LLC include the following:

- A business entity formed under a federal or state statute or under a statute of a federally recognized Indian tribe if the statute describes or refers to the entity as incorporated or as a corporation, body corporate, or body politic

- An association under regulations section 301.7701-3

- A business entity formed under a federal or state statute if the statute describes or refers to the entity as a joint stock association

- A state-chartered business entity conducting banking activities if any of its deposits are insured by the FDIC

- A business entity wholly owned by a state of political subdivision thereof, or a business entity wholly owned by a foreign government or other entity described in regulations section 1.892.2-T

- A business entity taxable as a corporation under a provision of the code other than section 7701(a)(3)

- Certain foreign entities (see form 8832 instructions)

- An insurance company

If an LLC does not fall into one of these categories, then it should file form 8832 and elect a classification for filing of the federal tax returns. If a business has at least two members, it can elect to be classified as either a corporation or a partnership. A business entity with a single member can elect to be classified as either a sole proprietorship, an association taxable as a corporation, or as a business that is disregarded as an entity separate from its owner, a **disregarded entity**. The latter has the effect of filing as a sole proprietor. The form elected can be changed from year to year by filing a new form 8832. If an LLC fails to submit form 8832, default rules apply and the IRS will determine the classification for the business. Under the default rules, if the LLC has at least two members and is not required to be classified as a corporation, it will be treated as a partnership. An LLC that has only a single member and does not elect is assigned the classification of disregarded entity. The disregarded entity files as a sole proprietorship.

If the LLC elects or is assigned partnership status, it should file its return according to the rules for a partnership. However, if it elects corporate status, it should file a U.S. Corporation Income Tax Return using form 1120. It is important to note that as a corporation filing form 1120, there are no pass-through items to a 1040. The corporation return is separate from the individual and taxes are assessed. Additional taxes may be assessed against the income the owners receive from the corporation as returns of capital (capital gains) or dividends. Another option is for the LLC to elect filing as an S-corporation. This more closely parallels many of the LLCs formed under state laws. When this is done, the LLC should file a form 1120-S, U.S. Income Tax Return for an S-corporation. With this method, each owner reports their specific share of corporate income, credits, and deductions on their personal return. This is the most common method and it will be discussed in this chapter.

Form 1120-S used for electing LLCs and S-corporations is very similar to form 1065 used for partnerships. It begins with identifying information. Like the 1065, the 1120-S follows with sections used to identify income and deductions. In some circumstances, the corporation might actually owe tax, even though it is, for the most part, a pass-through entity. Specifically, if the corporation has always been an S-corporation, there is no issue of excess net passive income tax. But if the corporation has accumulated earnings and profits determined as of the end of the tax year, has passive investment income for the tax year in an amount that exceeds

DISREGARDED ENTITY

A business that is disregarded as an entity separate from its owner.

25 percent of the corporations gross receipts, and has taxable income, the corporation must pay a tax on the excess net passive income. If the tax is not estimated and paid quarterly, there also could be associated penalties imposed.

Schedule A of the 1120-S is used to calculate the Cost of Goods Sold. The amount is calculated in the same manner as for other types of business. However, some questions specific to the 1120-S also must be answered. These are essentially informational questions and do not necessarily generate the need for additional forms or schedules. Like form 1065, 1120-S Schedule B asks questions that may very well result in the necessity of completing additional forms/schedules based on the answers. These include forms 8281, 1120-S Schedule L, M-1, M-2, and N, which are similar to those reported by partnerships in association with form 1065.

Finally, Schedule K is extremely similar to 1065 Schedule K. Like the partnership schedule, the S-corporation schedule identifies that information that will be necessary to summarize the activity of the business and properly apportion it to the owner(s). Once this is completed, forms 1120S/K-1(S) can be prepared and distributed to the owner or owners of the business.

3. Reporting Ownership Interest on Schedule C

As addressed in previous chapters, the sole proprietorship reports profit and/or loss, and ultimately taxable income, on the individual tax form 1040 Schedule C. This form also can be used as an election for an LLC in appropriate circumstances. Schedule C is the form that is used to calculate how much, if any, of the earnings of the business are subject to income tax. In addition, the completed form will provide the necessary amounts to be used on the forms 1040 and SE (Self-Employment) that is in turn paid toward Social Security and Medicare taxes. Also, depending on the expenses incurred, the Schedule C may generate the need for a number of additional forms and/or schedules to support the amounts claimed on Schedule C.

The first portion of the Schedule C is used to provide identifying information about the business. This not only distinguishes the business from other entities but also provides information to the government about the types and locations of various businesses around the country. Such information is essential to the proper management of economic resources and the tracking of business trends. This part of the form requires the name and address of the business as well as the category and IRS code for the particular type of business, and identifying number (either EIN or the owner's Social Security number).

The next section of Schedule C discloses information about the gross income generated by the business during the year. This also includes the COG. The subtraction of the COG from gross profit results in an income amount. However, this is not usually the taxable amount reported on the individual form 1040. A number of other deductible expenses are also subtracted in addition to the COG. These expenses, although deductible, are not part of the COG.

Form **1120S**

Department of the Treasury
Internal Revenue Service

U.S. Income Tax Return for an S Corporation

▶ Do not file this form unless the corporation has filed Form 2553
to elect to be an S corporation.
▶ See separate instructions.

OMB No. 1545-0130

2006

For calendar year 2006 or tax year beginning , 2006, ending , 20

A Effective date of S election	Use IRS label. Other-wise, print or type.	Name		C Employer identification number
		Number, street, and room or suite no. If a P.O. box, see instructions.		D Date incorporated
B Business activity code number (see instructions)		City or town, state, and ZIP code		E Total assets (see *instructions*) $

F Check if: **(1)** ☐ Initial return **(2)** ☐ Final return **(3)** ☐ Name change **(4)** ☐ Address change **(5)** ☐ Amended return
G Enter the number of shareholders in the corporation at the end of the tax year . . . . ▶
H Check if Schedule M-3 is required *(attach Schedule M-3)* . . . . ▶ ☐

Caution. *Include **only** trade or business income and expenses on lines 1a through 21. See the instructions for more information.*

Income

1a	Gross receipts or sales	**b** Less returns and allowances c Bal ▶	1c
2	Cost of goods sold (Schedule A, line 8)		2
3	Gross profit. Subtract line 2 from line 1c		3
4	Net gain (loss) from Form 4797, Part II, line 17 *(attach Form 4797)*		4
5	Other income (loss) *(see instructions—attach statement)*		5
6	**Total income (loss).** Add lines 3 through 5. . . . . ▶		6

Deductions (see instructions for limitations)

7	Compensation of officers		7
8	Salaries and wages (less employment credits)		8
9	Repairs and maintenance		9
10	Bad debts		10
11	Rents		11
12	Taxes and licenses		12
13	Interest		13
14	Depreciation not claimed on Schedule A or elsewhere on return *(attach Form 4562)*		14
15	Depletion **(Do not deduct oil and gas depletion.)**		15
16	Advertising		16
17	Pension, profit-sharing, etc., plans		17
18	Employee benefit programs.		18
19	Other deductions *(attach statement)*		19
20	**Total deductions.** Add lines 7 through 19 . . . . ▶		20
21	**Ordinary business income (loss).** Subtract line 20 from line 6		21

Tax and Payments

22a	Excess net passive income or LIFO recapture tax *(see instructions)*	22a		
b	Tax from Schedule D (Form 1120S)	22b		
c	Add lines 22a and 22b *(see instructions for additional taxes)* . .			22c
23a	2006 estimated tax payments and 2005 overpayment credited to 2006	23a		
b	Tax deposited with Form 7004.	23b		
c	Credit for federal tax paid on fuels *(attach Form 4136)* . . .	23c		
d	Credit for federal telephone excise tax paid *(attach Form 8913)*	23d		
e	Add lines 23a through 23d			23e
24	Estimated tax penalty *(see instructions)*. Check if Form 2220 is attached . . . . . ▶ ☐			24
25	**Amount owed.** If line 23e is smaller than the total of lines 22c and 24, enter amount owed . .			25
26	**Overpayment.** If line 23e is larger than the total of lines 22c and 24, enter amount overpaid .			26
27	Enter amount from line 26 **Credited to 2007 estimated tax** ▶ Refunded ▶			27

Sign Here

Under penalties of perjury, I declare that I have examined this return, including accompanying schedules and statements, and to the best of my knowledge and belief, it is true, correct, and complete. Declaration of preparer (other than taxpayer) is based on all information of which preparer has any knowledge.

▶ _____   _____   _____
Signature of officer   Date   Title

May the IRS discuss this return with the preparer shown below (see instructions)? ☐ Yes ☐ No

Paid Preparer's Use Only

Preparer's signature ▶		Date	Check if self-employed ☐	Preparer's SSN or PTIN
Firm's name (or yours if self-employed), address, and ZIP code	▶		EIN	
			Phone no. ( )	

For Privacy Act and Paperwork Reduction Act Notice, see separate instructions.   Cat. No. 11510H   Form **1120S** (2006)

EXHIBIT 10–3 Form 1120-S *(continues)*

Form 1120S (2006)   Page **2**

Schedule A   Cost of Goods Sold (see instructions)

1	Inventory at beginning of year	**1**
2	Purchases	**2**
3	Cost of labor	**3**
4	Additional section 263A costs (attach statement)	**4**
5	Other costs (attach statement)	**5**
6	**Total.** Add lines 1 through 5	**6**
7	Inventory at end of year	**7**
8	**Cost of goods sold.** Subtract line 7 from line 6. Enter here and on page 1, line 2	**8**

9a Check all methods used for valuing closing inventory: (i) ☐ Cost as described in Regulations section 1.471-3

     (ii) ☐ Lower of cost or market as described in Regulations section 1.471-4

     (iii) ☐ Other (Specify method used and attach explanation.) ▶

    b Check if there was a writedown of subnormal goods as described in Regulations section 1.471-2(c) . . . . ▶ ☐

    c Check if the LIFO inventory method was adopted this tax year for any goods (if checked, attach Form 970) . . . . . ▶ ☐

    d If the LIFO inventory method was used for this tax year, enter percentage (or amounts) of closing inventory computed under LIFO   **9d**

    e If property is produced or acquired for resale, do the rules of section 263A apply to the corporation? . . . . ☐ Yes ☐ No

    f Was there any change in determining quantities, cost, or valuations between opening and closing inventory? . . ☐ Yes ☐ No

     If "Yes," attach explanation.

Schedule B   Other Information (see instructions)

		Yes	No
1	Check accounting method: **a** ☐ Cash **b** ☐ Accrual **c** ☐ Other (specify) ▶		
2	See the instructions and enter the:		
	a Business activity ▶ .... **b** Product or service ▶		
3	At the end of the tax year, did the corporation own, directly or indirectly, 50% or more of the voting stock of a domestic corporation? (For rules of attribution, see section 267(c).) If "Yes," attach a statement showing: **(a)** name and employer identification number (EIN), **(b)** percentage owned, and **(c)** if 100% owned, was a QSub election made?		
4	Was the corporation a member of a controlled group subject to the provisions of section 1561?		
5	Has this corporation filed, or is it required to file, a return under section 6111 to provide information on any reportable transaction?		
6	Check this box if the corporation issued publicly offered debt instruments with original issue discount . . ▶ ☐		
	If checked, the corporation may have to file **Form 8281,** Information Return for Publicly Offered Original Issue Discount Instruments.		
7	If the corporation: **(a)** was a C corporation before it elected to be an S corporation **or** the corporation acquired an asset with a basis determined by reference to its basis (or the basis of any other property) in the hands of a C corporation **and (b)** has net unrealized built-in gain (defined in section 1374(d)(1)) in excess of the net recognized built-in gain from prior years, enter the net unrealized built-in gain reduced by net recognized built-in gain from prior years . . . . ▶ $		
8	Enter the accumulated earnings and profits of the corporation at the end of the tax year. $		
9	Are the corporation's total receipts (see instructions) for the tax year **and** its total assets at the end of the tax year less than $250,000? If "Yes," the corporation is not required to complete Schedules L and M-1.		

Note: If the corporation, at any time during the tax year, had assets or operated a business in a foreign country or U.S. possession, it may be required to attach **Schedule N (Form 1120),** Foreign Operations of U.S. Corporations, to this return. See Schedule N for details.

Schedule K   Shareholders' Pro Rata Share Items

			Total amount
	1	Ordinary business income (loss) (page 1, line 21)	**1**
	2	Net rental real estate income (loss) (attach Form 8825)	**2**
	3a	Other gross rental income (loss) **3a**	
	b	Expenses from other rental activities (attach statement) . **3b**	
	c	Other net rental income (loss). Subtract line 3b from line 3a	**3c**
Income (Loss)	4	Interest income	**4**
	5	Dividends: **a** Ordinary dividends	**5a**
		b Qualified dividends **5b**	
	6	Royalties	**6**
	7	Net short-term capital gain (loss) (attach Schedule D (Form 1120S))	**7**
	8a	Net long-term capital gain (loss) (attach Schedule D (Form 1120S))	**8a**
	b	Collectibles (28%) gain (loss) **8b**	
	c	Unrecaptured section 1250 gain (attach statement) . . . **8c**	
	9	Net section 1231 gain (loss) (attach Form 4797)	**9**
	10	Other income (loss) (see instructions) . . . . Type ▶	**10**

Form **1120S** (2006)

EXHIBIT 10–3   Form 1120-S (continued)

Form 1120S (2006)   Page **3**

	Shareholders' Pro Rata Share Items (continued)		Total amount
Deductions	**11** Section 179 deduction *(attach Form 4562)*	**11**	
	12a Contributions	**12a**	
	b Investment interest expense	**12b**	
	c Section 59(e)(2) expenditures **(1)** Type ▶_____ **(2)** Amount ▶	**12c(2)**	
	d Other deductions *(see instructions)* . . . . Type ▶	**12d**	
Credits	**13a** Low-income housing credit (section 42(j)(5))	**13a**	
	b Low-income housing credit (other)	**13b**	
	c Qualified rehabilitation expenditures (rental real estate) *(attach Form 3468)*	**13c**	
	d Other rental real estate credits *(see instructions)* Type ▶_____	**13d**	
	e Other rental credits *(see instructions)* . . . Type ▶_____	**13e**	
	f Credit for alcohol used as fuel *(attach Form 6478)*	**13f**	
	g Other credits *(see instructions)* . . . . . Type ▶	**13g**	
Foreign Transactions	**14a** Name of country or U.S. possession ▶_____		
	b Gross income from all sources	**14b**	
	c Gross income sourced at shareholder level	**14c**	
	Foreign gross income sourced at corporate level		
	d Passive	**14d**	
	e Listed categories *(attach statement)*	**14e**	
	f General limitation	**14f**	
	Deductions allocated and apportioned at shareholder level		
	g Interest expense	**14g**	
	h Other	**14h**	
	Deductions allocated and apportioned at corporate level to foreign source income		
	i Passive	**14i**	
	j Listed categories *(attach statement)*	**14j**	
	k General limitation	**14k**	
	Other information		
	l Total foreign taxes (check one): ▶ ☐ Paid ☐ Accrued	**14l**	
	m Reduction in taxes available for credit *(attach statement)*	**14m**	
	n Other foreign tax information *(attach statement)*		
Alternative Minimum Tax (AMT) Items	**15a** Post-1986 depreciation adjustment	**15a**	
	b Adjusted gain or loss	**15b**	
	c Depletion (other than oil and gas)	**15c**	
	d Oil, gas, and geothermal properties—gross income	**15d**	
	e Oil, gas, and geothermal properties—deductions	**15e**	
	f Other AMT items *(attach statement)*	**15f**	
Items Affecting Shareholder Basis	**16a** Tax-exempt interest income	**16a**	
	b Other tax-exempt income	**16b**	
	c Nondeductible expenses	**16c**	
	d Property distributions	**16d**	
	e Repayment of loans from shareholders	**16e**	
Other Information	**17a** Investment income	**17a**	
	b Investment expenses	**17b**	
	c Dividend distributions paid from accumulated earnings and profits	**17c**	
	d Other items and amounts *(attach statement)*		
Reconciliation	**18 Income/loss reconciliation.** Combine the amounts on lines 1 through 10 in the far right column. From the result, subtract the sum of the amounts on lines 11 through 12d and 14l	**18**	

Form **1120S** (2006)

EXHIBIT 10–3 Form 1120-S *(continued)*

Form 1120S (2006)   Page **4**

Schedule L	**Balance Sheets per Books**	Beginning of tax year		End of tax year	
	Assets	(a)	(b)	(c)	(d)
1	Cash				
2a	Trade notes and accounts receivable . .				
b	Less allowance for bad debts	( )		( )	
3	Inventories				
4	U.S. government obligations.				
5	Tax-exempt securities (see instructions) .				
6	Other current assets (attach statement) .				
7	Loans to shareholders				
8	Mortgage and real estate loans . . .				
9	Other investments (attach statement) .				
10a	Buildings and other depreciable assets . .				
b	Less accumulated depreciation . . .	( )		( )	
11a	Depletable assets				
b	Less accumulated depletion.	( )		( )	
12	Land (net of any amortization)				
13a	Intangible assets (amortizable only) . .				
b	Less accumulated amortization . . .	( )		( )	
14	Other assets (attach statement) . . .				
15	Total assets				
	Liabilities and Shareholders' Equity				
16	Accounts payable				
17	Mortgages, notes, bonds payable in less than 1 year .				
18	Other current liabilities (attach statement) .				
19	Loans from shareholders				
20	Mortgages, notes, bonds payable in 1 year or more .				
21	Other liabilities (attach statement) . . .				
22	Capital stock				
23	Additional paid-in capital				
24	Retained earnings				
25	Adjustments to shareholders' equity (attach statement)				
26	Less cost of treasury stock		( )		( )
27	Total liabilities and shareholders' equity . .				

Schedule M-1	**Reconciliation of Income (Loss) per Books With Income (Loss) per Return**
	Note: Schedule M-3 required instead of Schedule M-1 if total assets are $10 million or more—see instructions

1	Net income (loss) per books.		5	Income recorded on books this year not included on Schedule K, lines 1 through 10 (itemize):	
2	Income included on Schedule K, lines 1, 2, 3c, 4, 5a, 6, 7, 8a, 9, and 10, not recorded on books this year (itemize):			a Tax-exempt interest $	
3	Expenses recorded on books this year not included on Schedule K, lines 1 through 12 and 14l (itemize):		6	Deductions included on Schedule K, lines 1 through 12 and 14l, not charged against book income this year (itemize):	
a	Depreciation $		a	Depreciation $	
b	Travel and entertainment $			....	
			7	Add lines 5 and 6.	
4	Add lines 1 through 3.		8	Income (loss) (Schedule K, line 18). Line 4 less line 7	

Schedule M-2	**Analysis of Accumulated Adjustments Account, Other Adjustments Account, and Shareholders' Undistributed Taxable Income Previously Taxed** (see instructions)

		(a) Accumulated adjustments account	(b) Other adjustments account	(c) Shareholders' undistributed taxable income previously taxed
1	Balance at beginning of tax year			
2	Ordinary income from page 1, line 21. . .			
3	Other additions			
4	Loss from page 1, line 21	( )		
5	Other reductions	( )	( )	
6	Combine lines 1 through 5			
7	Distributions other than dividend distributions			
8	Balance at end of tax year. Subtract line 7 from line 6			

Form **1120S** (2006)

EXHIBIT 10–3 Form 1120-S (continued)

651106

☐ Final K-1	☐ Amended K-1	OMB No. 1545-0099

Schedule K-1
(Form 1065)

20**06**

Department of the Treasury
Internal Revenue Service

For calendar year 2006, or tax
year beginning _____ , 2006
ending _____ , 20____

Partner's Share of Income, Deductions,
Credits, etc.   ▶ See back of form and separate instructions.

Part I	Information About the Partnership

A   Partnership's employer identification number

B   Partnership's name, address, city, state, and ZIP code

C   IRS Center where partnership filed return

D   ☐ Check if this is a publicly traded partnership (PTP)
E   ☐ Tax shelter registration number, if any _____
F   ☐ Check if Form 8271 is attached

Part II	Information About the Partner

G   Partner's identifying number

H   Partner's name, address, city, state, and ZIP code

I   ☐ General partner or LLC   ☐ Limited partner or other LLC
      member-manager   member

J   ☐ Domestic partner   ☐ Foreign partner

K   What type of entity is this partner? _____
L   Partner's share of profit, loss, and capital:

	Beginning	Ending
Profit	%	%
Loss	%	%
Capital	%	%

M   Partner's share of liabilities at year end:
   Nonrecourse . . . . $ _____
   Qualified nonrecourse financing . . $ _____
   Recourse . . . . $ _____

N   Partner's capital account analysis:
   Beginning capital account . . . . $ _____
   Capital contributed during the year . $ _____
   Current year increase (decrease) . . $ _____
   Withdrawals & distributions . . . $ (_____)
   Ending capital account . . . . $ _____

   ☐ Tax basis   ☐ GAAP   ☐ Section 704(b) book
   ☐ Other (explain)

Part III	Partner's Share of Current Year Income, Deductions, Credits, and Other Items

1 Ordinary business income (loss)	15 Credits
2 Net rental real estate income (loss)	
3 Other net rental income (loss)	16 Foreign transactions
4 Guaranteed payments	
5 Interest income	
6a Ordinary dividends	
6b Qualified dividends	
7 Royalties	
8 Net short-term capital gain (loss)	
9a Net long-term capital gain (loss)	17 Alternative minimum tax (AMT) items
9b Collectibles (28%) gain (loss)	
9c Unrecaptured section 1250 gain	
10 Net section 1231 gain (loss)	18 Tax-exempt income and nondeductible expenses
11 Other income (loss)	
	19 Distributions
12 Section 179 deduction	
13 Other deductions	
	20 Other information
14 Self-employment earnings (loss)	

*See attached statement for additional information.

For IRS Use Only

For Privacy Act and Paperwork Reduction Act Notice, see Instructions for Form 1065.   Cat. No. 11394R   Schedule K-1 (Form 1065) 2006

EXHIBIT 10–4   Form 1120-S/K-1-S *(continues)*

Schedule K-1 (Form 1120S) 2006   Page **2**

This list identifies the codes used on Schedule K-1 for all shareholders and provides summarized reporting information for shareholders who file Form 1040. For detailed reporting and filing information, see the separate Shareholder's Instructions for Schedule K-1 and the instructions for your income tax return.

		Code		Report on
		L	Credit for increasing research activities	See the Shareholder's Instructions
		M	New markets credit	
		N	Credit for employer social security and Medicare taxes	
		O	Backup withholding	Form 1040, line 64
		P	Other credits	See the Shareholder's Instructions

1. Ordinary business income (loss). You must first determine whether the income (loss) is passive or nonpassive. Then enter on your return as follows:

	Report on
Passive loss	See the Shareholder's Instructions
Passive income	Schedule E, line 28, column (g)
Nonpassive loss	Schedule E, line 28, column (h)
Nonpassive income	Schedule E, line 28, column (j)

2. Net rental real estate income (loss)   See the Shareholder's Instructions

3. Other net rental income (loss)

Net income	Schedule E, line 28, column (g)
Net loss	See the Shareholder's Instructions

4. Interest income   Form 1040, line 8a

5a. Ordinary dividends   Form 1040, line 9a

5b. Qualified dividends   Form 1040, line 9b

6. Royalties   Schedule E, line 4

7. Net short-term capital gain (loss)   Schedule D, line 5, column (f)

8a. Net long-term capital gain (loss)   Schedule D, line 12, column (f)

8b. Collectibles (28%) gain (loss)   28% Rate Gain Worksheet, line 4 (Schedule D instructions)

8c. Unrecaptured section 1250 gain   See the Shareholder's Instructions

9. Net section 1231 gain (loss)   See the Shareholder's Instructions

10. Other income (loss)

Code		
A	Other portfolio income (loss)	See the Shareholder's Instructions
B	Involuntary conversions	See the Shareholder's Instructions
C	Sec. 1256 contracts & straddles	Form 6781, line 1
D	Mining exploration costs recapture	See Pub. 535
E	Other income (loss)	See the Shareholder's Instructions

11. Section 179 deduction   See the Shareholder's Instructions

12. Other deductions

Code		
A	Cash contributions (50%)	
B	Cash contributions (30%)	
C	Noncash contributions (50%)	
D	Noncash contributions (30%)	See the Shareholder's Instructions
E	Capital gain property to a 50% organization (30%)	
F	Capital gain property (20%)	
G	Investment interest expense	Form 4952, line 1
H	Deductions—royalty income	Schedule E, line 18
I	Section 59(e)(2) expenditures	See the Shareholder's Instructions
J	Deductions—portfolio (2% floor)	Schedule A, line 22
K	Deductions—portfolio (other)	Schedule A, line 27
L	Preproductive period expenses	See the Shareholder's Instructions
M	Commercial revitalization deduction from rental real estate activities	See Form 8582 Instructions
N	Reforestation expense deduction	See the Shareholder's Instructions
O	Domestic production activities information	See Form 8903 Instructions
P	Qualified production activities income	Form 8903, line 7
Q	Employer's W-2 wages	Form 8903, line 13
R	Other deductions	See the Shareholder's Instructions

13. Credits

Code		
A	Low-income housing credit (section 42(j)(5))	
B	Low-income housing credit (other)	See the Shareholder's Instructions
C	Qualified rehabilitation expenditures (rental real estate)	
D	Other rental real estate credits	
E	Other rental credits	
F	Undistributed capital gains credit	Form 1040, line 70, check box a
G	Credit for alcohol used as fuel	
H	Work opportunity credit	See the Shareholder's Instructions
I	Welfare-to-work credit	
J	Disabled access credit	
K	Empowerment zone and renewal community employment credit	Form 8844, line 3

14. Foreign transactions

A	Name of country or U.S. possession	
B	Gross income from all sources	Form 1116, Part I
C	Gross income sourced at shareholder level	

Foreign gross income sourced at corporate level

D	Passive	
E	Listed categories	Form 1116, Part I
F	General limitation	

Deductions allocated and apportioned at shareholder level

G	Interest expense	Form 1116, Part I
H	Other	Form 1116, Part I

Deductions allocated and apportioned at corporate level to foreign source income

I	Passive	
J	Listed categories	Form 1116, Part I
K	General limitation	

Other information

L	Total foreign taxes paid	Form 1116, Part II
M	Total foreign taxes accrued	Form 1116, Part II
N	Reduction in taxes available for credit	Form 1116, line 12
O	Foreign trading gross receipts	Form 8873
P	Extraterritorial income exclusion	Form 8873
Q	Other foreign transactions	See the Shareholder's Instructions

15. Alternative minimum tax (AMT) items

A	Post-1986 depreciation adjustment	
B	Adjusted gain or loss	See the Shareholder's Instructions and the Instructions for Form 6251
C	Depletion (other than oil & gas)	
D	Oil, gas, & geothermal—gross income	
E	Oil, gas, & geothermal—deductions	
F	Other AMT items	

16. Items affecting shareholder basis

A	Tax-exempt interest income	Form 1040, line 8b
B	Other tax-exempt income	
C	Nondeductible expenses	See the Shareholder's Instructions
D	Property distributions	
E	Repayment of loans from shareholders	

17. Other information

A	Investment income	Form 4952, line 4a
B	Investment expenses	Form 4952, line 5
C	Qualified rehabilitation expenditures (other than rental real estate)	See the Shareholder's Instructions
D	Basis of energy property	See the Shareholder's Instructions
E	Recapture of low-income housing credit (section 42(j)(5))	Form 8611, line 8
F	Recapture of low-income housing credit (other)	Form 8611, line 8
G	Recapture of investment credit	See Form 4255
H	Recapture of other credits	See the Shareholder's Instructions
I	Look-back interest—completed long-term contracts	See Form 8697
J	Look-back interest—income forecast method	See Form 8866
K	Dispositions of property with section 179 deductions	
L	Recapture of section 179 deduction	
M	Section 453(l)(3) information	
N	Section 453A(c) information	
O	Section 1260(b) information	
P	Interest allocable to production expenditures	See the Shareholder's Instructions
Q	CCF nonqualified withdrawals	
R	Information needed to figure depletion—oil and gas	
S	Amortization of reforestation costs	
T	Other information	

✸ Printed on recycled paper

EXHIBIT 10–4 Form 1120-S/K-1-S *(continued)*

They have to do with the operating of a business as opposed to costs associated with manufacture and/or preparation of a product inventory. These expenses are part of almost any business. But, for a service organization that does not sell products, it is an essential part of the determination of taxable income.

The most common expenses associated with general business operations are listed specifically on Schedule C. However, there is also a section provided in which "Other" expenses can be detailed. These must be legitimate business expenses not addressed in other sections of the schedule, and must be recognized as deductible by the IRS. Consequently, before listing an item in the section for "Other" expenses, it is wise to consult current IRS publications for rulings on the type of expenses the taxpayer intends to report. The expenses specifically listed on Schedule C include the following:

- Advertising
- Car and Truck Expenses (see discussion later in this chapter)
- Commissions and Fees
- Contract Labor (not employees)
- Depletion
- Depreciation (see discussion later in this chapter)
- Employee Benefit Programs
- Insurance (other than health)
- Interest
- Mortgage
- Legal and Professional Services
- Office Expenses
- Pension and Profit-Sharing Plans
- Rent or Lease
- Vehicles, machinery, equipment
- Other business property
- Repairs and Maintenance
- Supplies
- Taxes and Licenses
- Travel, Meals, Entertainment (see discussion later in this chapter)
    Travel Away from Home
    Deductible Meals/Entertainment (subject to limitations)
- Utilities
- Wages
- Other Expenses

Some of the sections mentioned here warrant more detailed discussions. First is the section for car and truck expenses. This is used to address vehicles driven off of the business property and not vehicular equipment, for example, a forklift. If the business has such expenses, then worksheets are necessary to determine the proper method for reporting the expenses. There are essentially two methods. The first involves calculating the actual expenses of operating vehicles. This includes operation, maintenance, upkeep, and possibly depreciation. This is known as the "Actual" method. The other option is the "Standard Mileage" method. This method involves a calculation based on the miles driven for the business. At first, these two methods may seem quite simplistic. However, there are numerous variables that play into the calculation including, but not limited to:

- the date each vehicle was placed into, or taken out of, service,
- the amount paid for the vehicle,
- whether there was a trade-in vehicle and its value,
- the percentage of business use for the vehicle versus other uses,
- whether the vehicle is used for any personal purpose,
- maintenance and repair expenses,
- gasoline purchases,
- the amount of miles driven for commuting, business, all other reasons, and
- whether the Actual or Standard Mileage method was used in the previous year for the vehicle

The answers to these questions will indicate which method the taxpayer should use. There are a variety of rules that apply to the calculation of car and truck expenses. As a result, it is essential that the taxpayer keep consistent written records for business use of vehicles. Without written documentation, the expenses may not be deductible and could result in a substantial increase in taxable income.

A related item is "travel away from home." There are numerous IRS rules that apply to the determination of the taxpayer's "tax home" and how expenses when traveling away from this location are computed. Limitations apply and the rules must be followed closely. Pub. 463 provides a detailed discussion and instructions on how the various expenses associated with business travel by someone who is self employed should be determined. These are not combined with expenses for local meals and entertainment that are calculated separately on Schedule C and discussed in greater detail later in this chapter.

With regard to the issue of depreciation, if this question is answered in the affirmative, that is, there are depreciable business items, the proper supporting worksheets must be prepared and attached to the return. This includes a depreciation schedule for each of the assets that detail the depreciation history for the assets, purchase dates, category of items, whether the items were sold or disposed of during the year and if so when, the method of depreciation, and so on. If a section 179 expense deduction is taken, it also must be addressed in terms of how it relates to the depreciation of the item.

Section 179 allows the taxpayer to deduct the expenses of an otherwise depreciable asset in the year of purchase rather than doing it over a period of several years. Although available to all businesses, this is an especially helpful tool for some small businesses that do not maintain substantial long-term assets and could benefit more from an immediate and larger deduction. It also helps young businesses that need to maximize deductions and thereby decrease taxable income as the business is getting on its feet. There are limitations on the amounts that can be expensed using a 179 election. But, for most sole proprietorships, these limits are high enough that they are not an issue.

Most of the other expense items are self-explanatory; however, IRS rulings are available for items that do not fall squarely within the definition of the item. For example, advertising includes not only items within the traditional forms of media but any expense reasonably expected to draw attention by the business toward potential consumers. This may include business cards, sponsorship of events, teams, and so on. Similarly, legal and professional services include everything from monies paid for legal representation to state licenses, and even tax preparation fees to the extent they were incurred to prepare business related documents. Taxes and licenses are separated out from legal and professional fees and should be detailed in the event of an audit. Office expenses can include items such as staplers, postage, and so on. When it comes to meals and entertainment, a number of special rules apply. Typically, only 50 percent of these items are deductible. If a related item such as a restaurant gift certificate, tickets to an event, and so on are given to someone outside the business rather than shared with the individual, it will be considered a gift. Gifts are limited to a total dollar amount per year, per recipient. As a result, no longer can someone get around the 50 percent limitation on meals and entertainment simply by giving the item to a potential business customer or associate. Very often, the gift

---

APPLICATION **10.3**

Bob decided to open a golf instruction business. He purchased $14,000 worth of golf equipment to use for his students. He had very little overhead, as he gave lessons at a public course. During his first year in business, he generated $28,000 in income. He wanted to maximize his income and minimize his tax liability. Also, he anticipated purchasing new equipment every 2–3 years as technology and trends in the sport advanced. As a result, he decided to expense the equipment under Section 179 all in one year rather than depreciate it over time. By doing so, he was able to reduce his table income by 50 percent. This deduction would be much less by using depreciation. And, because Bob intends to make similar purchases in future years, the expense method may be a more beneficial avenue for him.

limitation will be greater than the meals and entertainment limitation. Regardless of the type of expense, it is essential to clarify that it is one intended by the IRS to be included in the Schedule C calculation before actually calculating the result.

Once the COG of Part I and expenses of Part II have been determined, the form is not yet complete. For many sole proprietors, the most important part of the computation of taxable income is determined on line 30. If the sole proprietor maintains a part of their residence exclusively for business (with the exception of daycare that does not require exclusivity), this may be the most significant deductible expense. It is true that this expense is one that may generate attention by the IRS and possibly even an audit. However, if the taxpayer is truthful about the expense and can substantiate the amounts, there should be no cause for worry.

The business's use of home is determined by use of form 8829 and the result is reported on line 30 of Schedule C. Form 8829 requests information such as the location and size of the residence and the percentage of square footage used for business. Then, expenses associated with the residence are listed as either direct or indirect. Direct expenses are those identified exclusively with the business such as a private business phone line. Indirect expenses are those for the entire residence such as property taxes. The percentage of square footage is then multiplied against the indirect expenses to arrive at the amount of these expenses attributable to the business space. Even a very small area can be claimed if it is used for business. However, it is important that personal use not take place there. For example, costs of Internet service that is used for both personal and business reasons cannot be claimed as a business expense.

In addition to the expenses for the operation of the business portion of the residence, a home that is owned also can be depreciated. This, however, is subject to recapture. For example, if depreciation is taken on a business used portion of a residence and that residence is subsequently sold, part of the depreciation may be required to be added back into the sale of the house, thereby possibly increasing the profit and subsequently generating capital gains. As a result, any claim for depreciation of part of a residence for business use should be measured against the possible inclusion of depreciation amounts in into the ultimate profit determination on the sale of the house.

Finally, if the amount on line 31 of Schedule C is a net profit, the taxpayer is required to include the amount on line 12 of form 1040 and complete Schedule SE. This will determine if the taxpayer owes Social Security and Medicare tax. If a tax is owed, then SE also should be attached to the return and the proper amount is reported on form 1040. If the result of Schedule C is a net loss, this is also included on form 1040 line 12 and Schedule SE. If the business operates as a loss but some of the taxpayer's investment is not at risk of loss, form 6198 must be completed and submitted. It is important to recall that a loss for more than 3 of 5 years for a Schedule C business is likely to be treated by the IRS as a hobby rather than a business. In this event, none of the expenses are considered deductible.

SCHEDULE C
(Form 1040)

Department of the Treasury
Internal Revenue Service   (99)

Profit or Loss From Business

(Sole Proprietorship)

▶ **Partnerships, joint ventures, etc., must file Form 1065 or 1065-B.**

▶ **Attach to Form 1040, 1040NR, or 1041.**   ▶ **See Instructions for Schedule C (Form 1040).**

OMB No. 1545-0074

20**06**

Attachment
Sequence No. **09**

Name of proprietor   Social security number (SSN)

A	Principal business or profession, including product or service (see page C-2 of the instructions)	**B** Enter code from pages C-8, 9, & 10 ▶
C	Business name. If no separate business name, leave blank.	**D** Employer ID number (EIN), if any

E   Business address (including suite or room no.) ▶
    City, town or post office, state, and ZIP code

F   Accounting method: **(1)** ☐ Cash   **(2)** ☐ Accrual   **(3)** ☐ Other (specify) ▶

G   Did you "materially participate" in the operation of this business during 2006? If "No," see page C-3 for limit on losses   ☐ Yes   ☐ No

H   If you started or acquired this business during 2006, check here   . . . . ▶ ☐

Part I   **Income**

1	Gross receipts or sales. **Caution.** If this income was reported to you on Form W-2 and the "Statutory employee" box on that form was checked, see page C-3 and check here . . . . . . ▶ ☐	**1**
2	Returns and allowances	**2**
3	Subtract line 2 from line 1	**3**
4	Cost of goods sold (from line 42 on page 2)	**4**
5	**Gross profit.** Subtract line 4 from line 3	**5**
6	Other income, including federal and state gasoline or fuel tax credit or refund (see page C-3) . . ▶	**6**
7	**Gross income.** Add lines 5 and 6 . . . . ▶	**7**

Part II   **Expenses.** Enter expenses for business use of your home **only** on line 30.

8	Advertising	**8**	**18**	Office expense	**18**
9	Car and truck expenses (see page C-4)	**9**	**19**	Pension and profit-sharing plans	**19**
			20	Rent or lease (see page C-5):	
10	Commissions and fees . .	**10**	**a**	Vehicles, machinery, and equipment .	**20a**
11	Contract labor (see page C-4)	**11**	**b**	Other business property . . .	**20b**
12	Depletion	**12**	**21**	Repairs and maintenance . .	**21**
13	Depreciation and section 179 expense deduction (not included in Part III) (see page C-4)	**13**	**22**	Supplies (not included in Part III) .	**22**
			23	Taxes and licenses . . .	**23**
			24	Travel, meals, and entertainment:	
			a	Travel	**24a**
14	Employee benefit programs (other than on line 19) .	**14**	**b**	Deductible meals and entertainment (see page C-6)	**24b**
15	Insurance (other than health) .	**15**	**25**	Utilities	**25**
16	Interest:		**26**	Wages (less employment credits) .	**26**
a	Mortgage (paid to banks, etc.) .	**16a**	**27**	Other expenses (from line 48 on page 2)	**27**
b	Other	**16b**			
17	Legal and professional services	**17**			

28	**Total expenses** before expenses for business use of home. Add lines 8 through 27 in columns . ▶	**28**
29	Tentative profit (loss). Subtract line 28 from line 7	**29**
30	Expenses for business use of your home. Attach **Form 8829**	**30**
31	**Net profit or (loss).** Subtract line 30 from line 29. • If a profit, enter on both **Form 1040, line 12,** and **Schedule SE, line 2,** or on **Form 1040NR, line 13** (statutory employees, see page C-6). Estates and trusts, enter on Form 1041, line 3. • If a loss, you **must** go to line 32.	**31**
32	If you have a loss, check the box that describes your investment in this activity (see page C-6). • If you checked 32a, enter the loss on both **Form 1040, line 12,** and **Schedule SE, line 2,** or on **Form 1040NR, line 13** (statutory employees, see page C-6). Estates and trusts, enter on Form 1041, line 3. • If you checked 32b, you **must** attach **Form 6198.** Your loss may be limited.	**32a** ☐ All investment is at risk. **32b** ☐ Some investment is not at risk.

For Paperwork Reduction Act Notice, see page C-8 of the instructions.   Cat. No. 11334P   **Schedule C (Form 1040) 2006**

EXHIBIT 10–5   Schedule C *(continues)*

Schedule C (Form 1040) 2006
Page **2**

Part III **Cost of Goods Sold** (see page C-7)

33 Method(s) used to
value closing inventory: **a** ☐ Cost **b** ☐ Lower of cost or market **c** ☐ Other (attach explanation)

34 Was there any change in determining quantities, costs, or valuations between opening and closing inventory?
If "Yes," attach explanation . . . . ☐ **Yes** ☐ **No**

35 Inventory at beginning of year. If different from last year's closing inventory, attach explanation . .	35	
36 Purchases less cost of items withdrawn for personal use	36	
37 Cost of labor. Do not include any amounts paid to yourself	37	
38 Materials and supplies	38	
39 Other costs	39	
40 Add lines 35 through 39	40	
41 Inventory at end of year	41	
42 **Cost of goods sold.** Subtract line 41 from line 40. Enter the result here and on page 1, line 4 . .	42	

Part IV **Information on Your Vehicle.** Complete this part **only** if you are claiming car or truck expenses on line 9 and are not required to file Form 4562 for this business. See the instructions for line 13 on page C-4 to find out if you must file Form 4562.

43 When did you place your vehicle in service for business purposes? (month, day, year) ▶ ..../........../........

44 Of the total number of miles you drove your vehicle during 2006, enter the number of miles you used your vehicle for:

a Business .... **b** Commuting (see instructions) .... **c** Other ....

45 Do you (or your spouse) have another vehicle available for personal use?. . . . . ☐ **Yes** ☐ **No**

46 Was your vehicle available for personal use during off-duty hours? . . . . ☐ **Yes** ☐ **No**

47a Do you have evidence to support your deduction? . . . . ☐ **Yes** ☐ **No**

b If "Yes," is the evidence written? . . . . ☐ **Yes** ☐ **No**

Part V **Other Expenses.** List below business expenses not included on lines 8–26 or line 30.

....	
....	
....	
....	
....	
....	
....	
....	
....	
48 **Total other expenses.** Enter here and on page 1, line 27	48	

Schedule C (Form 1040) 2006

EXHIBIT 10–5 Schedule C *(continued)*

ASSIGNMENT 10.2

Consider the following items incurred by a self-employed individual and determine where they should be reported. Specifically identify whether the amount should be included on each of the following: form 1040, Schedule C, form 8829, Worksheet, Depreciation Schedules, 179 Expense Calculation, SE.

a. Cost of business cards

b. Cost of telephone service for office on business property

c. Cost of preparation of Schedule C and supporting documents

d. Money paid to a legal investigator who was an independent contractor

e. Money paid to full-time secretary

f. Deduction of cost of business machinery over 4 years

g. Deduction of cost of new computer in a single year

h. Cost of driving personal vehicle for 12,000 business miles during the year

i. Season tickets to local baseball stadium given to customer providing the most revenue for the year

j. $1,500 utility bill for house that contains home office occupying 10 percent of square footage of house

k. Net profit of $18,500 for business

ETHICAL QUESTION

Sanjay has his own business in the form of an LLC. The attorney who prepared the LLC documents also offers tax services to its small business clients. Sanjay is one such client. For the past 3 years, the firm has prepared Sanjay's taxes. Sanjay operates a frozen custard business in the community and elects to file as a sole proprietor. This year, Sanjay has stated that he also wants to claim a home office where he claims he does much of the work for his business. However, he and his wife are the only ones who work in the business. In the calculation, Sanjay claims that the entire 1,000 square feet of his finished basement is his home office. The square footage of the house including the basement is 2,300 square feet and is occupied by Sanjay, his wife, and three teenage children. Sanjay owns one computer and has Internet service. He claims all is 100 percent business use. He wants to expense the computer under Section 179. His Internet service bill is $750 for the year. How should Sanjay be advised about these items?

SUMMARY

This chapter demonstrates the many nuances of small business income tax returns. There are a variety of forms applicable to the various types of business ownership. It is essential that the proper forms and schedules be prepared not only for the business but for the individual as well. Even though many small business entities do not prepare separate income tax returns, the information about the business activity still must be reported and correspond to that reported by the individual owners on their personal returns. In addition to the forms for the business, it is likely that several additional supporting forms will be required regardless of the form of business entity. Close attention to the most current IRS rules is essential to properly prepare the returns and calculate any associated credits, deductions, or tax liability resulting from the net profit/loss of the business.

▌ KEY TERMS

informational return

For additional resources, visit our Web site at www.westlegalstudies.com

CHAPTER 11

Preparation of the Fiduciary Return

▪ OBJECTIVES

After completing this chapter, you will be able to:

❑ Describe the role of accounting in probate cases

❑ Distinguish decedent's estates from guardianship estates

❑ Discuss the documents commonly prepared in probate of a decedent's estate

❑ Discuss the documents commonly prepared in a guardianship estate

❑ Identify information required for the following types of tax returns: Estate Tax, Gift Tax, and Trust Tax

WHAT IS PROBATE AND ESTATE ACCOUNTING?

The purpose of accounting in the field of Probate and Estate law is to properly handle the assets of individuals who have either died or become incapacitated. The methods employed in the accounting for a probate estate are the same as those in other accounting situations. There are debits and credits, and financial statements, and so on. The difference is that for most individual estates, the accounting takes into account a great deal of assets that have not been formally valued as they would have in a business situation. Additionally, the best source of necessary information, the owner of the assets, is quite often gone, unable to adequately communicate, or unable to make informed decisions. As a result, probate and estate accounting often involves advanced research and estimating skills. Once the assets and liabilities are properly identified and valued, the accounting process is very similar to other accounting situations in terms of maintaining assets or liquidating them.

B. ESTATES

1. Procedures

■ ESTATES

All of the valuable things an individual owns, such as real estate, art collections, collectibles, antiques, jewelry, investments and life insurance.

■ DECEDENT

A deceased person.

Probate courts are assigned the task of administrating the **estates** of those who are deceased as well as those living under legal guardianship. Legal guardianship is when one or more persons is appointed to oversee the interests of someone who does not have the ability to protect their own interests. This may be in the case of a minor who does not have living parents with legal rights over the child, or someone who is mentally incapacitated (short term or long term). Whether the probate is for a **decedent** or one who has no legal capacity, the result is the same. The party cannot be responsible for his or her own legal issues including financial and tax matters. Consequently, the probate court oversees these on behalf of the decedent or incapacitated party. This is usually done through appointment of a person or persons

---

APPLICATION   11.1

Barbara and Gerry have lived together (unmarried) for about 12 years. They are involved in a car accident in which Gerry is killed and Barbara is left totally unable to care for herself. As a decedent, Gerry's estate required probate. This would include an accounting of his assets, liabilities, and a plan for payment of creditors, possible liquidation, and distribution of remaining assets. For Barbara, it is necessary to establish a probate estate to manage her liabilities and assets including any she might have shared with, or inherited from, Gerry through his will. If Gerry did not have a valid will, Barbara may have had no inheritance rights. The ownership and valuation of assets may be done in different ways based on the circumstances and the law of the jurisdiction. It would be necessary to determine what documents Barbara and Gerry may have had in place such as a will, power of attorney, and so on. These documents can provide helpful information as to how the parties intended that their estates be handled in the event of death and/or incapacitation.

to administrate the estate and report to the court. The title used for these individuals may vary from state to state and by type of probate. For the sake of discussion, the more common term of "administrator" will be used here.

In a probate case, it is first necessary to identify the needs of the party who is the subject of the probate and appoint appropriate persons to conduct the actual steps necessary to protect the rights and interests of property involved. If the individual is deceased, it must be determined if there was a valid will, a nominee for administering the estate, and a plan for handling the assets and liabilities of the decedent. If there was no valid will, state law will apply in the determination of who is entitled to inherit and how the net assets, after liabilities are satisfied, will be distributed.

The probate courts are also responsible to act in a supervisory role for incapacitated adults and minors whose parents do not have full parental rights and responsibilities. Once a guardianship is established, the guardian is required to periodically report to the courts with respect to the guardianship and the status of the incapacitated person and their estate. The frequency of reports often depend on the age and condition of the individual as well as the size of the estate.

Originally, each state developed laws of probate. These laws established formal procedures for the handling of assets, evaluation, and payment of persons claiming to be creditors, and management or distribution of the remaining assets after debts are paid. With the increasing mobility of our society, it is no longer unusual for an individual's assets to be scattered throughout several states. Laws of property generally require that real property be governed by the law where it is located. However, the law of estates often requires the probate to take place in the jurisdiction of domicile for the decedent or person subject to guardianship. In response to these and similar potential conflicts, the Uniform Probate Code was adopted. A wide majority of states have adopted the Code, which establishes identical probate procedures and standards in each adopting state. With this Code, rights are determined in the same manner, irrespective of where the property of the estate is located.

The procedure for probating an estate typically follows some common steps. When probate is begun, as the result of death or for the purpose of guardianship, a petition is filed with the probate court seeking that an estate be established. Once this petition is accepted, state law often requires that all assets be frozen (businesses owned by the subject of the probate may be permitted to continue). All bank accounts, stocks, bonds, and other financial transactions in the name of the decedent or person subject to guardianship, commonly known as a "ward," are frozen until such time as the court has determined the status of the assets within the estate in terms of control and/or ownership. Eventually, the court will institute a plan to administer the estate long term or to liquidate the assets.

Most jurisdictions have special provisions in place for estates that are considered relatively small in terms of value. In these cases, a simplified process is in place to limit the amount of money expended to administer the estate. One example might be a very small estate in which the court sets the estate of a decedent aside and allows the heirs to essentially take over the responsibility for the debts and any remaining assets after debts are paid. However, the majority of estates presented to probate courts require the various stages of procedure to ensure that the assets and debts of the estate are properly handled.

2. Preparation of Documents

To establish a case in the probate courts, it is necessary to file various documents. These include things such as the petition, which seeks the action of the court and notices to affected parties that probate of an estate has been formally requested. Once the case has been established, the court will order various steps to occur depending on whether the case is for the probate of an estate for a decedent or for an incapacitated person. Early on, the administrator is appointed and with this the wheels of probate begin to turn. One stage common to both types of case is an **Inventory of the Estate**. This is very much as it sounds. The administrator is ordered by the court to take a complete financial inventory of all assets and liabilities of the party who is the subject of the probate.

■ **INVENTORY OF THE ESTATE**

A complete financial inventory of all assets and liabilities of the party who is the subject of the probate.

3. Inventory and Valuation of the Estate

Inventory and valuation of an estate is often a substantial task. Typically, individuals do not maintain a complete written inventory of all their property. This would include all real property and personal property ranging from financial interests to household goods. Additionally, all of the property must be identified as to its current fair market value. Along with the assets, the inventory also must include all financial liabilities. Finally, any property that included the right of survivorship must be addressed. Property with a valid right of survivorship, for example, joint tenancy owners of an interest in real estate, is not part of the estate. This property interest literally passes at the moment of death to the other joint tenants. Any property of the decedent that was held in joint tenancy must be excluded from the inventory and the joint tenants notified of the death of the decedent. Identification of creditors, notice to heirs and joint tenants of the death in the case of a decedent probate is done through publication in a newspaper within the county of where the decedent was last domiciled. Some jurisdictions require similar publications for guardianship estates. The publication is typically required to be for a specified period of time and a subsequent amount of time is allowed for the creditors and others to come forward with their claims. Once this is accomplished, the administrator can prepare the Inventory of the Estate, which is similar in accounting to an accounting Statement of Assets and Liabilities.

In the formal preparation of an inventory, it is first necessary to identify all property held jointly between the party who is the subject of the estate and anyone else. If the property was held by valid joint tenancy or tenancy by the entireties (between spouses) with rights of survivorship and the probate subject is deceased, that property interest is passed at the moment of death to the surviving joint tenant. All other multiple ownership properties must be assessed not only in terms of value but also the percentage of ownership and possible debt associated with the property.

Jurisdictions typically will have an established form for conducting and reporting the inventory of the estate. The document is used to present an organized picture of the estate of the subject of probate. Most often, the inventory is distinguished by the type of property such as real property, financial assets, tangible personal property, and so on. In addition to the assets, liabilities must be disclosed as well. If the estate is one of an ongoing nature, such as that for a guardianship, it also may be necessary to itemize continuing periodic expenses. In Exhibit 11–1, a sample form is included to demonstrate how the information for an estate might be reported.

EXHIBIT 11–1   INVENTORY OF AN ESTATE

IN THE _____ COURT
OF _____ COUNTY
STATE OF _____

In the Matter of Probate/Guardianship Case No._____
of _____
an Incapacitated/Deceased Person.

In accordance with the laws of the State of _____ I,
_____, administrator of the Estate of _____, declare under penalty of perjury that the following is true and correct to the best of my knowledge:

The assets and liabilities of _____ as of the date of the Order Appointing Administrator are as follows:

PART I.
A. For Each Item of Real Property
Address:
Legal Description:
Lienholder:
Appraised Value:
Insurer and Date of term of Insurance:
Amount of Lien:

B. For All Types of Financial Accounts
Financial Institution (Name, Branch, Address):
Names on Account:

(continues)

EXHIBIT 11–1   INVENTORY OF AN ESTATE *(continued)*

Account Number:
Type of Account:
Balance/Value on _____ (date):

C. Stocks, Bonds, Securities, Cash Value Insurance Policies (Not Listed Above)

D. Personal Property (provide general value of collective items valued less than $1,000)
Household Furnishings
Automobiles
Boats/Recreational Vehicles, etc.
Other (including specific items of value great than $1,000 in value)
E. INCOME
WAGES
PENSIONS
INTEREST
DIVIDENDS
ANNUITY PAYMENTS (INCLUDE PRINCIPAL AMOUNT AND INCOME OVER PAST 12 MONTHS AS WELL AS SPECIFIC PERIODIC PAYMENT AMOUNT)
SOCIAL SECURITY PAYMENTS
VETERANS BENEFITS
RENTS & ROYALTIES
PENSIONS, IRAS, OTHER RETIREMENT ACCOUNTS
STOCKS AND BONDS (INCLUDE PRINCIPAL VALUE AS WELL AS INCOME NOT REPORTED ELSEWHERE).
OTHER

PART II. LIABILITIES AND DEBTS
A. Mortgages and Liens (List Mortgage/Lien holder, account number, principal balance, any periodic payment amount)

B. Installment Loans and Notes (List Lender, account number, principal balance, any periodic payment amount)

C. Credit Cards (List company, account number, principal balance, any periodic payment amount)

(continues)

EXHIBIT 11–1   INVENTORY OF AN ESTATE *(continued)*

D. Debts unsecured by written contract (List creditor, basis for debt, principal balance, any agreed-on periodic payment amount)

Signed_____

   Administrator of the above named Estate

Printed Name_____

Date_____

Notary Public:_____

_____

4. Documents to Finalize the Estate—Disposition or Periodic Reports

Once the accounting has been completed and accepted by the court, it is necessary to finalize the estate. In the case of a decedent estate, all valid creditors must be satisfied before the remaining property can be distributed. This includes the tax return for the estate, which is discussed further later in this chapter.

In the case of a decedent, the assets of the estate are distributed. In a situation involving an incapacitated person, there may be additional steps to protect the estate for the benefit of the individual. These steps are somewhat more complicated. In either case, the court will establish and oversee the estate. Generally, the first real step toward this is the submission of a plan for the estate submitted by the administrator.

In a decedent estate, it must be determined how assets will be distributed. First and foremost is the payment of creditors. This is usually done with liquid funds that are not affected by specific bequests in the event of a valid will. If there is a valid will that includes specific bequests or property, priorities must be established. Those assets identified as more valuable intact rather than liquidated to cash may be set aside in favor of assets that are less unique. For example, consider a will that includes a bequest of mutual funds and stocks along with a bequest of a family heirloom painting dating back centuries. It could be argued that the value of the painting is much greater and will appreciate more if it is kept within the family tradition. If the court accepts the argument, the more liquid assets, the mutual funds and stocks, may be converted to cash in order to pay creditors. In the event that the court is required to liquidate assets of the estate to pay creditors, there is an attempt toward fairness to the heirs in the distribution of the remaining estate. In some cases, there are bequests for specific items and others may include cash values. As a result, additional liquidation of nonidentified assets may be necessary to satisfy all of the bequests. Finally, the tangible assets are recommended for distribution.

The case is slightly different in a probate of an incapacitated person. Creditors are identified and debts paid. If there are ongoing expenses, such as for the care of the individual, educational expenses, and so on, the plan includes details of how this is to be accomplished and who is to be responsible for managing the assets of the estate and, ensuring that timely payments are made. There may or may not be the necessity of liquidation of assets for the benefit of the incapacitated person.

Once the plan for administering the estate is complete, one of two things occurs. In the case of a decedent, the plan is executed and a final accounting is filed with the court along with a request to close the probate. In the case of an incapacitated person, the administrator is put in charge of implementing the plan, including meeting the needs of the incapacitated person, and periodically filing a detailed report with the court as to how the estate is progressing. This process may be for a set term or may last indefinitely. A minor child under the supervision of the court may have a case open in probate until he or she is legally emancipated. A mentally incapacitated person may be under the oversight of the probate court for the rest of his or her life.

An additional part of the duties of the administrator are to see that the proper tax documents are filed for the decedent or ward. In the next section, various types of special returns are addressed, including those for estates in probate. The circumstances of each situation may affect to some degree when and how the returns are filed. However, this discussion introduces the common elements of such returns.

ASSIGNMENT 11.1

Consider the scenario discussed in Application 11.1. Now add the following information: The accident occurred on January 1, 2006. The probate for his estate was not closed until November 1, 2006. Gerry had a valid will in which he left all of his personal property and financial assets to Barbara. However, he directed his real property (including the home they had shared) be sold and net proceeds given to his children from a previous relationship. Below is a list of assets and liabilities for Barbara and Gerry. Barbara had a power of attorney in place. In it, she named Gerry as her guardian.

1. Outline the necessary steps of probate for each of the estates.

2. Create a plan for management and distribution of Gerry's estate.

Gerry's assets included a savings and brokerage account with a value of $265,000, on which Barbara was named as primary beneficiary and joint tenant with right of survivorship. He had real property valued at $160,000 subject to a $100,000 mortgage. He also had household goods and personal property including a collection of antiques and several valuable pieces of art. The fair market value of the household goods was $3,500. The antiques were valued at $23,000, and the artwork was appraised for $72,000. In addition to his mortgage, he owed $18,000 to the local bank on an automobile loan for the car that was

(continues)

ASSIGNMENT **11.1** *(continued)*

destroyed in the accident. The insurance paid $16,000 for the fair market value of the car, leaving a debt of $2,000. No other cars were involved in the accident. The household bills after Gerry's death including utilities, insurance, and property taxes totaled $500 per month. The mortgage payment was $600 per month. At the time of his death, Gerry had $4,000 in a savings account and $2,000 in a checking account, both solely in his name. He also had accrued wages, sick pay, and vacation pay of $5,200. His house sold for the market value on October 31. However, there were realtor's fees and closing costs of $8,800.

    Barbara went from the hospital to a nursing home. She had health insurance that paid all but $2,000 of her hospital medical bills. Barbara was placed on disability, which covered the costs of her nursing home residency. However, it did not cover costs for clothing and personal items. Her personal care costs included $100 per month for hairdresser, personal hygiene products and an average of $40 per month for clothing. At the time of the accident, Barbara had a vehicle valued at $14,000 with no debt attached. She had a credit card bill of $1,100. She had accrued wages, sick time, and vacation pay of $3,100. She had no pension but had an IRA account valued at $75,000. The total of her personal property solely in her name was $4,500. She had a checking account with a balance of $750 and a savings account with a balance of $8,300.

C. SPECIAL RETURNS

1. Probate Returns for Decedents and Incapacitated Persons

    An individual who is incapacitated and under the guardianship of another files their tax return just as any other taxpayer. The return is signed by the individual with power of attorney. This return will typically include information regarding the disability or legal incompetence of the individual. If the taxable income for the individual is below the required filing amount, a return may not even be required. However, for purposes of integrity, it is generally wise for a guardian to file a return for any individual with income for whom the guardian is responsible to avoid the appearance of impropriety. If the individual is receiving income from a trust established for their benefit, the trust may be required to file a separate turn. This is discussed later in this chapter.

    The disabled person may be eligible to be claimed as a dependent on another person's return if dependency requirements are satisfied. The alternative is for the individual to file as a taxpayer. Each situation is different and the outcome may change from year to year. For this reason, it is important to evaluate the manner in which the individual files each year. For those filing as a taxpayer, the tax credit for elderly and disabled persons may be available to reduce tax liability in some circumstances. For more detail on how this affects a ward, review the more detailed discussion in Chapter 10.

With respect to the return of a decedent, the process of filing taxes may become somewhat more complicated. First, if the decedent was married, the spouse is entitled to continue filing married filing jointly for the year in which the death of the spouse occurred. Following the year of the death of the spouse, the status of qualifying widow(er) may be used for filing income taxes under certain conditions. This status is generally more beneficial in terms of tax liability than single or head of household status. However, it can only be used for two years and in limited circumstances. Qualifying widow(er) status can be claimed only if *all* of the following apply:

- The spouse died in and the taxpayer did not/will not remarry during the tax year.

- The taxpayer has a child, adopted child, stepchild, or foster child who will be claimed as a dependent.

- This child will live in the taxpayer's home for all of the tax year.

- The taxpayer will pay over half the cost of keeping up the home.

- The taxpayer could have filed a joint return with his/her spouse the year he or she died, even if he/she did not actually do so.

This addresses the issue of a surviving spouse. However, a return must generally be filed for the estate of the decedent as well. The surviving spouse, if any, will report income of the decedent up to the date of death. Subsequent income such as accrued wages and so on is filed by the estate as income to the estate. This would be along with any other income that would have been paid to the decedent. The estate tax return must be filed for each year that the estate remains open.

There are a number of guidelines and requirements that should be followed when preparing an estate tax return.

The administrator of a decedent's estate should use form 706 to figure the estate tax due, if any. This tax is levied on the entire taxable estate, not just on shares received by beneficiaries. However, not every estate is required to file a return. The amounts involved are periodically adjusted so it is important to consult the proper requirements for the year of death of the decedent which is not necessarily the year in which a return is filed. Form 706 must be filed for the estates of decedents who were either U.S. citizens or U.S. residents at the time of death. This includes those who had a domicile (intended permanent place of residence) in the United States at the time of death. If a nonresident decedent became a U.S. citizen only because of his or her connection with a possession, then the decedent is considered a nonresident alien decedent for estate tax purposes, and form 706-NA is appropriate. If a decedent became a U.S. citizen wholly independently of his or her connection with a possession, then the decedent is considered a U.S. citizen for estate tax purposes. The situations in which an estate return must be filed are specifically described by the IRS.

For decedents who died in 2006, form 706 must be filed by the executor for the estate of every U.S. citizen or resident whose gross estate, plus adjusted taxable gifts and specific exemption, is more than $2,000,000. To determine if a return must be filed for the estate, include:

- The adjusted taxable gifts (under section 2001(b)) made by the decedent after December 31, 1976;

- Total specific exemption allowed under Section 2521 (as in effect before its repeal by the Tax Reform Act of 1976) for gifts made by the decedent after September 8, 1976; and

- The decedent's gross estate valued at the date of death

The gross estate includes all property in which the decedent had an interest (including real property outside the United States). It also includes: certain transfers made during the decedent's life without commensurate and appropriate consideration of money or money's worth, annuities, the includible percentage of joint estates with right of survivorship, the includible percentage of tenancies by the entirety, certain life insurance proceeds, property over which the decedent possessed a general power of appointment, dower or courtesy (or statutory estate) of the surviving spouse, and community property to the extent of the decedent's interest, if any.

Form 706 to report an estate should be filed within 9 months after the date of the decedent's death unless an extension of time to file is approved. Form 4768, Application for Extension of Time To File a Return and/or Pay U.S. Estate Taxes, is used to apply for an extension of time to file. The estate taxes are due within 9 months after the date of the decedent's death unless an extension of time for payment has been granted, or unless an election under Section 6166 to pay in installments or under Section 6163 to postpone the part of the tax attributable to a reversionary or remainder interest is granted. This may require supporting documentation. If there is more than one executor, all listed executors are responsible for the 706 return and are liable for penalties in the event of errors, however, only one signature is required.

If the decedent was a citizen or resident and died testate, attach a certified copy of the will to the return. If one cannot be obtained, a copy of the will should be attached with an explanation of why it is not certified. In addition, other related forms should be attached, including but not limited to forms 712, 709, and 706-CE, trust and power of appointment instruments, death certificate, and state certification of payment of death taxes. If these documents are not filed with the return, the processing of the return will be delayed.

Form **706**
(Rev. October 2006)

Department of the Treasury
Internal Revenue Service

United States Estate (and Generation-Skipping Transfer) Tax Return

Estate of a citizen or resident of the United States (see separate instructions).
To be filed for decedents dying after December 31, 2005, and before January 1, 2007.

OMB No. 1545-0015

1a Decedent's first name and middle initial (and maiden name, if any)	**1b** Decedent's last name

2 Decedent's Social Security No.

3a County, state, and ZIP code, or foreign country, of legal residence (domicile) at time of death	**3b** Year domicile established **4** Date of birth **5** Date of death

6b Executor's address (number and street including apartment or suite no. or rural route; city, town, or post office; state; and ZIP code) and phone no.

6a Name of executor (see page 4 of the instructions)

6c Executor's social security number (see page 4 of the instructions)

Phone no. (   )

7a Name and location of court where will was probated or estate administered

7b Case number

8 If decedent died testate, check here ▶ ☐ and attach a certified copy of the will.   **9** If you extended the time to file this Form 706, check here ▶ ☐

10 If Schedule R-1 is attached, check here ▶ ☐

Part 1—Decedent and Executor

Part 2—Tax Computation

1	Total gross estate less exclusion (from Part 5—Recapitulation, page 3, item 12)	**1**
2	Tentative total allowable deductions (from Part 5—Recapitulation, page 3, item 22)	**2**
3a	Tentative taxable estate (before state death tax deduction) (subtract line 2 from line 1)	**3a**
b	State death tax deduction	**3b**
c	Taxable estate (subtract line 3b from line 3a)	**3c**
4	Adjusted taxable gifts (total taxable gifts (within the meaning of section 2503) made by the decedent after December 31, 1976, other than gifts that are includible in decedent's gross estate (section 2001(b)))	**4**
5	Add lines 3c and 4	**5**
6	Tentative tax on the amount on line 5 from Table A on page 4 of the instructions	**6**
7	Total gift tax paid or payable with respect to gifts made by the decedent after December 31, 1976. Include gift taxes by the decedent's spouse for such spouse's share of split gifts (section 2513) only if the decedent was the donor of these gifts and they are includible in the decedent's gross estate (see instructions)	**7**
8	Gross estate tax (subtract line 7 from line 6)	**8**
9	Maximum unified credit (applicable credit amount) against estate tax . **9**	
10	Adjustment to unified credit (applicable credit amount). (This adjustment may not exceed $6,000. See page 6 of the instructions.) **10**	
11	Allowable unified credit (applicable credit amount) (subtract line 10 from line 9)	**11**
12	Subtract line 11 from line 8 (but do not enter less than zero)	**12**
13	Credit for foreign death taxes (from Schedule(s) P). (Attach Form(s) 706-CE.) **13**	
14	Credit for tax on prior transfers (from Schedule Q) **14**	
15	Total credits (add lines 13 and 14)	**15**
16	Net estate tax (subtract line 15 from line 12)	**16**
17	Generation-skipping transfer (GST) taxes payable (from Schedule R, Part 2, line 10)	**17**
18	Total transfer taxes (add lines 16 and 17)	**18**
19	Prior payments. Explain in an attached statement	**19**
20	Balance due (or overpayment) (subtract line 19 from line 18)	**20**

Under penalties of perjury, I declare that I have examined this return, including accompanying schedules and statements, and to the best of my knowledge and belief, it is true, correct, and complete. Declaration of preparer other than the executor is based on all information of which preparer has any knowledge.

Signature(s) of executor(s)   Date

Signature of preparer other than executor   Address (and ZIP code)   Date

For Privacy Act and Paperwork Reduction Act Notice, see page 28 of the separate instructions for this form.   Cat. No. 20548R   Form **706** (Rev. 10-2006)

EXHIBIT 11–2   IRS Form 706 (partial) *(continues)*

Form 706 (Rev. 10-2006)

Estate of:

Part 3—Elections by the Executor

Please check the "Yes" or "No" box for each question (see instructions beginning on page 6).

Note. Some of these elections require the posting of bonds or liens.

			Yes	No
1	Do you elect alternate valuation?	1		
2	Do you elect special-use valuation? If "Yes," you must complete and attach Schedule A-1.	2		
3	Do you elect to pay the taxes in installments as described in section 6166? If "Yes," you must attach the additional information described on pages 9 and 10 of the instructions. **Note. By electing section 6166, you agree to provide security for estate tax deferred under section 6166 and interest in the form of a surety bond or a section 6324A special lien.**	3		
4	Do you elect to postpone the part of the taxes attributable to a reversionary or remainder interest as described in section 6163?	4		

Part 4—General Information

(Note. Please attach the necessary supplemental documents. **You must attach the death certificate.**) (see instructions on page 11)

Authorization to receive confidential tax information under Regs. sec. 601.504(b)(2)(i); to act as the estate's representative before the IRS; and to make written or oral presentations on behalf of the estate if return prepared by an attorney, accountant, or enrolled agent for the executor:

Name of representative (print or type)	State	Address (number, street, and room or suite no., city, state, and ZIP code)

I declare that I am the ☐ attorney/ ☐ certified public accountant/ ☐ enrolled agent (you must check the applicable box) for the executor and prepared this return for the executor. I am not under suspension or disbarment from practice before the Internal Revenue Service and am qualified to practice in the state shown above.

Signature	CAF number	Date	Telephone number

1 Death certificate number and issuing authority (attach a copy of the death certificate to this return).

2 Decedent's business or occupation. If retired, check here ▶ ☐ and state decedent's former business or occupation.

3 Marital status of the decedent at time of death:
☐ Married
☐ Widow or widower—Name, SSN, and date of death of deceased spouse ▶ ....
....
☐ Single
☐ Legally separated
☐ Divorced—Date divorce decree became final ▶

4a Surviving spouse's name	4b Social security number	4c Amount received (see page 11 of the instructions)

5 Individuals (other than the surviving spouse), trusts, or other estates who receive benefits from the estate (do not include charitable beneficiaries shown in Schedule O) (see instructions).

Name of individual, trust, or estate receiving $5,000 or more	Identifying number	Relationship to decedent	Amount (see instructions)

All unascertainable beneficiaries and those who receive less than $5,000 . . . . ▶

Total . . . .

Please check the "Yes" or "No" box for each question.

		Yes	No
6	Does the gross estate contain any section 2044 property (qualified terminable interest property (QTIP) from a prior gift or estate) (see page 11 of the instructions)?		
7a	Have federal gift tax returns ever been filed? If "Yes," please attach copies of the returns, if available, and furnish the following information:		

7b Period(s) covered	7c Internal Revenue office(s) where filed

(continued on next page)   **Page 2**

EXHIBIT 11–2 IRS Form 706 (partial) *(continued)*

Form 706 (Rev. 10-2006)

Part 4—General Information (continued)

If you answer "Yes" to any of questions 8–16, you must attach additional information as described in the instructions.	Yes	No
8a Was there any insurance on the decedent's life that is not included on the return as part of the gross estate?		
b Did the decedent own any insurance on the life of another that is not included in the gross estate?		
9 Did the decedent at the time of death own any property as a joint tenant with right of survivorship in which **(a)** one or more of the other joint tenants was someone other than the decedent's spouse, and **(b)** less than the full value of the property is included on the return as part of the gross estate? If "Yes," you must complete and attach Schedule E		
10 Did the decedent, at the time of death, own any interest in a partnership or unincorporated business or any stock in an inactive or closely held corporation?		
11 Did the decedent make any transfer described in section 2035, 2036, 2037, or 2038 (see the instructions for Schedule G beginning on page 13 of the separate instructions)? If "Yes," you must complete and attach Schedule G		
12a Were there in existence at the time of the decedent's death any trusts created by the decedent during his or her lifetime? . .		
b Were there in existence at the time of the decedent's death any trusts not created by the decedent under which the decedent possessed any power, beneficial interest, or trusteeship?		
c Was the decedent receiving income from a trust created after October 22, 1986 by a parent or grandparent?		
If "Yes," was there a GST taxable termination (under section 2612) upon the death of the decedent?		
d If there was a GST taxable termination (under section 2612), attach a statement to explain. Provide a copy of the trust or will creating the trust, and give the name, address, and phone number of the current trustee(s).		
e Did decedent at any time during his or her lifetime transfer or sell an interest in a partnership, limited liability company, or closely held corporation to a trust described in question 12a or 12b?		
If "Yes," provide the EIN number to this transferred/sold item. ▶		
13 Did the decedent ever possess, exercise, or release any general power of appointment? If "Yes," you must complete and attach Schedule H		
14 Was the marital deduction computed under the transitional rule of Public Law 97-34. section 403(e)(3) (Economic Recovery Tax Act of 1981)?		
If "Yes," attach a separate computation of the marital deduction, enter the amount on item 20 of the Recapitulation, and note on item 20 "computation attached."		
15 Was the decedent, immediately before death, receiving an annuity described in the "General" paragraph of the instructions for Schedule I or a private annuity? If "Yes," you must complete and attach Schedule I		
16 Was the decedent ever the beneficiary of a trust for which a deduction was claimed by the estate of a pre-deceased spouse under section 2056(b)(7) and which is not reported on this return? If "Yes," attach an explanation		

Part 5—Recapitulation

Item number	Gross estate		Alternate value	Value at date of death
1	Schedule A—Real Estate	1		
2	Schedule B—Stocks and Bonds	2		
3	Schedule C—Mortgages, Notes, and Cash	3		
4	Schedule D—Insurance on the Decedent's Life (attach Form(s) 712) . . .	4		
5	Schedule E—Jointly Owned Property (attach Form(s) 712 for life insurance)	5		
6	Schedule F—Other Miscellaneous Property (attach Form(s) 712 for life insurance)	6		
7	Schedule G—Transfers During Decedent's Life (att. Form(s) 712 for life insurance)	7		
8	Schedule H—Powers of Appointment	8		
9	Schedule I—Annuities	9		
10	Total gross estate (add items 1 through 9)	10		
11	Schedule U—Qualified Conservation Easement Exclusion	11		
12	Total gross estate less exclusion (subtract item 11 from item 10). Enter here and on line 1 of Part 2—Tax Computation	12		

Item number	Deductions		Amount
13	Schedule J—Funeral Expenses and Expenses Incurred in Administering Property Subject to Claims	13	
14	Schedule K—Debts of the Decedent	14	
15	Schedule K—Mortgages and Liens	15	
16	Total of items 13 through 15	16	
17	Allowable amount of deductions from item 16 (see the instructions for item 17 of the Recapitulation) . . .	17	
18	Schedule L—Net Losses During Administration	18	
19	Schedule L—Expenses Incurred in Administering Property Not Subject to Claims	19	
20	Schedule M—Bequests, etc., to Surviving Spouse	20	
21	Schedule O—Charitable, Public, and Similar Gifts and Bequests	21	
22	Tentative total allowable deductions (add items 17 through 21). Enter here and on line 2 of the Tax Computation	22	

Page 3

EXHIBIT 11–2 IRS Form 706 (partial) (continued)

Form 706 (Rev. 10-2006)

Estate of:

SCHEDULE A—Real Estate

- For jointly owned property that must be disclosed on Schedule E, see the instructions on the reverse side of Schedule E.
- Real estate that is part of a sole proprietorship should be shown on Schedule F.
- Real estate that is included in the gross estate under section 2035, 2036, 2037, or 2038 should be shown on Schedule G.
- Real estate that is included in the gross estate under section 2041 should be shown on Schedule H.
- If you elect section 2032A valuation, you must complete Schedule A and Schedule A-1.

Item number	Description	Alternate valuation date	Alternate value	Value at date of death
1				
	Total from continuation schedules or additional sheets attached to this schedule . .			
	TOTAL. (Also enter on Part 5—Recapitulation, page 3, at item 1.)			

(If more space is needed, attach the continuation schedule from the end of this package or additional sheets of the same size.)

(See the instructions on the reverse side.)

Schedule A—Page 4

EXHIBIT 11-2 IRS Form 706 (partial) *(continued)*

Generally, before an estate will be closed in the probate courts, the administrator must submit a copy of the filed return as a final step in probate. If the decedent was a U.S. citizen but not a resident of the United States, the following must be attached to the following documents to the return:

- A copy of the inventory of property and the schedule of liabilities, claims against the estate, and expenses of administration filed with the foreign court of probate jurisdiction, certified by a proper official of the court;

- A copy of the return filed under the foreign inheritance, estate, legacy, succession tax, or other death tax act, certified by a proper official of the foreign tax department, if the estate is subject to such a foreign tax; and

- If the decedent died testate, a certified copy of the will

At the time of publication, Congress had established some modifications to the estate tax that will likely take effect in coming years. Some of the expected changes include but are not limited to the following:

- In 2009: the size of the estate tax exclusion increases to $3,500,000 in assets;

- The highest estate tax rate will be 45 percent for the portion of the estate that exceeds $3,500,000.

- In 2010: there will be no estate tax and consequently no applicable tax rates.

- In 2011: the estate tax exclusion amount returns to $1,000,000, unless Congress passes an extension on the ban on estate taxes;

- Unless there is further action by Congress, the highest estate tax rate will be as much as 55 percent for estates exceeding $1,000,000.

2. Federal Gift Tax Return

Most taxpayers are not aware that the gift tax is something that is paid by the giver and not the recipient of the gift. This is because the tax is designed to limit the ability of individuals from emptying their estate in an attempt to avoid estate taxes at death. The recipient of the gift has no control over the estate of the giver and so they are not required to pay the gift tax. However, in certain circumstances, the gift may generate income tax liability. For tax purposes, a gift is a transfer of property for less than its full value. If the owner is not compensated adequately the transfer is treated as a gift. There are some exclusions from gift tax. For example, as of 2006, a donor may make a gift of up to $11,000 to per person without generating any gift tax liability. During the lifetime of the donor, up to 1,000,000 total can be made in gifts before incurring gift tax as long as the gifts are not in excess of the annual gift per person limitation. But the amount of gifts made also may be added back and included in the estate of the owner to defeat avoidance of estate taxes through lifetime gifts.

APPLICATION **11.2**

Carney and Keith were married. They wanted to make gifts to their children. In 2006, they gave $44,000 to their married daughter and husband, and $22,000 to their son for total gifts of $66,000. None of the gifts were taxable because Carney and Keith are each entitled to give $11,000 to each person before gift tax is incurred.

These gifts would be considered in the following manner for tax purposes:

- Carney to daughter $11,000

- Keith to daughter $11,000

- Carney to son-in-law $11,000

- Keith to son-in-law $11,000

- Carney to son $11,000

- Keith to son $11,000

- TOTAL $66,000

Additional gifts that do not count as gifts included in the $1,000,000 lifetime total include charitable gifts and gifts to a spouse who is a U.S. citizen. Gifts to foreign spouses are subject to an annual limit of $117,000 ($120,000 for 2006), indexed for inflation. Also, nontaxable gifts include certain items related to educational expenses. To qualify for the unlimited exclusion for qualified education expenses, the payment must be made directly to the educational institution for tuition only. Books, supplies, and living expenses do not qualify. Nontaxable gifts of payment for medical expenses are somewhat limited. Medical payments must be paid directly to the health care provider providing the care in order to qualify for the unlimited exclusion. Qualifying medical expenses include:

- Diagnosis and treatment of disease

- Procedures affecting a structure or function of the body

- Transportation primarily for medical care

- Medical insurance, including long-term care insurance

Gifts by parents to minor children up to $11,000 to each child each year do not count toward the $1,000,000 of allowable gifts before the gift tax is triggered. Gifts that fall within this definition include the following:

- Gifts made outright to the minor

- Gifts made through a custodial account such as that under the Uniform Gifts to Minors Act (UGMA), the Revised Uniform Gifts to Minors Act, or the Uniform Transfers to Minors Act (UTMA). However, a disadvantage of using custodial accounts is that the minor must be given absolute control over the funds at maturity, as defined by state law (generally age 18 or 21).

A parent's support payments for a minor are not gifts if they are required as part of a legal obligation. They can be considered a gift if the payments are not legally required.

Other transactions that are not considered gifts include the addition of someone as a joint tenant to a bank or brokerage account or to a U.S. Savings Bond unless the new joint tenant withdraws funds.

When determining whether to transfer substantially valued property by gift or inheritance, it is important to consider the tax effects of each. The primary difference in the gift tax and estate tax is the basis. This is the amount invested by the taxpayer in property, real or personal, which is excluded from tax. For example, if a taxpayer buys a house for $50,000 and invests $10,000 in permanent repairs to the property, the basis is $60,000. If the taxpayer sells the house for $100,000, then $60,000 ($50,000 + $10,000) is excluded from tax. If the taxpayer gives the property away, the tax basis for the recipient is that same as that of the donor ($60,000). But, if the taxpayer dies and someone inherits the property, the tax basis would be the fair market value of the property on the date the donor dies. If the person who inherits and then sells the property at a loss, the tax basis becomes the lower of the donor's basis or the fair market value on the date of the gift. That can mean a great deal when the property is sold in terms of calculating capital gain tax.

APPLICATION **11.3**

Maria bought a house for $150,000. Over time, the house appreciates to a value of $250,000. Maria is elderly and wants to know what will be the tax consequences of giving the house to her children or leaving it to them in her will.

- If Maria's children receive the house as a gift and sell it for $250,000, the potential taxable gain on the sale is $100,000 ($250,000 minus $150,000).

- If Maria's children receive the house by inheritance and sell it for $250,000, the potential taxable gain on the sale is $0 ($250,000 minus $250,000).

For the purposes of determining the taxability, rate, and appropriate time to report a gift on a tax return, the following rules apply:

- Checks are effective on the date that the donor gives the check to the recipient. The donor must still be alive when the donor's bank pays the check. (This rule prevents people from making "deathbed gifts" to avoid estate taxes.)

- Adding a joint tenant to real estate ownership becomes a taxable gift if the new joint tenant has the right under state law to sever his interest in the joint tenancy and receive half of the property. Note that the recipient does not need to exercise this right but only to have it for the transaction to be considered a gift.

- Loans of $10,000 or more at below than the market rate of interest also known as the Prime Rate. The value of the gift is based on the difference between the interest rate charged and the applicable federal rate. Applicable federal rates are revised monthly. This rule does not apply to loans of $10,000 or less.

- Debt cancellation.

- Payment of the debt of another. This is effective on the date of the payment.

- Making a gift as an individual to a corporation. Such a donation is considered to ultimately be a gift to the individual shareholders of the corporation unless there is a valid business reason for the gift. Because the gift is not a present-interest gift, it does not qualify for the $11,000 per person per year exclusion.

- Gifts of foreign real estate by a U.S. citizen.

- Gifts of real or tangible property located in the United States, regardless of citizenship of the donor or recipient.

If a taxable gift is made, form 709, U.S. Gift (and Generation-Skipping Transfer) Tax Return, must be filed by April 15 of the following year. Even if no gift tax is owed because the taxpayer has not reached the $1,000,000 limit, the return is still required if the taxpayer made a gift that does not qualify as excludable. The IRS tracks the running total of the $1,000,000 lifetime exemption. Similarly, the recipient is required to report the taxable amount of the gift as income and thus these figures should correspond with the gifts reported by the donor.

Unlike the income tax that allows married couples to file together, only individuals file form 709. If a married couple gives a gift, each spouse has to file form 709. If one spouse gives a gift, the couple may elect "gift-splitting" in order to each use the $11,000 exclusion in that year. Gift-splitting requires that each spouse file a gift tax return and sign his or her consent.

On a gift tax return, the fair market value of the gift on the date of the transfer is reported as well as the donor's tax basis in the gift and the identity of the recipient. It is also necessary to attach supplemental documents that support the valuation of the

Form **709**	United States Gift (and Generation-Skipping Transfer) Tax Return	OMB No. 1545-0020
Department of the Treasury Internal Revenue Service	(For gifts made during calendar year 2006) ▶ **See separate instructions.**	**2006**

Part 1—General Information

1 Donor's first name and middle initial	2 Donor's last name	3 **Donor's social security number**
4 Address (number, street, and apartment number)		5 Legal residence (domicile) (county and state)
6 City, state, and ZIP code		7 Citizenship

		Yes	No
8	If the donor died during the year, check here ▶ ☐ and enter date of death		
9	If you extended the time to file this Form 709, check here ▶ ☐		
10	Enter the total number of donees listed on Schedule A. Count each person only once. ▶		
11a	Have you (the donor) previously filed a Form 709 (or 709-A) for any other year? If "No," skip line 11b		
11b	If the answer to line 11a is "Yes," has your address changed since you last filed Form 709 (or 709-A)? . . .		
12	**Gifts by husband or wife to third parties.** Do you consent to have the gifts (including generation-skipping transfers) made by you and by your spouse to third parties during the calendar year considered as made one-half by each of you? (See instructions.) (If the answer is "Yes," the following information must be furnished and your spouse must sign the consent shown below. **If the answer is "No," skip lines 13–18 and go to Schedule A.)**		
13	Name of consenting spouse	14 SSN	
15	Were you married to one another during the entire calendar year? (see instructions)		
16	If 15 is "No," check whether ☐ married ☐ divorced or ☐ widowed/deceased, and give date (see instructions) ▶		
17	Will a gift tax return for this year be filed by your spouse? (If "Yes," mail both returns in the same envelope.)		
18	**Consent of Spouse.** I consent to have the gifts (and generation-skipping transfers) made by me and by my spouse to third parties during the calendar year considered as made one-half by each of us. We are both aware of the joint and several liability for tax created by the execution of this consent.		

Consenting spouse's signature ▶   Date ▶

Part 2—Tax Computation

1	Enter the amount from Schedule A, Part 4, line 11	1	
2	Enter the amount from Schedule B, line 3	2	
3	Total taxable gifts. Add lines 1 and 2	3	
4	Tax computed on amount on line 3 (see *Table for Computing Gift Tax* in separate instructions) .	4	
5	Tax computed on amount on line 2 (see *Table for Computing Gift Tax* in separate instructions) .	5	
6	Balance. Subtract line 5 from line 4	6	
7	Maximum unified credit (nonresident aliens, see instructions)	7	345,800 00
8	Enter the unified credit against tax allowable for all prior periods (from Sch. B, line 1, col. C)	8	
9	Balance. Subtract line 8 from line 7	9	
10	Enter 20% (.20) of the amount allowed as a specific exemption for gifts made after September 8, 1976, and before January 1, 1977 (see instructions)	10	
11	Balance. Subtract line 10 from line 9	11	
12	Unified credit. Enter the smaller of line 6 or line 11	12	
13	Credit for foreign gift taxes (see instructions)	13	
14	Total credits. Add lines 12 and 13	14	
15	Balance. Subtract line 14 from line 6. Do not enter less than zero	15	
16	Generation-skipping transfer taxes (from Schedule C, Part 3, col. H, Total)	16	
17	Total tax. Add lines 15 and 16	17	
18	Gift and generation-skipping transfer taxes prepaid with extension of time to file	18	
19	If line 18 is less than line 17, enter **balance due** (see instructions)	19	
20	If line 18 is greater than line 17, enter **amount to be refunded**	20	

Sign Here

Under penalties of perjury, I declare that I have examined this return, including any accompanying schedules and statements, and to the best of my knowledge and belief, it is true, correct, and complete. Declaration of preparer (other than donor) is based on all information of which preparer has any knowledge.

▶ Signature of donor	Date

Paid Preparer's Use Only

Preparer's signature ▶	Date	Check if self-employed ▶ ☐
Firm's name (or yours if self-employed), address, and ZIP code ▶		Phone no. ▶ ( )

Attach check or money order here.

For Disclosure, Privacy Act, and Paperwork Reduction Act Notice, see page 12 of the separate instructions for this form.   Cat. No. 16783M   Form **709** (2006)

EXHIBIT 11–3   IRS Form 709 *(continues)*

Form 709 (2006)　　　　　　　　　　　　　　　　　　　　　　　　　　　　　　　　Page **2**

SCHEDULE A　　**Computation of Taxable Gifts** (Including transfers in trust) (see instructions)

A　Does the value of any item listed on Schedule A reflect any valuation discount? If "Yes," attach explanation　.　.　.　.　. Yes ☐　No ☐

B　☐　◄ Check here if you elect under section 529(c)(2)(B) to treat any transfers made this year to a qualified tuition program as made ratably over a 5-year period beginning this year. See instructions. Attach explanation.

Part 1—Gifts Subject Only to Gift Tax. Gifts less political organization, medical, and educational exclusions. See instructions.

A Item number	B • Donee's name and address • Relationship to donor (if any) • Description of gift • If the gift was of securities, give CUSIP no. • If closely held entity, give EIN	C	D Donor's adjusted basis of gift	E Date of gift	F Value at date of gift	G For split gifts, enter ½ of column F	H Net transfer (subtract col. G from col. F)
1							

Gifts made by spouse—*complete **only** if you are splitting gifts with your spouse and he/she also made gifts.*

Total of Part 1. Add amounts from Part 1, column H　.　.　.　.　.　.　.　.　.　.　.　.　.　.　.　.　. ► | |

Part 2—Direct Skips. Gifts that are direct skips and are subject to both gift tax and generation-skipping transfer tax. You must list the gifts in chronological order.

A Item number	B • Donee's name and address • Relationship to donor (if any) • Description of gift • If the gift was of securities, give CUSIP no. • If closely held entity, give EIN	C 2632(b) election out	D Donor's adjusted basis of gift	E Date of gift	F Value at date of gift	G For split gifts, enter ½ of column F	H Net transfer (subtract col. G from col. F)
1							

Gifts made by spouse—*complete **only** if you are splitting gifts with your spouse and he/she also made gifts.*

Total of Part 2. Add amounts from Part 2, column H　.　.　.　.　.　.　.　.　.　.　.　.　.　.　.　.　. ► | |

Part 3—Indirect Skips. Gifts to trusts that are currently subject to gift tax and may later be subject to generation-skipping transfer tax. You must list these gifts in chronological order.

A Item number	B • Donee's name and address • Relationship to donor (if any) • Description of gift • If the gift was of securities, give CUSIP no. • If closely held entity, give EIN	C 2632(c) election	D Donor's adjusted basis of gift	E Date of gift	F Value at date of gift	G For split gifts, enter ½ of column F	H Net transfer (subtract col. G from col. F)
1							

Gifts made by spouse—*complete **only** if you are splitting gifts with your spouse and he/she also made gifts.*

Total of Part 3. Add amounts from Part 3, column H　.　.　.　.　.　.　.　.　.　.　.　.　.　.　.　.　. ► | |

(If more space is needed, attach additional sheets of same size.)　　　　　　　　　　　　　　　　Form **709** (2006)

EXHIBIT 11–3　IRS Form 709 *(continued)*

Form 709 (2006)   Page **3**

Part 4—Taxable Gift Reconciliation

1	Total value of gifts of donor. Add totals from column H of Parts 1, 2, and 3	**1**
2	Total annual exclusions for gifts listed on line 1 (see instructions)	**2**
3	Total included amount of gifts. Subtract line 2 from line 1	**3**

Deductions (see instructions)

4	Gifts of interests to spouse for which a marital deduction will be claimed, based on item numbers _____ of Schedule A . .	**4**
5	Exclusions attributable to gifts on line 4	**5**
6	Marital deduction. Subtract line 5 from line 4	**6**
7	Charitable deduction, based on item nos. _____ less exclusions .	**7**
8	Total deductions. Add lines 6 and 7	**8**
9	Subtract line 8 from line 3	**9**
10	Generation-skipping transfer taxes payable with this Form 709 (from Schedule C, Part 3, col. H, Total)	**10**
11	**Taxable gifts.** Add lines 9 and 10. Enter here and on page 1, Part 2—Tax Computation, line 1 . . .	**11**

Terminable Interest (QTIP) Marital Deduction. (See instructions for Schedule A, Part 4, line 4.)

If a trust (or other property) meets the requirements of qualified terminable interest property under section 2523(f), and:

    a. The trust (or other property) is listed on Schedule A, and

    b. The value of the trust (or other property) is entered in whole or in part as a deduction on Schedule A, Part 4, line 4, then the donor shall be deemed to have made an election to have such trust (or other property) treated as qualified terminable interest property under section 2523(f).

If less than the entire value of the trust (or other property) that the donor has included in Parts 1 and 3 of Schedule A is entered as a deduction on line 4, the donor shall be considered to have made an election only as to a fraction of the trust (or other property). The numerator of this fraction is equal to the amount of the trust (or other property) deducted on Schedule A, Part 4, line 6. The denominator is equal to the total value of the trust (or other property) listed in Parts 1 and 3 of Schedule A.

If you make the QTIP election, the terminable interest property involved will be included in your spouse's gross estate upon his or her death (section 2044). See instructions for line 4 of Schedule A. If your spouse disposes (by gift or otherwise) of all or part of the qualifying life income interest, he or she will be considered to have made a transfer of the entire property that is subject to the gift tax. See *Transfer of Certain Life Estates Received From Spouse* on page 4 of the instructions.

12 Election Out of QTIP Treatment of Annuities

    ☐ ◄ Check here if you elect under section 2523(f)(6) **not** to treat as qualified terminable interest property any joint and survivor annuities that are reported on Schedule A and would otherwise be treated as qualified terminable interest property under section 2523(f). See instructions. Enter the item numbers from Schedule A for the annuities for which you are making this election ► _____

SCHEDULE B   **Gifts From Prior Periods**

If you answered "Yes" on line 11a of page 1, Part 1, see the instructions for completing Schedule B. If you answered "No," skip to the Tax Computation on page 1 (or Schedule C, if applicable).

A Calendar year or calendar quarter (see instructions)	**B** Internal Revenue office where prior return was filed	**C** Amount of unified credit against gift tax for periods after December 31, 1976	**D** Amount of specific exemption for prior periods ending before January 1, 1977	**E** Amount of taxable gifts

1	Totals for prior periods	**1**	
2	Amount, if any, by which total specific exemption, line 1, column D, is more than $30,000	**2**	
3	Total amount of taxable gifts for prior periods. Add amount on line 1, column E and amount, if any, on line 2. Enter here and on page 1, Part 2—Tax Computation, line 2	**3**	

(If more space is needed, attach additional sheets of same size.)   Form **709** (2006)

EXHIBIT 11–3   IRS Form 709 *(continued)*

Form 709 (2006)   Page **4**

SCHEDULE C   **Computation of Generation-Skipping Transfer Tax**

Note. Inter vivos direct skips that are completely excluded by the GST exemption must still be fully reported (including value and exemptions claimed) on Schedule C.

Part 1—Generation-Skipping Transfers

A Item No. (from Schedule A, Part 2, col. A)	B Value (from Schedule A, Part 2, col. H)	C Nontaxable portion of transfer	D Net Transfer (subtract col. C from col. B)
1			

Gifts made by spouse (for gift splitting only)

Part 2—GST Exemption Reconciliation (Section 2631) and Section 2652(a)(3) Election

Check here ▶ ☐ if you are making a section 2652(a)(3) (special QTIP) election (see instructions)

Enter the item numbers from Schedule A of the gifts for which you are making this election ▶ ....

1	Maximum allowable exemption (see instructions)	**1**
2	Total exemption used for periods before filing this return	**2**
3	Exemption available for this return. Subtract line 2 from line 1	**3**
4	Exemption claimed on this return from Part 3, column C total, below	**4**
5	Automatic allocation of exemption to transfers reported on Schedule A, Part 3 (see instructions)	**5**
6	Exemption allocated to transfers not shown on line 4 or 5, above. **You must attach a Notice of Allocation.** (see instructions)	**6**
7	Add lines 4, 5, and 6	**7**
8	Exemption available for future transfers. Subtract line 7 from line 3	**8**

Part 3—Tax Computation

A Item No. (from Schedule C, Part 1)	B Net transfer (from Schedule C, Part 1, col. D)	C GST Exemption Allocated	D Divide col. C by col. B	E Inclusion Ratio (subtract col. D from 1.000)	F Maximum Estate Tax Rate	G Applicable Rate (multiply col. E by col. F)	H Generation-Skipping Transfer Tax (multiply col. B by col. G)
1					46% (.46)		
					46% (.46)		
					46% (.46)		
					46% (.46)		
					46% (.46)		
					46% (.46)		

Gifts made by spouse (for gift splitting only)

					46% (.46)		
					46% (.46)		
					46% (.46)		
					46% (.46)		
					46% (.46)		
					46% (.46)		

Total exemption claimed. Enter here and on Part 2, line 4, above. May not exceed Part 2, line 3, above		**Total generation-skipping transfer tax.** Enter here; on page 3, Schedule A, Part 4, line 10; and on page 1, Part 2—Tax Computation, line 16	

(If more space is needed, attach additional sheets of same size.)   Form **709** (2006)

♻ *Printed on recycled paper*

EXHIBIT 11–3   IRS Form 709 *(continued)*

gift, such as financial statements in the case of a gift of stock in a closely held corporation or appraisals for real estate. If property or family heirlooms are sold to children of the taxpayer for full fair market value, there is no requirement to file a gift tax return. However, if there is any chance that the IRS could suspect that the transaction is undervalued, it may be wise to file the return. As with an income tax return, a transaction reported on a return is subject to audit and review for 3 years. If no return is filed, the transaction is subject to audit and review indefinitely.

3. The Trust Return

A trust is a financial arrangement whereby money is given by one party to be held by someone (often a financial institution) for the benefit of another. The person who provides the funds initially is known as the **Settlor**. The settlor transfers assets, usually money or property, to the **Trustee**. The trustee then holds the assets in trust for the **Beneficiary**(s) of the trust. This can be designated for specific individuals or for the support of a legally recognized purpose, for example, a foundation for charitable works, scholarships, and so on. There should be a signed trust deed (agreement) that acknowledges the transfer, known as a **Settlement**, but it is possible to establish a trust verbally.

The trustee is responsible to maintain the property of the trust for the beneficiary, and to administer the trust as directed by the settlement. Someone may be a trustee solely for the purpose of a trust. However, personal administrators of estates are also considered trustees. A trustee need not be an individual but can also be a company or other organization. It is very common for financial institutions to act as trustees.

The trustee is required to file an income tax return for the estate or trust each year. This is separate from the trustee's own personal tax return and from the personal return of the beneficiary. The tax return for the trust is filed using form 1041. Not every trust is required to file a return. There are basic threshold requirements, just as with individual returns. For a trust return, the requirements are based on income of the trust. Although the levels are relatively low, trusts that fall below these levels are not required to file. The levels are based on 2005 requirements. There are additional exceptions for what are known as "Grantor Trusts," in which the trust is controlled by the grantor or settlor, including retention of the power to revoke the trust.

A trust return is required for any trust with one or more of the following:

- Any taxable income
- Gross income of $600 or more
- A nonresident alien beneficiary

SETTLOR

One that makes a business or financial settlement or a settlement of property.

TRUSTEE

An individual who holds or manages assets for the benefit of another.

BENEFICIARY

A person or entity named in a will or a financial contract as the inheritor of property when the property owner dies.

SETTLEMENT

A signed trust deed (agreement) that acknowledges the transfer of funds.

Form **1041** Department of the Treasury—Internal Revenue Service

U.S. Income Tax Return for Estates and Trusts   2006   OMB No. 1545-0092

A Type of entity (see instr.):	For calendar year 2006 or fiscal year beginning , 2006, and ending , 20	
☐ Decedent's estate	Name of estate or trust (If a grantor type trust, see page 12 of the instructions.)	**C** Employer identification number
☐ Simple trust		
☐ Complex trust	Name and title of fiduciary	**D** Date entity created
☐ Qualified disability trust		
☐ ESBT (S portion only)	Number, street, and room or suite no. (If a P.O. box, see page 12 of the instructions.)	**E** Nonexempt charitable and split-interest trusts, check applicable boxes (see page 13 of the instr.):
☐ Grantor type trust		
☐ Bankruptcy estate–Ch. 7		☐ Described in section 4947(a)(1)
☐ Bankruptcy estate–Ch. 11	City or town, state, and ZIP code	☐ Not a private foundation
☐ Pooled income fund		☐ Described in section 4947(a)(2)

B Number of Schedules K-1 attached (see instructions) ▶

F Check applicable boxes: ☐ Initial return ☐ Final return ☐ Amended return ☐ Change in trust's name
☐ Change in fiduciary ☐ Change in fiduciary's name ☐ Change in fiduciary's address

G Pooled mortgage account (see page 14 of the instructions): ☐ Bought ☐ Sold Date:

Income

1	Interest income	1	
2a	Total ordinary dividends	2a	
b	Qualified dividends allocable to: **(1)** Beneficiaries .... **(2)** Estate or trust		
3	Business income or (loss). Attach Schedule C or C-EZ (Form 1040)	3	
4	Capital gain or (loss). Attach Schedule D (Form 1041)	4	
5	Rents, royalties, partnerships, other estates and trusts, etc. Attach Schedule E (Form 1040)	5	
6	Farm income or (loss). Attach Schedule F (Form 1040)	6	
7	Ordinary gain or (loss). Attach Form 4797	7	
8	Other income. List type and amount .... ▶	8	
9	**Total income.** Combine lines 1, 2a, and 3 through 8 . . . . ▶	9	

Deductions

10	Interest. Check if Form 4952 is attached ▶ ☐	10	
11	Taxes	11	
12	Fiduciary fees	12	
13	Charitable deduction (from Schedule A, line 7)	13	
14	Attorney, accountant, and return preparer fees	14	
15a	Other deductions **not** subject to the 2% floor (attach schedule)	15a	
b	Allowable miscellaneous itemized deductions subject to the 2% floor	15b	
16	Add lines 10 through 15b . . . . ▶	16	
17	Adjusted total income or (loss). Subtract line 16 from line 9 . . . 17		
18	Income distribution deduction (from Schedule B, line 15). Attach Schedules K-1 (Form 1041)	18	
19	Estate tax deduction including certain generation-skipping taxes (attach computation) . .	19	
20	Exemption	20	
21	Add lines 18 through 20 . . . . ▶	21	

Tax and Payments

22	Taxable income. Subtract line 21 from line 17. If a loss, see page 20 of the instructions	22	
23	**Total tax** (from Schedule G, line 7)	23	
24	**Payments: a** 2006 estimated tax payments and amount applied from 2005 return . . .	24a	
b	Estimated tax payments allocated to beneficiaries (from Form 1041-T)	24b	
c	Subtract line 24b from line 24a	24c	
d	Tax paid with Form 7004 (see page 20 of the instructions)	24d	
e	Federal income tax withheld. If any is from Form(s) 1099, check ▶ ☐	24e	
f	Credit for federal telephone excise tax paid. Attach Form 8913	24f	
	Other payments: **g** Form 2439 .... ; **h** Form 4136 .... ; Total ▶	24i	
25	**Total payments.** Add lines 24c through 24f, and 24i . . . . ▶	25	
26	Estimated tax penalty (see page 20 of the instructions)	26	
27	**Tax due.** If line 25 is smaller than the total of lines 23 and 26, enter amount owed . . .	27	
28	**Overpayment.** If line 25 is larger than the total of lines 23 and 26, enter amount overpaid	28	
29	Amount of line 28 to be: **a** Credited to 2007 estimated tax ▶ ; **b** Refunded ▶	29	

Sign Here

Under penalties of perjury, I declare that I have examined this return, including accompanying schedules and statements, and to the best of my knowledge and belief, it is true, correct, and complete. Declaration of preparer (other than taxpayer) is based on all information of which preparer has any knowledge.

▶ Signature of fiduciary or officer representing fiduciary   Date   ▶ EIN of fiduciary if a financial institution

May the IRS discuss this return with the preparer shown below (see instr.)? ☐ **Yes** ☐ **No**

Paid Preparer's Use Only

Preparer's signature		Date	Check if self-employed ☐	Preparer's SSN or PTIN
Firm's name (or yours if self-employed), address, and ZIP code	▶		EIN	
			Phone no. ( )	

For Privacy Act and Paperwork Reduction Act Notice, see the separate instructions.   Cat. No. 11370H   Form **1041** (2006)

EXHIBIT 11–4 IRS Form 1041 (continues)

Form 1041 (2006)   Page **2**

Schedule A   **Charitable Deduction.** Do not complete for a simple trust or a pooled income fund.

1	Amounts paid or permanently set aside for charitable purposes from gross income (see page 21)	1
2	Tax-exempt income allocable to charitable contributions (see page 21 of the instructions) .	2
3	Subtract line 2 from line 1	3
4	Capital gains for the tax year allocated to corpus and paid or permanently set aside for charitable purposes	4
5	Add lines 3 and 4	5
6	Section 1202 exclusion allocable to capital gains paid or permanently set aside for charitable purposes (see page 21 of the instructions)	6
7	**Charitable deduction.** Subtract line 6 from line 5. Enter here and on page 1, line 13 . . .	7

Schedule B   **Income Distribution Deduction**

1	Adjusted total income (see page 22 of the instructions)	1
2	Adjusted tax-exempt interest	2
3	Total net gain from Schedule D (Form 1041), line 15, column (1) (see page 22 of the instructions)	3
4	Enter amount from Schedule A, line 4 (minus any allocable section 1202 exclusion) . . .	4
5	Capital gains for the tax year included on Schedule A, line 1 (see page 22 of the instructions)	5
6	Enter any gain from page 1, line 4, as a negative number. If page 1, line 4, is a loss, enter the loss as a positive number	6
7	**Distributable net income (DNI).** Combine lines 1 through 6. If zero or less, enter -0- . .	7
8	If a complex trust, enter accounting income for the tax year as determined under the governing instrument and applicable local law 8	
9	Income required to be distributed currently	9
10	Other amounts paid, credited, or otherwise required to be distributed	10
11	Total distributions. Add lines 9 and 10. If greater than line 8, see page 22 of the instructions	11
12	Enter the amount of tax-exempt income included on line 11	12
13	Tentative income distribution deduction. Subtract line 12 from line 11	13
14	Tentative income distribution deduction. Subtract line 2 from line 7. If zero or less, enter -0-	14
15	**Income distribution deduction.** Enter the smaller of line 13 or line 14 here and on page 1, line 18	15

Schedule G   **Tax Computation** (see page 23 of the instructions)

1 **Tax: a**	Tax on taxable income (see page 23 of the instructions) . .	1a
b	Tax on lump-sum distributions. Attach Form 4972	1b
c	Alternative minimum tax (from Schedule I, line 56)	1c
d	**Total.** Add lines 1a through 1c . . . . ▶	1d
2a	Foreign tax credit. Attach Form 1116	2a
b	Other nonbusiness credits (attach schedule)	2b
c	General business credit. Enter here and check which forms are attached: ☐ Form 3800 ☐ Forms (specify) ▶	2c
d	Credit for prior year minimum tax. Attach Form 8801	2d
3	**Total credits.** Add lines 2a through 2d . . . . ▶	3
4	Subtract line 3 from line 1d. If zero or less, enter -0-.	4
5	Recapture taxes. Check if from: ☐ Form 4255 ☐ Form 8611	5
6	Household employment taxes. Attach Schedule H (Form 1040)	6
7	**Total tax.** Add lines 4 through 6. Enter here and on page 1, line 23 . . . . ▶	7

Other Information   Yes | No

1	Did the estate or trust receive tax-exempt income? If "Yes," attach a computation of the allocation of expenses Enter the amount of tax-exempt interest income and exempt-interest dividends ▶ $ ....
2	Did the estate or trust receive all or any part of the earnings (salary, wages, and other compensation) of any individual by reason of a contract assignment or similar arrangement? . . . .
3	At any time during calendar year 2006, did the estate or trust have an interest in or a signature or other authority over a bank, securities, or other financial account in a foreign country? . . . . See page 25 of the instructions for exceptions and filing requirements for Form TD F 90-22.1. If "Yes," enter the name of the foreign country ▶ ....
4	During the tax year, did the estate or trust receive a distribution from, or was it the grantor of, or transferor to, a foreign trust? If "Yes," the estate or trust may have to file Form 3520. See page 25 of the instructions .
5	Did the estate or trust receive, or pay, any qualified residence interest on seller-provided financing? If "Yes," see page 25 for required attachment . . . .
6	If this is an estate or a complex trust making the section 663(b) election, check here (see page 25) . ▶ ☐
7	To make a section 643(e)(3) election, attach Schedule D (Form 1041), and check here (see page 25) . ▶ ☐
8	If the decedent's estate has been open for more than 2 years, attach an explanation for the delay in closing the estate, and check here ▶ ☐
9	Are any present or future trust beneficiaries skip persons? See page 25 of the instructions . . . . .

Form **1041** (2006)

EXHIBIT 11–4   IRS Form 1041 *(continued)*

Form 1041 (2006)   Page **3**

Schedule I	**Alternative Minimum Tax (AMT)** (see pages 26 through 32 of the instructions)	

Part I—Estate's or Trust's Share of Alternative Minimum Taxable Income

1	Adjusted total income or (loss) (from page 1, line 17)	1	
2	Interest	2	
3	Taxes	3	
4	Miscellaneous itemized deductions (from page 1, line 15b)	4	
5	Refund of taxes	5 (	)
6	Depletion (difference between regular tax and AMT)	6	
7	Net operating loss deduction. Enter as a positive amount	7	
8	Interest from specified private activity bonds exempt from the regular tax	8	
9	Qualified small business stock (see page 27 of the instructions)	9	
10	Exercise of incentive stock options (excess of AMT income over regular tax income) . . .	10	
11	Other estates and trusts (amount from Schedule K-1 (Form 1041), box 12, code A) . . .	11	
12	Electing large partnerships (amount from Schedule K-1 (Form 1065-B), box 6)	12	
13	Disposition of property (difference between AMT and regular tax gain or loss)	13	
14	Depreciation on assets placed in service after 1986 (difference between regular tax and AMT)	14	
15	Passive activities (difference between AMT and regular tax income or loss)	15	
16	Loss limitations (difference between AMT and regular tax income or loss)	16	
17	Circulation costs (difference between regular tax and AMT)	17	
18	Long-term contracts (difference between AMT and regular tax income)	18	
19	Mining costs (difference between regular tax and AMT)	19	
20	Research and experimental costs (difference between regular tax and AMT)	20	
21	Income from certain installment sales before January 1, 1987	21 (	)
22	Intangible drilling costs preference	22	
23	Other adjustments, including income-based related adjustments	23	
24	Alternative tax net operating loss deduction (See the instructions for the limitation that applies.)	24 (	)
25	Adjusted alternative minimum taxable income. Combine lines 1 through 24	25	
	Note: *Complete Part II below before going to line 26.*		
26	Income distribution deduction from Part II, line 44 . . . . . [26]		
27	Estate tax deduction (from page 1, line 19) . . . . [27]		
28	Add lines 26 and 27	28	
29	Estate's or trust's share of alternative minimum taxable income. Subtract line 28 from line 25	29	

If line 29 is:

- • $22,500 or less, stop here and enter -0- on Schedule G, line 1c. The estate or trust is not liable for the alternative minimum tax.
- • Over $22,500, but less than $165,000, go to line 45.
- • $165,000 or more, enter the amount from line 29 on line 51 and go to line 52.

Part II—Income Distribution Deduction on a Minimum Tax Basis

30	Adjusted alternative minimum taxable income (see page 30 of the instructions)	30	
31	Adjusted tax-exempt interest (other than amounts included on line 8)	31	
32	Total net gain from Schedule D (Form 1041), line 15, column (1). If a loss, enter -0- . . .	32	
33	Capital gains for the tax year allocated to corpus and paid or permanently set aside for charitable purposes (from Schedule A, line 4)	33	
34	Capital gains paid or permanently set aside for charitable purposes from gross income (see page 30 of the instructions)	34	
35	Capital gains computed on a minimum tax basis included on line 25	35 (	)
36	Capital losses computed on a minimum tax basis included on line 25. Enter as a positive amount	36	
37	Distributable net alternative minimum taxable income (DNAMTI). Combine lines 30 through 36. If zero or less, enter -0-.	37	
38	Income required to be distributed currently (from Schedule B, line 9)	38	
39	Other amounts paid, credited, or otherwise required to be distributed (from Schedule B, line 10)	39	
40	Total distributions. Add lines 38 and 39	40	
41	Tax-exempt income included on line 40 (other than amounts included on line 8)	41	
42	Tentative income distribution deduction on a minimum tax basis. Subtract line 41 from line 40	42	
43	Tentative income distribution deduction on a minimum tax basis. Subtract line 31 from line 37. If zero or less, enter -0-	43	
44	**Income distribution deduction on a minimum tax basis.** Enter the smaller of line 42 or line 43. Enter here and on line 26	44	

Form **1041** (2006)

EXHIBIT 11–4 IRS Form 1041 *(continued)*

Form 1041 (2006)   Page **4**

Part III—Alternative Minimum Tax

45	Exemption amount		45	$22,500 00
46	Enter the amount from line 29	46		
47	Phase-out of exemption amount	47	$75,000 00	
48	Subtract line 47 from line 46. If zero or less, enter -0-	48		
49	Multiply line 48 by 25% (.25)		49	
50	Subtract line 49 from line 45. If zero or less, enter -0-		50	
51	Subtract line 50 from line 46		51	
52	Go to Part IV of Schedule I to figure line 52 if the estate or trust has qualified dividends or has a gain on lines 14a and 15 of column (2) of Schedule D (Form 1041) (as refigured for the AMT, if necessary). Otherwise, if line 51 is—			
	• $175,000 or less, multiply line 51 by 26% (.26).			
	• Over $175,000, multiply line 51 by 28% (.28) and subtract $3,500 from the result		52	
53	Alternative minimum foreign tax credit (see page 31 of the instructions)		53	
54	Tentative minimum tax. Subtract line 53 from line 52		54	
55	Enter the tax from Schedule G, line 1a (minus any foreign tax credit from Schedule G, line 2a)		55	
56	**Alternative minimum tax.** Subtract line 55 from line 54. If zero or less, enter -0-. Enter here and on Schedule G, line 1c		56	

Part IV—Line 52 Computation Using Maximum Capital Gains Rates

Caution: *If you did not complete Part V of Schedule D (Form 1041), the Schedule D Tax Worksheet, or the Qualified Dividends Tax Worksheet, see page 32 of the instructions before completing this part.*

57	Enter the amount from line 51		57	
58	Enter the amount from Schedule D (Form 1041), line 22, line 13 of the Schedule D Tax Worksheet, or line 4 of the Qualified Dividends Tax Worksheet, whichever applies (as refigured for the AMT, if necessary)	58		
59	Enter the amount from Schedule D (Form 1041), line 14b, column (2) (as refigured for the AMT, if necessary). If you did not complete Schedule D for the regular tax or the AMT, enter -0-	59		
60	If you did not complete a Schedule D Tax Worksheet for the regular tax or the AMT, enter the amount from line 58. Otherwise, add lines 58 and 59 and enter the **smaller** of that result or the amount from line 10 of the Schedule D Tax Worksheet (as refigured for the AMT, if necessary)	60		
61	Enter the **smaller** of line 57 or line 60		61	
62	Subtract line 61 from line 57		62	
63	If line 62 is $175,000 or less, multiply line 62 by 26% (.26). Otherwise, multiply line 62 by 28% (.28) and subtract $3,500 from the result ▶		63	
64	Maximum amount subject to the 5% rate	64	$2,050 00	
65	Enter the amount from line 23 of Schedule D (Form 1041), line 14 of the Schedule D Tax Worksheet, or line 5 of the Qualified Dividends Tax Worksheet, whichever applies (as figured for the regular tax). If you did not complete Schedule D or either worksheet for the regular tax, enter -0-	65		
66	Subtract line 65 from line 64. If zero or less, enter -0-	66		
67	Enter the **smaller** of line 57 or line 58	67		
68	Enter the **smaller** of line 66 or line 67	68		
69	Multiply line 68 by 5% (.05) ▶		69	
70	Subtract line 68 from line 67	70		
71	Multiply line 70 by 15% (.15) ▶		71	
	If line 59 is zero or blank, skip lines 72 and 73 and go to line 74. Otherwise, go to line 72.			
72	Subtract line 67 from line 61	72		
73	Multiply line 72 by 25% (.25) ▶		73	
74	Add lines 63, 69, 71, and 73		74	
75	If line 57 is $175,000 or less, multiply line 57 by 26% (.26). Otherwise, multiply line 57 by 28% (.28) and subtract $3,500 from the result		75	
76	Enter the **smaller** of line 74 or line 75 here and on line 52		76	

Form **1041** (2006)

EXHIBIT 11–4 IRS Form 1041 *(continued)*

If the trust has a taxable income and resulting tax liability, estimated payments of that tax liability may be required throughout the year preceding the filing of the trust return. Estimated payments are required if tax is $1,000 or more. Estimated payments are not required if the entity had no tax liability for the full 12-month tax year. Safe harbor rules similar to those for individuals apply to estates and trusts. A trust is also required to obtain an EIN separate from the EIN or Social Security number of the trustee or the beneficiaries. A grantor-type trust that is not required to file form 1041 does not need an EIN. Additional exceptions to the required EIN include trusts required to distribute all income if the income is less than $300, and trusts that accumulate less than $100 in income.

Trust returns are assumed to use the calendar year and have the same filing deadlines as individuals. If a Grantor Trust operates under a fiscal year, this election must be made in advance with the IRS. When it appears that a trust return is not going to be filed in a timely manner, form 8736 is used to request a 3-month extension. An additional 3-month extension may be granted with a second form 8736. Neither extension is automatic. If the trust is not filed on time, there may be penalties. The late filing penalty is 5 percent of the tax liability each month up to 25 percent plus late payment penalties and interest. If a return is more than 60 days late, the minimum late filing penalty is the smaller of $100 or the tax due. The penalty may be waived if an explanation showing reasonable cause for the delay is attached to the return.

In the trust return, the trustee is required to disclose:

- All income received by the trust
- Any tax credits relating to that income
- An allocation of income between beneficiary and trustee income
- Taxable distributions made to beneficiaries or on behalf of the trust

As part of the return, the trustee also is required to calculate the tax payable on the beneficiary income, trustee income, and taxable distributions. This tax is then paid with the return. In turn, the beneficiaries can claim a credit for tax paid on their beneficiary income. However, the beneficiary may be responsible for taxable distributions on their own personal income tax returns if the income was not previously taxed and satisfied in the trust return.

If a beneficiary receives income from a trust, or a taxable distribution from a foreign trust, a return is required if other filing requirements are met. Trust income should be included in the income in the personal tax return and is taxed at normal rates. A payment credit can be claimed for any tax the trust has deducted before the income was paid to the taxpayer. Foreign trusts have some additional requirements that should be consulted before filing the return.

Trusts are treated for tax purposes similar to guardianships. The trust must complete periodic financial reports. If the trust's balance date is not March 31, the trustee must include any income from the trust in the tax return for the year that corresponds with the trust's accounting year. It is not required to make any separate calculations to allow for a difference in balance dates. If beneficiary income or taxable distributions from a foreign or nonqualifying trust are received, the details of the trust income should be included on a schedule of beneficiary's estate or trust income form. The form should then be included with the trust return.

ASSIGNMENT 11.2

Research the state and federal filing requirements for the current tax year for the following:

1. Decedent's Estate Return

2. Gift Tax Return

3. Trust Return

ETHICAL QUESTION

Assume that you are employed by a medium-sized law firm that has a small business and individual clientele. One of the clients of the firm owns a local business that provides personal service. The owner is a single woman who is a gifted artist and portrait painter. She has been diagnosed with an illness that will likely claim her life within 2 to 4 years. It most certainly will end her business as the primary asset is her personal talent. Over the years, the owner has accumulated substantial personal assets in the form of well-known and highly valued paintings. She also has substantial debt from living a lifestyle above her means. She has informed the firm of her situation and her intent to give her adult children the entire collection of paintings before her death. The firm advised her of the tax consequences for this. You have personal knowledge that the gifts were in fact made. However, neither the woman nor her adult children to your knowledge have reported the transaction. For many years, the firm has prepared the taxes for the woman. But, when she is contacted, she states that her intent is to no longer file taxes and let the IRS figure it out when she dies. What should the next ethical step for the firm be?

SUMMARY

The primary focus of this chapter was the special situations that arise at some point in the life of most taxpayers and that require particular attention with regard to tax effects. This includes death of a family member, the incapacitation of someone leaving them unable to manage their own finances, gifts, and money held for the benefit of another. Each of these require particular steps to be completed in order to legally manage and/or distribute the money involved both for the benefit of the owner of the funds, any other persons they identify, and the tax consequences associated with the event. A decedent's estate requires careful handling of the assets of the estate until such time as the assets are fully distributed according to the law. Guardianships may be short-term or lifelong, depending on the circumstances. The guardian is a fiduciary of the ward but is also legally accountable to the courts and the IRS. When the settlor sets up a fund for the benefit of another, a trust occurs. This typically requires the inclusion of a trustee as a fiduciary for the advantage of the beneficiary. If someone makes a substantial gift to another, the grantor (gift-giver) or grantor's estate may be responsible to pay tax on the gift either at the time it is given or on the probate of the estate of the grantor, depending on the circumstances. Each of these situations produces unique tax considerations and requires the preparation of specific forms in addition to the associated individual returns that might be due.

KEY TERMS

estates	Settlor	Settlement
decedent	Trustee	
Inventory of the Estate	Beneficiary	

For additional resources, visit our Web site at www.westlegalstudies.com

Glossary

A

accounting A system of setting up financial record books, especially for tax purposes; a full explanation of a transaction or of an entire business.

Adjusted Gross Income Allows certain deductions against income before the determination for certain tax benefits is made.

adjusting entries Often include items such as incorrect mathematical computations and improper recording of numbers such as transpositions.

adjustments Allow the taxpayer to remove certain portions of gross income from the taxable income computation.

B

balance sheet The summary of all accounts of the business.

beneficiary A person or entity named in a will or a financial contract as the inheritor of property when the property owner dies.

C

calendar year Begins on January 1 and ends on December 31.

capital transaction Occurs when ownership of stock in a corporation changes.

cash-flow statement Shows every source of income and the way in which a company's money is expended during the accounting period.

chart of accounts A listing of the accounts used to track financial transactions of the business.

closing entries The closing out of all temporary accounts into the more general permanent accounts following the Adjusted Trial Balance.

contingent fee billing Typically used for the types of cases that have an uncertain outcome associated with a monetary result.

corporation Recognized by the law as a person or entity in and of itself.

correction An additional entry made to amend an error and correct the affected accounts.

cost advance Costs paid by a law firm for items deemed necessary to facilitate forward movement of a case. The firm will ultimately seek reimbursement of these costs from the client.

cost of goods sold Presale expenditures for a product in the retail or merchandising business.

credit A "from" or "minus" entry.

credits A dollar-for-dollar reduction of taxes owed. Differs from a deduction, which reduces the amount of income subject to tax.

D

debit A "to" or "plus" entry.

decedent A deceased person.

direct expenses Expenses that are exclusive to the business.

disregarded entity A business that is disregarded as an entity separate from its owner.

double entry accounting Recording both elements of each financial transaction affecting a business.

double entry A method of bookkeeping that records both the credit and debit elements of each financial transaction affecting a business.

E

earned income Consists of the money paid to a person who is employed.

employee A person who works for a business on a regular basis and who is generally subject to the direct supervision and control of the employer.

enrolled agent An individual who has demonstrated proficiency and advanced technical competence in the areas of taxation.

escrow A financial instrument (Securities, funds and other assets) held by a third party on behalf of the other two parties in a transaction. The funds are held by the escrow service until it receives the appropriate written or oral instructions confirming the obligations concerning the transaction have been fulfilled.

estates All of the valuable things an individual owns, such as real estate, art collections, collectibles, antiques, jewelry, investments and life insurance.

F

fair market value The price that a given property or asset would fetch in the marketplace, assuming prospective buyers and sellers are reasonably knowledgeable about the asset; they are behaving in their own best interests and are free of undue pressure to trade.

fiduciary Any relationship between persons in which one person acts for another in a position of trust.

filing status Can greatly affect tax liability.

financial statements Documents that reflect the overall health and activity of a business, prepared for the end of an accounting period.

flat fee billing An established fee for certain types of cases that have a fairly predictable investment of time.

Form W-4 An IRS document that helps determine the proper amount of an individual's pay to withhold for income tax purposes.

G

general journal Contains the Chart of Accounts, and is a place in which the specific transactions are recorded by date, amount, and accounts affected.

general partnership Consists of two or more general partners and personal liability is unlimited.

H

Head of Household An individual who is responsible for the support of certain other individuals.

hourly billing Billing based on tracking the time spent and attributed to the client for whom the time is expended.

I

income statement Used to disclose the financial activity over a period of time.

income Money received by a person or organization because of effort (work) or from return on investments.

independent contractor Usually employed on a project-by-project basis and is responsible for completing the task assigned independently.

indirect expenses Expenses that are included with the rest of the home such as real property taxes.

information form The primary method used by the government to track and assess taxes due by individuals and businesses.

Information Return A separate return is also filed for the partnership.

informational return A return filed by a business if it operates and engages in any sort of financial transaction.

Injured Spouse A co-signer of a joint tax return whose tax refund is used to pay one spouse's past-due child and/or spousal support, a past-due federal debt, or form 8379.

Innocent Spouse A co-signer of a joint tax return who is deemed to have been unaware of the understatement of tax made by his or her spouse and thus should not be held liable.

internal control A safeguard for accuracy and honesty.

inventory of the estate A complete financial inventory of all assets and liabilities of the party who is the subject of the probate.

letter of protection/lien letter A written document that acknowledges a debt and guarantees that the debt of the client will be paid directly by the firm on behalf of the client at the time a monetary award or settlement is received.

limited liability company Individuals who are not members of the profession that is the basis for the business may be owners of an LLC.

limited partnership Protects the personal assets of the limited partner from liability.

M

Married Filing Jointly A filing status for married couples that have wed before the end of the tax year. Both spouses record their respective incomes, exemptions, and deductions on the same tax return. Best if only one spouse has a significant income. In most cases, "married filing jointly" offers the most tax savings, especially when the spouses have different income levels.

Married Filing Separate A filing status for married couples who choose to record their respective incomes, exemptions, and deductions on separate tax returns. Best when both spouses work and the income and itemized deductions are large and very unequal.

Modified Adjusted Gross Income Allows even more deductions against income before the determination for certain tax benefits is made.

N

nonrefundable Tax credits that cannot reduce tax liability below $0.

P

partnership An entity shared in ownership by more than one individual.

pass-through Businesses that report income; however, the income itself is passed through the business and to the individual owner(s) for purposes of determining taxation.

passive income Typically something that regularly produces income for the owner with minimal involvement such as a rental property, a businesses ownership interest in which the taxpayer does not materially participate in the business operations, or authorship by the taxpayer of a creative work that produces royalties.

periodic accounting The regular and systematic process of tallying the accounts and preparation of such documents as Worksheets, Trial Balances, a Balance Sheet, and Income Statements for a specified period of time.

personal exemption Portion of income allowed to each person in a household that is exempt from being taxed.

professional corporation/professional service corporation Created for licensed professionals whose business was to provide services rather than ordinary types of commercial business.

Q

qualifying person A dependent or other individual who is eligible for a given tax credit or deduction through the fulfillment of certain IRS criteria.

Qualifying Widow(er) A tax status available to widows and widowers for up to two years following their spouse's death provided they have at least one dependent and meet certain IRS criteria concerning their previous filing status.

R

refundable Tax credits that can reduce tax liability below $0, resulting in a tax refund.

retainer An advance payment made to get representation underway.

reversing entries For each adjusting entry to close out a balance of a temporary account, a mirror image reversing entry is prepared to restore any balance that is carried over into another accounting period.

reversing entry An expense or revenue item covering more than one accounting period.

S

Saver's Credit Some contributions to a retirement plan, including an IRA, which can result in additional tax savings for the taxpayer.

settlement A signed trust deed (agreement) that acknowledges the transfer of funds.

settlor One that makes a business or financial settlement or a settlement of property.

short year An accounting cycle of a business that occurs for a period of less than 12 months.

single status The filing status used by a taxpayer who is unmarried and does not qualify for any other filing status.

sole proprietorship The entire ownership interest of the business is vested in a single individual.

SS-8 Determination of Worker Status for Purposes of Federal Employment Taxes and Income Tax Withholding An IRS form used to determine whether a person is considered an employee or independent contractor.

Standard Deduction The amount that each taxpayer(s) is eligible to claim on the return.

Statement of Capital Used to show changes in the owner's capital accounts over time.

T

tax avoidance Legal use of the terms of the tax code to one's own advantage.

tax evasion Occurs when efforts are made by individuals and other entities to dodge the payment of taxes by breaking the law.

tax year An annual accounting period for keeping records and reporting income and expenses. An annual accounting period does not include a short tax year. A tax year can be based on either the calendar year or the fiscal year.

taxable income The amount of net income used in calculating income tax.

trial balance The final tally or balance for every account in the Chart of Accounts.

Trustee An individual who holds or manages assets for the benefit of another.

W

worksheets or working papers Documents used to see the activity of the business, the net changes in the assets, liabilities, and equity, as well as the revenue trends.

Y

year-end The process of closing the books for the entire accounting year.

Index